The Palestine Yearbook of International Law, Volume 21 (2018)

The Palestine Yearbook of International Law

Editor-in-Chief

Ardi Imseis

Consulting Editor

Anis F. Kassim

Editors

Reem Al-Botmeh
Ata R. Hindi

Editorial Board

Anis F. Kassim	Camille Mansour
Asem Khalil	Ata R. Hindi
Ardi Imseis	Reem Al- Botmeh

Advisory Board

Georges M. Abi-Saab	Ahmed Abouelwafa
Abdallah Alashaal	Badriya Al-Awadhi
Mohammed Bedjaoui	Salah Dabbagh
Riad Daoudi	Nabil Elaraby
Awn Al-Khasawneh	Mahmoud Mubarak
Mohammad K. Al-Musa	Anis M. Al-Qasem
Muhammad M. Al-Saleh	Moufid M. Shehab
Muhammad Y. Olwan	Muhammad Aziz Shukri

VOLUME 21

The titles published in this series are listed at *brill.com/pyil*

The Palestine Yearbook of International Law, Volume 21 (2018)

Edited by

Ardi Imseis

BRILL
NIJHOFF

LEIDEN | BOSTON

The *Palestine Yearbook of International Law* is published in cooperation with the Birzeit University Institute of Law, under whose auspices it is edited. Established in 1993, the Institute of Law is research based and aims to contribute to the modernization of Palestinian legal structures both at the academic and professional levels.

All e-mail correspondence concerning the Yearbook should be sent to the Editor-in-Chief at: iol.pyil@birzeit.edu. Posted correspondence may be sent to: Attn: *Palestine Yearbook of International Law*, BZU Institute of Law. P.O. Box 14, Birzeit. Palestine. Telecommunication may be directed to the Institute of Law, at: Tel: (972) (2) 298-2009; Fax: (972) (2) 298-2137.

Typeface for the Latin, Greek, and Cyrillic scripts: "Brill". See and download: brill.com/brill-typeface.

ISSN 1386-1972
E-ISSN 2211-6141 (e-book)
ISBN 978-90-04-42731-0 (hardback)

Copyright 2020 by Koninklijke Brill NV, Leiden, The Netherlands.
Koninklijke Brill NV incorporates the imprints Brill, Brill Hes & De Graaf, Brill Nijhoff, Brill Rodopi, Brill Sense, Hotei Publishing, mentis Verlag, Verlag Ferdinand Schöningh and Wilhelm Fink Verlag.
All rights reserved. No part of this publication may be reproduced, translated, stored in a retrieval system, or transmitted in any form or by any means, electronic, mechanical, photocopying, recording or otherwise, without prior written permission from the publisher.
Authorization to photocopy items for internal or personal use is granted by Koninklijke Brill NV provided that the appropriate fees are paid directly to The Copyright Clearance Center, 222 Rosewood Drive, Suite 910, Danvers, MA 01923, USA. Fees are subject to change.

This book is printed on acid-free paper and produced in a sustainable manner.

Contents

Introduction XI
    Ardi Imseis

PART 1
Articles

Israeli Territory, Settlements, and European Union Trade: How Does the Legal and Territorial Jurisdictional Regime that Israeli Imposes throughout Israel-Palestine affect the EU-Israel Association Agreement and the EU-Palestinian Authority Association Agreement? 3
    Marco Guasti

The Legality of the Use of Force for Self-Determination 32
    Sean Shun Ming Yau

The Right to Return: Drafting Paragraph 11 of General Assembly Resolution 194 (III), December 11, 1948 77
    Terry Rempel

PART 2
Book Review

Mazen Masri, *The Dynamics of Exclusionary Constitutionalism: Israel as a Jewish and Democratic State* (2017)

Nimer Sultany, *Law and Revolution: Legitimacy and Constitutionalism after the Arab Spring* (2017) 201
    Emilio Dabed

PART 3
Materials

SECTION A
United Nations

General Assembly

G.A. Res. 73/256, Assistance to the Palestinian People (Dec. 20, 2018)   219

G.A. Res. 73/255, Permanent Sovereignty of the Palestinian People in the Occupied Palestinian Territory, including East Jerusalem and of the Arab Population in the Occupied Syrian Golan and Their Natural Resources (Dec. 20, 2018)   226

G.A. Res. 73/158, The Right of the Palestinian People to Self-Determination (Dec. 17, 2018)   232

G.A. Res. 79/99, Israeli Practices Affecting the Human Rights of the Palestinian People in the Occupied Palestinian Territory, including East Jerusalem (Dec. 18, 2018)   234

G.A. Res. 73/98, Israeli Settlements in the Occupied Palestinian Territory, including East Jerusalem, and Occupied Syrian Golan (Dec. 18, 2018)   244

G.A. Res. 73/97, Applicability of the Geneva Convention Relative to the Protection of Civilian Persons in Time of War, of 12 August 1949, to the Occupied Palestinian Territory, including East Jerusalem, and the Other Occupied Arab Territories (Dec. 7, 2018)   251

G.A. Res. 73/96, Work of the Special Committee to Investigate Israeli Practices Affecting the Human Rights of the Palestinian People and Other Arabs of the Occupied Territories (Dec. 7, 2018)   254

G.A. Res. 73/95, Palestine Refugees' Properties and Their Revenues (Dec. 7, 2018)   260

G.A. Res. 73/94, Operations of the United Nations Relief and Works Agency for Palestine Refugees in the Near East (Dec. 7, 2018)   262

G.A. Res. 73/93, Persons Displaced as a Result of the June 1967 and Subsequent Hostilities (Dec. 7, 2018)   275

G.A. Res. 73/92, Assistance to Palestine Refugees (Dec. 7, 2018)   277

G.A. Res. 73/89, Comprehensive, Just and Lasting Peace in the Middle East, U.N. Doc. A/RES/73/89 (Dec. 6, 2018)   280

G.A. Res. 73/22, Jerusalem (Nov. 30, 2018)   281

G.A. Res. 73/21, Division for Palestinian Rights of the Secretariat (Nov. 30, 2018)   284

G.A. Res. 73/20, Special Information Programme on the Question of Palestine of the Department of Public Information of the Secretariat (Nov. 30, 2018)   286

G.A. Res. 73/19, Peaceful Settlement of the Question of Palestine (Nov. 30, 2018)   289

G.A. Res. 73/18, Committee on the Exercise of the Inalienable Rights of the Palestinian People (Nov. 30, 2018)   301

Human Rights Council

H.R.C. Rs. 37/37, Ensuring Accountability and Justice for All Violations of International Law in the Occupied Palestinian Territory, including East Jerusalem (Mar. 23, 2018)   309

H.R.C. Res. 37/36, Israeli Settlements in the Occupied Palestinian Territory, including East Jerusalem, and in the Occupied Syrian Golan, A/HRC/RES/37/36 (Mar. 23, 2018)   314

H.R.C. Res. 37/35, Human Rights Situation in the Occupied Palestinian Territory, including East Jerusalem (Mar. 23, 2018)   325

H.R.C. Res. 37/34, Right of the Palestinian People to Self-Determination (Mar. 23, 2018)   335

SECTION B
United Nations Reports

Right of Peoples to Self-Determination, Report of the Secretary-General, U.N. Doc. A/73/329 (2018)   341

Report of the Special Rapporteur on the Situation of Human Rights in the Palestinian Territories Occupied since 1967, U.N. Doc. A/HRC/37/75 (June 14, 2018)   359

Database of All Business Enterprises Involved in the Activities Detailed in Paragraph 96 of the Report of the Independent International Fact-Finding Mission to Investigate the Implications of the Israeli Settlements on the Civil, Political, Economic, Social and Cultural Rights of the Palestinian People throughout the Occupied Palestinian Territory, including East Jerusalem, U.N. Doc. A/HRC/37/39 (Feb. 1, 2018)   388

SECTION C
International Criminal Court

Office of the Prosecutor, Report on Preliminary Examinations 2018 (Dec. 5, 2018) [Excerpts]   413

Referral by the State of Palestine Pursuant to Articles 13(a) and 14 of the Rome Statute (May 15, 2018)   427

SECTION D
International Court of Justice

ICJ, Relocation of the United States Embassy to Jerusalem (Palestine v. United States of America), Application Instituting Proceedings, Sep. 28, 2018   445

ICJ, Relocation of the United States Embassy to Jerusalem (Palestine v. United States of America), Order, Sep. 28, 2018   458

SECTION E
Cases

United States, Koontz v. Watson, 283 F. Supp. 3d 1007 (D. Kan. 2018)   465

United States, Jordahl v. Brnovich, 336 F Supp. 3d 1016 (D. Ariz. 2018)   486

SECTION F
Legislation

Israel

Basic Law: Israel The Nation State of the Jewish People (July 25, 2018)   521

United States

S. 2946, Anti-Terrorism Clarification Act of 2018   525

Index   529

Introduction

Since 2008, I have had the distinct privilege of serving as the Editor-in-Chief of the *Palestine Yearbook of International Law*. As all good things must come to an end, this volume represents my last. Looking back, it is hard not to marvel at just how much has changed during the past decade, and across a multiplicity of landscapes, both legal and political.

At the local level, we bore witness during this period to a marked regression in the situation faced by the people of occupied Palestine. This included: the ongoing blockade and siege of the Gaza Strip, punctuated by a continuous series of armed aggressions by the Occupying Power, rendering the place "unlivable" according to the United Nations (UN),[1] to say nothing of the thousands killed and injured, and hundreds of thousands displaced;[2] the continued colonization of the West Bank, including East Jerusalem, through the ongoing settlement by the Occupying Power of its civilian population in the territory, now numbering between 620,000–670,000 people (or approximately 23–25% of the total population of the territory);[3] and the ongoing physical and administrative fragmentation of occupied Palestine, whether through the reification of the 'interim' Oslo framework (*e.g.* the Palestinian Authority; Areas A, B, C; etc.), the wall and its associated regime, and the intensification of Israel's system of racial segregation[4] and apartheid;[5] or the ongoing split between rival

---

1 U.N. OCHA, *Gaza in 2020: A Livable Place?* (Aug. 2012), http://gaza.ochaopt.org/2012/08/gaza-in-2020-a-liveable-place/. *See also*, U.N., *Gaza 'Unlivable', UN Special Rapporteur for the Situation of Human Rights in the OPT Tells Third Committee – Press Release*, Seventy-Third Session, 31st and 32nd Meetings (AM & PM), U.N. Doc. GA/SHC/4242 (Oct. 24, 2018), https://www.un.org/unispal/document/gaza-unliveable-un-special-rapporteur-for-the-situation-of-human-rights-in-the-opt-tells-third-committee-press-release-excerpts/.
2 *See, e.g.*, *Report of the United Nations Fact Finding Mission on the Gaza Conflict*, U.N. Doc. A/HRC/12/48 (Sept. 25, 2009); *Report of the Independent International Commission of Inquiry Established Pursuant to Human Rights Council Resolution S/21-1*, U.N. Doc. A/HRC/28/79 (Mar. 26, 2015).
3 ICC-CPI, *Prosecution Request Pursuant to Article 19(3) for a Ruling on the Court's Territorial Jurisdiction in Palestine*, Situation in the State of Palestine, No. ICC-01/18 (Jan. 22, 2020), at n307, https://www.icc-cpi.int/CourtRecords/CR2020_00161.PDF [*hereinafter* ICC Prosecution Request].
4 U.N. CERD, *Concluding Observations of the Committee for the Elimination of Racial Discrimination, Israel*, U.N. Doc. CERD/ISR/CO/14-16 (Apr. 3, 2012), para. 24 [*hereinafter* CERD Concluding Observations].
5 U.N. ESCWA, *Israeli Practices Towards the Palestinian People and the Question of Apartheid*, U.N. Doc. E/ESCWA/ECRI/2017/1 (2017), https://www.middleeastmonitor.com/wp-content/uploads/downloads/201703_UN_ESCWA-israeli-practices-palestinian-people-apartheid

Palestinian authorities in the West Bank and Gaza Strip and the continued atrophy suffered by the Palestine Liberation Organization (PLO). The situation of that portion of the Palestinian people who remain inside Israel has become worse, as their civil, political, economic, social and cultural rights continue to be violated, as evidenced by the numerous laws that discriminate against them in all areas of life (*e.g.* equal access to land and property, social and economic benefits, citizenship and entry, and family unification),[6] epitomized by the July 2018 passage by the Knesset of the *Basic Law: Israel as the Nation-State of the Jewish People*, through which racial and religious discrimination has been consolidated as a constitutional norm.[7] At the same time, the plight of the Palestine refugees has continued to fester, both within the occupied Palestinian territory (oPt) and in the host States, with little promise that they will ever realize their inalienable rights under international law.

During the same period, the situation was hardly better at the regional level. Despite the initial hope wrought by the 'Arab Spring,' we have witnessed the virtual collapse of large portions of what was an already enfeebled Arab State system. Multiparty civil wars in Libya, Syria, and Yemen have produced human catastrophes that the world has not witnessed since the Second World War, with millions of civilians given no quarter from the effects of armed conflict. Early success stories in Tunis and Cairo have also not borne the fruit promised by the revolutions that once took hold of them. All of this has resulted in an even greater exposure of the Arab world to geo-political intervention from without. As a result of its political implosion, the Arab region remains a laboratory for regional and international superpowers, including for the 'progressive development' of international laws shaped by them and their proxies (think, for example, the ostensibly 'legal' justifications for the 'war on terror,' 'preemptive' self-defense, and autonomous drone warfare). In this context, while ordinary people in the Arab street have been increasingly alienated from those who purport to rule in their name, public perceptions of the value of international law have never been as low. For Palestine refugees, the complete disarray that has engulfed the region has understandably resulted in even greater levels of insecurity, vulnerability, and despair, whether in Lebanon, Syria, Jordan, or farther afield.

-occupation-english.pdf. *See also* John Dugard & J. Reynolds, *Apartheid, International Law and the Occupied Palestinian Territory*, 24 Eur. J. Int'l. L. 867 (2013).

6 CERD Concluding Observations.

7 Adalah – The Legal Center for Arab Minority Rights in Israel, *Position Paper: The Basic Law: Israel – The Nation State of the Jewish People* (Nov. 2018), https://www.adalah.org/uploads/uploads/Final_2_pager_on_the_JNSL_27.11.2018%20.pdf.

INTRODUCTION   XIII

Internationally, the past decade has also witnessed a gradual decline in respect for the primacy of the international rule of law. In addition to the expanding number of regional wars and growing socio-economic gaps between North and South, this has been most apparent in an increase in the antagonistic policies adopted by the United States (US) under the Trump administration in areas as wide-ranging as climate change and protection, nuclear non-proliferation, the World Trade Organization, the International Criminal Court (ICC), and the UN. Nor has Palestine been spared in this concerted attack on the multilateral order, once championed by Washington. In its case, this attack has taken a particularly cruel turn, as the US has unashamedly turned its back on the two-state framework it once sponsored, severing diplomatic ties with the PLO, ceasing all funding of the United Nations Relief and Works Agency for Palestine Refugees (UNRWA), questioning the very existence and legal status of the Palestine refugees, recognizing Israeli sovereignty over Jerusalem and the occupied Syrian Golan, and declaring Israeli settlements in these occupied territories to be 'legal.'[8]

A rather dismal state of affairs, one might say. But all is most certainly not lost. Given the façade of the claim of the US as the 'honest broker' for Middle East peace, one might be forgiven for feeling relieved at the emperor's clothes having finally been removed by none other than Washington itself. There can be no doubt, if there ever was one, that the US today stands not only in the position of underwriter of Israel's internationally wrongful acts in Palestine, but also as co-conspirator to those acts. If anything, this has provided Palestine with an opportunity to recalibrate its positions and tactics. The most obvious of these rests in the PLO's strategic decision to utilize the multilateral order as a means both for seeking redress for the ongoing and systematic victimization of its people, as well as for asserting the international legal personality of the State of Palestine. One of the great highlights of this period, therefore, has been the series of moves made by the State of Palestine to impose a cost on the occupation by making creative use of the multilateral system. This began with Palestine's upgrade by the UN General Assembly to non-member Observer State in November 2012,[9] followed accession to over 90 multilateral treaties and membership in a number of international bodies whose membership is reserved only for States. This included accession to the Four Geneva Conventions of 1949 and their Additional Protocols of 1977, most major international human rights treaties, the Vienna Convention on Diplomatic Relations (VCDR), and

---

8   U.S. White House, *Peace to Prosperity: A Vision to Improve the Lives of the Palestinian and Israeli People* (Feb. 2020), https://www.whitehouse.gov/peacetoprosperity/.
9   G.A. Res. 67/19 (Nov. 29, 2012).

the Rome Statute of the ICC.[10] These accessions have allowed Palestine to commence a number of actions on the international plane aimed at protecting its rights. Foremost of these has been an April 2015 referral of the situation in Palestine to the ICC Prosecutor, an April 2018 inter-state communication against Israel for breaches of its obligations under the International Covenant on the Elimination of All Forms of Racial Discrimination (a precedent, as the mechanism had hitherto never been invoked by any State party), and a September 2018 institution of proceedings against the US in the International Court of Justice (ICJ) on the basis that the US has violated its obligations under the VCDR by moving its embassy to Israel from Tel Aviv to Jerusalem in May 2018. Perhaps most significantly, as at the time of writing, over 138 states (of 193 Members of the UN) recognize the State of Palestine.[11]

For many, the above noted developments taken by the State of Palestine have brought to a head a debate that has gained strength over the past decade, one that has taken on existential proportions for those vested in the Palestinian liberation struggle. The debate demands participants to take one or the other side of a number of related binaries: Are you for one or two States? Do you believe in a top-down, statist approach at all? Or is it better to focus on a bottom-up grassroots approach to achieving justice?

For those who continue to work within a statist, two-State framework, Palestinian moves at the UN and other international organizations and tribunals have been the last line of defense for the realization of Palestinian national rights on the international plane. The value of these developments rests in a fundamental acceptance of the legitimacy of the multilateral rules-based international order, as established by and at the UN, despite the glaring inequities of doing so. Among these is the historic compromise by the PLO in 1988 to accept the 1947 partition UN General Assembly Resolution 181(II) and the two-State framework, recognize Israel within 78% of mandate Palestine, and acquiescing to a just and agreed resolution of the Palestine refugee problem. This position was/is rooted in a realist approach to the Palestinian situation, one that recognizes that in the face of overwhelming military, economic, and political odds of hegemonic actors, the only way to salvage at least a modicum of justice for the subaltern Palestinians is to be found within the multilateral statist framework at the UN and other international organizations and tribunals.

---

10   For a summary of Palestine's treaty accessions and membership in international organizations, *see* ICC Prosecution Request, paras. 124–134.
11   *Id.*

INTRODUCTION   XV

Those who prefer to work within a bottom-up grassroots, one-State framework regard the two-State protagonists as people who are caught in a "sovereignty trap."[12] In the face of the cold hard facts on the ground faced by the Palestinians – which signify an increase, not a decrease, of Palestinian precarity in the material world – they rightfully question the value of the statist frame of reference. Despite high sounding principles of international law that purportedly underscore the "temporariness" of Palestine's festering predicament (*i.e.* occupation, forced exile, etc.), they beseech us to accept that the likelihood of the establishment of an independent sovereign State of Palestine in the oPt has long been dead, that fate having been sealed by over half a century of unimpeded Israeli colonization. In this material world, the 'bantustanization' of the oPt, and the fragmentation of the Palestinian people as a whole, has been the result of the false hope placed by the PLO in the two-State framework and the multilateral order. The facts on the ground reveal that in fact one State already exists, they argue, only that it is an apartheid State in which the indigenous people of Palestine have but one obvious path toward freedom and dignity – a civil, as opposed to a people's, rights movement, aimed at the establishment of an old idea: one democratic State for all of its citizens, Palestinian, Israeli, Jewish, Christian, Muslim.

Without purporting to pick a side, as it were, I take the liberty to try to briefly note the merits and demerits of these positions.

Those considerations that mitigate in favour of the statist, two-State approach have to do with the fact that that it provides the Palestinians with the moral high-ground of international legitimacy. This legitimacy is located in the countless resolutions of the principle political and judicial organs of the United Nations, as informed by well-established international law, including international humanitarian law, human rights law and general principles of law. In this respect, three particular factors stand out as things that are now axiomatic in how the world understands Palestine and its people on the international legal plane. The first of these is the existence, as a matter of international law, of the Palestinian people as such. When one considers the long and sordid history of the imperial and neo-imperial effort to deprive this people of its international legal standing, this achievement is no small matter. As affirmed by the ICJ in 2004, "the existence of the Palestinian people is no longer in issue."[13] The second factor concerns the legal corollary of peoplehood, namely that its existence necessarily implies a right to self-determination. In the context of

---

12 *See* NOURA EREKAT, JUSTICE FOR SOME: LAW AND THE QUESTION OF PALESTINE (2019).
13 Legal Consequences of the Construction of a Wall in the Occupied Palestinian Territory, Advisory Opinion, 2004 I.C.J. Rep. 136, para. 118 (July 9).

the international law on decolonization, including as it pertains to Palestine, this right entails the license to political and territorial independence to the exclusion of all others in a State of one's own. Again, given the experience of Palestine as a place long-coveted by others without regard to the interests of its indigenous people, this achievement is not insignificant. Related to these is the third factor, namely the international community's universal acceptance of the oPt as the self-determination unit within which the Palestinian people are legally entitled to exercise its self-determination.[14] The status of the territory as occupied has particularly important normative value, as Occupying Powers are barred under international law from legitimately claiming rights of sovereignty over such territory. Being so barred, international law requires the Occupying Power (and all other States) to do nothing to permanently impede the right of the people of the territory to exercise its self-determination right, and indeed must take positive steps to protect and ensure the exercise of that right. The problem with all of this, of course, is that without an effective means of law enforcement on the international plane, these international legal norms continue to be honored only in their breach. As such, they have remained in the realm of the discursive, shaping the contours of what is regarded as legitimate, until such time as the requisite political will can be summoned by the relevant stakeholders to bring them to fruition.

Those considerations that mitigate in favour of the grassroots one-State approach are also rooted in international legal norms and a realism, only of a different sort. Its proponents argue that, in the face of the unrealized promise of the international law underpinning the two-State approach, the only way to maximize the realization of rights for both Israelis and Palestinians is within the framework of one democratic state encompassing the whole of the former mandate of Palestine (*i.e.* what is today Israel and the oPt). The legal norms underpinning this vision rely more on the wide array of the civil, political, economic, social, and cultural rights vested in individuals under human rights law – *i.e.* one person, one vote – and the re-imagination of the collective right of peoples to self-determination, Israeli or Palestinian, in such a manner that envisions both existing in the same space simultaneously. Whether this comes in the form of a binational or federal set up is not important. Rather what this viewpoint envisions is a different way to understand both group and peoples' rights in mandate Palestine that guards against the xenophobic, exclusivist, and racist foundations of the settler-colonialism that presently reigns in the land. For its adherents, the realism that underpins this view accepts Israeli colonization of the oPt as having been so thorough, so complete, so successful,

---

14 G.A. Res. 67/19 (Nov. 29, 2012).

that any effective rights-based approach must acknowledge this fact and begin afresh. At best, they argue, a 'two-State' solution would offer the Palestinians a rump-State, unable to defend itself, forever beholden to Israel. But therein lies the problem: for all of its appeal, the one democratic State ideal, whether in the federal or binational form, offers no realistic way to ensure that any relinquishment of the above-mentioned international legitimacy gained by the Palestinian people over the decades will be met with an equally historic concession on the part of Israel. Quite the opposite. With the exception of a negligible number of Israeli Jews (and supporters in the diaspora) who reject settler-colonialism's imperative of the 'elimination of the native,' to borrow from Patrick Wolfe's classic formulation,[15] there is little in today's world to suggest that the powers that be in Tel Aviv will ever relinquish their superiority, which they equally regard as a thing no less hard fought for and won. What we would be left with in such a circumstance would be more, not less, apartheid; only the principles advanced in support of this view would find less adherents in a State-centric world that, for good or ill, still predominates and has shown itself easily given to looking the other way when it comes to the 'internal affairs' of States.

It is clear that this introduction is no place to take a firm position on one or the other of these positions in the debate now raging. I set them out here because they are going concerns, which I am certain will increasingly shape the debate on Palestine's engagement with international law in years to come. Rest assured, no matter how things evolve in this respect, the *Palestine Yearbook of International Law* will continue to serve as a forum for debate on these and other issues. Uncertain though the future may be, what is clear is the imperative for all who care about international law to ensure that justice be given its appropriate due, and placed at the forefront of our engagement with the discipline. Law and justice are far from the same thing. In this regard, I have every confidence that under its new leadership, the *Yearbook* will continue to serve as a site for critical engagement with international law, with an emphasis on ensuring that new and fresh voices are heard, particularly from the global south.

>
> Editor in Chief
> *Ardi Imseis*

---

15   Patrick Wolfe, *Settler Colonialism and the Elimination of the Native*, J. Genocide Res. 387 (2006).

PART 1

Articles

∵

Israeli Territory, Settlements, and European Union Trade: How Does the Legal and Territorial Jurisdictional Regime that Israeli Imposes throughout Israel-Palestine affect the EU-Israel Association Agreement and the EU-Palestinian Authority Association Agreement?

Marco Guasti[*]

Contents

I   Introduction
II Territoriality: Israeli Borders and Borderlands
    A   *Israel and International Borders*
    B   *Israeli Jurisdiction and Annexation*
III The Illegality of the Israeli Territorial and Jurisdictional Regime
    A   *Israel and International Law*
    B   *Third-Party State Responsibility*
IV Israel and EU Trade
    A   *Israeli Settlement Goods and European Union Law*
    B   *The Israeli Economy and EU Trade*
V   Conclusion
    Bibliography

---

[*] Marco Guasti is a lawyer with a Bachelor's of Law and a Bachelor's of International Relations from the Pontifical Catholic University of São Paulo (Brazil) and holds an LLM in Human Rights Law from University College London (UK). He worked as a lawyer in different law firms in Brazil and lived in Palestine assisting Al-Haq (a Palestinian NGO) in monitoring human rights violations carried out by the State of Israel. Marco also studied critical theory, philosophy and psychoanalysis at Birkbeck University. He speaks Portuguese, English, Spanish, and Italian.

I Introduction

In 2000, the European Union (EU) and the State of Israel signed and ratified an Association Agreement (EU-Israel AA) that establishes the way in which goods and services transit between their territories and provides for the gradual elimination of tariffs and trade restrictions between them. The territoriality clause contained in the EU-Israel AA has been the subject of much debate, since Israel and the EU diverge in their interpretation of the extent of the Israeli territory. Whilst Israel has increasingly considered the settlements it maintains in the occupied Palestinian territory (oPt) to be part of Israeli territory, the EU has consistently refuted this position. Issues relating to "rules of origin" of Israeli goods thus require an understanding of what the Israeli territory is, from the perspective of international law, EU law, and Israeli law.

This study relies on the Hague Regulations (HRs), Geneva Conventions (GCs), United Nations (UN) resolutions, international treaties, and rulings of the International Court of Justice (ICJ) to reveal the legal extent of Israeli territory from the perspective of international law. By examining the different legal instruments Israel has instituted throughout Israel-Palestine, it will show that Israeli law defines the Israeli territory in very broad terms, progressively incorporating Palestinian land into it and extending its national jurisdiction over it. An analysis of the legal, jurisdictional, and territorial regime that Israel has established throughout the region will explain how this regime works mostly for the benefit of the Israeli population and economy, to the detriment of the lives, economy, and state of the Palestinian people, in violation of the applicable norms of international law.

The EU has tried to deal with these Israeli violations by establishing a "differentiation" policy in relation to the Israeli territory, aimed at distinguishing between Israel's pre-1967 borders and its post-1967 borders (*i.e.* following the 1949 Armistice or "Green Line"). As will be explained, however, this distinction is not possible in economic terms and does not take into consideration the actual territorial and jurisdictional regime Israel has imposed on the region. Whilst it will be shown that an import ban on Israeli settlement goods produced in the oPt is legally feasible and can be considered a first step towards addressing third-State responsibilities in relation to Israeli violations in the oPt such a ban still relies on the differentiation policy that fails to consider the legal and factual nature of the Green Line and of the regime instituted by Israel on both sides of it.

Finally, a systemic analysis of EU-Israel-Palestine relations will show how the free-trade zone currently in place between Israel and the EU helps sustain the discriminatory jurisdictional/territorial regime imposed by Israel throughout Israel-Palestine. This regime affects the Palestinian people's right to self-determination, sovereignty over their land and natural resources, and right to return to illegally appropriated lands. As will be seen, this regime also adversely impacts the implementation of the EU-Palestinian Authority Association Agreement (EU-PA AA), which established a free-trade zone between the EU and the Palestinian Authority (PA), with further legal implications for the EU and its Member States. Ultimately, if the EU and its Member States wish to uphold their obligations under international law and under the EU-PA AA, they must urgently reassess the nature of their economic and commercial dealings with Israel.

II   Territoriality: Israeli Borders and Borderlands

Most of the issues related to international trade with Israel stem from questions of territoriality and, more specifically, interpretations as to the extent of the Israeli territory. Whilst most of the international community agrees that the Israeli territory is confined to the area on the Israeli side of the "Green Line", Israel has instituted multiple legal instruments throughout that area and the oPt (*i.e.* Israel-Palestine) in order to incorporate Palestinian lands into its territory. As will be seen, the legal trend Israel established from 1948 onwards inside the Green Line was applied to the rest of the Palestinian territory (West Bank, including East Jerusalem, and Gaza Strip) after its occupation in 1967.

The means by which Israel expropriated Palestinian lands in both cases are the same: military emergency (land was requisitioned for military use); absentee status (land was expropriated from absent persons or persons deemed "absent"); and State lands (State land or land converted into State land was appropriated by Israel). By using different legal instruments, Israel eventually incorporated Palestinian lands into its own territory and legal system, extending its jurisdiction and applying its laws to them. The final status of these incorporated lands, both inside and outside the Green Line, is the same in Israeli law: they are considered to be under Israeli jurisdiction and part of the Israeli territory, though different mechanisms are used to constitute them as such. This has severe implications for countries and international entities that have established trade relationships with Israel and the PA.

A   *Israel and International Borders*

During WWI, the armed forces of the United Kingdom (UK) and France occupied the Ottoman Empire. The League of Nations granted these States mandatory powers to oversee the administration of the occupied regions in benefit of the local population, on the "principle that the well-being and development of such peoples form a sacred trust of civilization."[1] The British Mandate of Palestine was thus established by the League of Nations in 1922 to safeguard "the civil and religious rights of all the inhabitants of Palestine, irrespective of race and religion,"[2] as well as to "secure the establishment of a Jewish national home."[3]

In the wake of WWII, the UN General Assembly (UNGA) adopted Resolution 181 (II) and approved a "Partition Plan" for Palestine. The Plan demarcated 56% of the territory of Mandatory Palestine for the creation of a Jewish State, 43% for the creation of an Arab State, and 1% for the international city of Jerusalem.[4] Resolution 181 (II) also determined that the British Mandate would terminate no later than August 1948.[5] In May 1948, the UK terminated its Mandate and disengaged its forces from the region. One day later, the Declaration of the Establishment of the State of Israel was proclaimed by David Ben Gurion. It provided that Israel was "prepared to cooperate with the agencies and representatives of the [UN] in implementing the resolution of the [UNGA]"[6] but did not explicitly define its borders as those set forth in Resolution 181 (II).

That same year, Arab States decided to intervene in the civil war that broke out between the Arabs and Jews in Palestine following the approval of Resolution 181 (II). During the war, Israel occupied territory beyond the borders originally set forth in Resolution 181 (II) and established control over 77% of Mandatory Palestine, Jordan occupied (and subsequently annexed) the West Bank and East Jerusalem, and Egypt occupied the Gaza Strip.[7] The 1949 Armistice Agreements between the different belligerent parties and Israel set up the basic contours of the Armistice Demarcation Line (*i.e.* the Green Line). As made explicit in the Egyptian-Israeli Armistice Agreement, the Green Line was "not to be considered in any sense a political or territorial boundary and is delineated without prejudice to [...] the ultimate settlement of the Palestine

---

1 Covenant of the League of Nations, art. 22.
2 The Palestine Mandate, League of Nations, art. 2.
3 Id.
4 Joel Beinin & Lisa Hajjar, *Palestine, Israel and the Arab-Israeli Conflict*, Middle East Research and Information Project (2014) [*hereinafter* Beinin & Hajjar], https://merip.org/palestine-israel-primer.
5 G.A. Res. 181 (II), *Future Government of Palestine*, art. I(A)(1) (Nov. 29, 1947).
6 Declaration of the Establishment of the State of Israel, para. 13 (1948).
7 Beinin & Hajjar.

question."[8] From 1949 to 1967, neither Israel nor the other Armistice countries recognized the Green Line as an international border.[9]

In 1967, the Six-Day War resulted in Israel's occupation of the remainder of the Palestinian territory (West Bank, including East Jerusalem and the Gaza Strip) and the Syrian Golan Heights. From 1967 onwards, Israel would thus effectively control the borders of the entire territory of the former Mandate of Palestine. The subsequent 1979 peace treaty between Israel and Egypt established that the permanent border between them was "the recognized international boundary between Egypt and the former mandated territory of Palestine […] without prejudice to the issue of the status of the Gaza Strip."[10] The 1994 Peace Treaty between Israel and Jordan also established their permanent "international boundary […] without prejudice to the status of any territories that came under Israeli military government control in 1967."[11] These treaties demarcated the borders between Israel & Jordan and Israel & Egypt, respectively. They did not, however, address the issue of the border between the oPt & Israel and the oPt & Jordan and Egypt.

The UN Security Council (UNSC) addressed the Israeli military occupation of the oPt beyond the Green Line in multiple resolutions, most notably UNSC Resolution 242 (1967), which demanded the "withdrawal of Israeli armed forces from territories occupied in the recent [1967] conflict,"[12] and UNSC Resolution 2334 (2016), which explicitly condemned:

> … all measures aimed at altering the demographic composition, character and status of the Palestinian Territory occupied since 1967, including […] the construction and expansion of settlements, transfer of Israeli settlers, confiscation of land, demolition of homes and displacement of Palestinian civilians, in violation of international humanitarian law and relevant resolutions.[13]

The recent Resolution explicitly claims that UN Member States do not recognize any changes made to the territorial disposition of Palestine after 1967, *other than those agreed by the parties through negotiations*. It is worth mentioning, in

---

8   Israel and Egypt General Armistice Agreement art. V(2), Feb. 24, 1949.
9   Foundation for Middle East Peace, *Borders* (2016), http://www.merip.org/primer-palestine-israel-arab-israeli-conflict-new.
10 Egypt and Israel Treaty of Peace, art. II, Mar. 26, 1979.
11 Treaty of Peace between the State of Israel and the Hashemite Kingdom of Jordan art. 3(2), Oct. 26, 1994.
12 S.C. Res. 242, para. 1(i) (Nov. 22, 1967).
13 S.C. Res. 2334, preamble para. 4 (Dec. 23, 2016).

this regard, that all negotiations and treaties between the parties have always explicitly contained safeguards as to final-status negotiations on borders. One such example is found in the Israeli-Palestinian Interim Agreement (Oslo II), the last major Agreement signed between Israel and Palestinian representatives, where the "two sides agree that West Bank and Gaza Strip territory, *except for issues that will be negotiated in the permanent status negotiations*, will come under the jurisdiction of the Palestinian Council [...]."[14] Oslo II, an interim agreement supposed to last five years pending the "outcome of permanent status negotiations,"[15] was explicit in determining that neither party renounced "any of its existing rights, claims or positions."[16] Nevertheless, the majority of the international community currently considers the Green Line to be the closest thing Israel has to legitimate international borders.

On the other hand, Israel has consistently adopted policies and legislation in order to expand its territory and national jurisdiction well beyond the Green Line over the oPt. The gap between the way Israel views its borders, the way the international community recognizes them, and their legal status under international law is central to the issue of trading with Israel, since it relates not only to the applicable "rules of origin" and forms of labelling, but also to the legality of producing settlement goods and the possibility of instituting import bans on them.

B *Israeli Jurisdiction and Annexation*

The laws, military orders, and regulations enacted by Israel on both sides of the Green Line reveal a consistent use of legal instruments to appropriate Palestinian land, particularly for building Israeli-Jewish settlements, into the territory of the State of Israel. By understanding the process through which Israel appropriated, incorporated, and integrated parts of the oPt into its own, and the way it exerts control over the totality of the oPt, it will become clear why establishing a free-trade zone and a preferential tariffs regime with Israel is tenuous from the point of view of international law: because Israel does not consider its territory to be legally or otherwise restricted in relation to the territory of Palestine. This can already be seen by Israel's "Basic Law: Israel Lands," which establishes that "Israel Lands" are "the lands in Israel of the State, the Development Authority (DA) or the Jewish National Fund (JNF), [which]

---

14   Israeli-Palestinian Interim Agreement on the West Bank and the Gaza Strip, art. XI (2), Sept. 28, 1995 [emphasis added].
15   Id., art. XXXI(6).
16   Id.

shall not be transferred either by sale or in any other manner."[17] The specific wording of the Basic Law should not go unnoticed, since it defines the territory of Israel through double-reflexivity: the *Israeli territory is the territory in Israel* of the lands owned by the State, DA, and JNF. This unique way in which Israeli law defines its own territory has vast implications for the way Israeli jurisdiction has been extended throughout the region under its control, as it makes no reference to defined borders or international treaties.

Israel initiated the process of integrating and extending its jurisdiction over Palestinian lands in the oPt through the "Orders Regarding the Management of Regional Councils and of Local Councils," which virtually replicate Israeli law in the settlements by regulating them in matters of elections, budgets, planning, building, education, establishment of local courts and composition of Regional and Local (Settlement) Councils.[18] These Settlement Councils are subject to the Internal Affairs Officer of the Israeli Civil Administration, which has been under the direct authority of the Israeli Ministry of the Interior since 1996, and has a status equivalent to that of those districts inside the Green Line.[19] Each of these Settlement Councils has jurisdiction over the entire area within their municipal boundaries, which together encompass all the land Israel has appropriated inside the oPt.[20] Through the "Order Regarding Security," Israel also declared settlement areas to be "closed military areas,"[21] but explicitly established that "the provisions of this declaration do not apply to Israelis."[22] It is interesting to note that the definition of "Israelis" in that Order encompasses not only citizens or residents of Israel, but also any person who is "eligible to immigrate to Israel in accordance with the Law of Return 5710-1950" (*i.e.* Jews).[23] Local Palestinians, however, remain excluded from most of their territory in the oPt.

Furthermore, in 1967, the Israeli Minister of Defense implemented Emergency Regulation 5727, which extended Israeli law to all Israeli citizens in the oPt and determined that any offenses committed by Israeli citizens (including settlers) must be tried in Israeli civilian courts.[24] Two years later, the

---

17 Basic Law: Israel Lands (1960) [Isr.].
18 Yehezkel Lien, *Land Grab: Israel's Settlement Policy in the West Bank*, B'Tselem (2002), at 67 [*hereinafter* Lien], https://www.btselem.org/download/200205_land_grab_eng.pdf.
19 Id., at 68.
20 Id.
21 Order Regarding Security (Judea and Samaria) (No. 378) 5730 Declaration of the Closure of an Area (Israeli Communities) (1970) [Isr.]; *in* Lien, at 70.
22 Id.
23 Id.
24 Emergency Regulations (Offenses in the Administered Territories – Jurisdiction and Legal Assistance) 5727 (1967) [Isr.]; *in* Lien, at 65.

Israeli Minister of Justice enacted the Rules of Civil Procedure, which extends the jurisdiction of Israeli civilian courts to all matters between settlers (and Israelis in general) and Palestinians, as well as between settlers themselves.[25] These courts operate in accordance to Israeli law, rather than the local law that should be applicable in the oPt.[26] It is interesting to note that an Addendum to Regulation 5727, which was enacted directly by the Knesset (the Israeli parliament) in 1984, also extends the jurisdiction of Israeli civilian courts to all Jews who move to the settlements in accordance with the Law of Return, even if they do not have Israeli citizenship.[27] This Addendum was part of a package of laws passed directly by the Knesset to impose a series of Israeli laws on Israeli settlers in relation to military service, Income Tax Ordinance, Population Registry, National Insurance, etc., bringing them further into Israeli jurisdiction.[28]

In 1988, the Knesset further expanded its jurisdiction over the settlements/settlers by amending the Israeli "Development Towns and Areas Law," extending its application to "local authorities and Israeli citizens"[29] in the oPt. The significance of this amendment should not go unnoticed, since it expanded the application of an Israeli law directly to the settlement authorities and the territory under their administration, as well as to Israeli citizens therein, without any recourse to military rules or ordinances. Finally, the settlements were also given the status of "National Priority Areas" under Israeli law, and receive financial incentives from the Ministry of Construction and Housing (for purchasing and building homes), the Israel Lands Administration (on construction leasing fees), the Ministry of Education (on tuition fees), the Ministry of Industry and Trade (through income-tax benefits), the Ministry of Labor and Social Affairs (via increased benefits for social workers) and the Ministry of Finance (by providing income-tax reductions).[30]

> Settlers elect their local or regional council, participate in Knesset elections, pay taxes, National Insurance and health insurance, and enjoy all the social rights granted by Israel to its citizens. If suspected of an offense

---

25 Rules of Civil Procedure (Furnishing of Documents for the Administered Territories) 5730 (1969) [Isr.]; *in* Lien, at 65.
26 Lien, at 70.
27 Amendment and Extension of the Validity of the Emergency Regulations (Judea and Samaria, the Gaza Strip, Sinai and South Sinai – Jurisdiction and Legal Assistance) Law 5744, art. 6 (1984) [Isr.].
28 Lien, at 66.
29 Development Towns and Areas Law 5748, art. 3(E) (1988) [Isr.].
30 Lien, at 70–72.

under the law, they are arrested by the civilian police and tried in civilian courts in accordance with the law applying in Israel.[31]

As Tobias Kelly explains, territorial and jurisdictional regimes should not be understood solely as government laws that regulate "lines on maps or fences on the ground, but [also] as governmental techniques that produce status differences."[32] For the author, jurisdiction is not only about separating territory, but also about separating groups of people and creating different configurations of rights therein. While Israeli citizens in the West Bank are subject to the jurisdiction of Israeli civilian courts and are judged according to Israeli domestic law, Palestinians are ruled by a blend of military law (in Israeli military courts) and local civil law. Kimmerling describes this as "an extremely original Israeli invention, providing a personal sovereignty that accompanies each settler wherever he or she goes."[33]

While Israeli settlers move freely between the settlements and the territory within the Green Line (and even benefit from the EU-Israeli visa regime), the movement of Palestinians in the West Bank is limited by hundreds of checkpoints and by the Segregation Wall. For this reason, Del Sarto considers that it is better to talk about a "borders regime" between Israel-Palestine than a border itself: "largely administered by Israel on the Israeli-Palestinian side, these borders are not defined according to contiguous territory, but rather apply to different categories of people."[34] As summed up by Human Rights Watch, Israel has created a two-tier system of laws and norms that operate in the West Bank and provide preferential services, development and benefits for Jewish-Israeli settlers while imposing harsh conditions on Palestinian-Arabs: "such different treatment, on the basis of race, ethnicity, and national origin [...] violates the fundamental prohibition against discrimination under human rights law."[35]

The legal instruments Israel imposes on the region have established Israel's border and jurisdictional regime as a complex mechanism of land

---

31 Id., at 67.
32 Tobias Kelly, *Jurisdictional Politics in the Occupied West Bank: Territory, Community and Economic Dependency in the Formation of Legal Subjects*, 31 L. & Soc. Inquiry 39, 43 (2006) [*hereinafter* Kelly].
33 Baruch Kimmerling, Clash of Identities: Explorations in Israeli and Palestinian Societies 195 (2012).
34 Raffaella Del Sarto, *Visa Regimes and the Movement of People across the EU and Israel-Palestine*, in Fragmented Borders, Interdependence and External Relations: The Israel-Palestine-European Union Triangle 55 (Raffaella Del Sarto ed., 2015) [*hereinafter* Del Sarto].
35 Human Rights Watch, *Separate and Unequal* (Dec. 2010), at 1, https://www.hrw.org/news/2010/12/19/israel/west-bank-separate-and-unequal.

appropriation and group segregation that encompasses the entire territory of the Mandate of Palestine and beyond, within which Israel has created cantons of relative autonomy for the Palestinian people. To quote Brynjar Lia, the region's "extreme territorial fragmentation [is] sometimes sarcastically described as Swiss cheese: Israel kept the cheese and left the holes for the Palestinians."[36]

This is the main point that States and regional and international organizations do not take into consideration when dealing with Israel. They assume there is a hard border to be found somewhere between Israel and Palestine – whether it is the Green Line, what had been established in UN Resolution 181 (II), or what was envisioned in Oslo II – that will enable them to clearly demarcate Israel proper from the oPt and allow them to deal with Israel in one and not in the other. This border, however, does not exist for Israel, Israelis, and the Israeli economy, though its shifting nature is felt by Palestinians on a daily basis.

III   The Illegality of the Israeli Territorial and Jurisdictional Regime

A   *Israel and International Law*

In order to address the legality of establishing a preferential tariffs regime or a free-trade zone with Israel, between its territory and the territory of another country or regional entity, one must first consider if the extent of the Israeli territory and the jurisdictional regime it has created therein is legal, for it is this territory (and the goods produced therein) that will be subjected to a free-trade zone (and the goods produced therein that will obtain a preferential treatment in relation to tariffs). It is therefore telling that the methods used by Israel to appropriate Palestinian lands violate multiple obligations contained in the HRs, such as: "private property cannot be confiscated,"[37] "pillage is formally forbidden,"[38] and that the Occupying Power [(OP)] must ensure respect for "the laws in force in the country"[39] and act only "as administrator and usufructuary of public buildings, real estate, forests and agricultural estates."[40] As to the rules of usufruct, these were extensively addressed in *USA vs. Friedrich Flick*, where the Nuremburg Military Tribunal convicted the owner

---

36   Brynjar Lia, A Police Force without a State 283 (2006).
37   Hague Convention IV – Laws and Customs of War on Land art. 46, Oct. 18, 1907, 36 Stat. 2277, 1 Bevans 631, 205 Consol T.S. 277, 3 Martens Nouveau Recueil (ser. 3) 461 [*hereinafter* Hague Regulations].
38   Id., art. 47.
39   Id., art. 43.
40   Id., art. 55.

of a German industrial conglomerate for participating in property appropriation in territories occupied by Germany. The Tribunal found a violation of Article 55 "wherever the [OP] acts or holds itself out as owner of the public property owned by the occupied country."[41] For Antonio Cassese, an OP may not exploit the inhabitants, resources, or other assets of the territory under its control for the benefit of its own territory, population or economy.[42] Israel, as the occupying State, is also forbidden from changing the character, nature, and purpose of State land, except for strict security purposes.[43]

Authors such as Salman Abu Sitta and Yehezkel Lien also consider that Israel's systematic application of different legal mechanisms to appropriate, territorially integrate, lease, and sell Palestinian lands are means of permanently expropriating these properties from their legal owners. They violate Article 147 of Fourth Geneva Convention (GCIV), which states that the "extensive destruction and appropriation of property"[44] is a grave breach of that Convention. The ICJ also confirmed that both the HRs and the GCs codify "intransgressible principles of international customary law [...] to be observed by all States whether or not they have ratified the conventions that contain them."[45] James Crawford referenced the ICJ's decision in his analysis of third-party obligations towards Israeli settlements by stating that, "according to the principles of occupation set out in these documents, an occupant acquires only temporary authority, not sovereignty, over an occupied territory."[46] Any purported annexations of occupied territory are thus ineffective in altering the international status of that territory.

On the other hand, David Kretzmer addresses this point by explaining that neither the appropriation of Palestinian land from 1948 onwards nor the "Basic Law: Israel Lands" mean that Israel holds legal ownership of the land, nor that its territory encompasses it.[47] According to Wortley, for a State or authority to acquire any title via expropriation, several conditions must be satisfied: the method of expropriation must be legal under international law;

---

41   *U.S.A. v Friedrick Flick* (US Military Tribunal at Nuremberg) (1947) *in* United Nations War Crimes Commission, Law Report of Trials of War Criminals (1949).
42   Antonio Cassese, The Human Dimension of International Law 421 (2008).
43   Id.
44   Geneva Convention Relative to the Protection of Civilian Persons in Time of War, art. 147, Aug. 12, 1949, 75 U.N.T.S 287 [*hereinafter* Fourth Geneva Convention].
45   Legality of the Threat or Use of Nuclear Weapons, Advisory Opinion, 1996 I.C.J. Rep. 226, para. 257 (July 8).
46   James Crawford, *Third-Party Obligations with Respect to Israeli Settlements in the Occupied Palestinian Territories*, Opinion (2012), at 7 [*hereinafter* Crawford], https://www.tuc.org.uk/sites/default/files/tucfiles/LegalOpinionIsraeliSettlements.pdf.
47   David Kretzmer, The Legal Status of the Arabs in Israel 62 (2002).

done in accordance with the public interest of the local population; provide for remedies and compensation; and cannot be validated retroactively if the original act of expropriation was invalid (as Israel attempted to do with "Land Acquisition (Validation of Acts and Compensation) Law").[48]

The particular way in which Israeli law combines land ownership with national territory has severe implications for its policies in the region. Because the Basic Law establishes that lands held by the Israeli State, the DA, and the JNF *are* the territory of Israel under Israeli law, any lands found to have been illegally appropriated therein and returned to their original owners (or their legal heirs) as required under international law would therefore no longer constitute part of the territory of Israel (under Israeli law). This is the particular point of inflection that helps clarify the way Israel understands the extent of its territory: Israeli law considers the lands it acquired and appropriated to be an integral part of its territory, and does not distinguish between pre-48, pre-67, or post-67 borders in its Basic Law of territoriality. In fact, Israeli law makes no reference to international borders in defining its territory in relation to Palestine. In part, this is why Israel does not consider the oPt to be a belligerently occupied territory and why it has extended its jurisdiction to the Jewish-Israeli settlements and settlers therein. The Israeli High Court of Justice, for example, has never formally recognized the occupation of the oPt nor ruled whether the GCIV applies therein, though it has occasionally referred to the law of occupation.[49]

Authors like Benedetta Voltolini and James Crawford explain that the existence of settlements in the oPt are a breach of Article 49(6) of GCIV, which explicitly prohibits the OP from "[transferring] parts of its own civilian population into the territory it occupies."[50] As noted in the ICJ's *Wall* Advisory Opinion, this provision prohibits "measures taken by an [OP] in order to organize or encourage transfers of parts of its own population into the occupied territory."[51] In its Advisory Opinion, the ICJ also found that Articles 46 and 52 of the HRs and Articles 49 and 53 of GCIV had been breached by Israel in constructing the Segregation Wall that encapsulates many settlements in the oPt.

Ultimately, the ICJ concluded "that the Israeli settlements in the [oPt] (including East Jerusalem) have been established in breach of international law."[52]

---

48   B.A. Wortley, Expropriation in International Law 27–35 (1947).
49   Benedetta Voltolini, *Territorial Borders and Functional Regimes*, *in* Del Sarto 70 [*hereinafter* Voltolini].
50   Fourth Geneva Convention art. 49 para. 6.
51   Legal Consequences of the Construction of a Wall in the Occupied Palestinian Territory (Advisory Opinion), 2004 I.C.J. Rep 136, para. 120 (July 9) [*hereinafter* ICJ Wall].
52   Id.

Even though the Advisory Opinion does not have binding force, Crawford explains that it constitutes a declaration of international law and cannot be disregarded by the UN Members.[53] Furthermore, UNGA Resolution ES-10/15 (2004), which addresses the ICJ's findings, calls upon all UN Member States "to comply with their legal obligations as mentioned in the Advisory Opinion."[54] All EU Member States voted in favor of the Resolution, thus committing themselves even further to what they themselves defined as the "legal obligations" set out in the Advisory Opinion.

If all these illegalities surround Israel and its occupation of the oPt, there is little doubt third party States have the responsibility not to assist Israel in committing these violations, though the extent of the measures they must undertake to do so must be further fleshed out.

B   Third-Party State Responsibility

In the Advisory Opinion, the ICJ confirmed that Palestinians have a right to self-determination, that all States party to GCIV have an obligation to "ensure compliance by Israel with international humanitarian law",[55] and that all States are under an obligation not to recognize the illegal situation resulting from the construction of the Segregation Wall (which largely separates the settlements from the rest of the oPt) or "render aid or assistance in maintaining the situation created by such construction."[56] In relation to the right to self-determination contained in the International Covenant on Civil and Political Rights (ICCPR) and the International Covenant on Economic, Social, and Cultural Rights (ICESCR),[57] authors like Antonio Cassese[58] and Malcom Shaw[59] have classified it as a *jus cogens* right, and the ICJ confirmed its *erga omnes* character.[60] The UN Human Rights Committee's interpretation of the right to self-determination in the ICCPR clearly states: "this right entails corresponding duties for all States and the international community."[61] Tom Moerenhout adds, consistent with the ICJ's Advisory Opinion, that the right

---

53   Crawford, at 6.
54   G.A. Resolution ES-10/15, para. 71 (Aug. 2, 2004).
55   ICJ Wall, para. 159.
56   Id.
57   International Covenant on Economic, Social and Cultural Rights, Dec. 16, 1966, 993 U.N.T.S. 3; International Covenant on Civil and Political Rights, Dec. 16, 1966, 999 U.N.T.S. 171.
58   Antonio Cassese, International Law 65 (2nd ed., 2005).
59   Malcolm Shaw, International Law 808 (6th ed., 2008).
60   Crawford, at 11–13.
61   UN Human Rights Comm., *General Comment No.12: The right to self-determination of peoples (Art. 1)*, at para. 5 (Mar. 13, 1984).

to self-determination, the prohibition of acquiring territory by force, the violation of core humanitarian norms and the prohibition of instituting apartheid all "constitute *jus cogens* violations in the case of Israel's settlement enterprise in Palestine."[62]

The importance of the ICJ's decision therefore lies in its finding that third States are under the obligation not to recognize, aid or assist Israel in relation to the settlements. In its reading of GCIV Art. 1, the ICJ concluded that "every State party to that Convention […] is under an obligation to ensure that the requirements of the instruments in question are complied with."[63] Whilst Sassòli argues that third States must claim cessation and reparation from the responsible State in the interest of the injured State, Crawford takes a more conservative position, claiming third States only breach international law when they directly aid or assist the commission of an internationally wrongful act (apropos Art. 16 of the International Law Commission (ILC) Articles on State Responsibility).[64] It is important to note, however, that State practice does not impose "upper limits on how a State may 'ensure respect'" for the GCIV.[65] For Crawford, nevertheless, State action should be limited to non-recognition, imposition of economic measures, exclusion from international organization, or the creation of investigative committees.[66]

In relation to non-recognition, the ICJ's *Namibia* Advisory Opinion determined that States are under an obligation not to recognize an unlawful situation as lawful.[67] The Court also explained that States must not enter into treaty relations with (or apply existing treaties to) an unlawful regime with regard to the disputed territory, except for multilateral conventions invoked in benefit of the occupied population, and should refrain from diplomatic relations that imply recognition of the unlawful regime's authority over the occupied territory.[68] The Court also determined that States had an obligation to refrain from "lending any support or any form of assistance to South Africa

---

62 Tom Moerenhout, *The Consequence of the UN Resolution on Israeli Settlements for the EU: Stop Trade with Settlements*, EJIL: Talk! (Apr. 4, 2017), https://www.ejiltalk.org/the-consequence-of-the-un-settlements-resolution-for-the-eu-stop-trade-with-settlements/.
63 ICJ Wall, para. 168.
64 Crawford, at 17–18.
65 Marco Sassòli, *Implementation Mechanisms*, in How does Law protect in War?, ICRC, https://casebook.icrc.org/law/implementation-mechanisms.
66 Crawford, at 17.
67 *See* Legal Consequences for States of the Continued Presence of South Africa in Namibia (South West Africa) notwithstanding Security Council Resolution 276 (Advisory Opinion), 1971 I.C.J. Rep. 16 (June 21).
68 Id., para. 123.

with reference to its occupation of Namibia"[69] and to "abstain from entering into economic and other forms of relationship or dealings with South Africa [...] which may entrench its authority over the Territory."[70] While the Court explained that third-States may recognize routine administrative decisions by the breaching State (*e.g.* registration of births, deaths and marriages) or decisions taken by it solely in the benefit of the local population, they must not regard as valid any acts and transactions relating to public property or public concessions. In the words of Ronen, under Article 41(2) of the ILC Articles on State Responsibility, "[a] state which does recognize as lawful a situation created through violation of a peremptory norm is itself in violation of the obligation of non-recognition."[71]

As for non-assistance, Crawford explains that this obligation encompasses acts that help preserve the illegal situation. In the case of Israel, it would extend to acts that assist in preserving: "(a) Israel's *de facto* annexation of the West Bank and other occupied territories in breach of the right to self-determination, (b) Israel's breach of Article 49(6) of [GCIV] prohibiting the transfer of populations or (c) Israel's potential breach of Article 55 of the Hague Regulations."[72] Crawford thus correctly asserts that maintaining certain economic and commercial dealings with Israel can be considered a breach of the obligation of non-recognition and amount to aid or assistance in committing an internationally wrongful act.

For him, one clear example of such economic dealings is the import of agricultural settlement goods. Since these goods rely on an irrigation system that is largely based on water appropriated from the Jordan River Basin (which has been redirected to Israel and Israeli settlements in direct violation of local[73] and international law[74]), Crawford asserts that the import and purchase of these goods amounts to aiding and assisting the commitment of an internationally unlawful act. His argument relies on Article 43 of the HRs (the OP must respect the laws in force in the country) to assert that the appropriation of water supplies constitutes a violation. Whilst his argument is sound from the position of international law, the obligation not to recognize, aid or assist these Israeli breaches of international law extends well beyond trading in agricultural settlement produce.

---

69   Id., para. 119.
70   Id., para. 124.
71   Yael Ronen, *Illegal Occupation and its Consequences*, 41 Isr. L. Rev. 201, 233 (2008).
72   Crawford, at 32.
73   Jordanian Law No. 40 (1952) [Jordan].
74   Hague Regulations, art. 42.

The question of the distribution of water within Israel-Palestine illustrates this point: whilst settlers in the oPt receive an average of 370 liters/day (*per capita*) and Israelis receive 290 liters/day, Palestinians in the West Bank receive 79 and those in Gaza get 80 (most of which they must purchase from Israel).[75] To put these values in perspective, the World Health Organization recommends a minimum of 100 (*per capita*).[76] Israel is able to guarantee this discriminatory distribution of water by maintaining military control over the two main aquifers in Palestine, as well as the Jordan River basin, and exploiting them via Israeli-State-owned company Mekorot (which provides 90% of Israel's drinking water and 70% of its general water).[77] The water Israel appropriates from the oPt constitutes approximately 60% of Israel's total water supply and permeates every aspect of Israeli life and economy.[78] In the words of the UN Secretary General, "Palestinians have virtually no control over the water resources in the West Bank."[79] While Crawford considers that third-States must refrain from trading in agricultural Israeli settlement goods because they are dependent on water acquired in breach of Article 43 of the Hague Regulations, a consistent argument can be made that most of the water Israel uses throughout its economy (on both sides of the Green Line) results from this very same breach.

Though Palestinians have a right to permanent sovereignty over their land and natural resources (gas, oil, water, minerals, etc.), as set forth in ICCPR Article 1.2, Israel has taken significant steps to curtail that sovereignty and use these lands and resources for its own benefit and for the benefit of its population within and beyond the Green Line. Whilst an import ban on (agricultural or other) Israeli settlement goods can be seen as a first step for third States to fulfil their obligations under international law, a deeper examination of the Israeli economy will reveal the legal and practical shortcomings of addressing Israeli violations in the region only by means of a ban on settlement goods.

---

75   Institute for Middle East Understanding, *Water Consumption, Israeli Settlers vs Palestinians in the Occupied Palestinian Territories* (Mar. 22, 2014), https://imeu.org/article/water-consumption-israeli-settlers-vs.-palestinians-in-the-occupied-palesti.
76   Camilla Corradin, *Israel: Water as a Tool to Dominate Palestinians*, Al Jazeera (June 23, 2016), http://www.aljazeera.com/news/2016/06/israel-water-tool-dominate-palestinians-160619062531348.html.
77   *Israel's Water Company Mekorot: Nurturing Water Apartheid in Palestine*, Stop the Wall, https://stopthewall.org/sites/default/files/Mekorot%20Factsheet%20Final.pdf.
78   Ramzi El-Houry, *The Israeli-Palestinian Water Conflict*, Muftah (2010), https://muftah.org/the-israeli-palestinian-water-conflict-by-ramzi-el-houry-3/.
79   *Israeli settlements in the Occupied Palestinian Territory, including East Jerusalem, and the occupied Syrian Golan*, Report by the Secretary-General, U.N. Doc. A/67/375 (Sept. 18, 2012), at para. 14.

IV Israel and European Union Trade

A *Israeli Settlement Goods and EU Law*

The EU-Israel AA of 2000, in its territoriality clause, restricts the free-trade zone between both parties to the "territory of Israel"[80] and to the territory of the EU.[81] The European Court of Justice (ECJ) addressed the issue of the applicability of this clause in *Brita v Hauptzollamt* by stating that "products originating in the West Bank do not fall within the territorial scope of that agreement and do not therefore qualify for preferential treatment under that agreement."[82] The Court's reasoning was centered on the existence of another trade agreement, namely the EU-PA AA, which is applicable "to the territory of the West Bank and the Gaza Strip."[83]

The ECJ recognized that the competent customs authorities of Palestine are responsible for issuing certificates of origin in the territory where Israeli settlement goods (ISGs) are produced; allowing Israeli customs authorities to issue such certificates is the equivalent of imposing a duty on the PA to refrain from its obligations under the EU-PA AA. For the ECJ, this creates an obligation for a third party (the PA) without its consent, which is incompatible with Art. 34 of the Vienna Convention on the Law of Treaties.[84] The ECJ thus concluded that ISGs should not receive any benefits under the EU-Israel AA, not because these goods are produced as a result of Israeli violations of international law, but because they are incompatible with other EU trade obligations in the region. Unfortunately, the Court did not address the legality of producing ISGs in the first place, or of importing them into the EU. This has opened up the space for much discussion in Europe around issues of "labelling" and "rules of origin."

In relation to "rules of origin," the EU entered into a technical arrangement with Israel establishing that all Israeli imports must contain the postal code and name of the city where production has taken place. Goods produced "within the territories brought under Israeli administration since June 1967"[85] are not to receive preferential treatment. The technical arrangement has allowed

---

[80] O.J. (L. 143/3), Euro-Mediterranean Agreement establishing an Association between the European Communities and their Member States and the State of Israel, art. 83 (2000).

[81] *See* Eugene Kontorovich, *Economic Dealings with Occupied Territories*, 53(1) Colum. J. Transnat'l L. 584–638 (2015).

[82] Case C-386/08, Brita GmbH v Hauptzollamt Hamburg-Hafen, 2010 E.C.R. I-01289, paras. 1–2.

[83] O.J. (L. 187), Euro-Mediterranean Interim Association Agreement between the European Community and the Palestine Liberation Organization (PLO), art. 73 (1997).

[84] Vienna Convention on the Law of Treaties art. 34, May 23, 1969, 1155 U.N.T.S. 331.

[85] O.J. (C 232/5), Notice to Importers, Imports from Israel to EU, para. 1 (2012).

Israel to continue exporting ISGs to the EU without having to recognize that these goods are produced in settlements, since Israel must only cite the city of production and can maintain its legal position that there is no distinction between its territory and the settlements. Furthermore, Israeli companies often provide post codes from offices and PO boxes located in cities within the Green Line as a way to hide the real origins of goods produced in settlements. EU Member States' customs authorities are left with the responsibility of verifying which Israeli goods have been produced in the settlements and which have been produced inside the Green Line, often with access to confusing or misleading information.

Despite the fact that the technical arrangement still imposes the same non-consenting obligation on the PA (to refrain from issuing origin certificates in most of the West Bank, since these are issued by Israel in relation to ISGs, and not the PA), the main argument raised against it is that it places EU consumers in a vulnerable position, since they cannot easily distinguish between products "Made in Israel" and products "Made in Israeli Settlements" simply by reading a post code and the name of a city. This resulted in a push within EU law towards labelling ISGs. The rationale behind labelling relies on Article 12 and 169 of the Treaty on the Functioning of the EU (TFEU) and the ECJ's ruling in *Rau v Smedt*,[86] which established that labelling constitutes an effective form of consumer protection. The European Commission thus issued an Interpretive Notice declaring that Member States may label ISGs with "expressions such as 'product from the Golan Heights (Israeli settlement)' or 'product from the West Bank (Israeli settlement)'."[87] Whilst labelling indubitably addresses certain EU consumer rights, it does very little to address the rights of Palestinians or the obligations of third States under international law. Furthermore, it postpones the need to determine whether Israeli settlement goods should be imported to the EU at all and whether the EU has an obligation to ban them. Ultimately, it transfers the burden of that decision from EU Member States to consumers, which must make use of their position in the market to attempt to ensure Israel's compliance with international law, an obligation unknown to international law.

According to Voltolini, all these factors help show that the EU-Israel AA and the free-trade zone it creates are inconsistent both with third State obligations under international law and with the EU's own definition of the territorial regime that should exist in the region (*i.e.* one based upon the need

---

86 Case 261/81, Walter Rau Lebensmittelwerke v De Smedt PVBA, 1982 E.C.R. 03961.
87 C (2015) 7834, Eur. Comm., Interpretive Notice on Indication of Origin of Goods from the Territories Occupied by Israel since June 1967 (2015), par. 10.

to differentiate between Israel and the oPt).[88] In order to rectify this position, Article 215(1) of the TFEU authorizes the European Council to provide for the "interruption or reduction, in part or completely, of economic and financial relations with one or more third countries."[89] These reductions could take the form of arms embargoes, restrictions on financial transactions, or import bans. It is worth mentioning that Art. 21 of the Treaty of the EU also imposes on the EU the obligation to ensure consistency between its different areas of external action, implying that EU trade policy should run in accordance with its human rights policy and its foreign policy.[90]

For an import ban on ISGs to be instituted at EU level, under Art. 24 and Art. 30 of the TFEU, it would have to be proposed by a Member State or by the High Representative and adopted unanimously by the European Council.[91] Though the EU has increasingly used sanctions as instruments of foreign policy (*e.g.* the current import ban on goods produced in Russian-occupied Crimea that do not have Ukrainian certificates of origin),[92] Member States are also free to take action individually against the import of ISGs.

Art. 24(2) of EU Regulation 260/2009 established that Member States may impose import prohibitions on "grounds of public morality, public policy or public security; the protection of health and life of humans."[93] Crawford explains that the obligation to comply with the requirements of international law and of non-recognition can be legally justified on said "public policy" grounds. Furthermore, he claims that no EU laws would be breached if a Member State acted to ban the import of ISGs on such grounds. States would also be able to rely on Article 2 of the EU-Israel AA, which establishes that the relationship between the Parties and the provisions of the Agreement "shall be based on respect for human rights and democratic principles, which guides their *internal and international policy*,"[94] to show how such a ban is compatible with the agreement.

Crawford also claims that an import ban on ISGs would not be in breach of obligations undertaken under General Agreement on Tariffs and Trade

---

88   Voltolini, at 82.
89   O.J. C 326, Treaty on the Functioning of the European Union art. 215(1), Dec. 13, 2007,
90   Voltolini, at 80.
91   Agnes Bertrand-Sanz, *EU-Israel Relations: Promoting and Ensuring Respect for International Law*, Euro-Mediterranean Human Rights Network (Feb. 2012), at 46, http://www.refworld.org/pdfid/51500ed42.pdf.
92   *See* O.J. (L. 229/1), Council Regulation (EU) No. 833/2014 (2014).
93   *See* O.J. (L. 84/1), Council Regulation (EC) 260/2009 of 26 Feb. 2009 on the common rules for imports (2009).
94   EU-Israel AA, art.2 [emphasis added].

(GATT) or World Trade Organization (WTO) agreements. Even though GATT Article I requires that Israel receive most favored nation treatment due to it being a WTO Member and GATT Art. XI forbids restrictions such as import bans on such nations, these provisions refer only to "products originating in the 'territory' of another WTO Member; [and] the West Bank and Gaza cannot be considered to be Israel's territory."[95] Furthermore, even if GATT was mistakenly applied to Israeli settlements in the oPt by the WTO Panel or Appellate Body, States could still rely on GATT Article XX and XXI to legally impose restrictive measures such as import bans on grounds of public morality or public security, or to comply with laws and regulations, "including those relating to customs enforcement."[96]

Despite third State obligations under international humanitarian law (IHL) and international human rights law (IHRL), and the legality of instituting an import ban on all ISGs in international and European trade law, the EU and its Member States have taken few steps in this direction. At both levels, legal action has focused mostly on instituting forms of labelling ISGs and collecting non-beneficial customs duties on them. As Crawford rightly concludes, all the legal tools for instituting an import ban exist, but the lack of political will to implement them renders the applicable norms of international law ineffective. Nevertheless, Crawford explains that the status of international law does not change because of this, and retains the potential of being actualized in reality.[97]

The work of Georg Hegel can help elucidate this point. In *Philosophy of Right*, Hegel explains that international law only exists in reality through States themselves: "[i]nternational law arises out of the relation to one another of independent states."[98] For Hegel, international law exists only in and through States, even if they institute international organizations that establish primacy over international law in certain matters (*e.g.* UNSC). When a decision by such an organization is deemed to be the law (*e.g.* a binding UNSC Resolution), this law can only be actualized through State-activity (*e.g.* by undertaking the actions prescribed in the resolution). Ultimately, only States can enact international law, even if by constituting and funding international organizations or international courts; States' collective assistance and compliance with decisions by such institutions are what bring international law into the world.

---

95 Crawford, at 57.
96 General Agreement on Tariffs and Trade, art. XX(d), Oct. 30, 1947, 61 Stat. A-11, 55 U.N.T.S. 194.
97 Crawford, at 58.
98 Georg Hegel, Philosophy of Right para. 330 (2005).

Hegel adds that "[e]ach self-dependent state has the standing of a particular will; and it is on this alone that the validity of treaties depends."[99] If States do not respect the treaties to which they are bound, hold each other accountable to norms of international law, abide by the decisions undertaken by international courts or undertake action prescribed by the UNSC, international law itself is prevented from having actual existence. This helps explain why Israeli violations of international law remain greatly unchecked: collective measures have been undertaken mainly without individual or regional State-action. For Boisson, the ICJ's Advisory Opinion shows how the obligation to ensure respect for IHL is "incumbent on the entire international community and on all States: the objective is not limited to not recognizing illegal situations; everyone must take positive action to put an end to them, by using all available and admissible legal means."[100]

B   *The Israeli Economy and EU Trade*

The distribution of land, natural resources, and legal rights within Israel-Palestine must be understood in the context of the territorial and jurisdictional regime Israel imposes therein. Whilst Israel's territorial laws attempt to incorporate all the territory under its direct control into Israel's national territory (including Area C of the West Bank), its jurisdictional laws help extend these boundaries by creating distinct categories of people out of the populations throughout the entire region.[101] The conflict between Palestinian claims to territorial sovereignty and the economic integration of the Palestinian territory, population and natural resources into the Israeli economy "have created a shifting jurisdictional regime, which has included effective annexation for Israeli citizens and a combination of military rule and partial, if extremely limited, autonomy for Palestinian subjects."[102]

According to Richard Ford, jurisdictional regimes can help legitimate social hierarchies and economic inequality, and can be used to understand how the relationship between territory, subjects and individual rights are organized in a particular context.[103] In relation to Israel-Palestine, Tobias Kelly sums up

---

99   Id., para. 336.
100   Laurence Boisson and Luigi Condorelli, *Quelques remarques à propos de l'obligation des Etats de "respecter et faire respecter" le droit international humanitaire*, in Études et essais sur le droit international humanitaire et sur les principes de la Croix-Rouge en l'honneur de Jean Pictet 2 (Christophe Swinarski ed., 1984).
101   Kelly, at 68.
102   Id.
103   *See* Richard T. Ford, *Law's Territory (A History of Jurisdiction)*, 97 Mich. L. Rev. 843–930 (1999).

what the Israeli jurisdictional regime has established in the region: "the spaces of Israeli citizenship and rights depend on the nonspaces, noncitizens and nonrights of West Bank Palestinians."[104] This analysis should be extended to the entire region, not only to the West Bank, since Israel's regime applies itself to the entire territory of the Mandate of Palestine and beyond (*e.g.* the Syrian Golan Heights).

In this regard, it is worth noting that Israel does not have two separate economies, one within the Green Line and one in the oPt. As cited by Gordon and Prado, a study by Israeli NGO "Who Profits" shows how Israeli banks within the Green Line provide "the financial infrastructure for all activities of companies, governmental agencies and individuals in the continuing occupation of Palestine and the Syrian Golan Heights."[105] As seen with the case of water, natural resources from the oPt are also used extensively for the benefit of the Israeli population and economy, regardless of the Green Line. Furthermore, the customs and monetary regimes imposed by Israel are the same on both sides of the Green Line, and most companies operating in the oPt have headquarters and industrial facilities within it, allowing them to continue avoiding EU customs duties by providing postal codes within the Green Line for goods produced in the oPt. As Gordon and Pardo explain,

> By promulgating the notion that Israel's economy is severed from the occupation, the Rules of Origin provide the EU with normative legitimation to deepen its trade ties with Israel despite its displeasure with Israel's settlement project, since the EU can accurately proclaim that it is simultaneously sanctioning Israeli industry in the OPT. The problem with this strategy is that the use of customs rules to reassert a non-existent economic border can reinforce the existing *status quo*.[106]

The implementation of the territoriality clause in the EU-Israeli AA through the technical arrangement has provided Israel's economy with normative legitimacy by inserting an imaginary distinction between Israel's economy inside the Green Line and its economy in the oPt, whilst simultaneously permitting Israel to continue to ignore this distinction. This distinction cannot be upheld because Israel's conception of territory, legal jurisdiction and economic system extends itself throughout the entire region. The role for Palestinians, within

---

104   Kelly, at 69.
105   Who Profits, *Financing the Israeli Occupation* (2010), at 6, https://whoprofits.org/report/financing-the-israeli-occupation/.
106   Neve Gordon & Sharon Pardo, *Bordering Disputed Territories*, in Del Sarto 97.

this system, is relegated to providing various forms of support for the Israeli market, especially via "an offshore structure that relies on the much cheaper Palestinian labour costs [...] which average less than 70% of those of the Israelis."[107]

As Del Sarto explains, the legal instruments Israel has instituted in Israel-Palestine aim at promoting "inclusive exclusions."[108] Economically, Israel inclusively-excludes the oPt within a "customs envelope" (or complete customs union), being responsible for collecting taxes and customs duties on behalf of the PA (and with powers to withhold them). Israel's intersecting territorial and jurisdictional borders therein ensure that it maintains control over the flow of people, goods, and capital in and out of the areas that are still under relative Palestinian control. One can thus conceive of Palestine-Israel-EU relations in terms of one extensive borderland: on one side, Palestine is confined by Israel; in the middle, Israel benefits from its control over Palestine and from a free-trade zone with the EU; on the other side, the EU trades with both entities and attempts to mediate the tensions that result from the structural imbalances that exist between them.

For Helga Tawil-Souri, Palestinians are the ones who paradoxically need more borders in order to protect themselves from the unrestricted access that Israel enjoys over the entirety of Palestine-Israel.[109] Without such borders, it is impossible for Palestinians to exercise their right to self-determination and to sovereignty over land and natural resources, and the PA cannot fulfil its duties and exercise its rights in relation to the EU-PA AA. In fact, as shown by the ECJ's ruling in *Brita*, the trade regime currently in place between Israel and the EU still imposes on the PA an obligation to which it has not consented (the obligation not to issue certificates of origin for ISGs produced in most of the territory of the West Bank). This illegal state of affairs has instituted itself because bilateral and multilateral agreements, especially those related to international trade, generally presuppose the existence of 'hard national borders' between the parties (which can then be "opened").[110] As seen, Palestinians have been deprived of such borders by Israel, and are consequently unable to exercise their rights under international law.

According to figures provided by the Israeli Foreign Ministry to the World Bank in 2012, approximately 2% of all Israeli exports to the EU are of comprised

---

107   Helga Tawil-Souri, *Between Digital Flows and Territorial Borders*, in Del Sarto 118 [*hereinafter* Tawil-Souri].
108   Del Sarto, at 6.
109   Tawil-Souri, at 118.
110   Id.

of ISGs (€230m/year).[111] In comparison, the total value of Palestinian exports to the EU in 2016 amounted to €17m.[112] Total Israeli exports to the EU for the same year were of €34b.[113] The World Bank also estimates that the Israeli occupation costs the Palestinian economy approximately €2.9b/year, and has shattered the living conditions of Palestinians in the oPt.[114] Because Israel's territorial and jurisdictional control extends itself towards all aspects of spatial politics in Israel-Palestine – from borders to infrastructure, economic sovereignty to trade agreements, exercise of individual rights to national self-determination – trade relations between the EU and Israel have only strengthened the *status quo* in the region, legitimized Israel's discriminatory economic system, and allowed Israel to maintain the same *modus operandi* of continually appropriating Palestinian land and natural resources.[115]

The EU has been largely unable to open borders with Palestine because these borders are controlled by Israel, who acts as the gatekeeper of "mutual" relations with Palestine (which can therefore hardly be characterized as mutual).[116] The issue at hand, therefore, is not the existence of multilateral and cross-border agreements in the region *per se*, but the way in which these agreements have left the unequal and repressive laws and structures instituted by Israel therein intact and unchallenged, inhibiting Palestinians to exercise their rights under international law. In the absence of a permanent and final agreement between the parties that establishes a Palestinian State with international borders and sovereignty over its lands and natural resources, the EU should seriously consider revising its trade policy with Israel, not only because it helps legitimize the illegal territorial and jurisdictional policies that Israel instituted throughout the entire region, but also because it inhibits Palestinians from exercising their (trade) rights under international law.

The EU's differentiation policy thus places the EU in an ultimately untenable position. On the one hand, it attempts to differentiate between the Israel inside the Green Line and the Israel outside the Green Line, but does

---

111 World Bank, *The Imperative for Economic Cohesion in the Palestinian Territories* (2012), at 12, http://documents.worldbank.org/curated/en/350371468141891355/pdf/760230WP0GZ0AH02Box374357B00PUBLIC0.pdf.
112 European Commission, *Palestine*, http://ec.europa.eu/trade/policy/countries-and-regions/countries/palestine/index_en.htm.
113 European Commission, *Israel*, http://ec.europa.eu/trade/policy/countries-and-regions/countries/israel/.
114 Akiva Eldar, *The profitable business of Israeli occupation*, Al-Monitor (Jan. 28, 2016), http://www.al-monitor.com/pulse/originals/2016/01/palestinians-settlements-west-bank-plants-employment-poverty.html.
115 Tawil-Souri, at 120.
116 Frederica Bicchi, *On Borderlands, Borders and Bordering Practices*, in Del Sarto 186.

not effectively apply any restrictions on the goods Israel produces outside the Green Line except for demanding a loosely-imposed and rarely-verified labelling policy on those goods. On the other hand, it effectively recognizes and accepts Israel's regime and its extension from the Mediterranean to the Jordan River, with all its implications for Palestine and Palestinians, since it continues to trade and maintain full diplomatic relations with an Israel that makes no differentiation between the territory it has acquired inside and outside the Green Line and with an Israeli economy that is both fully integrated and highly dependent on the resources it appropriates from the oPt on a daily basis.

The EU is thus faced with clear options: (i) institute a ban on Israeli settlement goods and support a differentiation policy based on a difference that does not exist on the ground; (ii) impose sanctions on Israel as a whole until such a differentiation exists (and a Palestinian State with hard international borders can be differentiated from an Israeli State with hard international borders); or (iii) continue trading with and recognizing Israel on the terms it has so far, ignoring its obligations under international law, until Palestine no longer exists.

V   Conclusion

The EU has committed itself to the rule of law, the universality and indivisibility of human rights and fundamental freedoms, the principles of equality and solidarity, and the principles of the UN Charter and international law.[117] The EU Guidelines on IHL include the use of restrictive measures and sanctions by the EU as "an effective means of promoting compliance with IHL."[118] The free-trade relations the EU currently has with Israel undermines a series of Palestinian rights, third State obligations, and the possibility of altering the *status quo* in the region in favor of a permanent solution. For Israel, whose main trading partner is the EU, the perpetuation of these trade relations is essential to give it international legitimacy and financial stability. While the EU attempts to push for a policy of "differentiation" between Israeli goods produced within and beyond the Green Line, this border does not exist (*de facto*), is not an international border (*de jure*), and only serves to obfuscate the real nature of the discriminatory territorial and jurisdictional regime Israel has instituted throughout Israel-Palestine.

---

117   Treaty on the European Union art. 2, Oct. 26, 2012, O.J. (C 326), 1.
118   O.J. (C/303 12), EU Guidelines on Promoting Compliance with International Humanitarian Law, art. 16(d) (2009).

As much as EU "differentiation policy" attempts to find a way to both reprimand Israel's illegal land and resource appropriations in the oPt *and* recognize Israel in all its capacities within the region, it is ultimately unable to address Palestinian rights and third State obligations in relation to Israeli violations. Whilst an EU import ban on ISGs is legally feasible and can be considered a first step towards addressing Israeli violations in the region, it will not be able to address the structural and economic inequalities resulting from the territorial/jurisdictional regime Israel has instituted therein because it still attempts to uphold the non-existent Green Line.

Until a final agreement is reached between Israel and Palestine, the EU should not treat the Green Line as an international border within which Israel has complete sovereignty. In order for this sovereignty to be recognized, a permanent-status agreement must be reached by Israel and Palestine. In a world where international law prohibits States from solving conflicts through the use of force (though "peoples' struggle for self-determination and liberation from colonial and foreign domination"[119] is legitimate), trade restrictions and sanctions are one of the most effective political instruments available for States and regional organizations to use against breaches of international law.

Since its establishment, Israel has constantly demanded that its right to exist be recognized. Seventy years after its Declaration of Independence, the question still begs: within which borders does Israel want the right to exist? Until this issue is resolved, the EU and its Member States should re-evaluate their trade relations with the State of Israel as a whole if they wish to fully comply with their international obligations and allow Palestinians to exercise their rights under international law. The EU and its Member States have the international legitimacy and legal mechanisms required to institute restrictions on their trade with Israel. They should do so if they wish to help steer the region towards permanent-status negotiations that could enable some form of peaceful resolution to the occupation of Palestine.

Bibliography

Abu Ayyash, Abdul-Ilah, *Israeli Planning Policy in the Occupied Territories*, 11 J. Palestine Stud. 111–123 (1981).

---

[119] G.A. Res. 2782 (XXVI), *Importance of universal realization of the right of peoples to self-determination and of the speedy granting of independence to colonial countries and peoples for the effective guarantee and observance of human rights*, art. 1 (Dec. 6, 1971).

Abu Sitta, Salman, *Israel's Seizure, Confiscation and Sale of Palestinian Property* (Palestine Land Society, 2009).

Abu-Lughod, Janet, *Israeli Settlements in Occupied Arab Lands: Conquest to Colony*, 11 J. Palestine Studies 16–54 (1982).

Aronson, Geoffrey ed., *Settlement Monitor*, 40 J. Palestine Stud. 167–176 (2010).

Beinin, Joel & Lisa Hajjar, *Palestine, Israel and the Arab-Israeli Conflict*, Middle East Research and Information Project, 2014 [*hereinafter* Beinin & Hajjar], https://merip.org/palestine-israel-primer.

Bertrand-Sanz, Agnes, *EU-Israel Relations: Promoting and Ensuring Respect for International Law*, Euro-Mediterranean Human Rights Network (Feb. 2012), http://www.refworld.org/pdfid/51500ed42.pdf.

Bicchi, Frederica, *On Borderlands, Borders and Bordering Practices*, in Fragmented Borders, Interdependence and External Relations: The Israel-Palestine-European Union Triangle (Raffaella Del Sarto ed., 2015).

Boisson, Laurence and Luigi Condorelli, *Quelques remarques à propos de l'obligation des Etats de "respecter et faire respecter" le droit international humanitaire*, in Études et essais sur le droit international humanitaire et sur les principes de la Croix-Rouge en l'honneur de Jean Pictet 2 (1984).

Boris, Dimitris, *EU-Palestinian Security Cooperation after Oslo*, in Fragmented Borders, Interdependence and External Relations: The Israel-Palestine-European Union Triangle (Raffaella Del Sarto ed., 2015).

Bronner, Stephen S & Michael J. Thompson, The Logos Reader: Rational Radicalism and the Future of Politics (2005).

Cassese, Antonio, International Law (2005).

Cassese, Antonio, The Human Dimension of International Law (2008).

Corradin, Camilla, *Israel: Water as a Tool to Dominate Palestinians*, Al Jazeera (June 23, 2016), http://www.aljazeera.com/news/2016/06/israel-water-tool-dominate-palestinians-160619062531348.html.

Crawford, James, *Third Party Obligations with Respect to Israeli Settlements in the Occupied Palestinian Territories*, Opinion (Jan. 24, 2012), https://www.tuc.org.uk/sites/default/files/tucfiles/LegalOpinionIsraeliSettlements.pdf.

D'Amato, Anthony, *Israel's Borders under International Law*, Northwestern Public Law Research Paper No. 06–34 (Jan. 11, 2007), http://dx.doi.org/10.2139/ssrn.956143.

Del Sarto, Raffaella, *Visa Regimes and the Movement of People across the EU and Israel-Palestine*, in Fragmented Borders, Interdependence and External Relations: The Israel-Palestine-Euyropean Union Triangle 55 (Raffaella Del Sarto ed., 2015).

Diplomatic Mission of Palestine, Lisbon – Portugal, *Loss of Land* (Nov. 29, 2014) http://dmop.pt/category/maps/.

Dubuisson, François, *The International Obligations of the European Union and its Member States with regard to Economic Relations with Israeli Settlements*, Université Libre de Bruxelles (Feb. 2014).

Eldar, Akiva, *The profitable business of Israeli occupation*, Al-Monitor (Jan. 28, 2016), http://www.al-monitor.com/pulse/originals/2016/01/palestinians-settlements-west-bank-plants-employment-poverty.html.

El-houry, Ramzi, *The Israeli-Palestinian Water Conflict*, Muftah (2010), https://muftah.org/the-israeli-palestinian-water-conflict-by-ramzi-el-houry-3/.

European Commission, *Israel*, http://ec.europa.eu/trade/policy/countries-and-regions/countries/israel/.

European Commission, *Palestine*, http://ec.europa.eu/trade/policy/countries-and-regions/countries/palestine/index_en.htm.

Ford, Richard, *Law's Territory (A History of Jurisdiction)*, 97 Mich. L. Rev. 843–930 (1999).

Foundation for Middle East Peace, *Borders*, 2016, http://www.merip.org/primer-palestine-israel-arab-israeli-conflict-new.

Gordon, Neve & Sharon Pardo, *Bordering Disputed Territories*, in Fragmented Borders, Interdependence and External Relations: The Israel-Palestine-European Union Triangle (Raffaella Del Sarto ed., 2015).

Gordon, Neve & Sharon Pardo, *The European Union and Israel's Occupation: Using Technical Customs Rules as Instruments of Foreign Policy*, 69 The Middle East J. 74–90 (2015).

Hegel, Georg, Philosophy of Right (2005).

Human Rights Watch, *Separate and Unequal* (Dec. 2010), https://www.hrw.org/news/2010/12/19/israel/west-bank-separate-and-unequal.

Institute for Middle East Understanding, *Water Consumption, Israeli Settlers vs Palestinians in the Occupied Palestinian Territories* (Mar. 22, 2014), https://imeu.org/article/water-consumption-israeli-settlers-vs.-palestinians-in-the-occupied-palesti.

Jabareen, Yosef, *The Geo-Political and Spatial Implications of the New Israel Land Administration Law on the Palestinians*, Adalah Newsletter, Vol. 62 (July 2009), https://www.adalah.org/uploads/oldfiles/newsletter/eng/jul09/Yosef_English_on_new_ILA_law%5B1%5D.pdf.

Kelly, Tobias, *Jurisdictional Politics in the Occupied West Bank: Territory, Community and Economic Dependency in the Formation of Legal Subjects*, 31 L. & Soc. Inquiry 39–74 (2006).

Kimmerling, Baruch, Clash of Identities: Explorations in Israeli and Palestinian Societies (2012).

Kontorovich, Eugene, *Economic Dealings with Occupied Territories*, 53(1) Colum. J. Transnat'l L. 584–638 (2015).

Kretzmer, David, The Legal Status of the Arabs in Israel (2002).

Larudee, Paul, *Is the Custodian of Absentee Property Awaiting the Absentees?*, Dissident Voice (Apr. 8, 2013), http://dissidentvoice.org/2013/04/is-the-custodian-of-absentee-property-awaiting-the-absentees.

Levinson, Chaim, *Just 0.7% of State Land in the West Bank Has Been Allocated to Palestinians, Israel Admits*, Ha'aretz (Mar. 28, 2013), http://www.haaretz.com/

israel-news/just-0-7-of-state-land-in-the-west-bank-has-been-allocated-to-palestinians-israel-admits.premium-1.512126.

Lia, Brynjar, A Police Force without a State (2006).

Lien, Yehezkel, *Land Grab: Israel's Settlement Policy in the West Bank*, B'Tselem (2002), https://www.btselem.org/download/200205_land_grab_eng.pdf.

Lovatt, Hugh & Mattia Toaldo, *EU Differentiation and Israeli Settlements* (July 2015), European Council on Foreign Relations, http://www.ecfr.eu/publications/summary/eu_differentiation_and_israeli_settlements3076.

Moerenhout, Tom, *Just Trade and Foreign Policy: Case Study of the Legal Permissibility and Political Feasibility of Ceasing Trade with Israeli Settlements in Occupied Territories* (SSRN, Oct. 31, 2012) https://ssrn.com/abstract=2168748.

Moerenhout, Tom, *The Consequence of the UN Resolution on Israeli Settlements for the EU: Stop Trade with Settlements*, EJIL: Talk! (Apr. 4, 2017), https://www.ejiltalk.org/the-consequence-of-the-un-settlements-resolution-for-the-eu-stop-trade-with-settlements/.

Ronen, Yael, *Illegal Occupation and its Consequences*, 41 Isr. L. Rev. 201–245 (2008).

Rosen, Steven J., *A European Boycott of Israel?*, The Middle East Quarterly (Spring 2014) http://www.meforum.org/3747/europe-boycott-israel.

Sassòli, Marco, *Implementation Mechanisms*, in How does Law protect in War?, ICRC, https://casebook.icrc.org/law/implementation-mechanisms.

Shaw, Malcolm, International Law 808 (6th ed., 2008).

Stop the Wall, *Israel's Water Company Mekorot: Nurturing Water Apartheid in Palestine*, https://stopthewall.org/sites/default/files/Mekorot%20Factsheet%20Final.pdf.

Tawil-Souri, Helga, *Between Digital Flows and Territorial Borders*, in Fragmented Borders, Interdependence and External Relations: The Israel-Palestine-European Union Triangle (Raffaella Del Sarto ed., 2015).

Tonutti, Alessandro, *Feasting on the Occupation: Illegality of Settlement Produce and the Responsibility of EU Member States under International Law*, Al-Haq (2013), http://www.alhaq.org/publications/Feasting-on-the-occupation.pdf.

Tute, R.C., The Ottoman Land Laws (1927).

Voltolini, Benedetta, *Territorial Borders and Functional Regimes*, in Fragmented Borders, Interdependence and External Relations: The Israel-Palestine-European Union Triangle (Raffaella Del Sarto ed., 2015).

Who Profits, *Financing the Israeli Occupation* (2010), https://whoprofits.org/report/financing-the-israeli-occupation/.

World Bank, *The Imperative for Economic Cohesion in the Palestinian Territories* (2012), http://documents.worldbank.org/curated/en/350371468141891355/pdf/760230WP0GZ0AH02Box374357B00PUBLIC0.pdf.

Wortley, B.A., Expropriation in International Law (1947).

The Legality of the Use of Force for Self-Determination

Sean Shun Ming Yau[*]

Contents

I Introduction
II Self-Determination as a Positive Right
   A *Historical Emergence of Self-Determination as a Principle of Law*
   B *Self-Determination as an Enforceable Right*
   C *The Typology of Self-Determination*
III The Continued Relevance of Self-Determination in Today's World
IV The Use of Force for Self-Determination and International Law
   A *Peoples as the Beneficiaries of Self-Determination*
      1 People as the *sine qua non*
      2 Representative Entities
      3 The Issue of "Puppet Regimes"
   B *The Prohibition on the Use of Force and the Principle of Territorial Integrity*
      1 The Applicability Question
      2 The "Fluidity" of the Notion of Sovereignty
      3 Territorial Integrity as a Rebuttable Presumption
   C *The Use of Force as a Derivative Right*
      1 Self-Defense
      2 By Necessary Implication
   D *Reappraisal*
      1 The Neutrality of International Law
      2 The Contingency of Illegality
V Conclusion

---

[*] Researcher, Amsterdam Center for International Law, University of Amsterdam. Research Assistant, International Law Commission. LLM (Leiden). LLB (Hong Kong). The author wishes to thank Professors John Dugard and Pavel Šturma for the insightful discussions.

I Introduction

Self-determination is a complex animal. It is the only principle in international law which is so antithetical to State centricity – the premise of the legal architecture – and yet is one of the most fundamental principles of the discipline. More than 70 years after the adoption of the United Nations (UN) Charter, when the principle of self-determination first became black-letter law, today almost every aspect of its scope and content remains highly unsettled. To some, this concern is immaterial because they consider the principle obsolete and no longer applicable in today's world. Over the past decade, the International Court of Justice (ICJ), in its Advisory Opinions on *Kosovo* and recently on *Chagos*, has shown otherwise. It not only left the door open whether international law permits a right to secession; even more, it demonstrated that the process of decolonization might be void if unlawfully completed.

The article taps into one of the biggest nuances in this area of law: the use of force in the exercise of the right to self-determination, with a particular reference to Palestine. This is not least because the use of force has often been the means resorted to in historical attempts to achieve self-determination. Nonetheless, neither courts and tribunals nor academic scholars have seriously studied the issue.[1] The question *whether or not the use of force for self-determination is lawful* is also particularly interesting from a legal perspective. It is one of the few phenomena of international life where two legal norms, both with a hierarchical superiority – namely the prohibition on the use of force and the right to self-determination – seem to collide. But as this article will argue, both norms do not generate the definitive prohibition or permission

---

1 The issue of the use of force for self-determination has been discussed in literature. *See, e.g.*, Aureliu Cristescu, UN Special Rapporteur of the Sub-Commission on Prevention of Discrimination and Protection of Minorities, *The Right to Self-Determination: Historical and Current Development on the Basis of United Nations Instruments* (1981) [hereinafter Cristescu]; Heather Wilson, International Law and the Use of Force by National Liberation Movements (1988) [*hereinafter* Wilson]; Elizabeth Chadwick, Self-Determination, Terrorism, and the International Humanitarian Law of Armed Conflict (1996); Antonio Cassese, Self-Determination of Peoples: A Legal Reappraisal 193 ff (1995) [*hereinafter* Cassese]; Christine Gray, International Law and the Use of Force 63 (2008) [*hereinafter* Gray]; Elizabeth Chadwick, *National Liberation in the Context of Post- and Non-Colonial Struggles for Self-Determination*, in The Oxford Handbook of the Use of Force in International Law 841 (Marc Weller ed.; 2015); John Dugard, *The OAU and Colonialism: An Inquiry into the Plea of Self-Defence as a Justification of the Use of Force in the Eradication of Colonialism*, 46 Int' l & Comp. L. Q. 157, 172 ff (1967) [*hereinafter* Dugard]; Kieran O'Reilly and Noelle Higgins, *The Use of Force, Wars of National Liberation and the Right to Self-Determination in the South Ossetian Conflict*, 9 Int'l Crim. L. Rev. 567 (2009); Georges Abi-Saab, *Wars of National Liberation and the Laws of War*, 3 Annals Int'l Stud. 93 (1972).

concerning the use of force for self-determination. Thus, we are in a grey area of law where a specific act is unregulated.

II Self-Determination as a Positive Right

The last century has seen the transformation of self-determination originally from a political concept void of legal meaning, to a principle of law capable of generating a positive right for its beneficiaries (*Part A*). As the right to self-determination became enforceable, its legal consequences had crystallized under customary international law as a result of a process of norm-formation within the UN and through State practice (*Part B*). In this process, international law has universalized the principle of self-determination by developing its external and internal dimensions. While external self-determination may be realized through independence or the free association/integration with another State, internal self-determination ensures that a requisite degree of self- or representative government is put in place within the territorial borders of an already existing State (*Part C*).

A   *Historical Emergence of Self-Determination as a Principle of Law*

The term "self-determination" started to gain traction during the First World War.[2] Lenin was the first forceful proponent for a principle of self-determination at the international level.[3] He produced *On Imperialism* in 1915 with a socialist focus on the liberation of oppressed peoples, and *Theses on the Socialist Revolution and the Right of Nations to Self-Determination* in 1916, which enunciated the principle of self-determination comprehensively for the first time.[4] Lenin understood the principle of self-determination to entail two things: first, the principle was to be applied after inter-State conflicts for the allocation of territories, thereby prohibiting any annexation against the will of the peoples concerned; second, the principle was to grant ethnic or national groups the right to freely decide their destiny, including the "complete freedom to agitate for secession and for a referendum on secession by the

---

2   Manfred Lachs, *The Right of Self-Determination*, in Collected Courses of the Hague Academy of International Law, Vol. 169 45 (1980) [*hereinafter* Lachs] (pointing out that before the WWI, the principle of self-determination had been applied, albeit conceptually, such as in the Declaration of the Rights of Man).
3   To be sure, in 1913, Stalin had written a detailed pamphlet on the subject. *See* Ian Brownlie, *An Essay in the History of the Principle of Self-Determination*, in Grotian Society Papers 1968: Studies in the History of the Law of Nations 93 (Charles H. Alexandrowicz ed., 1968).
4   Vladimir Lenin, Selected Works 157, 159 (1969).

seceding nations."[5] According to this latter point, liberating peoples from oppressive regimes was necessary in pursuing a socialist integration of fragmented independent States.[6]

In 1918, former United States (US) President Woodrow Wilson delivered his "Fourteen Points" speech as a proposal for a post-WWI peace settlement. The concept of self-determination was most manifest in Point 5, which proposed "[a] free, open-minded, and absolutely impartial adjustment of all colonial claims, based upon a strict observance of the principle that in determining all such questions of sovereignty the interests of the populations concerned must have equal weight with the equitable claims of the government whose title is to be determined." The concept was extended to the proposed restructuring of the central European States from the Ottoman and Austro-Hungarian empires, which, in Wilson's view, demanded the creation of new States and autonomies (*e.g.* Poland, Romania, Serbia and Montenegro).[7] Beyond the external dimension of self-determination, Wilson further constructed the notion of "self-government." In particular, Point 6 stressed Russia's "independent determination of her own political development and national policy."[8]

The Covenant of the League of Nations unfortunately did not encapsulate *per se* the concept of self-determination as the big powers did not pursue its codification.[9] In order to consolidate the then existing sovereigns, Article 10 of the Covenant required that "[t]he Members of the League undertake to respect and preserve as against external aggression the territorial integrity and existing political independence of all Members...". Even though the League was frequently called upon to deal with questions involving group rights, including allocating territorial sovereignty under the Versailles Peace Treaty, it did not have opportunities to develop the "law" of self-determination in a significant way.[10] The International Commission of Jurists in the *Aland Islands* case thus observed that, at the time, "[t]he recognition of this principle [of self-determination] in a certain number of international treaties cannot be

---

5   Id., at 159.
6   Id., at 160.
7   Points 9–13. *See* Woodrow Wilson, *Fourteen Points speech of 8 January 1918*, reprinted in Saul K. Padover, Wilson's Ideals 109 (1942).
8   On Wilson's notion of "self-government", *see* Michla Pomerance, *The United States and Self-Determination: Perspectives on the Wilsonion Conception*, 70 Am. J. Int'l L. 1 (1976).
9   Lansing noted that the idea of self-determination was not consistently pursued by Wilson and the US delegation, and was opposed by the United Kingdom. *See* Robert Lansing, The Peace Negotiations 94 (1921); Alfred Cobban, National Self-Determination 11 (1949).
10 For the result of the territorial delimitation post-Versailles, *see* The Versailles Treaty, Part III, June 28, 1919.

considered as sufficient to put it upon the same footing as a positive rule of the Law of Nations."[11]

This silence lasted until the San Francisco Conference in April 1945.[12] The attempt to formulate the principle of self-determination in the UN Charter was met with divided views. The Soviet Union, supported by the Afro-Asian States, insisted on inserting the text on self-determination.[13] The provision was introduced in the First Committee and confronted by a number of States with reservations.[14] For instance, the Belgian delegation pointed to the legal uncertainty of the principle, such as whether States were duty-bound to intervene in furtherance of self-determination.[15] The Colombian delegation formally declared to only accept it on the condition that self-determination meant "self-government", and for it to connote "a right of withdrawal or secession" would be "international anarchy."[16] At the end of the Conference, it was agreed that "an essential element of the principle [of self-determination] is free and genuine expression of the will of the people."[17] In finalizing draft Article 1, the First Committee attached the clarification that the principle only implied a right of self-government of peoples, rather than a right of secession.[18] Article 1 of the Charter now provides:

11 *See* Rapport de la Commission Internationale de jurists chargée par le Conseil de la Société des Nations de donner un avis consultative sur certains aspects juridiques de la question des iles d'Aland, in La question des lies d'Aland. Documents diplomatiques publies par le Ministeérés Affaires Étrangères (1920), at 68–70.
12 This is despite the fact that a number of agreements were concluded after the WWI between newly independent States and their parent States. *See* Lachs, at 43.
13 *See* Ruth B. Russell, A History of the United Nations Charter 62 (1958).
14 Documents de la Conférence des Nations Unies sur l'Organisation international, Vol. VI, 1945, at 296 [*hereinafter* UNCIO].
15 Id., at 300 (Belgium issuing a memorandum proposing to strike out the entire draft provision).
16 Minutes of the First Committee, First Commission of the San Francisco Conference, May, 14–151945, at 20, 24 (Egypt warning the potential manipulation of the principle of self-determination in cases of military invasion and annexations) [*hereinafter* Minutes].
17 UNCIO, Vol. VI, 1945, at 296, 455. *See also* Minutes, at 12 (Syria stating that self-determination could be achieved only if the people concerned was able to express its genuine will).
18 UNCIO, Vol. VI, 1945, at 298 ("On a déclaré que ce principe n'était compatible avec les butsde la Charte que dans la mesure où il impliquait, pour les peuples, le droit des'administrer eux-mêmes, mais non pas le droit de secession"). This was confirmed by the Syrian delegation that the possibility was ruled out to rely on Article 1(2) in order to recognize the right of national minority groups to secede from sovereign States. *See* UNCIO, Vol. VI, 1945, at 455.

THE LEGALITY OF THE USE OF FORCE FOR SELF-DETERMINATION   37

> The Purposes of the [UN] are:…(2) To develop friendly relations among nations based on respect for the principle of equal rights and self-determination of peoples, and to take other appropriate measures to strengthen universal peace;[19]

Accordingly, Article 1(2) is the result of a process of converting self-determination as a political concept into a principle of law, albeit not so much as a *legal right* in 1945 when the text was drafted.[20] Furthermore, the provision did not seem to contemplate its application to colonial situations. No explicit reference to colonialism was made either during the negotiations or in the early years of the UN.[21]

B *Self-Determination as an Enforceable Right*

While the content of Article 1(2) remained disputed, its codification assisted the principle of self-determination to later evolve into a positive right under international law. In the early 1950s and the 1960s, with the strong support of the developing countries, the principle of self-determination was repeatedly invoked within the UN to call upon the termination of colonial rule. As the Western countries gradually gave way to this trend, there emerged an international consensus for customary obligations to decolonize and to transmit information to the UN on political progress.[22] This consensus was reflected in two important resolutions adopted by the UN General Assembly (UNGA) in 1960.

The first one was Resolution 1514(XV) ("Declaration on Granting Independence to Colonial Countries and Peoples").[23] It provides that "[a]ll

---

19   U.N. Charter, art. 1. Separately, U.N. Charter art. 55(c) in Chapter IX further stresses the promotion of human rights and fundamental freedoms "based on respect for the principle of equal rights and self-determination of peoples."

20   Rosalyn Higgins, Problems and Process: International Law and How We Use It 112 (1995) [*hereinafter* Higgins] ("The concept of self-determination did not then [in 1945], originally, seem to refer to a right of dependent peoples to be independent, or, indeed, even to vote."). *See also* Legal Consequences of the Separation of the Chagos Archipelago from Mauritius in 1965, Advisory Opinion, 2019 I.C.J. Rep. Gen. List 169, paras. 150–153 (Feb. 25) [*hereinafter* ICJ Chagos] (reviewing that a *right* to self-determination emerged under customary in the 1950s to 1960s).

21   The uncertainty of Article 2(1) was reflected in the ICJ's silence in *Portugal v. India* in 1957, where the Court avoided answering on the impact of the principle of self-determination on Portugal's alleged right of passage in a colonial territory. *See* Right of Passage over Indian Territory (Portugal v. India), Preliminary Objections, 1957 I.C.J. Rep. 125 (Nov. 26).

22   Higgins, at 113.

23   Proclaiming "the necessity of brining to a speedy and unconditional end colonialism in all its forms and manifestations." Passed by a vote of 89 to 0, with 9 abstentions (Australia,

peoples have the right to self-determination; by virtue of that right they freely determine their political status and freely pursue their economic, social and cultural development."[24] Recently, in its Advisory Opinion on *Chagos*, the ICJ considered Resolution 1514 (XV) to be "a defining moment in the consolidation of State practice on decolonization."[25] The second one was Resolution 1541 (XV) (annexing the "Principles which should guide Members in determining whether or not an obligation exists to transmit the information called for in Article 73(e) of the Charter of the [UN]").[26] Like Resolution 1514 (XV), it similarly stressed the "free and voluntary choice by the peoples of the territory concerned" as the prerequisite.[27]

The subsequent practice on Article 1(2) of the UN Charter, namely the repeated adoption of resolutions[28] applying it specifically to colonial and dependent peoples, created the legal normativity for the principle of self-determination to eventually crystallize into a positive right.[29] Writing in 1963, Rosalyn Higgins observed that the dynamics within the UN had converted the principle of self-determination into "a legal right enforceable here and now."[30] Cherif Bassiouni observed that "'[s]elf-determination' is a catch-all concept which exists as a principle, develops into a right under certain circumstances, unfolds as a process and results in a remedy."[31]

Belgium, Dominican Republic, France, Portugal, Spain, South Africa, the United Kingdom and the United States).

24 G.A. Res. 1514(XV), *Declaration on the Granting of Independence to Colonial Countries and Peoples* (Dec. 14, 1960), para. 2.

25 ICJ Chagos, para. 150.

26 Passed by a vote of 69 to 2 (Portugal and South Africa), with 21 abstentions (mostly socialist and some Western countries). *See* G.A. Res. 1541(XV), *Principles which should guide members in determining whether or not an obligation exists to transmit the information called for under Article 73e of the Charter* (Dec. 15, 1960).

27 Annex, Principle VII (a). However, the free will requirement is not without exception. For instance, the ICJ in *Western Sahara* acknowledged that "in certain cases the [UNGA] has dispensed with the requirement of consulting the inhabitants of a given territory [...] in view of special circumstances." *See* Western Sahara, Advisory Opinion, 1975 I.C.J. Rep. 12, para. 59 (Oct. 16) [*hereinafter* ICJ Western Sahara].

28 In addition to Resolutions 1514(XV) and 1541(XV), *see* G.A. Res. 1471(XIV) (Dec. 12, 1959); G.A. Res. 637(VII) (Dec. 16, 1952); G.A. Res. 738(VIII) (Nov. 28, 1953); G.A. Res. 1188(XII) (Dec. 11, 1957).

29 *See* Lachs, at 47 (taking the view that the right to self-determination was already in positive law; the UN Charter was to simply "give it a more precise formulation").

30 Rosalyn Higgins, Development of International Law through the Political Organs of the United Nations 100 (1963).

31 Charles W. Yost and M. Cherif Bassiouni, *'Self-Determination' and the Palestinians* 65 Am. J. Int'l L. 31, 33 (1971) [*hereinafter* Bassiouni]. *See also* Cassese, at 72 (noting that "in the 1960s there evolved in the world community a set of general standards specifying the

To be sure, the principle of self-determination had only been applied to colonies (a term often used interchangeably with "non-self-governing territories").[32] Between 1945 and 1965, already more than 50 countries benefited from the process of decolonization and gained independence. The ICJ in its *Namibia* Advisory Opinion summarized the legal position and held that: "[t]he subsequent development of international law in regard to non-self-governing territories, as enshrined in the Charter of the [UN], made the principle of self-determination applicable to all of them."[33] In addition to *Namibia*, the ICJ subsequently applied the principle of self-determination to other colonial territories to generate a legal entitlement (*i.e.* a right) for the people concerned, including in the *Western Sahara* and *Wall* Advisory Opinions, and the cases concerning *Burkina Faso v. Mali* and *Guinea-Bissau v. Senegal*.[34]

C   *The Typology of Self-Determination*

It should be noted that the established right to self-determination in the (colonial) situations discussed so far is of an external dimension, *i.e.* the freedom to determine the external political status of a territory. Resolution 1541(XV) thus enunciates three possible modes of implementation in the exercise of the people's right, namely: "(*a*) Emergence as a sovereign independent State; (*b*) Free association with an independent State; or (*c*) Integration with an independent State."[35]

A subsequent – often regarded as foundational – resolution of the UNGA in 1970, Resolution 2625, reaffirmed these modes of implementation.[36]

---

principle of self-determination enshrined in the [UN] Charter, with special regard to colonial peoples").

[32] The term "non-self-governing territories" has a broader connotation to include all territories that generally "have not yet attained independence." *See* ICJ Chagos, at 31.

[33] Legal Consequences for States of the Continued Presence of South Africa in Namibia (South West Africa) notwithstanding Security Council Resolution 276 (1970), Advisory Opinion, 1971 I.C.J. Rep. 16, at 31 (June 21) [*hereinafter* ICJ Namibia]. *See also* ICJ Western Sahara, para. 162 (speaking of "the principle of self-determination as a right of peoples, and its application for the purpose of bringing all colonial situations to a speedy end").

[34] ICJ Namibia at 63; ICJ Western Sahara, paras. 55, 61, 62; Legal Consequences of the Construction of a Wall in the Occupied Palestinian Territory, Advisory Opinion, 2004 I.C.J. Rep. 136, paras. 87, 118, 122, 149, 155, 159 (July 9) [*hereinafter* ICJ Wall]; Frontier Dispute (Burk. Faso v. Mali), Judgment, 1986 I.C.J. Rep. 554 (Dec. 22) [ICJ Frontier Dispute]; Arbitral Award of 31 July 1989 (Guinea-Bissau v. Sen.), Judgment, 1991 I.C.J. Rep. 53, at 423 (Nov. 21) [ICJ Arbitral Award].

[35] G.A. Res. 2625(XXV), *Declaration on Principles of International Law Concerning Friendly Relations and Co-operation among States in Accordance with the Charter of the United Nations* (Oct. 24, 1970), Principle V [*hereinafter* Friendly Relations Declaration].

[36] Friendly Relations Declaration, Principle V, para. 4.

Resolution 2625, entitled the "Declaration on Principles of International Law Concerning Friendly Relations and Co-operation among States in Accordance with the Charter of the [UN]", reaffirms in its Principle V, paragraph 1, that "all peoples have the right freely to determine, without external interference, their political status and to pursue their economic, social and cultural development." Paragraph 2 provides that this right is "in order to bring a speedy end to colonialism ... bearing in mind that subjection of peoples to alien subjugation, domination and exploitation constitutes a violation of the principle [of self-determination]." This *external* dimension of self-determination, having particular regard to colonial and subjugated peoples, is to be viewed against the separate development in international law which, not long after, recognized *internal* self-determination.

The two 1966 human rights Covenants are indicative of this development. During the negotiations of the International Covenant on Civil and Political Rights (ICCPR) and the International Covenant on Economic, Social and Cultural Rights (ICESCR), there was an attempt to insert a provision on the right to self-determination in the Third Committee of the UNGA. Despite the consensus in favor of the provision, States were divided on the question of who were the beneficiaries. While some focused only on colonial peoples,[37] those who proposed that the right extend to all the peoples opposed by their governments received strong support.[38] Ultimately, Soviet Union's draft proposal to limit the right to self-determination to the territories of dependent peoples was rejected and replaced by Egypt's amendment to cover "all countries without exception."[39] This broad construction, however, came with the understanding that self-determination meant self-government, *i.e.* the freedom from an authoritarian regime.[40] The final text of Article 1(1) in both Covenants provides that "All peoples have the right of self-determination. By virtue of that right

---

37 *See e.g.* U.N. Doc. A/C.3/SR.310 (Nov. 10, 1950), paras. 7–11 [Mexico]; U.N. Doc. A/C.3/SR.367 (Dec. 12, 1951), para. 42; U.N. Doc. A/C.3/SR.398 (Jan. 22, 1952), paras. 32–34; U.N. Doc. A/C.3/SR.400 (Jan. 23, 1952), para. 9 [Liberia].

38 *See e.g.* U.N. Doc. A/C.3/SR.309 (Nov. 9, 1950), para. 53 [Afghanistan]; U.N. Doc. A/C.3/SR.399 (Jan. 23, 1951), para. 4 [India]; U.N. Doc. A/C.3/SR.364 (Dec. 10, 1951), para. 19 [United States]; U.N. Doc. A/C.3/SR.645 (Oct. 27, 1955), para. 24 [El Salvador]; U.N. Doc. A/C.3/SR.649 (Nov. 1, 1955), paras. 29–30 [Lebanon]; U.N. Doc. A/C.3/SR.649 (Nov. 1, 1955), para. 9 [New Zealand]; U.N. Doc. A/C.3/SR.652 (Nov. 4, 1955), para. 24 [United Kingdom]; U.N. Doc. A/C.3/SR.677 (Nov. 30, 1955), para. 27 [Denmark].

39 U.N. Doc. A/C.4/SR.255 (May 9, 1952), para. 10.

40 *See e.g.* U.N. Doc. A/C.3/SR.310 (Nov. 10, 1950), para. 14 [India] (explaining that "individual and political rights could not be implemented if the people to whom they had been granted lived under a despotic regime" and that "the will of the people should be the basis of the authority of government"); U.N. Doc. A/C.3/SR.397 (Jan. 21, 1951), para. 5 [Syria];

they freely determine their political status and freely pursue their economic, social and cultural development."

While the provision directly adopted the language in UNGA Resolution 1514(XV), the right to self-determination in these two instruments entailed different scopes of application, with Resolution 1514(XV) granting external political choice, *i.e.* independence, to colonial peoples, and the Covenants having the extended consequence of self-government of all peoples in an internal socio-political context.[41] This internal/external dichotomy of self-determination within the remit of Article 1(1) of the Covenants has been confirmed by the opinion of the Human Rights Committee.[42] Subsequent human rights instruments[43] have likewise included a provision on self-determination, in a broad sense, to all peoples, legitimizing the view that the right to self-determination is "free-standing" and "universal" notwithstanding decolonization.[44]

U.N. Doc. A/C.3/SR.253 (Apr. 30, 1952), para. 13 [Pakistan]; U.N. Doc. A/C.3/SR.254 (Apr. 30, 1952), para. 9 [Lebanon].

[41] Higgins, at 117. India's Declarations: "the right of self-determination appearing in [this article] apply only to the peoples under foreign domination and that these words do not apply to sovereign independent States or to a section of a people or nation." This was objected by France, the Netherlands, Germany, and Pakistan.

[42] Regarding external self-determination, *see e.g. Gillot et al. v. France*, U.N. Hum. Rts. Comm., Commc'n No. 932/2000, U.N. Doc. CCPR/C/75/D/932/2000 (July 21, 2002), para. 14.7 (holding that, with respect to the referendum in New Caledonia, the cut-off points for the length of residence criterion "are not excessive inasmuch as they are in keeping with the nature and purpose of these ballots, namely a self-determination process involving the participation of persons able to prove sufficiently strong ties to the territory whose future is being decided"); U.N. Hum. Rts. Comm., Commc'n No. 1962/2010, U.N. Doc. CCPR/C/107/D/1962/2010 (May 13, 2013) (inadmissible complaint concerning southern Cameroon). Regarding internal self-determination, *see, e.g., Mahuika et al. v. New Zealand*, U.N. Hum. Rts. Comm., Commc'n No. 547/1993, U.N. Doc. CCPR/C/70/D/547/1993 (Nov. 16, 2000), para. 9.2 (holding that "the provisions of article 1 may be relevant in the interpretation of other rights protected by the Covenant, in particular article 27 [on the right of minorities]"). *See also Tiina Sanila-Aikio v. Finland*, U.N. Hum. Rts. Comm., Commc'n No. 2668, 2015, U.N. Doc. CCPR/C/199/D/2668/2015 (Oct. 16, 2018), para. 8.6 (with respect to the right to control tribal fisheries, rejecting the complainant's claim on Article 1 because "an author, as an individual, cannot claim under the Optional Protocol to be a victim of a violation of the right of self-determination enshrined in article 1 of the Covenant, which deals with rights conferred upon peoples, as such").

[43] Helsinki Final Act art. VIII, Aug. 1, 1975, 14 I.L.M. 1292; African Charter on Human and Peoples' Rights art. 20, June 27, 1981, 21 I.L.M. 59.

[44] *See e.g.* U.N. Secretary-General, *Annotations on the Text of the Draft International Covenants on Human Rights*, U.N. Doc. A/2929 (July 1, 1955), at 14; Higgins, at 117; Lachs, at 50.

However, the binary understanding of internal/external self-determination may oversimplify the actual practice, which has proved more complex. In the absence of any institutional arrangement, the right of a people to determine their external political fate may be rendered meaningless. In the case of Palestine, the Israeli-Palestinian Interim Agreement stipulates in Articles I and V(2) that the process of determining the international status of the Palestinian territories will be the outcome of internal Palestinian self-determination, among others. It is therefore appropriate to say that internal self-determination may be a *stepping-stone* to the exercise of external self-determination.[45] An analogous example is Kosovo. Pursuant to Resolution 1244 (1999), the UN Security Council (UNSC) decided to set up the UN Interim Administration Mission in Kosovo (UNMIK) to, *inter alia*, "[develop] provisional institutions for democratic and autonomous self-government pending a political settlement, including the holding of elections."[46]

In sum, the principle of self-determination initially codified in Article 1(2) of the UN Charter was thereafter applied, by subsequent instruments and customary practice, not only to (i) colonial and dependent peoples free to determine their political status *externally*, including but not limited to independence, but also to (ii) all peoples within established sovereign States free to determine their political status *internally*, e.g. democratic governance.[47] This means that modes of exercising external self-determination, *e.g.* secession from parent States, are not squarely available for national minorities, as a matter of law.[48] In many instances, international law has thus centered the right of minorities to self-determination upon, *inter alia*, their enjoyment of cultural, economic and socio-political rights as well as their right to natural resources.[49]

---

45 Cassese, at 241.
46 S.C. Res. 1244 (June 10, 1999), para. 11(a).
47 Accordance with International Law of the Unilateral Declaration of Independence in Respect of Kosovo, Advisory Opinion, 2010, I.C.J. Rep. 403, 523 (22 July) [*hereinafter* ICJ Kosovo); separate opinion of Judge Cancade Trindade, para. 174; Lachs, at 46.
48 "As a matter of law" because some jurists and scholars have treated secession as a pure international reality. *See e.g.* Alain Pellet, *Avis juridique sur certaines questions de droit international soulevées par le renvoi* (Dec. 2, 1997), *Amicus Curiae* submitted to the Canadian Supreme Court on 18 December 1997, para. 26 ("no principle of international law excludes the right of a people to secede, and when such is the case, the law of nations simply takes notice of the existence of the new state") [*hereinafter* Pellet]; Opinion No. 1 of the Badinter Arbitration Commission, para. 1(c), 31 I.L.M., 1992, at 1497 ("the existence or disappearance of the state is a matter of fact").
49 Lachs, at 55.

III The Continued Relevance of Self-Determination in Today's World

The focus of this paper – whether use of force in realization of a self-determination claim is lawful – presumes that the right to self-determination remains applicable to our understanding of the modern international legal system. Indeed, the inquiry is just as relevant to the decolonization context as it is to today. Notwithstanding the territories[50] whose process of decolonization has not begun, there were officially 17 non-self-governing territories listed by the UN Secretariat as of 2018.[51] This is in addition to other *ad hoc* territories whose people have been deemed entitled to external self-determination, such as the Palestinian people in the Occupied Palestinian territory (oPt).[52]

With regard to Palestine, the UN has repeatedly affirmed the "alienable rights of the people of Palestine"[53] who are "entitled to equal rights and self-determination, in accordance with the Charter of the UN."[54] On 22 November 1974, following the October 1973 Arab-Israeli war, the UNGA passed Resolution 3236 (XXIX) (by 89 votes to 8 with 37 abstentions), a major instrument that reaffirmed the right of Palestinians to self-determination. Since then, the ICJ[55] as well as the majority of States[56] have explicitly recognized the

---

50 In Africa, for instance, territories remain under the possession of colonial powers include Glorious Islands, Mayotte, the Chagos, Ceuta and Melilla, the Alhucemas Islands, Chafarinas and Peñón de Vélez de la Gomera. *See e.g.* Mamadou Hebie, *Was There Something Missing in the Decolonization Process in Africa?: The Territorial Dimension*, 28 Leiden J. Int'l L. 529–556 (2015).

51 *See* the updated list post-2018 session published by the UN Special Committee on Decolonization, http://www.un.org/en/decolonization/nonselfgovterritories.shtml.

52 H.R.C. Res. 31/34 (Apr. 20, 2016), para. 1; H.R.C. Res. 31/33 (Apr. 20, 2016), para. 1; H.R.C. Res. 31/36 (Apr. 20, 2016), para. 8; Michael Lynk, *Report of the Special Rapporteur on the Situation of Human Rights in the Palestinian Territories Occupied Since 1967*, U.N. Doc. A/71/554 (Oct. 19, 2016), paras. 39, 43.

53 G.A. Res. 2535/B (XXIV) (Dec. 10, 1969).

54 G.A. Res. 2672/C (XXV) (Dec. 8, 1970). *See also, e.g.,* G.A. Res. 2649 (XXV) (Nov. 30, 1970), para. 5 ("Condemns those Governments that deny the right to self-determination of peoples recognized as being entitled to it, especially of the peoples of southern Africa and Palestine."); G.A. Res. 2792D (XXVI) (Dec. 9, 1971), para. 1 ("Recognizes that the people of Palestine are entitled to equal rights and self-determination"); G.A. Res. 2963E (XXVII) (Dec. 13, 1972); G.A. Res. 3089D (XXVIII) (Dec. 7, 1973).

55 ICJ Wall, para. 118.

56 *See e.g.* U.N. Doc. A/C.3/38/SR.16 (Oct. 19, 1983), at 20 [United States] (recognizing "the legitimate rights of the Palestinian people"). *See also* U.N. Doc. A/C.3/43/SR.7 (Oct. 13, 1988), at 7 [Australia] (recognizing "the right to self-determination of, among others, the people of Namibia, Palestine, Kampuchea and Afghanistan"); id., at 8 [Japan] (comprehensive peace to attained by *inter alia* the "recognition of the right to self-determination of the Palestinian people, including the establishment of an independent Palestinian

right of Palestinians to self-determination, including Israel.[57] Notwithstanding the various alleged legal bases,[58] the more accurate view is that Palestinians are entitled to a right to self-determination by virtue of their status as a "people" on a non-self-governing territory.[59]

Whether any situations beyond the aforementioned are entitled to a right to self-determination is case-specific. Such analysis is not so much about proving that modern claims for self-determination are "bogus" claims, as it is ultimately a legal assessment left to a judicial body to make. A narrow construction of self-determination being solely confined to colonial territories is erroneous for three reasons.

Firstly, the right to self-determination has acquired a general character under international law. We may recall that the ICJ has made numerous pronouncements to declare the right to self-determination as a general principle

State"); U.N. Doc. A/C.3/43/SR.10 (Oct. 17, 1988), at 7 [Ireland] (recognizing "the right of the Palestinian people to self-determination, including their right to an independent State if they so wished"); U.N. Doc. A/C.3/43/SR.13 (Oct. 19, 1988), at 4 [Turkey] ("it would be impossible to achieve a just and lasting peace unless the legitimate rights of the Palestinians, including their right to self-determination, were recognised"); U.N. Doc. A/C.3/43/SR.23 (Oct. 27, 1988) at 25 [Greece, speaking on behalf of the Twelve Members of the European Economic Community] ("lasting peace could only be achieved if ... the right of the Palestinian people to self-determination [...] was also fully recognized"). For a summary of separate government statements to this effect, see Cassese, at 239 n 36.

57 See the Israeli-Palestinian Interim Agreement on the West Bank and the Gaza Strip of 28 September 1995, referring numerous times to the Palestinian people and its "legitimate rights" (Preamble, paras. 4, 7, 8; Article II, para. 2; Article III, paras. 1, 3; Article XXII, para. 2).

58 Cassese, at 239 (the right of Palestinians has its basis not on the rule relating to decolonization but to foreign military occupation). *Cf.* Speech of former Chairman of the Palestine Liberation Organization Yasser Arafat to the UNGA on Nov. 13, 1974, making the claim that the right of Palestinians to self-determination was based on (i) "colonialism", (ii) "racial discrimination" and (iii) "foreign domination." See G.A.O.R., XXIXth Session, 2282nd Mtg, U.N. Doc. A/PV.2282 and Corr. 1 (Nov. 13, 1974), paras. 26–28, 38–40.

59 ICJ Wall, para. 88 (recalling that the right to self-determination is applicable to all non-self-governing territories). Foreign occupation *stricto sensu* is not a legal basis for generating a right to self-determination but only an aggravating factor impeding its implementation. See G.A. Res. 48/94 (Dec. 20, 1993), para. 3 ("Reaffirms also the inalienable right of the Palestinian people and all peoples under foreign occupation and colonial domination to self- determination"); H.R.C. Res. 37/34, preamble (on the question of Palestine, recalling "the right of self-determination of all peoples and especially those subject to foreign occupation"). *See also* Friendly Relations Declaration, para. 2 (providing that the right to self-determination is "in order to bring a speedy end to colonialism ... bearing in mind that subjection of peoples to alien subjugation, domination and exploitation constitutes a violation of the principle [of self-determination]."

of law (*i.e.* a principle "recognized by civilized nations")[60] as well as "one of the essential principles of *contemporary* international law."[61] This is notwithstanding its insertion in Article 1 of the UN Charter as part of the "purposes and principles" of the UN, thereby setting itself apart from Chapter XII of the Charter specifically on the trusteeship system.[62] It may be said that the broad scope of Article 1(2) of the UN Charter, in accordance with the textual approach to interpretation, is unambiguous.[63] This is reaffirmed by the intent of the drafters of for a generic formulation, who did not have colonialism in their contemplation back then.[64] It was not until the 1960s that colonialism became the subject of the principle's application by way of customary practice at the UN and among States. The fact that a principle is of a general character "recognized by civilized nations" is strong evidence that the principle itself is evolutionary and universal, *i.e.* able to stand the test of time.[65] Here, it is useful to note that a principle of law must be coherently applied in order to legitimate.[66] Furthermore, the international community continues to progressively develop – in modern contexts – the *jus cogens*[67] and customary

---

60   Statute of the International Court of Justice, Article 38(1)(c). On the right to self-determination as a general principle of law, see ICJ Chagos, para. 155; ICJ Western Sahara, para. 59. *See also* Theodor Meron, Human Rights and Humanitarian Norms as Customary Law 97, 134 (1989) [*hereinafter* Meron]; Bruno Simma and Philip Alston, *The Sources of Human Rights Law: Custom, Jus Cogens, and General Principles*" 12 Aust. Y.B. Int'l L. 82, 93 (1988).

61   East Timor (Portugal v. Australia), Judgment, 1995 I.C.J. Rep. 90, para. 29 (June 30) [emphasis added] [*hereinafter* ICJ East Timor].

62   Article 76 lists "[t]he basic objectives of the trusteeship system, in accordance with the Purposes of the [UN] laid down in Article 1 of the present Charter."

63   Competence of the General Assembly Regarding Admission to the United Nations, Advisory Opinion, 1950 I.C.J. Rep. 4, 8 (Mar. 3) ("If the relevant words in their natural and ordinary meaning make sense in their context, that is the end of the matter").

64   U.N. Doc. A/C.3/SR.310 (Nov. 10, 1950), paras. 7–11.

65   Lord McNair, *The General Principles of Law Recognized by Civilized Nations*, 33 Brit. Y.B. Int'l L. 1, 10 (1957) (making the point that general principles of law are the default law applicable between States).

66   Thomas M. Franck, The Power of Legitimacy among Nations (1990).

67   On the *jus cogens* status of the right to self-determination, see *e.g.* Dire Tladi, Special Rapporteur on peremptory norms of general international law (*jus cogens*), Third Report, U.N. Doc. A/CN.4/714 (Feb. 12, 2018), paras. 31, 96, 97 [*hereinafter* Tladi]; Commentary to Article 26 of the draft Articles on Responsibility of States for Internationally Wrongful Acts, [2001] Y.B. Int'l L. Comm'n, U.N. Doc. A/CN.4/SER.A/2001/Add.1 (Part 2), paras. 5 and corrigendum, paras. 76–77 [*hereinafter* ARSIWA]. *See also* Giorgio Gaja, *Jus cogens beyond the Vienna Convention*, in Collected Courses of The Hague Academy of International Law Vol. 172 271–316, 282 (1981-III); Gros Espiell, *Self-Determination as Jus Cogens*, in UN Law/Fundamental Rights: Two Topics in International Law 168 (Antonio Cassese ed., 1979).

law status[68] for the right to self-determination as well as for certain consequences arising therefrom (*e.g.* obligations *erga omnes* owed by other States).[69] Overall, these developments tend to disprove the position that the right only materialized for colonial and other dependent peoples.

Secondly, the right to external self-determination, despite its historical application, is not exclusive to colonial peoples. A better view is that the changing international legal order has not completely dismissed the relevance of the right to self-determination.[70] In Namibia, the ICJ analyzed the then *lex lata* of the law relating to self-determination and stated that "its interpretation cannot remain unaffected by the subsequent development of law, through the Charter of the [UN] and by way of customary law."[71] There, the Court applied the broad principle of self-determination to engender the obligation of the administering powers to decolonize. It would thus seem artificial to construe the colonial application as limiting the actual scope of the principle itself.[72]

The fact that subsequent development of law may modify, by custom, the scope of its application and create new consequences beyond a particular time in history was again seen in *Kosovo*. Throughout the *Kosovo* proceedings, numerous States in their submissions applied the principle of self-determination to explain the phenomenon of secession in international law.[73] The Court considered the question of whether there existed a right of secession irrelevant to the request of the UNGA and simply took cognizance of the parties' arguments. If it was true that external self-determination had become obsolete and void of modern application, the Court could have said so. Rather, a number of judges in their opinions have convincingly argued for a positive right

---

68   On its customary law status, *see* recently ICJ Chagos, paras. 152, 155, 158. *See also* Meron, at 97, 134.

69   On the *erga omnes* character of the right to self-determination, *see* ICJ East Timor, para. 29; ICJ Wall, paras. 155–159. Regarding Palestine, the ICJ has stressed the *erga omnes* obligation of all States owed to the realization of the right of Palestinians. *See* ICJ Wall, paras. 155, 159 ("It is also for all States, while respecting the [UN] Charter and international law, to see to it that any impediment, resulting from the construction of the wall, to the exercise by the Palestinian people of its right to self-determination is brought to an end").

70   Lachs, at 50.

71   ICJ Namibia, at 31.

72   ICJ Chagos, para. 144 ("The Court is conscious that the right to self-determination, as a fundamental human right, has a broad scope of application"). *See also* David Raic, Statehood and the Law of Self-determination 227 (2002); Michla Pomerance, Law of Self-Determination in Law and Practice 37 (1982) [*hereinafter* Pomerance].

73   *See, e.g.,* Written submissions of the Netherlands, I.C.J. Doc. CR 2009/32 (Dec. 10, 2009), at 8, 11, 13, 16; Germany (Apr. 15, 2009), para. VI.2; Albania (Apr. 14, 2009), para. 81 (recognizing secession "where no government representing the whole people belonging to the territory without distinction as to race, creed or colour exists").

to secession derivable from the law of self-determination.[74] This suggests that international law may be moving towards recognizing the right of secession as an extended consequence of the principle of self-determination under exceptional circumstances.[75] Albeit still unsettled, this argument has been applied by eminent jurists to at least indigenous populations[76] and certain arguable individual cases, such as Tibet and Kashmir.[77] In certain instances, secessionist claims have been dismissed because they did not rise to the requisite level of severity. This was precisely the reason why the African Commission on Human and People's Rights rejected the complaint by Katanga of Zaire in *Katangese Peoples' Congress v. Zaire*, holding that internal means of self-determination had not been exhausted.[78]

Last but not least, international law has come to confer the right to external self-determination, in theory, not only on new entities (*e.g.* secessionists) but also to peoples to re-exercise their right. This is possible in at least two situations. The first concerns the unlawful process of decolonization. In this situation, any unlawful implementation of a verified right to self-determination (*e.g.* incomplete or wrongful restitution) would be void, thereby allowing the right to be re-exercised.[79] In this regard, Manfred Lachs noted in 1980 the examples of "dependence and foreign control […] even with regard to those territories which have acquired independence."[80] In the recent *Chagos* Advisory Opinion, the ICJ confirmed that the detachment of Chagos Archipelago "was

---

74 *See* ICJ Kosovo, separate opinion of Judge Cançado Trindade, at 523; dissenting opinion of Judge Bennouna, at 500; separate opinion of Judge Yusuf, at 618. *C.f.* some authors have however understood the Advisory Opinion as rejecting the doctrine of "remedial secession." *See* Olivier Corten, *Territorial Integrity Narrowly Interpreted: Reasserting the Classical Inter-State Paradigm of International Law*, 24 Leiden J. Int'l L. 87 (2011) [*hereinafter* Corten].

75 Stefan Oeter, *Self-Determination*, in The Charter of the United Nations: A Commentary, Vol. I para. 30 (Bruno Simma et al eds., 3rd ed., 2012) [*hereinafter* Oeter] ("but in cases of brute and violent oppression, it might also convert into a claim for independent statehood, *i.e.* 'secession'"). *C.f.* Higgins, at 117–118.

76 Oeter, para. 32 ("The indigenous populations of colonial entities had only limited citizenship rights … Self-determination, in the sense of self-government on the basis of equality, could accordingly only be achieved by forming an independent State").

77 Oeter, at 329.

78 *Katangese Peoples' Congress v. Zaire*, African Comm'm Hum. People's Rts., Commc'n. No. 75/92 (1995).

79 On the position that an internationally act which conflicts a *jus cogens* norm is void, *see* Tladi, draft conclusion 16, para. 146 ("It would make little sense if States were precluded from assuming obligations in conflict with jus cogens through treaties, but permitted to assume those same obligations through unilateral acts").

80 Lachs, at 53. *See also* Louis Henkin, International Law: Politics, Values and Functions 168 (1989).

not based on the free and genuine expression of the will of the people" and the United Kingdom (UK) committed "an unlawful act *of a continuing character.*"[81] Accordingly, Mauritius was permitted to complete the decolonization with a modality to be decided by the UNGA.[82]

The second situation is the unlawful abolition of self-determination arrangements. For instance, where a people has historically exercised their right to self-determination by joining another established State, but the specific sub-State arrangement was later revoked (*e.g.* abolishing an autonomy), it has been argued that their previous right "does not perish completely" and "might lead to a resurgence of the right of self-determination."[83] This argument was raised by a number of States with regard to the situation of Kosovo, according to which the illegal removal of its autonomy – together with the atrocious human rights violations against the people of Kosovo – created the *sui generis* circumstance necessary for secession.[84]

Lastly, self-determination is relevant, if not the most relevant, with regard to internal governance. After a people have implemented their external self-determination, they continue to enjoy internal self-determination as "an ongoing right", including a high degree of democratic and representative government.[85] The beneficiaries of this right cover the populations within a constituted States but also minorities in particular.[86] Antonio Cassese thus correctly noted that "the right to internal self-determination is neither destroyed nor diminished by its having already once been invoked and put into effect."[87]

IV The Use of Force for Self-Determination and International Law

Having ascertained the scope and content of the right to self-determination, the next question is: how can the people entitled to self-determination enforce such a right? The political reality remains that secession at the consent of the oppressive State is unlikely, making forcible action a means to likely be

---

81   ICJ Chagos, paras. 172, 177 [emphasis added].
82   Id., paras. 178–180.
83   Oeter, para. 34. *Cf.* Cassese, at 101 (stating that external self-determination "ceases to exist under customary international law once it is implemented").
84   *See, e.g.*, Written submissions of Finland, I.C.J. Doc. CR2009/30 (Dec. 8, 2009,) paras. 61, 64; Croatia, I.C.J. Doc. CR 2009/29 (Dec. 7, 2009), at 57.
85   Higgins, at 120; Cassese, at 101; Pomerance, at 37.
86   Oeter, para. 30 (noting that internal self-determination grants the possibility to minorities of certain arrangements and guarantees of self-government).
87   Cassese, at 101.

resorted to. But does international law permit the use of force to achieve the implementation of self-determination? The nuances in this question are manifest in the definitional components of the right to self-determination: not only must a group of persons who wish to claim such right qualify as a "people," but the subsequent exercise of self-determination – including by a use of force – must be a result of their free and genuine will (*Part A*). But even if the force is attributable to the people for the purpose of self-determination, the issue regarding the general prohibition on the use of force still needs to be dispensed with (*Part B*). Finally, it is important to consider whether international law provides for a permissive rule in this specific situation (*Part C*).

A *Peoples as the Beneficiaries of Self-Determination*
1 People as the *sine qua non*

International law confers rights and obligations on peoples who are the sole beneficiaries of the principle of self-determination. Thus, in order for a forcible exercise of self-determination to be legal, the use of force must be carried out by the people themselves. In reality, this creates certain problems for the legality question. The first problem is definitional: what constitutes a "people"?[88] Since the use of force is often administered and executed by part of the people concerned – and possibly with the involvement of third States – the issue of attribution also needs to be convincingly tackled.

It may be recalled that the right to self-determination, though historically applied to the peoples of colonial and non-self-governing territories, extends beyond the decolonization context. With regard to "non-self-governing territories", the ICJ has held that the list of the UN Special Committee on Decolonization was not exhaustive and the term generally means territories which "have not yet attained independence."[89] There has been post-colonial State practice recognizing the right to self-determination of peoples in an established State, including Kashmir and Kosovo.[90] In legal doctrine, an important strand of scholarship argues that the qualification as a "people" is a hybrid subjective/objective test. A group of persons bound together by common *objective* characteristics, like language, culture, religion and/or race, might qualify as

---

[88] As put by Sir Robert Jennings in 1956: "On the surface, it seemed reasonable: let the people decide. It was in fact ridiculous, because the people cannot decide until someone decides who are the people." *See* Sir Robert Jennings, The Approach to Self-Government 55–56 (1956); quoted in Anthony Whelan, *Wilsonian Self-determination and the Versailles Settlement*, 43 Int'l Comp. L. Q., 99 (1994).

[89] ICJ Chagos, at 31.

[90] On Kashmir, *see* S.C. Res. 91 (1951) and 122 (1957) (stressing the free will of the people of Kashmir to determine their political status by a UN-administered plebiscite).

a "people", so long as such group also has a common *subjective* understanding of belonging and being distinct from other surrounding groups.[91] In addition, it has been suggested that such people must possess a degree of territoriality, *i.e.* they must be constitutive of a certain territorial entity historically formed over time.[92] In practice, the territoriality requirement has been treated as part of the objective test.[93]

2   Representative Entities

But even if a group of persons qualify as a "people" for the purpose of self-determination, it remains to be decided whether the use of force is attributable to them. In most cases, a self-claimed representative entity, such as a liberation movement, would be the one carrying out the forcible measures. Previous practice of the UN and judicial decisions have defined the principle of self-determination as "the need to pay regard to the freely expressed will of peoples."[94] In the *Chagos* Advisory Opinion, the Court once again stressed that the exercise of self-determination "must be the expression of the free and genuine will of the people concerned."[95] In exceptional circumstances, this requirement may be dispensed by the UNGA.[96]

As such, in order to claim and exercise the right to self-determination, the entity must actually be representative of "the free and genuine will of the people concerned."[97] Although no particular legal test has been developed on this matter, it appears that either a proximate nexus between the entity and the represented people, or the recognition by the international community, is required.[98] The practice of international organizations is instructive to the

---

91   Dov Ronen, The Quest for Self-Determination 39–45 (1979); Oeter, at 325.
92   Thomas M. Franck, *Clan and Superclan: Loyalty, Identity and Community in Law and Practice*, 90 Am. J. Int'l L. 359 (1996); Jane A. Hofbauer, Sovereignty in the Exercise of the Right to Self-Determination 31 (2016).
93   *Kevin Mgwanga Gunme v. Cameroon*, African Comm'n Hum. and Peoples' Rts., Commc'n No. 75/92, Recommendations of Oct. 1995; *Katangese Peoples' Congress v. Zaire*, African Comm'n Hum. and Peoples' Rts., Commc'n No. 75/92 (1995). Economic and Social Council, *International Meeting of Experts on Further Study of the Concept of the Rights of Peoples: Final Report and Recommendations* (Feb. 22, 1990), para. 22, UNESCO Doc. SHS-89/CONF.602/7.
94   ICJ Western Sahara, at 12, para. 59; ICJ Chagos, para. 158.
95   ICJ Chagos, para. 157.
96   ICJ Western Sahara, para. 71 ("The right of self-determination leaves the [UNGA] a measure of discretion with respect to the forms and procedures by which that right is to be realized"). ICJ Chagos, paras. 157–158.
97   Cassese, at 146–147.
98   On the theory of recognition in relation to liberation movements, *see* Malcolm Shaw, *The International Status of National Liberation Movements*, 5 Liverpool L. Rev. 23 (1983)

theory of recognition. The UNGA has previously recognized national liberation movements – including those in Angola, Guinea-Bissau, Cape Verde and Mozambique – as the "authentic representatives of the true aspirations of the peoples" of those territories.[99] It also declared Frente Polisario as the representative of the people of Western Sahara.[100] The ECOSOC, as provided by its procedural rules, similarly allowed liberation movements "to participate, without the right to vote, in its deliberations on any matter of particular concern to that movement."[101]

It should also be pointed out that self-determination is a collective right.[102] Individuals not representative of the people as a whole may not invoke any rights in international law for the purposes of exercising self-determination. Therefore, in the case concerning *Tiina Sanila-Aikio v. Finland,* the UN Human Rights Committee refused to entertain the claim on self-determination because the complainant "as an individual, cannot claim under the Optical Protocol [of ICCPR] to be a victim of a violation of the right of self-determination enshrined in article 1 of the Covenant, which deals with rights conferred upon peoples, as such."[103]

In the case of Palestine, the ICJ has unequivocally found that "the existence of a 'Palestinian people' is no longer in issue."[104] The Palestine Liberation Organization (PLO) has been widely accepted as the representative of the Palestinian people. Former Chairman of the PLO Yasser Arafat in the speech to the UN on November 13, 1974 declared that the PLO "in its capacity as the sole representative of the Palestinian people" has the right "to establish

[*hereinafter* Shaw] ("The main criteria for recognition centres upon the effectiveness of the struggle of the organisation concerned and the degree of support it enjoys").

99   G.A. Res. 2918 (XXVII (Nov. 14, 1972).
100 G.A. Res. 34/37 (Nov. 21, 1979) (declaring the Front Polisario as "the representative of the people of Western Sahara"); S.C. Res. 690 (April 29, 1991). *See also* Case T-512/12, Front Polisario v. Council of the European Union, General Court, 2015 E.C.R. 953, paras. 73, 208 [*hereinafter* Front Polisario v. Council of the EU].
101 For instance, under the Economic and Social Council's procedural rules, it may invite "any national liberation movement recognised by or in accordance with resolutions of the [UNGA] to participate, without the right to vote, in its deliberations on any matter of particular concern to that movement." *See* Economic and Social Council Res. 1949 (LVIII) (May 8, 1975), rule 73. Other agencies also produce programs in cooperation with liberation movements, in particular UNESCO, the Food and Agriculture Organization, the World Health Organization and the International Labor Organization.
102 Oeter, at 315 ("Subsequent development in the UN ... transformed the old (political) principle of self-determination into a collective right").
103 *Tiina Sanila-Aikio v. Finland*, para. 8.6.
104 ICJ Wall, para. 118.

an independent national State on all liberated Palestinian territory."[105] The UNGA, in its Resolutions 3210 and 3236 (1974) accordingly recognized the PLO as the "representative of the Palestinian people."[106] In Resolution 3237 of November 22, 1974, it "invite[d] the PLO to participate in the sessions and the work of the [UNGA] in the capacity of observer" and other international conferences.[107] Notably, the PLO participated in the *travaux preparatoires* of the 1977 Protocols Additional to the 1949 Geneva Conventions.[108] In the exchange of letters of September 9, 1993, Israeli Prime Minister Yitzhak Rabin communicated to Yasser Arafat that "the Government of Israel has decided to recognize the PLO as the representative of the Palestinian people," thereby implying a recognition of the Palestinian people's right to self-determination.

3   The Issue of "Puppet Regimes"

The issue becomes complicated when a third State uses force against another State, under the pretext of assisting a right to self-determination of the people therein. An arguable example is Russia's intervention in the Crimean Peninsula in support of the alleged self-determination of Crimean people to secede from Ukraine, with the view to joining Russia. Does international law prohibit the use of force by Crimea/Russia against Ukraine? To the extent that the foreign intervention is not at the request of the people concerned, the people's "free and genuine will" is thereby vitiated, rendering the forcible action unlawful.

On one hand, the principle of self-determination entails certain *erga omnes* obligations for third States.[109] These include not only the obligations not to

---

105   G.A.O.R., XXIXth Session, 2283nd Mtg, U.N. Doc. A/PV.2282 and Corr. 1 (Nov. 13, 1974), paras. 26–28.
106   G.A. Res. 3210 (Oct. 14, 1974) and 3236 (Nov. 22, 1974).
107   G.A. Res. 3237 (XXIX) (Nov. 22, 1974), with 95 votes to 17, and 19 abstentions. *See also* G.A. Res. 67/19 (Nov. 29, 2012), with 138 votes to 9, and 41 abstentions, conferring upon Palestine the status of "non-member observer State." During the *travaux preparatoires* of Resolution 67/19, States continued to agree the representation of the Palestinian people by the PLO. *See, e.g.,* U.N. Doc. A/67/PV.44, 44th plenary meeting (Nov. 29, 2012), at 21 (Norway); id., at 2 (Sudan, requesting the UNGA "to accord Palestine non-member observer State status in the [UN], without prejudging the rights, privileges and role accorded the Palestine Liberation Organization as representative of the Palestinian people"). Currently, Palestine has a Permanent Observer Mission to the UN.
108   Marco Sassòli, *Legal mechanisms to improve compliance with international humanitarian law by armed groups*, in Proceedings of the Bruges Colloquium: Improving Compliance with International Humanitarian Law, Sept. 11–12, 2003, Collegium special edition, No. 30, Winter 2004, at 98.
109   ICJ Wall, paras. 155–159 ("The obligations *erga omnes* violated by Israel are the obligation to respect the right of the Palestinian people to self-determination, and certain of its obligations under international humanitarian law"). *See also* ICJ East Timor, para. 29.

forcibly suppress or deprive people of the right to self-determination and not to recognize any unlawful situation in violation of the right,[110] but also the obligation to support and assist the right to self-determination of peoples when lawfully invoked.[111] Whether third States have a duty to assist is a delicate question, at least to the extent that international law has no dispute settlement procedure to verify self-determination claims. This paradox can be explained in the context of the Friendly Relations Declaration. While foreign support is permitted – or even obligated – in its paragraphs 2–3 ("the duty to promote, through joint and separate action, realization of the principle of equal rights and self-determination of peoples"), paragraphs 7–8 prohibits any action that would impair the territorial integrity of established States who conduct themselves in compliance with the principle of self-determination.[112]

This careful caveat in the Friendly Relations Declaration demonstrates that, in situations involving the intervention of third States in support of an alleged right to self-determination, the question is not so much on the legality of the use of force, but is preceded by the validity of the self-determination claim. Nonetheless, the Declaration seems to have left the assessment entirely to the discretion of States on whether to assist, without further legal safeguards.

Some observations are in order. Where the use of force is carried out by an entity or a third States claiming to represent the people, the element of "the free and genuine will of the people" is necessary. In other words, the forcible implementation of self-determination must be attributable to the people in whom the self-determination right vests. In the past, the nuances in this free will requirement have made the legal assessment particularly difficult, bearing in mind historical attempts to establish so-called "puppet States" at the intervention of third States.

---

110   ARSIWA art. 41 provides that "No State shall recognize as lawful a situation created by a serious breach." The ILC commentary contains a specific reference to self-determination: "The obligation applies to 'situations' created by these breaches, such as, for example, attempted acquisition of sovereignty over territory through the denial of the right of self-determination of peoples. It not only refers to the formal recognition of these situations, but also prohibits acts which would imply such recognition." *See also* Friendly Relations Declaration, Principle V; ICJ Chagos, para. 180.

111   Friendly Relations Declaration, Principle V, paras. 2–3 ("Every State has the duty to promote, through joint and separate action, realization of the principle of equal rights and self-determination of peoples").

112   Paragraph 7 of the Friendly Relations Declaration provides that: "Nothing in the foregoing paragraphs shall be construed as authorizing or encouraging any action which would dismember or impair, totally or in part, the territorial integrity or political unity of sovereign and independent States *conducting themselves in compliance with the principle of equal rights and self-determination of peoples* ..." [emphasis added].

But even assuming that the group is a people entitled to a right to external self-determination, it should not be the end of the matter. The use of force against the existing State is unlawful if it falls outside the permissible aim, such as to bring about a regime change with the assistance of a third State. There must thus be a nexus between the force and the purpose of achieving self-determination. Otherwise, the forcible action, for instance to bring about a regime change, would not be justified under the principle of self-determination but a breach of the prohibition on the use of force and of the principle of non-intervention.[113] In practice, however, the line between unlawful intervention and assistance to lawful self-determination can be tenuous.

B   The Prohibition on the Use of Force and the Principle of Territorial Integrity

1   The Applicability Question

The first universal attempt to codify the prohibition on the use of force – the foundational rule in *jus ad bellum* – dates back almost a century. The Covenant of the League of Nations obliged its Members "to respect and preserve against external aggression the territorial integrity and existing political independence of all Members."[114] This obligation not to resort to war was later reiterated in other international arenas among States.[115] After WWII, this rule was made more explicit in Article 2(4) of the UN Charter. It provides that:

> All Members shall refrain in their international relations from the threat or use of force against the territorial integrity or political independence of any state, or in any other manner inconsistent with the Purposes of the [UN].

In *Nicaragua*, the ICJ proclaimed that the content of Article 2(4) reflected the customary law prohibiting the unlawful use of force in international relations.[116] Because of the customary character, it is thus a general rule the

---

113   U.N. Charter art. 2(4), 2(7).
114   Covenant of the League of Nations arts. 12, 13, 15. Commentators have understood this obligation as "a maximum commitment of members." See Charter of the United Nations: Commentary and Document 44 (Leland M. Goodrich et al., 3rd ed., 1969) [*hereinafter* Goodrich].
115   For example, at Bumbarton Oaks, the conferees were unanimous in including the obligation of members to refrain from "the use or threat of force in their international relations in any manner inconsistent with the purposes of the Organization." See *Dumbarton Oaks Proposals*, Chapter II, para. 4.
116   Military and Paramilitary Activities in and against Nicaragua (Nicar. v. U.S.), Judgment, 1986 I.C.J. Rep. 392, paras. 187–190 (Nov. 26) [*hereinafter* ICJ Nicaragua].

effect of which applies to all States.[117] Later in *Armed Activities*, the Court reaffirmed the significance of the rule considering it to be "a cornerstone of the [UN] Charter."[118]

The question before us is whether the prohibition applies *mutatis mutandis* to non-State actors, and in particular to peoples in their exercise of self-determination. To begin with, Article 2(4) in its ordinary meaning addresses UN "Members" *inter se* in the context of their "international relations."[119] At the time of drafting, despite the significant number of dependent territories and non-UN Member States, the discussion on Article 2(4) was not meant to have universal application, at least not for non-States. This is evident from the *travaux preparatoires* that the terms "against the territorial integrity or political independence of any state" was an assurance by the major powers in response to the demand of smaller States.[120] Most commentators are thus of the view that Article 2(4) of the UN Charter was limited to inter-State relations.[121]

This view is reinforced by other parallel developments. The International Law Commission (ILC), in its discussion of the "Declaration on the Rights and Duties of States," held the same view that self-determination "had no connexion with the rules of conduct governing relations between States."[122] The 1974 Definition of Aggression – basing the Charter prohibition on the use of force as the constitutive element of "aggression" – explicitly contains a "without prejudice" clause exempting self-determination. It provides that: "[n]othing in this Definition could in any way prejudice the right to self-determination ... particularly peoples under colonial and racist regimes or other forms of alien domination."[123] Other UN-commissioned reports have taken the same stand.[124]

---

117   Id.
118   Armed Activities on the Territory of the Congo (Dem. Rep. Congo v. Uganda), Judgment, 2005 I.C.J. Rep. 168, para. 148 (Dec. 19).
119   Vienna Convention on the Law of Treaties art. 31(1), May, 23, 1969, 1155 U.N.T.S. 331. U.N. Charter art. 1(2).
120   UNCIO, *Documents*, VI, at 342–46.
121   Goodrich, at 50; Gray, at 63.
122   First session, 10th meeting, [1949] Y.B. Int'l L. Comm'n 113, UN Doc. A/CN.4/SR.14 (Feb. 5, 1947).
123   G.A. Res. 3314 (XXIX) (Dec. 14, 1974). *See also* Bernard V. A. Röling, *The 1974 UN Definition of Aggression*, in The Current Legal Regulation of the Use of Force 413–21 (Antonio Cassese ed., 1986).
124   *See, e.g.,* Cristescu, paras. 207–8 ("the use of force by peoples under colonial domination is not a derogation from the principle of non-use of force stated in Article 2, paragraph 4, of the Charter").

More to the point, the ICJ in the early *Corfu Channel* case stressed that "between *independent States* respect for territorial sovereignty is an essential foundation of *international relations*."[125] In *Military and Paramilitary Activities in and against Nicaragua*, it again stressed "[t]he duty of *every State* to respect the territorial sovereignty of others."[126] In the course of the proceedings in the *Wall* Advisory Opinion, Israel argued that customary international law has developed to render the prohibition on the use of force applicable to non-State actors, and thus lending the use of the self-defense exception to the State under attack. The ICJ nonetheless dismissed the argument and made clear that the law of *jus ad bellum* must be between two States.[127] In this regard, James Crawford explained that "the reason why seceding groups are not bound by the international law rule of territorial integrity [...] is simply that such groups are not subjects of international law at all, in the way that States are."[128]

Those who opposed the legal operation of self-determination have additionally relied on the principle of territorial integrity. According to this position, the use of force to achieve external self-determination – with the purpose of terminating territorial ties with an existing State – would necessarily violate the territorial integrity of that State. The primary basis of this allegation is the Friendly Relations Declaration.[129] In particular, paragraphs 7–8 of Principle V provides the following:

> Nothing in the foregoing paragraphs shall be construed as authorizing or encouraging any action which would dismember or impair, totally or in part, the territorial integrity or political unity of sovereign and independent States conducting themselves in compliance with the principle of equal rights and self-determination of peoples as described above and thus possessed of a government representing the whole people belonging to the territory without distinction as to race, creed or colour.
>
> Every State shall refrain from any action aimed at the partial or total disruption of the national unity and territorial integrity of any other State or country.

---

125 Corfu Channel (U.K. v. Alb.), Judgment, 1949 I.C.J. Rep. 4, 35 (Apr. 9) [emphasis added].
126 ICJ Nicaragua, para. 213 [emphasis added].
127 Id., para. 139.
128 James Crawford, *The Right of Self-Determination in International Law: Its Development and Future*, in Peoples' Rights 50 (Philip Alston ed., 2001) [*hereinafter* Crawford].
129 G.A. Res. 2626 (XXV) (Oct. 24, 1970).

The ICJ has held that the principle of self-determination as contained in the Declaration reflected customary international law.[130] But like Article 2(4) of the UN Charter, it is not immediately clear why the Declaration could produce any effect upon non-State actors. The Declaration is concerned with "Friendly Relations *among States*" and is therefore addressed to States. A contextual reading of the Declaration and in particular Principle V – almost all paragraphs starting with "States" – suggests that States are the sole addressees of the Declaration, including the above paragraphs 7 and 8. This point was confirmed by its early *travaux preparatoires*.[131] Therefore, a proper interpretation of paragraph 7 is that, together with paragraph 8, they are specifically directed at situations where a third State renders unlawful assistance to unfounded claims of self-determination. With regard to well-founded claims, the latter part of paragraph 7 attaches a condition, namely "States conducting themselves in compliance with the principle of equal rights and self-determination of peoples." It further clarifies that such condition is satisfied by "a government representing the whole people belonging to the territory without distinction as to race, creed or colour." Insofar as a right to self-determination exists, paragraph 5 obliges States "to refrain from any forcible action which deprives peoples ... of their right to self-determination and freedom and independence."

It is on this basis that the Declaration appears to permit – or at least does not prohibit – a people to take actions that would *prima facie* impair the territorial integrity of an established State if that State were not conducting itself in compliance with the principle of equal rights and self-determination of peoples, including through the provision of representative government without distinction as to race, creed or color. In other words, the principle of territorial integrity simply does not apply in such circumstances. The impression that international law tends to favor States by virtue of the significance it attaches to the territorial integrity of established States is misleading. At most, the principle of territorial integrity allows States to take lawful steps to maintain their own territorial integrity.[132] This includes employing forcible measures to

---

130   ICJ Chagos, para. 155.
131   See Report of the Special Committee on Principles of International Law concerning Friendly Relations and Co-operation among States, G.A.O.R., 2th Sess., 1965, U.N. Doc. A/5746 (Nov. 16, 1964), Annexes, agenda items 90 and 94, at 83–104 [*hereinafter* Special Committee Report]. *See also* John Dugard, *The Secession of States and Their Recognition in the Wake of Kosovo*, The Hague Academy of International Law (2013), at 135–136.
132   James Crawford thus explained: "international law, both in principle and as evidenced in state practice, favours the territorial integrity of the predecessor state. It does so, not in the sense of offering any ultimate guarantee against separation or dissolution, but in the sense that for significant and often very substantial periods of time, it allows the central

suppress internal violence, until the point when the right to self-determination can be well-enough founded. It is, however, not a prohibitive norm overriding the rights of peoples.

2   The "Fluidity" of the Notion of Sovereignty

Any discussion of sovereignty as a fluid notion in present international law must proceed with considerable caution. The progressiveness of this discussion is, however, relatively safer in the instance of post-colonial secession ("remedial secession") on the basis of widespread and large-scale human rights violations. In such instance, whilst the secessionist group remains subject to the jurisdictional sovereign of the oppressing State, one can no longer confidently speak *stricto sensu* of the territorial integrity of that State. In academic writings, nonetheless, scholars have advanced the understanding that territorial integrity and sovereignty are "fluid" notions.[133]

At the ICJ, the proceedings of the *Kosovo* Advisory Opinion are particularly insightful. A handful of States averred that the principle of territorial integrity "forms a part of the corpus of international law" and bars secession.[134] In their view, the principle is applicable within States and has "an absolute character."[135] Serbia asserted that "the obligation to respect territorial integrity extends beyond States and binds non-State actors in situations of non-consensual attempts to violate the territorial integrity of independent States."[136] Libya also claimed that "the commitment to the principle of the territorial integrity … gives absolute sovereignty to States over their regions."[137]

On the other hand, the supporters of Kosovo considered that the territorial integrity of Serbia was irrelevant. For instance, Switzerland argued that the principle of territorial integrity "only applies to international relations,

---

government to seek to preserve the territorial integrity of the state." Crawford, at 50; Marc Weller, Escaping the Self-Determination Trap 44 (2008) [*hereinafter* Weller].

133   Marcelo G. Kohen, *Is the Notion of Territorial Sovereignty Obsolete?* in Borderlands under Stress 35 (Martin Pratt and Janet Allison-Brown eds., 1998); Alfred Van Staden, *The Erosion of State Sovereignty: Towards a Post-territorial World?* in State, Sovereignty, and International Governance (Gerard Kreijen et al, 2002); Jens Bartelson, *The Concept of Sovereignty Revisited*, 17 Eur. J. Int'l L. 463 (2006). *C.f.* Malcolm N. Shaw, International Law 409 (2003).

134   Written statement of Slovakia, para. 3.13.

135   Written statements of Islamic Republic of Iran, para. 4.2; Romania, para. 97.

136   Written statement of Serbia, para. 1040. *See also* Written statements of Iran, paras. 3.1–3.6; Egypt, paras. 46–50; Venezuela, at 3.

137   Written statement of Libyan Arab Jamahiriya, at 2.

and thus does not apply within a State."[138] This view was shared by others.[139] Specifically, the UK observed that "the protection of the territorial integrity of States is a protection in 'international relations'. It is not a guarantee of the permanence of a State as it exists at any given time."[140] Some other States adopted a softer tone and observed that the conflict between territorial integrity and self-determination was not absolute but called for a balancing exercise.[141] In this regard, Russia accepted the possibility of lawful secession in a remedial sense.[142] The US submitted that territorial integrity is not absolute and may be overridden.[143]

Whether this State practice has the effect of translating into customary law still depends on the requisite *opinio juris* (*i.e.* "a belief that the practice is rendered obligatory by the existence of a rule of law requiring it").[144] For now it suffices to say that positions taken by States that are motivated by policy rather than law should have no impact on the customary scope of the principle of territorial integrity.[145] In any event, in the *Kosovo* Advisory Opinion, the ICJ came to the conclusion that the prohibition on the use of force and the preservation

---

138 Written statement of Switzerland, para. 98.
139 *See also* written statements of France, para. 2.6: "in international law, the principle of territorial integrity relates not to relations between a State and its own population, but to relations between the States"; Albania, para. 113. Even States who held firmly the importance of territorial integrity also conceded on its non-applicability within States. *See* written statements of Azerbaijan, paras. 20–22; Spain, para. 26: "In this respect, suffice it to recall that the Helsinki Final Act, of 1 August 1975, confirmed the opinion juris concerning recognition of sovereignty and territorial integrity of States as a principle currently ruling mutual relations among the States participating in the above-cited Conference."
140 Written statement of United Kingdom, para. 5.9. *See also* written statements of Denmark, at 12, para. 37: "The proclamation of independence in the Declaration does not contradict general international law, which does not prohibit any part of a population of a State to declare its independence. As such it is not subject to the obligation to respect the territorial integrity of States."
141 Written statement of Slovenia, at 2.
142 Written statement of Russia, para. 88. *See also* written statement of Finland, para. 7 (stating that the principle of territorial integrity "may be overriden in exceptional cases").
143 Written statement of United States, at 72. *See also* written statements of Poland, para. 6.9; Luxembourg, para. 26.
144 North Sea Continental Shelf Cases (Germ. v. Den.; Germ./Neth.), Judgment, 1969 I.C.J. Rep. 3, at 44, para. 77 (Feb. 20); ICJ Nicaragua, para. 201 [*hereinafter* ICJ Continental Shelf].
145 Case Concerning Right of Passage over Indian Territory (Port. v. India), Preliminary Objections, 1957 I.C.J. Rep. 125, at 42 (Nov. 26) (holding that "[t]he practice predicates that the territorial sovereign *had the discretionary power to withdraw or to refuse permission*" and thus did not contribute to customary law).

of territorial integrity – pursuant to the Friendly Relations Declaration – apply to States *inter se*. It held:

> This resolution [2625(XXV)] then enumerated various obligations incumbent upon States to refrain from violating the territorial integrity of other sovereign States. In the same vein, the Final Act of the Helsinki Conference on Security and Co-operation in Europe of 1 August 1975 (the Helsinki Conference) stipulated that '[t]he participating *States* will respect the territorial integrity of each of the participating *States'* (Art. IV). *Thus, the scope of the principle of territorial integrity is confined to the sphere of relations between States.*[146]

This holding is important. While the Court confirmed the non-applicability of territorial integrity to the legality question regarding Kosovo's declaration of independence, it was in effect pronouncing on the impact of territorial integrity upon the means of implementing self-determination. In other words, the principle of territorial integrity does not bind – in general – a people who are qualified for a right to self-determination. After all, it would seem artificial as a matter of law to argue that the principle would now apply if Kosovo had implemented self-determination differently through a forcible means.

3   Territorial Integrity as a Rebuttable Presumption

At a more general level, it can be said that a State against whom a self-determination claim is posed may not hide behind the shield of territorial integrity. This proposition is by no means taken from thin air. A solid example would be colonialism or analogous situations of foreign domination. The relevant legal position is that a territory entitled to the right to self-determination has "a status separate and distinct from the territory of the State administering it" until the right is exercised.[147] In the past, UNGA has called upon the administering/third States to respect the territorial integrity of the dependent territory.[148] In *Chagos*, the ICJ confirmed "the customary law character of the

---

[146]   ICJ Kosovo, para. 80 [emphasis added]. *See also* Corten, at 87.
[147]   ICJ Western Sahara, para. 149; ICJ Namibia, at 115 (separate opinion of Judge Padilla Nervo); ICJ East Timor, at 146 (dissenting opinion of Judge Skubiszewski); Friendly Relations Declaration, Principle V, para. 6.
[148]   G.A. Res. 2023(XX) (Nov. 5, 1965) and 2183(XXI) (Dec. 12, 1966) (Question of Aden); 3161 (XXVIII) (Dec. 14, 1973) and 3291(XXIX) (Dec. 13, 1974) (Question of the Comoro Archipelago); G.A. Res. 34/91 (Dec. 12, 1979) (Question of the islands of Glorieuses, Juan de Nova, Europa and Bassas da India).

right to territorial integrity of a non-self-governing territory as a corollary of the right to self-determination."[149] It further held that:

> The Court considers that the peoples of non-self-governing territories are entitled to exercise their right to self-determination in relation to their territory as a whole, *the integrity of which must be respected by the administering Power*.[150]

Indeed, it cannot be otherwise. If the law of self-determination is to confer a positive right upon a people, it must do so in conformity with the people's understanding of *its own specific territorial link* formed by an objective assessment of historical fact.[151] It would appear to be a *non sequitur* for a foreign power to preserve the integrity of its territory, which in fact belongs to the people.[152] Similarly, under international humanitarian law (*jus in bello*), the use of force for self-determination shall be classified as an international armed conflict.[153] In this sense, the presumption of the territorial integrity of the established State is rebuttable by the founded claim of self-determination by a people, provided that the latter has not consented to the detachment of the territory concerned.[154]

It is on this basis that the international obligation of non-use of force is *reversed*: it is the States themselves who must not use force to impede the exercise of self-determination. Thus, the UNGA has previously condemned the use of force by the administering powers, such as the Netherlands in Indonesia[155]

---

149 ICJ Chagos, para. 160 ("respect for territorial integrity of a non-self-governing territory is a key element of the exercise of the right to self-determination under international law").
150 Id.
151 As Cherif Bassiouni succinctly noted, "realistically, [the right to self-determination] is exercisable only when it can be actuated within a given territory susceptible of acquiring the characteristics of sovereignty which is a prerequisite for acquiring membership in the community of nations." See Bassiouni, at 34.
152 Oeter, at 326, para. 25.
153 See Article 1(4) of the First Protocol additional to the Geneva Conventions. However, it should be noted that the recognition of the belligerent status in an international armed conflict under the law of *jus in bello* has no impact on the legality of the use of force under *jus ad bellum*. See James Crawford, The Creation of States in International Law 419 (1977).
154 ICJ Chagos, para. 160 (finding that the people of Chagos Archipelago had not consented at any point in time the detachment of the territory and therefore continued to benefit from the principle of territorial integrity).
155 S.C. Res. 30 (Aug. 25, 1947); S.C. Res. 27 (Aug. 1, 1947). See also G.A. Res. 1514 (XV) (Dec. 14, 1960) (declaring that "armed action or repressive measures of all kinds directed against dependent peoples shall cease in order to enable them to exercise peacefully and freely

and Portugal in Angola.[156] Generally, an Occupying Power has no recourse to a claim of self-defense within the territory it occupies under Article 51 of the Charter, for the reason that there is simply no territorial integrity of its own to be violated.[157]

With regard to Palestine, the existence of its territorial integrity (save the question regarding delimitation) is no longer disputed. The bilateral agreements concluded between Palestine and Israel thus far have consistently affirmed this point. It suffices to point out the Oslo Accord signed on 13 September 1993, in which Article IV provides that "the two sides view the West Bank and the Gaza Strip as a single territorial unit whose integrity will be preserved during the interim period."[158] In his Separate Opinion to the *Wall* Advisory Opinion, Judge Elaraby concluded that Israel had "contractual undertakings to respect the territorial integrity of the territory."[159]

As a result, international law protects the territorial integrity of Palestine against any breach of Article 2(4) of the UN Charter.[160] In Resolution 242 (1967), the UNSC unanimously called for the "[w]ithdrawal of Israel armed forces from territories occupied."[161] In so deciding, the UNSC emphasized the principle of inadmissibility of acquisition of territory by war.[162] This emphasis was borne out in the subsequent Resolution 298 (1971), in which the

---

their right to complete independence, and the integrity of their national territory shall be respected").

156 Same was applied to condemn Portugal's action in Angola and called upon the Portuguese authorities to desist from repressive measures against "the people of Angola." *See* U.N. Doc. S/4835 (June 9, 1961); G.A. Res. 1742 (XVI) (Jan. 30, 1962).

157 Dugard, at 188.

158 *See also* the Camp David Accords, Sept. 17, 1978 and the Israeli-Palestinian Interim Agreement on the West Bank and the Gaza Strip, Sept. 28, 1995, in particular Article XXXI, para. 7.

159 ICJ Wall, separate opinion of Judge Elaraby, at 252, para. 2.4. Referring to the Disengagement Plan of Israel, he continued: "The clear undertakings to withdraw and to respect the integrity and status of the West Bank and Gaza legally debar Israel from infringing upon or altering the international legal status of the Palestinian territory" (at 121, para. 2.5).

160 In academic writings, the point that Israel is prohibited under international law from the use of force in contravention to the territorial integrity of the Palestinian people has been made in numerous contributions in this Journal. *See, e.g.,* Antonio Cassese, *Legal Considerations on the International Status of Jerusalem,* 3 Palestine Y.B. Int'l L. 13, 31–32 (1986); S.V. Mallison and W.T. Mallison Jr, *The Juridical Bases for Palestinian Self-Determination,* 1 Palestine Y.B. Int'l L. 36, 61 (1984).

161 S.C. Res. 242 (Nov. 22, 1967), para. 1(i).

162 S.C. Res. 242 (Nov. 22, 1967), preamble; reaffirmed in ICJ Wall, paras. 87, 117.

UNSC declared the attempt to modify the status of Jerusalem "totally invalid."[163] Along this specific line, the ICJ concluded that "the Israeli settlements in the Occupied Palestinian Territory (including East Jerusalem) have been established in breach of international law."[164] The Court's conclusion further demonstrated that the intrusion upon a people's territory integrity need not be permanent *per se*. Instead, it took the view that: "the construction of the wall and its associated régime create a 'fait accompli' on the ground that could well become permanent" in which case "it would be tantamount to *de facto* annexation."[165] It is in this sense that Israel's unilateral act had violated the territorial integrity of the people of Palestine and therefore frustrated the exercise of its right to self-determination.

C   The Use of Force as a Derivative Right
1   Self-Defense

During the decolonization period, developing countries and the socialist bloc considered that peoples living colonial rule were authorized to use force to achieve self-determination.[166] The UNGA has endorsed this position on numerous occasions. For instance, in Resolution 34/92 on Question of Namibia, the UNGA supported the exercise of self-determination by the Namibian people "by all means at their disposal, including armed struggle."[167] Resolution 32/14, with respect to Zimbabwe, Namibia, Djibouti, the Comoros and Palestine, stressed that their self-determination were to be implemented "by all available means, including armed struggle."[168] In Resolution 35/33, without specifying a particular situation, the UNGA "*reaffirms once again* its strong support for the national liberation struggle [...] and for the achievement of self-determination by all available means, including armed struggle."[169] This

---

163   S.C. Res. 298 (Sept. 25, 1971), para. 3. *See also* S.C. Res. 446 (Mar. 22, 1979); S.C. Res. 452 (July 20, 1979) and 465 (Mar. 1, 1980), condemning the illegal settlement as a "flagrant violation" of the Fourth Geneva Convention.

164   ICJ Wall, para. 120.

165   ICJ Wall, para. 121; *see also* separate opinion of Judge Koroma, at 204, para. 2 ("Israel is therefore not entitled to embark there on activities of a sovereign nature which will change their status as occupied territory").

166   Cassese, at 151.

167   G.A. Res. 34/92 (Dec. 12, 1979), para. 12 ("Supports the armed struggle of the Namibian people, led by the South West Africa People's Organisation, to achieve self-determination"); G.A. Res. 38/36 (Dec. 1, 1983), para. 4 ("reaffirms the legitimacy of their [Namibia's] struggle by all the means at their disposal, including armed struggle, against the illegal occupation of their territory by South Africa").

168   G.A. Res. 32/14 (Nov. 7, 1977), para. 2.

169   G.A. Res. 35/33 (Nov. 14, 1980), para. 4 (emphasis in original).

general language endorsing the legality of armed struggles was also found in Resolutions 3070 (XXVIII) and 3246 (XXIX).[170] More explicitly, the *travaux preparatoires* leading up to the Friendly Relations Declaration showed that the legal basis for the forcible exercise of self-determination against the colonial powers was "a right of self-defence."[171] Between 1967–1970, the issue was intensively discussed within the Sixth Committee. During the Committee's 65th meeting, for instance, Yugoslavia was of the view that "[t]he right of self-defence of peoples under colonial domination constituted an exception to the prohibition of the use of force, which for the Yugoslav delegation was the universal and absolute rule."[172]

Scholars also expressed the view that self-defense was an arguable justification.[173] It is worth noting that for Louis Henkin, the use of force by a people for self-determination was outright permissible in the context of Article 2(4) of the UN Charter, so that the discussion of self-defense was not necessary. He explained in the following terms:

> Self-defense against colonial domination' invoked by those suffering that domination is rhetoric, not international law, and the law of the Charter, surely, does not forbid a people to liberate itself from colonial yoke.[174]

---

170   G.A. Res. 3070 (XXVIII) (Nov. 30, 1973), para. 2 ("reaffirms the legitimacy of the peoples' struggle for liberation from colonial and foreign domination and alien subjugation by all available means, including armed struggle"); 3246(XXIX) (Nov. 29, 1974), para. 3. *See also* G.A. Res. 3162 (XXVII) (Dec. 14, 1973) ("Reaffirms [...] support for, the people of the Sahara in the struggle they are waging in order to exercise their right to self-determination and independence").

171   Many States proposed a right of self-defense against colonial domination, such as Algeria, Burma, Cameroon, Dahomey, Ghana, India, Kenya, Lebanon, Madagascar, Nigeria, Syria, The United Arab Republic and Yugoslavia. *See* Special Committee report, at 497.

172   The relationship between self-defense and self-determination was summarized by Yugoslavia's delegate in 1967: "The right of self-defence of peoples under colonial domination constituted an exception to the prohibition of the use of force, which for the Yugoslav delegation was the universal and absolute rule. The exception applied only in the event of repressive measures being taken by a colonial power against a people aspiring to SD." U.N. Doc. A/AC.125/SR.65 (Dec. 4, 1967), at 14. *See also*, U.N. Doc. A/AC.125/SR.64 (Dec. 4, 1967), at 5 (India); U.N. Doc. A/AC.125/SR.64 (1967), at 6–7 (Algeria); 23 G.A.O.R. (1968) 6th Comm., 1095th mtg., U.N. Doc. A/C.6/SR.1095), para 25 (Iraq); 25 G.A.O.R. (1970) 6th Comm., 1179th mtg., U.N. Doc. A/C.6/SR.1179 (Sept. 24, 1970), para 19; U.N. Doc. A/AC.125/SR.70 (1967), at 14 (Cameroon). *See also* Gray, 63.

173   For a summary, *see* Dugard.

174   Louis Henkin, *The Reports of the Death of Article 2(4) Are Greatly Exaggerated*, 65 Am. J. Int'l L. 546, 545–546 (1971).

To be sure, the affirmative language in favor of lawful armed struggles for self-determination was no longer explicit beyond the colonial context. Especially since the 1990s, a number of international declarations were drafted to reaffirm the right to self-determination. In doing so, they speak only of implementation by "any legitimate action." This was the case in the 1993 Vienna Declaration[175] and the 1995 UN Fiftieth Anniversary Declaration.[176]

2   By Necessary Implication

A systemic outlook on international law also lends itself to the idea that the use of force by a people can be derived from its right to self-determination. This contention is premised on the assumption that peoples – as rights-holders in international law – have a limited degree of international legal personality which, by necessity, bestow upon them the legal capacity to enforce their rights.[177] Sir Hersch Lauterpacht defined the subject of international law as "the persons, natural and juridical, upon whom the law confers rights and imposes duties."[178] James Crawford in reference to self-determination noted some subjects have "intermediate legal status, involving some legal capacity."[179]

In this regard, in *Front Polisario v. Council of the European Union* the European Court of Justice held that Polisario had the "functional and transitory legal personality" necessary for the exercise of Western Sahara's self-determination.[180] With respect to the PLO, the Italian Court of Cassation confirmed that it enjoyed "a limited legal capacity" and was therefore "granted *locus standi* in the international community for the limited purpose of discussing the means and terms for the self-determination of the peoples they politically control."[181]

The critical question is what such legal capacity would entail. In terms of the means of implementing external self-determination, must a people first employ peaceful means before forcible measures? Two approaches may be

---

175   Vienna Declaration and Programme of Action Adopted by the World Conference on Human Rights in Vienna on 25 June 1993: "the World Conference on Human Rights recognizes the right of peoples to take any legitimate action, in accordance with the Charter of the United Nations, to realize their inalienable right of self-determination."
176   G.A. Res. 50/6 (Oct. 24, 1995), para. 1: "recognize the right of peoples to take legitimate action in accordance with the Charter of the [UN] to realize their inalienable right of self-determination."
177   On the point that functional personality is granted to the extent necessary, *see* Reparation for Injuries Suffered in the Service of the United Nations, Advisory Opinion, 1949 I.C.J. Rep. 174, paras. 174, 178 (Apr. 11) [*hereinafter* ICJ Reparations].
178   International Law – Collected Papers, Vol. 1 136 (Elihu Lauterpacht ed., 1970).
179   Crawford, at 418.
180   Front Polisario v. Council of the European Union, para. 78.
181   Court of Cassation, Arafat and Salah, 28 June 1985, at 884–889 (It.).

discerned. As to the first, international law has not imposed upon a people, as a matter of principle, any prescribed means of implementing its right to self-determination. The law on self-determination is silent on the matter. As the ICJ recently held: "[t]he right to self-determination under customary international does not impose a specific mechanism for its implementation in all instances."[182] In so holding, the Court had in mind the UNGA's specific "functions relating to decolonization,"[183] in which case the UNGA had "a measure of discretion with respect to the forms and procedures by which that right [to self-determination] is to be realized."[184] Beyond decolonization, the general proposition remains that customary law imposes no specific mechanism for implementation.

The second approach postulates that peaceful means precede resort to force. It is recalled that a people entitled to a right to self-determination, or their representative entity,[185] ordinarily have the legal capacity to claim and exercise such right. In its Advisory Opinion on *Reparation for Injuries Suffered in the Service of the United Nations*, the ICJ made clear that a subject of international law, once created for certain rights and obligations, "must be deemed to have those powers ... conferred upon it by necessary implication as being essential to the performance of its duties."[186] As such, the legal personality of the people or its entity is functional, to the extent that it permits certain means of implementing self-determination *by necessary implication*.[187] It follows that forcible implementation is lawful, but only on the *proviso* that no other choices are available and that the use of force comports with the *jus in bello*.

Historically, this position was predominant among States in the Third Committee of the UNGA over the years of discussions on self-determination. For instance, Greece, on behalf of the Twelve Member States of the European

---

182   ICJ Chagos, para. 158.
183   Id., para. 179.
184   Id., para. 157 (referring to ICJ Western Sahara, para. 71).
185   Where such entities exist to exercise the right of the peoples concerned, it has been noted that these groups are "authorities in their own right in international law, capable of legitimately resorting to the use of force." *See* Wilson, at 117.
186   ICJ Reparations, at 182; 184 (further holding that "the capacity of the Organization to exercise a measure of functional protection of its agents arises by necessary intendment out of the Charter").
187   In any event, this proposition assumes that the self-determination claim has been substantiated. *See* James Crawford, *Response to Experts Reports of the Amicus Curiae*, in Self-determination in International Law: Quebec and Lessons Learned 157–158 (Anne F. Bayefsky ed., 2000) ("A group does not become a subject of international law simply by expressing its wish to secede" but only does so at "an advanced stage in the process").

THE LEGALITY OF THE USE OF FORCE FOR SELF-DETERMINATION 67

Economic Community, considered that "the [UN] should above all encourage peaceful solutions to international problems."[188] In respect of the situation in Namibia, Uganda was clear that the use of force was a last resort to "all peaceful means to end apartheid."[189] This view was echoed by other States.[190] In his report on self-determination, UN Special Rapporteur Aureliu Cristescu explained that "[t]he right of self-defence of peoples under colonial domination is the counterpart of the right of peoples to defend their national identity against acts of force or coercion *which leave them no alternative.*"[191] It is in this connection that a people's legal capacity to exercise self-determination must be qualified accordingly.[192]

One may wish to note in passing the basic legal notion of negotiation. Consonant with the duty to negotiate under international law, "the parties are under an obligation to enter into negotiations with a view to arriving at an agreement."[193] In so defining in the judgment of *North Sea Continental Shelf*, the ICJ intended to articulate a general principle of law – but only in so far as the subject matter concerns "international relations,"[194] just as Article 33 of the UN Charter subsumes negotiation as one of the methods for the peaceful settlement of international disputes.[195] Whether the customary nature of the duty to negotiate between States *inter se* has transpired to bind non-State actors is, to say the least, doubtful. Put in the context of the preceding

---

188 U.N. Doc. A/C.3/43/SR.23 (Oct. 27, 1988) at 25.
189 U.N. Doc. A/C.3/43/SR.13 (Oct. 19, 1988), at 5 ("they had tried all peaceful means to end apartheid and the international community must not betray them and leave them with only one weapon, the use of force").
190 U.N. Doc. A/C.3/43/SR.10 (Oct. 17, 1988), at 2 [Romania]; at 9 [Hungary]; at 11 [Zambia].
191 Cristescu, paras. 207–208 [emphasis added].
192 *See* Shaw, at 33–34 (despite their possession of international legal personality, peoples "have no automatic right under international law to turn to violent measures"); Cassese, at 147 (referred to the "peaceful process of negotiation between the parties concerned" as "the path suggested by international norms"); Antonio Cassese, *Legal Considerations on the International Status of Jerusalem*, 3 Palestine Y.B. Int'l L. 13, 24 (1986) (arguing that a forcible re-acquisition of territory is lawful if "all possible means for a peaceful settlement of the dispute have been used before resorting to armed violence").
193 ICJ Continental Shelf, para. 85.
194 Id., para. 86. *See also* Free Zones of Upper Savoy and the District of Gex, 1932 P.C.I.J. (ser. A) No. 22, at 13 (June 7) (holding that the judicial settlement of international disputes "is simply an alternative to the direct and friendly settlement of such disputes between the parties").
195 Article 33(1) of the Charter provides that "The parties to any dispute, the continuance of which is likely to endanger the maintenance of international peace and security, shall, first of all, seek a solution by negotiation, enquiry, mediation, conciliation, arbitration, judicial settlement, resort to regional agencies or arrangements, or other peaceful means of their own choice."

developments concerning a people's use of force as the last resort, negotiation with a view to achieving self-determination is not obligatory as a legal norm.[196] Regardless, one should be mindful that the hortatory character of negotiation in no way leads to the position that a right to self-determination is "conditioned," such as upon the consent of the administering power. The content of the right is *neither negotiable nor amendable* save where the people concerned so consents. As Judge Al-Khasawneh meticulously put it, in the context of self-determination:

> ... no one should be oblivious that negotiations are a means to an end and cannot in themselves replace that end. The discharge of international obligations including *erga omnes* obligations cannot be made conditional upon negotiations.[197]

In relation to the situation of Palestine, the need for negotiations has dominated the process of implementing the right of Palestinians. At the outset, under Articles I and V(2) of the Israeli-Palestinian Interim Agreement, the process of determining the international status of the Palestinian territories will be the outcome, in part, of negotiations with the Israeli authorities.[198] This was precisely the view of the ICJ in the *Wall* Advisory Opinion:

> The Court considers that it has a duty to draw the attention of the [UNGA], to which the present Opinion is addressed, to the need for these efforts to be encouraged with a view to achieving as soon as possible, *on the basis of international law, a negotiated solution* to the outstanding problems and the establishment of a Palestinian State, existing side by side with Israel and its other neighbours, with peace and security for all in the region.[199]

As the people of Palestine has been subjugated by arguably the longest foreign military occupation in the past century, the suggestion that it has exhausted

---

196 Kader Asmal, *The Legal Status of National Liberation Movements (with Particular Reference to South Africa)*, 15 Zam. L. J. 37, 41 (1983).
197 ICJ Wall, separate opinion of Al-Khasawneh, para. 13.
198 *See also* Cassese, at 241 (pointing out that under international law "the proper way of exercising self-determination in Palestine should consist in the holding of a referendum or plebiscite in the contested area, so as to offer to the population a range of fair and realistic choices").
199 ICJ Wall, para. 162.

all available peaceful means is not without merit.[200] It is proper to point to the numerous occasions where the UNSC has expressed "its grave concern that the people of Palestine has been prevented by Israel from enjoying its inalienable rights and from exercising its right to self-determination."[201]

D   *Reappraisal*

1   The Neutrality of International Law

The question whether or not the use of force for self-determination is lawful is far from settled. The starting point is that it is not prohibited by any existing rules of international law. Under treaty law, Article 1(2) of the UN Charter codifies the principle of self-determination but neither authorizes nor bans the use of force by peoples to that end. Separately, the rule of the prohibition on the use of force, as pursuant to Article 2(4) of the Charter, is a rule governing relations between States, *i.e.* the use of force by State A against State B.

At times, States have taken the principle of territorial integrity out of context from Article 2(4), and argue *de novo* that the principle in itself prohibits the use of force for self-determination. Such argument would appear to go through the backdoor of the primary rule of *jus ad bellum* in Article 2(4). What it does in effect is that the preservation of territorial integrity, if it were to apply to self-determination claims, would in most cases water down the self-determination of peoples to an empty right.[202] This is because the people are subjected to the domestic jurisdiction of the parent State and in most cases, unless implemented by force, the right to self-determination is only to be exercised in vacuum. In any event, there does not seem to be a sufficient amount of State practice to suggest that a customary rule exists to forbid the use of force for self-determination.

Because of the impracticability for the peoples to exercise their right to self-determination while under colonial or foreign domination, the UN in its resolutions has repeatedly endorsed – explicitly or otherwise – their armed struggle. It has done so not only with specific reference to particular situations such as in Namibia, Western Sahara and Palestine, but also in general language with respect to peoples who qualify for self-determination under international

---

200   This suggestion has been made, for example, by Judge Elaraby in his separate opinion in ICJ Wall: "this special responsibility [by the UN regarding Palestine] was discharged for five decades without proper regard for the rule of law" (at 247).

201   S.C. Res. 2963E (XXVII) (Dec. 13, 1972), para. 2; S.C. Res. 2792D (XXVI) (Dec. 6, 1971), para. 2; S.C. Res. 3089D (XXVIII) (Dec. 7, 1973), para. 2.

202   In the instance of Palestine, for example, the question of territorial integrity simply does not arise, because the Occupying Power (*i.e.* Israel) is not a sovereign of the territory. *See* Pellet, at 34–35.

law. While some States chose to characterize this legal entitlement to use force as "a right of self-defense," the inconsistency in practice suggests that a general right of self-defense to achieve self-determination did not fully crystallize in customary law; rather, it remains to be case-specific. This is in addition to the fact that post-colonial instances no longer saw the UN's approval for the use of force by modern self-determination units. The treatment by international law to the use of force has thus moved from "permissible" for the colonial and non-self-governing territories to "neutral" for the post-colonial claims.

The concept of legal neutrality denotes the lack of definitive rules to regulate a specific act under positive international law.[203] Traditionally, international lawyers tackle a question of legality regarding a specific act by searching for rules that prohibit or permit it. In the absence of any cogent prohibition, the act is considered permitted and lawful. This binary understanding of permission/prohibition reflects a positivist version of international law, which finds its root in the *Lotus* Judgment of the Permanent Court of International Justice. In *Lotus*, the Permanent Court famously held that it is not necessary to demonstrate a permissive rule so long as there is no prohibition.[204] In *Kosovo*, the ICJ adopted the same methodology and arrived at the conclusion that the declaration of independence of Kosovo was in accordance with international law because there was no rule prohibiting it. Judge Simma in his declaration criticized such an approach as reflecting "an old, tired view of international law."[205] He convincingly argued that:

> That an act might be "tolerated" would not necessarily mean that it is "legal", but rather that it is "not illegal". In this sense, I am concerned that the narrowness of the Court's approach might constitute a weakness, going forward, in its ability to deal with the great shades of nuance that permeate international law. [...] The neutrality of international law on a certain point simply suggests that there are areas where international law has not yet come to regulate, or indeed, will never come to regulate. There would be no wider conceptual problem relating to the coherence of the international legal order.[206]

To answer the question before us, therefore, the first view is that because of the lack of a specific prohibition on it, the use of force for self-determination

---

203   Pellet, at 104.
204   Case of the S.S Lotus (France v. Turkey), 1927 P.C.I.J. (ser. A) No. 10 (Sep. 7).
205   ICJ Kosovo, at 478 (declaration of Judge Simma), para. 2.
206   Id., para. 9.

is *ipso facto* lawful under international law. But the second – and perhaps better – view is that international law seems to be deliberately neutral on the legality of such use of force. This is also to save the situation where an applicable permissible/prohibitive rule may later develop to regulate the matter. In line of this view, Sir Hersch Lauterpacht was of the opinion that "[i]nternational law does not condemn rebellion or secession aiming at the acquisition of independence."[207] Antonio Cassese noted that:

> [A]lthough [peoples] do not possess a *legal right* to enforce their substantive right to self-determination by resort to war, nevertheless [they] have a *legal license* to do so. This notion is intended to encapsulate the idea that wars for self-determination are not ignored by international law, or left in a legal vacuum as being outside the realm of law *qua* mere factual occurrences. Rather, legal rules take these wars into account, without however upgrading them to the status of manifestations of *jus ad bellum* proper.[208]

2   The Contingency of Illegality

But to say that international law is neutral towards a use of force for self-determination should not be the end of the matter. The neutral position applies only in so far as the force is not carried out in a manner which is *ultra vires* the purpose of exercising self-determination. There are circumstances in which the use of force may be tainted with illegality, in the sense that its implementation violates other international law rules.[209] For instance, if a group of persons in a pursuit of secession (whether qualified as a "people" or not) fortuitously succeed in its forcible action and declare independence, the consequences arising from this process are nonetheless regulated by international law. The first question that arises is the legality of the creation of the new

---

207   Hersch Lauterpacht, Recognition in International Law 8 (1947).
208   Cassese, at 153–154. *See also* Antonio Cassese, *La guerre civile et le droit international*, 90 La Revue générale de droit international public 556–57 (1986); Olivier Corten, The Law Against War 128 (2010); Olivier Corten, *Are there gaps in the international law of secession?* in Secession: International Law Perspectives 234 (Marcelo G. Kohen ed., 2006) ("la neutralité juridique se traduisant par un refus de se prononcer sur la licéité ou l'illicéité du phénoméne sécessionniste. [...] Le rapport politique entre le groupe sécessionniste et l'Etat dont il cherche à se séparer n'est en revanche pas couvert par le système juridique, non pas en raison d'une quelconque lacune mais, plus simplement, parce que le droit international n'a aucune vocation à le régir, et nie dès lors la qualité même de sujet à l'entité sécessionniste.").
209   Crawford, at 268 ("Secession is neither legal nor illegal in international law, but a legally neutral act the consequences of which are regulated internationally").

State.[210] A fundamental principle at play here is the inadmissibility of forcible acquisition of territory. In the *Wall*, the ICJ reiterated the customary status of the prohibition on the use of force and "its corollary entailing the illegality of territorial acquisition from the threat or use of force."[211] This view has been widely supported in academic writings.[212] As succinctly put by Antonio Cassese:

> ... at present general international law has departed markedly from the principle of effectiveness: de facto situations brought by force of arms are no longer automatically endorsed and sanctioned by international legal standards. At present the principle of legality is overriding – at least at the normative level – and effectiveness must yield to it.[213]

In consequence, the unlawful use of force for an unfounded secessionist claim would render the territorial acquisition unlawful and the title to that territory invalid and void.[214]

The same is true when the territorial acquisition in the guise of self-determination is carried out by *a third State*. The default position of international law is that such forcible intervention, whether individually or jointly with a people, if not directed at a valid claim of self-determination, is unlawful. It violates the prohibition on the use of force and the principle of non-intervention.[215] The act of the third State thereby constitutes an internationally wrongful act that incurs State responsibility.

---

210 *See* Weller (making the point that self-determination claims can no longer be addressed only by the principle of self-determination but by the law governing the identity and creation of States).

211 ICJ Wall, para. 87. *See also* Friendly Relations Declaration, Principle I, para. 10 (stating that: "[t]he territory of a State shall not be the object of acquisition by another State resulting from the threat or use of force. No territorial acquisition resulting from the threat or use of force shall be recognized as legal").

212 In academic writings, *see* Sir Robert Jennings, The Acquisition of Territory in International Law 56 (1963) ("conquest as a title to territorial sovereignty has ceased to be a part of the law" whether or not force used for the purpose of seizing territory was lawful or unlawful under the U.N. Charter") [*hereinafter* Jennings]; Abdelhamid El Ouali, Territorial Integrity in a Globalizing World, quoted Jennings, at 51 ("It seems therefore impossible any longer to concede that the successful seizure of another's territory by force, i.e. conquest, or subjugation, may be itself a lawful title to the territory"); Weller, at 75.

213 Cassese, at 32.

214 An act in breach of a *jus cogens* norm (*e.g.* the prohibition on the use of force) is null and void. *See* ARSIWA Commentaries, at 112, n641; Tladi, para. 146.

215 U.N. Charter arts. 2(4), 2(7). In this regard, the ICJ in *Nicaragua* held that the United States had given to the rebels (the *Contras*) constituted an unlawful use of force and an infringement of the territorial sovereignty of Nicaragua. *See* ICJ Nicaragua, para. 251.

Thus, in respect of the situation of northern Cyprus, the UNGA in its Resolutions 33/15 (1978), 34/30 (1979) and 37/253 (1983) "demand[ed] the immediate withdrawal of all foreign armed forces and foreign military presence from the Republic of Cyprus."[216] Subsequently, the UNSC pronounced the declaration of independence by the Turkish Cypriot authorities as invalid.[217] Similarly, the UNSC previously also pronounced the declared statehood of Republika Srpska and Nagorno-Karabakh as invalid, and demanded the "immediate, complete and unconditional withdrawal of the occupying forces."[218] Having taken note of these previous resolutions, the ICJ in the *Kosovo* held that "the illegality attached to the declarations of independence thus stemmed not from the unilateral character of these declarations as such, but from the fact that they were, or would have been, *connected with the unlawful use of force*."[219]

With regard to a use of force to achieve a well-founded right to self-determination, the principle of the inadmissibility of forcible acquisition of territory *prima facie* does not apply. The user of force would have done no more than to repossess its own. That is to say, the people simply *re-acquire* the territory under the general principle of restitution.[220] This is also consistent with our previous conclusion that a people have a distinct status – including the territorial integrity of their own – separate from the subjugating State. This position is nonetheless limited by the principle of *uti possidetis iure*, according to which the boundaries of the new State as a result of self-determination must remain as the ones previously established.[221] If the people forcibly acquire territories which fall outside what the scope of their self-determination

---

216   G.A. Res. 34/30 (Nov. 20, 1979), para. 5; G.A. Res. 33/15 (Nov. 9, 1978), para. 3; 37/253 (May 13, 1983), paras. 7, 8.
217   S.C. Res. 541 (Nov. 18, 1983), para. 6.
218   S.C. Res. 853 (1993) (July 29, 1993); S.C. Res. 787 (Nov. 16, 1992).
219   ICJ Kosovo, para. 81 [emphasis added].
220   Cassese, at 24, arguing that where it is "undisputed that prior to the use of force sovereignty over the territory belonged to the same state which used foce to expel the unlawful occupant … it would be more correct to speak of 'reacquisition' of territory."
221   ICJ Frontier Dispute, para. 20 ("It is a general principle, which is logically connected with the phenomenon of obtaining independence, wherever it occurs"); ICJ Arbitral Award, at 53. *See also* Badinter Committee Opinion No. 3, 31 I.L.M., 1992, at 1497 (in which the Committee affirmed the right of self-determination of the Bosnian Serbs but denied that this gave them the right to use force to alter existing boundaries). *See also* Gray, at 64; Jan Klabbers and Rene Lefeber, *Africa: Lost between Self-Determination and Uti Possidetis*, in Peoples and Minorities in International Law 37–76 (Catherine Brolmann et al eds., 1993), pp. 37–76; Higgins, supra note 21, p. 121.

claim could confer, the use of force for that particular result becomes unlawful and the acquisition void.[222]

In this vein, the question on the use of force for self-determination is necessarily preceded by the issue of territory. In other words, the territorial delimitation of what belongs to a people pre-determines whether the purpose for which the use of force is specifically directed would be *ultra vires*. To buttress this proposition, the ICJ has recently re-affirmed that "the right to self-determination of the people concerned is defined by reference to the entirety of a non-self-governing territory" and therefore "the peoples of non-self-governing territories are entitled to exercise their right to self-determination in relation to their territory as a whole."[223] From this point of view, the right of the people does not terminate simply by the fact that it is no longer physically present on the territory concerned, such as when it has been forcibly displaced. This conclusion was remarked at the 1971 American Society of International Law Proceedings in the context of Palestine:

> It must be noted that what is claimed by the Palestinians is not a right of "self-determination" arising only in the present or after their displacement in 1948 from Palestine, but a right which existed at the time the mandate was established and never terminated. The main tenet of this position is that legitimate rights such as "self-determination" are not extinguishable by the coercive displacement (or preventing the return) of the "people" from the "territory" after the right has accrued to this very "people" on that very territory.[224]

For the foregoing reasons, despite the neutrality of international law on the matter, that a particular use of force may become illegal is *sui generis* depending on the circumstances attached to it. It is also useful to point out that a people in their use of force may violate rules of international humanitarian law (*jus in bello*) - or even commit international crimes such as war crimes. However, a violation of *jus in bello* in theory has no impact on the analysis under *jus ad bellum* and thus would not render the force illegal. It remains

---

222 Cassese, at 24 (arguing that the use of force to reacquire territory is lawful provided that "the use of force has not gone beyond the limited goal of restoring sovereign rights over the territory").
223 ICJ Chagos, para. 160. *See also* ICJ Wall, separate opinion of Judge Higgins, para. 31 ("'Peoples' necessarily exercise their right to self-determination within their own territory").
224 Bassiouni, at 38.

simply that if the new successor State, if later created, would be responsible for such internationally wrongful act.[225]

V Conclusion

The application of the right to self-determination, under the auspices of the UN, has resulted in the creation of over 100 States. Now that the process of decolonization has virtually been completed, the principle of self-determination – perhaps less visible nowadays – is alive and well. The need to appreciate and, to the extent necessary, reconceptualize the principle has been reflected in modern self-determination claims by aspiring peoples who use the principle in a variety of (novel) manners. These include: (i) situations of alien subjugation and foreign domination (*e.g.* Palestine and Western Sahara); (ii) the notion of "remedial secession" (*e.g.* Kosovo); and (iii) the possibility of re-exercising the unlawfully implemented right to self-determination (*e.g.* Chagos Archipelago).

The present discussion on the legality of the use of force for self-determination is necessarily incomplete. It has not, for example, addressed the use of force for internal self-determination. Internal self-determination denotes a representative government and in particular a sufficient degree of self-government for minorities within a State. It thus accords a wide discretion to States in putting the necessary internal arrangements in place, *e.g.* an autonomy. Article 2(7) of the UN Charter provides that "[n]othing contained in the present Charter shall authorize the [UN] to intervene in matters which are essentially within the domestic jurisdiction of any state."[226] In this context, domestic law seems to take primacy in regulating the use of force that seeks to attain a representative governance. This being said, the increasing recognition of the concept of "remedial secession" – buttressed by the ICJ in the *Kosovo* Advisory Opinion and the majority of the State submissions in its proceedings – suggested the legal possibility that a right to *internal* self-determination, in the exceptional circumstance of atrocious human rights violations, may be elevated to a right to *external* self-determination. This blurred line between the international/domestic law realms can be described as the "indeterminacy" of the legality of

---

225 *See* Bijelić v. Montenegro and Serbia, No. 11890/05, Eur. Ct. Hum. Rts. (Apr. 28, 2009), paras. 68–70; Pavel Šturma, Special Rapporteur on succession of States in respect of State responsibility, Second Report, U.N. Doc. A/CN.4/719 (Apr. 12, 2018), draft article 7. paras. 120–122.

226 U.N. Charter art. 2(7). *See* Georg Nolte, *Article 2(7)*, in The Charter of the United Nations: A Commentary, Vol. I 162 (3rd ed., 2012).

the use of force question.[227] More specifically, it would be extremely difficult to say with precision at what point international law rules begin to bind the action of the peoples *vis-à-vis* their State.

It is in this sense that the right to self-determination is not a straightjacket. It must be interpreted in light of the changing landscape of the political reality, taking into consideration the progressive development of international law. To borrow the wisdom of the former ICJ Judge Manfred Lachs, he remarked:

> Today's meaning [of self-determination] must be placed within the context of contemporary relevance. It is an anachronism if old criteria are attached to the meaning of today. Thus statehood and sovereignty constitute today an inseparable link with self-determination and rely upon it as the rock ad basic principle from which they derive their real force.[228]

---

[227] Martti Koskenniemi, *National Self-Determination Today: Problems of Legal Theory and Practice*, 43 Int'l Comp. L. Q. 241, 264 (1994) (arguing that the right to self-determination is inherently indeterminate because of the relative "self" qualifier).

[228] Lachs, p. 54.

The Right to Return: Drafting Paragraph 11 of General Assembly Resolution 194 (III), December 11, 1948

Terry Rempel

Contents

I   Introduction and Background
II   Phase One: The United Nations Mediator on Palestine
     A   *The Mediator's June Suggestions*
     B   *The British Provisional Draft Resolution*
     C   *The Mediator's September Report*
III   Phase Two: The Anglo-American-Acting Mediator Drafts
     A   *The First British Draft*
     B   *The American Draft*
     C   *The First Composite Draft*
     D   *The Bunche Draft*
     E   *The Second Composite Draft*
     F   *The Third Composite Draft*
IV   Phase Three: The First Committee (Political) Drafts
     A   *The First Revised American (Partial) Draft*
     B   *The Revised British Draft*
     C   *The American Amendments*
     D   *Additional Draft Resolutions and Amendments*
     E   *The First Revised British Draft Resolution*
     F   *Israeli Observations on the Revised British Draft and American Amendments*
     G   *The American Composite Draft*
     H   *The Second Revised British Draft Resolution*
     I   *Discussion of the Tabulation*
V   Phase Four: Revisions in the General Assembly's Plenary Session
     A   *Final Amendments*
VI   Conclusions

I Introduction and Background

On 11 December 1948, the United Nations (UN) General Assembly (UNGA), meeting, in its third session, adopted Resolution 194 setting out the parameters for "a peaceful adjustment of the future situation of Palestine."[1] The adoption of the resolution capped months of consultation, debate and negotiation inside and outside the halls of the UN intersecting at times with concurrent discussions about international peace and security, the development of international law and the delivery of humanitarian relief in the years that followed the Second World War. The ebb and flow of hostilities that accompanied the dissolution of Mandate Palestine and the establishment of the State of Israel, electoral politics in the United States (US) where President Harry Truman was vying for a second term in office, along with increasing Cold War tensions and growing pressure for decolonization provided the backdrop to the drafting process that began in the summer of 1948 and ended some four months later with the adoption of Resolution 194. Speaking before the UNGA on December 11th, Hector McNeil, the representative of the United Kingdom (UK) and sponsor of the resolution, acknowledged that even though "it was not, unfortunately, a strong resolution, and, in the circumstances, it could not be so [Resolution 194] was the best answer which many brains and good intentions could produce, and which those who had worked upon it thought most likely to secure adequate authority. What [the resolution] lacked in precision [McNeil] hoped it would command by its authority, the authority of the [UN]."[2]

UNGA Resolution 194 was the UN's second major "peace plan" for Palestine and a response to the collapse of its first, UNGA Resolution 181, recommending the division of the country into politically distinct yet economically linked "Arab" and "Jewish" States.[3] It was the adoption of the "partition plan" on November 29th, 1947, just over a year earlier, which sparked hostilities leading to the dissolution of Mandate Palestine, the establishment of a Jewish State in the country and the Arab region's first major refugee crisis of the twentieth

---

1 G.A. Res. 194 (Dec. 11, 1948), para. 1.
2 G.A.O.R., 3rd Sess., 184th plen. mtg. (Dec. 11, 1948), at 952.
3 G.A. Res. 181 (Nov. 29, 1947). On UNGA resolutions as agreements, *see* Blaine Sloan, *General Assembly Resolutions Revisited (Forty Years Later)*, 41 Brit. Y.b. Int'l. L. 41, 65 (1988) [*hereinafter* Sloan] (stating that "the text of a resolution may itself constitute an agreement among member States [...] the resolution could be drafted in terms that express a clear intent to constitute an agreement, or the intention might be found in statements made at the time of the vote.").

century.[4] Among the various procedural and substantive changes in the second UN peace plan was a new provision on forced displacement arising from the first Arab-Israeli war. Under paragraph 11 the UNGA resolved that:

> the refugees wishing to return to their homes and live at peace with their neighbours should be permitted to do so at the earliest practicable date, and that compensation should be paid for the property of those choosing not to return and for loss of or damage to property which, under principles of international law or in equity, should be made good by the Governments or authorities responsible.[5]

A second clause instructed a newly-established UN organ, the Conciliation Commission for Palestine, "to facilitate the repatriation, resettlement and economic and social rehabilitation of the refugees and the payment of compensation."[6]

In the aftermath of a second major Arab-Israeli war in 1967, which ended with Israel's military occupation of the remaining areas of Mandate Palestine, along with the Egyptian Sinai and the Syrian Golan, the UN Security Council (UNSC) adopted Resolution 242, the international organization's third "peace plan" in barely two decades.[7] Faced with a second major refugee crisis, the UNSC affirmed the necessity "for achieving a just settlement of the refugee

---

4 For a detailed discussion of the refugee situation arising from the 1948 war, *see*: Benny Morris, The Birth of the Palestinian Refugee Problem Revisited (2004) [*hereinafter* Morris 2004]; Ilan Pappe, The Ethnic Cleansing of Palestine (2006) [*hereinafter* Pappe]. There are few studies of Jewish displacement with estimates of the number of Jews evacuated or displaced during the war in Palestine ranging from 8,000–72,000. *See, generally*, Nurit Cohen Levinovsky, *The Evacuation of the Non-Combatant Population During the 1948 War: Three Kibbutizim as a Case Study*, 26 J. Israeli Hist. 1, 2 (2007); Moshe Naor, *Israel's 1948 War of Independence as a Total War*, 43 J. Contemp. Hist. 241, 255 (2008). On forced displacement in the Arab region, *see, e.g.*, Anita Fabos, *Refugees in the Arab Middle East: Academic and Policy Perspectives*, 24 Digest. Mid. East. Stud. 96 (2015); Dawn Chatty, Displacement and Dispossession in the Modern Middle East (2010).
5 G.A. Res. 194 (Dec. 11, 1948), para. 11.
6 Id.
7 S.C. Res. 242 (Nov. 22, 1967). On UNSC resolutions as peace agreements, *see* Christine Bell, On the Law of Peace: Peace Agreements and the Lex Pacificatoria 95–96 (2008) (stating that "[i]nterstate treaty consolidation up to the end of the Cold War pushed peacemaking practices in intrastate conflict into mechanisms [including Security Council resolutions] other than the treaty in its modern codified sense"). The principles affirmed in Resolution 242 and its companion resolution – S.C. Res. 338 (Oct. 22, 1973) – were elaborated further in the 1978 Framework for Peace in the Middle East, the 1993 Declaration of Principles on Interim Self-Government arrangements and related agreements.

problem" arising from the struggle over Palestine.[8] Less than a decade later, in response to growing support for the inalienable rights of the Palestinian people, including their right to self-determination and the "right of Palestinians to return to their homes and property," the UNGA adopted a set of principles – Resolution 3236 (1974) – which member States described as "indispensable for a solution to the question of Palestine."[9] These principles provided the framework for a fourth and lesser known "peace plan."[10] While UN member States have reaffirmed each of the above resolutions since their adoption, they continue to regard UNSC Resolution 242 – along with subsequent UNSC resolutions clarifying procedural and substantive elements of a "just and lasting peace in the Middle East" – as the primary if not sole framework for a political settlement.[11]

The UNGA's second peace plan, Resolution 194, nevertheless retains special significance when it comes to finding solutions for the millions of Palestinians displaced as a result of the struggle over Palestine/Israel.[12] This may be attributed, in part, to claims about the juridical effects of the

---

8   S.C. Res. 242 (Nov. 22, 1967), para. 2(b). The ambiguous language used in paragraph 2(b), not unlike other provisions in Resolution 242, spawned a significant debate among policymakers and scholars about the substantive meaning of "a just settlement of the refugee problem." For discussion of the drafting history, see John Quigley, *Security Council Resolution 242 and the Right of Repatriation*, 37 J. Pal. Stud. 49 (2007) [*hereinafter* Quigley 2007]. An opposing view, without reference to the drafting history, can be found in Ruth Lapidoth, *The Misleading Interpretation of* UN *Security Council Resolution 242 (1967)*, 23 Jew. Pol. Stud. Rev. 7 (2011).

9   G.A. Res. 3236 (Nov. 22, 1974), para. 3. The UNGA previously clarified that "the enjoyment by the Palestine Arab refugees of their right to return to their homes and property, recognized by the [UNGA] in Resolution 194 (III) of 11 December 1948 […] is indispensable for the achievement of a just settlement of the refugee problem and for the exercise by the people of Palestine of its right to self-determination." G.A. Res. 3089D (Dec. 7, 1973), para. 3.

10 *Report of the Committee on the Inalienable Rights of the Palestinian People*, U.N. Doc. S/12090 (May 29, 1976). The plan provides for a two-State solution based on Israel's complete withdrawal from the West Bank, East Jerusalem, and Gaza Strip with provision for a temporary international peace-keeping mission and the phased return of displaced Palestinians to the future Palestinian State and refugees to their homes of origin inside the State of Israel.

11 *See* S.C. Res. 1397 (Mar. 22, 2002); S.C. Res. 1515 (Nov. 19, 2003); S.C. Res. 1850 (Dec. 16, 2008). *See also* resolutions reaffirmed in: G.A. Res. 73/19 (Nov. 30, 2018) on the Peaceful Settlement of the Question of Palestine.

12 Palestinians displaced as a result of the 1948 Arab-Israeli war comprise the majority of Palestinian refugees and displaced persons. The principles set forth in paragraph 11 of Resolution 194 nevertheless apply to other groups of displaced Palestinians. For a useful summary of groups and related statistics, *see* Survey of Palestinian Refugees and Internally Displaced Persons 2013–2015 33 (Nidal al-Azza & Omaya al-Orzza eds., 2015).

resolution, notwithstanding differences over whether paragraph 11 gives rise to legal obligations along with disagreements among both scholars and policymakers about their substantive content.[13] Of central importance to refugee situations, generally, and the Palestinian case, in particular, is the duty of States to take back their nationals with the UNGA's December 1948 resolution on Palestine described as "[t]he genesis of a modern [and corresponding] claim for refugees' 'right to return'."[14] The legal scrutiny and related debates provoked by this assertion bring to fore a second and related reason for the continuing relevance of the UN's second peace plan in crafting durable solutions for displaced Palestinians.[15] The outcome of dialogue and deliberation among the community of States, UNGA resolutions, as the British representative and sponsor of Resolution 194 seemed to allude, may also have "an invaluable influence on the behavior of states and stigmatize or isolate the practice of states

---

13   On the effects of UNGA resolutions, *see* Sloan, at 105 (stating that "[t]he term 'effects' covers a very broad panorama including legal, hortatory, political, practical and other consequences. Legal effects themselves are not limited to force or obligation but cover a wide area including matters of status and operation.").

14   On the duty of States to take back their nationals, *see* Guy S. Goodwin-Gill and Jane McAdam, The Refugee in International Law 2 (2007) [*hereinafter* Goodwin-Gill and McAdam] (stating that "refugee-generating states owe certain responsibilities to [refugee receiving countries] based on the doctrine of abuse of rights of third states"). *See also* John Quigley, *Mass Displacement and the Individual Right of Return*, 68 Brit. Yb. Int'l. L. 65, 67 (1997). On Resolution 194 as the "modern genesis" of refugees' right to return, *see* Katy Long, The Point of No Return: Refugees, Rights, and Repatriation 46, 73 (2013) [*hereinafter* Long] (further stating that "repatriation has always been considered the international community's ideal solution to refugee crises. This is because organized repatriation emerged in the early twentieth century in parallel with the consolidation of the liberal nation state.").

15   For an overview of the literature and related arguments, *see* Terry Rempel, *The Right of Palestinian Refugees to Return to their Homes in Theory and in Practice*, in International Conference on Palestinian Refugees, Conditions and Recent Developments 235 (Huwaida Arraf & Adam Shapiro eds., 2009) [*hereinafter* Rempel]. For a broader discussion of Palestinian and Jewish Israeli positions, *see*, *e.g.*: Nur Masalha, *The PLO, Resolution 194 and the 'right of return': evolving Palestinian attitudes towards the refugee question from the 1948 Nakba to the Camp David summit of July 2000*, 7 YB. Islamic & Middle E. L. 127 (2000–2001); Nur Masalha, The Politics of Denial: Israel and the Palestinian Refugee Problem (2003) [*hereinafter* Masalha]; Orit Gal, *Israeli Perspectives on the Palestinian Refugee Issue*, Chatham House Briefing Paper [hereinafter Gal], https://www.chathamhouse.org/sites/default/files/public/Research/Middle%20East/0608palrefugees_gal.pdf; Abbas Shiblak, *The Palestinian Refugee Issue: A Palestinian Perspective*, Chatham House Briefing Paper [hereinafter Shiblak], https://www.chathamhouse.org/sites/default/files/public/Research/Middle%20East/bp0209_pri_shiblak.pdf.

that do not conform to [them]."[16] In other words, resolutions can have certain political effects. For both these reasons – legal and political – Resolution 194, paragraph 11 in particular, has been subject to numerous and often conflicting interpretations.[17]

This article focuses on the meaning of paragraph 11 of UNGA Resolution 194 with special reference to the language on refugee return. Described as "the most oft-cited international document in discussions of the right of return," the latter phrase, namely, right of return, is curiously absent from the paragraph which refers, in its two sub-paragraphs respectively, to the "return" and the "repatriation" of refugees without explicitly mentioning their "right" to do so.[18] This absence is curious, in part, because the phrase ("right to return") is used extensively in the Progress Report of the UN Mediator on Palestine

---

16 Celine Van Den Rul, *Why Have Resolutions of the United Nations General Assembly if They Are Not Legally Binding*, E-International Relations, https://www.e-ir.info/2016/06/16/why-have-resolutions-of-the-un-general-assembly-if-they-are-not-legally-binding (and sources cited). *See also* M.J. Peterson, *General Assembly*, in The Oxford Handbook on the United Nations 97, 101–2 (Sam Daws and Thomas G. Weiss eds., 2009) (stating that "the political influence of a resolution varies directly with both the breadth and the depth of support it attracts. Assessing the depth of support [...] begins with a close reading of the resolution to see whether support has been won by adopting vague or lowest common denominator statements. It also includes paying attention to statements made in debate or during the interval when delegations may offer explanations of their vote.").

17 This includes disagreements over the absence of an explicit reference to the phrase "right of return"; the relationship between return, resettlement and compensation; the meaning of the phrase "live in peace with their neighbours;" the timing of return with reference to "the earliest practicable date;" the definition of a "refugee;" and, the legal effects of the resolution. Rempel, at 256.

18 Megan Bradley, Refugee Repatriation: Justice, Responsibility and Redress 199 (2013). *See also*: Megan Bradley, *Liberal Democracies' Divergent Interpretations of the Right of Return: Implications for Free Movement*, in Democratic Citizenship and the Free Movement of People 195, 195–6 (William Maas ed., 2013) (stating that there is, nevertheless, "a surprising death of literature examining the origins, evolution and implications" of the right to return "[d]espite the centrality of this principle to contemporary human rights system." Bradley suggests this may be the case "because thousands of people around the world exercise this right every day with relatively little fanfare, when they re-enter their countries after travelling abroad, and return to their homes after moving freely about their own state. [...] Equally, researchers concerned with migration and free movement may have overlooked the significance of this principle because of what may be called an 'outbound bias' in the migration and freedom of movement literature."); Long, at 4–5 (stating that "[t]he vast majority of research on repatriation has been carried out in the past thirty years. This is in part because of the exponential growth in refugee and forced migration studies, but it also reflects the fact that from the 1950s until the early 1980s, repatriations were rarely organized, and when they did occur they were largely uncontroversial. It was the political and ethical controversies that followed the expansion of repatriation in practice that also fuelled the critical growth in the study of refugee return.").

whose seven basic premises and eleven specific conclusions comprised the basis for the international organization's second peace plan.[19] The adoption of the Universal Declaration of Human Rights codifying return as an individual right on Dec. 10th, 1948, one day earlier, appears to lend further mystery to the absence of similar language in paragraph 11 of Resolution 194.[20] The absence of this phrase, moreover, is among the arguments often deployed by policy-makers and scholars who favour the assimilation of Palestinian refugees into countries of new nationality through local integration in countries of first asylum or resettlement in third States.[21] While a review of the drafting history of Resolution 194 is unlikely to alter the positions of those opposed to the return of Palestinian refugees to their homes and places of origin inside the State of Israel, it does help to explain the meaning of paragraph 11, including provisions governing refugee return, and in so doing may also further research and discussion about its legal and political effects.

Given the absence of established rules for the interpretation of UNGA resolutions, the article draws upon general principles of treaty interpretation codified in the 1969 Vienna Convention of the Law of Treaties.[22] Bearing in mind differences between UNGA resolutions and international treaties, in both substantive content and drafting procedures, the Convention provides useful guidelines for the interpretation of the UNGA's second peace plan.[23] The article builds upon the small body of existing research on UNGA Resolution 194,

---

19   Progress Report of the United Nations Mediator on Palestine, submitted to the Secretary-General for transmission to the members of the UN, U.N. G.A.O.R., 3rd Sess., Supp. No. 11, U.N. Doc. A/648 (1948) [*hereinafter* Progress Report].

20   Universal Declaration of Human Rights art. 13(2), G.A. Res. 217A (Dec. 10, 1948) [*hereinafter* UDHR].

21   *See, e.g.*: Joseph B. Schechtman, The Refugee in the World: Displacement and Integration 227 (1963) (stating that "paragraph 11 does not confer on the refugees any 'right' to repatriation and does not even use this term") [*hereinafter* Schechtman]; Kurt René Radley, *The Palestinian Refugees: The Right to Return in International Law*, 72 Am. J. Int'l. L. 596, 601 (1978) [*hereinafter* Radley] (stating that the terms "'right' or 'rights' [...] are nowhere to be found in the paragraph itself").

22   Vienna Convention on the Law of Treaties art. 31(1), May 23, 1969, 1155 U.N.T.S. 331 [*hereinafter* VCLT] (stating that "[a] treaty shall be interpreted in good faith in accordance with the ordinary meaning to be given to the terms of the treaty in their context and in the light of its object and purpose"). Sloan, at 128 (stating that when a UNGA resolution "contains a binding decision expressly authorized by the Charter, or where it constitutes an agreement, it would be reasonable to apply the treaty rule on *travaux préparatoires*. The rule might also be relevant for the determination of the meaning of the text of a resolution and even in ascertaining the intent of the [UNGA] as an organ.").

23   For a useful discussion in relation to resolutions of the UNSC, *see* Michael C. Wood, *The Interpretation of Security Council Resolutions*, 2 Max Planck Yb. U.N. L. 73, 82 (1998) [*hereinafter* Wood].

much of which is found in a broader body of research – historical, political and legal – on Palestinian refugees.[24] First, it draws upon a significant body of primary documents from American, British, and UN archives including several previously unpublished texts of resolutions drafted in the months leading up to discussion of the UN Mediator's Progress Report in the UNGA's First Committee. Second, the article also places the drafting process in the context of events unfolding in Palestine/Israel, especially those relating to forced displacement, from the outbreak of hostilities following the adoption of the first peace plan to the conclusion of the second peace plan just over a year later. Finally, it situates the drafting history of paragraph 11 on refugees within the context of a number of significant and related developments – legal, political and humanitarian – outside of Palestine in the years leading up to and following the 1948 war.

The article is divided into four major sections covering four distinct yet overlapping phases in the drafting history of Resolution 194. While the UNGA's first peace plan, Resolution 181, and its particular elements arose repeatedly in discussions of the UNGA's second plan, the drafting history of the partition plan is beyond the scope of this article. The first section of the article, from June through September (Phase One), examines suggestions and conclusions by Count Folke Bernadotte, the UN Mediator on Palestine. The next section (Phase Two) explores previously unpublished draft resolutions prepared in the context of Anglo-American-UN consultations from late September until the end of the second truce in October. The third section (Phase Three) covers the drafting history of the resolution in the UNGA's First Committee from the end of the second truce through early December. The fourth and final section (Phase Four) examines final amendments to the resolution adopted

---

24   *See, e.g.*: Rony Gabbay, A Political Study of the Arab-Jewish Conflict: The Arab Refugee Problem (A Case Study) (1959); George Tomeh, *Legal Status of Arab Refugees*, 33 Law & Contemp. Probs. 110 (1968) [*hereinafter* Tomeh]; Radley; W. Thomas Mallison & Sally V. Mallison, *An International Law Analysis of the Major United Nations Resolutions Concerning the Palestine Question*, U.N. Doc. ST/SG/SER.F/4, Sales No. E/79/I/19 (Jan. 1, 1979) [Mallison and Mallison]; Ruth Eschelbacher Lapidoth, *The Right of Return in International Law, with Special Reference to the Palestinian Refugees*, 16 Isr. Yb. Hum. Rts. 103 (1986) [*hereinafter* Lapidoth]; John Quigley, *Displaced Palestinians and a Right of Return*, 31 Harv. Int'l L. J. 171 (1998); Gail Boling, The 1948 Palestinian Refugees and the Individual Right of Return: An International Law Analysis (2nd ed., 2007) [*hereinafter* Boling]; Yaffa Zilbershats, *International Law and the Palestinian Right of Return to Israel*, in Israel and the Palestinian Refugees 191 (Sari Hanafi et al. eds., 2007) [*hereinafter* Zilbershats]; Andrew Kent, *Evaluating the Palestinians' Claimed Right of Return*, 34 U. Pa. J. Int'l L. 149 (2012–2013) [*hereinafter* Kent]; Simon A. Waldman, Anglo-American Diplomacy and the Palestinian Refugee Problem 1948–51 (2015).

on December 11th over the course of several plenary meetings of the UNGA. The refugee issue received relatively little attention during the drafting process with the primary focus on territorial and procedural issues relating to the peaceful adjustment of the situation in Palestine. These latter issues are nevertheless important in understanding the evolution of language on refugees and the final wording of paragraph 11 of Resolution 194.

II   Phase One: the United Nations Mediator on Palestine

UNGA Resolution 194 was drafted over a period of several months in the fall and early winter of 1948 with Anglo-American discussions in September and October followed by UN debates in November and early December. It was the suggestions and specific conclusions drafted by the UN Mediator on Palestine, Count Folke Bernadotte, and his team of advisors between June and September, however, that essentially gave birth to what would become the UNGA's second peace plan for Palestine.[25] Replacing the UN Palestine Commission, the body set up to facilitate the implementation of the UNGA's first peace plan, Resolution 181 (commonly described as the "partition plan"), member States asked Bernadotte to help secure a truce, address the humanitarian consequences of the fighting and "promote a peaceful adjustment of the future situation of Palestine."[26] While each task implicated the evolving refugee crisis, it was the Mediator's latter efforts to facilitate a political solution that brought to fore issues relating to the return of refugees to their homes,

---

25 For additional discussion of the UN Mediator, see, e.g.: Joseph Heller, *Failure of a Mission: Bernadotte and Palestine, 1948*, 14 J. Contemp. Hist. 515 (1979) [hereinafter Heller]; Sune O. Persson, Mediation & Assassination: Count Bernadotte's Mission to Palestine 264–66 (1979) [hereinafter Persson]; Saadia Touval, The Peace Brokers: Mediator's in the Arab-Israeli Conflict, 1948–79 24–75 (1982) [hereinafter Touval]; Amitzur Ilan, Bernadotte in Palestine, 1948 81–2 (1989) [hereinafter Ilan]; Brian Urquhart, Ralph Bunche: An American Life (1993) [hereinafter Urquhart]; Elad Ben-Dror, *Ralph Bunche and the Establishment of Israel*, 14 Israel Aff. 519 (2008). See also Frank Brecher, American Diplomacy and the Israeli War of Independence 86 (2013) (stating that "the practice was for Bernadotte to remain uninvolved in the initial preparation by his staff of the peace proposals; only after the details were put on paper would he be 'orally consulted' on them (Bunche's 1950 description at Harvard) before their issuance under his name").

26 G.A. Res. 186 (S-2) (May 14, 1948). The five-member Palestine Commission was comprised of representatives from Bolivia, Czechoslovakia, Denmark, Panama, and the Philippines. Many of the Commission's senior advisors, including its principal secretary, Ralph Bunche, had worked for the Special Committee on Palestine, the body set up by the UNGA in 1947 to make recommendations on the future of Palestine, and would later work for the UN Mediator on Palestine.

lands and properties within territories controlled by the recently established Jewish State. The provisions of the first truce agreement negotiated in late May and early June along with Bernadotte's interventions in the UNSC and his discussions with Arab and Israel officials would nevertheless having a bearing on the suggestions and conclusions that would comprise the basis for paragraph 11 of Resolution 194.

A   The Mediator's June Suggestions

With a truce agreement scheduled to come into effect on June 11th, Bernadotte and his team refocused their efforts on drafting informal ideas which they hoped would prolong the truce and ultimately contribute to a peaceful adjustment of the situation in Palestine.[27] Having met with Arab and Israeli officials in their respective capitals, Bernadotte returned to the Mediterranean island of Rhodes in mid-June for consultations with his senior advisors before departing once again for a second round of regional meetings. Completed two weeks later and handed over to Arab and Israeli officials on June 28, the Mediator identified "partition, the establishment of a Jewish State, and Jewish immigration" as the basic issues which needed to be addressed with his nine suggestions "designed solely to explore the possible bases for further discussions and mediation, and to elicit from the parties their reactions and further views."[28] Apparently surprised to discover the refugee situation upon taking up his post, notwithstanding the fact that an estimated 400,000 Palestinians had already been displaced, the future of the refugees appeared last among the Mediator's list of suggestions for a peaceful adjustment of the situation of Palestine.[29] In his first effort to tackle the crisis, Bernadotte recommended that "recognition

---

27 The day after his appointment, the UNSC reiterated its call upon Israeli and Arab governments and authorities to issue ceasefire orders to their respective forces. S.C. Res. 49 (May 22, 1948), para. 1. A week later the UNSC called for a four-week truce and stipulated for the first time that if the parties rejected, or having accepted later repudiated or violated the ceasefire, "the situation in Palestine [would] be reconsidered with a view to action under Chapter VII of the Charter of the [UN]." S.C. Res. 50 (May 29, 1948), para. 1. Another week would pass before the UN Mediator secured an agreement to end the fighting by which time the number of refugees had increased by around a quarter. For the text of the agreement, see Folke Bernadotte, To Jerusalem 66 (1951).

28 *Text of Suggestions Presented by the United Nations Mediator on Palestine to the Two Parties on 28 June 1948, Part I*, U.N. Doc. S/863 (June 28, 1948), paras. 4 and 8 [*hereinafter* Suggestions].

29 The figures for refugees used throughout the article, unless otherwise noted, are derived from Salman Abu Sitta, The Atlas of Palestine, 1917–1966 (2010) [*hereinafter* Abu Sitta]. *See also* Janet Abu-Lughod, *The Demographic Transformation of Palestine*, in The Transformation of Palestine: Essays on the Origin and Development of the Arab-Israeli Conflict 139 (Ibrahim Abu-Lughod ed., 1971).

be accorded to the *right* of residents of Palestine who, because of conditions created by the conflict there have left their normal places of abode, *to return to their homes* without restriction and to regain their property."[30] While the Mediator would amplify the terms of his June suggestions over the summer, including allowance for certain restrictions that aimed to secure the return of at least a portion of the refugees pending a peaceful adjustment of the situation, his position on the right to return would remain constant throughout his four months of service. The Mediator's suggestion on refugees was only one of two – the second (appearing eighth in his list of suggestions) relating to the status of minority and religious communities – that called for the protection of a specific right with the latter having added importance for refugees.[31] Guaranteeing the rights of minority populations would not only help to prevent further displacement, it would also facilitate the reintegration of returnees in their places of origin. Consistent with principles of international refugee law, with the Constitution of the International Refugee Organization (IRO) affirming that its main task "as regards displaced persons [was] to encourage and assist in every way possible their early return to their country of origin,"[32] the suggestion was also in line with international practice with the UN Relief and Rehabilitation Administration (UNRRA) having facilitated the return of an estimated seven million refugees after the end of the Second World War.[33] It was the unwillingness of certain refugees, including an estimated 250,000 European Jews, along with a new category of refugees fleeing individualized

---

30 Suggestions, Part II, para. 9 [emphasis added]. *See also* Persson, at 287 (stating that "[t]his clause, to become so important in future developments of the Palestine question, was not inserted in the 25 or 26 June drafts. And in all signed memoranda, produced by Bernadotte and his staff in preparation for the 27 June suggestions, there is not one word dealing with the Palestinian Arab refugees and their fate. What eventually made the Mediator finally add this clause to his first plan is unknown. But we know that this was one of the four Arab demands put forward by the Arab experts, among whom were two Palestinian Arab nationalists, available at Rhodes while the Mediator worked out his suggestions.").

31 Suggestions, Part II, para. 8 (recommending that "religious and minority rights be fully protected by each member of the Union and guaranteed by the [UN]").

32 Constitution of the International Refugee Organization, preamble, annexed to G.A. Res. 62 (Dec. 15, 1946). *See also* Louise W. Holborn, The International Refugee Organization, A Specialized Agency of the United Nations: Its History and Work 1946–1952 (1956).

33 Louise W. Holborn, Refugees, A Problem of Our Time: The Work of the United Nations High Commissioner for Refugees 1951–72 24 (1975). This included the repatriation of a small number of European Jews who had found asylum in Palestine during the war and wished to return to their countries of origin following the cessation of hostilities. Ori Yehudai, *Displaced in the National Home: Jewish Repatriation from Palestine to Europe, 1945–48*, 20 Jewish Soc. Stud. 69 (2014).

persecution in parts of Europe, that contributed to the post-war shift with the IRO eventually facilitating the resettlement of the vast majority of refugees falling under its mandate.

Israel's provisional government had already come to advocate the latter as the primary if not sole solution for the burgeoning number of Palestinian refugees notwithstanding significant differences between the two cases.[34] Two days before acceding to the truce agreement, David Ben Gurion, Israel's first Prime Minister, approved a plan (Retroactive Transfer: A Scheme for the Solution of the Arab Question in the State of Israel) formalizing measures already put in place back in the spring.[35] While the initial focus would be on measures to prevent the return of refugees, from the destruction and settlement of Jews in their villages to the adoption of legislation and dissemination of propaganda against their return, the plan also provided for resettlement of the refugees outside the State of Israel.[36] Meeting on 16 June, just over a month after the Jewish State came into being, Israel's cabinet agreed, despite reticence among some coalition members, that "[the provisional government] must prevent at all costs [the] return [of the refugees]."[37] Moshe Sharett, the Israeli Foreign Minister, described the forcible displacement of Palestinians as "one of those revolutionary changes after which [the clock of] history [could not] be turned back" comparing the situation in Palestine to the exchange of

---

34　United Kingdom Delegation to Foreign Office, No. 542, Aug. 4, 1948, NA, FO 371-68578 E10435 (stating that in response to a request for assistance in June 1948 from the Arab Higher Committee, the *de facto* representative of Palestine's Arab majority, the IRO stated that "in their opinion [the refugee situation] [was] fundamentally a relief and not a refugee problem"). *See also* Gerard Daniel Cohen, In War's Wake: Europe's Displaced Persons in the Post-War Order 146 (2012) [*hereinafter* Cohen] (stating that in October 1949, a year and a half later, "[t]he IRO legal division argued that 'Arab refugees were the result of war operations and did not fall within the wording "persecution or fear based on reasonable ground of persecution", the criterion otherwise used to evaluate the claims of [displaced persons] in Europe. But because they were 'willing' to return home but 'unable' to do so, Palestinian refugees could plausibly be considered political refugees: this inability, the IRO legal experts suggested, was potentially equivalent to 'fear of persecution'.").

35　Morris 2004, at 313.

36　The provisional government also authorized the use of force to prevent what it described as "infiltration" of the Jewish State by refugees seeking to re-establish themselves in their villages and towns of origin. Benny Morris, Israel's Border Wars, 1949–1956: Arab Infiltration, Israeli Retaliation and the Countdown to the Suez War 118 (1993).

37　Morris 2004, at 309–10 and 319–20. Four days after the truce came into effect, Mapam, the ruling Mapai's coalition partner, issued a policy paper expressing opposition to many of the policies and practices outlined in the retro-active transfer plan suggesting that the cabinet "issue a call to peace-minded Arabs 'to stay in their places'." Benny Morris, *The Crystallization of Israeli Policy Against a Return of the Arab Refugees: April–December 1948*, 6 J. Israeli Hist. 85, 94 (1985) [*hereinafter* Morris 1985].

minorities between Greece and Turkey twenty-five years earlier and the transfer of Sudeten Germans from Czechoslovakia at the end of the Second World War.[38] Such comparisons had been made before the war and would continue long after the signing of armistice agreements that ended the hostilities.

In public statements, however, Israeli officials avoided what the Foreign Minister described as "unequivocal statements" on the refugee situation emphasizing that "so long as the war continu[ed], there [could] be no talk of allowing return."[39] This position would evolve slightly over the coming weeks with Sharett explaining to the Mediator later in July that "[a]ny question of [the refugees'] return would ultimately have to be raised in the context of a general peace settlement."[40] Writing about "ways by which the Mediator's policy could be defeated or at least made 'unable to bring about any decisive effect'," Walter Eytan, Director-General of Israel's Ministry of Foreign Affairs, described a "two-pronged-tactic [of] adher[ing] to UN decisions [on the one hand] and [creating] *fait accomplis* [on the other]."[41] Having consulted with Israeli officials the day after the cabinet concluded that refugees would not be allowed to return, Bernadotte and his team may have been readily aware of the challenges ahead when they recommended that recognition be accorded to the right of refugees to return to their homes. What also appeared to be implicit in the June suggestion, moreover, was that the refugees, if not quite nationals of the Jewish State in the ethnic or sociological sense of the term were nevertheless nationals in the legal sense of the term and therefore entitled to return.[42]

---

38   Morris 2004, at 320.
39   Id. Implying that return would be considered once an armistice had been reached, this approach "eased the task of Israeli officials both with representatives of the UN and of the U.S." who had since begun to explore solutions to the refugee situation that involved their return. It also enabled the provisional government to navigate "[the] exigencies of Israeli coalition politics and national unity [which] demanded [a similar] element of flexibility." Morris 1985, at 93.
40   Meeting: M. Shertok – Count Bernadotte and Assistants (Tel Aviv, July 26, 1948), in Documents on the Foreign Policy of Israel Vol. 1, 412 (Yehoshua Freundlich ed., 1981). *See also* Morris 1985, at 96 (stating that by establishing a link between a political settlement and the possibility of return "refugees [had] thus [become] bargaining counters in Israel's question for recognition and peace in the region"); Memorandum by the Director of the Office of United Nations Affairs (Rusk) to the Under Secretary of State (Lovett), Aug. 20, 1948, in FRUS Vol. 5 (1948), at 1331 (stating that "the Provisional Government of Israel may be using the fate of these unfortunate people to enhance its bargaining position in connection with eventual settlement of the Palestine problem").
41   Ilan, at 170.
42   While Bernadotte did not consider himself strictly bound by the terms of the UNGA's first peace plan, Resolution 181 may have had contradictory implications with regard to the question of nationality/citizenship and the future status of Arab Palestinian refugees.

The challenge that the UN Mediator and his team of advisers never really appeared to confront, despite being raised repeatedly by Palestinian and other Arab representatives later in the summer and through the fall, was how the individual rights affirmed in his June suggestions melded with the national identity of the Jewish State and the concomitant sense of collective belonging.

Bernadotte's further suggestion that recognition also be accorded to the "right of residents of Palestine [...] to regain possession of their property," not unlike his suggestion on their right to return, was not so much an innovation as a reflection of the evolving body of international law under discussion at the UN.[43] Article 14 of the draft "International Declaration of Human Rights," for example, affirmed "the right [of everyone] to own such property as meets the essential needs of decent living, that helps to maintain the dignity of the individual and of the home, and shall not be arbitrarily deprived of it."[44] With both urban and rural refugees suffering loss of home, lands and other properties, the particular formulation of the right to property under the draft declaration in the summer of 1948 appeared especially relevant to the latter group who comprised the majority of refugees. To the extent that the repossession of property would facilitate the return and reintegration of refugees, however, Bernadotte's suggestion failed to account for Israel's emerging land regime with its emphasis on collective, that is to say, Jewish, ownership and use of the land.[45] One

---

On the one hand, the plan affirmed that the inhabitants of Mandate Palestine were entitled, *ipso facto*, to citizenship in the Arab and Jewish States to be set up under Resolution 181 according to their place of residence. On the other hand, framing the struggle over Palestine as a conflict between two national movements masked its settler colonial origins and concomitant efforts by the Zionist movement to resolve what officials described as their "Arab [majority] problem" through population transfer and exchange. *See, further*, Dan Freeman-Maloy, *The International Politics of Settler Self-Governance: Reflections on Zionism and 'Dominion' Status within the British Empire*, 8 Settler Col. Stud. 80 (2018); Patrick Wolfe, *Settler Colonialism and the Elimination of the Native*, J. Genocide Research 437 (2006) [*hereinafter* Wolfe]. On the Zionist movement and population transfer, *see* Nur Masalha, Expulsion of the Palestinians: The Concept of "Transfer" in Zionist Political Thought, 1882–1948 (1992) [*hereinafter* Masalha 1992].

43   Suggestions, Part II, para. 9.
44   *Report of the Drafting Committee to the Commission on Human Rights*, Annex A – Draft International Declaration on Human Rights, art. 14, U.N. Doc. E/CN.4/95 (May 21, 1948).
45   Alexandre (Sandy) Kedar, *The Jewish State and the Arab Possessor, 1948–1967*, in The History of Law in a Multicultural Society 311, 324 (Ron Harris ed., 2003) (further stating that "[t]he new land regime was based on 1) Nationalization and Judaization of the land, 2) centralized control of this land by State and Jewish institutions (mainly the JNF) and 3) selective and unequal possessory rights to Jews"). *See also* Alexandre (Sandy) Kedar, *The Legal Transformation of Ethnic Geography: Israeli Law and the Palestinian Landholder 1948–1967*, 33 N.Y.U. J. Int'l. L. & Pol. 923 (2000–2001) (stating that "[s]ettling ethnocracies attempt to extend or preserve the control of a 'founding' group over a contested

week before the truce came into effect, Israel's provisional council adopted an Abandoned Property Ordinance regulating the Israel's control of refugee property with an Abandoned Areas Ordinance, adopted three days later, extending Israeli jurisdiction to "any area or place conquered by or surrendered to armed forces or deserted by all or part of its inhabitants, and which [had] been declared by order to be an abandoned area."[46] As these ordinances appeared to suggest, the borders of the Jewish State would not be determined by international fiat, but through the creation of *fait accomplis* which Zionist leaders had spoken about long before the first Arab-Israeli war.[47] This also meant that Arab Palestinians outside the Jewish State as delineated under the UNGA's partition plan would be vulnerable to the same forces that displaced those within the State. The Mediator would address these issues in more detail in his subsequent report at the end of the summer.

While Bernadotte's suggested solution to the refugee crisis provoked division and debate, it was his recommendation that "Palestine [and] Transjordan might [...] form a Union comprising two members, one Arab and one Jewish" with either member "entitled to request the Council of the Union to review

---

multi-ethnic territory. Frequently, this Charter group controls most of the land resource; immigrants usually only receive a small portion; and indigenous and alien groups, who often serve as the main contributors of land, generally are denied a fair share."); Wolfe, at 388 (stating that "the primary motive for elimination [of the native] is not race (or religion, ethnicity, grade of civilization, etc.) but access to territory. Territoriality is settler colonialism's specific, irreducible element.").

46 Abandoned Property Ordinance, June 21, 1948, 1 L.S.I 25 (1948) [Isr.]; Abandoned Areas Ordinance, June 24, 1948, 1 L.S.I 25 (1948) [Isr.]. The first of four phases in the development of Israel's land regime, legislation in phase one created a temporary legal basis for the expropriation and reallocation of land seized during the war. Geremy Foreman and Alexandre (Sandy) Kedar, *From Arab Land to "Israel Lands": The Legal Dispossession of the Palestinians Displaced by Israel in the Wake of 1948*, 22 Environ. Planning D: Soc. Space 809 (2004) *hereinafter* Foreman and Kedar].

47 The establishment of the Jewish State through a series of *fait accomplis* was debated over and again in the UNGA's First Committee. The linkage between the creation of "facts" and the "reconstitution" of a Jewish State in Palestine is evident in the Basle Declaration under which the Zionist movement set out its basic objectives. The Basel Program, First Zionist Congress, Basle, Aug. 31, 1897, reprinted in, 1 Documents on Palestine 9 (Mahdi Abdul Hadi ed., 2007) (stating that "[t]he aim of Zionism is to create for the Jewish people a home in Palestine secured by public law. The congress contemplates the following means to the attainment of this end: 1. The promotion, on suitable lines, of the *colonization* of Palestine by Jewish agricultural and industrial works. 2. The organization and binding together of the whole Jewry by means of *appropriate institutions*. 3. The strengthening and fostering of Jewish *national sentiment* and consciousness. 4. Preparatory steps to obtaining *Government consent*, where necessary, to the attainment of Zionism.") [emphasis added].

the immigration policy of the other member and to render a ruling thereon in terms of the common interests of the Union" that undermined support for his nine suggestions.[48] His revised set of conclusions at the end of the summer would suffer the same fate. An apparent effort to create more homogenous and integrated States, the Mediator and his advisors suggested that the Negev be re-allocated to the Arab member of the proposed union with the Western Galilee re-allocated to the Jewish member.[49] As the Syrian Foreign Minister, Muhsin al-Barazi, would later point out, Bernadotte's suggestion may have unwittingly "augmented the danger" of forced displacement by creating an Arab majority that undermined the very *raison d'etre* of the Jewish State.[50] It also appeared to ignore the Jewish State's unilateral declaration of independence and subsequent recognition by other States back in May which rendered the control of immigration a largely domestic affair.[51] While the Mediator's sug-

---

48 Suggestions, at Part II, para. 1–2 and 7 (further stating that "[i]n the event of the inability of the [UNSC] to reach a decision on the matter, the issue could be referred by either member to the Economic and Social Council of the [UN] whose decision, taking into account the principle of economic absorptive capacity, would be binding on the member whose policy is at issue").

49 Id. Under the partition plan the Negev was part of the Jewish State with the Western Galilee part of the Arab State. The suggestions also provided for the incorporation of the city of Jerusalem into the Arab member of the union, consideration of the status of Jaffa and free ports (sea and air) in Haifa and Lydda. The city of Jerusalem was an international zone under the partition plan, Jaffa was an Arab enclave within the Jewish State while Haifa was part of the Jewish State with Lydda part of the Arab State. G.A. Res. 181. *See also* Pappe, at 35 (stating that "the UN map was an assured recipe for the tragedy that began to unfold the day after Resolution 181 was adopted. As theoreticians of ethnic cleansing acknowledged later, where an ideology of exclusivity is adopted in a highly charged ethnic reality, there can be only one result: ethnic cleansing. By drawing the map as they did, the UN members who voted in favour of the Partition Resolution contributed directly to the crime that was about to take place.").

50 Damascus (Keeley) to Secretary of State, No. 620, Sept. 26, 1948, National Archives and Records Administration [*hereinafter* Keeley], 501.BB Palestine-9-2648. Addressing the UNGA's First Committee in the fall, the representative of Pakistan, Zafarullah Khan, estimated that Bernadotte's plan would create a Jewish State in which 525,000 of its 975,000 citizens or fifty-four percent were of Arab Palestinian origin. U.N. G.A.O.R., 3rd Sess., First Comm., 210th [emphasis added] at 733, U.N. Doc. A/C.1/SR.210 (Nov. 24, 1948).

51 Israeli officials would raise the latter issue repeatedly in UNSC debates during the war, especially in relation to the immigration of displaced Jews held in detention camps in Cyprus. Between one-third and a half of all immigrants in 1948 enlisted in the Jewish State's war effort. Hannah Torok-Yablonka, *The Recruitment of Holocaust Survivors During the War of Independence*, 13 Stud. Zionism 44–5 (1992); Colin Schindler, A History of Modern Israel 55 (2nd ed., 2013). The International Refugee Organization suspended its resettlement operations in Palestine after the beginning of the inter-State war in mid-May with assistance to displaced European Jews limited to those residing in camps in

gestion placed a greater portion of land under Arab control, it also set aside the establishment of an independent Palestinian State in at least part of the country. By retaining a certain degree of international oversight the former may have facilitated the return of refugees to their homes of origin, however, the latter may have in turn militated against the refugee situation slowly "sorting itself out" as the humanitarian crisis arising from partition of the Indian sub-continent appeared to do.[52] In the absence of political will to uphold the right to return, moreover, the concomitant absence of a Palestinian State effectively transformed Arab Palestinians into what the Mahmoud Fawzi, the Egyptian representative, would later describe as a "refugee nation" characterized by the lack of a national home to call their own.[53] As Ahmad Shuqayri, one of several members of the Arab Higher Committee taking part in the drafting of the UNGA's second peace plan, noted in the fall, efforts to rectify this situation in the past had inevitably led to suggestions for the transfer and/or exchange of the country's Arab population.[54] Appearing to inspire early thinking in Washington and London about how to resolve the growing refugee crisis

---

Germany, Austria and Italy. Cohen, at 143. These issues, namely, the future of Europe's displaced Jews, immigration and Israeli sovereignty, would continue to intersect with the plight of Palestinian refugees over the coming months.

52 Aristide R. Zolberg et al., Escape from Violence: Conflict and the Refugee Crisis in the Developing World 227 (1989) [*hereinafter* Zolberg]. *See also* Indira Priyadarshini Ravindran, Narrative Silences, Institutional Ambiguities and the Historiography of International Refugee Law 54 (Oct. 2007) (unpublished Ph.D. dissertation, John Hopkins University) (on file with ProQuest) (commenting on Grahl-Madsen's study stating that "[r]efugees from India, Pakistan, and Korea (along with those in Vietnam, Italy and Turkey) were considered as con-nationals, since they enjoyed the protection of a state, despite being displaced from their places of habitual residence").

53 G.A.O.R., 3rd Sess., First Comm., 226th mtg., U.N. Doc. A/C.1/SR.226 (Dec. 3, 1948), at 912. *See also* Zolberg, at 240.

54 G.A.O.R., 3rd Sess., First Comm., 201st mtg., U.N. Doc. A/C.1/SR.201 (Nov. 16, 1948), at 648. *See, e.g.,* Palestine Royal (Peel) Commission Report, Cmd. 5479 (1937), at 389 (stating that "[i]f partition is to be effective in promoting a final settlement it must mean more than drawing a frontier and establishing two states. Sooner or later there should be a transfer of land and, as far as partition, an exchange of population." Identifying the exchange of minorities between Greece and Turkey as a model, the Commission also acknowledges that "the analogy breaks down at one essential point. In Northern Greece a surplus of cultivable land was available or could rapidly be made available for the settlement of the Greeks evacuated from Turkey. In Palestine there is at present no such surplus. Room exists or could soon be provided within the proposed boundaries of the Jewish State for the Jews now living in the Arab Area. It is the far greater number of Arabs who constitute the major problem; and, while some of them could be re-settled on the land vacated by the Jews, far more land would be required for the re-settlement of all of them."). *See also* Masalha 1992.

arising from the struggle over Palestine, this idea would reappear, albeit in a significantly revised form, in the Mediator's September report.

The wholesale rejection of Bernadotte's June suggestions by Israel, the Palestinians, and Arab States not only set back UN efforts to facilitate a peaceful adjustment of the situation, it also contributed to the eventual collapse of the truce on July 8th with the hostilities that followed further exacerbating the refugee crisis in Palestine. Appearing before the UNSC in New York five days later, the UN Mediator used the opportunity to emphasize that "[s]*pecial attention* ought to be given to ensuring the *right to return to their homes* of the substantial number of Arab refugees who fled from the Jewish-occupied areas because of war conditions."[55] By the time the truce was restored ten days later, the number of refugees had increased by more than 100,000 with the mass expulsion of Palestinians from Ramle and Lydda, towns allocated to the Arab State under the UNGA's partition plan, more than doubling the number of Palestinians displaced since the collapse of the truce.[56] In a memo to the State Department three days after the truce was restored, Philip Jessup expressed concern that "[the] Arab refugee problem [was] likely to become more acute in the near future" further noting that Israel's policy was likely to "further complicate negotiations for a political settlement in Palestine."[57] The American representative to the UNGA gave no indication of the reasons for his concern, however, several days later Israeli forces launched the first of several military operations "to clear rear and front lines of active, potentially hostile populations" with almost all Palestinian villages regarded as a potential "fifth column."[58] Such operations not only resulted in the ongoing displacement of the country's indigenous Arab population, they also led to further interventions by the Mediator demanding that Israel allow the refugees to return to their homes. In the aftermath of several UN investigations which found Israeli

---

55 S.C.O.R., 3rd yr, 333rd mtg., U.N. Doc. S/PV.333 (July 13, 1948), at 9. The UNSC (Res. 54, July 15, 1948) subsequently "[d]etermin[ed] that the situation in Palestine constitut[ed] a threat to peace within the meaning of Article 39 of the Charter of the [UN]" and "[o]rder[ed] the Governments and authorities concerned, pursuant to Article 40 of the Charter, to desist from further military action and to this end to issue cease-fire orders to their military and paramilitary forces." S.C. Res. 54 (July 15, 1948), para. 1–2 [emphasis added].

56 Benny Morris, *Operation Dani and the Palestinian Exodus from Lydda and Ramle in 1948*, 40 Middle East J. 82 (1986).

57 New York (Jessup) to Secretary of State, No. 933, July 21, 1948, NARA, 501.BB Palestine/7-2148.

58 Morris 2004, at 438–445. Jessup's additional suggestion for an "evaluation of the extent to which Arab interests and property [were] being respected in Jewish-held territory" may also explain his apparent concern that the refugee crisis would yet get worse.

forces responsible for the depopulation and destruction of some of the last remaining Palestinian villages – Ijzim, Jaba' and 'Ayn Ghazal – in the coastal plain, for example, Bernadotte decided that the inhabitants should "be allowed to return forthwith and that the Israeli Government should rehabilitate the Arab inhabitants of the villages."[59] Raphael Cilento, an Australian-born refugee expert from the Department of Social Affairs tasked with carrying out a humanitarian survey, described the refugee situation in Palestine at the beginning of August as "more helpless than anywhere else in the world except China" where upwards of thirty million people had been uprooted by war and revolution.[60] With a population of around half a billion, however, it was the scope of displacement in Palestine where around a third of the Arab population had been displaced by the middle of the summer that appeared to set it apart from other cases including India and Pakistan where partition had uprooted around half the number of displaced persons in China.

B *The British Provisional Draft Resolution*

In early August, the American Ambassador in London, Lewis Douglas, cabled the American Secretary of State, George Marshall, a summary of British ideas about a peaceful adjustment of the situation of Palestine being developed in the Foreign Office for discussion with their American counterparts.[61] Drafted by officials in the Foreign Office, a Suggested Heads of Assembly Resolution, comprised what appeared to be the first in a series of draft resolutions that would eventually culminate in the UNGA's second major effort to facilitate a solution to the struggle over Palestine. With its substantive content dependent in large part on the outcome of Bernadotte's forthcoming progress report, the provisional nature of the draft resolution nevertheless differed from the more definitive drafts that would follow. Weighing the merits of a resolution mapping out a "provisional solution" designed to smooth the way for a "definitive solution" later on, British officials believed that the former was more likely to find Arab support given that the latter would entail their recognition of the

---

59 Persson, at 186; Morris 2004, at 438; Pappe, at 164. While the provisional government eventually allowed a small number of families to return, the Israeli military expelled the returning inhabitants at the end of the year and once again resettled the three villages with Jewish immigrants.

60 Donald Neff, Fallen Pillars: US Policy Towards Palestine and Israel Since 1945 66 n54 (1996).

61 London (Douglas) to Secretary of State, No. 3484, Aug. 2, 1948, NARA, 501.BB Palestine/8-248; The Secretary of State (Marshall) to the Embassy in the United Kingdom, No. 3187, Aug. 12, NARA, 501.BB Palestine/8-1248.

Jewish State.[62] Approaching the issue from a different perspective, Philip Jessup, the American representative to the UNGA, observed that a definitive solution was the better option because it offered the possibility of falling back on a provisional solution later on.[63] American officials would return to this idea in early December when it appeared that the draft resolution approved by the First Committee (Political) might not obtain the required two-thirds support when voted on by members in the UNGA's plenary. Part of an ongoing reassessment of policy that had begun on both sides of the Atlantic after Bernadotte's appointment as UN Mediator, the exchange of ideas over the summer of 1948 would comprise the basis for more elaborate Anglo-American cooperation into the fall. The UK Foreign Office nevertheless expressed concern that joint sponsorship of a resolution might prove impossible in light of "[the] special difficulties with which the [American government] [might] be faced in the next few months."[64] Responding to British concerns about the potential impact of the upcoming presidential election on American policy, Jessup noted that since both political parties, Democratic and Republic, were "irrevocably committed to support of the [provisional government of Israel]," it was unlikely that there would be "any substantial change in [the American] position with regard to a peaceful settlement in Palestine."[65] As the British would eventually discover, this would turn out otherwise later in the fall.

Comprised of a short preamble followed by a series of recommendations, the British draft resolution called upon the Mediator to "continue [carrying] out his task of seeking a peaceful solution of the Palestine question" with the assistance of "the Jewish and Arab authorities in Palestine and the Governments of the Arab States [and] all other powers."[66] These consultations would continue into August and resume later in September after the Mediator's return from a Red Cross conference in Stockholm where he would also appeal for emergency relief. In line with Bernadotte's June suggestions, the draft resolution further recommended that "both parties should take such action as may be necessary to ensure the proper administration of the territory which they control[led]

---

62 Douglas (further stating that "[a]dvantages of a positive resolution are: (A) It would remove [the] possibility of further dispute over [the] location [of the] frontier; (B) UN guarantees of [the] frontier could come into force at once; (C) It would obviate either side jockeying to improve its position").

63 New York (Jessup), to Secretary of State (Marshall), No. 1000, Aug. 6, 1948, NARA, 501.BB Palestine/6-848.

64 London (Douglas) to Secretary of State, No. 3484.

65 New York (Jessup) to Secretary of State, No. 1000.

66 Foreign Office Minute (Burrows) [Suggested Heads of Assembly Resolution on Palestine], July 29, 1948, National Archives, FO 371-68579 E10680; London (Douglas) to Secretary of State, No. 3485, Aug. 2, 1948, NARA, 501.BB Palestine/8-248.

with due regard to the position of minorities and to the fulfillment of normal international obligations."[67] This provision was not insignificant with the Mediator's advisers admonishing Foreign Minister Sharett several weeks later that certain policies and practices, including the expulsion of Arab civilians and the detention of men of military age in "concentration camps," contravened the Hague Convention and its annexed Regulations.[68] On the same day Sharett sent a letter to Chaim Weizmann, Israel's President, emphasizing that the provisional government was "determined [...] to explore all possibilities of getting rid, once and for all, of the huge Arab minority which originally threatened us."[69] In its final part, the draft resolution recommended that the UN Mediator give "particular and urgent attention" to a number of specific problems instructing Bernadotte "[i]nsofar as [the question of Jewish and Arab refugees] [was] not being dealt with by specialized organs of the [UN]" to "examine how far it [would] be possible for these refugees to be settled in Palestine and to the extent that this [was] not possible, to make recommendations in conjunction with the appropriate organ of the [UN] for their disposal elsewhere."[70] Speaking in the UNSC on the same day that Douglas relayed the Foreign Office ideas on ways forward in Palestine, Alexander Cadogan, the British Ambassador to the UN, similarly recommended that the UNSC "call the matter [of displaced Jews] to the urgent attention of the Economic and Social Council [...] to give a powerful impetus in the direction of speedy and effective action" and request the UN Mediator "to investigate the problem of Arab displaced persons and to make proposals for dealing with it."[71] The Heads of Assembly Resolution on Palestine would be the first and last draft resolution

---

67   Foreign Office Minute (Burrows) [Suggested Heads of Assembly Resolution on Palestine] (further recommending that "pending the conclusion of a settlement by agreement between the parties, or failing this, further action by the [UNGA] at its next annual meeting, none of the parties concerned in Palestine should take any step to alter in any way the position as described in the Mediator's report with regard to the control of territory in Palestine, i.e. neither party shall try to deprive the other of control over territory described in the Mediator's report as being in the other's control at the present time.").

68   Persson, at 186.

69   Masalha 1992, at 193 (the Foreign Minister added that "[w]hat can be achieved in this period of storm and stress will be quite unattainable once conditions get established.").

70   Foreign Office Minute (Burrows) [Suggested Heads of Assembly Resolution on Palestine].

71   U.N. S.C.O.R., 3rd yr, 343rd mtg., U.N. Doc. S/PV.343 (Aug. 2, 1948). The meeting was the first of several wide-ranging discussions on the situation of displaced European Jews and Arab refugees. *See* Foreign Office to New York, No. 3160, July 27, 1948, NA, FO 371-68573 E9495; Foreign Office to New York, No. 3161, July 27, 1948, NA, FO 371-68573 E9495; Foreign Office to New York, No. 3162, July 27, 1948, NA, FO 371-68573 E9495. Initially opposed by the US, in part, because officials fear that it would harm administration efforts to secure Congressional support for relaxing restrictions on the entry of displaced Jews, the State

on a peaceful adjustment of the situation to address the status of displaced European Jews which appeared to "sort itself out" in part through immigration and resettlement in the newly-established Jewish State.

Introducing the option of resettlement, which Bernadotte would subsequently address in his September progress report, the Suggested Heads of Assembly Resolution on Palestine appeared to reflect a prevailing view among British officials that many of the refugees were unlikely to wish to return or in the case of Arab refugees would be prevented by Israel from doing so.[72] The Mediator expressed similar doubts in a cable to Trygve Lie, the UN Secretary-General, barely a week early after failing to secure Israel's agreement to the initial return of an estimated 150,000 refugees to the coastal cities of Haifa and Jaffa which Israeli military forces had depopulated during the first months of the war.[73] Having already lowered expectations about prospects for the large-scale return of refugees, however, the British Middle East Office in Cairo added that "[n]ow that the initial difficulty of persuading the Arabs of Palestine to leave their homes has been overcome by Jewish terrorism and Arab panic it seems possible that the solution may lie in their transference to Iraq and Syria."[74] The cable further noted that "[t]he Jews [had] quite recently, though not officially, given some publicity to the suggestion that the Arabs in the Jewish area, especially those who [had] fled, should be exchanged with the Jewish subjects in Arab states."[75] The consideration of population transfer appeared, in turn, to correlate with an emerging trans-Atlantic consensus on the reallocation of territory from that delineated under the UNGA's first peace plan in order to create what Robert McClintock and Philip Jessup described as a more "compact and homogenous [Jewish] state."[76] According to Bernard

---

Department eventually relented to the meeting with the British agreeing to limit their comments on the situation of displaced Jews.

72   British Middle East Office (Cairo) to Foreign Office, No. 28, Aug. 3, 1948, NA, FO 371-68578 E10456 (reporting that "there [was] little chance of the Arab refugees being able to return to their villages." Noting that this was partly due to Israeli plans for Jewish immigration, with the provisional government likely "to put every obstacle in the way of the return of the Arabs," the Office added that it was also due "to the fear of the Arabs as to what their future [was] likely to be under Jewish rule.").

73   Meeting: M. Shertok – Count Bernadotte and Assistants (Tel Aviv, July 26, 1948). In line with restrictions already imposed on Jewish immigration, the Mediator sought to assure Israeli officials that "among those [refugees] who [might] wish to return differentiation may be made between men of military age and all others in recognition of security considerations."

74   British Middle East Office (Cairo) to Foreign Office, No. 28.

75   Id.

76   Memorandum by Mr. Robert M. McClintock to the Director of the Office of United Nations Affairs (Rusk), July 1, 1948, in FRUS Vol. 5 (1948) at 1171; The Acting United States

THE RIGHT TO RETURN 99

Burrows, head of the Foreign Office's Eastern Department, the establishment of a more "compact and defensible" Jewish State had two main advantages: it would solve the question of immigration since "[t]he authorities would not wish to cause over population and unemployment" and it "would [also] provide a much better protection against Jewish or communist expansion [than the] Arab areas of Palestine [alone]."[77] As Burrows went on to explain, this also meant that "the boundaries [of the two entities] would have to be ruthlessly changed [and that] there would have to be a *large exchange of populations* [...] so that a considerable part of Western Galilee might become Jewish."[78] With the Western Galilee comprised of 98 Palestinian villages and only 3 Jewish colonies, it appeared that the scope of such an exchange would indeed be quite large.[79] Secretary Marshall appeared to take a slightly different approach emphasizing the need for "discussion of [an] exchange of populations *in certain cases*" adding that discussions should also focus on "[the] desirability of permitting [the] *return of refugees so desiring*, including assistance in effecting resettlement and property restoration, and appropriate civil rights guarantees."[80] The only hitch, as McClintock would note, was that the "[American] government could not agree to any diminution of [Israel's] sovereignty except with the consent of the Government of Israel," a position that would have an impact on the drafting of the UNGA's second peace plan once the presidential election heated up in the fall.[81] Acknowledging that the mass resettlement of

---

Representative at the United Nations (Jessup) to the Secretary of State, June 30, 1948, in FRUS Vol. 5 (1948), at 1161.

77 Foreign Office Minute, Mr. Burrows [Notes on the Ultimate Settlement of Palestine], June 10, 1948, NA, FO 371-68566 E8524; Foreign Office Minute, Mr. Wright, Probable Solutions to the Palestine Problem, June 10, 1948, NA, FO 371-68566 E8526; Foreign Office Minute, Mr. Wright, Proposed Possible Solutions of the Palestine Problem, June 15, 1948, NA, FO 68650 E8409 (further recommending the negotiation of burden-sharing agreements under which "Jewish immigrants [would] either be limited to defined numbers or regulated by the economic absorptive capacity of the country [while] homes for a given number of displaced Jews [would] be found by member states elsewhere than in Palestine").

78 Foreign Office Minute [Notes on the Ultimate Settlement of Palestine], id. [Emphasis added].

79 Abu Sitta.

80 The Secretary of State (Marshall) to the Embassy in the United Kingdom, No. 3187. [Emphasis added].

81 Memorandum by Mr. Robert M. McClintock [Peaceful Adjustment of the Future Situation of Palestine], June 23, 1948, in FRUS Vol. 5 (1948), at 1134 (further stating that "[i]t is pertinent to quote excerpts from the official Republican Party Platform for 1948, Section VI: 'We welcome Israel into the family of nations and take pride in the fact that the Republican Party was the first to call for the establishment of a free and independent Jewish commonwealth. [...] Subject to the letter and spirit of the [UN] Charter, we

the refugees would "cost large sums of money" the British Middle East Office concluded that the costs "should in justice be for the [UN] who are primarily responsible for the present state of affairs, to find."[82] The idea that a transfer or exchange of populations could resolve the Arab refugee situation nevertheless appeared to fade from view even as the size and scope of the humanitarian crisis arising from the struggle over Palestine continued to grow.

On August 3rd, the day after the UNSC opened discussion on the situation of Arab refugees and displaced European Jews, Philip Jessup cabled the Secretary of State from New York requesting further clarification of American policy in light of Israel's revised position on a solution to the refugee situation. In discussions with the UN Mediator just over a week earlier, Moshe Sharett had laid out three justifications for Israel's refusal to consider return outside the context of a comprehensive political settlement beginning with the assertion that "[the] return [of the refugees] was a *political* question of the first magnitude."[83] Israel's Foreign Minister went on to explain that "[i]f they were allowed back they would have the opportunity of organising a fifth column on a vast scale" and that the "economic aspect [...] would greatly complicate the return of the refugees even under normal (i.e., peacetime) conditions."[84] Refuting Bernadotte's assertion that "the 'world would not understand' Israel's position" in a cabinet meeting several days later, Moshe Sharett argued that "[t]he world, which understood the uprooting of the Sudeten [Germans] from Czechoslovakia, would also understand [what Israel had done]."[85] Israel's Foreign Ministry subsequently cabled the State Department updating American officials about Israel's views on a solution to the refugee situation.[86] Jessup wanted to know whether the Department "agree[d] with the position that economic, political and military factors render[ed] impossible the immediate return of these refugees to Israel and that the matter should be dealt with

---

pledge to Israel full recognition, with its boundaries as sanctioned by the [UN] and aid in developing its economy. [...] The Democratic Party Platform will undoubtedly include equivalent references to the State of Israel.").

82 British Middle East Office (Cairo) to Foreign Office, No. 28.
83 Meeting: M. Shertok – Count Bernadotte and Assistants (Tel Aviv, July 26, 1948). *See also* Jacob Tovy, Israel and the Palestinian Refugee Issue: The Formulation of a Policy, 1948–1956 15 (2014) (quoting similar remarks by Moshe Sharett in June stating that "[t]here will be a need to explain the tremendous importance of this transformation that took place from a settlement perspective, from a security perspective, from the perspective of the robustness of the state's structure and solution to vital social and very grave political problems that have cast their shadow on the entire future of the state").
84 Id.
85 Morris 2004, at 324.
86 New York (Jessup) to Secretary of State (Marshall), No. 972, July 27, 1948, NARA, 501.BB Palestine/7-2748.

[only] as part of the future settlement assuming that property and other rights of [the] refugees [would] be fully protected."[87] While Secretary Marshall had been among the handful of American officials who had mused about a possible exchange of populations, there was little if any trace of that thinking in his response to Jessup just over a week later. Beginning with general directives, Marshall stated that "[the] UN should continue to *induce* [the provisional government of Israel] to accept [the] return [of] Arab refugees initially in small numbers but increasing movement as experience demonstrat[ed] [that the] security and economy [of Israel were] not endangered in fact."[88] In a cable to the American Embassy in London the previous day, the Secretary emphasized that the US "consider[ed] [that a] solution Arab [displaced person] problem [was] intrinsic to negotiations and [a] settlement [of the Palestine question]."[89] The Secretary then responded in a further telegram to each of the provisional government's justifications against return arguing that "under [the] supervision [of the] Mediator [a] substantial number [of] refugees so desiring could be permitted gradually to return to their homes and resume their occupations without prejudicing [the] maintenance [of the] internal security [of] Israel."[90] Dismissing concerns that Israel would be unable to absorb the returnees, the Secretary observed that the country was "now demonstrating its ability to absorb large numbers [of] European [displaced persons] monthly" with more than 100,000 Jewish immigrants having entered the country by the end of the year.[91] "From a political standpoint," Marshall concluded that "action by [the provisional government] to permit [the] gradual return of Arab refugees would provide Arabs with tangible assurance of [the provisional government's] desire to establish cooperative relations with Arab states on a long range basis."[92] Several days later, President Truman approved a memorandum on relief of

---

87 New York (Jessup) to Secretary of State, No. 984, Aug. 3, 1948, NARA, 501.BB Palestine/8-348.

88 Department of State (Marshall) to New York, No. 531, Aug. 13, 1948, NA, 501.BB Palestine/8-34 [emphasis added].

89 Id. *See also* Department of State (Marshall) to the American Embassy in London, No. 3187. This is the same cable mentioned earlier in which the Secretary raised the possibility of discussions of a population transfer in certain cases.

90 Department of State (Marshall) to the United States Delegation at the United Nations in New York, No. 534, Aug. 14, 1948, NA, 501.BB Palestine/8-348.

91 Id.

92 Id. *See also* Department of State (Marshall) to New York, No. 531 (further stating that "[the] Mediator should be urged by [the UNSC] to estimate as soon as he can numbers and locations of Arab refugees, [the] number desiring to return to their homes and those for whom immediate resettlement might prove practical, food and other supplies required, sources and costs thereof, food costs per person per diem and currencies in which supplies can be procured. [The] Mediator should also be encouraged to make interim practical proposals for meeting problem.").

Arab and Jewish refugees which recommended "the need for repatriating Arab and Jewish refugees under conditions which [would] not imperil the internal security of the receiving states."[93] Coming on the heels of a high-level meeting of Israeli officials who once again unanimously agreed "to do everything possible to prevent the return of the [Arab] refugees [to the Jewish state]," the latter included plans for the construction of Jewish settlements on and expropriation of refugee lands with the Jewish Agency granting approval for resettlement of Jewish immigrants in the Palestinian village of Deir Yassin where a massacre by Jewish forces back in April contributed to the mass exodus of refugees that continued into the summer.[94] The Israeli Prime Minister, David Ben Gurion, subsequently informed the American representative in Tel Aviv that "there were two issues on which Israel would never compromise (1) independence of the state, and (2) any action which involved a threat to national security."[95] According to James McDonald, the latter "refer[ed] to [the] danger of allowing [the] mass return [of] Arab refugees prior to peace."[96]

By the end of August, initial thinking in London about a peaceful adjustment of the situation of Palestine had coalesced around an "outline plan" and a series of "tactical suggestions" related to its implementation which Douglas subsequently relayed to Marshall in Washington.[97] Reiterating a position set out in Foreign Office ideas relayed by Douglas to the State Department earlier in the month, the outline plan recommended that "[t]he [d]ivision between Arab and Jewish areas should follow very generally the lines now held by the forces of either side."[98] Holding that Palestinian and other Arab representatives

---

93 Memorandum by the Director of the Office of United Nations Affairs (Rusk) to the Under Secretary of State (Lovett).

94 Morris 2004, at 328; Arnon Golan, *The Transfer to Jewish Control of Abandoned Arab Lands During the War of Independence*, *in* Israel: The First Decade of Independence 403, 418 (Ilan S. Troen and Noah Lucas, eds., 1995); Michael Fischbach, Records of Dispossession: Palestinian Refugee Property and the Arab-Israeli Conflict 11, 18 (2003) [*hereinafter* Fischbach].

95 The Special Representative in Israel (McDonald) to the Secretary of State, Aug. 20, 1948, in FRUS Vol. 5 (1948), at 1334.

96 Id.

97 London (Douglas) to Secretary of State (Marshall), No. 3878, Aug. 27, 1948, in FRUS Vol. 5 (1948), at 1352; London (Douglas) to Secretary of State (Marshall), No. 3879, Aug. 27, 1948, in FRUS Vol. 5 (1948), at 1354.

98 London (Douglas) to Secretary of State (Marshall), No. 3880, Aug. 27, 1948, in FRUS Vol. 5 (1948), at 1354. The exchange of ideas between London and Washington, nevertheless, appeared to result in two changes with Jerusalem once again designated as an international zone and Jaffa re-allocated to the Jewish State. *See* New York (Jessup) to Secretary of State, No. 1000; Department of State (Marshall) to the American Embassy in London, No. 3468, Sept. 1, 1948, NARA, 501.BB Palestine/9-148.

would be unlikely to reach agreement on the future of areas not placed under Jewish control, the Foreign Office recommended that "general principles on which [these areas] should be disposed of must be laid down by [the] UN" with the added suggestion for their incorporation into Transjordan.[99] While the UNGA's first peace plan had raised a number of unresolved legal questions, which the Syrian representative, Faris el-Khouri raised once again back in July in the context of UNSC deliberations to restore the truce, the British suggestions raised yet another, namely, the acquisition of territory by force.[100] Similar to discussions about the future of Palestine a year earlier, this was not one which the majority of UNGA members appeared willing to entertain. Noting that the Mediator's upcoming recommendations would probably include "some action as to the Arab refugees" which would "depend largely on [...] the numbers of refugees and the proportion of them who wish[ed] to move back to Jewish areas," the Foreign Office suggested in language similar to Marshall's directive just over a week earlier that Bernadotte could possibly recommend "that as part of [the] boundary settlement, the Jewish authorities *should be made to allow* refugees to come back or to give them compensation for the property which they have left behind."[101] The establishment of a "Committee for Removal and Expulsion" in late August tasked with drafting "a proposal about possibilities of settling the Arabs of the Land of Israel in the Arab states" indicated once again that the Jewish State had other ideas in mind.[102] Describing the refugee situation as "one involving [the] life or death of some 300,000 people," Secretary Marshall emphasized that "[t]he leaders of

---

99   London (Douglas), to Secretary of State (Marshall), No. 3880.
100 U.N. S.C.O.R., 3rd yr, 334th mtg., U.N. Doc. S/PV.334 (July 13, 1948). The UNSC rejected the Syrian draft resolution by a vote of 6 in favor, 1 against (Ukrainian SSR) with 4 abstentions including the US and the Soviet Union. For discussion of legal questions and requests for an advisory opinion during discussion of the partition plan, *see* Victor Kattan, From Co-Existence to Conflict: International Law and the Origins of the Arab-Israeli Conflict, 1891–1949 149–150 (2009).
101 London (Douglas) to Secretary of State (Marshall), No. 3880 [emphasis added].
102 Masalha 1992, at 194. *See also* Fischbach, at 41–42 (stating that the committee was tasked with studying resettlement possibilities for the refugees in neighboring Arab countries, recent population transfers including the transfer of Armenians from Turkey, Sudetan Germans from Czechoslovakia and Assryians from Iraq along with the scope and value of refugee property). *See also* Benny Morris, *Yosef Weitz and the Transfer Committees, 1948–49*, 22 Middle East Stud. 522, 549 (1986) (stating that "[t]he committee's terms of appointment at the end of August had been restricted apparently to theoretical evaluation, investigation and recommendations concerning the fate of Arabs who had already moved out of Israel. But during the autumn of 1948 the committee as a body and its members individually remained active as consultants and lobbyists regarding the possible fate of various Arab communities. The committee acted as a pressure group, albeit of experts,

Israel would make a grave miscalculation if they thought callous treatment of this tragic issue could pass unnoticed by world opinion."[103] In an updated report on Possible Developments from the Palestine Truce filed at the end of August the Central Intelligence Agency observed that "Israel's decision not to allow the refugees to return to their homes has greatly exacerbated Arab bitterness against the Jews" further describing the refugee situation as "[t]he most serious population upheaval since the termination of WWII."[104]

Turning to tactical matters, the UK Foreign Office recommended that Washington and London advise the UN Mediator to make a recommendation to the UNSC in line with the above-mentioned plan which in turn would be asked for its endorsement.[105] Taking a position that was in part contrary to the one held by their counterparts in the State Department, officials in the Foreign Office argued that the UNSC could deal with the plan as a matter of international peace and security.[106] Failure to obtain a majority in support of the plan or the prospect that it would be vetoed, however, may require consideration of the plan by the UNGA. In a memorandum to Dean Rusk, Director of the Office of UN Affairs at the State Department, Robert McClintock advised that "it would be inexpedient to bring [the plan] before the [UNSC], because of almost certain Soviet opposition to any just settlement" and that "[i]t would be similarly inexpedient to ventilate the issue further in the [UNGA] unless there were prior acquiescence by both Arabs and Jews."[107] They nevertheless con-

---

urging the IDF brass and the country's political leadership to expel Arabs and move refugees away from the new, expanding borders.").

103 The Secretary of State (Marshall) to the Special Representative of the United States in Israel (McDonald), Sept. 1, 1948, in FRUS Vol. 5 (1948), at 1366 (further stating that "Jewish authorities in Palestine [had made statements] promising safeguards for [the] Arab minority in areas under Jewish control"). *See also* Foreign Office (London), to Washington, No. 9949, Sept. 4, 1948, NA, FO 371-68585 E11806.

104 Irene Gendzier, Dying to Forget: Oil, Power, Palestine and the Foundations of US Policy in the Middle East 135 (2015) [*hereinafter* Gendzier].

105 London (Douglas) to Secretary of State (Marshall), No. 3881, Aug. 27, 1948, in FRUS Vol. 5 (1948), at 1358.

106 Id.

107 Memorandum by Mr. Robert M. McClintock to the Director of the Office of United Nations Affairs (Rusk), in FRUS Vol. 5 (1948), at 1372. This also led to a series of cables with American officials in Stockholm where Bernadotte was attending the above-mentioned Red Cross conference due to concerns that the Mediator would recommend placing the peaceful adjustment of the future of Palestine on the agenda of the UNGA's upcoming fall session. *See* Department of State (Marshall) to the American Embassy in Sweden, No. 634, Aug. 24, 1948, NARA, 501.BB Palestine/8-2448; Sweden (Matthews) to Secretary of State, Aug. 26, 1948, NARA, 501.BB Palestine/8-2648; Department of State (Marshall) to the American Embassy in London, No. 3468, Sept. 1, 1948, NARA, 501.BB Palestine/9-148.

curred that they should be prepared for a "full-dress debate in [the] event [that] some other delegation lodg[ed] [the] Palestine problem before [the] [UNGA] in Paris."[108] While the UK Foreign Office acknowledged that an "induced" solution was "less attractive" than a negotiated one, it remained convinced that "direct negotiations [were] in present circumstances impractical" and that "neither party in Palestine [was] at all likely to make a positive act of acceptance of the kind of settlement to be proposed by [the] Mediator."[109] Officials surmised that "both parties might well acquiesce in it if it were put into effect with sufficient determination."[110] According to Ernest Bevin, the British Foreign Secretary, this was "possibly the most important difference" between London and Washington on how to handle the peaceful adjustment of the situation of Palestine.[111] Respective views on this issue, acquiescence to a solution versus a negotiated one, would threaten to undermine Anglo-American cooperation through the fall with the compromise eventually reached having unforeseen and unintended consequences on provisions for a solution to the refugee situation in the UNGA's second peace plan. Hoping that "if all [went] well" the five stage process might conclude around 20 September with the UNSC's endorsement of the Mediator's report, the Foreign Office subsequently recommended an abbreviated timetable after learning that the State Department had shared the substance of Anglo-American thinking with Israeli officials in Tel Aviv.[112] As one official put it, "[n]ow [that] the cat [was] half out of [the] bag, [the] quick [the] bag [was] handed off in the hands of [the] Mediator the better."[113]

---

108   The Secretary of State (Marshall), to the Embassy in the United Kingdom, No. 3468.
109   London (Douglas) to Secretary of State (Marshall), No. 3881.
110   Id.
111   London (Douglas) to Secretary of State, No. 3879. This was a principle which the Americans had made clear back in February when the UNSC first began to contemplate an alternative way forward once it appeared that neither Palestinians nor other Arab States would acquiesce to the UNGA's partition plan. U.N. S.C.O.R., 3rd yr, 253rd [emphasis added] at 267, U.N. Doc. S/PV.253 (Feb. 24, 1948) (the American ambassador, Warren Austin, stating that "[the] Charter of the [UN] [did] not empower the [UNSC] to enforce a political settlement whether it [was] pursuant to a recommendation of the [UNGA] or of the [UNSC] itself").
112   London (Douglas) to Secretary of State, No. 3927, Sept. 1, 1948, NARA, 501.BB Palestine/9-148.
113   London (Douglas) to Secretary of State, No. 3962, Sept. 3, 1948, NARA, 501.BB Palestine/9-348 (further stating that it is "important that from moment proposals become known they should carry as label 'Mediator – Made in Sweden'"). *See also* Department of State (Marshall) to the American Embassy in London, No. 3544, Sept. 8, 1948, NARA, 501. BB Palestine/9-848.

C *The Mediator's September Report*

In early September, Bernadotte met with Bunche in Stockholm before returning to Rhodes with a brief stop in Paris to pick up a small staff to work on the humanitarian situation and see Secretary-General Lie who asked the Mediator to submit a progress report no later than one week before the opening of the UNGA's fall session. Following a brief round of further consultations in the region, the two returned to Rhodes where Bunche and his team began to draft the Mediator's progress report. Joined by Robert McClintock from the State Department and John Troutbeck from the British Middle East Office who were keen to ensure a common approach towards the peaceful adjustment of the situation in Palestine, Philip Jessup and John Ross, Warren Austin's deputy at the UN, were in London hoping to secure British support in delaying discussion of the Mediator's report until after the American presidential election. On September 15th, the Mediator and his team completed the draft report which was signed and transmitted to Paris the following day. The next morning Bernadotte left for Jerusalem with Bunche scheduled to join him the next day from where the two would depart for Paris for the UNGA. Divided into three parts, the Mediator's Progress Report, addressing political, security and humanitarian aspects of the question of Palestine, informed the directives on assistance to refugees and solutions to their situation approved by the UNGA later in the year.[114] Calling upon member States to take action, Bernadotte argued that it would be a "mistake of tragic consequences if [the question of Palestine was] not considered and necessary decisions [were] not taken" further warning that it was a "dangerous complacency to assume that the truce could be maintained with no settlement in sight."[115] The Progress Report reiterated the three basic factors that Bernadotte felt needed to be addressed for a peaceful adjustment of the situation of Palestine, namely, partition, the Jewish State, and immigration, adding that since the adoption of the UNGA's first peace plan "[a] new and difficult element [had] entered into the Palestine problem."[116] Summarizing the impact of the war on the civilian population, Bernadotte noted that "[o]f a population of somewhat more than 400,000 Arabs prior to the outbreak of hostilities, the number presently estimated as remaining in Jewish-controlled territory [was] approximately 50,000."[117] Turning to the

---

114   Progress Report.
115   Id., at 3–4.
116   Id., at 7.
117   Id., at 47. In some areas of the country controlled by Israeli military forces not a single Palestinian village remained intact. This included parts of the former sub-districts of Jaffa and Ramle conquered during the first phase of the war and between the first and second truce. The former sub-districts of Beersheba and Gaza would suffer the same fate

Jewish population, Bernadotte estimated that "some 7,000 Jewish women and children from Jerusalem and various areas occupied by the Arabs [had] sought refuge within Jewish-controlled territory."[118] In contrast to the situation of Arab Palestinian refugees, their situation had been largely "sorted out" with the establishment of the Jewish State notwithstanding individual claims that might arise in the context of a political settlement.[119] In the conclusion (Section VIII) of the first part of the report, the Mediator listed seven basic premises for a peaceful adjustment of the situation in Palestine. In contrast to his June suggestions, Bernadotte acknowledged that "[a] Jewish State called Israel [now] exist[ed] in Palestine and there [were] no sound reasons for assuming that it [would] not continue to do so."[120] The Mediator nevertheless reiterated his previous suggestion that "[t]he boundaries of this new State must finally be fixed either by formal agreement between the parties concerned or failing that, by the [UN]" and that "the principle of geographical homogeneity and integration [...] should be the major objective of the boundary arrangements."[121] This conclusion would be one of several focal points of disagreement later in the fall. No longer last on the list, as it had been in June, the fifth premise ("Right of Repatriation") recommended that "[t]he *right* of innocent people, uprooted from their homes by the present terror and ravages of war, *to return to their homes*, should be affirmed and made effective, with assurance of adequate compensation for the property of those who may choose not to return."[122]

Similar to the Mediator's June suggestions in that it affirmed a "right" to return, the premise put forward in September represented a significant evolution in Bernadotte's thinking about a solution to the refugee situation. Explicit in the use of the term "repatriation" was that the refugees would be going back to their *patria*, that is to say, their native country or homeland, even though a new country, that is to say, the State of Israel, had since been established in its place. Moreover, refugees would be returning on the basis of a right rather than on sufferance with the latter central to Israel's subsequent agreement to

---

later in the fall. For additional information, *see* Toward the De-Arabization of Palestine/Israel, 1945–1977 (Basheer K. Nijim ed., 1984); All That Remains, The Palestinian Villages Occupied and Depopulated by Israel in 1948 (Walid Khalidi, ed., 1992); Abu Sitta.

118   Progress Report, at 47.
119   On potential claims, *see* Eyal Benvenisti and Eyal Zamir, *Private Claims to Property Rights in the Future Israeli-Palestinian Settlement*, 89 Am. J. Int'l L. 295 (1995). *See also* Michael R. Fischbach, Jewish Property Claims Against Arab Countries 84–8 (2008).
120   Progress Report, at 17.
121   Id.
122   Id. [emphasis added].

allow small-scale family reunification after the war.[123] Going beyond his previous suggestion, Bernadotte emphasized that the right to return should not only be affirmed, he also emphasized that the right to return should also be made effective. That the right to return should be made effective appears especially significant given Israel's repeated rejection of Bernadotte's numerous appeals over the summer for the return of at least a portion of the refugees in order to alleviate the humanitarian situation.[124] Referring to the uprooting of "innocent people", a phrase which Bernadotte used in communications with the UN Secretary-General, the Mediator appeared to underscore a distinction between civilians and combatants that he had also made in previous months in the context of securing Israeli agreement to the initial return of a portion of the refugees.[125] This also appeared to challenge Israel's position that the refugees comprised a potential fifth column, which effectively subsumed all refugees, the vast majority of whom comprised women, children and the elderly, under the category of enemy nationals.[126] In a further contrast with his June suggestions, Bernadotte also appeared to draw a distinction between the "indirect" causes of forced displacement and the more "direct" ones associated with Israeli efforts to "cleanse" areas under their control along ethnic, national and religious lines.[127] This apparent distinction is further clarified in Part Five ("Refugees") of the report which states that Arab refugees "[had] been dislodged by the *hazards* and *strategy* of the armed conflict between

---

123 *See, e.g.*, the discussion of early family reunification in: Don Peretz, Israel and the Palestine Arabs (1958).

124 In August, Bernadotte sought Israeli approval for the return of certain categories or groups of refugees including those originating from Israeli controlled territory outside the borders of the Jewish State delineated under the partition plan, from villages that remained intact, refugees who had sought shelter in the town of Nazareth, owners of orange groves and others who had ready access to employment along with special cases on humanitarian grounds. *See* Points for Discussion with Mr. Shertok on Refugee Problem, undated, UN Archives, Series? Box 1, File 16, DAG 13/3.3.0. *See also* the Mediator's appeal in July for the return of refugees to the coastal cities of Haifa and Jaffa: Meeting: M. Shertok – Count Bernadotte and Assistants (Tel Aviv, July 26, 1948).

125 Cablegram dated 1 August 1948 from the United Nations Mediator to the Secretary General Concerning Arab Refugees, Press Release, U.N. Doc. PAL/236 (Aug. 5, 1948).

126 Progress Report, at 48

127 Pappe, at 71–2 (stating that "[t]he word cleansing, '*tihur*', was used economically in the Consultancy's [an 11-member committee that advised David Ben-Gurion, the chairman of the Jewish Agency who became Israel's first Prime Minister and Defense Minister] meetings, but appears on every order the High Command passed down to the units on the ground. It means in Hebrew what it means in any other language: the expulsion of entire populations from their villages and towns."). *See also* Morris 2004, at 217, 236, 464 and 518 (citing specific military orders that calling for the cleansing ('*tihur*') of Palestinian villages).

Arabs and Jews in Palestine."[128] While the former might comprise flight from generalized fear arising from the war, the latter appears to pinpoint certain policies and practices set out in military plans and operational orders. Plan D which governed Jewish/Israeli operations from April 1948 onwards, for example, included a list of policies and related practices such as the destruction and depopulation of villages that were among the more direct causes for force displacement during the war.[129] The Israeli military's own assessment of the first phase of the war, that is to say, until the establishment of the Jewish State in mid-May, found that the forcible displacement of indigenous population was due, primarily, to "[d]irect, hostile Jewish [Haganah/IDF] operations against Arab [Palestinian] settlements," followed by the effect of operations on nearby villages and towns along with operations by militias like the Irgun and Lehi.[130] In more explicit terms, the following paragraph of the Progress report explain[ed] that "[t]he exodus of Palestinian Arabs resulted from panic created by fighting in their communities, by rumours concerning real or alleged acts of terrorism, or expulsion."[131] As noted earlier, the Mediator's advisors had raised serious concerns about such policies and practices with the Israeli Foreign Minister earlier in the summer. This might also explain Bernadotte's emerging

---

128 Id., at 14 [emphasis added].
129 Walid Khalidi, *Plan Dalet: Master Plan for the Conquest of Palestine*, 18 J. Pal. Stud. 4 (1988). *See also* Pappe, at 82 and 129 (further stating that "Plan D had two very clear objectives, the first being to take swiftly and systematically any installation, military or civilian, evacuated by the British. The second, and far more important, objective of the plan was to cleanse the future Jewish state of as many Palestinians as possible."); Morris 2004, at 164 (stating that "Plan D was not a political blueprint for the expulsion of Palestine's Arabs: it was governed by military considerations and was geared to achieving military ends. But, given the nature of the war and the admixture of the two populations, securing the interior of the Jewish State for the impending battle along its borders in practice meant the depopulation and destruction of villages that hosted hostile local militia and irregular forces."). *See also* Jaap C. Bosma, *Plan Dalet in the Context of the Contradictions of Zionism*, 9 Holy Land Stud. 209 (2010) (explaining that Morris drew his conclusion based on the short text of Plan Dalet, while Pappe examined the thousands of orders related to its implementation).
130 Benny Morris, *The Causes and Character of the Arab Exodus from Palestine: The Israel Defence Forces Intelligence Branch Analysis of June 1948*, 22 Middle East Stud. 5 (1986). Additional causes listed in the report, by order of ranking, included orders given by Arab leaders, psychological warfare, expulsion orders, fear of retaliation, the presence of irregular Arab forces, fear of the consequences of an Arab invasion, isolation and various local factors along with generalized fear about the future. *See also* Abu Sitta, at 108–16 (for tabulation of the six major causes of forced displacement by village and by district along with a comparison with figures tabulated by Israeli history Benny Morris at the district level).
131 Progress Report, at 14.

recognition dating back to July that some refugees might choose not to return and that they should be compensated for their losses. Having already drawn attention of Israeli officials to the fact that certain military practices violated the rules of war, the Progress Report appeared to draw upon language used in the Hague Convention and its annexed Regulations in reference to "numerous reports from reliable sources of large-scale looting, pillaging and plundering, and of instances of destruction of villages *without apparent military necessity*."[132] Commenting on his visit to Palestine in later summer, Bernadotte noted that "[h]e had seen [Haganah] organizing and supervising [the] removal [of] contents [of] Arab houses in Ramle which he understood was being distributed among newly arrived Jewish immigrants."[133] The scope of this provision would be the subject of discussion later in the fall with the representatives of some States expressing concern that certain refugees might favor compensation due to fears about their treatment should they return to the Jewish State. In a paragraph that the British would later draw upon in a revised draft resolution in the fall, Bernadotte concluded that "[t]he liability of the Provisional Government of Israel to restore private property to its Arab owners and to indemnify those owners for property wantonly destroyed [was] clear."[134]

Bernadotte then enumerated eleven specific conclusions which he regarded as "a reasonable, equitable and workable basis for [a political] settlement."[135] With his above-mentioned basic premises having unilaterally removed two of the three "basic factors" for a peaceful adjustment of the situation of Palestine from the negotiating table, namely, the existence of the Jewish State and Jewish immigration, the Mediator's specific conclusion on partition focused on the re-allocation of territory providing more specific directives on the Western Galilee and the Negev.[136] Having concluded that an independent Arab State was no longer viable in light of ongoing Palestinian and Arab opposition to partition and the unlikelihood of an economic union should an Arab State come into being, the Mediator recommended that "[t]he disposition of the territory of Palestine not included within the boundaries of the Jewish State

---

132   Id., at 14.
133   The Charge in Egypt (Patterson) to the Secretary of State, Aug. 7, 1948, in FRUS Vol. 5 (1948), at 1295. *See also* Memorandum by the Department of State to President Truman, undated [drafted August 19], in FRUS Vol. 5 (1948), at 1324 (stating that "[t]hus far the Provisional Government of Israel has refused to admit the Arab refugees to their former homes, which have in some cases been destroyed by fighting and in others pre-empted by Jewish immigrants").
134   Progress Report, at 14.
135   Id., at 18.
136   Id.

should be left to the Governments of the Arab States in full consultation with the Arab inhabitants of Palestine."[137] In line with his past suggestions, not to mention the prevailing view in both London and Washington, Bernadotte further recommended that "in view of the historical connexion and common interests of Transjordan and Palestine there would be compelling reasons for merging the Arab territory of Palestine with the territory of Transjordan, subject to such frontier rectifications regarding other Arab States as may be found practicable and desirable."[138] These were significant shifts from the Mediator's June suggestions in the sense that their removal from the search for a peaceful adjustment of the situation of Palestine, in whole or in part, essentially appeared to foreclose discussion of the very issues, namely, self-determination and its corollaries of sovereignty and non-intervention in the domestic affairs of States along with the prohibition of the acquisition of territory by force that would need to be addressed in finding solutions for the refugees. In the ninth conclusion (paragraph 4(i)) on refugees, Bernadotte recommended that "[t]he *right* of the Arab refugees to *return to their homes* in Jewish-controlled territory at the earliest possible date should be affirmed by the [UN]."[139] That the Mediator further specified that the refugees had a right to return to "Jewish-controlled territory" appeared to arise from Israel's ongoing conquest of land beyond the borders of the Jewish State delineated under the partition plan. In Bernadotte's view, moreover, the creation of *fait accomplis* in Jewish-controlled territory, what Israel's government had described back in June as "retro-active transfer," did not appear to comprise a barrier to their return. Addressing the humanitarian consequences of the refugee crisis in the third part of his report, the Mediator observed that "[e]ven though in many localities their homes had been destroyed, and their furniture and assets dispersed, it was obvious that a solution for their difficulties could be more readily found there than elsewhere."[140] Having already emphasized in his related premise that the right to return should be affirmed, the specific conclusion on refugees further elaborated how it should be made effective. In contrast to his June suggestions, the Mediator recommended that "[the] repatriation, resettlement and economic and social rehabilitation [of the refugees], and payment of adequate compensation for the property of those choosing not to return, should be supervised and assisted by the [UN] conciliation

---

137 Id., at 6.
138 Id., at 14.
139 Id., at 18.
140 Id., at 48.

commission."[141] The establishment of a conciliation commission to "employ its good offices to make such recommendations to the parties or to the [UN] [...] with a view to ensuring the continuation of the peaceful adjustment of the situation in Palestine" appeared to underscore Bernadotte's view that while responsibility for resolving the refugee situation lay with the State of Israel, it was also an international one which stemmed in large part from the UNGA's initial recommendation to divide the country into separate Arab and Jewish States.[142] Indeed, numerous officials had warned that partition would lead to armed conflict and forced displacement of the country's indigenous Arab population.[143] Implicit in the instructions given to the conciliation commission, moreover, was that the implementation of the right to return involved giving refugees a choice, a principle which Bernadotte had already set forth in the above-mention premise on the right to repatriation. Absent from his June suggestions, the evolution in the Mediator's recommendation appears to have arisen in part from doubts expressed over the summer about whether and how many refugees might wish to return with his report explicitly emphasizing that "in any case their *unconditional right to make a free choice* should be fully respected."[144] The principle of refugee choice was also implicit in a related conclusion which appeared to resurrect an Anglo-American idea raised back in the summer with the conciliation commission directed to "lend its good offices, on the invitation of the parties, to any efforts toward exchanges of populations with a view to troublesome minority problems, and on the basis of

---

141 Id., at 18 [emphasis added].
142 Id., at 18–19. *See also* David P. Forsythe, United Nations Peacemaking: The United Nations Conciliation Commission For Palestine 26 (1971) (further stating that "Bernadotte believed that the [UN] had continuing responsibility in the Arab-Zionist conflict, but he was dissatisfied with the political stalemate that had persisted in sight of his peacemaking efforts. He thought a commission might succeed where he had not. Also contributing to his view that another form of peacemaking was needed was his feeling that personality conflicts had developed between himself and certain of those with whom he was dealing. He felt that in such situations it was the Mediator's job to expendable."). *See also* Touval, at 44.
143 Speaking before the UNGA's Ad Hoc Committee one year earlier, Sir Muhammad Zafrullah Khan, Pakistan's representative, warned fellow members that "[t]he effect of partition," something he was all too familiar with, "would be to force the entire Arab population of the Jewish State," around half a million people, "to migrate into the neighbouring Arab States." U.N. G.A.O.R., 3rd Sess., Ad Hoc Comm. on the Palestine Question, 7th mtg. (Oct. 7, 1947), at 38. British Foreign Secretary Bevin and Loy Henderson, Director of the Office of Near Eastern Affairs at the American State Department, offered similar warnings. Gendzier, at 61 and 68.
144 Progress Report, at 14 [emphasis added].

adequate compensation for property owned."[145] In contrast to previous suggestions for a population exchange, however, the one proposed by Bernadotte would have to be agreed upon, that is to say, it had to involve consent, a principle that had defeated past attempts to resolve the struggle over Palestine through partition and the transfer of its indigenous Arab population. Reiterating a point he had made just over a month earlier after surveying the situation in Palestine, the Mediator emphasized that "[i]t would be an offence against the principles of elemental justice if these innocent victims of the conflict were denied the right to return to their homes while Jewish immigrants flow into Palestine, and, indeed, at least offer the threat of permanent replacement of the Arab refugees who have been noted in the land for centuries."[146] Finally, Bernadotte's specific conclusion on refugees stipulated that implementation of the right to return also involved the economic and social integration of the refugees in their homes and places of origin in what he referred to as Jewish-controlled territories. Noting that "[t]he vast majority of the refugees may no longer have homes to return to," the Mediator acknowledged that "their resettlement in the State of Israel present[ed] an economic and social problem of special complexity."[147] Whether they returned to their homes and places of origin or chose to resettle elsewhere, "a major question to be faced [was] that of placing them in an environment in which they [could] find employment and the means of livelihood."[148] Underscoring a core principle of the draft "International Declaration on Human Rights," which affirmed that "[a]ll men are born free and equal in dignity and rights,"[149] Bernadotte further emphasized that "[t]he political, economic, social and religious rights of all Arabs in the Jewish territory of Palestine and of all Jews in the Arab territory of Palestine should be fully guaranteed and respected by the authorities."[150] This provision

---

145   Id., at 18.

146   Id., at 14. Reflecting on his visit to Palestine in the summer after the restoration of the truce, Bernadotte similarly concluded that "it seemed [an] anomaly for Jews to base [their] demand for [a] Jewish state on [the] need to find [a] home [for] Jewish refugees and that they should demand [the] migration to Palestine of Jewish [displaced persons] when they refused to recognize [the] problem of Arab refugees they had created." The Charge in Egypt (Patterson) to the Secretary of State.

147   Progress Report.

148   Id.

149   Report of the Drafting Committee to the Commission on Human Rights, Draft International Declaration on Human Rights art. 3(1), UN Doc. E/CN.4/95, May 21, 1948 (stating that "[e]veryone is entitled to all the rights and freedoms set forth in this Declaration, without distinction of any kind, such as race (which includes colour), sex, language, religion, political or other opinion, property status, or national or social origin").

150   Progress Report, at 18.

is further expanded upon on the third part of the report on refugee assistance stating that "[t]he refugees on return to their homes are entitled to adequate safeguards for their personal security, normal facilities for employment, and adequate opportunity to develop in the community without racial, religious or social discrimination."[151] This principle would the focus of debate over the coming weeks and months. Three days after submitting his report to Secretary-General Trygve Lie, Bernadotte was dead, killed by Jewish assassins on his way to a meeting in Jerusalem. Aware of the difficulties that lay ahead, the Foreign Office felt that "[the] report should be published immediately as a monument to Bernadotte" further noting that "[the] Stern Gang [had] done more to galvanize support for the plan that the US and UK could have done in weeks of work."[152] Alluding to the challenges, Lewis Douglas, the American Ambassador in London, noted that the progress made to date "was not far from being a miracle."[153]

III Phase Two: the Anglo-American-Acting Mediator Drafts

On 21 September, Trygve Lie, the UN Secretary-General requested that the agenda for the third regular session of the UNGA include the item "Progress report of the [UN] Mediator on Palestine." On the same day, the Americans and the British simultaneously issued statements urging Israel, the Arab States and members of the UNGA to accept Bernadotte's conclusions "in their entirety."[154] Reiterating support for the Mediator's conclusions in the UNGA's general debate two days later, Secretary Marshall called for "[a] Palestine free from strife and the threat of strife."[155] In setting out a number of principles for a peaceful settlement, Marshall once again emphasized American support for "the repatriation of refugees who *wished to return* and *live in peace* with their neighbours," reaffirming principles introduced over the spring and summer that would eventually find their way into the UNGA's second peace plan

---

151 Id., at 52.
152 London (Douglas) to Secretary of State, DELGA 4167, Sept. 18, 1948, NARA, 501.BB Palestine/9-1848. *See also*, Heller, at 525 (quoting the Israeli Foreign Minister, Moshe Sharett, warning the provisional government that "a dead Bernadotte might be more powerful and influential than Bernadotte alive").
153 The Ambassador in the United Kingdom (Douglas) to the Secretary of State, Sept. 17, 1948, in FRUS Vol. 5 (1948), at 1409–12.
154 The Acting Secretary of State to Certain Diplomatic and Consular Offices, Sept. 21, 1948, in FRUS Vol. 5 (1948), at 1416; London (Bliss) to Secretary of State, No. 4219, Sept. 21, 1948, NA, FO 371-68585 E12288.
155 U.N. G.A.O.R., 3rd Sess., 139th mtg., U.N. Doc. A/PV.139 (Sept. 23, 1948), at 41.

for Palestine.[156] Concurring with their American counterparts that "the main political resolution [on Palestine] should reaffirm the right of the Arabs to return to their homes,"[157] British officials nevertheless continued to believe that it "seem[ed] almost certain [...] that the great majority of the refugees [would] either not wish or [would] not be able to return to their homes" and that their "[r]esettlement [would] almost certainly have to take place elsewhere."[158] With officials on both sides of the Atlantic in agreement that the Mediator's Progress Report should be addressed in the UNGA's First Committee (Political), previous warnings about the potential consequences of the mass resettlement of displaced European Jews in Palestine against the wishes of the country's indigenous population appeared to have come to fruition.[159] Speaking in the UNGA's Third Committee (Social) in debate over the establishment of the International Refugee Organization just over two years earlier, Charles Malik had cautioned that "the future Organization should not be allowed to be used as a political tool for political ends."[160] In a prescient comment, the Lebanese representative added that "[i]t would indeed be ironical if, after having solved the international refugee problem in the Third Committee [...], another Committee, the First Committee for example, were subsequently faced with another international problem raised through the settlement of the present problem."[161] On September 24th, the same day that the UNGA referred a draft of the

---

156 Id. [emphasis added].
157 Washington to Foreign Office, No. 4592, Sept. 27, 1948, NA, FO 371-68589 E12574.
158 Foreign Office to United Nations General Assembly, Paris (United Kingdom Delegation), No. 65, Sept. 25, 1948, NA, FO 371-68678.
159 Foreign Office (London) to Washington, No. 10746, Sept. 25, 1948, NA, FO 371-68589 E12587; Washington to Foreign Office (London), No. 4592.
160 U.N. G.A.O.R., 3rd Sess., Third Comm., 18th mtg., U.N. Doc. A/C.3/SR.18 (Nov. 9, 1946), at 96. The representatives of Iraq, Egypt and Syria expressed similar concerns.
161 Id. The Foreign Office offered a similar perspective back in July when it instructed its delegation at the UN to initiate in the UNSC the above-mentioned discussion about displaced European Jews and Arab refugees. See Foreign Office to New York, No. 3162 (stating that "[the] last fifteen years [of] British mandatory administration in Palestine [had been] greatly complicated by the Jewish refugee problem resulting from the Nazi persecution," the Foreign Office argued that "it was this new factor in the situation which finally destroyed the hope [...] that a Jewish National Home [in Palestine] would develop in such a way as to enable it to play a harmonious part in the development of the Middle East as a whole." The Office further acknowledged that "[b]y attempting to '[solve] the problem of Jewish displaced persons in Europe' through the division of Palestine into separate Arab and Jewish States the [UNGA] had 'creat[ed] an even larger problem of Arab displaced persons in the Middle East'."). The Foreign Office was notably silent, however, on the UK's own role through the British cabinet's support for the Balfour Declaration which give imprimatur to the Jewish colonization of Palestine and through its concomitant restrictions on Jewish asylum in the UK.

"International Declaration of Human Rights" to the Third Committee, where discussions would also intersect with the situation in Palestine, the UNGA's General Committee referred the Mediator's report to the First Committee for further consideration. With discussion of the report scheduled for the end of the month there was little time for preparation of a draft resolution.

A   *The First British Draft*

On 28 September, after consultations with colleagues in the Foreign Office in London, Harold Beeley, an official in the Eastern Department and one of Foreign Secretary Bevin's closest advisors on Palestine, forwarded a draft resolution to the American delegation in Paris.[162] The first of a handful of drafts exchanged between American, British and UN officials over the following two weeks, the draft resolution set out the principles for what British officials had earlier described as a "definitive" solution to the situation of Palestine. Comprised of two parts, the body of the draft resolution "[a]ccept[ed] the specific conclusions contained in Part One, Section VIII, paragraph 4, of the Mediator's report as the basis for a settlement in Palestine" and established a UN Conciliation Commission for Palestine "to *give effect* to the Mediator's proposals."[163] Bernadotte's specific conclusions including those relating to the re-allocation of territory and a solution to the refugee situation were set out in the annex to the resolution. In line with paragraph 4(i) of the Mediator's report, which recommended that the UN should affirm the right of Arab refugees to return to their homes, the draft stipulated that "[t]he Palestinian refugees displaced from their homes since 29 November 1947 [the date of the partition plan] *shall be entitled* to return to their homes at the earliest possible date."[164] It then tasked the Conciliation Commission with "supervis[ing] and assist[ing] their repatriation, resettlement, social and economic rehabilitation, and the payment of adequate compensation for the property of those choosing not to return."[165] This basic structure, with the first sentence setting out relevant principles for a solution to the refugee situation and the second addressing their implementation, was preserved throughout the remainder of the drafting process. It was also consistent with the above-mentioned principles and practice which governed solutions to refugee situations elsewhere. While repatriation was a right, reflected in the draft resolution's affirmation that refugees were

---

162   London (Bliss) to Secretary of State, No. 4286, Sept. 28, 1948, NARA, 501.BB Palestine/9-2848.
163   Discussion between Mr. Beeley and the American Delegation about the Draft Resolution on Palestine, Sept. 28, 1948, NA, FO 371-68590 E12716 [emphasis added].
164   Id. [emphasis added].
165   Id.

"entitled" to return, resettlement was an option subject to the sovereign discretion of countries of first asylum and third States in cases of onward movement. The American delegation at the UN accepted the British draft as a working paper and offered to prepare an alternative resolution.[166]

B *The American Draft*

A revised American draft, forwarded to the Foreign Office the following day, dispensed with the annex in favour of a single text comprised of twelve unnumbered paragraphs. While the number of paragraphs in subsequent drafts would vary – up to a total of seventeen – the new format, that is to say, without the annex, remained constant through the remainder of the drafting process. "Endorsing" rather than "accepting" Bernadotte's specific conclusions, the draft resolution limited the role of the technical boundaries commission to be set up under the plan "to assist[ing] [the parties] in delimiting in detail the frontiers in Palestine."[167] This would be an ongoing source of dispute that appeared to stem, in part, from the above-mentioned Anglo-American differences over the principle of acquiescence and direct negotiations between Israel and its Arab neighbours. Instead of having an executive function, moreover, the American text authorized the Commission to "*establish machinery* to supervise and assist their repatriation, resettlement and economic and social rehabilitation [and] arrange for the payment of adequate compensation for the property of those choosing not to return."[168] Thus, in contrast to the British draft, the Commission was empowered "to *give effect* to the Mediator's specific conclusions *in the light of the present resolution*."[169] Beeley, who had since returned to Paris for the UNGA's fall session, informed colleagues back at the Foreign Office that a third revision was being prepared and would be sent as soon as it

---

166 Paris (Jessup) to Secretary of State, DELGA 154, Sept. 29, 1948, NARA, 501.BB Palestine/9-2948; Discussion between Mr. Beeley and the American Delegation about the Draft Resolution on Palestine. *See also* Foreign Office to Washington, No. 10865, Sept. 29, 1948, NA, FO 371-68589 E12574.

167 United Nations General Assembly, Paris (United Kingdom Delegation) to Foreign Office, No. 52, Sept. 29, 1948, NA, FO 371-68590 E12690. The British draft stipulated that "[i]f the parties directly concerned do not agree upon the recognition of these frontiers, they shall nevertheless be regarded as *de facto* international frontiers." Similarly, with regard to the future of Arab Palestine the British draft determined that "[i]n the event of disagreement, [the] Conciliation Commission shall make recommendations to the next session of the [UNGA]." Discussion between Mr. Beeley and the American Delegation about the Draft Resolution on Palestine, Sept. 28, 1948.

168 United Nations General Assembly, Paris (United Kingdom Delegation) to Foreign Office, No. 52 [emphasis added].

169 Id. [emphasis added].

was available.[170] Having met the initial deadline for a draft resolution, the First Committee subsequently voted to delay discussion of the Mediator's Progress Report for several weeks with Arab representatives requesting more time to "properly study" Bernadotte's conclusions and "consult one another."[171] In a cable to the British delegation the following day, the Foreign Office expressed three major concerns about the delay: that the situation in Palestine would likely deteriorate in the absence of diplomatic action, that Jewish pressure on the American government would continue to grow as the presidential election drew nearer and that Latin American States who comprised a third of committee members might vote against the British proposal.[172] While these issues would continue to trouble British officials through the remainder of drafting process, the delay nevertheless provided more time to further hone and build support among Committee members for Bernadotte's recommendations.

C The First Composite Draft

By the first week in October a series of meetings between the British and American delegations in Paris had produced an agreed upon draft resolution which "[e]ndorsed the specific conclusions contained in part I, section VIII, paragraph 4 of the Mediator's report" and incorporated the American draft language on territory and a solution to the refugee situation.[173] The third draft resolution thus "[d]etermin[ed] that the Palestinian refugees displaced from their homes since November 29, 1947, shall be entitled to return to their homes at the earliest possible date" and that the proposed Conciliation Commission "shall establish machinery to supervise and assist their repatriation, resettlement and economic and social rehabilitation, and shall arrange for the payment of adequate compensation for the property of those choosing not to return."[174] British consultations with members of the fifteen-member Western bloc in the Committee indicated "agree[ment] in principle" with the Anglo-American draft resolution pending further instructions from their respective delegations.[175] Officials in the Foreign Office nevertheless expressed

---

170 United Nations General Assembly, Paris (United Kingdom Delegation) to Foreign Office, No. 49, Sept. 29, 1948, NA, FO 371-68589 E12657.
171 U.N. G.A.O.R., 3rd Sess., First Comm., 143rd, mtg. U.N. Doc. A/C.1/SR.143 (Sept. 29, 1948), at 4 [emphasis added].
172 Foreign Office to United Nations General Assembly, Paris (United Kingdom Delegation), No. 102, Sept. 30, 1948, NA, FO 371-68590 E12893. Latin American States comprised just over a third of Committee and UNGA members.
173 Paris (Marshall) to Secretary of State, DELGA 220, Oct. 6, 1948, NARA, 501.BB Palestine/10-648.
174 Id.
175 Id.

concern about Arab efforts to delay discussion of the Mediator's report, a tactic which, in their view, had been "harmful to [the] Arab cause."[176] Responding to Anglo-American statements back in September calling upon the parties to accept the Mediator's report in its entirety, Mahmoud Fawzi had warned that "if the [UNGA] attempted to push through a solution based on an all-out acceptance of the Bernadotte recommendations, the Arab Delegations would refuse to have anything to do with the matter and would regard the solution as one imposed upon them."[177] The Egyptian representative further emphasized that "the primary basis for a settlement would be the return of Arab refugees to their homes in Israel [and that] monetary compensation [for their property] would not serve as a substitute."[178] Reiterating that "[i]t was essential that [the refugees] should be permitted to return," a demand Arab representatives had made repeatedly in the UNSC since the spring, Fawzi offered a lukewarm endorsement of the Mediator's specific conclusion on refugees which he described as "satisfactory in this respect."[179] British officials expressed equal, if not greater, alarm, however, over Israel's "forceful and widespread" efforts to amend Bernadotte's plan, noting that "[the] Israeli strategy appear[ed] to be that once [the] principle [had] been established that [the plan could] be amended regarding [the] Negeb it [would] be possible for them to bring about other amendments [...] which would very shortly put [the] situation back in pre-Bernadotte days."[180] Speaking in Israel's Provisional Council barely a week earlier, Foreign Minister Sharett had declared his government's "[intent] to fight [the Mediator's] report and bring about its rejection by the [UN]."[181] Describing how this would be done, Sharett referred to Prime Minister Ben Gurion's "theory of force" explaining that "one [had] to distinguish between a country's opposition to something and its readiness to use force."[182] While Israeli military forces had conquered parts of the northern Negev after

---

176 London (Holmes) to Secretary of State, No. 4382, Oct. 4, 1948, NARA, 501.BB Palestine/10-448.
177 Memorandum of Conversation by Mr. Henry S. Villard of the Advisory Staff of the United Nations Delegation to the General Assembly, Sept. 26, 1948, in FRUS Vol. 5 (1948), at 1423.
178 Id.
179 Id.
180 London (Holmes) to Secretary of State, No. 4421, Oct. 7, 1948, NARA, 501.BB Palestine/10-748. *See also* London (Holmes) to Secretary of State, No. 4455, Oct. 11, 1948, NARA, 501.BB Palestine/10-1148.
181 Sitting 20 of the Provisional Council of State, Sept. 27, 1948 Major Knesset Debates, 1948–1981 288 (Daniel J. Elazar ed., 1993).
182 Id., 269. *See also* Morris 2004, at 360 (quoting Ben Gurion in February 1948 stating that "the war will give us the land. The concept of 'ours' and 'not ours' are only concepts in peacetime and during war they lose their meaning."); Pappe, at 36–7 n14 (stating that the

the collapse of the first truce in July, they had failed to secure control over Jewish colonies that remained in territories under Egyptian control and continued to harass the Arab population in the area leading to ongoing cycles of displacement.[183] Commenting on Ben Gurion's theory of force in relation to the refugees, Sharett further emphasized Israel had "the strength not to return the refugees [b]ecause [it] control[led] all the places [that] the Arabs [had] abandoned, and [that] it [was] only by force that they [could] be given back to [the refugees] against [the government's] will."[184] With the Mediator's report having yet to be taken up by the First Committee, the Foreign Office expressed further concern that in the weeks since the Mediator's assassination "a good deal of emotional appeal and drive behind the Bernadotte Plan [had] dissipated" and that "steps [would] have to be taken to refocus [the] attention of [the] world on [the] uneasy character of [the] truce in Palestine and [the] vital need for [the] fair and equitable settlement offered by [the] Bernadotte Plan."[185]

D *The Bunche Draft*

Ralph Bunche, who had since become the Acting Mediator after Bernadotte's assassination, had also provided the British and the Americans with the draft resolution they requested back in September during talks in Rhodes. "Approv[ing] the progress report of the late UN Mediator, and adopt[ing] the conclusions to part one of that report [...] as the basic plan for the peaceful settlement of the situation in Palestine", the Bunche draft, in language similar to the previous Anglo-American draft, instructed the proposed Conciliation Commission to "carry out the functions assigned to it by [the] resolution in accordance with the provisions of the basic plan."[186] The Acting Mediator, however, also made a number of changes beginning with his explicit recognition that the refugees had a "right" to return, a principle that had until then

---

"borders [of the state], given the Palestinian and Arab rejection, said Ben Gurion, will be determined by force and not by the partition resolution").

183 Morris 2004, at 436 and 462 (stating that Bernadotte's report "compelled the Israeli political and military leadership to focus attention on the south, where the surrounded, poorly supplied enclave of less than two dozen settlements was cut off from the core of the Yishuv by Egyptian forces holding the Majdal – Faluja – Beit Jibrin – Hebron axis").
184 Sitting 20 of the Provisional Council of State, Sept. 27, 1948, at 288.
185 London (Holmes) to Secretary of State, No. 4421.
186 Paris (Austin) to Secretary of State, DELGA 284, Oct. 11, 1948, NARA, 501.BB Palestine/10-1148; Paris (Austin) to Marshall, DELGA 289, Oct. 11, 1948, NARA, 501.BB Palestine/10-1148. The UN archives include several undated drafts with the earliest dated draft prepared more than a week prior to the US delegation forwarding a copy of the Bunche draft to the State Department. The Bunche draft was also the first draft to introduce numbered paragraphs.

only been implicit in previous drafts through endorsement of the specific conclusion in Part One, Section VIII, paragraph 4(i) of the Mediator's report and through subsequent Anglo-American determination that the refugees were "entitled" to return to their homes. Paragraph 11 of the Bunche draft thus "[r]ecogniz[ed] fully the *right* of refugees from the conflict in Palestine to *return to their homes* at the earliest possible date [...] and [then] instruct[ed] the Conciliation Commission to assist and supervise the repatriation of such refugees as may *choose* to exercise this right, and their resettlement."[187] The day after Warren Austin, the American Ambassador at the UN, sent the Acting Mediator's draft to Secretary Marshall, the Lebanese representative on the Third Committee, Karim Azkhoul, introduced an amendment on freedom of movement to the draft "International Declaration on Human Rights" adding the phrase "and to return to his country" to sub-paragraph 2 of article 11 which affirmed "[everyone's] right to leave any country, including his own."[188] In a second major contrast with Bernadotte's specific conclusion and the previous Anglo-American draft resolution, both of which provided for the payment of adequate compensation for the property of those choosing not to return, the Bunche draft "[r]ecogniz[ed] fully the *right* of refugees [...] to be adequately compensated *for any losses* suffered by them *as a result of confiscation or destruction of property not resulting from military necessity*."[189] Similar to the language in Part One, Section V, paragraph 7 of the late Mediator's report, emphasizing Israel's liability to restore private property and compensate refugees for the destruction of their property without military necessity, the Acting Mediator's text also appeared to reference the Hague Convention. Article 23 of the annexed Regulations, for example, stipulated that it was forbidden "[t]o destroy or seize the enemy's property, unless such destruction or seizure be imperatively demanded by the necessities of war."[190] Israel's military strategy and its retro-active transfer plan, as noted earlier, both provided for the destruction of property as a means of clearing out unwanted populations and preventing their return. Article 25 prohibited "[t]he attack or bombardment, by whatever means, of towns, villages, dwellings, or buildings which are undefended."[191]

---

187 Paris (Austin) to Secretary of State, DELGA 284 [emphasis added].
188 Lebanon: Amendments to Draft Declaration E/800, U.N. Doc. A/C.3/260 (Oct. 12, 1948); ECOSOC, *Report of the Third Session of the Commission on Human Rights*, U.N. Doc. E/800 (June 28, 1948). Cuba and Egypt also introduced amendments using slightly different language that similarly affirmed the right to return.
189 Paris (Austin) to Secretary of State, DELGA 284 [emphasis added].
190 Convention (IV) Respecting the Laws and Customs of War on Land and its Annex: Regulation concerning the Laws and Customs of War on Land, Oct. 18, 1907, 187 C.T.S. 227.
191 Id.

This had also been a major part of Israel's war effort beginning with the bombardment of Lydda after the collapse of the first truce which together with military operations in the neighboring town of Ramle, as noted earlier, led to the single largest expulsion of Palestinians during the 1948 war. A report by the US Central Intelligence Agency subsequently noted that Israeli operations in the two towns "were designed to induce civilian panic and flight – as a means of precipitating military collapse and possibl[y] also as an end itself."[192] Having recognized compensation as a right, the Bunche draft also affirmed, in contrast to the late Mediator's specific conclusion and the previous Anglo-American draft, that its exercise was equally applicable to those refugees who chose to exercise their right to return to their homes. These changes would be the source of Anglo-American difference in the following weeks.

In a further innovation, Bunche introduced a second and related paragraph addressing the situation of refugees who did not wish to exercise their right to return. Consistent with the emphasis on choice in the Mediator's Progress Report, not to mention Bernadotte's apparent uncertainty about whether and how many refugees might choose to return to their homes in "Jewish-controlled territory," paragraph 12 of the draft resolution "[r]ecogniz[ed] that for various reasons numbers of refugees *may not exercise the right to return to their former homes*."[193] It therefore instruct[ed] the Conciliation Commission to establish as urgent measures appropriate machinery to study the problem and to take such action as it may deem appropriate to facilitate the resettlement of refugees elsewhere."[194] In line with the Mediator's Progress Report and the previous Anglo-American draft resolution, the paragraph further instructed the Commission "to supervise the payment of adequate compensation for the property of those choosing not to return to their homes."[195] By introducing an additional paragraph, moreover, the Acting Mediator was able to more ac-

---

192 Gendzier, at 133. *See also* Saleh Abdel Jawad, *Zionist Massacres: The Creation of the Palestinian Refugee Problem in the 1948 War*, in Israel and the Palestinian Refugees 59 (Sari Hanafi et al ed., 2007) [*hereinafter* Jawad] (stating that "the bombing of civilian areas with airplanes acquired illegally during the truce 'brought the 'industrialization of massacres' (mass killings on a wide and speedy basis from a distance) to the Middle East").

193 Paris (Austin) to Secretary of State, DELGA 284. *See also* Cablegram dated 1 August 1948 from the United Nations Mediator to the Secretary General Concerning Arab Refugees, Press Release, U.N. Doc. PAL/236 (Aug. 5, 1948) (stating that "the strife in Palestine [had] created conditions which might well make it impracticable, for security and other reasons, the return of all or the preponderance of these innocent victims of a needless conflict" further noting that he was unsure "how many of these persons [might] *wish* to return before peace is permanently restored in Palestine") [emphasis added].

194 Paris (Austin) to Secretary of State, DELGA 284 [emphasis added].

195 Id.

curately address the different responsibilities and functions associated with a solution to the refugee crisis. Thus, in the case of repatriation the Commission would offer "assistance" and "supervision", not unlike the UN Relief and Rehabilitation Administration, the international body set up three years earlier to facilitate the repatriation of persons displaced as a result of the Second World War. This contrasted with Commission's role with regard to those who did not wish to return, which required the "establishment of machinery" and further "study", and may have been more similar, in part, to operations of the International Refugee Organization, notwithstanding its concomitant responsibility as noted earlier for repatriation of the smaller number of refugees wishing to return to their countries of origin. As the UN Mediator noted in his September report, this latter option appeared to be considerably more complex, not to mention more costly, as British officials observed back in the summer. The introduction of separate paragraphs also enabled a distinction between compensation of returnees, which fell within the domestic jurisdiction of the State of Israel, and compensation for non-returnees as one of several matters requiring international protection and oversight.

Bunche made two further changes of significance to the refugee situation. In contrast to the Anglo-American composite draft described above, the Bunche draft deleted reference to the Mediator's conclusion that "[t]he disposition of the territory of Palestine not included within the boundaries of the Jewish State should be left to the Governments of the Arab States in full consultation with the Arab inhabitants of Palestine."[196] Explaining his rationale to British officials, the Acting Mediator noted that the establishment of an "All Palestine Government" and its declaration of an independent State in all of Mandate Palestine several weeks earlier had changed the situation and that the only "feasible" way to avoid "consultation of the Gaza leaders" was to omit reference to the Mediator's recommendation.[197] Aside from the major differences between Palestine and other partitions that led to widespread displacement, the removal of the above clause appeared to remove possibilities for the refugee situation slowly "sorting itself out" through their integration in a future Palestinian State. Finally, in line with Bernadotte's recommendation that

---

196 Progress Report, at 18; Paris (Austin) to Secretary of State, DELGA 284.

197 United Nations General Assembly, Paris (United Kingdom Delegation) to Foreign Office, No. 135, Oct. 12, 1948, NA FO 371-68591 E13256; Foreign Office to United Nations General Assembly, Paris (United Kingdom Delegation), No. 211, Oct. 13, 1948, NA, FO 371-68591 E13257. For additional discussion of the All Palestine Governent, *see, e.g.*, Avi Shlaim, *The Rise and Fall of the All-Palestine Government in Gaza*, 20 J. Pal. Stud. 37 (1990); Johanna Caldwell, *Inter-Arab Rivalry and the All-Palestine Government of 1948*, 62 Jerusalem Q. 50 (2015)

"political, economic, social and religious rights [...] should be fully guaranteed and respected by the authorities", the Bunche draft contained a new paragraph which "[d]eclar[ed] that, within the respective political entities of Palestine, Arabs and Jews shall enjoy *equal political, economic, social and religious rights*."[198] Important for the social and economic rehabilitation of refugees that Bernadotte had envisaged, securing equal treatment, a protection which by this time had been removed from Israel's evolving draft constitution, would have provided an additional safeguard against further displacement.[199] This principle would nevertheless add to the growing list of disputes that would have to be resolved if the UNGA was going to approve a second peace plan.

E   *The Second Composite Draft*

The American delegation in Paris subsequently produced a composite text based on the Bunche draft and the first Anglo-American composite draft resolution. Incorporating the Acting Mediator's paragraphs on a solution to the refugee situation, the composite draft re-inserted the Mediator's recommendation on the future of "Arab areas of Palestine" not included in the Jewish State with a new clause allowing for "adjustments" in Bernadotte's recommended re-allocation of territory "as may promote agreement between the Arabs and the Jews."[200] The two delegations met with Bunche during the second week of October to discuss the composite text. In the meeting on October 13th and in discussions of subsequent drafts the primary difference on a solution to the refugee situation, which appeared to have arisen as a result of the changes introduced by the Acting Mediator several days earlier, related to the question of compensation rather than return. Not so much a fissure in Anglo-American relations, this nevertheless added to what appeared to be a growing list of transatlantic disagreements about the way forward. In a cable to the American delegation in Paris, Robert Lovett, the Acting Secretary of State while Marshall

---

198   Paris (Austin) to Secretary of State, No. 284. In his role as principal secretary of the UN Special Committee on Palestine, whose recommendations led to the adoption of the UNGA's first peace plan, Bunche had observed that the "[d]anger in any arrangement [was] that a caste system [would] develop with backward [sic] Arabs as the lower caste." Urquhart, at 146 [emphasis added].

199   Amihai Radzyner, *A Constitution for Israel: The Design of the Leo Kohn Proposal, 1948*, 54 Israel Stud. 9 (2010) (describing changes in Israel's evolving constitution and stating that by October 1948 "sections detailing [...] relations with the State's Arab citizens and the residents of Jerusalem [had] been omitted").

200   United Nations General Assembly, Paris (United Kingdom Delegation) to the Foreign Office [Text of the New United States Draft Resolution on Palestine], Oct. 12, 1948, NA, FO 371-67591 E13257; Paris (Marshall) to the Secretary of State, DELGA 318, Oct. 13, 1948, NARA, 501.BB Palestine/10-1348.

was taking part in the UNGA's third session, expressed concern that the phrase "not resulting from military necessity," introduced by Bunche, "[would] produce unlimited and acrimonious debate when actual cases of compensation [were] taken up, since [the] gov't against which [such] claims are made will be tempted to assert that all destruction was due to military necessity."[201] Lovett also reiterated the American position that operational aspects of resettlement and compensation should be delegated to subsidiary organs such as a "Palestine Refugee Compensation Committee," since otherwise the "main task of [the] Conciliation Commission [would] be much hindered by these vexatious problems."[202] This was addressed in the second paragraph of the Bunche draft which instructed the Commission to set up machinery to study the problem of those refugees not wishing to return to their homes. Officials in the Foreign Office, meanwhile, felt that Bunche's text "[did] not make it absolutely clear that compensation [was] to be paid by the Jewish authorities" and "[left] open the position of refugees who [were] not in fact allowed to return home."[203] While it is unclear why British officials seemed "almost certain" that large numbers of refugees would not return, aside from the measures that Israel was taking to foreclose their right to do so, the above comment on paragraph 12 of the Bunche draft appeared to derive from this concern. Two days before the Foreign Office cabled its delegation at the UN, Israel's provisional government had adopted additional emergency legislation which empowered the Minister of Agriculture to assume control of land which he deemed to be uncultivated.[204] In tandem with restrictions on freedom of movement under the Defense Emergency Regulations, the regulations on the cultivation of fallow land enabled Israel to assume control over land owned and used by refugees and by Palestinians who remained within areas controlled by the Jewish State.[205] Acknowledging that it would be "difficult to provide for something to

---

201 Department of State to the American Embassy (Paris), GADEL 192, Oct. 13, 1948, NARA, 501.BB Palestine/10-1148.
202 Id.
203 Foreign Office to United Nations General Assembly, Paris (United Kingdom Delegation), No. 211.
204 Emergency Regulations for the Cultivation of Fallow land and the Use of Unexploited Water Sources, 27 Official Gazette 3 (1948).
205 Defense (Emergency) Regulations, 1442 Palestine Gazette (1945). *See also* Foreman and Kedar, at 814 (stating that the Emergency Regulations for the Cultivation of Fall Land "[were] the first to legalize the seizure and reallocation of appropriated Arab land and served as a key component of the sophisticated mechanism that gradually turned temporary possession into unrestricted Jewish-Israeli ownership. The regulations were characteristic of most early legislation on the appropriated Arab land in that they legalized its past and future transfer to Jewish possession.").

be done in the event of the Jews not obeying the [UN] resolution," and without ideas of their own, Foreign Office officials suggested that Beeley discuss the matter further in Paris.[206]

The Foreign Office also recommended omission of Bunche's paragraph on equal rights arguing that "declarations of this kind [were] impossible to enforce or supervise and [would] cause far more trouble than they [were] worth."[207] The suggestion marked a significant departure from the UNGA's first peace plan and from initial truce proposals back in the spring along with Bernadotte's June suggestions and his September Progress Report. It was also significant in light of the evolving situation inside Israel where developments increasingly reflected the State's settler colonial origins in contrast to its liberal democratic status. Explaining that the paragraph might lead to a situation in which "Jews in [the] territory acquired by Transjordan and Egypt were under special [UN] protection, whereas Jews in other parts of the territory of those States would not be under such protection [which] would lead to all kinds of practical difficulties and anomalies," the Foreign Office suggested that its delegation in Paris might explain the proposed omission by arguing that "these rights should be covered by [the UN] Charter and [the] Human Rights declaration."[208] The proposed omission, however, may have also reflected British anxiety about having "racially discriminatory policies" debated in the UNGA with Commonwealth countries having played a key role in drafting Charter provisions that prohibited external interference in matters falling within the domestic jurisdiction of States.[209] Meanwhile, as the fall session of the UNGA progressed it seemed increasingly clear to the Americans that "even under the most favorable circumstances with the US and UK standing shoulder to shoulder" it was going to be difficult "to obtain a 2/3 majority for the Bernadotte proposals in the

---

206   Foreign Office to United Nations General Assembly, Paris (United Kingdom Delegation), No. 211.

207   Id.

208   Id. For additional discussion of the treatment of Jewish citizens of Arab countries during the period, *see, e.g.*, Fischbach.

209   Lorna Floyd, *"A Most Auspicious Beginning": The 1946 United Nations General Assembly and the Question of the Treatment of Indians in South Africa*, 16 Rev. Int'l. Stud. 131 (1990). *See also* Mark Mazower, *The Strange Triumph of Human Rights, 1933–1950*, 47 Historical J. 379, 391 (2004) (stating that "[t]he British in particular regarded talk of rights as an unfortunate American obsession which must not be allowed to get out of hand"). Two years later, however, the UNGA affirmed the principle of equality in a resolution clarifying the mandate of the Conciliation Commission. G.A. Res. 394 (Dec. 14, 1950), para. 3 (calling upon "the governments concerned to undertake measures to ensure that refugees, whether repatriated or resettled, will be treated without any discrimination either in law or in fact").

[UNGA]."[210] Having failed to secure a further delay in discussion of the Mediator's report until after the American presidential election, moreover, Ambassador Douglas informed the Foreign Office that in light of the "extreme Jewish pressure on the administration [i]t [might] be necessary [for the American delegation] to make a statement that they leave open the possibility of making an adjustment in [Bernadotte's] plan."[211] Marking the beginning of a significant fissure in Anglo-American cooperation, the Foreign Office "strongly urged against such a statement [which would] disturb [in its view] the essential equilibrium of the Bernadotte proposals as a whole."[212]

F   The Third Composite Draft

On October 15th, the First Committee resumed discussion of the Mediator's report, with initial discussion focused on whether Jordan and Israel, neither of whom were member States, would be allowed to take part in the forthcoming deliberations. Bunche also provided a brief overview of Bernadotte's report reiterating the late Mediator's recommendation that the UNGA "take a firm position" and adopt a resolution "so reasonable as to discourage any attempt to thwart it and to defy the [UNSC] [...] by the employment of armed force."[213] The Syrian representative, Faris el-Khouri, suggested that a representative of the Arab Higher Committee should be invited to take part in the discussion. With the Committee chairman engaged with the parties about ways forward on the Mediator's report, discussion in the First Committee briefly turned to the question of atomic energy. On the same day, the second truce collapsed after the Israeli cabinet decided to send a convoy of trucks to supply Jewish colonies in parts of the Negev under Egyptian control. Accompanied by more than a dozen massacres over the following weeks, Israeli military operations led to another outflow of Palestinians primarily from those areas Bernadotte

---

210   London (Douglas) to Secretary of State, No. 4503, Oct. 14, 1948, NARA, 501.BB Palestine/10-1448. *See also* London (Douglas) to Secretary of State, No. 4524, Oct. 15, 1948, NARA, 501.BB Palestine 10-1548. The UN Charter stipulates that UNGA decisions on important questions, including the maintenance of international peace and security, shall be made by a two-thirds majority of the members present and voting.

211   The Secretary of State (Marshall) to the Acting Secretary of State, DELGA 319, Oct. 13, 1948, NARA, 501.BB Palestine/10-1348; Foreign Office to Washington, No. 11292, Oct. 14, 1948, NA, FO 371-82197 E13367.

212   Foreign Office to Washington, No. 11292, Oct. 14, 1948.

213   U.N. G.A.O.R., 3rd Sess., 161st mtg., U.N. Doc. A/C.1/SR161 (Oct. 15, 1948), at 162. Drawing a contrast with the UNGA's first peace plan, the Acting Mediator further noted that while "it [was not] advisable to draw up a detailed plan [...] the [specific] conclusions reached by the [late] Mediator [in Part One, Section VIII, paragraph 4 of his report] might form the basis for such an overall solution." Id., at 164–5.

had recommended for re-allocation in his report, namely, the Western Galilee and the Negev. Describing the Israeli action as a "serious breach of the truce", the Acting Mediator further observed that the military operations "[were] on a scale which could only be undertaken after considerable preparation, and could scarcely be explained as a simple retaliatory action for an attack on a convoy."[214] With the population of Gaza more than doubling to around a quarter of a million persons as refugees sought shelter from the fighting, the American special representative to Israel, James McDonald, in a cable to President Truman appealing for humanitarian assistance, observed that the refugee crisis was "rapidly reaching catastrophic proportions."[215] Despite the situation in Palestine descending into further chaos, American officials continued to lobby their British counterparts for support in postponing discussion of the Mediator's report with the question of Palestine estimated to come before the First Committee only a few days before the presidential election.[216]

Two days later, after further talks between Bunche and Beeley, taking into account views expressed by the State Department and the Foreign Office, Secretary Marshall, still in Paris for the fall session of the UNGA, cabled a revised draft resolution to the State Department. "[E]ndors[ing] the [Mediator's] specific conclusions [...] as a basis for the peaceful settlement of the situation in Palestine," the draft included minor revisions on the re-allocation of territory stipulating that any changes should maintain "the general equilibrium of the mediator's conclusion" and take into account "the nature of the terrain and the unity of village areas."[217] This would be the last Anglo-American draft resolution before the British introduced their own revised draft resolution roughly a month later when the First Committee began substantive discussion of the Mediator's Progress Report in the weeks that followed the American election. In a separate cable, Ambassador Austin explained that paragraphs 11 and 12 of the Bunche draft had been consolidated into a single paragraph "to

---

214   Fred J. Khouri, The Arab-Israeli Dilemma 87 (1976).
215   Morris, at 462 and 471; The Special Representative of the United States in Israel (McDonald) to Truman, Oct. 17, 1948, in FRUS Vol. 5 (1948) at 1486–7 (further appealing for a "comprehensive program and immediate action [of the kind] that dramatic and overwhelming calamities such as [a] vast flood or earthquake would invoke").
216   Paris (Austin) to Secretary of State, DELGA 367, Oct. 16, 1948, NARA, 501.BB Palestine/10-1648; United Nations General Assembly, Paris (United Kingdom Delegation) to Foreign Office, No. 172, Oct. 17, 1948, NA, FO 371-68592 E13430.
217   Paris (Marshall) to the Acting Secretary of State, DELGA 350, Oct. 15, 1948, NARA, 501.BB Palestine/10-1548; Paris (Marshall) to Secretary of State, DELGA 351, Oct. 15, 1948, in FRUS Vol. 5 (1948) at 1481–83; United Nations General Assembly, Paris (United Kingdom Delegation) to Foreign Office, No. 160, Oct. 16, 1948, NA, FO 371-68592 E13403.

conform more closely with Bernadotte's specific conclusions."[218] Under paragraph 12 of the consolidated draft, the UNGA "[r]ecogniz[ed] the *right* of the Arab refugees *to return to their homes* in Jewish-controlled territory at the earliest possible date; and the right of adequate compensation for property which has been lost as a result of pillage or confiscation or of destruction not resulting from military necessity."[219] Similar to previous drafts, the Anglo-American draft then "instruct[ed] the Conciliation Commission to facilitate the repatriation, resettlement, and economic and social rehabilitation of the Arab refugees and the payment of compensation."[220] Austin further explained that, despite previously stated concerns, the "[p]hrase concerning military necessity [was] retained at Secretariat request in order to maintain [a] realistic balance re: compensation."[221] This appeared to comprise an acknowledgment or at least acquiescence to the principle first introduced in the Bunche draft, namely, that the right to compensation applied to all refugees in contrast to Mediator's progress report and previous American drafts which limited compensation to those not choosing to return. With the added reference to "pillage", which the Mediator also referred to in Part One, Section V, paragraph 7 of his Progress Report, the composite draft appeared to draw once again from the Hague Convention and its annexed Regulations under which pillage was strictly prohibited. In keeping with the American delegation's previous position, however, the revised draft introduced a new paragraph authorizing the proposed Conciliation Commission "*to appoint such auxiliary bodies* and to employ such technical experts, acting under its authority, as it may find necessary to the effective discharge of its functions and responsibilities."[222] In addition to the previously mentioned "Palestine Refugee Compensation Committee," Austin noted without further explanation that this might also include a "Palestine Refugee Board."[223] The Foreign Office nevertheless persisted in its demand for more explicit language on compensation suggesting that this might be accomplished by referring to Part One, Chapter V, paragraph 7 of the Mediator's report, which emphasized "[t]he liability of the Provisional Government of Israel to restore private property to its Arab owners and to indemnify those owners

---

218 Paris (Austin) to Secretary of State, DELGA 367, Oct. 16, 1948.
219 Paris (Marshall) to Secretary of State, DELGA 351 [emphasis added].
220 Id.
221 Paris (Austin) to Secretary of State, DELGA 367, Oct. 16, 1948.
222 Paris (Marshall) to Secretary of State, DELGA 351 [emphasis added].
223 Id. The cable does not explain the difference between the two bodies, however, given the various tasks listed in the second sentence of the paragraph, one might assume that a "Refugee Board" would be responsible for matters relating to repatriation, resettlement and economic and social integration.

for property wantonly destroyed."[224] The Foreign Office requested its delegation in Paris to "ask [their] legal Advisers what would be the effect of [the] present re-draft if [the] Jews den[ied] liability to pay compensation."[225] With only weeks to go before the American election, efforts in Washington to delay discussion in the First Committee had in the meantime reached a fevered pitch with Truman "request[ing] that no statement be made or no action be taken on the subject of Palestine [...] without obtaining [his] specific authority."[226]

On October 20th, several days later, the First Committee once again agreed to delay discussion of the Mediator's report after Cuba proposed that a Mexican appeal to the Great Powers to renew efforts to resolve differences towards the establishment of a lasting peace be considered first. Over in London, meanwhile, officials in the Foreign Office, having acceded to the American request without having received assurances of future cooperation, worried that "by the time Palestine [was] discussed we shall find that the territorial position in Palestine [had] been so much changed that it [would] no longer be practicable to give effect to the Mediator's proposals."[227] Instructing its delegation in Paris, the Foreign Office thus suggested that, in order to "prevent [UN] authority as regards the Palestine question being still further weakened," the UNSC should continue efforts to bring about a cessation of hostilities in the south of the country with "early and constructive discussion of Arab refugees in [the Third Committee]."[228] The following day the UNSC "[r]emind[ed] the Governments and authorities concerned that all [of their] obligations and responsibilities [under previous resolutions] [were] to be discharged fully and in good faith" with a subsequent recommendation calling upon the parties "to undertake negotiation *through [UN] intermediaries or directly* as regards outstanding

---

224   Foreign Office to United Nations General Assembly, Paris (United Kingdom Delegation), No. 238, Oct. 16, 1948, NA, FO 371-68592 E13403.
225   Id.
226   The Acting Secretary of State to the Secretary of State at Paris, Telmar 72, Oct. 18, 1948, in FRUS Vol. 5 (1948), at 1489. *See also* Memorandum by the Acting Secretary of State to President Truman, Oct. 19, 1948, in FRUS Vol. 5 (1948) at 1494.
227   Foreign Office to United Nations General Assembly, Paris (United Kingdom Delegation), No. 242, Oct. 18, 1948, NA, FO 371-68592 E13430 (further stating that "[t]he essential point is that whenever Palestine is discussed, the Americans should be wholeheartedly with us as regards: (a) moving [an agreed upon] resolution; (b) recommending the approval of it to other delegations privately; [and] (c) adopting an agreed attitude with [the United Kingdom] in regard to all amendments").
228   Foreign Office to the United Nations General Assembly, Paris (United Kingdom Delegation), No. 270, Oct. 22, 1948, NA, FO 371-68592 E13539.

problems in the Negev."229 The construction of this phrase would also have implications for the UNGA's second peace plan in the coming weeks. Adopting a British motion, the Third Committee, meanwhile, agreed to place the question of refugee relief on its agenda with discussions over the following weeks leading to the establishment of the UN Relief for Palestine Refugees to coordinate relief efforts undertaken by voluntary organizations operating in Palestine (including Israel), Transjordan, Lebanon and Syria.230 Raphael Cilento, the Australian tasked with setting up an initial relief system, who previously described the refugee situation in Palestine as second only to the one in China now compared it to some "100,000,000 destitute Americans [suddenly having] to [rely] on outside help."231

On October 23rd, the same day that members of the UNGA's Sixth Committee (Legal) rejected a Syrian amendment to the draft Convention on the Prevention and Punishment of the Crime of Genocide under which forcible displacement would fall within the definition of genocide, the First Committee resumed deliberations on the situation of Palestine.232 Unable to agree on what the Iranian representative, Mostafa Adl, described as the "somewhat complicated [...] legal aspect of the problem of [All Palestine Government] participation," Committee members accepted his suggestion that it would be "wiser to give the delegations sufficient time to come to a decision with full knowledge of the facts."233 The American delegation described the delay as the "[l]ast possible postponement without losing self-respect and that of others" further noting that even though debate [on the Mediator's report] would resume before the presidential election initial discussions would focus on procedural

---

229   S.C. Res. 59 (Oct. 19, 1948), para. 3. In a strange twist that helps to explain, by way of analogy, the final wording of paragraph 11 of Resolution 194 a month-and-a-half down the road, a Syrian amendment to the Acting Mediator's recommendation on the truce led to the removal of a provision endorsing the return of "dislocated Arabs" to their lands in the Negev. This was not because members opposed the principle of return, but rather due to the desire of Arab representatives to exclude reference to other issues. U.N. S.C.O.R., 3rd yr, 367th mtg., U.N. Doc. S/PV.367 (Oct. 19, 1948) [emphasis added].
230   G.A. Res. 212, U.N. G.A.O.R., 3rd Sess., U.N. Doc. A/RES/212 (Nov. 19, 1948).
231   UN Relief Supplies on Way to Palestine Refugee Camps, Press Release, U.N. Doc. PAL/322 (Oct. 1, 1948).
232   Id.
233   U.N. G.A.O.R., 3rd Sess., Sixth Comm., 81st mtg., U.N. Doc. A/C.6/SR.81 (Oct. 22, 1948), at 176. This may have been due in part to concerns expressed by a number of States, including those involved in the mass transfer of ethnic Germans after the Second World War, that they might be found complicit in genocide under the Syrian amendment. See, e.g., Communication Received from the United States of America, Washington, Sept. 30, 1947, in The Genocide Convention: The Travaux Préparatoires Vol. I 347 (Hirad Abtahi and Philippa Webb, eds., 2008).

matters involving the All Palestine Government with the US not expected to speak until the end of the first week in November, that is to say, after the election.[234] Responding to criticism from the Republican presidential candidate, Thomas Dewey, the following day, President Truman released a statement announcing that the US "approv[ed] the claims of the State of Israel to the boundaries set forth in [Resolution 181] and consider[ed] that modifications thereof should be made only if fully acceptable to the State of Israel."[235] The fissure in Anglo-American cooperation that the British had expressed concern about back in August thus turned into what appeared to be a rupture. In a cable notifying the American delegation in Paris about the President's statement, Robert Lovett, the Acting Secretary of State, suggested that Marshall "[might] wish to inform [Ambassador] Douglas so he can batten down the hatches."[236] On October 28th, the same day that Truman described Israel as a "state with the highest standards of Western civilization" to campaign supporters in New York, Israeli military forces launched military operations in the north with a further spate of atrocities contributing to the forcible displacement of tens of thousands of Arab Palestinians from the upper Galilee which the Mediator had re-allocated to the Jewish State.[237] Writing from London, Ambassador Douglas described the situation as "probably as dangerous to our national interests as [the blockade] in Berlin" even though it had not received the same headlines.[238] The British delegation in Paris cabled the Foreign Office relaying a conversation with Robert Lovett from the State Department assuring them that "silly season [in the US] would be over by Wednesday."[239] Back in Washington President Truman issued a second directive reiterating that

---

234   U.N. G.A.O.R., 3rd Sess., 169th mtg., U.N. Doc. A/C.1/SR.169 (Oct. 23, 1948), at 241. The Committee adopted the Iranian motion by a vote of 19 in favour and 16 against.

235   The United States Delegation to the Acting Secretary of State, DELGA 462, Oct. 23, 1948, NARA, 501.BB Palestine/10-2348. The Acting Secretary of State to the Secretary of State, at Paris [Statement by the President], Telmar 97, Oct. 24, 1948, in FRUS Vol. 5 (1948), at 1512.

236   The Acting Secretary of State to the Secretary of State, at Paris, Telmar 92, Oct. 23, 1948, in FRUS Vol. 5 (1948), at 1507.

237   Address in Madison Square Gardens, New York, Oct. 28, 1948, Public Papers, Harry S. Truman, 1945–53, Harry S. Truman Presidential Library & Museum, https://www.trumanlibrary.org/publicpapers/index.php?pid=2013&st=&st1. *See also* Morris, at 481; Jawad.

238   London (Douglas) to Secretary of State, No. 4621, Oct. 26, 1948, in FRUS Vol. 5 (1948), at 1516.

239   United Nations General Assembly, Paris (United Kingdom Delegation) to Foreign Office, No. 258, Oct. 30, 1948, NA, FO 371-68594 E14108.

"every effort [should] be made to avoid taking [a] position on Palestine prior to [the election]."[240]

IV Phase Three: the First Committee (Political) Drafts

On November 2nd, the same day that voters in the US returned Truman to the White House, the UNGA's Third Committee resumed discussion of article 11 of the draft "International Declaration of Human Rights" relating to freedom of movement. Introduced back in October, Karim Azkhoul, the Lebanese representative, observed that if the Committee accepted his amendment, "the right to leave a country, already sanctioned in article 11 [of the draft declaration], would be strengthened by the assurance of the right to return."[241] Describing the Lebanese amendment as "sufficiently realistic," Eleanor Roosevelt, the American representative, stated that the US would vote for its adoption with the addition of the right to return subsequently approved without a negative vote.[242] Meeting two days later, the UNSC called upon the warring parties in Palestine to withdraw their forces to positions held before the collapse of the second truce and to establish permanent truce lines "through negotiations conducted *directly* between the parties, or, failing that, *through the intermediaries* [...] *of the* [UN]."[243] Having altered the phrasing of its recommendation issued two weeks earlier by prioritizing direct talks between the parties over negotiations mediated by the UN, the UNSC may have unwittingly provided a solution to one of several Anglo-American differences several weeks later. Three days after the American election, Chaim Weizmann, Israel's first president, congratulated Truman on his electoral victory before proceeding to discuss an issue that had been the subject of discussion in the UNSC over the summer. "While the eyes of the world have been turned to the battlefields in the south and the north [of the country]," wrote Weizmann, "we have succeeded in liquidating one refugee camp after another in Europe and bringing the chance of a new life [in Palestine] to thousands of ruined men and women whom the world has all but forgotten."[244] In a cable to Secretary Marshall the

---

240 The Acting Secretary of State (Lovett) to the Secretary of State, at London, No. 4158, Oct. 31, 1948, in FRUS Vol. 5 (1948), at 1535.
241 U.N. G.A.O.R., 3rd Sess., Third Comm., 120th mtg., U.N. Doc. A/C.3/SR.120 (Nov. 2, 1948), at 316.
242 Id. The Lebanese amendment was adopted by 33 votes to none with 8 abstentions.
243 S.C. Res. 61, (Nov. 4, 1948), para. 2 [emphasis added].
244 The President of the Provisional Government of Israel (Weizmann) to President Truman, Nov. 5, 1948, in FRUS Vol. 5 (1948), at 1549. Once the International Refugee Organization

previous day, James Keeley, the American representative in Syria, was less than impressed by Truman's "praise of Israel as [a] 'state with [the] highest standards of civilization'."[245] While the President was speaking in Madison Square Gardens, "[the] Israeli army (according to UN eye-witness accounts) was forcibly expelling Arabs from their homes in [the] Galilee and systematically looting their possessions."[246] With the onset of yet another wave of forced displacement characterized by the capture and expulsion of returnees and Palestinians residing in Israel's "border" regions along with the eviction and transfer of Palestinians within the Jewish State, the Red Cross officials in Gaza estimated that starvation and dysentery were contributing to the death of more than one hundred refugees every day.[247] Keeley recommended that "Israel should [...] be told that [the] continuation [of] US friendship [would] depend [upon] rectification [of its] shocking conduct."[248]

A The First Revised American (Partial) Draft

Two weeks after the American election, the UNGA's First Committee finally resumed discussion of the Mediator's report with initial meetings focused on participation of the Arab Higher Committee. Having dealt with procedural issues that in the end enabled the Arab Higher Committee to take part in discussions, albeit not as the recognized representative of the All Palestine Government,

---

had determined that "the war no longer hampered [the] firm re-establishment [of displaced European Jews] in areas controlled by Israel," moreover, the organization decided to "[make] budgetary provisions to retroactively pay for the emigration of 50,000 Jewish [displaced persons] independently transported [by Jewish organizations] since May 1948." Cohen, at 143–44 (further stating that "[the] proposal to retroactively pay for the transportation of Jewish [displaced persons] to Israel was hotly debated within the IRO Executive Committee. The American representative, George Warren, conceded that there was 'no positive proof that no refugee who had gone to Palestine was living in a house previously occupied by an Arab and unquestionably some were doing so'. He added, however, that 'the immigrants who had moved to Arab houses could be almost counted on the fingers of one hand' and that the vast majority of Jewish newcomers 'only worked in cooperatives and in areas where the Arab had not lived'. As recent research has established, this statement did not reflect the reality on the ground.").

245   Damascus (Keeley) to the Secretary of State, No. 688, Nov. 4, 1948, NARA, 501.BB Palestine/11-448.
246   Id.
247   Morris, at 525, 536 (further stating that "[e]xcluding the Negev beduin, it is probable that the number of Arabs kicked out of, or persuaded to leave, the country in the border-clearing operations and in the internal anti-infiltration sweeps during 1948–1950 was around 20,000. If one includes expelled northern Negev beduin, the total may have been as high as 30,000–40,000."); Benny Morris, *The Initial Absorption of the Palestinian Refugees in the Arab Host Countries, 1948–49* 37 (1991).
248   Damascus (Keeley) to the Secretary of State, No. 688.

Israel, the Arab Higher Committee and Arab States reiterated their respective positions on the Mediator's Progress Report and his specific conclusions on a peaceful adjustment of the situation in Palestine. The following day, Harold Beeley and John Beith from the British delegation met with John Ross and Dean Rusk at the American delegation's office in Paris to work on a revised draft resolution for the First Committee.[249] No longer endorsing the specific conclusions in Part One, Section VIII, paragraph 4 of the Mediator's Progress Report, the American draft which had yet to be finalized "call[ed] upon the Governments and authorities concerned to extend the scope of the negotiations provided for in the [UNSC's] 16 November resolution" on the establishment of an armistice and in similar language "recommended that [Arab-Israeli] negotiations be conducted either directly or through the Conciliation Commission."[250] Bringing to fore a difference first identified late in the summer – between acquiescence and a negotiated solution to the situation of Palestine – the American revision threatened a second rupture in Anglo-American cooperation with officials in London and Washington still trying to mend fences after Truman's statement on the modification of Israel's borders as delineated under the first peace plan. In a cable to the Foreign Office, the British delegation expressed alarm that the American revisions had "changed the entire character" of the Anglo-American draft resolution by undermining the principle of acquiescence and that "public opinion [would] inevitably interpret [the American] paragraph [on territory] as an abandonment of the Bernadotte plan."[251] Requesting input from London in advance of additional meetings with their American counterparts, the British delegation observed that in light of the above changes the introduction

---

249   United Nations General Assembly Paris (United Kingdom Delegation) to Foreign Office, No. 436, Nov. 16, 1948, NA, FO 371-68596 E14756.

250   United Nations General Assembly Paris (United Kingdom Delegation) to Foreign Office, No. 437, Nov. 16, 1948, NA FO 371-68596 E14756. *See also* S.C. Res. 62 (Nov. 16, 1948), para. 2 ("[c]alling upon the parties directly involved in the conflict in Palestine [...] to seek agreement forthwith, by negotiations conducted either directly or through the Acting Mediator, [...] [on] the immediate establishment of the armistice [in all sectors of Palestine]").

251   United Nations General Assembly Paris (United Kingdom Delegation) to Foreign Office, No. 436. *See also* Foreign Office to United Nations General Assembly, Paris (United Kingdom Delegation), No. 505, Nov. 23, 1948, NA, CO 537-3356 E25047 (stating that "if the basic principle of acquiescence was dropped and we were left with a recommendation for negotiation between the parties *either directly or through a Conciliation Commission* without any powers," the formulation used by the UNSC in its November 4th resolution, "the negotiating positions of [the] two parties would be quite different and we could foresee that sooner or later we should be asked to encourage and if necessary coerce the Arab states and in particular Transjordan to enter into negotiations contrary to their wishes").

of an Anglo-American resolution "[would] probably be impossible."[252] Having seen the new British draft resolution for a peaceful adjustment of the situation of Palestine, Secretary Marshall similarly concluded that "it appear[ed] improbable that [the] US and UK [could] harmonize their positions sufficiently to present a joint draft resolution" to the UNGA's First Committee.[253] The following morning the two delegations reached an agreement under which the British would introduce a draft resolution "incorporat[ing] as much of [the new American draft] as was in [their] view an improvement consistent with [the British] conception of the form the resolution should take."[254] The Americans would, in turn, make a statement in support of the British draft resolution, reserving the right to amend it at a later date while maintaining close contact throughout the subsequent debate to keep Anglo-American differences to a minimum.[255]

B   The Revised British Draft

Introduced on November 18th, the revised British draft resolution "[e]ndors[ed] the specific conclusions contained in Part I of [the Mediator's] Report as a basis for a peaceful settlement of the Palestine question" and directed the Conciliation Commission to "to carry out the functions assigned to it by [the] resolution in accordance with the specific conclusions of Part I of the [Mediator's] Report."[256] Incorporating language from the Anglo-American draft from mid-October on the re-allocation of territory, the British introduced new language on refugees which appeared to reflect their previous concern about compensation. Adding a "preamble" or "chapeau", paragraph 11 "[e]ndors[ed] the principle stated in Part I, Section V, Paragraph 7 of the Mediator's report" which affirmed Israel's obligation for both restitution of private property and compensation for property wantonly destroyed.[257] This was one of six provisions in the British draft resolution endorsing principles contained in the Mediator's Progress Report which would be the focus of discussion nearly three weeks later. In contrast to the previous draft resolution, which

---

252   United Nations General Assembly Paris (United Kingdom Delegation) to Foreign Office, No. 436.
253   Paris (Marshall) to the Secretary of State, DELGA 803, Nov. 17, 1948, NARA, 501.BB Palestine/11-1748. *See also* Paris (Marshall) to the Secretary of State, DELGA 797, Nov. 17, 1948, NARA, 501.BB Palestine/11-1748 (providing "alternative drafts" for paragraphs 2, 3 and 5 of the British draft resolution).
254   United Nations General Assembly Paris (United Kingdom Delegation) to Foreign Office, No. 41, Nov. 17, 1948, NA, FO 371-68597 E14812.
255   The Secretary of State (Marshall) to the Acting Secretary of State, DELGA 797.
256   U.N. G.A.O.R., 3rd Sess., U.N. Doc. A/C.1/394 (Nov. 18, 1948).
257   Id.

recognized the right of Arab refugees to return to their homes, the British draft appeared to emphasize Israel's corresponding obligation by "[r]esolv[ing] that the Arab refugees *should be permitted* to return to their homes at the earliest possible date and that adequate compensation should be paid for the property of those choosing not to return and for property which has been lost as a result of pillage, confiscation or of destruction."[258] While the Foreign Office did not appear to offer an explanation for the shift in language, it might be explained by Israel's refusal to consider the return of refugees outside a comprehensive settlement and its concomitant efforts to create *fait accomplis* against their return. This was an issue which appeared to vex British and American officials alike with the British Middle East Office in Cairo noting in mid-November that "the [Jews] had no intention of accepting at any rate [the] return of refugees to their homes or at least their adequate compensation."[259] As was becoming evident with respect to efforts in the UNSC, moreover, the Office added that it was "[e]qually clear the [UN was] incapable of imposing such conditions" that would enable the refugees to return.[260] Calling fellow members to task, Faris el-Khouri observed that "since the [UNSC had taken] control of the Palestine question" back in February, "half the population of Palestine [had] been scattered over the whole country,"[261] If the refugee crisis was an indicator of insecurity, the UNSC which had been almost completely silent in response to repeated requests by Arab representatives for a response to the refugee situation had failed miserably in its most fundamental task. Similar to the second composite resolution drafted back in October, the British draft resolution "instruct[ed] the Conciliation Commission to facilitate the repatriation, resettlement and economic and social rehabilitation of the Arab refugees and the payment of compensation."[262] Having introduced their own draft resolution, officials in the Foreign Office appeared apprehensive that American amendments "designed to remove the powers of the Conciliation Commission and to leave the boundaries open for negotiation between the parties" would garner greater support among Committee members.[263] In a cable to its delegation in Paris, the Foreign Office reiterated that "[w]e cannot get into a Munich situation in which we should be pressing, or at least be expected by the Americans

---

258 Id [emphasis added].
259 British Middle East Office (Cairo) to Foreign Office, No. 459, Nov. 13, 1948, NA, FO 371-68596 E14586.
260 Id.
261 U.N. S.C.O.R., 3rd yr, 381st mtg., U.N. Doc. S/PV.383 (Nov. 16, 1948), at 12–13.
262 U.N. G.A.O.R., 3rd Sess., U.N. Doc. A/C.1/394.
263 Foreign Office to the United Nations General Assembly Paris (United Kingdom Delegation), No. 519, Nov. 18, 1948, NA, FO 371-68597 E4828.

to press, Transjordan to accept certain conditions against its will."[264] Looking for a bridging formula, the Foreign Office decided that "the question of how a settlement [was] to reached and carried out [was] probably more important than the actual frontier line" between Israel and Arab Palestine whatever the future status of the latter.[265] Uncertain whether its resolution would find sufficient support in the Committee, the Foreign Office concluded that "the cooperation of the Arabs [would] be even more necessary to secure approval of [its] resolution" and given the time constraints "it seem[ed] essential [to] begin [British] action with the Arab states and representatives at once."[266] Describing Anglo-American differences as "a major crisis in US-UK relations" in a cable to Secretary Marshall, Ambassador Douglas still felt that "[the US] possess[ed] enough ingenuity and persuasiveness [to resolve] the most, if not most critical issue [it] now fac[ed] with the [UK]."[267]

C *The American Amendments*

Addressing the First Committee two days after the British submitted their draft resolution, Philip Jessup reiterated American support for the basic premises of the Mediator's conclusions which he described as "solid contributions to a settlement [of the Palestine question]."[268] As the American representative went on to explain, however, there was one significant caveat, which Robert McClintock had noted back in the summer, namely, that "modifications [...] to the boundaries [of the State of Israel] as set forth in the 29 November resolution [...] should be made only if acceptable to the State of Israel."[269] Commenting

---

264 Id.
265 Foreign Office to United Nations General Assembly, Paris (United Kingdom Delegation), No. 537, Nov. 19, 1948, NA, FO 371-68597 E4828. The Foreign Office also suggested prior Anglo-American agreement on frontiers or language that would empower the commission to determine borders if the parties were unable within a specified period of time to come to an agreement.
266 Foreign Office to Cairo, No. 1906, Nov. 19, 1948, NA, FO 371-68595 E14457.
267 The Ambassador to the United Kingdom (Douglas) to the Secretary of State, at Paris, No. 892, Nov. 18, 1948, in FRUS Vol. 5 (1948), at 1610; The Ambassador to the United Kingdom (Douglas), to the Secretary of State (Marshall), at Paris, No. 893, Nov. 18, 1948, in FRUS Vol. 5 (1948), at 1613.
268 U.N. G.A.O.R., 3rd Sess., First Comm., 205th mtg., U.N. Doc. A/C.1/SR.205 (Nov. 20, 1948), at 683. *See also* The Acting Secretary of State (Lovett) to the United States Delegation at Paris, GADEL 551, Nov. 22, 1948, NARA, 501.BB Palestine/11–2248 (stating that the draft resolution contained "many positive and constructive elements"). In subsequent meetings, the representatives of Canada and the Netherlands similarly described the Mediator's report as good basis for discussion.
269 U.N. G.A.O.R., 3rd Sess., First Comm., 205th mtg., at 683. *See also* Paris (Marshall) to Secretary of State, DELGA 641, Nov. 6, 1948, NARA, 501.BB Palestine/11-648 (stating

THE RIGHT TO RETURN   139

on the Mediator's fifth premise ("right of repatriation"), Jessup explained that "[t]he US Government believed that those who *wished* should be returned to their homes and that adequate compensation should be arranged for the property of those who [chose] not to return."[270] Several days later, Jessup introduced a series of amendments to the British draft resolution addressing the two primary issues – endorsement of the Mediator's report in its entirety [acquiescence] and modification of Israel's borders only with the latter's consent – that threatened to undermine Anglo-American cooperation in putting forward a second peace plan for Palestine.[271] Arguing that the British draft resolution "could be strengthened by reference to the principle adopted by the [UNSC] in its 16 November resolution," namely, expansion of the scope negotiations "conducted either directly or through the [UN]," Jessup reiterated that "[while] the matter of boundaries should be left to the Commission [...] any changes would be subject to Israel's consent."[272] In what would soon become an important caveat, however, the American representative further noted that "[i]f Israel wished to add territory [beyond that accorded to the Jewish state under the partition plan] it would have to offer an appropriate exchange, acceptable to the Arabs, through negotiations."[273] While there did not appear to be any discussion of a connection to the refugee issue at the time, the American caveat offered the possibility that at least a portion of the refugees would be able to return to their homes and places of origin through what essentially comprised a land swap, however, it also raised questions about the status of Palestinians in areas transferred to the Jewish State given existing concerns as noted earlier about their treatment.

---

        that the United States "[was] able to subscribe to all [of] the seven basic premises in the Bernadotte Plan and [to] all [of] his specific conclusions, with the exception of his specific recommendation regarding the boundaries of Israel").

270   Id. [emphasis added]. *See also*, id. at 686 (the Chinese representative, Mr. Liu Chieh, stating that he "endorsed the Mediator's conclusion that no settlement would be just or complete if recognition were not accorded to the *rights* of the Arab refugees to return to their homes [and that refugees] who did not wish to return should receive compensation for the properties which they had lost"); and, U.N. G.A.O.R., 3rd Sess., First Comm., 209th [emphasis added] at 729, U.N. Doc. A/C.1/SR.209 (Nov. 23, 1948) (the French representative, Alexandre Parodi, stating that "[t]here was one more point on which the commission should receive precise directives: the distressing problem of the Arab refugees, which another organ of the [UNGA] was also considering. Substantial aid must be given to those refugees to enable them to return home or, if they so preferred, to settle elsewhere.").

271   U.N. G.A.O.R., 3rd Sess., First Comm., 209th mtg., at 725.
272   Id., at 727.
273   Id.

Turning to the refugee situation, the American amendment, in language similar to Marshall's statement to the UNGA in September, "[r]esolv[ed] that the Arab refugees *wishing to return* to their homes and *live at peace* with their neighbors should be permitted to do so at the earliest possible date."[274] Implicit in previous draft resolutions through provisions offering refugees a choice of solutions and their concomitant economic and social rehabilitation, the American amendment brought to fore in more explicit terms two important "corollaries" of return, namely, that it should be "voluntary" and that it should be "safe." With antecedents in Truman's oral approval of repatriation back in August and Marshall's statement to the UNGA in September, the Mediator had emphasized similar principles in his September Progress Report albeit in different terms. The American amendment also removed certain references to compensation – pillage, confiscation and destruction – which State Department officials had expressed misgivings about since the beginning of the drafting process with the effect of limiting compensation to those refugees not wishing to return to their homes. Speaking in favour of the amendment, Jessup observed that the paragraph "endorsed a generally recognized principle and provided means for its implementation."[275] While Jessup did not explain further, it appears that he was referring to the return of refugees rather than their compensation. The American position from the beginning of the drafting process, as described above, was that compensation would be better dealt with through negotiations rather than in the specific directives contained in the draft resolution. As Jessup reminded Committee members: "[i]t was not necessary [...] to mention the purely technical question of compensation for losses incurred during the recent fighting [which] could be dealt with better by the parties concerned, perhaps with the assistance of a claims commission."[276] Writing to its delegation in Paris, the Foreign Office was adamant that "[it] would not (repeat not) agree to the American amendment of the refugee paragraph," which removed endorsement of the Mediator's report and limited compensation to non-returnees.[277] Disappointed by Jessup's statement and

---

274 U.N. G.A.O.R., 3rd Sess., First Comm., U.N. Doc. A/C.1/397 (Nov. 23, 1948) [emphasis added].
275 U.N. G.A.O.R., 3rd Sess., First Comm., 209th mtg., at 728.
276 Id.
277 Foreign Office to United Nations General Assembly, Paris (United Kingdom Delegation), No. 581, Nov. 23, 1948, NA, FO 371-68598 E15044. *See also* the Danish representative, Per Federspiel (stating that "[t]he question of compensation should not be considered as the least important point. In that connexion the [US] amendment to paragraph 11 of the United Kingdom draft resolution seemed inadequate."). U.N. G.A.O.R., 3rd Sess., First Comm., 211th mtg., U.N. Doc. A/C.1/SR.211 (Nov. 24, 1948), at 476.

the American amendments, but still convinced that it was "[n]ot too late to bridge differences with [the] US," the Foreign Office instructed its Washington delegation to further impress upon the Americans that "unless the [US was] allowed to make considerable advance from their present position [...] we shall probably have to vote on different sides."[278] As officials in London and Washington suspected only weeks before, once changes to the second composite resolution drafted back in October were made public "the flood gates would be open to amendments from all sources."[279] It remained to be seen, in the words of Lewis Douglas, the American Ambassador in London, whether "there would be little if any left of the cheese when the rats got through."[280]

D *Additional Draft Resolutions and Amendments*

On November 19th, the day after the British introduced their draft resolution in the First Committee, Secretary Marshall cabled the State Department from Paris informing officials that Israel wanted a "simplified resolution" which would "declare support for [the UNSC's] armistice effort and appoint a conciliation commission to assist [the] parties in reaching [a] settlement."[281] Reiterating Moshe Sharett's arguments in Knesset debate about the Mediator's report back in September, Michael Comay, a senior official from Israel's Foreign Ministry, explained that Israel's "strongest objection" to the British draft resolution was to the second operative paragraph which "[e]ndors[ed] the specific conclusions contained in Part I of that Report as a basis for a peaceful settlement of the Palestine question."[282] Speaking in the First Committee about Bernadotte's recommended re-allocation of territory on the same day that Jessup introduced the American amendments to the British draft resolution, Abba Eban, Israel's Ambassador to the UN, argued that "the reasons which had led the [UNGA] to

---

278 Foreign Office to Washington, No. 12443, Nov. 23, 1948, NA, FO 371-68598 E25047. *See also* Washington to Foreign Office, No. 5335, Nov. 23, 1948, NA, CO 537-3356 E25047 (stating that Acting Secretary of State Lovett "held out no likelihood of the USG modifying their attitude [on territory and negotiations] or altering the instructions set to Doctor Jessup"); Foreign Office to Washington, No. 12482, Nov. 24, 1948, NA, CO 537-3356 E25047 (stating that "Minister should see Lovett (or Marshall) again today and point out that it is by no means too late for further efforts to bridge the gap between us over the Bernadotte proposals").

279 The Ambassador in the United Kingdom (Douglas) to the Acting Secretary of State, No. 4849, Nov. 12, 1948, NARA, 501.BB Palestine/11-1248.

280 Id.

281 Paris (Marshall) to Secretary of State, No. 849, Nov. 19, 1948, NARA, 501.BB Palestine/11-1948. *See also* U.N. G.A.O.R., 3rd Sess., First Comm., 208th mtg., U.N. Doc. A/C.1/SR.208 (Nov. 23, 1948), at 711–19.

282 Paris (Marshall) to Secretary of State, No. 849.

accord [the Negev] to [the Jewish state under the partition plan] remained fully valid," namely, that it would "provide a reserve area for the development of the State's [Jewish] population and economy."[283] Turning to the situation in the north, Eban added that "the reasons which had led [the UNGA] to [exclude] the Western Galilee [from the Jewish state under the partition plan] no longer remained valid [because] the flight of Arabs during the war [had] reduced [the] problem of an Arab majority in the Jewish state."[284] Couched in diplomatic language, the Jewish State's so-called Arab majority problem had been resolved, as Israeli military and political officials had themselves acknowledged on more than one occasion, because the Arab population had been forced to leave their homes whether directly through expulsion or indirectly by generating a climate of fear not least of which stemmed from a growing list of atrocities. Speaking in the First Committee only days before, in terms that mirrored comments in Israel's provisional council back in September, Foreign Minister Sharett had noted that "if the Arabs of Palestine had accepted [the] partition [plan] and [had] cooperated with the Jewish state the latter would never have attempted to reduce its large Arab minority."[285] Turning to paragraph 11 of the British draft resolution, Comay recommended that "[t]he immediate problem of relief of [the] refugees [should] be dealt with on the basis of Committee Three recommendations," which as noted above led to the establishment of a new body, the UN Relief for Palestine Refugees, to oversee humanitarian assistance.[286] In Comay's opinion this would provide "breathing space" for the UN Economic and Social Council to "work out a permanent solution of the Arab refugee problem, in consultation with all interested governments, specialized agencies and voluntary organizations."[287] Israeli officials nevertheless characterized the above criticisms as little more than "quibbling," with the British draft resolution "so completely wrapped up in the Bernadotte plan that it would be a mistake to [even] try to amend it."[288] Commenting on Comay's suggestions, Robert Lovett informed the American delegation in Paris that the

---

283 U.N. G.A.O.R., 3rd Sess., First Comm., 208th mtg., U.N. Doc. A/C.1/SR.208 (Nov. 23, 1948), at 714.
284 Id.
285 U.N. G.A.O.R., 3rd Sess., First Comm., 200th mtg., U.N. Doc. A/C.1/SR.200 (Nov. 15, 1948), at 646. *See also* Major Knesset Debates, 1948–1981.
286 Paris (Marshall) to Secretary of State, No. 849.
287 Id.
288 Id.; Paris (Marshall) to Secretary of State, DELGA 857, No. 21, 1948, NARA, 501.BB Palestine/11-2048.

State Department "[did] not (repeat not) feel receptive to [the] Israeli suggestion for such a resolution at this time."[289]

Underscoring the growing divisions within the First Committee about the peaceful adjustment of the situation in Palestine, Australia and Poland introduced their own draft resolutions several days later which affirmed Resolution 181, including its allocation of territory to the Jewish and Arab States to be set up under the partition plan, as "the basic starting point of settlement by the [UNGA] of the Palestine question."[290] Recognizing that the situation in Palestine had changed substantially since the UNGA adopted its first peace plan, the Australian draft added that the delineation of borders should also "take into account subsequent proposals including those in the Mediator's report."[291] These differences with the British draft resolution would be the focus of significant debate in the First Committee and in the UNGA's plenary over the next two weeks. Turning to the refugee situation, the Australian and Polish draft resolutions directed the proposed Conciliation Commission "[t]o call into consultation all those organized agencies of the [UN] which may assist in working out plans both for the resettlement of Palestinian refugees and displaced persons and for their repatriation where feasible in the areas from which they come."[292] Reversing the order of solutions with the primary emphasis on resettlement, neither resolution addressed the meaning of "feasible" return nor did they include provision for compensation. With the International Refugee Organization having already clarified that the refugee situation in Palestine fell outside its mandate and the Economic and Social Council's agenda for its work year already set, it was also unclear which agencies might have assisted in working out a solution to the refugee situation. While Abba Eban thought that the Australian draft "established many signposts towards a final solution in Palestine," the British delegation described the Australian draft as "worse than we could have believed possible."[293] In a cable to the Foreign Office, the delegation recommended that the Australian

---

289 The Acting Secretary of State (Lovett) to the United States Delegation at Paris, GADEL 551, Nov. 22, 1948, NARA, 501.BB Palestine/11-2248.
290 U.N. G.A.O.R., 3rd Sess., First Comm., UN Doc. A/C.1/396 (Nov. 23, 1948); U.N. G.A.O.R., 3rd Sess., First Comm., U.N. Doc. A/C.1/400 (Nov. 25, 1948).
291 U.N. G.A.O.R., 3rd Sess., First Comm., UN Doc. A/C.1/396.
292 Id.; U.N. G.A.O.R., 3rd Sess., First Comm., U.N. Doc. A/C.1/400.
293 U.N. G.A.O.R., 3rd Sess., First Comm., 208th mtg., U.N. Doc. A/C.1/SR.208 (Nov. 23, 1948), at 719; Foreign Office to United Nations General Assembly, Paris (United Kingdom Delegation), No. 581, Nov. 23, 1948, NA, FO 371-68598 E15044.

draft "should be resisted by all possible means" further noting that "[t]he [US] amendments seem[ed] by comparison not nearly so bad [after all]."[294]

Arguing that the British draft was "too rigid in form and needed to take into account the facts," Jorge García Granados, the Guatemalan representative, recommended deleting operative paragraph two which endorsed Bernadotte's specific conclusions and replacing it with a paragraph from the Australian draft resolution which "[r]equest[ed] the [UNSC] to give sympathetic consideration to an application for the admission of the State of Israel to the [UN]."[295] Sympathetic to the Zionist project of reconstituting a Jewish State in Palestine, Granados had previously observed in debate leading up to the adoption of the UNGA's first peace plan that "[i]n twenty-five years [of British Mandate rule], the Jewish people had left upon Palestine the indelible mark of an outstanding culture" and that "Palestine was not more Arab than certain Spanish countries of Latin America were Indian."[296] In the days ahead the Guatemalan recommendation to delete reference to the Mediator's specific conclusions would provide at least a partial solution towards conciliating divisions within the Committee without which it would have been impossible to obtain a majority in support of the draft resolution. Concurring with his Australian and Polish counterparts that the delineation of borders should be "in conformity with the principles of [Resolution 181] without excluding any territorial settlement mutually acceptable to the parties," Granados' amendment further stipulated in reference to the future of "Arab areas" not under Jewish control that "[n]o annexation to a neighboring State shall be decreed without the consent of the people, freely and legally expressed."[297] In contrast to the Mediator's recommendation over the summer that "[once] an armistice [had been reached], all those Arabs who want[ed] to return should have the right to do so," Granados recommended that the return of the refugees to their homes should be linked to "the proclamation of peace between the contending parties in Palestine, including the Arab States."[298] Compared to his previous recommendation,

---

294 Foreign Office to United Nations General Assembly, Paris (United Kingdom Delegation), No. 581.
295 U.N. G.A.O.R., 3rd Sess., First Comm., U.N. Doc. A/C.1/398 (Nov. 24, 1948). The Polish draft resolution included a similar provision.
296 U.N. G.A.O.R., 2nd Sess., Ad Hoc Committee on the Palestinian Question, 190th mtg., U.N. Doc. A/AC.14/SR.10 (Oct. 10, 1947), at 56 (further stating in defense of his support for the establishment of a Jewish state in Palestine where the Jewish population comprised a third of the population that "what characterized a nation was its culture and not the number of inhabitants").
297 U.N. G.A.O.R., 3rd Sess., First Comm., U.N. Doc. A/C.1/398.
298 U.N. S.C.O.R., 3rd yr, 334th mtg., at 20; U.N. G.A.O.R., 3rd Sess., First Comm., U.N. Doc. A/C.1/398.

this one would be the focus of significant and at times acrimonious debate during the final drafting stage of the UNGA's second peace plan. Hoping to reconcile the diversity of views within the Committee, Colombia introduced its own draft resolution on a peaceful adjustment of the situation of Palestine which was an amalgam of elements from each of the above draft resolutions and amendments.[299]

E   The First Revised British Draft Resolution

On 25 November, the British introduced a revised draft resolution in response to some of the major criticisms expressed by Committee members over the previous week. Addressing concerns that its first draft "did not make sufficient provision for settlement by direct negotiations," the revised draft introduced by Hector McNeil further instructed the proposed commission, in language similar to the American amendment, "[t]o enter into consultations with the Governments and authorities concerned with a view to achievement of all questions outstanding between them."[300] Responding to additional concerns raised by other Committee members, including Australia and Poland, that "the discretion of the [...] commission had been unduly limited by the instruction that it should *give effect* to the recommendations contained in Part I of the Mediator's report," the revised draft further stipulated that the resolution of outstanding questions should also address those raised "in the [UNGA] resolution of 29 November 1947."[301] Combining elements from its own draft resolution with those from the American amendment in light of the above revisions, the British recommended a territorial solution that would include elements common to the partition plan and the Mediator's report "in [keeping with] the general equilibrium envisaged in [Resolution 181], [and] the Mediator's comments thereon in [his basic premises and specific conclusions]."[302] Unable to accept the American amendment on refugees, which removed the "preamble" from paragraph 11 (which became paragraph 10 under the revised draft) referring to Israel's liability to compensate refugees, McNeil explained that "the [UNGA] should give the utmost authority possible to those whose task it would be to *maintain the rights* of the refugees and to *secure for them some redress*

---

299   U.N. G.A.O.R., 3rd Sess., First Comm., U.N. Doc. A/C.1/399 (Nov. 24, 1948).
300   U.N. G.A.O.R., 3rd Sess., First Comm., U.N. Doc. A/C.1/394/Rev.1 (Nov. 24, 1948); U.N. G.A.O.R., 3rd Sess., First Comm., 212th mtg., U.N. Doc. A/C.1/SR.212 (Nov. 25, 1948), at 760.
301   Id. [emphasis added].
302   Id. This included the principle of geographic homogeneity and integration in the creation of "continuous frontiers" which comprised one of the Mediator's premises for a peaceful adjustment of the situation. Progress Report, at 17.

for the suffering which they had borne as a result of the Palestine conflict."[303] In a comment that might explain Egypt's lukewarm endorsement of the late Mediator's specific conclusion on refugees months earlier, Mahmoud Fawzi argued that operative paragraph ten of the revised British draft resolution was still too weak since it failed to clarify "whether the refugees [would] be allowed not merely to return to Palestine, but *to return to a Palestine they could consider their own country.*"[304] Speaking to the same Committee several days earlier, Henry Cattan, another member of the Arab Higher Committee had made a similar point with Palestinian and other Arab members continuing to press the issue in the days to come.[305] Remarks by Fawzi and Cattan essentially pinpointed the primary obstacle to return which few if any of the First Committee members, whether for historical, political, legal or humanitarian reasons, appeared willing to address. As Moshe Sharett explained to the provisional council back in September in a disparaging debate on the UN Mediator's Progress Report, "[a]s far as [Israel] [was] concerned [the refugee issue] [was] a matter concerning nations [and] not individuals," that is to say, Israel was a nation State for the Jews and the refugees would thus have to find homes elsewhere, a point that Israeli officials would continue to hammer away at over the coming months and years.[306] The only change to the paragraph which the British delegation was willing to accept was a French proposal "instruct[ing] the conciliation commission to cooperate with the Director of the [UN] Relief for Palestine Refugees […] in order to avoid any appearance of conflict between the recommendations of the First Committee and those of the Third Committee on the same subject."[307] Writing to the Foreign Office later the same day, the British delegation explained that its language in operative paragraph two endorsing the Mediator's report, recommended by Granados for deletion, was "almost certainly to be defeated" with prospects for carrying its preferred language on

---

303 U.N. G.A.O.R., 3rd Sess., First Comm., 212th mtg., at 760–3 [emphasis added].
304 Id., at 756–7 [emphasis added].
305 U.N. G.A.O.R., 3rd Sess., First Comm., 207th [emphasis added] at 699, U.N. Doc. A/C.1/SR.207 (Nov. 22, 1948) (Henry Cattan stating that "it was not only to their homes that those refugees should return but to their country as well; and it was unthinkable that certain delegations and the [UN] itself could imagine that the Arab refugees might be willing to sell the country left them by their ancestors, and be offered a choice between life under Jewish domination and expropriation").This also explains comments by another member of the Arab Higher Committee, Ahmad Shuqayri, using language that would reappear decades later. U.N. G.A.O.R., 3rd Sess., First Comm., 201st mtg., at 652 (stating that "[the] refugees would return as liberators, which was their inalienable right").
306 Major Knesset Debates, 1948–1981, at 272.
307 U.N. G.A.O.R., 3rd Sess., First Comm., 212th mtg., at 762–3; U.N. G.A.O.R., 3rd Sess., First Comm., 209th mtg., at 729.

territory in the fourth operative paragraph "difficult to calculate."[308] The delegation nevertheless believed that it "[stood] a chance of carrying [its] draft [language in operative paragraph ten] dealing with the refugees."[309] Having identified negotiations as its primary concern, the Foreign Office explained in a cable to its delegation in Paris that "while the American paragraph 2 [spoke] of 'negotiations directly or through the Conciliation Commission' [...] the alternative", that is to say, through the Commission or directly, "should sufficiently safeguard the Arab position."[310] The UNSC's reformulation of the phrase in previous weeks, as described above, thus appeared to have provided British officials with a potential way forward.

When the Committee began discussion of its next steps the following day, Philip Jessup noted that while "[he] was gratified that the revised UK draft incorporated many of the US amendments," the American delegation "could not [...] agree to the wording of paragraphs 2, 4(b) and 10 of the revised draft resolution and regarded the acceptance of its amendments to those paragraphs as essential."[311] As Jessup further explained, the second operative paragraph of the revised British draft resolution continued to limit the discretionary powers of the proposed conciliation commission, while the fourth one failed to "[give] the correct degree of emphasis to [Resolution] 181 and the Mediator's report."[312] Turning to operative paragraph ten on the refugees, Jessup reiterated the American view that it "would unnecessarily complicate matters if the [UNGA] took a definite decision in respect of compensation to be given to Arab refugees [and that it] would be far more reasonable to entrust the problem to a subsidiary body."[313] Jorge García Granados, meanwhile, submitted a revised amendment which stipulated that the "delimiting [of] frontiers in Palestine" should "[take] into account the actual situation in Palestine."[314] This added provision may help to explain Granados' comment several days earlier that the first British draft resolution was too rigid in form and needed to take into account the actual facts in Palestine. A last minute draft resolution

---

308 United Nations General Assembly, Paris (United Kingdom Delegation) to Foreign Office, No. 542, Nov. 25, 1948, NA, FO 371-68599 E15143.
309 Id.
310 Id.
311 U.N. G.A.O.R., 3rd Sess., First Comm., 214th mtg., U.N. Doc. A/C.1/SR.214 (Nov. 26, 1948), at 780.
312 Id.
313 Id.
314 U.N. G.A.O.R., 3rd Sess., First Comm., U.N. Doc. A/C.1/394/Rev.1 (Nov. 27, 1948). The amendment also instructed the proposed commission "[t]o use its good offices with the Governments and authorities concerned with a view to achievement of a final settlement of all questions outstanding between them."

submitted by Faris el-Khouri called for the establishment of a five-member commission to prepare proposals for the establishment of a single democratic State under which "the Arab refugees would have the necessary assurance if they were to return to their homes."[315] A long-standing demand of Palestinian and other Arab representatives, the "assurance" which el-Khouri referred to appeared to relate not only to respect for the individual rights of the refugees, but also to their national identity and collective belonging, that is to say, they would be returning not just to their homes but also to their homeland. What this meant for the Jewish inhabitants of Palestine, whether indigenous, immigrants, colonizers or native born was not made clear. After a lengthy debate on ways forward, members of the First Committee voted in favor of a suggestion by Lester Pearson, the Canadian representative, to set up a working group to prepare a consolidated tabulation of the various resolutions and amendments introduced over the previous week to facilitate discussion.

F   *Israeli Observations on the Revised British Draft and American Amendments*

On November 27th, two days after Israel's second transfer committee completed their Report on a Settlement of the Arab Refugee issue, the American delegation in Paris forwarded to Secretary Marshall a lengthy text of Israeli observations on the British draft resolution taking into account the amendments submitted by the US. Drawing attention to Israel's major concerns, the letter first identified three major "omissions" in the draft, namely, recognition of Israel's existence as a State, that its boundaries as delineated under Resolution 181 could not be altered without its consent and American support for Israel's early admission to the UN.[316] This latter issue, namely, Israel's request to become a member State, would also intersect with the adoption of the UNGA's second peace plan in the coming days. Israel's second concern was that the British draft resolution accorded "no greater status or validity [to Resolution 181] than the Mediator's progress report."[317] In contrast to the latter, which Abba Eban later characterized as little more than "the views of a distinguished individual," Israeli officials regarded the partition plan, which also happened to be one of the State's founding documents, as a "valid

---

315   U.N. G.A.O.R., 3rd Sess., First Comm., U.N. Doc. A/C.1/402 (Nov. 26, 1948); U.N. G.A.O.R., 3rd Sess., First Comm., 214th mtg., at 742.
316   Paris (Dulles) to Secretary of State, NIACT DELGA 977, Nov. 27, 1948, NARA, 501.BB Palestine/11-2748.
317   Id.

instrument of international law."³¹⁸ Turning to the refugee situation, Israeli officials expressed what appeared to be a certain degree of relief that removal of the "preamble," citing the late Mediator on Israel's "liability [...] to restore private property to its Arab owners and to indemnify those owners for property wantonly destroyed," along with references to pillage, confiscation and destruction in his September report "[made] the [British draft] resolution more non-committal on the question of compensation and claims."³¹⁹ That relief may have been more than palpable given the Mediator's assessment, as noted earlier, that certain Israeli policies and practices during the war comprised violations of the laws of war. At the same time, officials appeared to express alarm that the American amendment which "[r]esolv[ed] that the refugees *wishing to return* and *live at peace* with their neighbours should be permitted to do so at the earliest possible date [...] still establish[ed] the principle of *absolute and unrestricted return*, and urg[ed] permission for its exercise at the earliest possible date."³²⁰ Describing the UN Mediator's attempt "to establish the right of Arab individuals to return to their homes in Israel" during debate in the provisional council back in September as something "very negative" for the Jewish State, Foreign Minister Sharett nevertheless acknowledged that "[i]t [was] not so nice or humanitarian to oppose something which [was] so basic, so simple: a person's right to return to the home from which he [had] been driven out by force."³²¹ Reiterating Abba Eban's remarks several days earlier, the Israeli letter emphasized that "[t]here [was] far more realism and equity in the Australian draft resolution which 'call[ed] into consultation all the organs and agencies of the UN which may assist in working out plans for the resettlement of Palestinian refugees and for their repatriation where feasible'."³²²

G   *The American Composite Draft*

In the meantime, members of the American delegation along with Dean Rusk from the State Department's Office of [UN] Affairs, working at staff level, had drafted a composite resolution which they hoped the British would accede to.³²³ Calling upon the parties to extend the scope of armistice negotiations and "to seek agreement by negotiations conducted either directly or through

---

318   U.N. G.A.O.R., 3rd Sess., First Comm., 216th mtg., U.N. Doc. A/C.1/SR.216 (Nov. 29, 1948), at 804.
319   Paris (Dulles) to Secretary of State, NIACT DELGA 977.
320   Id. [emphasis added].
321   Major Knesset Debates, 1948–1981 269, at 181.
322   Paris (Dulles) to Secretary of State, NIACT DELGA 977.
323   Paris (Dulles) to Secretary of State, NIACT DELGA 976, Nov. 27, 1948, NARA, 501.BB Palestine/11-2748.

the conciliation commission," the composite draft identified Resolution 181 as "the basic starting point for a settlement" with the UN Mediator's report comprising "a basic for a renewed effort to bring about a peace adjustment [of the situation]."[324] Emphasizing the importance of elements common to the resolution and the report, the draft resolution recommended "modifications in the territorial arrangements [of Resolution 181] [...] taking into account [the Mediator's specific conclusions]."[325] Similar to the American amendment to the British draft resolution, the composite draft "consider[ed] that the refugees wishing to return to their homes and live at peace with their neighbours should be permitted to do so at the earliest possible date."[326] Attempting to bridge Anglo-American differences on compensation, however, the text affirmed that "adequate compensation should be paid for the property of those choosing not to return *and* for property which has been lost as a result of pillage, expropriation or wanton destruction."[327] It further added that this would be "*subject to principles and procedures* to be established by the conciliation commission pursuant to agreement between the governments and authorities concerned."[328] The composite text then "instruct[ed] the conciliation commission to facilitate the repatriation, resettlement and economic and social rehabilitation of the refugees and the payment of compensation *and* to maintain close contact with the Director of the [UN] Relief for Palestine Refugees."[329] In a meeting with the American delegation that afternoon, Harold Beeley "recognized [the] improvement reflected [in] paragraph 4(f) concerning refugees [but] objected [to the] phrase 'pursuant to agreement between the governments and authorities concerned' as being unrealistic and depriving [the] paragraph of any meaning."[330] As Hector McNeil had previously explained in response to the American amendment, the British delegation strongly felt that the proposed commission should have sufficient authority to maintain the rights of and secure some redress for the refugees. Beeley nevertheless observed that with regard to the principle of acquiescence and Israeli consent in the modification of its borders as set forth in the partition plan the composite text "had [the] effect [of] widening [the] gap between

---

324 Id.
325 Id.
326 Id.
327 Id. [emphasis added].
328 Id. [emphasis added].
329 Id. [emphasis added].
330 Id.

[the] US-UK."³³¹ Summarizing the outcome of the meeting, John Foster Dulles concluded that "[the] British [were] not yet quiet [sic] prepared to consider [the] composite approach."³³² Going forward, both delegations acknowledged that in addition to reconciling their own differences, it would also be necessary to resolve disputes with Australia, Guatemala and others in order to ensure requisite support for the UNGA's second peace plan for Palestine.³³³

H The Second Revised British Draft Resolution

On November 29th, one year to the day that the [UNGA had recommended the partition of Mandate Palestine into politically distinct but economically integrated Arab and Jewish States, the First Committee's working group submitted its tabulation of draft resolutions and amendments. With only days before a final decision would have to be taken on a draft resolution, the British and American delegations in Paris had yet to find solutions for the primary issues that divided them. In a mid-day cable to the Foreign Office, having discovered that there was "little chance" that amendments being offered by the American delegation in Paris would be accepted by officials back in Washington, the British delegation concluded that the time may have come to part ways with the US in the First Committee in the hope of "reaching a last minute agreement" in advance of the plenary debate.³³⁴ With meetings scheduled with the Brussels powers (Belgium, France, Luxembourg, Netherlands) and with the US, the delegation sought further instruction from the Foreign Office. The following day, however, cables from each of the delegations to London and Washington, respectively, announced that Anglo-American agreement had nearly been reached with a compromise on operative paragraphs 2 and 4(b) of the revised British revised draft resolution worked out in discussions between Ambassador Douglas and officials in the Foreign Office.³³⁵ Agreeing to delete endorsement of the Mediator's specific conclusions in the second operative paragraph, the British obtained American agreement on revised language calling for negotiations "'either through the Conciliation Commission

---

331 Paris (Dulles) to Secretary of State (Marshall), No. 981, Nov. 27, 1948, NARA, 501.BB Palestine/11-2748.
332 Id.
333 Id.; Paris (Dulles) to Secretary of State, No. 972, Nov. 27, 1948, NARA, 501.BB Palestine/11-2748.
334 Id.
335 United Nations General Assembly, Paris (United Kingdom Delegation) to Foreign Office, No. 603, Nov. 30, 1948, NA, CO 537-3356 E25047; Paris (Dulles) to Secretary of State, DELGA 996, Nov. 30, NARA, 501.BB Palestine/11/-3048.

or directly' *instead of the other way round.*"336 In turn, the British accepted the American language on territory "that certain modifications in the territorial arrangements of [Resolution 181] should be considered taking into account Part One, Section VIII, paragraph 4(b) of the [Mediator's Progress Report]," while the latter agreed that any adjustments should be "based on reciprocity and mutual interest."337 Explaining the addition of this phrase, the British delegation noted that the agreed upon aim was to "prevent Jews [from] getting the best of both worlds," that is to say, "if they gain[ed] [territory] in one place there [had to] be a compensatory adjustment elsewhere."338 As noted earlier, this had potentially contradictory implications for the refugee situation. Appearing to have assumed that the Americans supported British language on refugees in operative paragraph 10, the Foreign Office subsequently informed its delegation that their American counterparts in Paris had in the meantime "propos[ed] to work out agreed wording [on refugees with them]."339 "We do not want to spoil agreement by insisting on our wording," the Foreign Office noted, "but we do not see why we should give away any points of substance on this paragraph" especially since "[o]n this point the Americans are not tied by any election pledge so far as we know."340 The two sides nevertheless agreed to refer the matter to their legal advisors who produced a revised text with two major changes. First, in the preamble, they replaced endorsement of Part One, Section V, paragraph 7 of the Mediator's report on "[t]he liability of the Provisional Government of Israel to restore private property to its Arab owners and to indemnify those owners for property wantonly destroyed" with Part One, Section VIII, paragraph 4(i) on "the right of the Arab refugees to return to their homes in Jewish-controlled territory."341 This change was significant not only because it appeared to underscore Anglo-American support for the late Mediator's specific conclusion on the "right" to return, the amended language followed Israel's complaint that the American amendment introduced a week earlier which resolved that refugees wishing to return to their homes and live at peace with their neighbours had already established the principle of "absolute and unrestricted" return. Second, on compensation they added the phrase: "and for loss of or damage to property which under principles of

---

336 Id. [emphasis added].
337 Id.
338 *Id. See also* Department of State, to American Embassy in London, No. 4485, Dec. 1, 1948, NARA, 501.BB Palestine/12-148.
339 Foreign Office to United Nations General Assembly, Paris (United Kingdom Delegation), No. 660, Nov. 29, 1948, NA, CO 537-3356 E25047.
340 Id.
341 Paris (Dulles) to Secretary of State, DELGA 997, Nov. 30, 1948, NARA, 501.BB Palestine/11-3048.

international law or in equity should be made good by the governments or authorities responsible."[342] The new phrase appeared to strike a balance between British emphasis on Israel's liability to compensate refugees, with the terms "loss" (pillage and expropriation), "damage" (wanton destruction) and "principles of international law" (without military necessity) replacing more specific terms; and, American emphasis on negotiations through the introduction of new terms – "in equity" (mixed claims commissions) and "governments or authorities responsible" (as used in UNSC truce resolutions). The American delegation subsequently withdrew its amendment to the revised British draft resolution. In order to retain priority on the Committee's agenda, however, the UK remained the sole sponsor of the revised "Anglo-American" draft resolution.[343] While the refugee paragraph underwent further changes, the above language on compensation remained in the final text of Resolution 194. On the same day, one year after the adoption of the UNGA's first peace plan, and two weeks after raising the issue with the State Department, Israel submitted a request for membership in the UN, which threatened to unravel the entire deal.

The American delegation's prediction a week earlier that it might yet prove possible to bring the British closer to their positions nevertheless appeared to have come to fruition. Having accepted American amendments to their draft resolution for what they described as "small concessions in return," the British delegation observed that "a weaker resolution [was] better than no resolution at all."[344] Instructing its missions in the Arab region to offer a "frank" explanation of the revised draft resolution, the Foreign Office directed its diplomats to emphasize that while the British "[had] given up the general endorsement of Bernadotte's proposals, the specific conclusions of Bernadotte's report [were] all referred to in various paragraphs of the resolution and in most cases without qualification."[345] This position would be restated with the introduction of final amendments during plenary discussion of the British draft resolution just over a week later. Noting that the "greatest difficulty [had] been in dealing with the general feeling in the [UNGA] that the parties should be called upon to negotiate directly," a concern expressed at the outset of Committee meetings

---

342 Id.
343 Paris (Dulles) to Secretary of State, DELGA 996, Nov. 30, NARA, 501.BB Palestine/11/-3048; United Nations General Assembly, Paris (United Kingdom Delegation) to Foreign Office, No. 603, Nov. 30, 1948, NA, CO 537-3356 E25047; Foreign Office to Cairo, No. 1967, Dec. 1, 1948, NA, CO 537-3356 E25047.
344 United Nations General Assembly Paris (United Kingdom Delegation) to Foreign Office, No. 603. See also Foreign Office to the United Nations General Assembly, Paris (United Kingdom Delegation), No. 581.
345 Foreign Office to Cairo, No. 1967.

in mid-November, the Foreign Office further instructed its missions to emphasize that "with great difficulty" the British had secured new wording under which the parties were called upon to negotiate "either with the Commission or directly *instead of* directly or through the Commission."[346] Officials further acknowledged that British concessions had produced language on territory that "[was] not as strong as they [had] wished," but emphasized that according to the agreed upon interpretation of the revised language "the Jews [could not] have the best of both plans and that, e.g., if they gain[ed] in Western Galilee, they must lose elsewhere."[347] With the instructions silent on the revised paragraph on refugees, it appeared that the Foreign Office assumed that the provisions were still generally acceptable to Arab States as they had indicated to American officials back in September in response to the Mediator's specific conclusions. Summing up, the Foreign Office observed that "[t]he inescapable conclusion seem[ed] to [...] be that the Arabs must rely on getting the least bad [UNGA] resolution that [was] possible in the circumstances and then making the best possible use of this in negotiating with the Conciliation Commission."[348] While the American delegation began lobbying for Latin American support, warning that a lengthy debate would decrease the likelihood of the resolution's adoption, the debate over a peaceful adjustment of the situation in Palestine was not quite yet over. Faris el-Khouri requested once again, as the Syrian representative had done in July, that the International Court of Justice render an advisory opinion on "the power of the [UNGA] under the Charter to partition Palestine [...] against the wishes of the majority of the Palestine population [and on] the international status of Palestine upon the termination of the Mandate on 15 May 1948."[349] The Guatemalan and Australian representatives submitted amendments to the revised British draft resolution while the Polish representative submitted an amendment to the Australian amendment each reiterating changes requested during previous meetings.[350] In a tersely worded cable to the British delegation in Paris, the Foreign Office emphasized that the

---

346 Id. [emphasis added].
347 Id.
348 Id.
349 U.N. G.A.O.R., 3rd Sess., First Comm., U.N. Doc. A/C.1/405 (Nov. 30, 1948). The Syrian representative also tabled an amendment to the preamble of the British draft resolution recalling that "[Resolution 181] was rejected by the Arabs of Palestine as well as by the neighbouring Arab states and gave birth to serious disturbances in the Holy Land" and that "the proposals in [the Mediator's] report [were] based on partitioning Palestine – proposals which [had] been flatly rejected by the Arabs and proved to be far from being able to be peacefully implemented."
350 U.N. G.A.O.R., 3rd Sess., First Comm., U.N. Doc. A/C.1/398/Rev.2 (Dec. 1, 1948); U.N. G.A.O.R., 3rd Sess., First Comm., U.N. Doc. A/C.1/408/Rev.1 (Dec. 1, 1948); U.N. G.A.O.R., 3rd Sess., First Comm., U.N. Doc. A/C.1/409/Rev.1 (Dec. 2, 1948).

latter amendments "[were] not (repeat not) acceptable."[351] By early December as the war in Palestine had reached its final stage it thus appeared that changes to the Anglo-American draft resolution in the UNGA's First Committee had finally reached a conclusion.

I *Discussion of the Tabulation*

In the three days that it took to examine and vote on the draft resolutions and amendments tabled in previous weeks, Committee members focused primarily on sections three to five of the consolidated tabulation covering general principles, the composition and appointment of the proposed conciliation commission and the delineation of boundaries. It was these elements of the proposed peace plan that had nearly led to the collapse of Anglo-American efforts to put forward a joint draft resolution on a peaceful settlement of the situation of Palestine. The first potential hurdle in moving the second revised British draft resolution forward in the First Committee was cleared after members approved all four paragraphs of the preamble which referred to Resolution 181, the Mediator's Progress Report along with the UNSC resolutions calling for a truce including the directive on negotiations conducted directly or through the UN.[352] While the British delegation's decision to delete operative paragraph two of its first revised draft resolution which endorsed the Mediator's specific conclusions removed a second potential obstacle, several operative paragraphs of the Anglo-American draft resolution still referred to Resolution 181 and the Mediator's specific conclusions over which committee members remained divided.[353] This included paragraph 2(c) calling upon the conciliation commission to enter into consultations with the parties to resolve all questions outstanding between them; paragraph 4 directing the commission to facilitate a solution to the delimitation of borders between Jewish and Arab-controlled areas of Palestine; paragraph 5 on the disposition of those territories not included in the Jewish State; and, paragraph 11 on a solution to the

---

351 Foreign Office to United Nations General Assembly, Paris (United Kingdom Delegation), No. 700, Dec. 1, 1948, NA, CO 537-3356 E25047.

352 U.N. G.A.O.R., 3rd Sess., First Comm., 221st mtg., U.N. Doc. A/C.1/SR.221 (Dec. 1, 1948). The Committee rejected the above-mentioned Syrian amendments to the preambular paragraphs. For detailed discussion of voting records on the draft resolutions and amendments, *see* U.N. G.A.O.R., 3rd Sess., *Report of the First Committee, Palestine: Progress Report of the United Nations Mediator*, U.N. Doc. A/776 (Dec. 7, 1948) [*hereinafter* First Committee Report].

353 The Committee cleared yet another hurdle after members rejected an Australian amendment making Resolution 181 the basic starting point of a settlement by the UNGA of the Palestine question. The Australian representative subsequently withdrew its paragraph requesting the UNSC to give sympathetic consideration to the application of the State of Israel for admission to the United Nations. *See also* First Committee Report.

refugee situation. Unable to reach agreement on revisions to paragraph 2(c), 4 and 5 of the revised British draft resolution, Committee members narrowly rejected the first two paragraphs with the latter paragraph rejected by a larger margin.[354] The Committee subsequently approved by a large margin an American amendment that replaced the fourth operative paragraph of the revised British draft resolution with a new paragraph which, as New Zealand had proposed the previous day, instructed the Conciliation Commission "to assist Governments and authorities concerned to achieve a final settlement of all questions outstanding between them."[355] Having scrubbed the paragraph of all references to Resolution 181 and the Mediator's Progress Report, this approach to obtaining majority support for the Anglo-American draft resolution would have a bearing on the final text of the UNGA's second peace plan later in December. The deletion of the fifth operative paragraph, on the other hand, not only removed the issue of Palestinian self-determination as one of several elements to be addressed in securing a peaceful adjustment of the situation of Palestine, it also appeared to transform what was in fact a political question into little more than one in need of humanitarian relief.

Having successfully cleared several hurdles that appeared to threaten the UNGA's second attempt at the peaceful adjustment of the situation of Palestine, Committee members turned their attention to what seemed to be the final challenge, securing support for paragraph 11 delineating the terms of a solution to the refugee crisis arising from the 1948 war. Endorsing the Mediator's specific conclusion on refugees in its preamble or chapeau, the paragraph once again brought to fore divisions among Committee members about the general principles or framework that would govern UN led efforts to facilitate a political settlement. Identifying Resolution 181 as the basic starting point for a solution, members had already rejected the Australian draft amendment which directed the proposed conciliation commission to bring together UN organs and agencies to help design plans for the resettlement and repatriation of the refugees.[356] While the debate in paragraph 11 of the second revised British draft resolution and the Guatemalan amendment linking the return of refugees to

---

354 U.N. G.A.O.R., 3rd Sess., First Comm., U.N. Doc. A/C.1/SR.223 (Dec. 2, 1948); U.N. G.A.O.R., 3rd Sess., First Comm., 224th mtg., U.N. Doc. A/C.1/SR.224 (Dec. 3, 1948). An American proposal to reconsider paragraph 2(c) failed to receive a two-thirds majority required under the Committee's relevant rules of procedure. Having reached what appeared to be a significant impasse, after members rejected paragraph 4, the Committee accepted an American motion to adjourn the meeting to allow the delegations time "to consider the effect on the resolution as a whole." *See also* First Committee Report.
355 U.N. G.A.O.R., 3rd Sess., First Comm., 224th mtg.
356 U.N. G.A.O.R., 3rd Sess., First Comm., 221st mtg. *See also* First Committee Report.

the proclamation of peace covered a range of inter-related issues, not a single member of the Committee spoke against the Mediator's specific conclusion on the right of refugees to return to their homes nor did members challenge the concomitant right of refugees to be compensated for loss and damage arising from their displacement. Responding to questions from Committee members about the definition of a refugee under the revised draft resolution, given the different terminology used during the drafting process (Palestinian refugees, Arab refugees, and refugees), Harold Beeley explained that the term "referred to all refugees, irrespective of race or nationality, provided they had been displaced from their homes in Palestine."[357] While the British delegation was responsible for the removal of provisions introduced by Bunche back in October that affirmed the fundamental right to equality, Beeley's understanding of the refugee definition under paragraph 11 appeared to suggest that equality and the corresponding principle of non-discrimination were implicit in the second revised draft resolution. In the specific context of paragraph 11 this meant that all refugees, Arab Palestinians, Jews and others "wishing to return to their homes and live at peace with their neighbours should be permitted to do so at the earliest possible date."[358] This fact would be lost in subsequent Israeli criticism of the UNGA's second peace plan with neither the concept of a Jewish refugee nor their concomitant right to return under paragraph 11 finding a place with the country's Zionist political narrative. The State would nevertheless apply the principle of return in at least a partial way as noted earlier after its consequent of the remaining lands of Mandate Palestine during the second Arab-Israeli war.

The same principle, as Beeley subsequently clarified, also applied to the following clause governing compensation for "those choosing not to return and for loss of damage to property which under principles of international law or in equity should be made good by the governments or authorities responsible."[359] Criticizing the Guatemalan amendment because it "because it omitted compensation for Arabs 'who [would] return to their homes and [find]

---

357   U.N. G.A.O.R., 3rd Sess., First Comm., 226th mtg., U.N. Doc. A/C.1/SR.226 (Dec. 3, 1948), at 904–6 (further stating that "the terms of paragraph 11 of the [UK] draft resolution would apply to all refugees and the Arabs who had previously been living in the New City of Jerusalem would be entitled either to return to their homes or to obtain adequate compensation for their losses").

358   U.N. G.A.O.R., 3rd Sess., First Comm., U.N. Doc. A/C.1/394/Rev. 2 (Nov. 30, 1948).

359   Id.; U.N. G.A.O.R., 3rd Sess., First Comm., 226th mtg., at 905–6 (responding to a question from the representative of New Zealand, Peter Fraser, Beeley further explained that "[t]he question of who was to pay the compensation was not answered in the resolution and was a matter to be determined under sub-paragraph 3 of paragraph 11 and under paragraph 12").

them damaged or destroyed,'" the British representative further explained that in addition to applying to both Arab and Jewish refugees displaced as a result of the war in Palestine, the State of Israel as the Foreign Office had insisted throughout the drafting process was liable to compensate refugees for losses and damages regardless of whether they chose to return or not.[360] While Israel had accepted this principle, at least in part, with Moshe Sharret noting back in June that the "proprietary rights [of the refugees] would certainly be respected," the Foreign Minister added that "all [of the refugee] lands and houses that remained [under Israeli control were] *spoils* of [the] war."[361] On the same day that Committee members were concluding the final debate on paragraph 11, Israel's Finance Minister, Eliezer Kaplan, signed into force the Emergency Regulations regarding Absentees' Property drawing on the concept of enemy nationals as justification for the wholesale expropriation of refugee homes, lands and properties.[362] While the shift from the status of the land to the status of its owners under the Regulations was new, the use of the enemy national concept was not with Israeli officials, as noted earlier, having characterized Arab Palestinians as a potential "fifth column" for months dating back at least to the beginning of the second truce.[363] The concept contradicted what was

---

360   U.N. G.A.O.R., 3rd Sess., First Comm., 226th mtg., at 905.
361   Morris 2004, at 319–20 [emphasis added]. *See also* Michael Kagan, *Destructive Ambiguity: Enemy Nationals and the Legal Enabling of Ethnic Conflict in the Middle East*, 38 Colum. Hum. Rts. L. Rev. 263, 295 (2006–2007) (stating that "Israel's June 1948 focus on conquest as a legal criterion for property confiscation was clearly rooted in the antiquated doctrine of war booty, in which conquest alone was enough to justify seizing property. This policy violated the Hague Regulations and likely fell under the definition of 'plunder' used at Nuremberg.").
362   1948 Emergency Regulations Concerning Absentee Property, 1 L.S.I. 8 (1948) [Isr.]. Foreman and Kedar, at 815 (stating that the Regulations "introduced a framework and terminology that would remain a central, permanent component of Israel's legal treatment of appropriated Arab land"). *See also* Kagan, at 264, 297 (further stating that "the enemy nationals concept is in theory an exceptional rule applicable only to a small set of foreigners and subject to substantial regulation." Drawing a distinction with the 1939 Trading with the Enemy Act on which the Regulations were based, Kagan further notes that the British Act "defined a person's enemy character in terms of his place of residence, not his nationality or permanent domicile (in law, domicile is more permanent, while residence can be temporary)" and that the purpose of the Act "was not to permanently seize the property (which would violate the Hague Regulations), but to hold it in escrow until the end of hostilities)." Kagan thus concludes that Israel's "policies are better understood as an application of the war booty doctrine, where conquest by Jewish forces alone effectively led to permanent dispossession").
363   The enemy national concept may also usefully explain the scope of forced displacement during the war in the sense that it blurred if not removed the distinction between civilians and combatants under the laws of war. *See, e.g.,* Salman Abu Sitta and Terry Rempel,

implicit in Bernadotte's June suggestions and later explicit in his September Progress Report, namely, that the Arab refugees were nationals of the Jewish State in the legal sense of the term. While the Regulations were in law temporary in nature, in practice the provisional government considered absentee properties as State properties.[364] Highlighting the fundamental lack of equality and related discrimination that was and remains at the root of forced displacement arising from the struggle over Palestine, the Regulations included a clause under which persons of "Jewish nationality," a concept used for domestic purposes to regulate differential and discriminatory treatment, whether overt and covert, with respect to membership in the political community, distribution and control of resources and access to power, were exempt from its application.[365] It was the Jewish State's treatment of its Arab inhabitants

---

The ICRC and the Detention of Palestinian Civilians in Israel's POW/Labor Camps, 43 J. Pal. Stud. 11, 13 (2014) [*hereinafter* Abu Sitta and Rempel] (describing the Red Cross appeal in March 1948 calling upon the Jewish Agency and the Arab Higher Committee in March 1948 "'to act in obedience to the traditional rules of international law, and to apply ... the principles embodied in the [Hague Conventions]' [...] which included 'security for all non-combatants, especially, women, children and the aged'." As noted earlier, Raphael Cilento's initial survey in August found that women, children and the elder comprised 85 percent of the refugees. While both parties agreed to comply with the appeal "the [Jewish Agency] tempered its agreement with a crucial proviso: the Zionist forces would protect the civilian population only 'to the extent that the [1929 Geneva] Conventions appli[ed] to civilians'. It hardly bears mention that the [Agency] was entirely conversant with the conventions' inadequacies with regard to civilian protection, and on 3 April 1948, the very same day that the [Agency] accepted the [Red Cross] appeal, the Zionist paramilitary organization, the Haganah, launched Plan Dalet, the military blueprint for the conquest of Palestine through the large-scale expulsion of the civilian population.").

364 Foreman and Kedar, at 815 (further stating that "[Prime Minister] Ben-Gurion and [Finance Minister] Kaplan negotiated the sale of one million dunams to the [Jewish National Fund] the following month. Ben-Gurion later noted the legal discrepancies involved with the JNF sale, acknowledging that 'the government does as it pleases with this property', despite the fact that 'the law limits the government in its efficient, permanent use'. This illegal sale reflected that, despite the temporary arrangements along the way, authorities had long-term plans for the permanent use of Palestinian refugee land and the transfer of its unrestricted ownership into Jewish hands").

365 The concept of "Jewish nationality" was debated in the UNSC and in the UNGA throughout the 1948 war, however, few representatives, aside from the representatives of Arab States and their allies were willing to address the controversy, whether generally or specifically in relation to the refugee situation. Central to the structured privilege without which the Zionist movement would have likely been unable to secure its objective in reconstituting a Jewish State in Palestine, the concept and related privileges were first enshrined in the League of Nations Mandate for Palestine and in the country's first "constitution" adopted several years later which included a clause that prohibited legislation which contradicted the (unequal) terms of the Mandate. It is here where one arguably finds the origins or root cause of forced displacement in Palestine over that

(not yet citizens in the absence of legislation governing their status) which the State Department had expressed concern about as far back as June with the Lebanese representative, Fouad Ammoun, noting that "[i]f the refugees feared bad treatment, they might prefer some form of compensation, and by those means the Jews might succeed in preventing the return of the Arabs."[366] Focusing once again on the scope of the paragraph 11, Mahmoud Fawzi, the Egyptian representative, felt that the loss and damage covered was insufficient because it excluded "[refugees] who were sick and suffering" with "provisions [for material losses] indefinite and illusory."[367]

The most heated debate revolved around the Guatemalan amendment which linked the exercise of return to the proclamation of peace. "[If] the Arabs were allowed to return to Jewish territory in Palestine while [the] war was continuing", argued Jorge García Granados, "they would only contribute to the ill-will between the parties."[368] Describing the amended language as even less acceptable than the revised British paragraph, Fawzi expressed concern that it "gave the Jews an opportunity to use the status of the Arab refugees as a bargaining point in the settlement of the Palestine question" as American and British officials had noted earlier in the summer.[369] The only restriction on return that the UN Mediator had accepted after the restoration of the truce back in July was limited to men of military age who comprise a small minority of the refugee population. Responding to his Guatemalan counterpart, the Lebanese representative argued that Granados "overlooked the fact that the refugees had fled from the homes of their forefathers without arms and would return unarmed to the Jewish area."[370] What was implicit in Ammoun's response was more explicit in comments by the representatives of Syria and Egypt with the discussion in the First Committee once again returning to the above-mentioned issues relating to the nature of the Jewish State. "If it were to be assumed that a Jewish State was recognized as existing," Faris el-Khouri observed, "the refugees who had fled from the Jewish occupied areas would be citizens of that State [so] it was difficult to understand why their return

last one hundred years. More recently, *see, e.g.*, David Kretzmer, The Legal Status of the Arabs in Israel (1990); Roselle Tekiner, *Race and the Issue of National Identity in Israel*, 23 Int. J. Middle E. Stud. 39 (1991); Don Handelman, *Contradictions between Citizenship and Nationality: Their Consequences for Ethnicity and Inequality in Israel*, 7 Int'l J. Pol. Cult. & Soc. 441 (1994); Mazen Masri, The Dynamics of Exclusionary Constitutionalism: Israel as a Jewish and Democratic State (2017).

366   U.N. G.A.O.R., 3rd Sess., First Comm., 226th mtg., at 908.
367   Id., at 911.
368   Id., at 904.
369   Id., at 904.
370   Id., at 911.

to their own country should depend upon a peace treaty."³⁷¹ Continuing in the same vein, Mahmoud Fawzi argued that "[t]here was a serious omission in the Guatemalan amendment: the word 'repatriation' did not appear" leaving the Egyptian representative wondering why "it seemed that the representative of Guatemala did not feel that the refugees should return as if to their own country."³⁷²

Reiterating concerns raised by Arab representatives in previous meetings, El-Khouri emphasized that "[t]he refugees should be enabled to return and *enjoy full rights in their own country* where their families had lived for centuries" with Ammoun criticizing the second revised British draft resolution for failing to address the "political rehabilitation [of] some 700,000 refugees [who] could not return without their *political rights*."³⁷³ Noting that the UNGA's first peace plan had provided for a right of option, that is to say, residents of the Arab and Jewish States were entitled to citizenship in the State in which they comprised a majority, Jose García Granados responded that "it was too early to say whether repatriation, *properly speaking*, would be involved."³⁷⁴ While the Guatemalan representative did not offer further explanation, what he appeared to suggest or at least question was whether the refugees could be considered nationals of the newly-established Jewish State. When asked about his government's view of repatriation, Abba Eban, Israel's Ambassador to the UN reiterated Israel's position that "demographic homogeneity should be achieved in order to avoid a minority problem," a position that Zionist leaders and most others including Palestinians and other Arabs would have disparaged when Jews comprised a minority of the population.³⁷⁵

Taking the discussion one step further, Harold Beeley hoped that his fellow Committee members "would not subscribe to the thesis that [minorities which disputed the rights of their governments or indeed of their State

---

371   Id., at 908–9.
372   Id., at 911.
373   Id., at 908–9. *See also* U.N. G.A.O.R., 3rd Sess., First Comm., 222nd mtg., U.N. Doc. A/C.1/SR.222 (Dec. 2, 1948), at 868 (the Egyptian representative, Mahmoud Fawzi, similarly stating that the revised British draft resolution and Australian amendment, "took too weak an attitude on the *economic, social and financial rights* of the displaced persons and committed a serious sin of omission by failing to mention the *political rights* of the Arab refugees" [emphasis added]. While the refugees had "the right to be assisted by the [UN], which was to some extent responsible for their plight," Fawzi emphasized as he had done in previous discussions, that "[the refugees] also had *political rights* which were safe-guarded by documents of major importance such as the Atlantic Charter, the Charter of the [UN] and the Declaration of Human Rights" [emphasis added].
374   U.N. G.A.O.R., 3rd Sess., First Comm., 226th mtg.
375   Id., at 907.

to exist] should be driven out as refugees into other countries because of differences of political opinion with the Governments of the countries in which they lived."[376] This was in fact the basic argument that the provisional government had tasked its second transfer committee to try to make in order "[to] confront every nation with a list of its own crimes [forcing them] to restrain," in what appeared to be an unintended acknowledgement of culpability, "their criticism of Israel's actions."[377] Responding to Beeley, Granados countered that "in war conditions minorities who favoured the enemy were placed in concentration camps or otherwise segregated" and that "[t]here was no reason why this practice should not be practiced by Israel and there seemed no point in sending thousands there to prison."[378] The British delegation nevertheless opposed the Guatemalan amendment because "it might be many years before a formal peace was established in Palestine [however] conditions of stability might be established in fact without any agreement on the terms of a formal peace."[379] Supporting the British position that the refugees "need not wait for the proclamation of peace before returning," reiterating a view expressed earlier in the summer, Dean Rusk observed that "[t]hese unfortunate people should not be made pawns in the negotiations for a final settlement."[380] Thinking more about the timing of return, Harold Beeley thought that reliance should be placed on the conciliation commission, in consultation with the Director of the UN Relief for Palestine Refugees, to properly interpret the words "at the earliest possible date."[381] As the discussion of paragraph 11 drew to a close, it is significant that even Jorge Granados, whose amendment sparked a prolonged and often heated debate in the First Committee, acknowledged that in the end "[t]he refugees should eventually be returned."[382] The vast majority of Committee members subsequently rejected the Guatemalan amendment linking their return to the proclamation of peace between the parties concerned.

The discussion ended with two minor changes to paragraph 11. The British delegation agreed to replace the above-mentioned phrase regulating the timing of return, that is to say, "as soon as possible", with the corresponding phrase "as soon as practicable" in order to make the UNGA's intention more clear.[383]

---

376 Id., at 910.
377 Yoav Gelber, Palestine, 1948: War, Escape and the Emergence of the Palestinian Refugee Problem 292 (2006).
378 U.N. G.A.O.R., 3rd Sess., First Comm., 226th mtg., at 911.
379 Id., at 905.
380 Id., at 909.
381 Id., at 905.
382 Id., at 910.
383 Id., at 910.

While Harold Beeley did not offer further explanation, the UN Mediator had used the same phrase over the summer when he had attempted to secure Israel's agreement to the return of certain groups of refugees once the truce had been restored. The views expressed by the British representative and other members of the First Committee in discussions about the Guatemalan amendment were consistent with Bernadotte's position. This contrasts with Abba Eban's suggestion early in the debate that a "qualifying phrase might be inserted in the resolution to emphasize to the parties that the consequences of war could only be settled at the end of the war."[384] In other words, it was the existence of a truce or an armistice rather than the conclusion of a permanent peace that would enable the organized repatriation of the refugees to their homes with the term practicable quite possibility introducing a more objective set of criteria. A brief phrase added to the second sentence, at the request of the Australian delegation, further directed the Conciliation Commission to maintain close relations "through [the UNRPR] with the appropriate organs and agencies of the [UN]."[385] Taking the floor before voting commenced, Mahmoud Fawzi, whose pleas in the UNSC and UNGA for intervention on behalf of the refugees had been met with arguably little response in relation to the scale of the crisis, observed that the situation in Palestine "was a clear case of practically a whole nation being driven out."[386] For the Egyptian representative, it was no less than "the principles of the [UN]" and the "security of civilized society" that were at stake.[387] In a vote by show of hands, the First Committee subsequently approved the revised text of paragraph 11 with 29 members in favour, 6 against and 13 abstentions. The First Committee ended its deliberations on the revised British draft resolution at mid-day on December 4, after more than thirty meetings of intense debate, narrowly adopting the revised text of the British draft resolution by a vote of 25 in favor and 21 against with 9 abstentions.

Later the same day, Australia, Colombia and Poland withdrew their draft resolutions with Committee members subsequently rejecting the Syria draft resolutions calling for the establishment of a commission to consider recognition of a single State in Palestine and an advisory opinion from the International Court of Justice on the status of Palestine and the legality of partition. Almost immediately the American delegation in Paris expressed concern about whether the draft resolution approved by the First Committee would receive the necessary two-thirds majority in the UNGA given unresolved differences over the general

---

384   Id., at 906–7.
385   Id., at 910.
386   Id., at 912.
387   Id.

principles for a peaceful adjustment of the situation in Palestine, that is to say, the principles elaborated in Resolution 181 and the late Mediator's Progress Report.[388] Writing to Secretary Marshall, John Foster Dulles, the acting chairman of the American delegation in Paris, explained that in order to secure a two-thirds majority it would be necessary to obtain six more affirmative votes and eliminate six negative votes and that American "[e]fforts [were] being directed towards Bolivia, Guatemala and Venezuela, all of whom abstained, and from Argentina, Costa Rica and Uruguay who were absent."[389] Dulles added that the delegation was also "trying to reduce negative votes by securing abstentions from Burma, Ethiopia, Greece, India, Iran and Turkey."[390] The British and French delegations, meanwhile, were trying to convince Arab States that "[the] complete absence of [a UNGA] resolution would greatly weaken [the] Arab position and expose them to more certain consolidation of a military status quo than would otherwise be the case."[391] Reiterating an argument put to Arab States by the British some weeks earlier, the delegations argued that "[the] Arab states should [therefore] either abstain or absent themselves from the vote."[392] Dulles concluded that "[t]here [was] no chance of affecting the vote of the eastern European bloc which insist[ed] upon literal adherence to [Resolution 181]."[393] The American delegation also put forward two fall back plans in the event that the resolution failed to achieve the requisite majority. The first would be a shorter resolution essentially setting up the Conciliation Commission without addressing any of the substantive issues and if this failed the delegation held that the May 14 resolution appointing a UN Mediator in Palestine would stand and a new Mediator would be appointed.

V   Phase Four: Revisions in the General Assembly's Plenary Session

Plenary discussion of the First Committee's draft resolution was scheduled for 11 December, one day after the UNGA was scheduled to vote on the draft "Universal Declaration of Human Rights" and two years to the day that the UNGA had called for the progressive development of international law,

---

388 Paris (Dulles) to Secretary of State, DELGA 1063, Dec. 4, 1948, NARA, 501.BB Palestine/12-448. *See also* Department of State (Lovett) to Paris, GADEL 693, Dec. 7, 1948, NARA, 501.BB Palestine/12-748.
389 Paris (Dulles) to Secretary of State, DELGA 1063.
390 Id.
391 Id.
392 Id.
393 Id.

affirmed the legal principles recognized by the Charter of the Nuremberg Tribunal and recognized genocide as a crime under international law.[394] Adopted by the Third Committee two days after the First Committee concluded debate on a peaceful adjustment of the situation in Palestine, article 14(2) of the draft "Declaration of Human Rights" now affirmed "the right [of everyone] to leave any country, including his own, *and* to return to his country."[395] Having affirmed two years earlier that "the main task concerning displaced persons is to encourage and assist in every way possible their early return to their countries of origin,"[396] the UNGA called upon Albania, Bulgaria, Yugoslavia, and Greece the following year to "cooperate in the settlement of the problems arising out of refugees in the four states concerned through voluntary repatriation wherever possible."[397] The draft resolution on the situation in Palestine now before the Plenary, however, would be the first UNGA resolution to address the right of a specific group of refugees to "return to their homes [with] compensation [...] paid for the property of those choosing not to return and for loss of damage to property which under principles of international law or in equity should be made good by the governments or authorities responsible."[398] The short delay between the conclusion of First Committee deliberations and the opening of Plenary discussions effectively gave the Foreign Office and the State Department a week to gather sufficient votes to secure a two-thirds majority vote for the draft resolution.

On December 9th, the same day that the UNGA adopted the Convention on the Prevention and Punishment of the Crime of Genocide with members have decided against inclusion of forced displacement as an act of genocide, a series of cables from John Foster Dulles to Secretary Marshall noted two significant events that would have implications for the upcoming vote on the British draft resolution. In the first cable, Dulles informed Marshall that a group of States, including Australia, Canada, China, and New Zealand, were planning to amend the draft resolution in order to "make it possible to obtain [the] broadest possible support for such [a] resolution."[399] The proposed amendments essentially aimed to further strip the draft resolution of all references

---

394 G.A. Res. 94 (Dec. 11, 1948); G.A. Res. 95 (Dec. 11, 1948); G.A. Res. 96 (Dec. 11, 1948).
395 U.N. G.A.O.R., 3rd Sess., Third Comm., Draft Universal Declaration of Human Rights, Text of Articles of the Draft Declaration as Adopted by the Sub-Committee 4, U.N. Doc. A/C.3/SC.4/20 (Dec. 3, 1948) [emphasis added].
396 U.N. Res. 8 (Feb. 12, 1946), para. 2(b).
397 U.N. Res. 109 (Oct. 21, 1947), para. 5.
398 U.N. G.A.O.R., 3rd Sess., U.N. Doc. A/C.1/394/Rev.2 (Nov. 30, 1948), at para. 11.
399 The Acting Chairman of the United States Delegation at Paris (Dulles) to the Secretary of State, DELGA 1122, Dec. 9, 1948, in FRUS Vol. 5 (1948), at 1656–57.

to Resolution 181 and the Mediator's Progress Report which had been the focus of considerable dispute and debate in the First Committee. The acting chairman of the American delegation explained that "these amendments [would] make it possible for [the] Arab States to abstain rather than to vote against [the draft resolution] and that [the] Middle East and Far East friends of Arabs [would] vote affirmatively for [the] resulting resolution."[400] Dulles also believed that the proposed changes "[would also] be acceptable to Israel."[401] The unintended consequence of the amendment, similar to what had taken place in the UNSC back in October, was to remove the reference to the Mediator's specific conclusion (Part I, Section VIII, paragraph 4(i)) recommending that "[t]he right of the Arab refugees to return to their homes in Jewish-controlled territory at the earliest possible date should be affirmed by the [UN]."[402] Later that evening, Dulles received word that the UNSC would take up Israel's membership request the following day when the UNGA would be discussing and voting on the draft Universal Declaration of Human Rights.[403] Arab delegations, including Lebanon and Egypt, informed Dulles that in the event of "favorable [UNSC] action on Israeli application [...] Arabs would vote against [the UNGA] resolution and [would] strongly urge [their] friends to do so."[404] The fate of what would become Resolution 194 once again hung in the balance.

A   *Final Amendments*

On the morning of December 11th, discussion of the draft resolution approved by the First Committee opened in the UNGA. After reports by the First Committee and the Fifth Committee on the financial implications of the draft resolution were tabled, John Hood, the Australian representative, introduced the amendments his delegation had co-sponsored with Brazil, Canada, China, Colombia, France, and New Zealand.[405] Noting that debates on the Mediator's Progress Report in the First Committee "had been prolonged and heated" and that the draft resolution "had been adopted by a very narrow margin," Hood explained that "many of the representatives had been apprehensive about the

---

400   Id.
401   Id.
402   Progress Report, at 18.
403   The Acting Chairman of the United States Delegation at Paris (Dulles) to the Secretary of State, DELGA 1139, Dec. 9, 1948, in FRUS Vol. 5 (1948) at 1657.
404   Id.
405   U.N. G.A.O.R., 3rd Sess., First Comm., U.N. Doc. A/776 (Dec. 7, 1948); U.N. G.A.O.R., 3rd Sess., Fifth Comm., U.N. Doc. A/786 (Dec. 8, 1948). The Committee approved a recommendation for a USD 3 million budget for the proposed Conciliation Commission; U.N. G.A.O.R., 3rd Sess., U.N. Doc. A/789 (Dec. 9, 1948).

ultimate result of the recommendation of that resolution to the [UNGA]."[406] Hood further observed that while "the sponsors of the amendments might differ on their interpretation of minor points, he was nevertheless sure that they would all be in accord on their understanding of the primary purpose of the amendments" which was "to make the intention set forth in the resolution adopted by the First Committee more specific and more practical [and] to see the stage of conciliation in Palestine approached in a practical and realistic fashion."[407] The Australian representative's explanation echoed remarks by John Foster Dulles in the First Committee's final meeting. Co-sponsors of the amendments similarly pointed out that the changes, in the words of the Brazilian representative, Joao Carlos Muniz, "made it possible to rally a large majority in support of the [draft] resolution adopted by the First Committee" where less than half of the members had voted for the text.[408] Noting that the situation in Palestine was a "direct development of [Resolution 181] passed by the [UNGA] the previous year" and that "the responsibility of the [UNGA for the situation in Palestine] still existed," Hood argued that the UNGA "should see that the next stages in the development of the Palestine question evolved under the cognizance of the [UN]."[409] The amendments to the draft resolution adopted by the First Committee thus intended "to bring about the collective responsibility of the [UN] and to ensure that a realistic policy would be followed."[410]

Turning to the substantive content, Hood explained that "[t]he object had been to modify the resolution without destroying its essential purpose, so as to specify more clearly what its intention was and to delete from it any polemical references."[411] This included all references to the UNGA's first peace plan and the Mediator's report "which might be held to be prejudicial to the intention of setting up a real conciliation commission."[412] Amendments thus proposed changes to the draft resolution's preamble and operative paragraphs 2, 4, 5, and 11 all of which had been the subject of considerable discussion in the First Committee. While Committee members had decided to retain reference to the late Mediator's report in paragraph 11, the specific conclusion calling upon the UNGA to affirm the "right of refugees to return to their homes" in Part I, Section VIII, paragraph 4(i) of his report was removed from the final

---

406   U.N. G.A.O.R., 3rd Sess., 184th plen. mtg., U.N. Doc. A/PV.184 (Dec. 11, 1948), at 937.
407   Id.
408   Id., at 940.
409   Id., at 938–9.
410   Id., at 937.
411   Id.
412   Id.

draft in order to scrub the resolution of all reference to Resolution 181 and the Mediator's report. Paragraph 11 of the resolution in its final form thus

> [r]esolv[ed] that the refugees wishing to return to their homes and live at peace with their neighbours should be permitted to do so at the earliest practicable date, and that compensation should be paid for the property of those choosing not to return and for loss of or damage to property which, under principles of international law or in equity, should be made good by the Governments or authorities responsible; [and]
>
> [i]nstruct[ed] the Conciliation Commission to facilitate the repatriation, resettlement and economic and social rehabilitation of the refugees and the payment of compensation, and to maintain close relations with the Director of the [UN] Relief for Palestine Refugees and, through him, with the appropriate organs and agencies of the [UN].[413]

According to Hood and other representatives who took the floor during the debate, such changes "would not materially affect the resolution, since some of the points covered in those paragraphs were repeated elsewhere in the resolution."[414] Addressing the change to paragraph 11 on refugees, Lester Pearson, the Canadian representative, described the first part of the paragraph which had been removed as "redundant" since "the objective it stated was adequately elaborated in the course of the paragraph which followed."[415] It was the first part of the paragraph "[r]esolv[ing] that the refugees wishing to return to their homes and live at peace with their neighbours should be permitted to do so," moreover, that Israeli officials had described as "establishing the principle of *absolute and unrestricted return*" with the latter phrase "at the earliest practicable date" revised to clarify that the return of refugees should not have to await "the proclamation of peace."

Wrapping up his remarks, Hood acknowledged that while "[t]he text was not perfect [it] offered the best prospect of leading to a further stage in the solution of the problem" with other delegations making similar appeals for support.[416] Hector McNeill conceded that the draft resolution before the plenary, which "differed greatly" from the first British draft, "[was] the best answer which many brains and good intentions could produce, and which those

---

413   G.A. Res. 194.
414   U.N. G.A.O.R., 3rd Sess., 184th plen. mtg., at 939.
415   Id., at 943.
416   Id., at 947.

who had worked upon it thought most likely to secure adequate authority."[417] Acknowledging that "[t]he terms and contents of the resolution might not be to the liking of all Member States," John Foster Dulles nevertheless emphasized that its terms were "basically sound" and held out hope of achieving its three main objectives: a peaceful settlement of the Palestine problem; protection of the Holy Places and provision of free access; and, the repatriation and resettlement of the refugees.[418] Lester Pearson whose procedural interventions had guided the draft resolution through the First Committee issued a more ominous warning: "Either [the UNGA] passed a resolution, such as the amended resolution at present before it, as the basis for a permanent peace settlement, or it decided to do nothing at all, with the probable result of encouraging violence, disorder and division in Palestine."[419] In advance of the vote, Peter Fraser, the representative of New Zealand, similarly warned that "[i]f the [UN] did not pass the resolution that day, it would be still another example of its helplessness and the world would be aghast at the fact that the problem of the government of an area of 10,000 square miles only could not be solved by all the brains and all the goodwill in the world."[420] Noting that "[i]t would be a lamentable failure for the [UN] if the [UNGA] did not reach an agreement and if it proved powerless to deal with a conflict which was restricted in its scale, but which had incalculable moral and political consequences," it was Robert Schuman, the French representative, who perhaps best summarized the sentiment behind the final version of paragraph of the resolution.

> Some 700,000 refugees were suffering untold hardships. Homeless, lacking food and clothing, they were, according to a neutral observer, living like animals. Many of the villages which they had been obliged to leave had been partly demolished by systematic action which was still continuing. [...] It was unthinkable that the horrors perpetrated during the war against the Jewish populations in Europe should be repeated or should be reproduced in respect of the Arab population. Such a situation, which was a disgrace to mankind, must be brought to a close.[421]

The joint amendment was thus adopted by a vote of 44 in favour with 8 abstentions. The draft resolution as amended was adopted 35 in favour, 15 against and

---

417   Id., at 952.
418   Id., at 954.
419   Id., at 944.
420   U.N. G.A.O.R., 3rd Sess., 185th plen. mtg., U.N. Doc. A/PV.185 (Dec. 11, 1948), at 977.
421   U.N. G.A.O.R., 3rd Sess., 184th plen. mtg., at 945–7.

8 abstentions. Presiding over the third session of the UNGA, the Australian Minister for External Affairs, H.V. Evatt, concluded that "the [UNGA] believed and hoped that success would attend [Conciliation Commission's] efforts and that, at least, there would be in that area not only peace, but justice."[422] That would, unfortunately, be another story.

VI   Conclusions

Seventy years later, Resolution 194, and paragraph 11 in particular, continues to be the focus of debates when it comes to finding solutions for refugees from the 1948 war who, with their descendants today, comprise well over half of the Palestinian people. With the first major legal studies of paragraph 11 published after the signing of the Framework for Peace in the Middle East between Egypt and Israel in the late 1970s, the launch of the Middle East Peace Process after Israel and the Palestine Liberation Organization (PLO) agreed to a Declaration of Principles on Interim Self-Government Arrangements led to the publication of additional legal research.[423] Both agreements, with the former comprising the genesis for the latter, provided for deferred or final status negotiations on the Palestinian refugee situation thus raising questions about their rights and future status including the unresolved issue of their return to homes and places of origin inside the State of Israel. Having previously considered return as a collective right to be exercised in tandem with the liberation of Palestine, the PLO's acceptance of the country's partition in 1988 leading to a two State solution and its subsequent call for a solution to the refugee situation in 1991 on the basis of the individual right to return affirmed in Resolution 194 appeared to heighten interest in the meaning of paragraph 11.[424] So did the Clinton administration's unsuccessful effort to repeal the resolution after the launch of negotiations between Israel and the PLO.[425] Israel's attempt to (re)define the

---

422   Id., 996.
423   *See, e.g.*, George Tomeh, *Legal Status of Arab Refugees*, 33 Law & Contemp. Probs. 110 (1968); and the counter arguments in: Radley. More recently, *see*, Boling; and the counter arguments made in: Zilbershats, at 191 (Sari Hanafi et al. eds. 2007). For additional discussion of the literature, *see* Rempel.
424   Masalha 2003; Shiblak. *See also* Menachem Klein, *Between Right and Return: The PLO and the Dialectics of 'The Right of Return'*, 11 J. Ref. Stud. 1 (1998).
425   Ambassador Madelaine K. Albright, Letter to Ambassadors to the United Nations, New York, Aug. 8, 1994, in 24 J. Pal. Stud. 153 (1995) (stating that "[the United States] also believ[es] that resolution language referring to 'final status' issues should be dropped, since these issues are now under negotiation by the parties themselves"). In what appeared to be a similar effort a decade later, the second Bush administration introduced a resolution (G.A. Res. 58/95 (Dec. 9, 2003)) on assistance to Palestine refugees which

substantive content of paragraph 11 through its unofficial working paper on refugees discussed during final status talks with the PLO in Taba, Egypt in 2001 similarly raised questions about the meaning of the paragraph as did the Arab peace initiative several years later which called for "a just solution to the Palestinian refugee problem to be agreed upon in accordance with [UNGA] Resolution 194."[426]

Given the ongoing significance of Resolution 194 when it comes to finding solutions for the millions of Palestinians including descendants forcibly displaced as a result of the 1948 war and the establishment of the State of Israel, it is somewhat surprising that comparatively little has been written about the meaning of paragraph 11, the right to return, in particular, relative to the much broader body of research on UNSC Resolution 242, the primary framework for negotiated political solution since the 1967 war, which calls for "a just settlement of the refugee problem."[427] This also appears somewhat odd given the apparent influence the drafting of paragraph 11 had on the codification of the right to return in the Universal Declaration of Human Rights which the UNGA adopted one day before Resolution 194.[428] Paragraph 11 also appeared to generate model language for UNGA resolutions addressing other refugee situations throughout most of the Cold War period.[429] In the context of UNGA

---

excluded reaffirmation of Resolution 194 as found in other annual resolutions on Palestinian refugees.

426   Masalha 2003; Gal. *See also Israeli Private Response to the Palestinian Refugee Proposal of 22 January 2001, "Non-Paper – Draft 2"*, 22 January 2001, 31 J. Pal. Stud. 148, 149 (2001) (stating that "8. Regarding return, repatriation and relocation, each refugee may apply to one of the following programs, thus fulfilling the relevant clause of [UNGA Resolution] 194: a. To Israel – capped to an agreed limit of XX refugees [...] b. To Israeli swapped territory [...] c. To the State of Palestine [...] d. Rehabilitation within existing host countries [...] e. Relocation to third countries"). The idea of redefining the meaning of paragraph 11 of Resolution 194 is similar to a proposal put forward by the Clinton administration nearly a decade earlier under which a bilateral agreement between Israel and the PLO would "constitute the implementation of Resolutions 242 and 338 in all their respects." Rempel. The language in the Arab peace initiative is slightly different from the relationship between resolutions 194 and 242 as discussed in the UNSC in 1967 and in UNGA Resolution 3089D adopted five years later. *See* Quigley 2007; G.A. Res. 3089D. 9. For discussion of the Arab initiative, *see* Marwan Muasher, The Arab Center: The Promise of Moderation 102 (2009).

427   *See* notes 7–8 and sources cited. Dozens of articles have been written about UNSC Resolution 242 while research on General Assembly Resolution 194, as noted above, is found largely in a broader body of research – historical, political and legal – on Palestinian refugees. *See* note 24 and sources cited.

428   *See* notes 188, 394 and related text. *See also*, Mary Ann Glendon, A World Made New: Eleanor Roosevelt and the Universal Declaration of Human Rights (2003).

429   *See, e.g.*, resolutions affirming the return of refugees to their homes in: G.A. Res. 1389 (Nov. 20, 1959) (Algeria); G.A. Res. 1671 (Dec. 18, 1961) (Angola); G.A. Res. 2790 (Dec. 6,

efforts to address the human rights causes of mass exodus and promote international cooperation to avert new flows of refugees in the 1980s and early 1990s, Resolution 194 informed principles contained in a series of declarations adopted by the International Law Association on mass expulsion and refugee compensation.[430] The more explicit reference to the right to return in UNGA resolutions along with Conclusions adopted by the Executive Committee of the UN High Commissioner for Refugees in the post-Cold War period, moreover, is remarkably similar to the language used by the UN Mediator in Palestine in his June 1948 Suggestions and in his Progress Report the following September with several draft resolutions in October likewise explicitly affirming the right to return.[431] While each of the above examples appear to demonstrate Resolution

---

1971) (East Pakistan (Bangladesh)); G.A. Res. 3212 (Nov. 1, 1974); (Cyprus) G.A. Res. 35/37 (Nov. 20, 1980) (Afghanistan); G.A. Res. 41/157 (Dec. 4, 1987). In a number of other cases, including Rwanda, South West Africa (Namibia), and, French Somaliland (Djibouti), however, the UNGA referred to the return and resettlement of all refugees, the return of political refugees who are natives, and, more simply, the return of all refugees.

430 Declaration of Principles of International Law on Mass Expulsion, 62nd International Law Association, Seoul, 24–30 August 1986, *reprinted in*, 6 Ref. Survey Q. 95 (1987) (Principle 5 stating that "[t]he reaffirmation by the [UNGA] each year of resolution 194 (III), paragraph 11 of 11 December 1948, which identifies certain matters as governed by 'principles of international law ... or equity', has over time imbued those matters with legal quality"); Cairo Declaration of Principles of International Law on Compensation to Refugees, 65th International Law Association, Cairo, Apr. 20–26, 1992, *reprinted in*, 87 Am. J. Int'l L. 157 (1993) (recalling that "the [UNGA] Resolution 194 (III) of 11 December 1948, which has been reaffirmed each year, resolved that 'the refugees wishing to return to their homes and live at peace with their neighbours should be permitted to do so at the earliest practicable date, and that compensation should be paid for the property of those choosing not to return and for loss of or damage to property which, under principles of international law or in equity, should be made good by the Governments or authorities responsible'"). Sloan identifies several additional reasons why repetition or re-citation is important. Sloan, at 132 (stating that "it demonstrates continuity and distinguishes those resolutions having stable support from those enjoying only an ephemeral majority. It also strengthens their evidential and precedential value and increases expectations of continued interest and support. It mobilizes public opinion and legal thinking, impresses the importance which States attach to the resolution, reinforces claims and confirms a persistent practice"). *See also* Samuel A. Bleicher, 63 *The Legal Significance of Re-Citation of General Assembly Resolutions*, 444 Am. J. Int'l. L. (1969).

431 *See, e.g.*, resolutions on the right of refugees to return: G.A. Res. 46/242 (Aug. 25, 1992) (Bosnia); G.A. Res. 49/43 (Dec. 9, 1994) (Croatia); G.A. Res. 54/96H (Dec. 15, 1999) (East Timor). The UNGA also affirmed the right to return of refugees on the context of the realization of the right to self-determination, G.A. Res. 48/93 (Dec. 20, 1993). These resolutions were preceded by a small number of additional resolutions in previous decades affirming refugees' right to return: G.A. Res. 3236 (Palestine); G.A. Res. 35/6 (Oct. 22, 1980) (Kampuchea (Cambodia)); International Cooperation to Avert New Flows of Refugees, adopted 32 years to day after Resolution 194, G.A. Res. 35/124 (Dec. 11, 1980). For the right

194's ongoing juridical effect, they also raise the question posed at the beginning of this article, namely, what happened to the explicit reference to the "right" of refugees to return to their homes in paragraph 11.[432]

First mentioned during the initial phase of the drafting process in the UN Mediator's June suggestions, which recommended that "recognition be accorded to the *right* of residents of Palestine who, because of conditions created by the conflict there have left their normal places of abode, *to return to their homes* without restriction and to regain their property," the UNGA had already affirmed repatriation as a solution for refugees from the Second World War along with those displaced by the conflict in the Balkans.[433] In similar language, the Mediator identified the "Right of Repatriation" as one of seven basic premises for a peaceful adjustment of the situation of Palestine emphasizing

---

to return in conclusions adopted by UNHCR's Executive Committee, *see, e.g.*, Conclusion No. 40 (XXVI) – Voluntary Repatriation, U.N. Doc. A/40/12/Add.1 (Oct. 18, 1985); Conclusion No. 74 (XLV) – General Conclusion on International Protection, U.N. Doc. A/49/12/Add.1 (Oct. 7, 1994); Conclusion No. 96 (LIV) – Return of Persons Found not to be in Need of International Protection, U.N. Doc. A/58/12/Add.1 (Oct. 10, 2003); Conclusion No. 109 (LV) – Protracted Refugee Situations, U.N. Doc. A/AC.96/1080 (Dec. 8, 2009).

432 The resolution has had a number of additional juridical effects, most notable, perhaps, being the establishment of operational agencies. This includes the establishment of the UN Conciliation Commission for Palestine which though inoperative continues to exist and submits to the UNGA a brief annual report stating that the Commission has nothing new to report. As a result of an American amendment, discussed above, the Commission is also authorized to establish subsidiary organs to facilitate its work. During the roughly ten years in which the UNCCP actively pursued its mandate, it established a number of subsidiary organs to facilitate the implementation of paragraph 11 of Resolution 194. This included a Technical Committee, an Economic Survey Mission, a Refugee Office, and a Technical and Valuation Office. The recommendations of the Economic Survey Mission led in turn to the establishment of the UN Relief and Works Agency for Palestine Refugees in the Near East (UNRWA). One of the primary operative effects of Resolution 194, therefore, was to create what is sometimes described as the Palestinian refugee regime comprised of the UNCCP and UNRWA. For additional discussion of the juridical effects of UNGA resolutions, *see* Sloan.

433 Suggestions, Part II, para. 9 [emphasis added]. U.N. Res. 8, para. (c)(iii) (stating that "the main task concerning displaced persons is to encourage and assist in every possible way their early return to their countries of origin"); U.N. Res. 109, para. 5 (calling upon Albania, Bulgaria, Yugoslavia and Greece "[to] cooperate in the settlement of the problems arising out of the presence of refugees in the four states concerned through voluntary repatriation wherever possible"). *See also*, Mallison and Mallison (stating that "[i]t is significant that Count Bernadotte did not recommend the creation of a new right, but instead recommended that the right to return 'be affirmed by the [UN]'. Consistent with this recommendation, subsequent resolutions of the [UNGA] have sought to affirm and make effective an existing right. The right of return, based on state practice, was apparently regarded as an established part of customary international law as well as one of 'the general principles of law recognized by civilized nations'.").

that "[t]he *right* of innocent people, uprooted from their homes by the present terror and ravages of war, *to return to their homes*, should be affirmed and made effective."[434] Bernadotte subsequently recommended in his specific conclusions that the UN should affirm "[t]he *right* of the Arab refugees to return to their homes in Jewish-controlled territory at the earliest possible date" which he described as "a reasonable, equitable and workable basis for [a political] settlement."[435] It was during the second phase of the drafting process in the fall of 1948 that the British Foreign Office and the American State Department decided to incorporate the Mediator's specific conclusion in their composite resolution on the basis of language drafted by Bernadotte's principal secretary Ralph Bunche which "[r]ecogniz[ed] fully the *right* of refugees from the conflict in Palestine to *return to their homes* at the earliest possible date."[436] It was also during this period that several major disagreements over the substantive content of Resolution 194 came to the fore with Anglo-American cooperation threatened by disputes over the general principles that would guide efforts by the Conciliation Commission to facilitate a peaceful adjustment of the situation. This included Israel's consent in the modification of borders of the Jewish State delineated under Resolution 181, endorsement of the Mediator's specific conclusions in his September report and compensation for Palestinians forcibly displaced as a result of the war.[437] All three of these disputes would have

---

434   Progress Report, at 17 [emphasis added].

435   Id., at 18 [emphasis added]. The Mediator further emphasized that "[i]t would be an offence against the *principles of elemental justice* if these innocent victims of the conflict were denied the *right to return* to their homes while Jewish immigrants flow into Palestine, and, indeed, at least offer the threat of permanent replacement of the Arab refugees who have been noted in the land for centuries" [emphasis added]. Id., at 14. The US similarly described the return of refugees to their homes as "intrinsic to negotiations and [a] settlement [of the Palestine question]." Department of State (Marshall) to New York, No. 531.

436   Paris (Austin) to Secretary of State, DELGA 284 [emphasis added]; United Nations General Assembly, Paris (United Kingdom Delegation) to the Foreign Office [Text of the New United States Draft Resolution on Palestine]. The third composite draft which consolidated the two paragraphs on refugees in the Bunche draft in a single paragraph maintained the explicit reference to the right to return. Paris (Marshall) to the Acting Secretary of State, DELGA 351. The initial drafts prepared by the Foreign Office and by the State Department in late September along with the first composite draft stipulated that refugees were "entitled" to return. As noted earlier, that the UNGA "determined" that the refugees were "entitled" to return appeared to respond to the Mediator's recommendation that the UN should affirm the right of refugees to return to their homes. Discussion between Mr. Beeley and the American Delegation about the Draft Resolution on Palestine; United Nations General Assembly, Paris (United Kingdom Delegation) to Foreign Office, No. 52; and, Paris (Marshall) to Secretary of State, DELGA 220.

437   *See* discussion in section III (E).

implications for the final provisions of paragraph 11 of Resolution 194 during the third and final phases of the drafting process.

The third phase of the drafting process in the UNGA's First Committee revolved around Anglo-American efforts to promote their respective draft language and concomitant efforts to find solutions to each of the above-mentioned disagreements that threatened a joint approach to the peaceful adjustment of the situation of Palestine. This resulted initially in the submission of a British-sponsored draft resolution which in contrast to the last composite draft appeared to emphasize Israel's corresponding obligations to the refugees by resolving "that the Arab refugees *should be permitted* to return to their homes at the earliest possible date" with the addition of a chapeau endorsing the Mediator's recommendation on Israel's liability to compensate refugees for loss and damage.[438] Drawing upon its initial draft resolution from late September along with statements by American officials that aimed to amend the British text, the US introduced amended language – "[r]esolving that the Arab refugees *wishing to return* to their homes and *live at peace* with their neighbors should be permitted to do so at the earliest possible date" – subsequently incorporated into composite American draft resolution and in the final text of paragraph 11.[439] Unable to support the amended language on refugees, the British nevertheless attempted to the bridge the gap with the Americans on other issues of dispute through a revised draft resolution which introduced language on negotiations and referred to Resolution 181 as a further basis for resolving outstanding questions aimed to secure Australian and eastern bloc support.[440] With the weight of Committee opinion not in their favour, the British decided that the process through which an agreement on a peaceful adjustment of the situation of Palestine was reached was more important than the actual demarcation of borders separating the Jewish State from territories to be merged with one or more Arab States.[441] Having failed to secure support for their revised draft resolution, the British introduced further revisions agreeing to forego endorsement of the Mediator's report in exchange

---

438 U.N. G.A.O.R., 3rd Sess., U.N. Doc. A/C.1/394 [emphasis added].
439 U.N. G.A.O.R., 3rd Sess., First Comm., U.N. Doc. A/C.1/397 [emphasis added]. *See also* U.N. G.A.O.R., 3rd Sess., 139th mtg., at 41; United Nations General Assembly, Paris (United Kingdom Delegation) to Foreign Office, No. 52; Paris (Dulles) to Secretary of State, NIACT DELGA 976. The primary change on refugees in the American composite draft resolution related to compensation.
440 U.N. G.A.O.R., 3rd Sess., First Comm., U.N. Doc. A/C.1/394/Rev.1. *See also* note 303.
441 Foreign Office to United Nations General Assembly, Paris (United Kingdom Delegation), No. 537; United Nations General Assembly, Paris (United Kingdom Delegation) to Foreign Office, No. 542.

for American agreement on language that prioritized negotiations under the Conciliation Commission's auspices rather than direct talks between the parties involved.[442] In return for agreeing to the principle of Israel's consent in the modification of borders delineated under Resolution 181, the Americans offered an interpretation under which Israel would have to give up territory in one area if it wished to gain territory in another.[443] Finally, the British agreed to American language which replaced the existing chapeau with new language endorsing the Mediator's specific conclusion calling upon the [UN] to affirm "the right of the Arab refugees to return to their homes in Jewish-controlled territory."[444]

While these changes resolved Anglo-American disagreements, they failed to resolve disputes with other members of the First Committee. These disagreements which essentially revolved around the general principles guiding a peaceful adjustment of the situation of Palestine, were addressed in part during discussion of the tabulation of draft resolutions and amendments. The above-mentioned disputes were resolved through two inter-related mechanisms, namely, removal of references to Resolution 181 and the Mediator's progress report along with removal of several "offending" paragraphs themselves from the draft resolution.[445] This also resulted in the rejection of draft language introduced by Australia and Poland and supported by Israel which appeared to prioritize resettlement over repatriation further stipulating that the latter would have to be feasible without defining the meaning of the term.[446] The above-mentioned paragraph on refugees agreed upon by the British and the Americans nevertheless remained intact including its chapeau with its reference to the Mediator's progress report. While amendments made to the second revised British draft resolution during discussion of the tabulation of draft resolutions and amendments did not resolve all the disagreements over

---

442   United Nations General Assembly, Paris (United Kingdom Delegation) to Foreign Office, No. 603; Paris (Dulles) to Secretary of State, DELGA 996.
443   Id.; Department of State, to American Embassy in London, No. 4485.
444   Paris (Dulles) to Secretary of State, DELGA 997.
445   U.N. G.A.O.R., 3rd Sess., First Comm., 221st mtg.; U.N. G.A.O.R., 3rd Sess., First Comm., 223rd mtg.; U.N. G.A.O.R., 3rd Sess., First Comm., 224th mtg., and related text. It appears that references to the Mediator's progress report and Resolution 181 in the preamble of the draft resolution initially survived due to the inoperative character of the paragraphs. *See, e.g.*, Wood, at 86–7 (stating that preambles need to be treated with care because they "tend to be used as dumping ground for proposals that are not acceptable in the operative paragraphs").
446   U.N. G.A.O.R., 3rd Sess., First Comm., U.N. Doc. A/C.1/396; U.N. G.A.O.R., 3rd Sess., First Comm., U.N. Doc. A/C.1/400. *See also* Paris (Dulles) to Secretary of State, NIACT DELGA 977.

the Anglo-American draft resolution, the above mechanisms provided a solution to resolve remaining problems during the fourth phase in which members of the UNGA considered the draft adopted by the First Committee in plenary session. This resulted in both the removal of preambular language referring to the Mediator's progress report and Resolution 181 as well as the chapeau to paragraph 11 which endorsed Bernadotte's specific conclusion calling upon the UN to affirm "[t]he *right* of the Arab refugees to return to their homes in Jewish-controlled territory at the earliest possible date."[447] The final version of paragraph 11 thus resolved without explicit reference to the "right" to return, that "the refugees *wishing to return* to their homes and live at peace with their neighbours should be permitted to do so at the earliest practicable date."[448]

It has since been argued that paragraph 11 of UNGA Resolution 194 does not provide a legal basis for the return of Palestinian refugees to their homes and places of origin inside the State of Israel because the paragraph does not state explicitly that the refugees have a "right" to return.[449] This argument has been addressed in part through the assertion that paragraph 11 reaffirms an existing principle, namely, the right to return, already considered to be part of international customary law at the time of the 1948 war making the return of refugees a binding obligation regardless of the precise language used in Resolution 194.[450] Jessup's description of the American amendment to paragraph 11 during discussion of the British sponsored draft resolution in the First Committee in the fall of 1948 appears to underscore this argument. Speaking

---

447 Progress Report, at 18 [emphasis added].
448 G.A. Res. 194, para. 11 [emphasis added].
449 Schechtman; Radley. Radley's article is commonly cited by other scholars who draw a similar conclusion. *See, e.g.*, Lapidoth; Zilbershats; and Kent. Given its wide citation, Radley's article poses somewhat of a mystery as the author does not appear to have published other research nor has this author been able to trace Radley's biography. Correspondence with the American Journal of International Law failed to shed further light on the issue.
450 *See, e.g.*, Mallison and Mallison; Quigley; Boling. The most detailed argument can be found in Boling who identifies relevant State practice and applicable norms of international custom under the law of nationality and State succession, international humanitarian law and international human rights law. *See also* Sloan, at 68–9 and sources cited (stating that "to the extent that a resolution is actually declaratory of existing law, its provisions are clearly obligatory; but their binding force comes from customary law." Sloan further observes that "[c]ustom by its very nature, being derived from diffuse practice, may lack the precision of a text. Resolutions will define, formulate, clarify, specify and authenticate text and corroborate the rule contained therein. Where in fact a text does exist, as in the case of the Nuremberg Principles, resolutions affirm or confirm, and this removes doubts concerning its legal status." Moreover, "under the guise of formulation, they may interpret, elaborate and in fact develop the law while maintaining the umbrella of customary international law.").

in favor of the amendment which "[r]esolved that the Arab refugees *wishing to return* to their homes and *live at peace* with their neighbors should be permitted to do so at the earliest possible date," the American diplomat, scholar and jurist observed that the paragraph "endorsed a *generally recognized principle* and provided means for its implementation."[451] The widespread support for the Lebanese amendment to the draft Universal Declaration of Human Rights which completed provisions on freedom of movement by adding the right to return to the right to leave is consistent with Jessup's description of the right to return as a "generally recognized principle."[452] Concerns expressed by the Mediator and his senior advisors that certain Israeli practices during the 1948 war, including the expulsion of Arab civilians and the destruction of their property without military necessity, contravened the Hague Convention and its annexed Regulations appear to further evidence the claim that paragraph 11 endorsed a principle already considered part of international customary law.[453] Having achieved customary status well before the 1948 war in Palestine, the Convention and its Regulations concerning the Laws and Customs of War on Land are said to "constitute the foundational source of the general right of return in customary humanitarian law of *all* displaced persons to return to their homes of origin following the cessation of hostilities."[454] That paragraph

---

451 U.N. G.A.O.R., 3rd Sess., First Comm., 209th mtg., at 728 [emphasis added]. As noted above, Jessup did not explain further, however, it appears that he was referring to the return of refugees rather than their compensation given the American position that compensation would be better dealt with through negotiations rather than in the specific directives contained in the draft resolution.

452 *See*, the discussion in note 188, 241–42 and related text.

453 Persson, at 186. Theodor Meron, *The Geneva Conventions as Customary Law*, 81 Am. J. Int'l L. 348 (1987). Having already drawn attention of Israeli officials to the fact that certain military practices violated the rules of war, the Progress Report appeared to draw upon language used in the Hague Convention and its annexed Regulations in reference to "numerous reports from reliable sources of large-scale looting, pillaging and plundering, and of instances of destruction of villages *without apparent military necessity*." The Bunche draft "[r]ecogniz[ed] fully the *right* of refugees […] to be adequately compensated *for any losses* suffered by them *as a result of confiscation or destruction of property not resulting from military necessity*."

454 Boling, at 50–53 (further stating that "[t]he Article 43 rule requiring a belligerent occupant to let the local population continue its normal existence with a minimum of interference would logically necessarily include a requirement that the local population be permitted to remain in or return to their homes of origin following the cessation of hostilities. Thus, the rule of Article 43 is the foundation of the general right of return in humanitarian law. […] While the Hague Regulations do not specifically articulate the obligation of a state to repatriate *civilian* (i.e., non-combatant) habitual residents of the territory who may have become temporarily displaced during the conflict, it must be immediately obvious that the entire purpose of the Hague Regulations – as is clearly stated

11 which "[r]esolv[ed] that refugees wishing to return to their homes and live at peace with their neighbours should be permitted to do so at the earliest practicable date" endorsed a customary norm of international law also appears evident in the Conciliation Commission's subsequent conclusion on the legal status of returnees under Israeli law.[455] Drafted by Paolo Contini, a legal advisor to the UNRRA and the IRO before his employment by the Conciliation Commission, Contini's conclusion that "[t]he temporary exodus from Israel of those refugees who will return legally to that country would not seem to change their citizenship status" was consistent with the customary norm that in situations of State succession habitual residents *ipso facto* acquire the nationality of the successor State under the law of nationality.[456]

The principles of treaty interpretation provide a useful tool to further probe the meaning of paragraph 11 with respect to the right to return keeping in mind the distinction between treaties and resolutions adopted by the UNGA. Setting aside for now the question of good faith, the language used in the final draft of the paragraph which "resolves that refugees wishing to *return* to their homes and live at peace with their neighbours should be allowed to do so at

---

in the Preamble to the Hague Convention – and indeed of all humanitarian law generally is to 'mitigate' the 'severity' of war as much as possible and to spare the local inhabitants (i.e., the habitual residents) to the maximum extent possible. [...] Accordingly, Article 20 of the Hague Regulations must be interpreted as incorporating, by logical necessity, the right of return of *all* habitual residents to a territory following the cessation of hostilities (and not just prisoners of war, or combatants, who are, in any case, specifically covered by the express language of Article 20)"). *See also* Alfred de Zayas, Forced Population Transfer, Max Planck Encyc. Publ. Int'l L., Oct. 2010 [*hereinafter* de Zayas] (stating that "[f]orced population transfers would necessarily breach [...] Art. 46 1907 Hague Convention IV which stipulates that 'family honour and rights, the lives of persons, and private property, as well as religious practice must be respected. Private property can not be confiscated', and Art. 50 1907 Hague Convention IV according to which '[n]o general penalty, pecuniary or otherwise, shall be inflicted upon the population.'").

455 UNCCP, Legal Aspects of the Problem of Compensation to Palestine Refugees, annexed to, Letter and Memorandum dated 22 November 1949, Concerning Compensation, received by the Chairman of the Conciliation Commission from Mr. Gordon R. Clapp, Chairman, United Nations Economic Survey Mission for the Middle East, Working Paper No. 35 10 U.N. Doc. A/AC.25/W.32 (Jan. 19, 1950).

456 Id. (further stating that "[i]t appears [...] that Arabs should be regard as having the same citizenship status as Jews, both at the time of their displacement and upon their re-admission to Israeli territory"). Contini drafted the opinion to determine responsibility for compensation claims. *See also* Boling, at 29–30 (stating that "[u]nder the law of state succession, when territory undergoes a change of sovereignty, the law of state succession requires that inhabitants (commonly referred to as 'habitual residents') of the geographical territory coming under new sovereignty be offered nationality by the new state. This rule represents a customary norm and is binding upon all states.").

the earliest practicable date" should be interpreted within the ordinary meaning of the relevant terms.[457] The qualifying or contingent phrases, namely, "live at peace", "should be permitted" and "the earliest practicable date" are important in understanding the meaning of the term "return" in paragraph 11, however, the meaning of these phrases based on the drafting history of Resolution 194 have been addressed elsewhere.[458] The question that remains to be addressed is whether the removal of the term "right" as used in the UN Mediator's suggestions and specific conclusions in addition to several draft resolutions in the fall of 1948 changed the meaning of paragraph 11 with respect to the return of refugees to their homes. In other words, was it the position of those involved in drafting the paragraph that the refugees displaced by the 1948 war in Palestine did not have a "right" to return to their homes under international law. While the UN Mediator along with officials in the Foreign Office and in the State Department from time to time expressed doubts about the viability of return, citing Israeli measures to prevent refugees from going back to their homes and related fears stemming from Israeli policies and practices that led to their displacement, the drafting record does not support the assertion that those taking part meant anything other than the actual return of refugees to their homes.[459] Having initially considered a population exchange, the State

457   *See* VCLT.
458   UNCCP, *Analysis of Paragraph 11 of the General Assembly's Resolution of 11 December 1948*, Working Paper Prepared by the Secretariat, 4–7 U.N. Doc. A/AC.25/W.45 (May 15, 1950) (stating that "[a]t first sight it would appear that [the] phrase ['live at peace'] was intended to place a limiting condition upon the return of the refugees, i.e., an obligation on the part of the returning refugees and a right on the part of in whose territory the refugees would be re-establishing themselves. On further examination, however, it becomes evident that the reverse is also true. [...] In connection with the right of refugees to live at peace with their neighbours, the injunction ['should be permitted'] is addressed to the Government in whose territory the refugees will be settling and impose an obligation on this Government to ensure the peace of the returning refugees and protect them from any elements seeking to disturb that peace. [...] It would appear indisputable that such conditions [for the return of refugees to their homes 'at the earliest practicable date'] were established by the signing of the four Armistice Agreements."). The Commission did not address the absence of the term "right" in its 1950 working paper, however, a subsequent working paper, as detailed below, affirms the assertion that with the removal of the term the representatives of States did not intend to imply that the refugees did not have a right to return.
459   British Middle East Office (Cairo) to Foreign Office, No. 28; The Ambassador in London (Douglas) to the Secretary of State, No. 3851, Aug. 25, 1948, in FRUS Vol. 5 (1948), at 1342; Foreign Office to United Nations General Assembly, Paris (United Kingdom Delegation), No. 65; Paris (Marshall) to Secretary of State, No. 158, Sept. 29, 1948, NARA, 501.BB Palestine/9-29. In at least one cable, however, British officials noted that while refugees from "Arab Palestine", that is to say, that part of the country not under the control of

Department and the Foreign Office subsequently concluded, respectively, that Israel should be "induced" and "made to allow" the refugees to return.[460] In a point-by-point rebuttal, the State Department rejected the assertion made by the Israel's provisional government that economic, security and political reasons militated against the return of Palestinian refugees to their homes inside the Jewish State outside the context of a comprehensive peace agreement.[461] Throughout the drafting history, moreover, the representatives of States repeatedly referred to the "right" of the refugees to return to their homes; at no point in the drafting history did the representatives of States suggest or state that the refugees did not have a "right" to return to their homes.[462] Even Guatemala which repeatedly lobbied for amended language conditioning the return of Palestinian refugees to the proclamation of peace did not dispute the widespread consensus apparent within the First Committee that the refugees had a right to return to their homes inside the State of Israel. In observations on the American amendment to paragraph 11 of the first British draft resolution submitted to the First Committee, Israeli officials explicitly stated that the first part of the paragraph under which the UNGA "[r]esolv[ed] that the refugees *wishing to return* and live at peace with their neighbours should be permitted to do so at the earliest possible date [...] *establish[ed] the principle of absolute and unrestricted return.*"[463] Commenting later on the substantive content of paragraph 11, the Conciliation Commission observed that "[a]mong

---

Jewish military forces, should be encouraged to return, resettlement of those originating from the latter area "probably offer[ed] the best chance for their prosperity and for [the] solution of the problem of the Jewish state." Jerusalem to Foreign Office (London), No. 332, July 29, 1948, NA, FO371-68577 E10235.

460 See the discussion in notes 72–82 and related text. *See also* Department of State (Marshall) to New York, No. 531; London (Douglas) to Secretary of State (Marshall), No. 3880.

461 Department of State (Marshall) to the United States Delegation at the United Nations in New York, No. 534.

462 *See, e.g.*, British Middle East Office (Cairo) to Foreign Office, No. 276, July 28, 1948, NA, FO371-68577 E10220; London (Douglas), to Secretary of State (Marshall), No. 4132, Sept. 15, 1948, 501.BB NARA, Palestine/9-1548; Washington to Foreign Office, No. 4592. *See also* Ahmad Shukayri (Arab Higher Committee), U.N. G.A.O.R., 3rd Sess., First Comm., 201st mtg., U.N. Doc. A/C.1/SR.201 (Nov. 16, 1948), at 652; Liu Chieh (China), U.N. G.A.O.R., 3rd Sess., First Comm., 205th mtg., U.N. Doc. A/C.1/SR.205 (Nov. 20, 1948), at 686; Roberto Urdaneta Arbalaez (Colombia), U.N. G.A.O.R., 3rd Sess., First Comm., 209th mtg., U.N. Doc. A/C.1/SR.209 (Nov. 23, 1948), at 724; Enrique Rodriguez Fabregat (Uruguay), U.N. G.A.O.R., 3rd Sess., 210th mtg., U.N. Doc. A/C.1/SR.210 (Nov. 24, 1948), at 740; Mahmoud Fawzi (Egypt), U.N. G.A.O.R., 3rd Sess., 212th mtg., U.N. Doc. A/C.1/SR.756-7 (Nov. 25, 1948), at 756–7; Hector McNeil (United Kingdom), U.N. G.A.O.R., 3rd Sess., 212th mtg., U.N. Doc. A/C.1/SR.761 (Nov. 25, 1948), at 761.

463 Paris (Dulles) to Secretary of State, NIACT DELGA 977.

the rights conferred on refugees [under Resolution 194], one of the most important is undoubtedly the return to their homes of refugees who desire it."[464] Subsequent UN resolutions on the situation in Palestine appear to adopt the same meaning of the term "return to homes," that is to say, that the refugees have a "right" to return to their homes, notwithstanding the different language used. This includes UNSC Resolution 242 calling for "a just settlement of the refugee problem" and UNGA Resolution 3236 affirming the inalienable right of the refugees to return to their homes and to recover their properties.[465] Finally, appearing to provide model language for subsequent resolutions adopted by the UN in other refugee situations, there is no indication that by referring to the "return of refugees to their homes" without reference to their "right" to do so that Member States intended to reject the principle that the refugees in other cases had a right to return to their homes under relevant sources of international law.[466]

Turning to context and purpose, the primary purpose of UNGA Resolution 194 was to facilitate a peaceful adjustment of the situation in Palestine including the problem of forced displacement arising from the 1948 war.[467] Having rejected population transfer and exchange as workable solutions to the refu-

---

464   UNCCP, *Memorandum on the Relations between the United Nations Relief and Works Agency for Palestine Refugees and the Conciliation Commission*, Working Paper No. 42, U.N. Doc. A/AC.25/W.42 (Mar. 30, 1950) (further stating that "[f]or that purpose the first paragraph of Article 11 of the resolution of 11 December 1948 lays down the three following principles: (1) Refugees wishing to return to their homes and live at peace with their neighbours should be permitted to do so at the earliest practicable date; (2) Refugees not choosing to return shall be entitled to compensation for the property they have abandoned; (3) Refugees shall be compensated for all loss of or damage to property which, under principles of international law or in equity, should be made good by the Governments or authorities responsible. Those three principles derive from general rules of law.").

465   Quigley 2007, at 59 (stating that "[r]epatriation as called for in Resolution 194 is what was contemplated by the 'just settlement' phrase in Resolution 242. The conclusion on this point reached some years ago by international law specialists Sally and Tom Mallison, authors of a major work on legal aspects of the Palestine question, is borne out by the evidence, as recounted above, of UN activity on the issue. The Mallisons noted that "[t]here are no elements of such a just settlement stated in the resolution [242] and the only authoritative principles adopted by the [UN] on this subject remain the [UNGA] resolutions"). Resolution 194 was also mentioned frequently in plenary sessions that led to the adoption of the [UNGA] resolution in the inalienable rights of the Palestinian people, including the "right of Palestinians to return to their homes and property." G.A. Res. 3236, para. 3.

466   *See*, selected resolutions above. On the practice of return, *see, e.g.,* Long; Holborn.

467   G.A. Res. 186 (S-2), para. 1(iii) (empowering the UN Mediator to "[p]romote a peaceful adjustment of the situation of Palestine"). It was the UN Mediator's specific conclusions

gee crisis arising from the struggle over Palestine, the US "consider[ed] [that a] solution Arab [displaced person] problem [was] intrinsic to negotiations and [a] settlement [of the Palestine question]."[468] Introducing his September progress report which provided the foundation for the UNGA's second peace plan for Palestine, the UN Mediator described his eleven specific conclusions as "a reasonable, equitable and workable basis for [a political] settlement [of the situation of Palestine]."[469] This included his ninth conclusion on forced displacement which called upon the UN to affirm "[t]he right of the Arab refugees to return to their homes in Jewish-controlled territory at the earliest possible date."[470] Having secured British support for the above-mentioned amended language which "[r]esolv[ed] that the refugees *wishing to return* and live at peace with their neighbours should be permitted to do so at the earliest possible date," American officials explained that they had worked with their British counterparts to "deal [with the refugee problem] in a practical manner" and that "an effort had been made to express the principles [relevant to resolving the refugee crisis] simply."[471] The primary obstacle that they faced in securing the support of a majority of the UNGA's member States for a second peace plan required resolving the dispute over general principles. More specifically, the difference related disagreements over the "balance" and "equilibrium" between Resolution 181, the UNGA's first peace plan, and the Mediator's Progress Report.[472] This involved questions relating to geopolitical interests, but it also involved legal questions relating to self-determination following the Jewish People's Council's unilateral declaration of independence and recognition of the State by the US and the Soviet Union. The dispute over general principles, in turn provided the context for the removal of the chapeau to paragraph 11, inserted on the basis of an Anglo-American compromise, that endorsed the Mediator's specific conclusion on the right to return.[473] As the co-sponsors of the amendment explained, the purpose was to make the resolution more ac-

---

as set forth in his September Progress Report, as noted above, which provided the basis for the UNGA's second peace plan delineated in Resolution 194.
468 Department of State (Marshall) to New York, No. 531.
469 Progress Report.
470 Id., at 18.
471 U.N. G.A.O.R., 3rd Sess., First Comm., 226th mtg., U.N. Doc. A/C.1/SR.226 (Dec. 3, 1948), at 909.
472 Foreign Office to Washington, No. 11292, Oct. 14, 1948; Paris (Marshall) to the Acting Secretary of State, DELGA 350, Oct. 15, 1948; Paris (Marshall) to Secretary of State, DELGA 351, Oct. 15, 1948; and, United Nations General Assembly, Paris (United Kingdom Delegation) to Foreign Office, No. 160; U.N. G.A.O.R., 3rd Sess., First Comm., 212th mtg., at 760.
473 See discussion in section V(A).

ceptable to majority of members in order to secure the required two-thirds majority necessary under the UN Charter for decisions on important matters.[474] They further clarified that the removal of all references to the UNGA's first peace plan and the Mediator's progress report "would not materially affect the resolution, since some of the points covered in those paragraphs were repeated elsewhere in the resolution."[475] In other words, the language in paragraph 11 should be interpreted as fulfilling the Mediator's specific conclusion, referenced in the paragraph's chapeau introduced as a result of Anglo-American compromise in the British delegation's second revised draft, calling upon the UN to affirm "[t]he right of the Arab refugees to return to their homes."[476]

Returning then to the question of good faith, Israeli officials as noted above initially interpreted the American amendment to paragraph 11, which "[r]esolv[ed] that the refugees wishing to return and live at peace with their neighbours should be permitted to do so at the earliest possible date," as "establishing the principle of absolute and unrestricted return."[477] Explaining two months earlier that the UN Mediator's attempt to "establish the right of Arab individuals to return to their homes in Israel" was something "very negative" for the Jewish State, Moshe Sharett, Israel's Foreign Minister, nevertheless acknowledged that "[i]t [was] not so nice or humanitarian to oppose something which [was] so basic, so simple: a person's *right to return* to the home from which he [had] been driven out by force."[478] Six months after the UNGA adopted Resolution 194, in the context of the Jewish State's second attempt to become a member of the UN, Israeli officials offered a different interpretation of the above-mentioned language in paragraph 11. The exchange between Abba Eban, Israel's Ambassador, and members of the UNGA's *Ad Hoc* Political Committee is insightful in light of the above-mentioned statements and is worth quoting at length. Noting that "[q]uestions raised in connexion with Israel's application for membership in the [UN] were being discussed in light of the compliance of Israel with the relevant resolutions of the [UNGA]",

---

474   *See* discussion in section V(A).
475   U.N. G.A.O.R., 3rd Sess., 184th plen. mtg., at 937. Lester Pearson, the Canadian representative, as noted earlier, described the chapeau which had been removed as "redundant" since "the objective it stated was adequately elaborated in the course of the paragraph which followed." Id., at 943.
476   Progress Report.
477   Paris (Dulles) to Secretary of State, NIACT DELGA 977.
478   Major Knesset Debates, 1948–1981 at 269 [emphasis added].

THE RIGHT TO RETURN   185

Eban offered his country's interpretation of paragraph 11 of Resolution 194.[479] According to the Israeli Ambassador,

> the restrictive conditions laid down by the [UNGA] itself, such as that those who wished to 'live in peace with their neighbours', should be permitted to return to their homes, clearly presupposed a situation of peace and excluded the possibility of a renewal of hostilities. Similarly, the reference [...] to the 'earliest practicable date' was also a definite acknowledgment of the fact that the restoration of normal conditions was essential to any fruitful discussion on the proportion of refugees willing and able to return.[480]

Eban nevertheless informed the Committee that his government "had not taken any irrevocable decision."[481] This was clearly not the case with the cabinet having already decided almost one year earlier to "prevent at all costs [the] return [of the refugees]" and an approved plan for "retro-active transfer" providing for the destruction and settlement of Jews in their villages to the adoption of legislation and dissemination of propaganda against their return along with the resettlement of the refugees outside the State of Israel.[482]

Meeting the following day, Per Federspiel, the representative of Denmark, asked Eban to clarify whether his remarks the previous day "[meant] that

---

479 U.N. G.A.O.R., 3rd Sess., *Ad Hoc* Political Committee, 45th mtg., at 227, U.N. Doc. A/AC.24/SR.45 (May 5, 1949).
480 Id., at 238. *See also* Jacob Tovy, Israel and the Palestinian Refugee Issue: The Formulation of a Policy, 1948–1956 26 (2014) (quoting Foreign Minister Moshe Sharett speaking to the Knesset on 15 June 1949 one year after the cabinet decided against the return of the refugees that "again they buffet us with the 11 December resolution. But even that resolution which seemingly requires the return of the refugees who want to [return], qualifies on the spot this obligation with two provisos. First of all, only peace-seekers are entitled to return. Who will examine the sincerity of the desire for peace among returning masses, and who will guarantee the stability of this desire? Secondly, [the refugees] should be returned 'at the earliest practical date'. Who decided that this possible date has already arrived?"). *See, however,* the Conciliation Commission's interpretation of the provisos. The Ambassador's interpretation of these provisos should also be read in the context of insecurity and abnormal conditions created among others by policies and practices associated with retro-active transfer and the establishment of a military government to administer the lives of Palestinians remaining within the State of Israel.
481 Id., at 239. Eban added that his government nevertheless "contended that resettlement in neighbouring areas should be considered as the main principle of solution." Id., at 240.
482 *See,* notes 36–37 and related text. A high-level meeting of Israeli officials at the end of August 1948 once again unanimously agreed "to do everything possible to prevent the return of the [Arab] refugees [to the Jewish state]," at note 94.

the Government of Israel [would] not accept the provision set forth in paragraph 11 [...] which says that the refugees who might desire to return to their homes and live at peace with their neighbours should be permitted to do so."[483] Responding that "[he] did not think that [was] a correct interpretation of what [he had] said," Eban explained that Prime Minister Ben Gurion had "[made] it quite clear that he rejected no principle laid down by the [UNGA], but that the question of return hinged upon [...] the restoration of peace [and] the extent to which the return of the refugees [was] practicable."[484] Pushing the Ambassador for additional clarification, Federspiel asked whether "[he] [was] right in understanding that the Government of Israel [would] neither accept nor reject paragraph 11 of [Resolution 194]?"[485] Appearing to deflect the question, Eban responded that "[he] should rather like to deal in concrete terms rather than words."[486] Unwilling to let the matter rest, the Danish representative "stress[ed] that this [was] a question of principle. The UNGA resolution of 11 December 1948 treated the Arab refugees as individuals having *individual rights* of resettlement in their country of origin."[487] Federspiel thus asked Eban whether the Israeli government "consider[ed] the *rights* of Arab refugees as *rights of individuals*, or as a subject of negotiation between states," which the Ambassador once again appeared to try to deflect responding that "[he] [was] less concerned with legal principles than with *facts*."[488] Eban's response was not entirely inaccurate, as noted above, from the moment the provisional government decided that the refugees would not be allowed to return to their homes, officials focused their attention on the creation of a series of *fait accomplis* that aimed to preclude their return. At the same time, as Sharett's initial response to the UN Mediator's progress report back in September 1948 and Israel's assessment of the American amendment to paragraph 11 of the British draft resolution two months later evidenced, the provisional government was clearly concerned about legal principles when it came to a solution to the refugee crisis arising from the 1948 war.

"If the Government of Israel [did] not accept the principles of *individual rights* of property and of living in their own country of refugee Arabs," Federspiel pressed Eban to explain how "the Government of Israel would reconcile that

---

483 U.N. G.A.O.R., 3rd Sess., *Ad Hoc* Political Committee, 47th mtg., U.N. Doc. A/AC.24/SR.45 (May 6, 1949), at 281–2.
484 Id., at 282.
485 Id.
486 Id.
487 Id., at 282–83 [emphasis added].
488 Id., [emphasis added].

attitude with the principle laid down in Article 1, paragraph 2 of the [UN] Charter, dealing with the principle of equal rights and self-determination of peoples?"[489] For the third time, the Ambassador tried to avoid giving a direct answer responding that "[he] [was] again being plunged into a juridical debate, of which [he] frankly [did] not feel technically qualified."[490] In a related question, Joseph Nisot, the Belgian representative, asked Eban whether Israel "would agree to cooperate subsequently with the [UNGA] in settling [...] the refugee problem" if granted membership in the UN "or whether, on the contrary, it would invoke, Article 2, paragraph 7 of the Charter which [dealt] with the domestic jurisdiction of states?"[491] Affirming that his government would "cooperate with the [UNGA] in seeking a solution [to the refugee problem]," the Ambassador once again reiterated in slightly different words that "[he] [did] not wish rashly to commit [himself] to legal theories, being perhaps the least juridically versed of any [members of the committee]."[492] Nisot nevertheless pressed Eban for additional clarification of Israel's position on Article 2, paragraph 7 in relation to the refugee situation. Opting to give what he described as his "personal opinion" in yet another apparent attempt to evade Nisot's question, the Ambassador observed that "the principle of the sovereignty of Israel [was] more applicable in the case of refugees, since it affect[ed] the territory of Israel itself, than it could be in relation to the territory of Jerusalem, which [did] not [have] the same juridical status as the territory of Israel."[493] In what

---

489   Id., [emphasis added]. U.N. Charter art. 1, para. 2 (stating that "[t]he purposes of the [UN] are: To develop friendly relations among nations based on respect for the principle of equal rights and self-determination of peoples, and to take other appropriate measures to strengthen universal peace"). Federspiel did not explain further, however, he appeared to be referring to the "doctrine of abuse of rights of third states" under which "refugee-generating states owe certain responsibilities to [refugee receiving countries]." Goodwin-Gill and McAdam, at 2.

490   Id.

491   Id., at 286. U.N. Charter art. 2, para. 7 (stating that "[t]he Organization and its Members, in pursuit of the Purposes stated in Article 1, shall act in accordance with the following Principles. Nothing contained in the present Charter shall authorize the [UN] to intervene in matters which are essentially within the domestic jurisdiction of any state or shall require the Members to submit such matters to settlement under the present Charter; but this principle shall not prejudice the application of enforcement measures under Chapter VII.").

492   Id.

493   Id., at 286–87. The comparison with Jerusalem is interesting in that it appeared to comprise acknowledgement of the international status of Jerusalem as delineated under both Resolution 181 and Resolution 194, the UNGA's first and second peace plans for Palestine.

appeared to be a response to the Danish representative's prior question, Eban added that in his view

> it would be a mistake for any of the Governments concerned to take refuge, with regard to their refugee problem, in their *legal right* to exclude people from their territories, and that it would be right for them to make a constructive effort to expedite the resettlement and rehabilitation of such numbers as are agreed upon amongst themselves, without worrying whether they are legally compelled to accept them or not.[494]

Eban's cleverly worded response suggested two things. First, the Ambassador was not entirely unversed in the juridical nature of the questions as he claimed to be, at least to the extent that he appeared to be aware of the fact that the neighbouring Arab States where the majority of the refugees had found temporary refuge were not legally obligated to grant them asylum under international law.[495] Second, while Israel's provisional government had yet to adopt legislation governing the acquisition of citizenship in the Jewish State, with Prime Minister Ben Gurion continuing to reject draft bills "fearing that any universal law that treated Arabs and Jews uniformly would enable refugees abroad to claim Israeli residency and citizenship by virtue of their prior nationality as 'Palestinians,'" Eban's response which appeared to equate the right of host States to exclude non-nationals as equivalent to Israel's refusal to allow the refugees to return implied that while a citizenship law had yet to be approved Israel had already denationalized the refugees.[496] Perhaps aware that his attempt to equate Israel's treatment of the refugees with the legal rights of Arab

---

494 Id. [emphasis added].

495 This is another issue where the situation in Palestine arising from the 1948 war appeared to influence the codification of related principles in the Universal Declaration of Human Rights. Johannes Morsink, The Universal Declaration of Human Rights: Origins, Drafting, and Intent 78 (1999) (stating that "[the] war [in Palestine] caused four separate waves of refugees, the last of which, in October and November 1948, overlapped with the discussions and votes in the Third Committee on the right to asylum. This explains why the teeth were taken out of the article as it had been proposed by the Third Session.").

496 Shira Robinson, Citizen Strangers: Palestinians and the Birth of Israel's Liberal Settler State 71 (2013). *See also* Masalha 1992, at 176 (stating that "JAE meeting in early November 1947, consensus denying citizenship to as many Arabs as possible, Ben Gurion, as Arab citizens they could be expelled for disloyalty, but as Israeli citizens only imprisoned, better then to expel them"). *See also* Anat Leibler and Daniel Breslau, *The Uncounted: Citizenship and Exclusion in the Israeli Census of 1948*, 28 Eth. & Rac. Stud. 880, 890–92 (2005) (stating that "[i]f the departure of Arab residents could be defined as a political act of renunciation, and an abandonment of property, the exclusion of an ethnic minority could be legitimated in terms of international norms regarding citizenship rights. The presence or absence

host States was little more than a ruse, Eban added that "[t]here [were] already enough obstacles in the way of solving this problem without there being any need to invoke legal rights to make the solution even more complicated."[497]

Responding to Per Federspiel's question relating to Article 2, paragraph 7 of the UN Charter and Israel's position on the refugee situation which was implicit in his above response to the Belgian representative the previous day, Eban drew upon one element of the provisional government's position that Moshe Sharett had already made clear in his response to the UN Mediator and in his closing remarks to the First Committee during the drafting of Resolution 194. According to the Ambassador, the above article "refer[ed] to the relations between groups, that is, either nations or peoples, and does not affect the duty of Governments in the rehabilitation of individual refugees."[498] This interpretation, in turn, enabled Eban to highlight another element of Israel's approach to the refugee situation that Foreign Minister Sharett had also made clear once the cabinet had decided against the return of the refugees back in June during the first truce of the 1948 war, namely, population exchange and transfer.[499] Similar to arguments made by high-ranking Israeli officials over the previous year, Eban argued that "[t]here [were] many instances of recent international history, both in Europe and in Asia, when the rehabilitation of refugees took place not on the basis of individual rights, but by agreements between the Governments concerned."[500] This included the minority exchange between Greece and Turkey during the interwar period, which, as noted earlier, Israeli officials would continue to raise as a model for resolving the Palestinian refugee situation in the years following the 1948 war.[501] While the initial years after the Second World War were characterized by a "Merry-Go-Round of demographic engineering," including the forced transfer of millions of ethnic Germans agreed to by Allied Powers at Potsdam, Eban could not but have been aware of the fact, despite his pleadings about lack of juridical knowledge, that international law had since moved on with Jews

---

of Palestinian Arabs within the borders of Israel was thereby defined as an acceptance or rejection of citizenship.").

497 Id.
498 U.N. G.A.O.R., 3rd Sess., *Ad Hoc* Political Committee, 48th mtg., U.N. Doc. A/C.1/SR.48 (May 7, 1948), at 301.
499 *See* note 38 and related text.
500 U.N. G.A.O.R., 3rd Sess., *Ad Hoc* Political Committee, 48th mtg., at 301.
501 *See* note 38 and related text. *See also* Christa Meindersma, *Population Exchanges: International Law and Practice – Part I*, 9 Int'l. J. Refugee. L. 335, 350 (1997) (stating that "70 years ago there were strong doubts about the compatibility of the Greek Turkish exchange with international law and treatment of minorities").

being one of the principle beneficiaries.[502] Two years to the day before the UNGA's adoption of Resolution 194, as noted earlier, member States affirmed that among the legal principles recognized by the Charter of the Nuremberg Tribunal the forced transfer of population was a crime against humanity.[503] It was the 1948 war in Palestine, in particular, the appeal to the warring sides by the International Committee of the Red Cross for the protection of women, children, and the elderly, that contributed to enhanced civilian protections under the Fourth Geneva Convention which codified the deportation of civilians as a war crime.[504] Meeting on 13 August, the day after delegates adopted by the above Convention, Rifki Zorlu, the Turkish representative to the Conciliation Commission reported that Israeli officials had explained that in the event that the government would allow the entry of refugees into the country "they would be treated as if they were new immigrants and would be settled according to the Government's economic plans."[505] Here, finally, was the answer to the Belgian representative's question about whether Israel would rely on the principle of sovereign equality and its corollary of non-intervention in the domestic affairs of States in order to bar Palestinian refugees from returning to their homes inside the Jewish State. Addressing the unresolved refugee situation a year later in the UNGA's *Ad Hoc* Political Committee, where representatives of Member States would debate the refugee in subsequent years, Abba Eban also appeared to answer at last the Danish representative's initial question as to whether Israel accepted the individual right of refugees to return to their homes, villages and towns of origin. No longer concerned, it seemed, about the implication of refusing to implement what the American representative to the UNGA, Philip Jessup, described as a "generally recognized principle" which Israeli officials themselves had characterized with reference to Resolution 194 as an "absolute" right, Eban was forthright, Israel "could not agree to give any special legal validity to paragraph 11."[506] In sum, light of all the above discussion this was hardly an interpretation of good faith.

---

502   De Zayas, at paras. 7 and 19 (stating that "the legality of the Potsdam Protocol under international law as well as the subsequent forced population transfer were vigorously contested at the time" and that "population transfers practised by the National Socialist authorities during World War II were condemned in the Nuremberg judgment as 'war crimes' and as 'crimes against humanity'").
503   G.A. Res. 96. *See also* Mélanie Jacques, Armed Conflict and Forced Displacement: The Protection of Refugees and Displaced Persons Under International Humanitarian Law 23–5 (2008).
504   *See* Abu Sitta and Rempel, and related text.
505   UNCCP, Summary Record, 89th mtg., U.N. Doc. A/AC.25/SR.89 (Aug. 13, 1949).
506   U.N. G.A.O.R., *Ad Hoc* Political Committee, 36th mtg., U.N. Doc. A/AC.38/SR.36 (Nov. 7, 1950). At 216.

Resolution 194 – Draft Language on Refugees

United Kingdom, Suggested Heads of Assembly Resolution on Palestine, July 29, 1948
Recommends that
(6) the Mediator should give particular and urgent attention to the following problems:

(a) Insofar as this is not being dealt with by specialized organs of the United Nations, the question of Jewish and Arab refugees. The Mediator should examine how far it will be possible for these refugees to be settled in Palestine and to the extent that this is not possible, to make recommendations in conjunction with the appropriate organ of the United Nations for their disposal elsewhere.

United Kingdom, Palestine: Draft Resolution, Sept. 28, 1948
Annex
The Palestinian refugees displaced from their homes since the 29th November 1947 shall be entitled to return to their homes at the earliest possible date. The United Nations Conciliation Commission shall supervise and assist their repatriation, resettlement and economic and social rehabilitation, and the payment of adequate compensation for the property of those choosing not to return.

United States, Draft Resolution, Sept. 29, 1948
determines that the Palestinian refugees displaced from their homes since November 29th 1947 shall be entitled to return to their homes at the earliest possible date; and that the Palestine Conciliation Commission shall establish machinery to supervise and assist their repatriation, resettlement and economic and social rehabilitation, and shall arrange for the payment of adequate compensation for the property of those choosing not to return;

Ralph Bunche files, Draft Resolution, no date
11. RECOMMENDS fully the right of refugees form the conflict in Palestine to return to their homes at the earliest possible date and to be adequately compensated for any losses suffered by them as a result of confiscation or destruction of property not resulting from military necessity, and INSTRUCTS the Conciliation Commission to assist and supervise the repatriation of such refugees as may choose to exercise this right and their resettlement.

12. RECOGNIZES that some refugees may not exercise the right to return to their former homes, and therefore INSTRUCTS the Conciliation Commission

to establish as an urgent measure appropriate machinery to study the problem and to take such action as it may deem appropriate to facilitate the resettlement of refugees elsewhere, and to supervise the payment of adequate compensation for the property of those choosing not to return to their homes.

Ralph Bunche files, Second Draft Resolution, no date
11. RECOMMENDS fully the right of refugees form the conflict in Palestine to return to their homes at the earliest possible date and to be adequately compensated for any losses suffered by them as a result of confiscation or destruction of property not resulting from military necessity, and INSTRUCTS the Conciliation Commission to assist and supervise the repatriation of such refugees as may choose to exercise this right and their resettlement.

12. RECOGNIZES that some refugees may not exercise the right to return to their former homes, and therefore INSTRUCTS the Conciliation Commission to establish as an urgent measure appropriate machinery to study the problem and to take such action as it may deem appropriate to facilitate the resettlement of refugees elsewhere, and to supervise the payment of adequate compensation for the property of those choosing not to return to their homes.

Provisional Draft of Palestine Resolution for Committee I, Oct. 2, 1948
Determines that the Palestinian refugees displaced from their homes since November 29, 1947 shall be entitled to return to their homes at the earliest possible date; and that the Palestine Conciliation Commission shall establish machinery to supervise and assist their repatriation, resettlement and economic and social rehabilitation, and shall arrange for the payment of adequate compensation for the property of those choosing not to return;

DELGA 220, Draft Resolution, Oct. 6, 1948
Determines that the Palestinian refugees displaced from their homes since November 29, 1947, shall be entitled to return to their homes at the earliest possible date; and that the Palestine Conciliation Commission shall establish machinery to supervise and assist their repatriation, resettlement and economic and social rehabilitation, and shall arrange for the payment of adequate compensation for the property of those choosing not to return;

DELGA 284, Draft Resolution, Oct. 11, 1948
11. Recognizes fully the right of refugees from the conflict in Palestine to return to their homes at the earliest possible date and to be adequately compensated for any losses suffered by them as a result of confiscation or destruction of

property not resulting from military necessity, and instructs the Conciliation Commission to assist and supervise the repatriation of such refugees as may choose to exercise this right, and their resettlement;

12. Recognizes that for various reasons numbers of refugees may not exercise the right to return to their former homes, and therefore instructs the Conciliation Commission to establish as urgent measures appropriate machinery to study the problem and to take such action as it may deem appropriate to facilitate the resettlement of refugees elsewhere, and to supervise the payment of adequate compensation for the property of those choosing not to return to their homes;

DELGA 318, Draft Resolution, Oct. 13, 1948
11. Recognizes fully the right of refugees from the conflict in Palestine to return to their homes at the earliest possible date and to be adequately compensated for any losses suffered by them as a result of confiscation or destruction of property not resulting from military necessity, and instructs the Conciliation Commission to assist and supervise the repatriation of such refugees as may choose to exercise this right, and their resettlement;

12. Recognizes that for various reasons numbers of refugees may not exercise the right to return to their former homes, and therefore instructs the Conciliation Commission to establish as urgent measures appropriate machinery to study the problem and to take such action as it may deem appropriate to facilitate the resettlement of refugees elsewhere, and to supervise the payment of adequate compensation for the property of those choosing not to return to their homes;

DELGA 351, Draft Resolution, Oct. 16, 1948
Twelve. Recognizes the right of the Arab refugees to return to their homes in Jewish-controlled territory at the earliest possible date; and the right of adequate compensation for the property of those choosing not to return and for property which has been lost as a result of pillage or confiscation or of destruction not resulting from military necessity; and instructs the conciliation commission to facilitate the repatriation, resettlement, and economic and social rehabilitation of the Arab refugees and the payment of compensation;

United Kingdom, Draft Resolution, UN Doc. A/C.1/394, Nov. 18, 1948
11. ENDORSES the principle stated in Part I, Section V, Paragraph 7 of the Mediator's Report and RESOLVES that the Arab refugees should be permitted

to return to their homes at the earliest possible date and that adequate compensation should be paid for the property of those choosing not to return and for property which has been lost as a result of pillage, confiscation or of destruction; and INSTRUCTS the Conciliation Commission to facilitate the repatriation, resettlement, and economic and social rehabilitation of the Arab refugees and the payment of compensation;

Australia, Draft Resolution, UN Doc. A/C.1/396, Nov. 23, 1948
Requests the Security Council to give sympathetic consideration to an application for the admission of the State of Israel to the United Nations if and when such application will be submitted establishes a Conciliation Commission for Palestine composed of not more than five members with the following functions:

(5) To call into consultation all those organized agencies of the United Nations which may assist in working out plans both for the resettlement of Palestinian and displaced persons and for their repatriation where feasible in the areas from which they have come;

United States of America: Amendment to the Draft Resolution of the United Kingdom (Document A/C.1/394), UN Doc. A/C.1/397, Nov. 23, 1948
D. Delete numbered paragraph eleven and substitute the following paragraph, numbered as indicated:

"10. RESOLVES that the Arab refugees wishing to return to their homes and live at peace with their neighbors should be permitted to do so at the earliest possible date and that adequate compensation should be paid for the property of those choosing not to return; and INSTRUCTS the Conciliation Commission to facilitate the repatriation, resettlement, and economic and social rehabilitation of the Arab refugees and the payment of compensation;"

United Kingdom, Revised Draft Resolution, UN Doc. A/C.1/394/Rev.1, Nov. 24, 1948
10. ENDORSES the principle stated in Part I, Section V, Paragraph 7 of the Mediator's Report and RESOLVES that the Arab refugees should be permitted to return to their homes at the earliest possible date and that adequate compensation should be paid for the property of those choosing not to return and for property which has been lost as a result of pillage, confiscation or of destruction; and INSTRUCTS the Conciliation Commission to facilitate the repatriation, resettlement, and economic and social rehabilitation of the Arab

refugees and the payment of compensation, and to enter into contact with the Director of the United Nations Relief for Palestine Refugees;

Colombia, Draft Resolution, UN Doc. A/C.1/399, Nov. 24, 1948
10. RESOLVES that the Arab refugees wishing to return to their homes and live at peace with their neighbors should be permitted to do so at the earliest possible date and that adequate compensation should be paid for the property of those choosing not to return; and INSTRUCTS the Conciliation Commission to facilitate the repatriation, resettlement, and economic and social rehabilitation of the Arab refugees and the payment of compensation;

Guatemala: Amendment to the United States amendment (Document A/C.1/397) to the draft resolution of the United Kingdom (Document A/C.1/394), UN Doc. A/C.1/398, Nov. 24, 1948
6. Paragraph 10: insert the following after: "... at the earliest possible date:"

"... after the proclamation of peace between the contending parties in Palestine, including the Arab States"

Poland, Draft Resolution, UN Doc. A/C.1/400, Nov. 25, 1948
ESTABLISHES a Commission of Conciliation for Palestine composed of representatives of ... (five states), with the following functions:

(4) To call into consultation all those organs and agencies of the United Nations which may assist in working out plans both for the resettlement of Palestinian refugees and displaced persons and for their repatriation where feasible in the areas from which they have come;

United States of America: Amendment to the Draft Resolution of the United Kingdom (Document A/C.1/394/Rev.1), UN Doc. A/C.1/397/Rev.1, Nov. 25, 1948
D. Delete numbered paragraph 10 and substitute the following:

"10. RESOLVES that the Arab refugees wishing to return to their homes and live at peace with their neighbors should be permitted to do so at the earliest possible date and that adequate compensation should be paid for the property of those choosing not to return; and INSTRUCTS the Conciliation Commission to facilitate the repatriation, resettlement, and economic and social rehabilitation of the Arab refugees and the payment of compensation;"

Guatemala: Revised amendments to the United States revised amendments (A/C.1/397/Rev.1) to the revised draft resolution of the United Kingdom (A/C.1/394/Rev.1), UN Doc. A/C.1/394/Rev.1, Nov. 27, 1948
6. Delete paragraph 10 and replace it with the following:

"10. RESOLVES that the Arab refugees wishing to return to their homes and live at peace with their neighbours should be permitted to do so at the earliest possible date after the proclamation of peace between the contending parties in Palestine, including the Arab States, and that adequate compensation should be paid for the property of those choosing not to return; and INSTRUCTS the Conciliation Commission to use its good offices to facilitate the repatriation, resettlement, and economic and social rehabilitation of the Arab refugees and the payment of compensation;"

United States, Composite Draft Resolution, DELGA 976, Nov. 27, 1948
4(f) Refugees. The GA considers that the refugees wishing to return to their homes and live at peace with their neighbours should be permitted to do so at the earliest possible date, and that adequate compensation should be paid for the property of those choosing not to return and for property which has been lost as a result of pillage, expropriation or wanton destruction, subject to principle and procedures to be established by the conciliation commission pursuant to agreement between the governments and authorities concerned. The GA instructs the conciliation commission to facilitate the repatriation, resettlement and economic and social rehabilitation of the refugees and the payment of compensation and to maintain close contact with the Director of the United Nations Relief for Palestine Refugees.

United Kingdom, Second Revised Draft Resolution, UN Doc. A/C.1/394/Rev. 2, Nov. 30, 1948
11. ENDORSES the conclusions stated in Part I, Section VIII, paragraph 4(I) of the Progress Report of the United Nations Mediator in Palestine, and

RESOLVES that the refugees wishing to return to their homes and live at peace with their neighbors should be permitted to do so at the earliest possible date, and that compensation should be paid for the property of those choosing not to return and for loss of damage to property which under principles of international law or in equity should be made good by the governments or authorities responsible; and

INSTRUCTS the Conciliation Commission to facilitate the repatriation, resettlement and economic and social rehabilitation of the refugees and the payment of compensation and to maintain close relations with the Director of the United Nations Relief for Palestine Refugees;

Australia: Amendment to the second revised draft resolution of the United Kingdom (A/C.1/394/Rev.2), UN Doc. A/C.1/394/Rev.2, Dec. 1, 1948
2. Delete paragraph 2 and insert the following paragraph:

"Establishes a Commission of Conciliation for Palestine composed of not more than five members, with the following functions:

"(5) To call into consultation all those organs and agencies of the United Nations which may assist in working out plans both for the resettlement of Palestinian refugees and displaced persons and for their repatriation where feasible in the areas from which they have come;

Guatemala: Revised amendment to the Second Revised Draft Resolution of the United Kingdom (A/C.1/394/Rev.2), UN Doc. A/C.1/394/Rev. 2, Dec. 1, 1948
5. Delete paragraph 11 and replace it with the following:

"11. RESOLVES that the Arab refugees wishing to return to their homes and live at peace with their neighbors should be permitted to do so at the earliest possible date after the proclamation of peace between the contending parties in Palestine, including the Arab States, and that adequate compensation should be paid for the property of those choosing not to return; and INSTRUCTS the Conciliation Commission to use its good offices to facilitate the repatriation, resettlement, and economic and social rehabilitation of the Arab refugees and the payment of compensation;"

Australia, Brazil, Canada, China, Colombia, France and New Zealand: Amendments to the draft resolution proposed by the First Committee, UN Doc. A/789, Dec. 9, 1948
6. Delete in paragraph 11 the following words:

"ENDORSES the conclusions stated in part one, section VIII, paragraph 4(i), of the Progress Report of the United Nations Mediator in Palestine;"

PART 2

Book Review

∴

Legal Structure, Practices, and Discourse in the Middle East

Mazen Masri, *The Dynamics of Exclusionary Constitutionalism: Israel as a Jewish and Democratic State* (2017)

Nimer Sultany, *Law and Revolution: Legitimacy and Constitutionalism after the Arab Spring* (2017)

Contents

I The Importance of Legality in the Analysis of Power
II Sultany's and Masri's Critical Legal Theory
III Constitutionalism as a Contextualized Theory of Practices
IV Law: Between Reflection of and Intervention in the Socio-Political Reality
V Conclusion

Mazen Masri's *"The Dynamics of Exclusionary Constitutionalism"* and Nimer Sultany's *"Law and Revolution"* tell us the most recent story of constitutionalism in the Middle East. Sultany takes on a number of Arab countries after the revolutions in 2011, and Masri addresses constitutional developments in Israel. They both know their objects in a somehow intimate way, as they are both Palestinian citizens of Israel, they are both legal scholars trained abroad and working in Europe and, by reading their books together, one also understands that they not only know each other but that they share a certain political history, intellectual background, and theoretical and methodological approaches. Not surprisingly, their respective books, their theoretical and methodological choices, their discoveries, and some of their conclusions present striking similarities.

It is along these commonalities that I intend to analyze their contributions, which should illustrate the main conclusions of my reading of their books: the idea that constitutionalism in Arab countries and in Israel – despite being arenas of divergences, contestation, struggle, and contradictory dynamics – tend to exclude certain political or ethnic groups from the national political fabric, favor anti-democratic practices, and facilitate the reproduction and legitimization of this status quo. From a contextualized, practice centered perspective – which is what Sultany and Masri offer – Israeli and Arab constitutionalism do not fit the binary relation through which they are frequently portrayed (*i.e.* modern-traditional, democratic-authoritarian); they are actually connected by similar dynamics, they can be seen as the two sides of a Janus-faced coin of imperial and colonial domination, and that future scholarship should put them in a position to more seriously explore these parallels, and to try to unveil the theoretical-political implications of their family resemblances, that is, their common traits.

I The Importance of Legality in the Analysis of Power

Firstly, Sultany's *Law and Revolution* and Masri's *The Dynamics of Exclusionary Constitutionalism* remind us of the central importance of legal structures and practices in the study of power. Perhaps inspired by a reductionist reading of Foucault, critical theory's analysis of power in general, including in the Middle East, has in recent decades privileged the study of other cultural and societal "disciplinary" mechanisms over state and law. Foucault's invitation to "cut off the head of the king" in political theory (the need to study power as not localized in the state and the law but, rather, circulating in the micromorph mechanisms of disciplinary power, power in its "extremities," in its "infinitesimal" non-sovereign forms), has been read as suggesting that state and law have lost their explanatory capacities regarding power dynamics.

In contrast, *The Dynamics of Exclusionary Constitutionalism* and *Law and Revolution* reintroduce one of Foucault's central theses into the discussion of power in the Middle East: the intertwinement of legal structures, processes, and practices on the one hand, with disciplinary power mechanisms on the other. Sultany and Masri's books are two fascinating illustrations of these imbrications, and the role of law and its complex, multiple, and contingent socio-political impact. Masri alerts us to this gap in critical theory: "Despite the marked increase in academic research that uses settler-colonialism [and other critical categories] to inform analysis about the Israeli state and society [...] lawyers and law as a discipline are lagging behind."[1] This is exactly one

---

[1] Mazen Masri, The Dynamics of Exclusionary Constitutionalism: Israel as a Jewish and Democratic State 22 (2017) [*hereinafter* Masri].

of the objectives that Sultany attributes to *Law and Revolution* from the very introduction of the book: to highlight the central role of law in the "political upheavals in the Arab world" whose "significance transcends the region as it provides a laboratory for examining scholarly ideas about revolutions, legitimacy, legality, constitutions, and more."[2]

In their contributions, Masri and Sultany show us how legal dispositive and constitutional structures and practices are not mere symbolic complements of power, epiphenomena of the political re-definition of Arab States after the revolutions of 2011, or of the construction of the ethno-national state of Israel. They develop a socio-legal analysis and a political history that puts legal dispositive and constitutional structure and practices at the very center of political divergences, negotiations and conflict, highlighting the fact that structures of legal authority and the creation of power hierarchies and dynamics are inextricably intertwined.

II   Sultany's and Masri's Critical Legal Theory

The gap in the legal literature that I refer to does not imply that legal scholars have been silent regarding constitutional developments after 2011 in Arab countries and in Israel. Rather, my point is that their analyses frequently hover around positivist or institutionalist perspectives that, though important, are insufficient and sometimes misleading. They tend to approach constitutional orders in light of a set of normative principles of political theory (*i.e.* separation of power, rule of law, protection of rights, etc.) against which the constitutional texts are evaluated. From this perspective – and depending on who writes about what – the constitutional texts appear suitable or unsuitable, in harmony or contradicting the normative assumptions of good governance theory, democratic and legitimate or exposing the gap between law and fact, that is, between democratization efforts and authoritarian status quo.

The *Dynamics of Exclusionary Constitutionalism* and *Law and Revolution* propose an alternative approach, that make a number of contributions in the field of critical legal theory: first, these works look at law in general and constitutional law in particular as social and historical formations whose intelligibility also depend on two elements that are often ignored – the historical and socio-political context in which constitutional orders emerge, and

---

2   Nimer Sultany, Law and Revolution: Legitimacy and Constitutionalism After the Arab Spring XXV (2017) [*hereinafter* Sultany].

legal-constitutional practices; second, they strongly highlight the mutually constitutive nature of the socio-political and the legal fields and; third, theirs is a perspective from which legal inconsistencies and indeterminacy are no longer understood as mere institutional inadequacy that needs reform but, rather, as being essential to the process of normative production.

III   Constitutionalism as a Contextualized Theory of Practices

Law and Revolution and *The Dynamics of Exclusionary Constitutionalism* propose an approach to constitutionalism whose basic assumption is that the analysis of a constitutional regime cannot be limited to a study of constitutional text. It requires an inquiry into the historical and socio-political context in which that text emerges, and the political and legal-constitutional practice by which it is defined.

Sultany sketches a political history of Arab constitutionalism from the Ottoman era to the Arab revolutions of 2011, one that reads Arab constitutional regimes through the socio-political conditions and legal practices of the Ottoman Empire, European colonial rule, Arab nationalism, the postcolonial regimes, and pre- and post-2011 revolutions. This ambitious project divides recent Arab constitutional experiences into two types: "revolutionary constitution-making" where he situates Egypt, Tunisia, and Libya, and "reformist constitution-making" in which he analyses the cases of Morocco, Jordan, Bahrain, Oman, and Algeria.

This socio-political history shows first, that "[c]onstitutional normativity cannot be deduced simply from the textual reading of the constitutional document [...] a proper understanding avoids the decontextualization of these constitutions and rejects a formalist understanding that would portray their weakness as inherent to the document and simply because of the 'strategic', 'ideological', 'instrumental' or 'temporary' design of the rulers."[3] Second, it shows that "the focus of a realistic constitutional theory should be on constitutional practice"[4] because, for Sultany, "it is insufficient [...] to focus on formal declarations (law-in-the-books) and ignore the law-in-action [...] judges make the law and do not mechanically apply it."[5] From this perspective, the book argues: that the binary of modern/traditional to capture the relation between

---

3 Sultany, at 95.
4 Id., at 69.
5 Id., at 73.

colonial law and native law is flawed; that the opposition continuity/rupture used to unpack the evolution from colonial rule to the post-independence Arab States, and the pre- and post-2011 constitutional developments, misrepresent the relation between law and revolution; and that the dichotomy between sovereign, unfettered constituent power and necessary constitutional limits "mystifies legal and constitutional practices in revolutionary moments."[6]

Early in his introduction, Masri explicitly adopts the same perspective: "[l]aw in general, and constitutional law in particular, cannot be understood in isolation from the political context."[7] He adds that within the Israeli political context, of central importance is Israel's settler-colonial nature: "[...] in order to understand many features of Israeli constitutionalism, especially (but not exclusively) the relationship between the state and Palestinians who are also Israeli citizens, we need to analyze the constitutional order through the lens of settler-colonialism."[8] The idea of law-in-action is also central to Masri's work: "[a]n examination of the ways the constitution is shaped and amended, and how legislation is enacted, interpreted and reviewed by courts, is in the essence an examination of the constitution in action."[9] Legal practice, that is, courts' interpretation of the law is central because "the process of interpretation gives meaning to the [legal] text."[10]

This is exactly what Masri offers, a socially and politically contextualized analysis of Israeli constitutional practices working to reconcile the two patently contradictory tenets of Israel's definition of itself as a "Jewish and democratic state." It starts with the Israeli declaration of 'independence,' its colonial framing, and the Israeli Supreme Court's upgrading of its legal status as central to the State's constitutional regime. It shows how this foundational document transformed a settler community "[...] into a collective of citizens in a state,"[11] and declared Israel the State not of its citizens but of the Jewish people. It finally explains how Israeli legislation (the citizenship law, the law of return, basic law of the Knesset, and other laws), court decisions (interpreting the law and exercising judicial review) and political arrangements (*i.e.* the Knesset rules of procedure and parliamentary dynamics), have articulated these contradictory principles of Israel as a democratic state but of the Jewish people only, within a practice that sacrifices democracy to secure its Jewishness.

6   Id., at xxxii.
7   Masri, at 15.
8   Id., at 21.
9   Id., at 24.
10 Id., at 181.
11 Masri, at 61.

IV Law: Between Reflection of and Intervention in the Socio-Political Reality

If, for Sultany and Masri, law cannot be extricated from its context, it is because the co-constitutive nature of the socio-political and the legal fields is central to their legal-constitutional theory. That fundamentally means two things.

First, law is a social and historical product, and not only norms explainable by formal-abstract procedures. As such, law is also a central "battlefield" of political struggle – that is, that the fight for political domination (in the Arab world, Israel or elsewhere) is never confined only to the streets, elite structures or elections, but rather that it is enacted over multiple fields, and the legal field is one of them. Changes taking place in the social and political realm are often translated into legal-constitutional strategies and reflected in legal structures. It is in this sense that the constitutional order can be understood as a sort of "metaphoric representation" of its social and political context.

Second, that – as Griffiths puts it – juridical phenomena "not only reflect but also produce and reinforce social processes."[12] Therefore, explaining the production of the law through social and political forces is only one part of Masri's and Sultany's analysis. The other part consists in highlighting the performative role of law, what Bourdieu refers to as the "force of law."[13] its capacity to create reality.[14] This is exactly why political divergences regarding the revolution, the limits of constituent power, or the negotiation over distribution of powers, for instance, systematically turned into conflicts over the nature and structure of political authority. Revolutionaries and counter-revolutionaries knew that they were not just struggling for symbolic markers, but over a central element of the very articulation of a new structure of power relations.

In chapter 2 of *The Dynamics of Exclusionary Constitutionalism* Masri discusses the different conceptions in play within the Israeli social and political spectrum regarding the question – critical to any constitutional order or debate on democracy – of "who is included in the People"?[15] In the Israeli settler-colonial context, they range from the ultra-nationalist approach for which only Jews can be citizens of Israel – where non-Jews are considered temporary

---

12   Anne M.O. Griffiths, *Academic Narratives: Models and Methods in the Search for Meanings*, in Moore Sally Falk, *Law and Anthropology: A Reader* 230 (2005).
13   Pierre Bourdieu, The Force of Law: Toward a Sociology of the Juridical Field, 38 *Hastings L.J.* 85 (1987).
14   Pierre Bourdieu, Raisons pratiques. Sur la théorie de l'action 125 (Editions du Seuil, 1994).
15   Masri, at 25.

residents, "lodgers not owners,"[16] a threat to the Jewishness of the state, and that proposes the forcible deportation of Palestinians – to the various manifestations of what is commonly referred to as 'liberal Zionism.' The first version of 'liberal Zionism' is what Masri calls the "nationalists of the Liberal nationalists"[17] for whom the "Jewish element is stronger than the weight they attach to liberal values"[18] but that, in an extraordinary twist of political theory, do not see, or want to see it, as contradictory with democratic principles. They understand the priority of the Jewishness of the State as a question of human rights, and "part of [Israel's] democratic character [because it] reflects the wishes of the majority of the population."[19] A second version of 'liberal Zionism' is what Masri calls "the pragmatists of the liberal nationalists" (including former Chief Justice of the Israeli Supreme Court, Aharon Barak), where the Jewish and democratic values have a normative constitutional status that is above the law"[20] and that, like any other tension between constitutional principles, they can and should be balanced and reconciled. A third version of 'liberal Zionism' is what Masri calls "the liberals of the liberal nationalists," who "take liberalism more seriously" but are still nationalists – either by prioritizing national-ethno-cultural self-determination within a State that cannot be neutral to identity and naturally owes a preferential treatment to the ethno-national majority, or by accepting a multi-national State but where Palestinian self-determination would be limited based on security concerns.[21]

From there, Masri's book goes on to show how the exclusionary character of the Israeli colonial context and the justificatory theories that it produces are mirrored in the legal field, both in the legislation and the courts' interpretation of it. He explains how the dissolution, exclusion, and control of the native community – which is inherent to any settler-colonial society – are articulated by the Israeli State not in spite of the law, but through it. The articulation of settler-colonial parameters is made possible through the crystallization into law of particular social and political realities. Chapter 3 analyses the creation of the polity, "The People" of Israel in the "Declaration of Independence," and how colonial domination is constitutionally normalized as a right and an imperative for Jewish self-determination. In chapters 4 and 5, Masri explores a number of performative legal mechanisms: the role of citizenship, immigration,

16   Id., at 26.
17   Id., at 28.
18   Id., at 28.
19   Id., at 27–28.
20   Id., at 35.
21   Id., at 40–41.

and residence laws and practices in the elimination, dissolution, and exclusion of the Palestinian native; the role of the "Law of Return" in the engineering of a settler nation into a State citizenry whose contours are defined by the exclusion of the native; and the consolidation of the settler society's dominance in terms of the State's identity and population numbers. Chapter 6 analyses the role of the electoral system and the Knesset basic law in constructing the limits and exclusions imposed upon the Palestinian minority's political representation and self-determination. In Masri's words, they "eliminate the indigenous population as a political unit [and] maintain its members as individuals with diluted political demands," limiting political representation "to those who agree with principles of Zionism and do not wish to challenge them."[22] Finally, chapter 7 describes the role of the "Jewish and democratic" constitutional self-definition of the Israeli State in consolidating Jewish dominance in the constitutional and law-making process, and other legislation. This entire analysis of the performative powers of law and legal practices is one of the most important contributions of Masri's work. He does not satisfy himself with naming colonialism; he offers a convincing explanation of how it actually works from a legal perspective.

Sultany's *Law and Revolution*, in turn, also embraces this perspective. According to him, "the constitutional struggle for rights, self-rule, and accountable government shapes and, at the same time, is shaped by socio-political conditions."[23] This dialectic relation emerges because "constitutions [operate] as a site for political and legal contestation in which differently situated parties accepted them for different reasons, placed in them conflicting hopes, and used them in a variety of ways."[24] Their political views are constantly translated into legal strategies, either legislative or interpretive. Since for Sultany "constitutions [are] embedded in social, political, and intellectual process,"[25] it is not surprising that what his book describes in the following chapters, among other things, is precisely this mirroring effect: "[t]he struggle between different visions over the formation of a new socio-political order,"[26] and how the different political contexts of the countries he analyses were reflected in both colonial and post-independence constitutional regimes, on the one hand,

---

22   Id., at 151.
23   Sultany, at 63–64.
24   Id., at 38.
25   Id., at 45.
26   Id., at xxvi.

and revolutionary and reformist legal-constitutional making after 2011, on the other hand.

In chapters 2 and 3, Sultany looks at Arab constitutions during colonial rule and post-independence through the concept of legitimacy. His analysis shows that "constitutional deficiencies of post-colonial states differ from their colonial predecessors only in degree"[27] and that "Arab constitutions [during colonial rule and in post-independence states as well] shared similar deficiencies of normative weakness, democratic exclusion, and incomplete sovereignty,"[28] reflecting in different ways their respective contexts. Chapter 4 explores the revolutions of 2011 and how they destabilized a number of concepts central to political theory: first, the relationship between revolution and legitimacy, because the 2011 revolutions, being the popular reaction to a lack of legitimacy, created other "legitimation deficits that resemble the pre-revolutionary deficits,"[29] second, the realities of the 2011 Arab revolutions problematize the very concept of revolution as a rupture, a new beginning because revolutions engender their own negation, the counter-revolution, and also produce continuities reflecting the play of political forces during the revolutionary moment.

The remaining chapters of Sultany's book look at post-2011 constitutional regimes through the notions of continuity/rupture, legal contradictions, and popular sovereignty. Notwithstanding the unconvincing analysis of the Egyptian constitutional crisis followed by the 3 February 2013 counterrevolutionary coup d'état, these chapters explain well how "despite the revolutionary upheavals, the judges of Egypt and Tunisia [but not only] generally maintained institutional continuity that hampered judicial reform, legal continuity that thwarted holding former regime officials accountable, and constitutional continuity that obstructed political re-constitution."[30] Since the revolutions did not fundamentally change the social and political forces at play, post-revolutionary constitutional regimes progressively re-asserted the status quo. In this process law and legal practices had an important performative role. This was manifest in at least four ways:

First, the inconsistencies and indeterminacy – which are proper to law and can "make it play in one way or another" – and the fact that "the judiciary that interprets and applies the law is part of the very social and political

---

27 Id., at 79.
28 Id., at 96.
29 Id., at 127.
30 Id., at xxvii.

conflicts it is supposed to resolve"[31] determine what law can render possible. Or, in Sultany's words, inconsistencies and indeterminacy can make of law an instrument of expression of the revolution but also the "revolution's enemy."[32] For instance, the author shows how the legal principle of "judicial independence," which was one revolutionary demand, could also be used to prevent judicial reform after the revolution (by denouncing it as an undue intervention in judiciary power) and help consolidate the status quo. The negation of inconsistencies and indeterminacy as an essential part of law, that is, the argument that law is coherent and requires the judges to decide in the way they do, characteristic of positivist legalism, obfuscates the political responsibility of judges by assuming that they only and mechanically apply the law. Sultany says "[l]egalism, whether deployed by the judges or their critics, reproduce the false rigid distinction between law and politics [these inconsistencies and indeterminacy] are deep seated because they are intertwined with competing conceptions of the community."[33] Second, according to Sultany, legal logic and practices tend to reduce "political injustice and tyranny to notions of [individual] criminality,"[34] making impossible the judgment of a decades-regime of oppression and dispossession. Third, another important element that Sultany's book foregrounds is the "ability of the old regime's bureaucracy (such as the police, prosecution, and the judiciary) to sabotage ordinary trials."[35] Fourth, and more crucially, courts and legal practices (in Egypt for instance) played a central role in redefining the very concept of "popular sovereignty" in several ways. One way was by opposing it to individual rights. While "rhetorically the SCC [Egyptian Supreme Constitutional Court] argued that political rights and popular sovereignty were symbiotic, it effectively deployed political rights to constrain popular sovereignty and undermine collective agency."[36] Another way was by opposing "popular sovereignty" to a particular, procedural conception of the principle of "rule of law." For instance, the SCC invalidated provisions of Law No. 17 of 2012 disqualifying former regime officials to run in elections on grounds that they constituted "retroactive punishment; punishment without a crime; violation of constitutionally protected political rights; and impermissible discrimination."[37] The deployment of these and other legal principles and mechanisms aimed at and did prevent changes in the political

---

31 Id., at 159.
32 Id., at xxvi.
33 Id., at 199.
34 Id., at 174.
35 Id., at 174.
36 Id., at 202.
37 Id., at 204.

and social system, demobilize popular political action, and subordinate popular sovereignty to a rather counter-revolutionary judicial control.

V   Conclusion

Masri and Sultany confront the recent socio-political history of constitutionalism in the Middle East with diverse political theories, but predominantly liberal: the names of John Rawls, Jurgen Habermas, Ronald Dworkin, Amartya Sen, Max Weber, Bruce Ackerman, etc., are followed by references to other authors inspired by them, or analyzing power through liberal concepts such as rule of law, separation of powers, popular sovereignty, contractualist political theory, and binaries such as democracy/authoritarianism, etc. An important part of Sultany's and Masri's theoretical analysis is the manner in which they indicate, and correctly so, that these political theories and concepts do not capture the much more complex dynamics of constitutionalism in the Middle East. The inadequacy of liberal theory to describe constitutionalism in the Middle East or elsewhere becomes obvious when one understands what Masri's and Sultany's work only indirectly expose: that liberal theory in general does not constitute a descriptive account of the source and functions of law and power, but a normative meta-theory founding the notions of a "just law" and "legitimate power." This means that liberal theory's aim is not to explain how law and power really arise in society, but rather to reconstruct the conditions upon which we would call a society a "just society." While fundamentally articulating the institutional principles under which political power can be rationally legitimized for its ability to embody social justice, liberal theories hardly examine or describe how social groups and conflicts emerge and how political power really arises and is exercised. They do not describe society, power and law, but rather, serve to normatively evaluate them.

This is why Masri's and Sultany's works would greatly benefit from a deeper engagement with critical (non-liberal) theory, and other theories of power that are key to understanding the social emergence, exercise and practice of power and its relations to law. These perspectives highlight: the notion of "domination" rather than popular sovereignty and freedoms; colonial studies and its power/knowledge relations rather than self-determination, constituent power, and democracy; ideas about the socio-political constitution of discursive formations rather than legitimacy; and an analysis of the performative powers of law and the production of "truth" rather than legal contradiction and indeterminacy. From such angles, the important question would not so much be *who* has the power and *what* does the subject do with it but, rather, what are the mechanisms by which power relations are expressed, exercised, and consolidated. These viewpoints would allow Masri and Sultany to better articulate all the analytical power of the conclusions that their works inspire.

Emilio Dabed[*]

---

[*] Emilio Dabed is a Palestinian-Chilean lawyer and political scientist (Science Po-Aix en Provence, France) specializing in constitutional matters, international law, and human rights. Currently, he is Adjunct Professor at Osgoode Hall Law School and Visiting Fellow at the Nathanson Center on Transnational Human Rights, Crime, and Security, at York University in Toronto. Previously, he was a Researcher and Visiting Professor at An-Najah National University Law School, Nablus, Palestine (2017–2018). In 2015–2016, he was the Palestine and Law Fellow and Adjunct Assistant Professor of Law at Columbia University Law School-Center for Palestine Studies. Between 2014 and 2015 he directed the International Law and Human Rights Program at Al-Quds/Bard College, Jerusalem, where he taught from 2011 to 2015. He also taught critical legal theory and philosophy of law in Diego Portales University, Santiago, Chile. His latest research and publications look at the relations between legal processes and discursive practices, on the one hand, and political and social changes, subjectivity, and identity formation on the other, with a particular focus on the disciplinary powers of law and the discourse of (human) rights in contemporary politics.

PART 3

Materials

SECTION A

United Nations

∴

General Assembly

G.A. Res. 73/256, Assistance to the Palestinian People (Dec. 20, 2018)

United Nations
General Assembly
A/RES/73/256
Distr.: General
Jan. 23, 2019
Seventy-third session
Agenda item 75(b)

Resolution adopted by the General Assembly on 20 December 2018

[*without reference to a Main Committee (A/73/L.69 and A/73/L.69/Add.1)*]

73/256. Assistance to the Palestinian people

The General Assembly,

Recalling its resolution 72/134 of 11 December 2017, as well as its previous resolutions on the question,

Recalling also the signing of the Declaration of Principles on Interim Self-Government Arrangements in Washington, D.C., on 13 September 1993, by the Government of the State of Israel and the Palestine Liberation Organization, the representative of the Palestinian people,[1] and the subsequent implementation agreements concluded by the two sides,

Recalling further all relevant international law, including humanitarian and human rights law, and, in particular, the International Covenant on Civil and Political Rights,[2] the International Covenant on Economic, Social and Cultural Rights,[2] the Convention on the Rights of the Child[3] and the Convention on the Elimination of All Forms of Discrimination against Women,[4]

---

1 A/48/486-S/26560, annex.
2 See resolution 2200 A (XXI), annex.
3 United Nations, *Treaty Series*, vol. 1577, No. 27531.
4 Ibid., vol. 1249, No. 20378.

Gravely concerned at the difficult living conditions and humanitarian situation affecting the Palestinian people, in particular women and children, throughout the occupied Palestinian territory, particularly in the Gaza Strip where economic recovery and vast infrastructure repair, rehabilitation and development are urgently needed, especially in the aftermath of the conflict of July and August 2014,

Conscious of the urgent need for improvement in the economic and social infrastructure of the occupied territory,

Welcoming, in this context, the development of projects, notably on infrastructure, to revive the Palestinian economy and improve the living conditions [p. 2] of the Palestinian people, stressing the need to create the appropriate conditions to facilitate the implementation of these projects, and noting the contribution of partners in the region and of the international community,

Aware that development is difficult under occupation and is best promoted in circumstances of peace and stability,

Noting the great economic and social challenges facing the Palestinian people and their leadership,

Emphasizing the importance of the safety and well-being of all people, in particular women and children, in the whole Middle East region, the promotion of which is facilitated, inter alia, in a stable and secure environment,

Deeply concerned about the negative impact, including the health and psychological consequences, of violence on the present and future well-being of children in the region,

Conscious of the urgent necessity for international assistance to the Palestinian people, taking into account the Palestinian priorities, and recalling in this regard the National Early Recovery and Reconstruction Plan for Gaza,

Expressing grave concern about the grave humanitarian situation in the Gaza Strip, and underlining the importance of emergency and humanitarian assistance and the need for the advancement of reconstruction in the Gaza Strip,

Welcoming the results of the Conference to Support Middle East Peace, convened in Washington, D.C., on 1 October 1993, the establishment of the Ad Hoc Liaison Committee for the Coordination of the International Assistance to Palestinians and the work being done by the World Bank as its secretariat and the establishment of the Consultative Group, as well as all follow-up meetings and international mechanisms established to provide assistance to the Palestinian people,

Underlining the importance of the Cairo International Conference on Palestine: Reconstructing Gaza, held on 12 October 2014, and urging the timely and full disbursement of pledges for expediting the provision of humanitarian assistance and the reconstruction process,

Recalling the International Donors' Conference for the Palestinian State, held in Paris on 17 December 2007, the Berlin Conference in Support of Palestinian Civil Security and the Rule of Law, held on 24 June 2008, and the Palestine Investment Conferences, held in Bethlehem from 21 to 23 May 2008 and on 2 and 3 June 2010, and the International Conference in Support of the Palestinian Economy for the Reconstruction of Gaza, held in Sharm el Sheikh, Egypt, on 2 March 2009,

Welcoming the ministerial meetings of the Conference on Cooperation among East Asian Countries for Palestinian Development, convened in Tokyo in February 2013 and in Jakarta in March 2014, as a forum to mobilize political and economic assistance, including through exchanges of expertise and lessons learned, in support of Palestinian development,

Welcoming also the latest meetings of the Ad Hoc Liaison Committee for the Coordination of the International Assistance to Palestinians, held in Brussels on 27 May 2015 and in New York on 25 September 2013, 22 September 2014, 30 September 2015, 19 September 2016, 18 September 2017 and 27 September 2018,

Welcoming further the activities of the Joint Liaison Committee, which provides a forum in which economic policy and practical matters related to donor assistance are discussed with the Palestinian Authority, [p. 3]

Welcoming the implementation of the Palestinian National Development Plan 2011–2013 on governance, economy, social development and infrastructure and the adoption of the Palestinian National Development Plan 2014–2016: State-building to Sovereignty, and stressing the need for continued international support for the Palestinian State-building process, as outlined in the summary by the Chair of the meeting of the Ad Hoc Liaison Committee held on 22 September 2014,

Stressing the need for the full engagement of the United Nations in the process of building Palestinian institutions and in providing broad assistance to the Palestinian people,

Recognizing, in this regard, the positive contribution of the United Nations Development Assistance Framework 2014–2016, which is aimed, inter alia, at enhancing developmental support and assistance to the Palestinian people and strengthening institutional capacity in line with Palestinian national priorities,

Welcoming steps to ease the restrictions on movement and access in the West Bank, while stressing the need for further steps to be taken in this regard, and recognizing that such steps would improve living conditions and the situation on the ground and could promote further Palestinian economic development,

Welcoming also the tripartite agreement facilitated by the United Nations regarding access to the Gaza Strip, and calling for its full implementation and complementary measures that address the need for a fundamental change in policy that allows for the sustained and regular opening of the border crossings for the movement of persons and goods, including for humanitarian and commercial flows and for the reconstruction and economic recovery of Gaza,

Stressing that the situation in the Gaza Strip is unsustainable and that a durable ceasefire agreement must lead to a fundamental improvement in the living conditions of the Palestinian people in the Gaza Strip and ensure the safety and well-being of civilians on both sides,

Stressing also the urgency of reaching a durable solution to the crisis in Gaza through the full implementation of Security Council resolution 1860 (2009) of 8 January 2009, including by preventing the illicit trafficking in arms and ammunition and by ensuring the sustained reopening of the crossing points on the basis of existing agreements, including the 2005 Agreement on Movement and Access between the Palestinian Authority and Israel,

Stressing, in this regard, the importance of the effective exercise by the Palestinian Authority of its full government responsibilities in the Gaza Strip in all fields, including through its presence at the Gaza crossing points,

Noting the active participation of the United Nations Special Coordinator for the Middle East Peace Process and Personal Representative of the Secretary-General to the Palestine Liberation Organization and the Palestinian Authority in the activities of the Special Envoys of the Quartet,

Reaffirming the necessity of achieving a comprehensive resolution of the Arab-Israeli conflict in all its aspects, on the basis of relevant Security Council resolutions, including resolutions 242 (1967) of 22 November 1967, 338 (1973) of 22 October 1973, 1397 (2002) of 12 March 2002, 1515 (2003) of 19 November 2003, 1850 (2008) of 16 December 2008 and 1860 (2009), as well as the terms of reference of the Madrid Conference and the principle of land for peace, in order to ensure a political solution, with two States – Israel and an independent, democratic, contiguous, sovereign and viable Palestinian State – living side by side in peace and security and mutual recognition, [p. 4]

Having considered the report of the Secretary-General,[5]

Expressing grave concern about continuing violence against civilians,

1. *Takes note* of the report of the Secretary-General;[5]

2. *Expresses its appreciation* to the Secretary-General for his rapid response and ongoing efforts regarding assistance to the Palestinian people, including with regard to the emergency humanitarian needs in the Gaza Strip;

3. *Also expresses its appreciation* to the Member States, United Nations bodies and intergovernmental, regional and non-governmental organizations that have provided and continue to provide assistance to the Palestinian people;

---

5 A/73/84-E/2018/72.

4. *Stresses* the importance of the work of the United Nations Special Coordinator for the Middle East Peace Process and Personal Representative of the Secretary-General to the Palestine Liberation Organization and the Palestinian Authority and of the steps taken under the auspices of the Secretary-General to ensure the achievement of a coordinated mechanism for United Nations activities throughout the occupied territories;

5. *Urges* Member States, international financial institutions of the United Nations system, intergovernmental and non-governmental organizations and regional and interregional organizations to extend, as rapidly and as generously as possible, economic and social assistance to the Palestinian people, in close cooperation with the Palestine Liberation Organization and through official Palestinian institutions;

6. *Welcomes* the meetings of the Ad Hoc Liaison Committee for the Coordination of the International Assistance to Palestinians of 25 September 2013, 22 September 2014, 27 May and 30 September 2015, 19 September 2016, 18 September 2017 and 27 September 2018, the outcome of the Cairo International Conference on Palestine: Reconstructing Gaza, held on 12 October 2014, and the generous donor response to support the needs of the Palestinian people, and urges the rapid disbursement of donor pledges;

7. *Stresses* the importance of following up on the results of the Cairo International Conference on Palestine: Reconstructing Gaza to effectively promote economic recovery and reconstruction in a timely and sustainable manner;

8. *Calls upon* donors that have not yet converted their budget support pledges into disbursements to transfer funds as soon as possible, encourages all donors to increase their direct assistance to the Palestinian Authority in accordance with its government programme in order to enable it to build a viable and prosperous Palestinian State, underlines the need for equitable burden sharing by donors in this effort, and encourages donors to consider aligning funding cycles with the Palestinian Authority's national budget cycle;

9. *Calls upon* relevant organizations and agencies of the United Nations system to intensify their assistance in response to the urgent needs of the Palestinian people in accordance with priorities set forth by the Palestinian side;

10. *Expresses its appreciation* for the work of the United Nations Relief and Works Agency for Palestine Refugees in the Near East, and recognizes the vital role of the Agency in providing humanitarian assistance to the Palestinian people, particularly in the Gaza Strip;

11. *Calls upon* the international community to provide urgently needed assistance and services in an effort to alleviate the difficult humanitarian situation

[p. 5] being faced by Palestinian women, children and their families and to help in the reconstruction and development of relevant Palestinian institutions;

12. *Stresses* the role that all funding instruments, including the European Commission's Palestinian-European Mechanism for the Management of Socioeconomic Aid and the World Bank trust fund, have been playing in directly assisting the Palestinian people;

13. *Urges* Member States to open their markets to exports of Palestinian products on the most favourable terms, consistent with appropriate trading rules, and to implement fully existing trade and cooperation agreements;

14. *Calls upon* the international donor community to expedite the delivery of pledged assistance to the Palestinian people to meet their urgent needs;

15. *Stresses*, in this context, the importance of ensuring free humanitarian access to the Palestinian people and the free movement of persons and goods;

16. *Also stresses* the need for the full implementation by both parties of existing agreements, including the Agreement on Movement and Access and the Agreed Principles for the Rafah Crossing, of 15 November 2005, to allow for the freedom of movement of the Palestinian civilian population, as well as for imports and exports, within and into and out of the Gaza Strip;

17. *Further stresses* the need to ensure the safety and security of humanitarian personnel, premises, facilities, equipment, vehicles and supplies, as well as the need to ensure safe and unhindered access by humanitarian personnel and delivery of supplies and equipment, in order to allow such personnel to efficiently perform their task of assisting affected civilian populations;

18. *Urges* the international donor community, United Nations agencies and organizations and non-governmental organizations to extend to the Palestinian people, as rapidly as possible, emergency economic assistance and humanitarian assistance, particularly in the Gaza Strip, to counter the impact of the current crisis;

19. *Stresses* the need for the continued implementation of the Paris Protocol on Economic Relations of 29 April 1994, fifth annex to the Israeli-Palestinian Interim Agreement on the West Bank and the Gaza Strip, signed in Washington, D.C., on 28 September 1995,[6] including with regard to the full, prompt and regular transfer of Palestinian indirect tax revenues;

20. *Requests* the Secretary-General to submit a report to the General Assembly at its seventy-fourth session, through the Economic and Social Council, on the implementation of the present resolution, containing:

(a) An assessment of the assistance actually received by the Palestinian people;

---

6   A/51/889-S/1997/357, annex.

(b) An assessment of the needs still unmet and specific proposals for responding effectively to them;

21. *Decides* to include in the provisional agenda of its seventy-fourth session, under the item entitled "Strengthening of the coordination of humanitarian and disaster relief assistance of the United Nations, including special economic assistance", the sub-item entitled "Assistance to the Palestinian people".

62nd plenary meeting
20 December 2018

G.A. Res. 73/255, Permanent Sovereignty of the Palestinian People in the Occupied Palestinian Territory, including East Jerusalem and of the Arab Population in the Occupied Syrian Golan and Their Natural Resources (Dec. 20, 2018)

United Nations
General Assembly
A/RES/73/255
Distr.: General
15 January 2019
Seventy-third session

Resolution adopted by the General Assembly on 20 December 2018

[*on the report of the Second Committee (A/73/546)*]

73/255. Permanent sovereignty of the Palestinian people in the Occupied Palestinian Territory, including East Jerusalem, and of the Arab population in the occupied Syrian Golan over their natural resources

The General Assembly,

  Recalling its resolution 72/240 of 20 December 2017, and taking note of Economic and Social Council resolution 2018/20 of 24 July 2018,

  Recalling also its resolutions 58/292 of 6 May 2004 and 59/251 of 22 December 2004,

  Reaffirming the principle of the permanent sovereignty of peoples under foreign occupation over their natural resources,

  Guided by the principles of the Charter of the United Nations, affirming the inadmissibility of the acquisition of territory by force, and recalling relevant Security Council resolutions, including resolutions 242 (1967) of 22 November 1967, 465 (1980) of 1 March 1980, 497 (1981) of 17 December 1981 and 2334 (2016) of 23 December 2016,

  Recalling its resolution 2625 (XXV) of 24 October 1970,

Bearing in mind its resolution 70/1 of 25 September 2015, entitled "Transforming our world: the 2030 Agenda for Sustainable Development",

Reaffirming the applicability of the Geneva Convention relative to the Protection of Civilian Persons in Time of War, of 12 August 1949,[1] to the Occupied Palestinian Territory, including East Jerusalem, and other Arab territories occupied by Israel since 1967, [p. 2]

Recalling, in this regard, the International Covenant on Civil and Political Rights and the International Covenant on Economic, Social and Cultural Rights,[2] and affirming that these human rights instruments must be respected in the Occupied Palestinian Territory, including East Jerusalem, as well as in the occupied Syrian Golan,

Recalling also the advisory opinion rendered on 9 July 2004 by the International Court of Justice on the legal consequences of the construction of a wall in the Occupied Palestinian Territory,[3] and recalling further its resolutions ES-10/15 of 20 July 2004 and ES-10/17 of 15 December 2006,

Recalling further its resolution 67/19 of 29 November 2012,

Taking note of the accession by Palestine to several human rights treaties and the core humanitarian law treaties, as well as to other international treaties,

Expressing its concern about the exploitation by Israel, the occupying Power, of the natural resources of the Occupied Palestinian Territory, including East Jerusalem, and other Arab territories occupied by Israel since 1967,

Expressing its grave concern about the extensive destruction by Israel, the occupying Power, of agricultural land and orchards in the Occupied Palestinian Territory, including the uprooting of a vast number of fruit-bearing trees and the destruction of farms and greenhouses, and the grave environmental and economic impact in this regard,

Expressing its grave concern also about the widespread destruction caused by Israel, the occupying Power, to vital infrastructure, including water pipelines, sewage networks and electricity networks, in the Occupied Palestinian Territory, in particular in the Gaza Strip during the military operations of July and August 2014, which, inter alia, has polluted the environment and which negatively affects the functioning of water and sanitation systems and the water supply and other natural resources of the Palestinian people, and stressing the urgency of the reconstruction and development of water and other

---

1 Reissued for technical reasons on 7 March 2019. United Nations, *Treaty Series*, vol. 75, No. 973.
2 See resolution 2200 A (XXI), annex.
3 See A/ES-10/273 and A/ES-10/273/Corr.1.

vital civilian infrastructure, including the project for the desalination facility for the Gaza Strip,

Expressing its grave concern further about the negative impact on the environment and on reconstruction and development efforts of unexploded ordnance that remains in the Gaza Strip as a result of the conflict in July and August 2014, and commending the efforts of the Mine Action Service of the United Nations for the safe removal of such ordnance,

Expressing its grave concern about the chronic energy shortage in the Gaza Strip and its detrimental impact on the operation of water and sanitation facilities, which threaten to further erode groundwater resources, of which only 5 per cent remains potable,

Recalling the 2009 report by the United Nations Environment Programme regarding the grave environmental situation in the Gaza Strip, and relevant reports by the United Nations country team, including "Gaza in 2020: a liveable place?", "Gaza: two years after" and "Gaza ten years later", and stressing the need for follow-up to the recommendations contained therein,

Deploring the detrimental impact of the Israeli settlements on Palestinian and other Arab natural resources, especially as a result of the confiscation of land and the forced diversion of water resources, including the destruction of orchards and crops and the seizure of water wells by Israeli settlers, and of the dire socioeconomic consequences in this regard, [p. 3]

Recalling the report of the independent international fact-finding mission to investigate the implications of the Israeli settlements on the civil, political, economic, social and cultural rights of the Palestinian people throughout the Occupied Palestinian Territory, including East Jerusalem,[4]

Aware of the detrimental impact on Palestinian natural resources being caused by the unlawful construction of the wall by Israel, the occupying Power, in the Occupied Palestinian Territory, including in and around East Jerusalem, and of its grave effect as well on the economic and social conditions of the Palestinian people,

Stressing the urgency of achieving without delay an end to the Israeli occupation that began in 1967 and a just, lasting and comprehensive peace settlement on all tracks, on the basis of Security Council resolutions 242 (1967), 338 (1973) of 22 October 1973, 425 (1978) of 19 March 1978, 1397 (2002) of 12 March 2002 and 2334 (2016), the principle of land for peace, the Arab Peace Initiative[5] and the Quartet performance-based road map to a permanent two-State solution

---

4   A/HRC/22/63.
5   A/56/1026-S/2002/932, annex II, resolution 14/221.

to the Israeli-Palestinian conflict,[6] as endorsed by the Council in its resolution 1515 (2003) of 19 November 2003 and supported by the Council in its resolution 1850 (2008) of 16 December 2008,

Stressing also, in this regard, the need for respect for the obligation upon Israel under the road map to freeze settlement activity, including so-called "natural growth", and to dismantle all settlement outposts erected since March 2001,

Stressing further the need for respect and preservation of the territorial unity, contiguity and integrity of all of the Occupied Palestinian Territory, including East Jerusalem,

Recalling that the Security Council, in its resolution 2334 (2016), underlined that it would not recognize any changes to the 4 June 1967 lines, including with regard to Jerusalem, other than those agreed by the parties through negotiations,

Recalling also the need to end all acts of violence, including acts of terror, provocation, incitement and destruction,

Taking note of the report prepared by the Economic and Social Commission for Western Asia on the economic and social repercussions of the Israeli occupation on the living conditions of the Palestinian people in the Occupied Palestinian Territory, including East Jerusalem, and of the Arab population in the occupied Syrian Golan, as transmitted by the Secretary-General,[7]

1. *Reaffirms* the inalienable rights of the Palestinian people and of the population of the occupied Syrian Golan over their natural resources, including land, water and energy resources;

2. *Demands* that Israel, the occupying Power, cease the exploitation, damage, cause of loss or depletion and endangerment of the natural resources in the Occupied Palestinian Territory, including East Jerusalem, and in the occupied Syrian Golan;

3. *Recognizes* the right of the Palestinian people to claim restitution as a result of any exploitation, damage, loss or depletion or endangerment of their natural resources resulting from illegal measures taken by Israel, the occupying Power, and Israeli settlers in the Occupied Palestinian Territory, including East Jerusalem, and expresses the hope that this issue will be dealt with within the framework of the final status negotiations between the Palestinian and Israeli sides; [p. 4]

4. *Stresses* that the wall and settlements being constructed by Israel in the Occupied Palestinian Territory, including in and around East Jerusalem,

---

6 S/2003/529, annex.

7 A/73/87-E/2018/69.

are contrary to international law and are seriously depriving the Palestinian people of their natural resources, and calls in this regard for full compliance with the legal obligations affirmed in the 9 July 2004 advisory opinion of the International Court of Justice[3] and in relevant United Nations resolutions, including General Assembly resolution ES-10/15;

5. *Calls upon* Israel, the occupying Power, to comply strictly with its obligations under international law, including international humanitarian law, and to cease immediately and completely all policies and measures aimed at the alteration of the character and status of the Occupied Palestinian Territory, including East Jerusalem;

6. *Also calls upon* Israel, the occupying Power, to bring a halt to all actions, including those perpetrated by Israeli settlers, harming the environment, including the dumping of all kinds of waste materials, in the Occupied Palestinian Territory, including East Jerusalem, and in the occupied Syrian Golan, which gravely threaten their natural resources, namely water and land resources, and which pose an environmental, sanitation and health threat to the civilian populations;

7. *Further calls upon* Israel to cease its destruction of vital infrastructure, including water pipelines, sewage networks and electricity networks, and to cease its demolition and confiscation of Palestinian homes and civilian infrastructure, agricultural lands and water wells, which, inter alia, have a negative impact on the natural resources of the Palestinian people, stresses the urgent need to advance reconstruction and development projects in this regard, including in the Gaza Strip, and calls for support for the necessary efforts in this regard, in line with the commitments made at, inter alia, the Cairo International Conference on Palestine: Reconstructing Gaza, held on 12 October 2014;

8. *Calls upon* Israel, the occupying Power, to remove all obstacles to the implementation of critical environmental projects, including sewage treatment plants in the Gaza Strip and the reconstruction and development of water infrastructure, including the project for the desalination facility for the Gaza Strip;

9. *Also calls upon* Israel not to impede Palestinian development and export of discovered oil and natural gas reserves;

10. *Calls for* the immediate and safe removal of all unexploded ordnance in the Gaza Strip and for support for the efforts of the Mine Action Service of the United Nations in this regard, and welcomes the extensive efforts exerted by the Mine Action Service to date;

11. *Encourages* all States and international organizations to continue to actively pursue policies to ensure respect for their obligations under international law with regard to all illegal Israeli practices and measures in the Occupied

Palestinian Territory, including East Jerusalem, particularly Israeli settlement activities and the exploitation of natural resources;

12. *Underscores*, in this regard, the call by the Security Council, in its resolution 2334 (2016), upon all States to distinguish, in their relevant dealings, between the territory of the State of Israel and the territories occupied since 1967;

13. *Requests* the Secretary-General to report to the General Assembly at its seventy-fourth session on the implementation of the present resolution, including with regard to the cumulative impact of the exploitation, damage and depletion by Israel of natural resources in the Occupied Palestinian Territory, including East Jerusalem, and in the occupied Syrian Golan, and with regard to the impact of such practices on [p. 5] the promotion of the Sustainable Development Goals,[8] and decides to include in the provisional agenda of its seventy-fourth session the item entitled "Permanent sovereignty of the Palestinian people in the Occupied Palestinian Territory, including East Jerusalem, and of the Arab population in the occupied Syrian Golan over their natural resources".

62nd plenary meeting
20 December 2018

---

[8] See resolution 70/1.

G.A. Res. 73/158, The Right of the Palestinian People to Self-Determination (Dec. 17, 2018)

United Nations
General Assembly
A/RES/73/158
Distr.: General
9 January 2019
Seventy-third session
Agenda item 73

Resolution adopted by the General Assembly on 17 December 2018

[*on the report of the Third Committee (A/73/588)*]

73/158. The right of the Palestinian people to self-determination

The General Assembly,

Aware that the development of friendly relations among nations, based on respect for the principle of equal rights and self-determination of peoples, is among the purposes and principles of the United Nations, as defined in the Charter,

Recalling, in this regard, its resolution 2625 (XXV) of 24 October 1970, entitled "Declaration on Principles of International Law concerning Friendly Relations and Cooperation among States in accordance with the Charter of the United Nations",

Bearing in mind the International Covenants on Human Rights,[1] the Universal Declaration of Human Rights,[2] the Declaration on the Granting of Independence to Colonial Countries and Peoples[3] and the Vienna Declaration and Programme of Action adopted at the World Conference on Human Rights on 25 June 1993,[4]

---

1 Resolution 2200 A (XXI), annex.
2 Resolution 217 A (III).
3 Resolution 1514 (XV).
4 A/CONF.157/24 (Part I), chap. III.

Recalling the Declaration on the Occasion of the Fiftieth Anniversary of the United Nations,[5]

Recalling also the United Nations Millennium Declaration,[6]

Recalling further the advisory opinion rendered on 9 July 2004 by the International Court of Justice on the legal consequences of the construction of a wall in the Occupied Palestinian Territory,[7] and noting in particular the reply of the Court, including on the right of peoples to self-determination, which is a right *erga omnes*,[8] [p. 2]

Recalling the conclusion of the Court, in its advisory opinion of 9 July 2004, that the construction of the wall by Israel, the occupying Power, in the Occupied Palestinian Territory, including East Jerusalem, along with measures previously taken, severely impedes the right of the Palestinian people to self-determination,[9]

Stressing the urgency of achieving without delay an end to the Israeli occupation that began in 1967 and a just, lasting and comprehensive peace settlement between the Palestinian and Israeli sides, based on the relevant resolutions of the United Nations, the Madrid terms of reference, including the principle of land for peace, the Arab Peace Initiative[10] and the Quartet road map to a permanent two-State solution to the Israeli-Palestinian conflict,[11]

Stressing also the need for respect for and preservation of the territorial unity, contiguity and integrity of all of the Occupied Palestinian Territory, including East Jerusalem, and recalling in this regard its resolution 58/292 of 6 May 2004,

Recalling its resolution 72/160 of 19 December 2017,

Recalling also its resolution 67/19 of 29 November 2012,

Affirming the right of all States in the region to live in peace within secure and internationally recognized borders,

1. *Reaffirms* the right of the Palestinian people to self-determination, including the right to their independent State of Palestine;

2. *Urges* all States and the specialized agencies and organizations of the United Nations system to continue to support and assist the Palestinian people in the early realization of their right to self-determination.

55th plenary meeting
17 December 2018

---

[5] Resolution 50/6.
[6] Resolution 55/2.
[7] See A/ES-10/273 and A/ES-10/273/Corr.1.
[8] Ibid., advisory opinion, para. 88.
[9] Ibid., para. 122.
[10] A/56/1026-S/2002/932, annex II, resolution 14/221.
[11] S/2003/529, annex.

G.A. Res. 79/99, Israeli Practices Affecting the Human Rights of the Palestinian People in the Occupied Palestinian Territory, including East Jerusalem (Dec. 18, 2018)

United Nations
General Assembly
A/RES/73/99
Distr.: General
18 December 2018
Seventy-third session
Agenda item 55

Resolution adopted by the General Assembly on 7 December 2018

[*on the report of the Special Political and Decolonization Committee (Fourth Committee) (A/73/524)*]

73/99. Israeli practices affecting the human rights of the Palestinian people in the Occupied Palestinian Territory, including East Jerusalem

The General Assembly,

Recalling the Universal Declaration of Human Rights,[1]

Recalling also the International Covenant on Civil and Political Rights, the International Covenant on Economic, Social and Cultural Rights[2] and the Convention on the Rights of the Child,[3] and affirming that these human rights instruments must be respected in the Occupied Palestinian Territory, including East Jerusalem,

---

1 Resolution 217 A (III).
2 See resolution 2200 A (XXI), annex.
3 United Nations, *Treaty Series*, vol. 1577, No. 27531.

Reaffirming its relevant resolutions, including resolution 72/87 of 7 December 2017, as well as those adopted at its tenth emergency special session,

Recalling the relevant resolutions of the Human Rights Council,

Recalling also the relevant resolutions of the Security Council, and stressing the need for their implementation,

Having considered the report of the Special Committee to Investigate Israeli Practices Affecting the Human Rights of the Palestinian People and Other Arabs of the Occupied Territories[4] and the report of the Secretary-General on the work of the Special Committee,[5] [p. 2]

Taking note of the report of the Special Rapporteur of the Human Rights Council on the situation of human rights in the Palestinian territories occupied since 1967,[6] as well as of other relevant recent reports of the Human Rights Council,

Taking note also of the recent report by the Economic and Social Commission for Western Asia on the economic and social repercussions of the Israeli occupation on the living conditions of the Palestinian people in the Occupied Palestinian Territory, including East Jerusalem, and the Arab population in the occupied Syrian Golan,[7]

Deeply regretting that 51 years have passed since the onset of the Israeli occupation, and stressing the urgent need for efforts to reverse the negative trends on the ground and to restore a political horizon for advancing and accelerating meaningful negotiations aimed at the achievement of a peace agreement that will bring a complete end to the Israeli occupation that began in 1967 and the resolution of all core final status issues, without exception, leading to a peaceful, just, lasting and comprehensive solution of the question of Palestine,

Aware of the responsibility of the international community to promote human rights and ensure respect for international law, and recalling in this regard its resolution 2625 (XXV) of 24 October 1970,

Recalling the advisory opinion rendered on 9 July 2004 by the International Court of Justice on the legal consequences of the construction of a wall in the Occupied Palestinian Territory,[8] and recalling also relevant General Assembly resolutions,

---

4 A/73/499.
5 A/73/420.
6 A/HRC/37/75.
7 A/73/87-E/2018/69.
8 See A/ES-10/273 and A/ES-10/273/Corr.1.

Noting in particular the Court's reply, including that the construction of the wall being built by Israel, the occupying Power, in the Occupied Palestinian Territory, including in and around East Jerusalem, and its associated regime are contrary to international law,

Taking note of its resolution 67/19 of 29 November 2012,

Noting the accession by Palestine to several human rights treaties and the core humanitarian law conventions, as well as other international treaties,

Reaffirming the principle of the inadmissibility of the acquisition of territory by force,

Reaffirming also the applicability of the Geneva Convention relative to the Protection of Civilian Persons in Time of War, of 12 August 1949,[9] to the Occupied Palestinian Territory, including East Jerusalem, and other Arab territories occupied by Israel since 1967,

Reaffirming further the obligation of the States parties to the Fourth Geneva Convention[9] under articles 146, 147 and 148 with regard to penal sanctions, grave breaches and responsibilities of the High Contracting Parties,

Recalling the statement of 15 July 1999 and the declarations adopted on 5 December 2001 and on 17 December 2014[10] by the Conference of High Contracting Parties to the Fourth Geneva Convention on measures to enforce the Convention in the Occupied Palestinian Territory, including East Jerusalem, aimed at ensuring respect for the Convention in the Occupied Palestinian Territory, including East Jerusalem, [p. 3]

Reaffirming that all States have the right and the duty to take actions in conformity with international law and international humanitarian law to counter deadly acts of violence against their civilian population in order to protect the lives of their citizens,

Stressing the need for full compliance with the Israeli-Palestinian agreements reached within the context of the Middle East peace process, including the Sharm el-Sheikh understandings, and the implementation of the Quartet road map to a permanent two-State solution to the Israeli-Palestinian conflict,[11]

Stressing also the need for the full implementation of the Agreement on Movement and Access and the Agreed Principles for the Rafah Crossing, both of 15 November 2005, to allow for the freedom of movement of the Palestinian civilian population within and into and out of the Gaza Strip,

Gravely concerned by the tensions and violence in the recent period throughout the Occupied Palestinian Territory, including East Jerusalem and including

---

9   United Nations, *Treaty Series*, vol. 75, No. 973.
10   A/69/711-S/2015/1, annex.
11   S/2003/529, annex.

with regard to the holy places of Jerusalem, including the Haram al-Sharif, and deploring the loss of innocent civilian life,

Recognizing that security measures alone cannot remedy the escalating tensions, instability and violence, and calling for full respect for international law, including humanitarian and human rights law, including for the protection of civilian life, as well as for the promotion of human security, the de-escalation of the situation, the exercise of restraint, including from provocative actions and rhetoric, and the establishment of a stable environment conducive to the pursuit of peace,

Expressing grave concern about the continuing systematic violation of the human rights of the Palestinian people by Israel, the occupying Power, including that arising from the excessive use of force and military operations causing death and injury to Palestinian civilians, including children, women and non-violent, peaceful demonstrators, as well as journalists, medical personnel and humanitarian personnel; the arbitrary imprisonment and detention of Palestinians, some of whom have been imprisoned for decades; the use of collective punishment; the closure of areas; the confiscation of land; the establishment and expansion of settlements; the construction of a wall in the Occupied Palestinian Territory in departure from the Armistice Line of 1949; the destruction of property and infrastructure; the forced displacement of civilians, including attempts at forced transfers of Bedouin communities; and all other actions by it designed to change the legal status, geographical nature and demographic composition of the Occupied Palestinian Territory, including East Jerusalem, and demanding the cessation of all such unlawful actions,

Gravely concerned by the ongoing demolition by Israel, the occupying Power, of Palestinian homes, as well as of structures, including schools, provided as international humanitarian aid, in particular in and around Occupied East Jerusalem, including if carried out as an act of collective punishment in violation of international humanitarian law, which has escalated at unprecedented rates, and by the revocation of residence permits and eviction of Palestinian residents of the City of Jerusalem,

Deploring the continuing and negative consequences of the conflicts in and around the Gaza Strip and the high number of causalities among Palestinian civilians in the recent period, including among children,

Gravely concerned about the disastrous humanitarian situation and the critical socioeconomic and security situation in the Gaza Strip, including that resulting from the prolonged closures and severe economic and movement restrictions that in effect amount to a blockade and deepen poverty and despair among the Palestinian civilian [p. 4] population, and about the short- and long-term detrimental impacts of this situation and the widespread destruction and continued impeding of the reconstruction process by Israel, the occupying Power, on the human rights situation,

Expressing grave concern about the alarming conditions and figures reflected in the United Nations country team reports, of 26 August 2016, entitled "Gaza: two years after", and of July 2017, entitled "Gaza ten years later",

Recalling the statement by the President of the Security Council of 28 July 2014,[12]

Stressing the need for the full implementation by all parties of Security Council resolution 1860 (2009) of 8 January 2009 and General Assembly resolution ES-10/18 of 16 January 2009,

Stressing also that the situation in the Gaza Strip is unsustainable and that a durable ceasefire agreement must lead to a fundamental improvement in the living conditions of the Palestinian people in the Gaza Strip, including through the sustained and regular opening of crossing points, and ensure the safety and well-being of civilians on both sides, and regretting the lack of progress made in this regard,

Gravely concerned by reports regarding serious human rights violations and grave breaches of international humanitarian law committed during the successive military operations in the Gaza Strip,[13] and reiterating the necessity for serious follow-up by all parties of the recommendations addressed to them towards ensuring accountability and justice,

Stressing the need for protection of human rights defenders engaged in the promotion of human rights issues in the Occupied Palestinian Territory, including East Jerusalem, to allow them to carry out their work freely and without fear of attacks and harassment,

Expressing deep concern also about the Israeli policy of closures and the imposition of severe restrictions, including through hundreds of obstacles to movement, checkpoints and a permit regime, all of which obstruct the freedom of movement of persons and goods, including medical and humanitarian goods, and the follow-up and access to donor-funded projects of development cooperation and humanitarian assistance, throughout the Occupied Palestinian Territory, including East Jerusalem, and impair the Territory's contiguity, consequently violating the human rights of the Palestinian people and negatively impacting their socioeconomic and humanitarian situation, which remains dire in the Gaza Strip, and the efforts aimed at rehabilitating and developing the Palestinian economy, and calling for the full lifting of restrictions,

---

12   S/PRST/2014/13; see *Resolutions and Decisions of the Security Council, 1 August 2013–31 July 2014* (S/INF/69).
13   See A/63/855-S/2009/250; S/2015/286, annex; A/HRC/12/48; and A/HRC/29/52.

Expressing grave concern that thousands of Palestinians, including many children and women, as well as elected representatives, continue to be held in Israeli prisons or detention centres under harsh conditions, including unhygienic conditions, solitary confinement, the extensive use of administrative detention of excessive duration without charge and denial of due process, lack of proper medical care and widespread medical neglect, including for prisoners who are ill, with the risk of fatal consequences, and denial of family visits, that impair their well-being, and expressing grave concern also about the ill-treatment and harassment and all reports of torture of any Palestinian prisoners,

Expressing deep concern about the hunger strikes by Palestinian prisoners in protest of the harsh conditions of their imprisonment and detention by the occupying [p. 5] Power, while taking note of agreements reached on conditions of detention in Israeli prisons and calling for their full and immediate implementation,

Recalling the United Nations Standard Minimum Rules for the Treatment of Prisoners (the Nelson Mandela Rules)[14] and the United Nations Rules for the Treatment of Women Prisoners and Non-custodial Measures for Women Offenders (the Bangkok Rules),[15] and calling for respect for those Rules,

Recalling also the prohibition under international humanitarian law of the deportation of civilians from occupied territories,

Deploring the practice of withholding the bodies of those killed, and calling for the release of the bodies that have not yet been returned to their relatives, in line with international humanitarian law and human rights law, in order to ensure dignified closure in accordance with their religious beliefs and traditions,

Stressing the need for the prevention of all acts of violence, harassment, provocation and incitement by extremist Israeli settlers and groups of armed settlers, especially against Palestinian civilians, including children, and their properties, including homes, agricultural lands and historic and religious sites, including in Occupied East Jerusalem, and deploring the violation of the human rights of Palestinians in this regard, including acts of violence leading to death and injury among civilians,

Convinced of the need for an international presence to monitor the situation, to contribute to ending the violence and protecting the Palestinian civilian population and to help the parties to implement the agreements reached,

---

14 Resolution 70/175, annex.
15 Resolution 65/229, annex.

and in this regard recalling the positive contribution of the Temporary International Presence in Hebron,

Stressing that the protection of civilians is a critical component in ensuring peace and security,

Taking note of the report of the Secretary-General on the protection of the Palestinian civilian population[16] and the observations made therein on ways and means for ensuring the safety, protection and well-being of the Palestinian civilian population under Israeli occupation,

Noting the continued efforts and tangible progress made in the Palestinian security sector, and noting also the continued cooperation that benefits both Palestinians and Israelis, in particular by promoting security and building confidence,

Urging the parties to observe calm and restraint and to refrain from provocative actions, incitement and inflammatory rhetoric, especially in areas of religious and cultural sensitivity, including in East Jerusalem, and to take every possible step to defuse tensions and promote conditions conducive to the credibility and success of the peace negotiations,

Emphasizing the right of all people in the region to the enjoyment of human rights as enshrined in the international human rights covenants,

1. *Reiterates* that all measures and actions taken by Israel, the occupying Power, in the Occupied Palestinian Territory, including East Jerusalem, in violation of the relevant provisions of the Geneva Convention relative to the Protection of Civilian Persons in Time of War, of 12 August 1949,[9] and contrary to the relevant resolutions of the Security Council, are illegal and have no validity; [p. 6]

2. *Demands* that Israel, the occupying Power, cease all measures contrary to international law, as well as discriminatory legislation, policies and actions in the Occupied Palestinian Territory that violate the human rights of the Palestinian people, including the killing and injury of civilians, the arbitrary detention and imprisonment of civilians, the forced displacement of civilians, including attempts at forced transfers of Bedouin communities, the destruction and confiscation of civilian property, including home demolitions, including if carried out as collective punishment in violation of international humanitarian law, and any obstruction of humanitarian assistance, and that it fully respect human rights law and comply with its legal obligations in this regard, including in accordance with relevant United Nations resolutions;

---

16   A/ES-10/794.

3. *Also demands* that Israel, the occupying Power, comply fully with the provisions of the Fourth Geneva Convention of 1949[9] and cease immediately all measures and actions taken in violation and in breach of the Convention;

4. *Calls for* urgent measures to ensure the safety and protection of the Palestinian civilian population in the Occupied Palestinian Territory, including East Jerusalem, in accordance with the relevant provisions of international humanitarian law and as called for by the Security Council in its resolution 904 (1994) of 18 March 1994;

5. *Takes note* of the report of the Secretary-General on the protection of the Palestinian civilian population,[16] notably the observations made therein, including the possible expansion of existing protection mechanisms to prevent and deter violations, and calls for continued efforts within the United Nations human rights framework regarding the legal protection and safety of the Palestinian civilian population;

6. *Calls for* full cooperation by Israel with the relevant special rapporteurs and other relevant mechanisms and inquiries of the Human Rights Council, including the facilitation of entry to the Occupied Palestinian Territory, including East Jerusalem, for monitoring and reporting on the human rights situation therein according to their respective mandates;

7. *Demands* that Israel, the occupying Power, cease all of its settlement activities, the construction of the wall and any other measures aimed at altering the character, status and demographic composition of the Occupied Palestinian Territory, including in and around East Jerusalem, all of which, inter alia, gravely and detrimentally impact the human rights of the Palestinian people, and the prospects for achieving without delay an end to the Israeli occupation that began in 1967 and a just, lasting and comprehensive peace settlement between the Palestinian and Israeli sides, and calls for the full respect and implementation of all relevant General Assembly and Security Council resolutions in this regard, including Security Council resolution 2334 (2016) of 23 December 2016;

8. *Calls for* urgent attention to the plight and the rights, in accordance with international law, of Palestinian prisoners and detainees in Israeli jails, including those on hunger strike, calls for efforts between the two sides for the further release of prisoners and detainees, and also calls for respect for the United Nations Standard Minimum Rules for the Treatment of Prisoners (the Nelson Mandela Rules)[14] and the United Nations Rules for the Treatment of Women Prisoners and Non-custodial Measures for Women Offenders (the Bangkok Rules);[15]

9. *Condemns* all acts of violence, including all acts of terror, provocation, incitement and destruction, especially any use of force by the Israeli occupying forces against Palestinian civilians in violation of international law, particularly

in the Gaza Strip, which have caused extensive loss of life and vast numbers of injuries, including among children and women; [p. 7]

10. *Also condemns* all acts of violence by militants and armed groups, including the firing of rockets, against Israeli civilian areas, resulting in loss of life and injury;

11. *Reiterates its demand* for the full implementation of Security Council resolution 1860 (2009);

12. *Demands* that Israel, the occupying Power, comply with its legal obligations under international law, as mentioned in the advisory opinion rendered on 9 July 2004 by the International Court of Justice[8] and as demanded in General Assembly resolutions ES-10/15 of 20 July 2004 and ES-10/13 of 21 October 2003, and that it immediately cease the construction of the wall in the Occupied Palestinian Territory, including in and around East Jerusalem, dismantle forthwith the structure situated therein, repeal or render ineffective all legislative and regulatory acts relating thereto, and make reparations for all damage caused by the construction of the wall, which has gravely impacted the human rights and the socioeconomic living conditions of the Palestinian people;

13. *Reiterates* the need for respect for the territorial unity, contiguity and integrity of all of the Occupied Palestinian Territory and for guarantees of the freedom of movement of persons and goods within the Palestinian territory, including movement into and from East Jerusalem, into and from the Gaza Strip, between the West Bank and the Gaza Strip, and to and from the outside world;

14. *Calls upon* Israel, the occupying Power, to cease its imposition of prolonged closures and economic and movement restrictions, including those amounting to a blockade on the Gaza Strip, and in this regard to fully implement the Agreement on Movement and Access and the Agreed Principles for the Rafah Crossing, both of 15 November 2005, in order to allow for the sustained and regular movement of persons and goods and for the acceleration of long overdue and massive reconstruction needs and economic recovery in the Gaza Strip, while noting the tripartite agreement facilitated by the United Nations in this regard;

15. *Urges* Member States to continue to provide emergency assistance to the Palestinian people to alleviate the financial crisis and the dire socioeconomic and humanitarian situation, particularly in the Gaza Strip;

16. *Urges* all States and the specialized agencies and organizations of the United Nations system to continue to support and assist the Palestinian people in the early realization of their inalienable human rights, including their right to self-determination, as a matter of urgency, in the light of the passage

of more than 50 years of the Israeli occupation and the continued denial and violation of the human rights of the Palestinian people;

17. *Emphasizes* the need to preserve and develop the Palestinian institutions and infrastructure for the provision of vital public services to the Palestinian civilian population and the promotion of human rights, including civil, political, economic, social and cultural rights, and urges in this regard the implementation of the agreement signed in Cairo on 12 October 2017,[17] which would be an important step towards achieving Palestinian unity and lead to the effective functioning of the Palestinian national consensus government, including in the Gaza Strip, under the leadership of President Mahmoud Abbas, consistent with the Palestine Liberation Organization commitments and the Quartet principles;

18. *Requests* the Secretary-General to report to the General Assembly at its seventy-fourth session on the implementation of the present resolution, including with regard to the applicability of the Fourth Geneva Convention to the Occupied Palestinian Territory, including East Jerusalem, and the other occupied Arab territories.

48th plenary meeting
7 December 2018

---

[17] S/2017/899, annex.

G.A. Res. 73/98, Israeli Settlements in the Occupied Palestinian Territory, including East Jerusalem, and Occupied Syrian Golan (Dec. 18, 2018)

United Nations
General Assembly
A/RES/73/98
Distr.: General
18 December 2018
Seventy-third session
Agenda item 55

Resolution adopted by the General Assembly on 7 December 2018

[*on the report of the Special Political and Decolonization Committee (Fourth Committee) (A/73/524)*]

73/98. Israeli settlements in the Occupied Palestinian Territory, including East Jerusalem, and the occupied Syrian Golan

The General Assembly,

Guided by the principles of the Charter of the United Nations, and affirming the inadmissibility of the acquisition of territory by force,

Recalling its relevant resolutions, including resolution 72/86 of 7 December 2017, as well as those resolutions adopted at its tenth emergency special session,

Recalling also the relevant resolutions of the Security Council, including resolutions 242 (1967) of 22 November 1967, 446 (1979) of 22 March 1979, 465 (1980) of 1 March 1980, 476 (1980) of 30 June 1980, 478 (1980) of 20 August 1980, 497 (1981) of 17 December 1981, 904 (1994) of 18 March 1994 and 2334 (2016) of 23 December 2016,

Reaffirming the applicability of the Geneva Convention relative to the Protection of Civilian Persons in Time of War, of 12 August 1949,[1] to the

---

1 United Nations, *Treaty Series*, vol. 75, No. 973.

Occupied Palestinian Territory, including East Jerusalem, and to the occupied Syrian Golan,

Affirming that the transfer by the occupying Power of parts of its own civilian population into the territory it occupies constitutes a breach of the Fourth Geneva Convention[1] and relevant provisions of customary law, including those codified in Additional Protocol I[2] to the four Geneva Conventions,[3]

Recalling the advisory opinion rendered on 9 July 2004 by the International Court of Justice on the legal consequences of the construction of a wall in the [p. 2] Occupied Palestinian Territory,[4] and recalling also General Assembly resolutions ES-10/15 of 20 July 2004 and ES-10/17 of 15 December 2006,

Noting that the International Court of Justice concluded that "the Israeli settlements in the Occupied Palestinian Territory (including East Jerusalem) have been established in breach of international law",[5]

Taking note of the recent reports of the Special Rapporteur of the Human Rights Council on the situation of human rights in the Palestinian territories occupied since 1967,[6]

Recalling the report of the independent international fact-finding mission to investigate the implications of the Israeli settlements on the civil, political, economic, social and cultural rights of the Palestinian people throughout the Occupied Palestinian Territory, including East Jerusalem,[7]

Recalling also the statement of 15 July 1999 and the declarations adopted on 5 December 2001 and on 17 December 2014[8] by the Conference of High Contracting Parties to the Fourth Geneva Convention on measures to enforce the Convention in the Occupied Palestinian Territory, including East Jerusalem, aimed at ensuring respect for the Convention in the Occupied Palestinian Territory, including East Jerusalem,

Recalling further the Declaration of Principles on Interim Self-Government Arrangements of 13 September 1993[9] and the subsequent implementation agreements between the Palestinian and Israeli sides,

Recalling the Quartet road map to a permanent two-State solution to the Israeli-Palestinian conflict,[10] and emphasizing specifically its call for a freeze

---

2   Ibid., vol. 1125, No. 17512.
3   Ibid., vol. 75, Nos. 970-973.
4   See A/ES-10/273 and A/ES-10/273/Corr.1.
5   Ibid., advisory opinion, para. 120.
6   A/HRC/34/70;; see also A/72/556.
7   A/HRC/22/63.
8   A/69/711-S/2015/1, annex.
9   A/48/486-S/26560, annex.
10   S/2003/529, annex.

on all settlement activity, including so-called natural growth, and the dismantlement of all settlement outposts erected since March 2001, and the need for Israel to uphold its obligations and commitments in this regard,

Recalling also its resolution 67/19 of 29 November 2012,

Noting the accession by Palestine to several human rights treaties and the core humanitarian law conventions, as well as other international treaties,

Aware that Israeli settlement activities involve, inter alia, the transfer of nationals of the occupying Power into the occupied territories, the confiscation of land, the forced transfer of Palestinian civilians, including Bedouin families, the exploitation of natural resources, the fragmentation of territory and other actions against the Palestinian civilian population and the civilian population in the occupied Syrian Golan that are contrary to international law,

Bearing in mind the extremely detrimental impact of Israeli settlement policies, decisions and activities on the ongoing regional and international efforts to resume and advance the peace process, on the prospects for the achievement of peace in the Middle East in accordance with the two-State solution of Israel and Palestine, living side by side in peace and security within recognized borders, on the basis of the pre-1967 borders, and on the viability and credibility of that solution, [p. 3]

Expressing grave concern about the continuation by Israel, the occupying Power, of settlement activities in the Occupied Palestinian Territory, including East Jerusalem, and condemning those activities as violations of international humanitarian law, relevant United Nations resolutions, the agreements reached between the parties and obligations under the Quartet road map and as actions in defiance of the calls by the international community to cease all settlement activities,

Deploring in particular Israel's construction and expansion of settlements in and around occupied East Jerusalem, including its so-called E-1 plan that aims to connect its illegal settlements around and further isolate occupied East Jerusalem, the continuing demolition of Palestinian homes and eviction of Palestinian families from the city, the revocation of Palestinian residency rights in the city, and ongoing settlement activities in the Jordan Valley, all of which further fragment and undermine the contiguity of the Occupied Palestinian Territory,

Deploring the plans to demolish the Palestinian village of Khan al-Ahmar, in contravention of international law, which would have serious consequences with regard to the displacement of its residents, severely threaten the viability of the two-State solution and undermine the prospect of peace, given the area's sensitive location and importance for preserving the contiguity of the Palestinian territory, and demanding the cessation of such plans,

Taking note of the Quartet report of 1 July 2016,[11] and stressing its recommendations, as well as its recent statements, including of 30 September 2015, 23 October 2015, 12 February 2016 and 23 September 2016, in which the Quartet members concluded that, inter alia, the continuing policy of settlement construction and expansion, designation of land for exclusive Israeli use and denial of Palestinian development, including the recent high rate of demolitions, are steadily eroding the two-State solution,

Deploring the continuing unlawful construction by Israel of the wall inside the Occupied Palestinian Territory, including in and around East Jerusalem, and expressing its concern, in particular, about the route of the wall in departure from the Armistice Line of 1949 and in such a way as to include the great majority of the Israeli settlements in the Occupied Palestinian Territory, including East Jerusalem, and which is causing humanitarian hardship and a serious decline of socioeconomic conditions for the Palestinian people, is fragmenting the territorial contiguity of the Territory and undermining its viability, and could prejudge future negotiations and make the two-State solution physically impossible to implement,

Condemning acts of violence and terror against civilians on both sides, and recalling the need to end all acts of violence, including acts of terror, provocation, incitement and destruction,

Condemning also all acts of violence, destruction, harassment, provocation and incitement by Israeli settlers in the Occupied Palestinian Territory, including East Jerusalem, against Palestinian civilians, including children, and their properties, including historic and religious sites, and agricultural lands, as well as acts of terror by several extremist Israeli settlers, and calling for accountability for the illegal actions perpetrated in this regard,

Taking note of the relevant reports of the Secretary-General, including pursuant to Security Council resolution 2334 (2016),[12] [p. 4]

Noting the special meeting of the Security Council convened on 26 September 2008, as well as the meeting of the Council of 18 February 2011,

1. *Reaffirms* that the Israeli settlements in the Occupied Palestinian Territory, including East Jerusalem, and in the occupied Syrian Golan are illegal and an obstacle to peace and economic and social development;

---

11 S/2016/595, annex.
12 A/73/357, A/73/364, A/73/410 and A/73/420.

2. *Calls upon* Israel to accept the de jure applicability of the Geneva Convention relative to the Protection of Civilian Persons in Time of War, of 12 August 1949,[1] to the Occupied Palestinian Territory, including East Jerusalem, and to the occupied Syrian Golan and to abide scrupulously by the provisions of the Convention, in particular article 49, and to comply with all of its obligations under international law and cease immediately all actions causing the alteration of the character, status and demographic composition of the Occupied Palestinian Territory, including East Jerusalem, and of the occupied Syrian Golan;

3. *Reiterates its demand* for the immediate and complete cessation of all Israeli settlement activities in all of the Occupied Palestinian Territory, including East Jerusalem, and in the occupied Syrian Golan, and calls in this regard for the full implementation of all the relevant resolutions of the Security Council, including, inter alia, resolutions 446 (1979), 452 (1979) of 20 July 1979, 465 (1980), 476 (1980), 1515 (2003) of 19 November 2003 and 2334 (2016);

4. *Recalls* the affirmation by the Security Council, in its resolution 2334 (2016), that it will not recognize any changes to the 4 June 1967 lines, including with regard to Jerusalem, other than those agreed by the parties through negotiations;

5. *Condemns* settlement activities in the Occupied Palestinian Territory, including East Jerusalem, and in the occupied Syrian Golan and any activities involving the confiscation of land, the disruption of the livelihood of protected persons, the forced transfer of civilians and the de facto annexation of land;

6. *Calls for* the consideration of measures of accountability, in accordance with international law, in the light of continued non-compliance with the demands for a complete and immediate cessation of all settlement activities, which are illegal under international law, constitute an obstacle to peace and threaten to make a two-State solution impossible, stressing that compliance with and respect for international humanitarian law and international human rights law is a cornerstone for peace and security in the region;

7. *Stresses* that a complete cessation of all Israeli settlement activities is essential for salvaging the two-State solution on the basis of the pre-1967 borders, and calls for affirmative steps to be taken immediately to reverse the negative trends on the ground that are imperilling the viability of the two-State solution;

8. *Demands* that Israel, the occupying Power, comply with its legal obligations, as mentioned in the advisory opinion rendered on 9 July 2004 by the International Court of Justice;[4]

9. *Reiterates its call for* the prevention of all acts of violence, destruction, harassment and provocation by Israeli settlers, especially against Palestinian civilians and their properties, including historic and religious sites and including in Occupied East Jerusalem, and their agricultural lands;

10. *Calls for* accountability for the illegal actions perpetrated by Israeli settlers in the Occupied Palestinian Territory, and stresses in this regard the need for the implementation of Security Council resolution 904 (1994), in which the Council called upon Israel, the occupying Power, to continue to take and implement measures, including the confiscation of arms, aimed at preventing illegal acts of violence by [p. 5] Israeli settlers, and called for measures to be taken to guarantee the safety and protection of the Palestinian civilians in the occupied territory;

11. *Stresses* the responsibility of Israel, the occupying Power, to investigate all acts of settler violence against Palestinian civilians and their properties and to ensure accountability for these acts;

12. *Calls upon* all States and international organizations to continue to actively pursue policies that ensure respect for their obligations under international law with regard to all illegal Israeli practices and measures in the Occupied Palestinian Territory, including East Jerusalem, particularly Israeli settlement activities;

13. *Recalls*, in this regard, the statement of 15 July 1999 and the declarations adopted on 5 December 2001 and on 17 December 2014[8] by the Conference of High Contracting Parties to the Fourth Geneva Convention on measures to enforce the Convention in the Occupied Palestinian Territory, including East Jerusalem, and welcomes in this regard initiatives by States parties, both individually and collectively, in accordance with article 1 of the Convention, aimed at ensuring respect for the Convention;

14. *Also recalls* that the Security Council, in its resolution 2334 (2016), called upon all States to distinguish, in their relevant dealings, between the territory of the State of Israel and the territories occupied since 1967;

15. *Calls upon* all States, consistent with their obligations under international law and the relevant resolutions, and bearing in mind the advisory opinion of the International Court of Justice of 9 July 2004, not to render aid or assistance in maintaining the situation created by illegal settlement activities;

16. *Calls upon* the relevant United Nations bodies to take all necessary measures and actions within their mandates to ensure full respect for and compliance with Human Rights Council resolution 17/4 of 16 June 2011,[13] concerning the Guiding Principles on Business and Human Rights[14] and other relevant international laws and standards, and to ensure the implementation of the United Nations "Protect, Respect and Remedy" Framework, which provides

---

13   See *Official Records of the General Assembly, Sixty-sixth Session, Supplement No. 53* (A/66/53), chap. III, sect. A.

14   A/HRC/17/31, annex.

a global standard for upholding human rights in relation to business activities that are connected with Israeli settlements in the Occupied Palestinian Territory, including East Jerusalem;

17. *Requests* the Secretary-General to report to the General Assembly at its seventy-fourth session on the implementation of the present resolution.

48th plenary meeting
7 December 2018

G.A. Res. 73/97, Applicability of the Geneva Convention Relative to the Protection of Civilian Persons in Time of War, of 12 August 1949, to the Occupied Palestinian Territory, including East Jerusalem, and the Other Occupied Arab Territories (Dec. 7, 2018)

United Nations
General Assembly
A/RES/73/97
Distr.: General
18 December 2019
Seventy-third session
Agenda item 55

Resolution adopted by the General Assembly on 7 December 2018

[*on the report of the Special Political and Decolonization Committee (Fourth Committee) (A/73/524)*]

73/97. Applicability of the Geneva Convention relative to the Protection of Civilian Persons in Time of War, of 12 August 1949, to the Occupied Palestinian Territory, including East Jerusalem, and the other occupied Arab territories

The General Assembly,

Recalling its relevant resolutions, including resolution 72/85 of 7 December 2017,

Bearing in mind the relevant resolutions of the Security Council,

Recalling the Regulations annexed to the Hague Convention IV of 1907, the Geneva Convention relative to the Protection of Civilian Persons in Time of

War, of 12 August 1949,[1] and relevant provisions of customary law, including those codified in Additional Protocol I[2] to the four Geneva Conventions,[3]

Having considered the report of the Special Committee to Investigate Israeli Practices Affecting the Human Rights of the Palestinian People and Other Arabs of the Occupied Territories[4] and the relevant reports of the Secretary-General,[5]

Considering that the promotion of respect for the obligations arising from the Charter of the United Nations and other instruments and rules of international law is among the basic purposes and principles of the United Nations,

Recalling the advisory opinion rendered on 9 July 2004 by the International Court of Justice,[6] and also recalling General Assembly resolution ES-10/15 of 20 July 2004, [p. 2]

Noting in particular the Court's reply, including that the Fourth Geneva Convention[1] is applicable in the Occupied Palestinian Territory, including East Jerusalem, and that Israel is in breach of several of the provisions of the Convention,

Recalling the Conference of High Contracting Parties to the Fourth Geneva Convention on measures to enforce the Convention in the Occupied Palestinian Territory, including East Jerusalem, held on 15 July 1999, as well as the declarations adopted by the reconvened Conference on 5 December 2001 and on 17 December 2014,[7] and the urgent need for the parties to follow up the implementation of those declarations,

Welcoming and encouraging the initiatives by States parties to the Convention, both individually and collectively, according to article 1 common to the four Geneva Conventions, aimed at ensuring respect for the Convention, as well as the continuing efforts of the depositary State of the Geneva Conventions in this regard,

Noting the accession by Palestine on 1 April 2014 to the Geneva Conventions and Additional Protocol I,

Stressing that Israel, the occupying Power, should comply strictly with its obligations under international law, including international humanitarian law,

1. *Reaffirms* that the Geneva Convention relative to the Protection of Civilian Persons in Time of War, of 12 August 1949,[1] is applicable to the Occupied

---

1 United Nations, *Treaty Series*, vol. 75, No. 973.
2 Ibid., vol. 1125, No. 17512.
3 Ibid., vol. 75, Nos. 970–973.
4 A/73/499.
5 A/73/357, A/73/364, A/73/410 and A/73/420.
6 See A/ES-10/273 and A/ES-10/273/Corr.1.
7 A/69/711-S/2015/1, annex.

Palestinian Territory, including East Jerusalem, and other Arab territories occupied by Israel since 1967;

2. *Demands* that Israel accept the de jure applicability of the Convention in the Occupied Palestinian Territory, including East Jerusalem, and other Arab territories occupied by Israel since 1967, and that it comply scrupulously with the provisions of the Convention;

3. *Calls upon* all High Contracting Parties to the Convention, in accordance with article 1 common to the four Geneva Conventions[3] and as mentioned in the advisory opinion of the International Court of Justice of 9 July 2004,[6] to continue to exert all efforts to ensure respect for its provisions by Israel, the occupying Power, in the Occupied Palestinian Territory, including East Jerusalem, and other Arab territories occupied by Israel since 1967;

4. *Notes* the reconvening by Switzerland, the depositary State, of the Conference of High Contracting Parties to the Fourth Geneva Convention on 17 December 2014, and calls for efforts to uphold the obligations reaffirmed in the declarations adopted on 5 December 2001 and 17 December 2014;[7]

5. *Welcomes* initiatives by States parties, in accordance with article 1 of the Convention, aimed at ensuring respect for the Convention;

6. *Reiterates* the need for speedy implementation of the relevant recommendations contained in the resolutions adopted by the General Assembly, including at its tenth emergency special session and including resolution ES-10/15, with regard to ensuring respect by Israel, the occupying Power, for the provisions of the Convention;

7. *Requests* the Secretary-General to report to the General Assembly at its seventy-fourth session on the implementation of the present resolution.

48th plenary meeting
7 December 2018

G.A. Res. 73/96, Work of the Special Committee to Investigate Israeli Practices Affecting the Human Rights of the Palestinian People and Other Arabs of the Occupied Territories (Dec. 7, 2018)

United Nations
General Assembly
A/RES/73/96
Distr.: General
18 December 2018
Seventy-third session
Agenda item 55

Resolution adopted by the General Assembly on 7 December 2018

[*on the report of the Special Political and Decolonization Committee (Fourth Committee) (A/73/524)*]

73/96. Work of the Special Committee to Investigate Israeli Practices Affecting the Human Rights of the Palestinian People and Other Arabs of the Occupied Territories

The General Assembly,

Guided by the purposes and principles of the Charter of the United Nations,

Guided also by international humanitarian law, in particular the Geneva Convention relative to the Protection of Civilian Persons in Time of War, of 12 August 1949,[1] as well as international standards of human rights, in particular the Universal Declaration of Human Rights[2] and the International Covenants on Human Rights,[3]

---

1 United Nations, *Treaty Series*, vol. 75, No. 973.
2 Resolution 217 A (III).
3 Resolution 2200 A (XXI), annex.

Recalling its relevant resolutions, including resolutions 2443 (XXIII) of 19 December 1968 and 72/84 of 7 December 2017, and the relevant resolutions of the Human Rights Council, including resolutions S-12/1 of 16 October 2009,[4] S-21/1 of 23 July 2014[5] and 29/25 of 3 July 2015,[6]

Recalling also the relevant resolutions of the Security Council, including resolution 2334 (2016) of 23 December 2016,

Taking into account the advisory opinion rendered on 9 July 2004 by the International Court of Justice on the legal consequences of the construction of a wall in the Occupied Palestinian Territory,[7] and recalling in this regard its resolution ES-10/15 of 20 July 2004, [p. 2]

Recalling the statement of 15 July 1999 and the declarations adopted on 5 December 2001 and on 17 December 2014[8] by the Conference of High Contracting Parties to the Fourth Geneva Convention, and welcoming initiatives by States parties, both individually and collectively, according to article 1 of the Convention and aimed at ensuring respect for the Convention in the Occupied Palestinian Territory, including East Jerusalem,

Recalling also its resolution 58/292 of 6 May 2004,

Taking note of the report of the independent international fact-finding mission to investigate the implications of the Israeli settlements on the civil, political, economic, social and cultural rights of the Palestinian people throughout the Occupied Palestinian Territory, including East Jerusalem,[9]

Convinced that occupation itself represents a gross and grave violation of human rights,

Noting with deep regret that 51 years have passed since the onset of the Israeli occupation, and stressing the urgent need for efforts to reverse the negative trends on the ground and to restore a political horizon for advancing and accelerating meaningful negotiations aimed at the achievement of a peace agreement that will bring a complete end to the Israeli occupation that began in 1967 and the resolution of all core final status issues, without exception, leading to a peaceful, just, lasting and comprehensive solution for the question of Palestine,

Recognizing that the occupation and ensuing persistent and systematic violations of international law by Israel, including international humanitarian

---

4 See *Official Records of the General Assembly, Sixty-fourth Session, Supplement No. 53A* (A/64/53/Add.1), chap. I.
5 Ibid., *Sixty-ninth Session, Supplement No. 53* (A/69/53), chap. VI.
6 Ibid., *Seventieth Session, Supplement No. 53* (A/70/53), chap. II.
7 See A/ES-10/273 and A/ES-10/273/Corr.1.
8 A/69/711-S/2015/1, annex.
9 A/HRC/22/63.

and human rights law, are considered to be the main sources of other Israeli violations and discriminatory policies against the Palestinian civilian population in the Occupied Palestinian Territory, including East Jerusalem,

Gravely concerned about the continuing detrimental impact of ongoing unlawful Israeli practices and measures in the Occupied Palestinian Territory, including East Jerusalem, including the excessive use of force by the Israeli occupying forces against Palestinian civilians, resulting in the death and injury of civilians and the widespread destruction of property and vital infrastructure, including during the Israeli military operations in the Gaza Strip in July and August 2014, as well as ongoing settlement activities and construction of the wall, the internal forced displacement of civilians, the imposition of collective punishment measures, particularly against the civilian population in the Gaza Strip, where continuing severe restrictions on movement amount to a blockade, and the detention and imprisonment of thousands of Palestinians,

Expressing grave concern about tensions, instability and violence in the Occupied Palestinian Territory, including East Jerusalem, due to the illegal policies and practices of Israel, the occupying Power, including, in particular, provocations and incitements regarding the holy places of Jerusalem, including the Haram al-Sharif,

Gravely concerned about all acts of violence, intimidation and provocation by Israeli settlers against Palestinian civilians and properties, including homes, mosques, churches and agricultural lands,

Gravely concerned also by reports regarding serious human rights violations and grave breaches of international humanitarian law,[10] [p. 3]

Recalling the report of the independent commission of inquiry established pursuant to Human Rights Council resolution S-21/1,[11] and stressing the imperative of ensuring accountability for all violations of international humanitarian law and international human rights law in order to end impunity, ensure justice, deter further violations, protect civilians and promote peace,

Having considered the report of the Special Committee to Investigate Israeli Practices Affecting the Human Rights of the Palestinian People and Other Arabs of the Occupied Territories[12] and the relevant reports of the Secretary-General,[13]

---

10   See A/63/855-S/2009/250 and A/HRC/12/48.
11   A/HRC/29/52.
12   A/73/499.
13   A/73/357, A/73/364, A/73/410 and A/73/420.

Recalling the Declaration of Principles on Interim Self-Government Arrangements of 13 September 1993[14] and the subsequent implementation agreements between the Palestinian and Israeli sides,

Stressing the urgency of bringing a complete end to the Israeli occupation that began in 1967, and thus an end to the violation of the human rights of the Palestinian people, and of allowing for the realization of their inalienable human rights, including their right to self-determination and their independent State,

Taking note of the application of Palestine for admission to membership in the United Nations, submitted on 23 September 2011,[15]

Recalling its resolution 67/19 of 29 November 2012, by which, inter alia, Palestine was accorded non-member observer State status in the United Nations, and taking note of the follow-up report of the Secretary-General,

Noting the accession by Palestine to several human rights treaties and the core humanitarian law conventions, as well as other international treaties,[16]

1. *Commends* the Special Committee to Investigate Israeli Practices Affecting the Human Rights of the Palestinian People and Other Arabs of the Occupied Territories for its impartiality and efforts in performing the tasks assigned to it by the General Assembly, in spite of the obstruction of its mandate;

2. *Reiterates its demand* that Israel, the occupying Power, cooperate, in accordance with its obligations as a State Member of the United Nations, with the Special Committee in implementing its mandate, and deplores the continued lack of cooperation in this regard;

3. *Deplores* those policies and practices of Israel that violate the human rights of the Palestinian people and other Arabs of the occupied territories, as reflected in the report of the Special Committee covering the reporting period;[12]

4. *Expresses grave concern* about the critical situation in the Occupied Palestinian Territory, including East Jerusalem, particularly in the Gaza Strip, as a result of unlawful Israeli practices and measures, and especially condemns and calls for the immediate cessation of all illegal Israeli settlement activities and the construction of the wall, the lifting of the blockade of the Gaza Strip, as well as a complete cessation of the excessive and indiscriminate use of force and military operations against the civilian population, settler violence, the destruction and confiscation of properties, including home demolitions as a measure of reprisal, the forced displacement of civilians, all measures of

---

14 A/48/486-S/26560, annex.
15 A/66/371-S/2011/592.
16 A/67/738.

collective punishment, and the detention and imprisonment of thousands of civilians; [p. 4]

5. *Requests* the Special Committee, pending complete termination of the Israeli occupation, to continue to investigate Israeli policies and practices in the Occupied Palestinian Territory, including East Jerusalem, and other Arab territories occupied by Israel since 1967, especially Israeli violations of the Geneva Convention relative to the Protection of Civilian Persons in Time of War, of 12 August 1949,[1] and to consult, as appropriate, with the International Committee of the Red Cross, according to its regulations, in order to ensure that the welfare and human rights of the peoples of the occupied territories, including prisoners and detainees, are safeguarded, and to report to the Secretary-General as soon as possible and whenever the need arises thereafter;

6. *Also requests* the Special Committee to submit regularly to the Secretary-General periodic reports on the current situation in the Occupied Palestinian Territory, including East Jerusalem;

7. *Further requests* the Special Committee to continue to investigate the treatment and status of the thousands of prisoners and detainees, including children, women and elected representatives, in Israeli prisons and detention centres in the Occupied Palestinian Territory, including East Jerusalem, and other Arab territories occupied by Israel since 1967, and expresses grave concern about harsh conditions and ill-treatment of prisoners and recent hunger strikes, stressing the need for respect for all applicable rules of international law, including the Fourth Geneva Convention,[1] the United Nations Standard Minimum Rules for the Treatment of Prisoners (the Nelson Mandela Rules)[17] and the United Nations Rules for the Treatment of Women Prisoners and Non-custodial Measures for Women Offenders (the Bangkok Rules);[18]

8. *Requests* the Secretary-General:

(a) To provide the Special Committee with all necessary facilities, including those required for its visits to the occupied territories, so that it may investigate the Israeli policies and practices referred to in the present resolution;

(b) To utilize his good offices to facilitate and support the Special Committee in carrying out its mandate;

(c) To continue to make available such staff as may be necessary to assist the Special Committee in the performance of its tasks;

(d) To circulate regularly to Member States the periodic reports mentioned in paragraph 6 above;

---

17   Resolution 70/175, annex.
18   Resolution 65/229, annex.

(e) To ensure the widest circulation of the reports of the Special Committee and of information regarding its activities and findings, by all means available, through the Department of Public Information of the Secretariat and, where necessary, to reprint those reports of the Special Committee that are no longer available;

9. *Decides* to include in the provisional agenda of its seventy-fourth session the item entitled "Report of the Special Committee to Investigate Israeli Practices Affecting the Human Rights of the Palestinian People and Other Arabs of the Occupied Territories".

48th plenary meeting
7 December 2018

G.A. Res. 73/95, Palestine Refugees' Properties and Their Revenues (Dec. 7, 2018)

United Nations
General Assembly
A/RES/73/95
Distr.: General
Dec. 18, 2018
Seventy-third session
Agenda item 54

Resolution adopted by the General Assembly on 7 December 2018

[*on the report of the Special Political and Decolonization Committee (Fourth Committee) (A/73/523)*]

73/95. Palestine refugees' properties and their revenues

The General Assembly,

Recalling its resolutions 194 (III) of 11 December 1948 and 36/146 C of 16 December 1981 and all its subsequent resolutions on the question,

Taking note of the report of the Secretary-General submitted pursuant to its resolution 72/83 of 7 December 2017,[1] as well as that of the United Nations Conciliation Commission for Palestine for the period from 1 September 2017 to 31 August 2018,[2]

Recalling that the Universal Declaration of Human Rights[3] and the principles of international law uphold the principle that no one shall be arbitrarily deprived of his or her property,

Recalling in particular its resolution 394 (V) of 14 December 1950, in which it directed the Conciliation Commission, in consultation with the parties

---

1 A/73/323.
2 A/73/296.
3 Resolution 217 A (III).

concerned, to prescribe measures for the protection of the rights, property and interests of the Palestine refugees,

Noting the completion of the programme of identification and evaluation of Arab property, as announced by the Conciliation Commission in its twenty-second progress report,[4] and the fact that the Land Office had a schedule of Arab owners and a file of documents defining the location, area and other particulars of Arab property, [p. 2]

Expressing its appreciation for the preservation and modernization of the existing records, including the land records, of the Conciliation Commission, and stressing the importance of such records for a just resolution of the plight of the Palestine refugees in conformity with resolution 194 (III),

Recalling that, in the framework of the Middle East peace process, the Palestine Liberation Organization and the Government of Israel agreed, in the Declaration of Principles on Interim Self-Government Arrangements of 13 September 1993,[5] to commence negotiations on permanent status issues, including the important issue of the refugees,

1. *Reaffirms* that the Palestine refugees are entitled to their property and to the income derived therefrom, in conformity with the principles of equity and justice;

2. *Requests* the Secretary-General to take all appropriate steps, in consultation with the United Nations Conciliation Commission for Palestine, for the protection of Arab property, assets and property rights in Israel;

3. *Calls once again upon* Israel to render all facilities and assistance to the Secretary-General in the implementation of the present resolution;

4. *Calls upon* all the parties concerned to provide the Secretary-General with any pertinent information in their possession concerning Arab property, assets and property rights in Israel that would assist him in the implementation of the present resolution;

5. *Urges* the Palestinian and Israeli sides, as agreed between them, to deal with the important issue of Palestine refugees' properties and their revenues within the framework of the final status peace negotiations;

6. *Requests* the Secretary-General to report to the General Assembly at its seventy-fourth session on the implementation of the present resolution.

48th plenary meeting
7 December 2018

---

4 *Official Records of the General Assembly, Nineteenth Session, Annexes, Annex No. 11*, document A/5700.
5 A/48/486-S/26560, annex.

G.A. Res. 73/94, Operations of the United Nations Relief and Works Agency for Palestine Refugees in the Near East (Dec. 7, 2018)

United Nations
General Assembly
A/RES/73/94
Distr.: General
Dec. 18, 2018
Seventy-third session
Agenda item 54

Resolution adopted by the General Assembly on 7 December 2018

[*on the report of the Special Political and Decolonization Committee (Fourth Committee) (A/73/523)*]

73/94. Operations of the United Nations Relief and Works Agency for Palestine Refugees in the Near East

The General Assembly,

Recalling its resolutions 194 (III) of 11 December 1948, 212 (III) of 19 November 1948, 302 (IV) of 8 December 1949 and all subsequent related resolutions, including its resolution 72/82 of 7 December 2017,

Recalling also the relevant resolutions of the Security Council,

Having considered the report of the Commissioner-General of the United Nations Relief and Works Agency for Palestine Refugees in the Near East covering the period from 1 January to 31 December 2017,[1]

Taking note of the letter dated 19 June 2018 from the Chair of the Advisory Commission of the Agency addressed to the Commissioner-General,[2] and noting the extraordinary meeting of the Commission held on 21 January and 16 August 2018,

---

1 *Official Records of the General Assembly, Seventy-third Session, Supplement No. 13* (A/73/13).
2 Ibid., pp. 6–7.

Underlining that, at a time of heightened conflict and instability in the Middle East, the Agency continues to play a vital role in ameliorating the plight of the Palestine refugees through the provision of, inter alia, essential education, health, relief and social services programmes and emergency assistance to a registered population of more than 5.4 million refugees whose situation has become extremely precarious, in mitigating the consequences of alarming trends, including increasing violence, marginalization and poverty, in the areas of operation, and in providing a crucial measure of stability in the region,

Deeply concerned about the extremely critical financial situation of the Agency, caused by the structural underfunding of the Agency, as well as by rising needs and expenditures resulting from the deterioration of the socio-economic and humanitarian [p. 2] conditions and the conflicts and rising instability in the region and their significant negative impact on the ability of the Agency to deliver essential services to the Palestine refugees, including its emergency, recovery, reconstruction and development programmes in all fields of operation,

Taking note of the report of the Secretary-General on the operations of the United Nations Relief and Works Agency for Palestine Refugees in the Near East,[3] submitted pursuant to resolution 71/93 of 6 December 2016, and the request contained therein for broad consultations to explore all ways and means, including through voluntary and assessed contributions, to ensure that the Agency's funding is sufficient, predictable and sustained for the duration of its mandate, and considering the recommendations contained in the report,

Taking note also of the report of 30 June 2017 of the Commissioner-General, submitted pursuant to paragraph 57 of the report of the Secretary-General and in follow-up to the update to the special report of 3 August 2015 of the Commissioner-General,[4] submitted pursuant to paragraph 21 of General Assembly resolution 302 (IV), regarding the severe financial crisis of the Agency and the negative implications for the continued delivery of core Agency programmes to the Palestine refugees in all fields of operation,

Expressing appreciation for the efforts of donors and host countries to respond to the Agency's unprecedented financial crisis, including through generous, additional contributions and, where possible, continued increases in voluntary contributions, while acknowledging the steadfast support of all other donors to the Agency,

Noting that contributions have not been predictable enough or sufficient to meet growing needs and remedy the persistent shortfalls, which have been

---

3   A/71/849.
4   A/70/272, annex.

exacerbated in 2018 by the suspension of the single largest voluntary contribution to the Agency, undermining the Agency's operations and efforts to promote human development and meet Palestine refugees' basic needs, and stressing the need for further efforts to comprehensively address the recurrent funding shortfalls affecting the Agency's operations,

Recognizing the Agency's extensive efforts to rapidly develop innovative and diversified ways to address its financial shortfall and mobilize resources, including through the expansion of the donor base and partnerships with international financial institutions, the private sector and civil society, including through special initiatives such as the "Dignity is priceless" campaign,

Commending the Agency for the measures taken to address the financial crisis, despite difficult operational circumstances, including through the implementation of the medium-term strategy for 2016–2021 and various internal measures to contain expenditures, reduce operational and administrative costs, maximize the use of resources and reduce the funding shortfalls, and expressing profound concern that, despite such measures, the Agency's programme budget, which is funded primarily by voluntary contributions from Member States and intergovernmental organizations, faces persistent shortfalls that are increasingly threatening the delivery of the Agency's core programmes of assistance to the Palestine refugees,

Encouraging the Agency to sustain those reform efforts, while also taking all possible measures to protect and improve the quality of access to and the delivery of core programmes of assistance, [p. 3]

Recalling its resolution 65/272 of 18 April 2011, in which it requested the Secretary-General to continue to support the institutional strengthening of the Agency,

Stressing the need to support the Agency's capacity to uphold its mandate and to avert the serious humanitarian, political and security risks that would result from any interruption or suspension of its vital work,

Recognizing that the recurring and growing financial shortfalls directly affecting the sustainability of the Agency's operations need to be remedied by examining new funding modalities designed to put the Agency on a stable financial footing to enable it to effectively carry out its core programmes in accordance with its mandate and commensurate with humanitarian needs,

Welcoming the affirmation in the New York Declaration for Refugees and Migrants, adopted by the General Assembly on 19 September 2016,[5] that, inter alia, the Agency, along with other relevant organizations, requires sufficient

---

5 Resolution 71/1.

funding to be able to carry out its activities effectively and in a predictable manner,

Bearing in mind the 2030 Agenda for Sustainable Development,[6] including the pledge that no one will be left behind, emphasizing that the Sustainable Development Goals apply to all, including refugees, and commending the efforts of the Agency's programmes to promote 10 of the 17 Goals, as indicated in the report of the Secretary-General,[3]

Welcoming the joint efforts of host countries and donors to mobilize support for the Agency, including through extraordinary ministerial meetings, inter alia, the extraordinary ministerial conference held in Rome on 15 March 2018 on the theme "Preserving dignity and sharing responsibility: mobilizing collective action for the United Nations Relief and Works Agency for Palestine Refugees in the Near East", chaired by Egypt, Jordan and Sweden, and the ministerial meeting convened at United Nations Headquarters in New York on 27 September 2018, hosted by Germany, Japan, Jordan, Sweden, Turkey and the European Union, aimed at urgently addressing the Agency's funding shortfall and expanding donor support for the Agency,

Welcoming also the decision taken by the Organization of Islamic Cooperation Council of Foreign Ministers at its forty-fifth session, held in Bangladesh in May 2018, and reaffirmed at the seventh extraordinary session of the Islamic Summit Conference, held in Turkey in May 2018, to establish a waqf fund to support Palestine refugees through enhanced support to the Agency,

Recalling Articles 100, 104 and 105 of the Charter of the United Nations and the Convention on the Privileges and Immunities of the United Nations,[7]

Recalling also the Convention on the Safety of United Nations and Associated Personnel,[8]

Recalling further its resolutions 72/131 of 11 December 2017 on the safety and security of humanitarian personnel and protection of United Nations personnel and 72/133 of 11 December 2017 on the strengthening of the coordination of emergency humanitarian assistance of the United Nations, calling upon, inter alia, all States to ensure respect for and the protection of all humanitarian personnel and United Nations and associated personnel, to respect the principles of humanity, neutrality, [p. 4] impartiality and independence for the provision of humanitarian assistance and to respect and ensure respect for the inviolability of United Nations premises,

---

6 Resolution 70/1.
7 Resolution 22 A (I).
8 United Nations, *Treaty Series*, vol. 2051, No. 35457.

Affirming the applicability of the Geneva Convention relative to the Protection of Civilian Persons in Time of War, of 12 August 1949,[9] to the Palestinian territory occupied since 1967, including East Jerusalem,

Aware of the continuing needs of the Palestine refugees in all fields of operation, namely Jordan, Lebanon, the Syrian Arab Republic and the Occupied Palestinian Territory,

Gravely concerned about the extremely difficult socioeconomic conditions being faced by the Palestine refugees in the Occupied Palestinian Territory, including East Jerusalem, particularly in the refugee camps in the Gaza Strip, as a result of the recurrent military operations, continuing prolonged Israeli closures, the construction of settlements and the wall, evictions, the demolition of homes and livelihood properties causing forced transfers of civilians, and the severe economic and movement restrictions that in effect amount to a blockade, which have deepened unemployment and poverty rates among the refugees, with potentially lasting, long-term negative effects, while taking note of developments with regard to the situation of access there,

Deploring the continuing and negative repercussions of the conflicts in and around the Gaza Strip and the high number of Palestinian causalities, including children, in the recent period,

Expressing grave concern in this regard about the lasting impact on the humanitarian and socioeconomic situation of the Palestine refugees in the Gaza Strip, including high rates of food insecurity, poverty, displacement and the depletion of coping capacities, and taking note in this regard of the United Nations country team reports of 26 August 2016, entitled "Gaza: two years after" and of July 2017, entitled "Gaza ten years later" and the alarming conditions and figures documented therein,

Deploring all attacks affecting United Nations installations, including Agency schools sheltering displaced civilians, and all other breaches of the inviolability of United Nations premises, including during the conflict in the Gaza Strip in July and August 2014, as reported in the summary by the Secretary-General of the report of the Board of Inquiry[10] and by the independent commission of inquiry established pursuant to Human Rights Council resolution S-21/1,[11] and stressing the imperative of ensuring accountability,

Recalling the temporary tripartite agreement facilitated by the United Nations in September 2014, and stressing the urgent need for the lifting of all

---

9   Ibid., vol. 75, No. 973.
10 S/2015/286, annex.
11 See A/HRC/29/52.

Israeli closures and restrictions on the Gaza Strip and for the reconstruction of destroyed homes and infrastructure,

Recalling also its resolution ES-10/18 of 16 January 2009 and Security Council resolution 1860 (2009) of 8 January 2009, as well as the Agreement on Movement and Access of 15 November 2005,

Calling upon Israel to ensure the expedited and unimpeded import of all necessary construction materials into the Gaza Strip and to reduce the burdensome cost of importation of Agency supplies, while taking note of the continued implementation of the tripartite agreement facilitated by the United Nations, [p. 5]

Expressing concern about the continuing classroom shortage, including in the Gaza Strip, and the consequent negative impact on the right to education of refugee children,

Stressing the urgent need for the advancement of reconstruction in the Gaza Strip, including by ensuring the timely facilitation of construction projects, including extensive shelter repair, and the need for the accelerated implementation of other urgent United Nations-led civilian reconstruction activities,

Welcoming contributions made to the Agency's emergency appeals, including for the Gaza Strip, and calling urgently upon the international community to continue its support, since needs persist and these appeals remain severely underfunded,

Urging the full disbursement of pledges made at the Cairo International Conference on Palestine: Reconstructing Gaza, held on 12 October 2014, for ensuring the provision of the necessary humanitarian assistance and accelerating the reconstruction process,

Stressing that the situation in the Gaza Strip is unsustainable and that a durable ceasefire agreement must lead to a fundamental improvement in the living conditions of the Palestinian people in the Gaza Strip, including through the sustained and regular opening of crossing points, and must ensure the safety and well-being of civilians on both sides,

Affirming the need to support the Palestinian national consensus Government in its assumption of full government responsibilities in both the West Bank and the Gaza Strip, in all fields, as well as through its presence at Gaza's crossing points,

Noting with appreciation the significant progress made towards rebuilding the Nahr el-Bared refugee camp, commending the Government of Lebanon, donors, the Agency and other parties concerned for the continuing efforts to assist affected and displaced refugees, and emphasizing the need for the funding required to complete the reconstruction of the camp and end without delay the displacement from the camp of thousands of residents whose shelters have not been rebuilt,

Expressing deep concern at the critical situation of Palestine refugees in the Syrian Arab Republic and at the impact of the crisis on the Agency's installations and its ability to deliver its services, and regretting profoundly the loss of life and widespread displacement among refugees and the killing of staff members of the Agency in the crisis since 2012,

Emphasizing the continuing need for assistance to Palestine refugees in the Syrian Arab Republic as well as those who have fled to neighbouring countries, and emphasizing the necessity of ensuring open borders for Palestine refugees fleeing the crisis in the Syrian Arab Republic, consistent with the principles of non-discrimination and non-refoulement under international law, and recalling in this regard the statement by the President of the Security Council of 2 October 2013[12] and the New York Declaration for Refugees and Migrants,

Aware of the valuable work done by the Agency in providing protection to the Palestinian people, in particular Palestine refugees, and recalling the need for the protection of all civilians in situations of armed conflict,

Deploring the endangerment of the safety of the Agency's staff and the damage and destruction caused to the facilities and properties of the Agency during the period [p. 6] covered by the report of the Commissioner-General, and stressing the need to maintain the neutrality and safeguard the inviolability of United Nations premises, installations and equipment at all times,

Deploring also the breaches of the inviolability of United Nations premises, the failure to accord the property and assets of the Organization immunity from any form of interference, incursions or misuse, the failure to protect United Nations personnel, premises and property and any disruption caused to Agency operations by such violations,

Condemning the killing, injury and detention contrary to international law of Agency staff members,

Condemning also the killing, wounding and detention contrary to international law of refugee children and women,

Affirming the need for accountability and compensation to victims of violations of international law in accordance with international standards by all sides,

Deeply concerned about the continuing imposition of restrictions on the freedom of movement and access of the Agency's staff, vehicles and goods, and the injury, harassment and intimidation of the Agency's staff, which

---

12   S/PRST/2013/15; see *Resolutions and Decisions of the Security Council, 1 August 2013–31 July 2014* (S/INF/69).

undermine and obstruct the work of the Agency, including its ability to provide essential basic and emergency services,

Recalling the statement of 15 July 1999 and the declarations adopted on 5 December 2001 and on 17 December 2014[13] by the Conference of High Contracting Parties to the Fourth Geneva Convention, including the call upon parties to facilitate the activities of the Agency, to guarantee its protection and to refrain from levying taxes and imposing undue financial burdens,

Aware of the agreement between the Agency and the Government of Israel,

Taking note of the agreement reached on 24 June 1994, embodied in an exchange of letters between the Agency and the Palestine Liberation Organization,[14]

1. *Reaffirms* that the effective functioning of the United Nations Relief and Works Agency for Palestine Refugees in the Near East remains essential in all fields of operation;

2. *Expresses its appreciation* to the Commissioner-General of the Agency, as well as to all the staff of the Agency, for their tireless efforts and valuable work, particularly in the light of the difficult conditions, instability and crises faced during the past year;

3. *Expresses special commendation* to the Agency for the essential role that it has played for almost seven decades since its establishment in providing vital services for the well-being, human development and protection of the Palestine refugees and the amelioration of their plight and for the stability of the region, and affirms the necessity for continuing the work of the Agency and its unimpeded operation and provision of services, pending the just resolution of the question of the Palestine refugees;

4. *Commends* the Agency for its extraordinary efforts, in cooperation with other United Nations agencies on the ground, to provide emergency humanitarian assistance, including shelter, food and medical aid, to refugees and affected civilians [p. 7] during periods of crisis and conflict, and recognizes its exemplary capacity to mobilize in emergency situations while continuously carrying out its core human development programmes;

5. *Expresses its grave concern* about attempts to discredit the Agency despite its proven operational capacity, record of effective provision of humanitarian and development assistance and consistent implementation of its mandate in accordance with relevant resolutions and its regulatory framework, even under the most difficult circumstances;

---

13 A/69/711-S/2015/1, annex.
14 *Official Records of the General Assembly, Forty-ninth Session, Supplement No. 13* (A/49/13), annex I.

6. *Reaffirms* the Agency's important role in providing humanitarian and development assistance to Palestine refugees, engaging with international human rights mechanisms, as appropriate, and in doing so contributing to the protection and resilience of Palestinian civilians, as outlined in the report of the Secretary-General on the protection of the Palestinian civilian population,[15] and contributing to regional stability;

7. *Expresses its appreciation* for the important support and cooperation provided by the host Governments to the Agency in the discharge of its duties;

8. *Also expresses its appreciation* to the Advisory Commission of the Agency, and requests it to continue its efforts and to keep the General Assembly informed of its activities;

9. *Takes note* of the report of the Working Group on the Financing of the United Nations Relief and Works Agency for Palestine Refugees in the Near East[16] and the efforts to assist in ensuring the financial security of the Agency, and requests the Secretary-General to provide the necessary services and assistance to the Working Group for the conduct of its work;

10. *Expresses its deep appreciation* to all donor countries and organizations that have, inter alia, sustained, accelerated or increased their contributions to the Agency, helping to alleviate its unprecedented financial crisis in 2018, to mitigate imminent risks to its core and emergency programming and to prevent an interruption of essential assistance to Palestine refugees;

11. *Commends* the Agency for its six-year medium-term strategy for 2016–2021 and the Commissioner-General for his continuing efforts to increase the budgetary transparency and efficiency of the Agency, as reflected in the Agency's programme budget for the biennium 2018–2019;[17]

12. *Also commends* the Agency for sustaining its robust internal reform efforts, despite difficult operational circumstances, and recognizes its implementation of maximum efficiency procedures to contain expenditures, reduce operational and administrative costs, reduce its funding shortfalls and maximize the use of resources;

13. *Takes note* of the report of the Secretary-General on the operations of the United Nations Relief and Works Agency for Palestine Refugees in the Near East[3] and the conclusions and recommendations contained therein;

14. *Appeals* to States and organizations for the maintenance of their voluntary contributions to the Agency, as well as an increase in contributions where

---

15   A/ES-10/794.
16   A/73/349.
17   *Official Records of the General Assembly, Seventy-second Session, Supplement No. 13A* (A/72/13/Add.1).

possible, in particular to the Agency's programme budget, including in the consideration of their allocation of resources for international human rights, peace and stability, development [p. 8] and humanitarian efforts, to support the Agency's mandate and its ability to meet the rising needs of the Palestine refugees and essential associated costs of operations;

15. *Appeals* to States and organizations not currently contributing to the Agency to urgently consider making voluntary contributions in response to the calls of the Secretary-General for expansion of the Agency's donor base, in order to stabilize funding and ensure greater sharing of the financial burden of supporting the Agency's operations, in accordance with the continuing responsibility of the international community as a whole to assist the Palestine refugees;

16. *Calls for* the provision by donors of early annual voluntary contributions, less earmarking, and multi-year funding, in line with the Grand Bargain on humanitarian financing announced at the World Humanitarian Summit, held in Istanbul, Turkey, in May 2016, in order to enhance the Agency's ability to plan and implement its operations with a greater degree of assurance regarding resource flows;

17. *Also calls for* the full and timely funding by donors of the Agency's emergency, recovery and reconstruction programmes as set out in its appeals and response plans;

18. *Requests* the Commissioner-General to continue efforts to maintain and increase traditional donor support and to enhance income from non-traditional donors, including through partnerships with public and private entities;

19. *Encourages* the Agency to explore financing avenues in relation to the implementation of the Sustainable Development Goals;[6]

20. *Urges* States and organizations to actively pursue partnerships with and innovative support for the Agency, including as recommended in paragraphs 47, 48 and 50 of the report of the Secretary-General,[3] including through the establishment of endowments, trust funds or revolving fund mechanisms and assistance to the Agency to access humanitarian, development and peace and security trust funds and grants;

21. *Welcomes* pledges by States and organizations to provide diplomatic and technical support to the Agency, including engagement with international and financial development institutions, including the World Bank and the Islamic Development Bank, and, where appropriate, to facilitate support for the establishment of financing mechanisms that can provide assistance to refugees and in fragile contexts, including to meet the needs of the Palestine refugees, and calls for serious follow-up efforts;

22. *Encourages* further progress with regard to the creation of a World Bank multi-donor trust fund, as well as by the Organization of Islamic Cooperation for the establishment of an Islamic Development Bank endowment fund (waqf) to support Palestine refugees through the Agency;

23. *Requests* the Agency to continue to implement efficiency measures through its medium-term strategy and the development of a five-year proposal for stabilizing the Agency's finances, including specific and time-bound measures, and to continue to improve its cost efficiency and resource mobilization efforts;

24. *Calls upon* the members of the Advisory Commission and the Working Group on the Financing of the United Nations Relief and Works Agency for Palestine Refugees in the Near East to consider the relevant recommendations in the report of the Secretary-General,[3] including to help the Agency to address resource mobilization challenges and to actively assist the Commissioner-General in the efforts to create sustainable, sufficient and predictable support for the Agency's operations; [p. 9]

25. *Takes note* of the recommendations of the Secretary-General regarding the support provided to the Agency from the regular budget of the United Nations;

26. *Endorses* the efforts of the Commissioner-General to continue to provide humanitarian assistance, as far as is practicable, on an emergency basis and as a temporary measure, to persons in the area who are internally displaced and in serious need of continuing assistance as a result of recent crises in the Agency's fields of operation;

27. *Encourages* the Agency to provide increased assistance, in accordance with its mandate, to affected Palestine refugees in the Syrian Arab Republic as well as to those who have fled to neighbouring countries, as detailed in the Syrian regional crisis response plans, and calls upon donors to urgently ensure sustained support to the Agency in this regard in the light of the continuing grave deterioration of the situation and the growing needs of the refugees;

28. *Welcomes* the progress made thus far by the Agency in rebuilding the Nahr el-Bared refugee camp in northern Lebanon, and calls for donor funding to enable the expeditious completion of its reconstruction, for the continued provision of relief assistance to those displaced following its destruction in 2007 and for the alleviation of their ongoing suffering through the provision of the necessary support and financial assistance until the reconstruction of the camp is complete;

29. *Encourages* the Agency, in close cooperation with other relevant United Nations entities, to continue to make progress in addressing the needs, rights and protection of children, women and persons with disabilities in its operations,

including through the provision of necessary psychosocial and humanitarian support, in accordance with the Convention on the Rights of the Child,[18] the Convention on the Elimination of All Forms of Discrimination against Women[19] and the Convention on the Rights of Persons with Disabilities;[20]

30. *Also encourages* the Agency to continue to reduce the vulnerability and improve the self-reliance and resilience of Palestine refugees through its programmes;

31. *Recognizes* the acute protection needs of Palestine refugees across the region, and encourages the Agency's efforts to contribute to a coordinated and sustained response in accordance with international law, including the Agency's development of its protection framework and function in all field offices, including for child protection;

32. *Commends* the Agency for its humanitarian and psychosocial support programmes and other initiatives that provide recreational, cultural and educational activities for children in all fields, including in the Gaza Strip, recognizing their positive contribution, as well as the detrimental impact of the funding shortfall on some emergency assistance provided by the Agency, calls for full support for such initiatives by donor and host countries, and encourages the building and strengthening of partnerships to facilitate and enhance the provision of these services;

33. *Calls upon* Israel, the occupying Power, to comply fully with the provisions of the Geneva Convention relative to the Protection of Civilian Persons in Time of War, of 12 August 1949;[9]

34. *Also calls upon* Israel to abide by Articles 100, 104 and 105 of the Charter of the United Nations and the Convention on the Privileges and Immunities of the United Nations[7] in order to ensure the safety of the personnel of the Agency, the [p. 10] protection of its institutions and the safeguarding of the security of its facilities in the Occupied Palestinian Territory, including East Jerusalem, at all times;

35. *Takes note* of the investigations into the incidents affecting the Agency's facilities during the conflict in the Gaza Strip in July and August 2014, and calls for ensuring accountability for all violations of international law;

36. *Urges* the Government of Israel to expeditiously reimburse the Agency for all transit charges incurred and other financial losses sustained as a result of the delays and restrictions on movement and access imposed by Israel;

---

18   United Nations, *Treaty Series*, vol. 1577, No. 27531.
19   Ibid., vol. 1249, No. 20378.
20   Ibid., vol. 2515, No. 44910.

37. *Calls upon* Israel particularly to cease obstructing the movement and access of the staff, vehicles and supplies of the Agency and to cease levying taxes, extra fees and charges, which affect the Agency's operations detrimentally;

38. *Reiterates its call upon* Israel to fully lift the restrictions impeding or delaying the import of necessary construction materials and supplies for the reconstruction and repair of the remaining damaged or destroyed refugee shelters, and for the implementation of suspended and urgently needed civilian infrastructure projects in refugee camps in the Gaza Strip, noting the alarming figures reflected in the United Nations country team reports of 26 August 2016, entitled "Gaza: two years after" and of July 2017, entitled "Gaza ten years later";

39. *Requests* the Commissioner-General to proceed with the issuance of identification cards for Palestine refugees and their descendants in the Occupied Palestinian Territory;

40. *Notes with appreciation* the positive contribution of the Agency's microfinance and job creation programmes, encourages efforts to enhance the sustainability and benefits of microfinance services to a greater number of Palestine refugees, especially in view of the high unemployment rates affecting them, and youth in particular, welcomes the Agency's efforts to streamline costs and increase microfinance services through internal reform efforts, and calls upon the Agency, in close cooperation with the relevant agencies, to continue to contribute to the development of the economic and social stability of the Palestine refugees in all fields of operation;

41. *Reiterates its appeals* to all States, the specialized agencies and non-governmental organizations to continue and to augment their contributions to the programme budget of the Agency, to increase their special allocations for grants and scholarships for higher education to Palestine refugees and to contribute to the establishment of vocational training centres for Palestine refugees, and requests the Agency to act as the recipient and trustee for the special allocations for grants and scholarships;

42. *Calls upon* the Commissioner-General to include, in the annual reporting to the General Assembly, assessments on the progress made to remedy the recurrent funding shortfalls of the Agency and ensure sustained, sufficient and predictable support for the Agency's operations, including through the implementation of the relevant provisions of the present resolution.

48th plenary meeting
7 December 2018

G.A. Res. 73/93, Persons Displaced as a Result of the June 1967 and Subsequent Hostilities (Dec. 7, 2018)

United Nations
General Assembly
A/RES/73/93
Distr.: General
18 December 2018
Seventy-third session
Agenda item 54

Resolution adopted by the General Assembly on 7 December 2018

[*on the report of the Special Political and Decolonization Committee (Fourth Committee) (A/73/523)*]

73/93. Persons displaced as a result of the June 1967 and subsequent hostilities

The General Assembly,

Recalling its resolutions 2252 (ES-V) of 4 July 1967, 2341 B (XXII) of 19 December 1967 and all subsequent related resolutions,

Recalling also Security Council resolutions 237 (1967) of 14 June 1967 and 259 (1968) of 27 September 1968,

Taking note of the report of the Secretary-General submitted in pursuance of its resolution 72/81 of 7 December 2017,[1]

Taking note also of the report of the Commissioner-General of the United Nations Relief and Works Agency for Palestine Refugees in the Near East covering the period from 1 January to 31 December 2017,[2]

Concerned about the continuing human suffering resulting from the June 1967 and subsequent hostilities,

---

1 A/73/338.
2 *Official Records of the General Assembly, Seventy-third Session, Supplement No. 13* (A/73/13).

Taking note of the relevant provisions of the Declaration of Principles on Interim Self-Government Arrangements of 13 September 1993[3] with regard to the modalities for the admission of persons displaced in 1967, and concerned that the process agreed upon has not yet been effected,

Taking note also of its resolution 67/19 of 29 November 2012,

1. *Reaffirms* the right of all persons displaced as a result of the June 1967 and subsequent hostilities to return to their homes or former places of residence in the territories occupied by Israel since 1967; [p. 2]

2. *Stresses* the necessity for an accelerated return of displaced persons, and calls for compliance with the mechanism agreed upon by the parties in article XII of the Declaration of Principles on Interim Self-Government Arrangements of 13 September 1993[3] on the return of displaced persons;

3. *Endorses*, in the meantime, the efforts of the Commissioner-General of the United Nations Relief and Works Agency for Palestine Refugees in the Near East to continue to provide humanitarian assistance, as far as practicable, on an emergency basis, and as a temporary measure, to persons in the area who are currently displaced and in serious need of continued assistance as a result of the June 1967 and subsequent hostilities, and requests the Commissioner-General to include information on relevant efforts in his annual report;

4. *Strongly appeals* to all Governments and to organizations and individuals to contribute generously to the Agency and to the other intergovernmental and non-governmental organizations concerned for the above-mentioned purposes.

48th plenary meeting
7 December 2018

---

[3] A/48/486-S/26560, annex.

G.A. Res. 73/92, Assistance to Palestine Refugees (Dec. 7, 2018)

United Nations
General Assembly
A/RES/73/92
Distr.: General
18 December 2018
Seventy-third session
Agenda item 54

Resolution adopted by the General Assembly on 7 December 2018

[*on the report of the Special Political and Decolonization Committee (Fourth Committee) (A/73/523)*]

73/92. Assistance to Palestine refugees

The General Assembly,

Recalling its resolution 194 (III) of 11 December 1948 and all its subsequent resolutions on the question, including resolution 72/80 of 7 December 2017,

Recalling also its resolution 302 (IV) of 8 December 1949, by which, inter alia, it established the United Nations Relief and Works Agency for Palestine Refugees in the Near East,

Recalling further the relevant resolutions of the Security Council,

Aware of the fact that, for more than six decades, the Palestine refugees have suffered from the loss of their homes, lands and means of livelihood,

Affirming the imperative of resolving the problem of the Palestine refugees for the achievement of justice and for the achievement of lasting peace in the region,

Acknowledging the essential role that the Agency has played for over 65 years since its establishment in ameliorating the plight of the Palestine refugees through the provision of education, health, relief and social services and ongoing work in the areas of camp infrastructure, microfinance, protection and emergency assistance,

Taking note of the report of the Commissioner-General of the Agency covering the period from 1 January to 31 December 2017,[1]

Taking note also of the report of the Commissioner-General of 31 May 2018, submitted pursuant to paragraph 57 of the report of the Secretary-General,[2] and expressing concern regarding the severe financial crisis of the Agency and the negative implications for the continued delivery of core programmes to the Palestine refugees in all fields of operation, [p. 2]

Aware of the growing needs of the Palestine refugees throughout all the fields of operation, namely, Jordan, Lebanon, the Syrian Arab Republic and the Occupied Palestinian Territory,

Expressing grave concern at the especially difficult situation of the Palestine refugees under occupation, including with regard to their safety, well-being and socioeconomic living conditions,

Expressing grave concern in particular at the grave humanitarian situation and socioeconomic conditions of the Palestine refugees in the Gaza Strip, and underlining the importance of emergency and humanitarian assistance and urgent reconstruction efforts,

Noting the signing of the Declaration of Principles on Interim Self-Government Arrangements on 13 September 1993 by the Government of Israel and the Palestine Liberation Organization[3] and the subsequent implementation agreements,

1. *Notes with regret* that repatriation or compensation of the refugees, as provided for in paragraph 11 of General Assembly resolution 194 (III), has not yet been effected, and that, therefore, the situation of the Palestine refugees continues to be a matter of grave concern and the Palestine refugees continue to require assistance to meet basic health, education and living needs;

2. *Also notes with regret* that the United Nations Conciliation Commission for Palestine has been unable to find a means of achieving progress in the implementation of paragraph 11 of General Assembly resolution 194 (III), and reaffirms its request to the Conciliation Commission to continue exerting efforts towards the implementation of that paragraph and to report to the Assembly on the efforts being exerted in this regard as appropriate, but no later than 1 September 2019;

3. *Affirms* the necessity for the continuation of the work of the United Nations Relief and Works Agency for Palestine Refugees in the Near East and the importance of its unimpeded operation and its provision of services,

---

1 *Official Records of the General Assembly, Seventy-third Session, Supplement No. 13* (A/73/13).
2 A/71/849.
3 A/48/486-S/26560, annex.

including emergency assistance, for the well-being, protection and human development of the Palestine refugees and for the stability of the region, pending the just resolution of the question of the Palestine refugees;

4. *Calls upon* all donors to continue to strengthen their efforts to meet the anticipated needs of the Agency, including with regard to increased expenditures and needs arising from conflicts and instability in the region and the serious socioeconomic and humanitarian situation, particularly in the Occupied Palestinian Territory, and those needs mentioned in recent emergency, recovery and reconstruction appeals and plans for the Gaza Strip and in the regional crisis response plans to address the situation of Palestine refugees in the Syrian Arab Republic and those Palestine refugees who have fled to countries in the region;

5. *Commends* the Agency for its provision of vital assistance to the Palestine refugees and its role as a stabilizing factor in the region and the tireless efforts of the staff of the Agency in carrying out its mandate;

6. *Decides* to admit, upon its request, Qatar, in accordance with the criterion set forth in General Assembly decision 60/522 of 8 December 2005, as a member of the Advisory Commission of the United Nations Relief and Works Agency for Palestine Refugees in the Near East.

48th plenary meeting
7 December 2018

G.A. Res. 73/89, Comprehensive, Just and Lasting Peace in the Middle East, U.N. Doc. A/RES/73/89 (Dec. 6, 2018)

United Nations
General Assembly
A/RES/73/89
Distr.: General
18 December 2018
Seventy-third session
Agenda item 38

Resolution adopted by the General Assembly on 6 December 2018

[*without reference to a Main Committee (A/73/L.49)*]

73/89. Comprehensive, just and lasting peace in the Middle East

The General Assembly,
  Recalling its relevant resolutions,
  Guided by the purposes and principles of the Charter of the United Nations,
  Reiterates its call for the achievement, without delay, of a comprehensive, just and lasting peace in the Middle East on the basis of the relevant United Nations resolutions, including Security Council resolution 2334 (2016) of 23 December 2016, the Madrid terms of reference, including the principle of land for peace, the Arab Peace Initiative[1] and the Quartet road map,[2] and an end to the Israeli occupation that began in 1967, including of East Jerusalem, and reaffirms in this regard its unwavering support, in accordance with international law, for the two-State solution of Israel and Palestine, living side by side in peace and security within recognized borders, based on the pre-1967 borders.

47th plenary meeting
6 December 2018

---

1 A/56/1026-S/2002/932, annex II, resolution 14/221.
2 S/2003/529, annex.

G.A. Res. 73/22, Jerusalem (Nov. 30, 2018)

United Nations
General Assembly
A/RES/73/22
Distr.: General
4 December 2018
Seventy-third session
Agenda item 38

Resolution adopted by the General Assembly on 30 November 2018

[*without reference to a Main Committee (A/73/L.29 and A/73/L.29/Add.1)*]

73/22. Jerusalem

The General Assembly,

Recalling its resolution 181 (II) of 29 November 1947, in particular its provisions regarding the City of Jerusalem,

Recalling also its resolution 36/120 E of 10 December 1981 and all its subsequent relevant resolutions, including resolution 56/31 of 3 December 2001, in which it, inter alia, determined that all legislative and administrative measures and actions taken by Israel, the occupying Power, which have altered or purported to alter the character and status of the Holy City of Jerusalem, in particular the so-called "Basic Law" on Jerusalem and the proclamation of Jerusalem as the capital of Israel, were null and void and must be rescinded forthwith,

Recalling further the Security Council resolutions relevant to Jerusalem, including resolution 478 (1980) of 20 August 1980, in which the Council, inter alia, decided not to recognize the "Basic Law" on Jerusalem,

Recalling Security Council resolution 2334 (2016) of 23 December 2016, in which the Council affirmed that it would not recognize any changes to the 4 June 1967 lines, including with regard to Jerusalem, other than those agreed by the parties through negotiations,

Recalling also the advisory opinion rendered on 9 July 2004 by the International Court of Justice on the legal consequences of the construction of a wall in the Occupied Palestinian Territory,[1] and recalling further its resolution ES-10/15 of 20 July 2004,

Expressing its grave concern about any action taken by any body, governmental or non-governmental, in violation of the above-mentioned resolutions,

Expressing its grave concern also, in particular, about the continuation by Israel, the occupying Power, of illegal settlement activities, including measures regarding the so-called E-1 plan, its construction of the wall in and around East Jerusalem, its [p. 2] restrictions on Palestinian access to and residence in East Jerusalem and the further isolation of the city from the rest of the Occupied Palestinian Territory, which are having a detrimental effect on the lives of Palestinians and could prejudge a final status agreement on Jerusalem,

Expressing its grave concern further about the continuing Israeli demolition of Palestinian homes and other civilian infrastructure in and around East Jerusalem, the revocation of residency rights, and the eviction and displacement of numerous Palestinian families from East Jerusalem neighbourhoods, including Bedouin families, as well as other acts of provocation and incitement, including by Israeli settlers, in the city, including desecration of mosques and churches,

Expressing its concern about the Israeli excavations undertaken in the Old City of Jerusalem, including in and around religious sites,

Expressing its grave concern, in particular, about tensions, provocations and incitement regarding the holy places of Jerusalem, including the Haram al-Sharif, and urging restraint and respect for the sanctity of the holy sites by all sides,

Reaffirming that the international community, through the United Nations, has a legitimate interest in the question of the City of Jerusalem and in the protection of the unique spiritual, religious and cultural dimensions of the city, as foreseen in relevant United Nations resolutions on this matter,

Reaffirming also the importance of the City of Jerusalem for the three monotheistic religions,

Having considered the report of the Secretary-General on the situation in the Middle East,[2]

1. *Reiterates its determination* that any actions taken by Israel, the occupying Power, to impose its laws, jurisdiction and administration on the Holy City of Jerusalem are illegal and therefore null and void and have no validity whatsoever, and calls upon Israel to immediately cease all such illegal and unilateral measures;

---

1 See A/ES-10/273 and A/ES-10/273/Corr.1.
2 A/73/322/Rev.1.

2. *Stresses* that a comprehensive, just and lasting solution to the question of the City of Jerusalem should take into account the legitimate concerns of both the Palestinian and Israeli sides and should include internationally guaranteed provisions to ensure the freedom of religion and of conscience of its inhabitants, as well as permanent, free and unhindered access to the holy places by people of all religions and nationalities;

3. *Also stresses* the need for the parties to observe calm and restraint and to refrain from provocative actions, incitement and inflammatory rhetoric, especially in areas of religious and cultural sensitivity, and expresses its grave concern in particular about the recent series of negative incidents in East Jerusalem;

4. *Calls for* respect for the historic status quo at the holy places of Jerusalem, including the Haram al-Sharif, in word and in practice, and urges all sides to work immediately and cooperatively to defuse tensions and halt all provocations, incitement and violence at the holy sites in the City;

5. *Requests* the Secretary-General to report to the General Assembly at its seventy-fourth session on the implementation of the present resolution.

43rd plenary meeting
30 November 2018

G.A. Res. 73/21, Division for Palestinian Rights of the Secretariat (Nov. 30, 2018)

United Nations
General Assembly
A/RES/73/21
Distr.: General
4 December 2018
Seventy-third session
Agenda item 39

Resolution adopted by the General Assembly on 30 November 2018

[*without reference to a Main Committee (A/73/L.34 and A/73/L.34/Add.1)*]

73/21.   Division for Palestinian Rights of the Secretariat

The General Assembly,

Having considered the report of the Committee on the Exercise of the Inalienable Rights of the Palestinian People,[1]

Taking note, in particular, of the action taken by the Committee and the Division for Palestinian Rights of the Secretariat in accordance with their mandates,

Recalling its resolution 32/40 B of 2 December 1977 and all its subsequent relevant resolutions, including its resolution 72/11 of 30 November 2017,

1. *Notes with appreciation* the action taken by the Secretary-General in compliance with its resolution 72/11;

2. *Considers* that, by providing substantive support to the Committee on the Exercise of the Inalienable Rights of the Palestinian People in the implementation of its mandate, the Division for Palestinian Rights of the Secretariat continues to make a constructive and positive contribution to raising international awareness of the question of Palestine and of the urgency of a peaceful settlement of the question of Palestine in all its aspects on the basis of international

---

1 *Official Records of the General Assembly, Seventy-third Session, Supplement No. 35* (A/73/35).

law and United Nations resolutions and the efforts being exerted in this regard and to generating international support for the rights of the Palestinian people;

3. *Requests* the Secretary-General to continue to provide the Division with the necessary resources and to ensure that it continues to effectively carry out its programme of work as detailed in relevant earlier resolutions, in consultation with the Committee and under its guidance;

4. *Requests* the Division, in particular, to continue to monitor developments relevant to the question of Palestine, to organize international meetings and activities in support of the Committee's mandate with the participation of all sectors of the [p. 2] international community and to ensure, within existing resources, the continued participation of eminent persons and international renowned experts in these meetings and activities, to be invited on a par with the members of the Committee, to liaise and cooperate with civil society and parliamentarians, including through the Working Group of the Committee, to develop and expand the "Question of Palestine" website and the documents collection of the United Nations Information System on the Question of Palestine, to prepare and widely disseminate the publications listed in paragraph 81 of the report of the Committee,[1] in the relevant official languages of the United Nations, and information materials on various aspects of the question of Palestine and to develop and enhance the annual training programme for staff of the Palestinian Government in contribution to Palestinian capacity-building efforts;

5. *Also requests* the Division, as part of the observance of the International Day of Solidarity with the Palestinian People on 29 November, to continue to organize, under the guidance of the Committee, an annual exhibit on Palestinian rights or a cultural event in cooperation with the Permanent Observer Mission of the State of Palestine to the United Nations, and encourages Member States to continue to give the widest support and publicity to the observance of the Day of Solidarity;

6. *Requests* the Secretary-General to ensure the continued cooperation with the Division of the United Nations system entities with programme components addressing various aspects of the question of Palestine and the situation in the Occupied Palestinian Territory, including East Jerusalem;

7. *Invites* all Governments and organizations to extend their cooperation to the Division in the performance of its tasks.

43rd plenary meeting
30 November 2018

G.A. Res. 73/20, Special Information Programme on the Question of Palestine of the Department of Public Information of the Secretariat (Nov. 30, 2018)

United Nations
General Assembly
A/RES/73/20
Distr.: General
4 December 2018
Seventy-third session
Agenda item 39

Resolution adopted by the General Assembly on 30 November 2018

[*without reference to a Main Committee (A/73/L.33 and A/73/L.33/Add.1)*]

73/20. **Special information programme on the question of Palestine of the Department of Public Information of the Secretariat**

The General Assembly,

Having considered the report of the Committee on the Exercise of the Inalienable Rights of the Palestinian People,[1]

Taking note, in particular, of the information contained in chapter VI of that report,

Recalling its resolution 72/12 of 30 November 2017,

Convinced that the worldwide dissemination of accurate and comprehensive information and the role of civil society organizations and institutions remain of vital importance in heightening awareness of and support for the inalienable rights of the Palestinian people, including the right to self-determination and independence, and for the efforts to achieve a just, lasting and peaceful settlement of the question of Palestine,

---

1 *Official Records of the General Assembly, Seventy-third Session, Supplement No. 35* (A/73/35).

Recalling the mutual recognition between the Government of the State of Israel and the Palestine Liberation Organization, the representative of the Palestinian people, as well as the existing agreements between the two sides,

Affirming its support for a comprehensive, just, lasting and peaceful settlement to the Israeli-Palestinian conflict on the basis of the relevant United Nations resolutions, the terms of reference of the Madrid Conference, including the principle of land for peace, the Arab Peace Initiative adopted by the Council of the League of Arab States at its fourteenth session,[2] and the Quartet road map to a permanent [p. 2] two-State solution to the Israeli-Palestinian conflict,[3] endorsed by the Security Council in its resolution 1515 (2003) of 19 November 2003,

Recalling the advisory opinion rendered on 9 July 2004 by the International Court of Justice on the legal consequences of the construction of a wall in the Occupied Palestinian Territory,[4]

Taking note of its resolution 67/19 of 29 November 2012,

Reaffirming that the United Nations has a permanent responsibility towards the question of Palestine until the question is resolved in all its aspects in a satisfactory manner in accordance with international legitimacy,

1. *Notes with appreciation* the action taken by the Department of Public Information of the Secretariat in compliance with its resolution 72/12;

2. *Considers* that the special information programme on the question of Palestine of the Department is very useful in raising the awareness of the international community concerning the question of Palestine and the situation in the Middle East and that the programme is contributing effectively to an atmosphere conducive to dialogue and supportive of peace efforts and should receive the necessary support for the fulfilment of its tasks;

3. *Requests* the Department, in full cooperation and coordination with the Committee on the Exercise of the Inalienable Rights of the Palestinian People, to continue, with the necessary flexibility as may be required by developments affecting the question of Palestine, its special information programme for 2019–2020, in particular, inter alia:

(a) To disseminate information on all the activities of the United Nations system relating to the question of Palestine and peace efforts, including reports on the work carried out by the relevant United Nations organizations, as well as on the efforts of the Secretary-General and his Special Envoy vis-à-vis the objective of peace;

---

2 A/56/1026-S/2002/932, annex II, resolution 14/221.
3 S/2003/529, annex.
4 See A/ES-10/273 and A/ES-10/273/Corr.1.

(b) To continue to issue, update and modernize publications and audiovisual and online materials on the various aspects of the question of Palestine in all fields, including materials concerning relevant recent developments, in particular the efforts to achieve a peaceful settlement of the question of Palestine;

(c) To expand its collection of audiovisual material on the question of Palestine, to continue the production and preservation of such material and to update, on a periodic basis, the public exhibit on the question of Palestine displayed in the General Assembly Building as well as at United Nations headquarters in Geneva and Vienna;

(d) To organize and promote fact-finding news missions for journalists to the Occupied Palestinian Territory, including East Jerusalem, and Israel;

(e) To organize international, regional and national seminars or encounters for journalists aimed, in particular, at sensitizing public opinion to the question of Palestine and peace efforts and at enhancing dialogue and understanding between Palestinians and Israelis for the promotion of a peaceful settlement to the Israeli-Palestinian conflict, including by fostering and encouraging the contribution of the media in support of peace between the two sides; [p. 3]

(f) To continue to provide assistance to the Palestinian people in the field of media development, in particular through its annual training programme for Palestinian broadcasters and journalists;

4. *Encourages* the Department to continue organizing encounters for the media and representatives of civil society to engage in open and positive discussions to explore means for encouraging people-to-people dialogue and promoting peace and mutual understanding in the region.

43rd plenary meeting
30 November 2018

G.A. Res. 73/19, Peaceful Settlement of the Question of Palestine (Nov. 30, 2018)

United Nations
General Assembly
A/RES/73/19
Distr.: General
5 December 2018
Seventy-third session
Agenda item 39

Resolution adopted by the General Assembly on 30 November 2018

[*without reference to a Main Committee (A/73/L.32 and A/73/L.32/Add.1)*]

73/19. Peaceful settlement of the question of Palestine

The General Assembly,
   Recalling its relevant resolutions, including those adopted at its tenth emergency special session,
   Recalling also its resolution 58/292 of 6 May 2004,
   Recalling further relevant Security Council resolutions, including resolutions 242 (1967) of 22 November 1967, 338 (1973) of 22 October 1973, 1397 (2002) of 12 March 2002, 1515 (2003) of 19 November 2003, 1544 (2004) of 19 May 2004, 1850 (2008) of 16 December 2008 and 2334 (2016) of 23 December 2016,
   Recalling the affirmation by the Security Council of the vision of a region where two States, Israel and Palestine, live side by side within secure and recognized borders,
   Expressing deep concern that it has been over 70 years since the adoption of its resolution 181 (II) of 29 November 1947 and 51 years since the occupation of Palestinian territory, including East Jerusalem, in 1967, and that a just, lasting and comprehensive solution to the question of Palestine has yet to be achieved,

Having considered the report of the Secretary-General submitted pursuant to the request made in its resolution 72/14 of 30 November 2017,[1]

Reaffirming the permanent responsibility of the United Nations with regard to the question of Palestine until the question is resolved in all its aspects in accordance with international law and relevant resolutions,

Recalling the advisory opinion rendered on 9 July 2004 by the International Court of Justice on the legal consequences of the construction of a wall in the [p. 2] Occupied Palestinian Territory,[2] and recalling also its resolutions ES-10/15 of 20 July 2004 and ES-10/17 of 15 December 2006,

Convinced that achieving a just, lasting and comprehensive settlement of the question of Palestine, the core of the Arab-Israeli conflict, is imperative for the attainment of comprehensive and lasting peace and stability in the Middle East,

Stressing that the principle of equal rights and self-determination of peoples is among the purposes and principles enshrined in the Charter of the United Nations,

Reaffirming the principle of the inadmissibility of the acquisition of territory by war,

Reaffirming also the applicability of the Geneva Convention relative to the Protection of Civilian Persons in Time of War, of 12 August 1949,[3] to the Occupied Palestinian Territory, including East Jerusalem,

Recalling its resolution 2625 (XXV) of 24 October 1970, and reiterating the importance of maintaining and strengthening international peace founded upon freedom, equality, justice and respect for fundamental human rights and of developing friendly relations among nations irrespective of their political, economic and social systems or the level of their development,

Bearing in mind its resolution 70/1 of 25 September 2015, entitled "Transforming our world: the 2030 Agenda for Sustainable Development", in particular Sustainable Development Goal 16,

Stressing the urgent need for efforts to reverse the negative trends on the ground and to restore a political horizon for advancing and accelerating meaningful negotiations aimed at the achievement of a peace agreement that will bring a complete end to the Israeli occupation that began in 1967 and the resolution of all core final status issues, without exception, leading to a peaceful, just, lasting and comprehensive solution to the question of Palestine,

---

1 A/73/346-S/2018/597.
2 See A/ES-10/273 and A/ES-10/273/Corr.1.
3 United Nations, *Treaty Series*, vol. 75, No. 973.

Reaffirming the illegality of the Israeli settlements in the Palestinian territory occupied since 1967, including East Jerusalem,

Expressing grave concern about the extremely detrimental impact of Israeli settlement policies, decisions and activities in the Occupied Palestinian Territory, including East Jerusalem, including on the contiguity, integrity and viability of the Territory, the viability of the two-State solution based on the pre-1967 borders and the efforts to advance a peaceful settlement in the Middle East,

Expressing grave concern also about all acts of violence, intimidation and provocation by Israeli settlers against Palestinian civilians, including children, and properties, including homes, mosques, churches and agricultural lands, condemning acts of terror by several extremist Israeli settlers, and calling for accountability for the illegal actions perpetrated in this regard,

Reaffirming the illegality of Israeli actions aimed at changing the status of Jerusalem, including settlement construction and expansion, home demolitions, evictions of Palestinian residents, excavations in and around religious and historic sites, and all other unilateral measures aimed at altering the character, status and demographic composition of the city and of the Territory as a whole, and demanding their immediate cessation, [p. 3]

Expressing grave concern about tensions, provocations and incitement regarding the holy places of Jerusalem, including the Haram al-Sharif, and urging restraint and respect for the sanctity of the holy sites by all sides,

Reaffirming that the construction by Israel, the occupying Power, of a wall in the Occupied Palestinian Territory, including in and around East Jerusalem, and its associated regime are contrary to international law,

Encouraging all States and international organizations to continue to actively pursue policies to ensure respect for their obligations under international law with regard to all illegal Israeli practices and measures in the Occupied Palestinian Territory, including East Jerusalem, particularly Israeli settlements,

Expressing deep concern about the continuing Israeli policies of closures and severe restrictions on the movement of persons and goods, including medical and humanitarian and economic, via the imposition of prolonged closures and severe economic and movement restrictions that in effect amount to a blockade, as well as of checkpoints and a permit regime throughout the Occupied Palestinian Territory, including East Jerusalem,

Expressing deep concern also about the consequent negative impact of such policies on the contiguity of the Territory and the critical socioeconomic and humanitarian situation of the Palestinian people, which remains a disastrous humanitarian crisis in the Gaza Strip, as well as on the international efforts and the efforts of the Palestinian Government aimed at rehabilitating and developing the damaged Palestinian economy, including reviving the agricultural and productive sectors, and, while recalling Security Council resolution 1860 (2009) of 8 January 2009, calling for the full lifting of restrictions on the movement and access of persons and goods, which are crucial for social and economic recovery,

Recalling the mutual recognition 25 years ago between the Government of the State of Israel and the Palestine Liberation Organization, the representative of the Palestinian people,[4] and stressing the urgent need for efforts to ensure full compliance with the agreements concluded between the two sides,

Recalling also the endorsement by the Security Council, in its resolution 1515 (2003), of the Quartet road map to a permanent two-State solution to the Israeli-Palestinian conflict[5] and the call in Council resolution 1850 (2008) for the parties to fulfil their obligations under the road map and to refrain from any steps that could undermine confidence or prejudice the outcome of negotiations on a final peace settlement,

Underscoring the demand by the Security Council, most recently in its resolution 2334 (2016), that Israel immediately and completely cease all settlement activities in the Occupied Palestinian Territory, including East Jerusalem, and that it fully respect all its legal obligations in this regard,

Recalling the Arab Peace Initiative, adopted by the Council of the League of Arab States at its fourteenth session, held in Beirut on 27 and 28 March 2002,[6] and stressing its importance in the efforts to achieve a just, lasting and comprehensive peace,

Urging renewed and coordinated efforts by the international community aimed at restoring a political horizon and advancing and accelerating the conclusion of a peace treaty to attain without delay an end to the Israeli occupation that began in 1967 [p. 4] by resolving all outstanding issues, including all core issues, without exception, for a just, lasting and peaceful settlement of the Israeli-Palestinian conflict, in accordance with the internationally recognized basis of the two-State solution, and ultimately of the Arab-Israeli conflict as a whole for the realization of a comprehensive peace in the Middle East,

Welcoming, in this regard, all regional and international efforts aimed at promoting meaningful negotiations and achieving a two-State solution based on the pre-1967 borders and on the long-standing terms of reference, as called for in Security Council resolution 2334 (2016),

---

4   See A/48/486-S/26560, annex.
5   S/2003/529, annex.
6   A/56/1026-S/2002/932, annex II, resolution 14/221.

Taking note of the report of the Quartet of 1 July 2016,[7] and stressing its recommendations as well as all its recent statements, in which, inter alia, grave concerns were expressed that current trends on the ground are steadily eroding the two-State solution and entrenching a one-State reality and in which recommendations were made to reverse those trends in order to advance the two-State solution on the ground and create the conditions for successful final status negotiations,

Reiterating its support for the convening of an international conference in Moscow, as envisioned by the Security Council in its resolution 1850 (2008) and the Quartet statement of 23 September 2011, and stressing the importance of multilateral support and engagement for the advancement and acceleration of peace efforts towards the fulfilment of a just, lasting and comprehensive solution to the question of Palestine,

Noting the important contribution to peace efforts of the United Nations Special Coordinator for the Middle East Peace Process and Personal Representative of the Secretary-General to the Palestine Liberation Organization and the Palestinian Authority, including within the framework of the activities of the Quartet and with regard to the trilateral agreement and recent developments regarding the Gaza Strip,

Welcoming the ongoing efforts of the Ad Hoc Liaison Committee for the Coordination of the International Assistance to Palestinians, chaired by Norway, and noting its recent meeting at United Nations Headquarters, on 27 September 2018, and the ongoing efforts to generate sufficient donor support in this critical period for urgently addressing the immense humanitarian, reconstruction and recovery needs in the Gaza Strip, bearing in mind the detailed needs assessment and recovery framework for Gaza developed with the support of the United Nations, the World Bank and the European Union, and furthering Palestinian economic recovery and development, [p. 5]

Recognizing the efforts being undertaken by the Palestinian Government, with international support, to reform, develop and strengthen its institutions and infrastructure, emphasizing the need to preserve and further develop Palestinian institutions and infrastructure, despite the obstacles presented by the ongoing Israeli occupation, and commending in this regard the ongoing efforts to develop the institutions of an independent Palestinian State, including through the implementation of the Palestinian National Policy Agenda: National Priorities, Policies and Policy Interventions (2017–2022),

Expressing concern about the risks posed to the significant achievements made, as confirmed by the positive assessments made by international

---

7 S/2016/595, annex.

institutions regarding readiness for statehood, including by the World Bank, the International Monetary Fund, the United Nations and the Ad Hoc Liaison Committee, owing to the negative impact of the current instability and financial crisis being faced by the Palestinian Government and the continued absence of a credible political horizon, [p. 5]

Recognizing the positive contribution of the United Nations Development Assistance Framework, which is aimed, inter alia, at enhancing development support and assistance to the Palestinian people and strengthening institutional capacity in line with Palestinian national priorities,

Recalling the ministerial meetings of the Conference on Cooperation among East Asian Countries for Palestinian Development convened in Tokyo in February 2013 and Jakarta in March 2014 as a forum for the mobilization of political and economic assistance, including via exchanges of expertise and lessons learned, in support of Palestinian development, and encouraging the expansion of such efforts and support in the light of worsening socioeconomic indicators,

Recognizing the continued efforts and tangible progress made in the Palestinian security sector, noting the continued cooperation that benefits both Palestinians and Israelis, in particular by promoting security and building confidence, and expressing the hope that such progress will be extended to all major population centres,

Recognizing also that security measures alone cannot remedy the tensions, instability and violence, and calling for full respect for international law, including for the protection of civilian life, as well as for the promotion of human security, the de-escalation of the situation, the exercise of restraint, including from provocative actions and rhetoric, and the establishment of a stable environment conducive to the pursuit of peace,

Gravely concerned over the negative developments that have continued to occur in the Occupied Palestinian Territory, including East Jerusalem, including the escalation of violence and excessive use of force, resulting in a large number of deaths and injuries, mostly among Palestinian civilians, including children and women, as well as the continued construction and expansion of settlements and the wall, the arbitrary arrest and detention of Palestinian civilians, the acts of violence, vandalism and brutality committed against Palestinian civilians by Israeli settlers in the West Bank, the widespread destruction of public and private Palestinian property, including religious sites, and infrastructure and the demolition of homes, including if carried out as a means of collective punishment, the internal forced displacement of civilians, especially among the Bedouin community, and the consequent deterioration of the socioeconomic and humanitarian conditions of the Palestinian people,

Deploring the continuing negative repercussions of the conflicts in and around the Gaza Strip and the large number of Palestinian civilian casualties in the recent period, including among children, and any violations of international law, and calling for full respect for the relevant principles of international humanitarian and human rights law, including the principles of legality, distinction, precaution, limitation and proportionality, as well as the need for independent and transparent investigation into the use of force,

Stressing the need to ensure accountability for all violations of international humanitarian law and international human rights law in order to end impunity, ensure justice, deter further violations, protect civilians and promote peace,

Emphasizing the importance of the safety, protection and well-being of all civilians in the whole Middle East region, stressing that Israel must respect the right to peaceful protest, and condemning all acts of violence and terror against civilians on both sides, including the firing of rockets by armed groups against Israeli civilian areas, resulting in loss of life and injury,

Deploring any actions that could provoke violence and endanger lives, and calling upon all actors to ensure that protests remain peaceful, [p. 6]

Expressing grave concern over the persisting disastrous humanitarian situation and socioeconomic conditions in the Gaza Strip as a result of the prolonged Israeli closures and severe economic and movement restrictions that in effect amount to a blockade, bearing in mind numerous United Nations agency reports, including the reports of the United Nations country team, and stressing that the situation is unsustainable and that urgent efforts are required to reverse the de-development trajectory in Gaza and respond adequately and immediately to the immense humanitarian needs of the civilian population,

Recalling the statement of the President of the Security Council of 28 July 2014,[8]

Stressing the need for calm and restraint by the parties, including by consolidating the ceasefire agreement of 26 August 2014, achieved under the auspices of Egypt, to avert the deterioration of the situation,

Reiterating the need for the full implementation by all parties of Security Council resolution 1860 (2009) and General Assembly resolution ES-10/18 of 16 January 2009,

Stressing that a durable ceasefire agreement must lead to a fundamental improvement in the living conditions of the Palestinian people in the Gaza Strip, including through the sustained and regular opening of crossing points, and ensure the safety and well-being of civilians on both sides,

---

[8] S/PRST/2014/13; see *Resolutions and Decisions of the Security Council, 1 August 2013–31 July 2014* (S/INF/69).

Expressing grave concern about the imprisonment and detention by Israel of thousands of Palestinians, including children, under harsh conditions, and all violations of international humanitarian law and human rights law that have occurred in this regard,

Emphasizing the importance of the safety, protection and well-being of all civilians in the whole Middle East region, and condemning all acts of violence and terror against civilians on both sides, including the firing of rockets,

Stressing the need for measures to be taken to guarantee the safety and protection of the Palestinian civilian population throughout the Occupied Palestinian Territory, consistent with the provisions and obligations of international humanitarian law, and taking note of the report of the Secretary-General on the protection of the Palestinian civilian population,[9]

Stressing also the need to respect the right of peaceful assembly,

Emphasizing the need for respect for and the preservation of the territorial integrity and unity of the Occupied Palestinian Territory, including East Jerusalem,

Affirming the need to support the Palestinian Government of national consensus, formed consistent with Palestine Liberation Organization commitments and the Quartet principles, in its assumption of full government responsibilities in both the West Bank and the Gaza Strip, in all fields, as well as through its presence at Gaza's crossing points, welcoming in this regard the efforts of Egypt to facilitate and support Palestinian unity, and taking note of the Quartet statement of 28 September 2017,

Stressing the urgent need for sustained and active international involvement and for concerted initiatives to support the parties in building a climate for peace, to assist the parties in advancing and accelerating direct peace process negotiations for the achievement of a just, lasting and comprehensive peace settlement that ends the [p. 7] occupation that began in 1967 and results in the independence of a democratic, contiguous and viable State of Palestine living side by side in peace and security with Israel and its other neighbours, on the basis of relevant United Nations resolutions, the terms of reference of the Madrid Conference, the Quartet road map and the Arab Peace Initiative,

Taking note of the application of Palestine for admission to membership in the United Nations, submitted on 23 September 2011,[10]

Taking note also of its resolution 67/19 of 29 November 2012, by which, inter alia, Palestine was accorded non-member observer State status in

---

9   A/ES-10/794.
10 A/66/371-S/2011/592, annex I.

the United Nations, and taking note further of the follow-up report of the Secretary-General,[11]

Acknowledging the efforts being undertaken by civil society to promote a peaceful settlement of the question of Palestine,

Recalling the findings by the International Court of Justice, in its advisory opinion, including on the urgent necessity for the United Nations as a whole to redouble its efforts to bring the Israeli-Palestinian conflict, which continues to pose a threat to international peace and security, to a speedy conclusion, thereby establishing a just and lasting peace in the region,[12]

Stressing the urgency of achieving without delay an end to the Israeli occupation that began in 1967,

Affirming once again the right of all States in the region to live in peace within secure and internationally recognized borders,

1. *Reaffirms* the necessity of achieving a peaceful settlement of the question of Palestine, the core of the Arab-Israeli conflict, in all its aspects, and of intensifying all efforts towards that end, and stresses in this regard the urgency of salvaging the prospects for realizing the two-State solution of Israel and Palestine, living side by side in peace and security within recognized borders, based on the pre-1967 borders, and making tangible progress towards implementing that solution and justly resolving all final status issues;

2. *Calls for* the full implementation of Security Council resolution 2334 (2016), and stresses, inter alia, the call upon all parties to continue, in the interest of the promotion of peace and security, to exert collective efforts to launch credible negotiations on all final status issues in the Middle East peace process and within the time frame specified by the Quartet in its statement of 21 September 2010;

3. *Calls once more for* the intensification of efforts by the parties, including through negotiations, with the support of the international community, towards the conclusion of a final peace settlement;

4. *Urges* in this regard the intensification and acceleration of renewed international and regional diplomatic efforts and support aimed at achieving, without delay, a comprehensive, just and lasting peace in the Middle East on the basis of the relevant United Nations resolutions, the Madrid terms of reference, including the principle of land for peace, the Arab Peace Initiative,[6] the Quartet road map[5] and an end to the Israeli occupation that began in 1967, and underscores in this regard the importance of the ongoing efforts, including by the European Union, the Russian Federation, the United Nations and the United States of America, as members of the [p. 8] Quartet, as well as efforts

---
11 A/67/738.
12 A/ES-10/273 and A/ES-10/273/Corr.1, advisory opinion, para. 161.

by the League of Arab States, Egypt, France, China and other concerned States and organizations;

5. *Stresses* the need for a resumption of negotiations based on the long-standing terms of reference and clear parameters and within a defined time frame aimed at expediting the realization of a just, lasting and comprehensive settlement;

6. *Calls for* the timely convening of an international conference in Moscow, as envisioned by the Security Council in its resolution 1850 (2008), for the advancement and acceleration of the achievement of a just, lasting and comprehensive peace settlement;

7. *Calls upon* both parties to act responsibly on the basis of international law and their previous agreements and obligations, in both their policies and actions, in order to, with the support of the Quartet and other interested parties, urgently reverse negative trends, including all measures taken on the ground that are contrary to international law, and create the conditions necessary for the launching of a credible political horizon and the advancement of peace efforts;

8. *Calls upon* Israel, the occupying Power, to comply strictly with its obligations under international law, including international humanitarian law, and to cease all of its measures that are contrary to international law and all unilateral actions in the Occupied Palestinian Territory, including East Jerusalem, that are aimed at altering the character, status and demographic composition of the Territory, including the confiscation and de facto annexation of land, and thus at prejudging the final outcome of peace negotiations, with a view to achieving without delay an end to the Israeli occupation that began in 1967;

9. *Stresses* the need, in particular, for an immediate halt to all actions contrary to international law that undermine trust and prejudge final status issues;

10. *Calls upon* the parties to observe calm and restraint and to refrain from provocative actions, incitement and inflammatory rhetoric, especially in areas of religious and cultural sensitivity, including in East Jerusalem, and calls for respect for the historic status quo at the holy places of Jerusalem, including the Haram al-Sharif, in word and in practice, and for immediate and serious efforts to defuse tensions;

11. *Stresses* the need for an immediate and complete cessation of all acts of violence, including military attacks, destruction and acts of terror;

12. *Underscores* the need for the parties to take confidence-building measures aimed at immediately improving the situation on the ground, promoting stability, building trust and fostering the peace process, and stresses the need, in particular, for an immediate halt to all settlement activities and home demolitions, ending violence and incitement and taking measures to address

settler violence and ensure accountability, and for the further release of prisoners and an end to arbitrary arrests and detentions;

13. *Stresses* the need for the removal of checkpoints and other obstructions to the movement of persons and goods throughout the Occupied Palestinian Territory, including East Jerusalem, and the need for respect for and preservation of the territorial unity, contiguity and integrity of all the Occupied Palestinian Territory, including East Jerusalem;

14. *Reiterates its demand* for the full implementation of Security Council resolution 1860 (2009);

15. *Reiterates* the need for the full implementation by both parties of the Agreement on Movement and Access and of the Agreed Principles for the Rafah Crossing, of 15 November 2005, and the need, specifically, to allow for the sustained [p. 9] opening of all crossings into and out of the Gaza Strip for humanitarian supplies, movement and access of persons and goods, as well as for commercial flows, including exports, and economic recovery;

16. *Reiterates its demand* for the complete cessation of all Israeli settlement activities in the Occupied Palestinian Territory, including East Jerusalem, and in the occupied Syrian Golan, calls for the full implementation of the relevant Security Council resolutions, including resolution 2334 (2016), and for the consideration of measures of accountability, in accordance with international law, including without limitation in relation to the continued non-compliance with the demands for a complete and immediate cessation of all settlement activities, and stresses that compliance with and respect for international humanitarian law and international human rights law is a cornerstone of peace and security in the region;

17. *Underscores* in this regard the affirmation by the Security Council in its resolution 2334 (2016) that it will not recognize any changes to the 4 June 1967 lines, including with regard to Jerusalem, other than those agreed by the parties through negotiations, and its call upon States to distinguish in their relevant dealings between the territory of the State of Israel and the territories occupied since 1967, as well as its determination to examine practical ways and means to secure the full implementation of its relevant resolutions;

18. *Reiterates* the need for Israel forthwith to abide by its road map obligation to freeze all settlement activity, including so-called "natural growth", and to dismantle settlement outposts erected since March 2001;

19. *Calls for* the cessation of all provocations, including by Israeli settlers, in East Jerusalem, including in and around religious sites;

20. *Demands* that Israel, the occupying Power, comply with its legal obligations under international law, as mentioned in the advisory opinion rendered on 9 July 2004 by the International Court of Justice[2] and as demanded in the relevant General Assembly resolutions;

21. *Reaffirms its commitment*, in accordance with international law, to the two-State solution of Israel and Palestine, living side by side in peace and security within recognized borders, based on the pre-1967 borders;

22. *Calls for*:

(a) The withdrawal of Israel from the Palestinian territory occupied since 1967, including East Jerusalem;

(b) The realization of the inalienable rights of the Palestinian people, primarily the right to self-determination and the right to their independent State;

23. *Stresses* the need for a just resolution of the problem of Palestine refugees in conformity with its resolution 194 (III) of 11 December 1948;

24. *Calls upon* all States, consistent with their obligations under the Charter of the United Nations and relevant Security Council resolutions, inter alia:

(a) Not to recognize any changes to the pre-1967 borders, including with regard to Jerusalem, other than those agreed by the parties through negotiations;

(b) To distinguish, in their relevant dealings, between the territory of the State of Israel and the territories occupied since 1967;

(c) Not to render aid or assistance to illegal settlement activities, including not to provide Israel with any assistance to be used specifically in connection with settlements in the occupied territories, in line with Security Council resolution 465 (1980) of 1 March 1980; [p. 10]

25. *Urges* Member States and the United Nations to continue and expedite the provision of economic, humanitarian and technical assistance to the Palestinian people and the Palestinian Government during this critical period in order to help to alleviate the serious humanitarian situation in the Occupied Palestinian Territory, including East Jerusalem, which is dire in the Gaza Strip, to rehabilitate the Palestinian economy and infrastructure and to support the development and strengthening of Palestinian institutions and Palestinian State-building efforts in preparation for independence;

26. *Requests* the Secretary-General to continue his efforts with the parties concerned, and in consultation with the Security Council, including with regard to the reporting required pursuant to resolution 2334 (2016), towards the attainment of a peaceful settlement of the question of Palestine and the promotion of peace in the region and to submit to the General Assembly at its seventy-fourth session a report on these efforts and on developments on this matter.

43rd plenary meeting
30 November 2018

G.A. Res. 73/18, Committee on the Exercise of the Inalienable Rights of the Palestinian People (Nov. 30, 2018)

United Nations
General Assembly
A/RES/73/18
Distr.: General
4 December 2018
Seventy-third session
Agenda item 39

Resolution adopted by the General Assembly on 30 November 2018

[*without reference to a Main Committee (A/73/L.31 and A/73/L.31/Add.1)*]

73/18. Committee on the Exercise of the Inalienable Rights of the Palestinian People

The General Assembly,

Recalling its resolutions 181 (II) of 29 November 1947, 194 (III) of 11 December 1948, 3236 (XXIX) of 22 November 1974, 3375 (XXX) and 3376 (XXX) of 10 November 1975, 31/20 of 24 November 1976 and all its subsequent relevant resolutions, including those adopted at its emergency special sessions and its resolution 72/13 of 30 November 2017,

Recalling also its resolution 58/292 of 6 May 2004,

Having considered the report of the Committee on the Exercise of the Inalienable Rights of the Palestinian People,[1]

Recalling the mutual recognition between the Government of the State of Israel and the Palestine Liberation Organization, the representative of the Palestinian people, as well as the existing agreements between the two sides and the need for full compliance with those agreements,

---

1 *Official Records of the General Assembly, Seventy-third Session, Supplement No. 35* (A/73/35).

Affirming its support for a comprehensive, just, lasting and peaceful settlement to the Israeli-Palestinian conflict on the basis of the relevant United Nations resolutions, the terms of reference of the Madrid Conference, including the principle of land for peace, the Arab Peace Initiative adopted by the Council of the League of Arab States at its fourteenth session[2] and the Quartet road map to a permanent two-State solution to the Israeli-Palestinian conflict,[3] endorsed by the Security Council in resolution 1515 (2003) of 19 November 2003,

Recalling the relevant Security Council resolutions, including resolution 2334 (2016) of 23 December 2016, and underscoring in this regard, inter alia, the call [p. 2] upon all parties to continue, in the interest of the promotion of peace and security, to exert collective efforts to launch credible negotiations on all final status issues in the Middle East peace process and within the time frame specified by the Quartet in its statement of 21 September 2010,

Recalling also the advisory opinion rendered on 9 July 2004 by the International Court of Justice on the legal consequences of the construction of a wall in the Occupied Palestinian Territory,[4] and recalling further its resolutions ES-10/15 of 20 July 2004 and ES-10/17 of 15 December 2006,

Taking note of the application of Palestine for admission to membership in the United Nations, submitted on 23 September 2011,[5]

Recalling its resolution 67/19 of 29 November 2012, by which, inter alia, Palestine was accorded non-member observer State status in the United Nations, and taking note of the follow-up report of the Secretary-General,[6]

Taking note of the accession by Palestine to several human rights treaties and the core humanitarian law conventions, as well as other international treaties,

Noting with deep regret the passage of 51 years since the onset of the Israeli occupation and over 70 years since the adoption of resolution 181 (II) on 29 November 1947 and the Nakba without tangible progress towards a peaceful solution, and stressing the urgent need for efforts to reverse the negative trends on the ground and to restore a political horizon for advancing and accelerating meaningful negotiations aimed at the achievement of a peace agreement that will bring a complete end to the Israeli occupation that began

---

2   A/56/1026-S/2002/932, annex II, resolution 14/221.
3   S/2003/529, annex.
4   See A/ES-10/273 and A/ES-10/273/Corr.1.
5   A/66/371-S/2011/592, annex I.
6   A/67/738.

in 1967 and the resolution of all core final status issues, without exception, leading to a peaceful, just, lasting and comprehensive solution to the question of Palestine,

Reaffirming that the United Nations has a permanent responsibility towards the question of Palestine until the question is resolved in all its aspects in a satisfactory manner in accordance with international legitimacy,

1. *Expresses its appreciation* to the Committee on the Exercise of the Inalienable Rights of the Palestinian People for its efforts in performing the tasks assigned to it by the General Assembly, and takes note of its annual report,[1] including the conclusions and valuable recommendations contained in chapter VII thereof, inter alia, the recommendations for the redoubling of international efforts aimed at achieving a peaceful settlement of the question of Palestine, for an expanded multilateral framework for the revitalization of peace efforts and for efforts to ensure fullest accountability and implementation of the long-standing parameters for peace in accordance with the relevant United Nations resolutions;

2. *Requests* the Committee to continue to exert all efforts to promote the realization of the inalienable rights of the Palestinian people, including their right to self-determination, to support the achievement without delay of an end to the Israeli occupation that began in 1967 and of the two-State solution on the basis of the pre-1967 borders and the just resolution of all final status issues and to mobilize international support for and assistance to the Palestinian people, and in this regard authorizes the Committee to make such adjustments in its approved programme of work as it may consider appropriate and necessary in the light of developments and to report thereon to the General Assembly at its seventy-fourth session and thereafter; [p. 3]

3. *Also requests* the Committee to continue to keep under review the situation relating to the question of Palestine and to report and make suggestions to the General Assembly, the Security Council or the Secretary-General, as appropriate;

4. *Further requests* the Committee to continue to extend its cooperation and support to Palestinian and other civil society organizations and to continue to involve additional civil society organizations and parliamentarians in its work in order to mobilize international solidarity and support for the Palestinian people, particularly during this critical period of political instability, humanitarian hardship and financial crisis, with the overall aim of promoting the achievement by the Palestinian people of their inalienable rights and a just, lasting and peaceful settlement of the question of Palestine, the core of the Arab-Israeli conflict, on the basis of the relevant United Nations resolutions,

the terms of reference of the Madrid Conference, including the principle of land for peace, the Arab Peace Initiative[2] and the Quartet road map;[3]

5. *Commends* the Committee on its efforts and activities in upholding its mandate, including through cooperative initiatives with Governments, relevant organizations of the United Nations system, intergovernmental organizations and civil society organizations;

6. *Commends* the Working Group of the Committee on its efforts in coordinating the efforts of international and regional civil society organizations regarding the question of Palestine;

7. *Requests* the United Nations Conciliation Commission for Palestine, established under General Assembly resolution 194 (III), and other United Nations bodies associated with the question of Palestine to continue to cooperate fully with the Committee and to make available to it, at its request, the relevant information and documentation that they have at their disposal;

8. *Invites* all Governments and organizations to extend their cooperation and support to the Committee in the performance of its tasks, recalling its repeated call for all States and the specialized agencies and organizations of the United Nations system to continue to support and assist the Palestinian people in the early realization of their right to self-determination, including the right to their independent State of Palestine;

9. *Requests* the United Nations Conference on Trade and Development to continue to report to the General Assembly on the economic costs of the Israeli occupation for the Palestinian people, and, while drawing attention to the alarming findings, as reflected in the recent reports[7] in this regard, calls for the exertion of all efforts for the provision of the resources necessary to expedite the completion and publication of the report, including the facilitation and coordination of pertinent inputs from the relevant organs, bodies and agencies of the United Nations system;

10. *Requests* the Secretary-General to circulate the report of the Committee to all the competent bodies of the United Nations, and urges them to take the necessary action, as appropriate;

11. *Requests* the Committee, bearing in mind the regrettable absence of tangible progress towards a peaceful solution, to continue to focus its activities throughout 2019 on efforts and initiatives to end the Israeli occupation that began in 1967 and to organize activities in this regard, within existing resources and in cooperation with Governments, relevant organizations of the United Nations system, intergovernmental organizations and civil society

---

7   A/71/174 and A/73/201.

organizations, aimed at raising international awareness and mobilizing diplomatic efforts to launch credible [p. 4] negotiations aimed at achieving without delay a just, lasting, comprehensive and peaceful solution to the question of Palestine in all its aspects;

12. *Requests* the Secretary-General to continue to provide the Committee with all the facilities necessary for the performance of its tasks.

43rd plenary meeting
30 November 2018

Human Rights Council

H.R.C. Rs. 37/37, Ensuring Accountability and Justice for All Violations of International Law in the Occupied Palestinian Territory, including East Jerusalem (Mar. 23, 2018)

United Nations
General Assembly
A/HRC/RES/37/37
Distr.: General
13 April 2018
Original: English
Human Rights Council
Thirty-seventh session
26 February–23 March 2018
Agenda item 7

Resolution adopted by the Human Rights Council on 23 March 2018

37/37. Ensuring accountability and justice for all violations of international law in the Occupied Palestinian Territory, including East Jerusalem

The Human Rights Council,

Guided by the purposes and principles of the Charter of the United Nations,

Recalling the relevant rules and principles of international law, including international humanitarian law and human rights law, in particular the Geneva Convention relative to the Protection of Civilian Persons in Time of War, of 12 August 1949, which is applicable to the Occupied Palestinian Territory, including East Jerusalem,

Recalling also the Universal Declaration of Human Rights and the other human rights covenants, including the International Covenant on Civil and Political Rights, the International Covenant on Economic, Social and Cultural Rights and the Convention on the Rights of the Child,

Recalling further the statement of 15 July 1999 and the declarations adopted on 5 December 2001 and 17 December 2014 at the Conference of High Contracting Parties to the Fourth Geneva Convention on measures to enforce the Convention in the Occupied Palestinian Territory, including East Jerusalem, at which the High Contracting Parties reaffirmed, inter alia, their commitment to uphold their obligation to ensure respect for the Convention in the Occupied Palestinian Territory, including East Jerusalem,

Recalling its relevant resolutions, including resolutions S-9/1 of 12 January 2009, 19/17 of 22 March 2012 and S-21/1 of 23 July 2014,

Recalling also the advisory opinion rendered on 9 July 2004 by the International Court of Justice on the legal consequences of the construction of a wall in the Occupied Palestinian Territory,

Expressing its appreciation to the independent commission of inquiry on the 2014 Gaza conflict, and all other relevant United Nations mechanisms, as well as the treaty bodies and other United Nations bodies, for their reports,

Recognizing the work of Palestinian, Israeli and international civil society actors and human rights defenders in documenting and countering violations of international law in the Occupied Palestinian Territory, including East Jerusalem,

Affirming the obligation of all parties to respect international humanitarian law and international human rights law, [p. 2]

Emphasizing the importance of the safety and well-being of all civilians and reaffirming the obligation to ensure the protection of civilians in armed conflict,

Gravely concerned by reports regarding serious human rights violations and grave breaches of international humanitarian law, including possible war crimes, including the findings of the United Nations Fact-Finding Mission on the Gaza Conflict, of the independent international fact-finding mission to investigate the implications of Israeli settlements on the civil, political, economic, social and cultural rights of the Palestinian people throughout the Occupied Palestinian Territory, including East Jerusalem, of the independent commission of inquiry on the 2014 Gaza conflict, and of the boards of inquiry convened by the Secretary-General,

Condemning all violations of human rights and of international humanitarian law, and appalled at the widespread and unprecedented levels of destruction, death and human suffering caused in the Occupied Palestinian Territory, including East Jerusalem,

Stressing the urgency of achieving without delay an end to the Israeli occupation that began in 1967, and affirming that this is necessary in order to uphold human rights and international law,

Deploring the non-cooperation by Israel with all Human Rights Council fact-finding missions and the independent commission of inquiry on the 2014 Gaza conflict, and the refusal to grant access to and cooperate with international human rights bodies and a number of United Nations special procedures seeking to investigate alleged violations of international law in the Occupied Palestinian Territory, including East Jerusalem,

Regretting the lack of implementation of the recommendations contained in the reports of the independent commission of inquiry on the 2014 Gaza conflict,[1] the independent international fact-finding mission to investigate the implications of Israeli settlements on the civil, political, economic, social and cultural rights of the Palestinian people throughout the Occupied Palestinian Territory, including East Jerusalem,[2] and the United Nations Fact-Finding Mission on the Gaza Conflict,[3] which follows a pattern of lack of implementation of recommendations made by United Nations mechanisms and bodies,

Alarmed that long-standing systemic impunity for international law violations has allowed for the recurrence of grave violations without consequence, and stressing the need to ensure accountability for all violations of international humanitarian law and international human rights law in order to end impunity, ensure justice, deter further violations, protect civilians and promote peace,

Regretting the lack of progress in the conduct of domestic investigations in accordance with international law standards, and aware of the existence of numerous legal, procedural and practical obstacles in the Israeli civil and criminal legal system contributing to the denial of access to justice for Palestinian victims and of their right to an effective judicial remedy,

Emphasizing the need for States to investigate and prosecute grave breaches of the Geneva Conventions of 1949 and other serious violations of international humanitarian law, to end impunity, to uphold their obligations to ensure respect and to promote international accountability,

Noting the accession by the State of Palestine on 2 January 2015 to the Rome Statute of the International Criminal Court,

1. *Welcomes* the report of the independent commission of inquiry on the 2014 Gaza conflict;[1]

2. *Calls upon* all duty bearers and United Nations bodies to pursue the implementation of the recommendations contained in the reports of the independent commission of inquiry on the 2014 Gaza conflict,[1] the independent

---

1 A/HRC/29/52.
2 A/HRC/22/63.
3 A/HRC/12/48.

international fact-finding mission to investigate the implications of Israeli settlements on the civil, political, [p. 3] economic, social and cultural rights of the Palestinian people throughout the Occupied Palestinian Territory, including East Jerusalem,[2] and the United Nations Fact-Finding Mission on the Gaza Conflict,[3] in accordance with their respective mandates;

3. *Notes* the importance of the work of the independent commission of inquiry on the 2014 Gaza conflict, the independent international fact-finding mission to investigate the implications of Israeli settlements on the civil, political, economic, social and cultural rights of the Palestinian people throughout the Occupied Palestinian Territory, including East Jerusalem, and the United Nations Fact-Finding Mission on the Gaza Conflict, and of the information collected regarding grave violations in support of future accountability efforts, in particular information on alleged perpetrators of violations of international law;

4. *Emphasizes* the need to ensure that all those responsible for violations of international humanitarian law and international human rights law are held to account through appropriate, fair and independent national or international criminal justice mechanisms, and to ensure the provision of effective remedy to all victims, including full reparations, and stresses the need to pursue practical steps towards these goals to ensure justice for all victims and to contribute to the prevention of future violations;

5. *Stresses* that all efforts to end the Israeli-Palestinian conflict should be grounded in respect for international humanitarian law and international human rights law and should ensure credible and comprehensive accountability for all violations of international law in order to bring about sustainable peace;

6. *Calls upon* the parties concerned to cooperate fully with the preliminary examination of the International Criminal Court and with any subsequent investigation that may be opened;

7. *Denounces* all acts of intimidation, threats and delegitimization directed at civil society actors and human rights defenders involved in documenting and countering violations of international law and impunity in the Occupied Palestinian Territory, including East Jerusalem, and calls upon all States to ensure their protection;

8. *Calls upon* all States to promote compliance with international law and all High Contracting Parties to the Fourth Geneva Convention to respect, and to ensure respect for, international humanitarian law in the Occupied Palestinian Territory, including East Jerusalem, in accordance with article 1 common to the Geneva Conventions, and to fulfil their obligations under articles 146, 147 and 148 of the said Convention with regard to penal sanctions, grave breaches and

the responsibilities of the High Contracting Parties, including by ensuring that their public authorities and private entities do not become involved in internationally unlawful conduct, inter alia, the provision of arms to end users that could use the arms to commit or facilitate serious violations of international humanitarian and/or human rights law;

9. *Recommends* that the General Assembly remain apprised of the matter until it is satisfied that appropriate action with regard to implementing the recommendations made by the United Nations Fact-Finding Mission on the Gaza Conflict in its report has been or is being taken appropriately at the national or international levels to ensure justice for victims and accountability for perpetrators;

10. *Requests* the United Nations High Commissioner for Human Rights to report on the implementation of the present resolution to the Human Rights Council at its fortieth session;

11. *Decides* to remain seized of the matter.

56th meeting
23 March 2018

[Adopted by a recorded vote of 27 to 4, with 15 abstentions. The voting was as follows:

In favour:

Afghanistan, Angola, Belgium, Brazil, Burundi, Chile, China, Côte d'Ivoire, Cuba, Ecuador, Egypt, Iraq, Kyrgyzstan, Nepal, Nigeria, Pakistan, Peru, Philippines, Qatar, Saudi Arabia, Senegal, Slovenia, South Africa, [p. 4] Switzerland, Tunisia, United Arab Emirates, Venezuela (Bolivarian Republic of)

Against:

Australia, Togo, United Kingdom of Great Britain and Northern Ireland, United States of America

Abstaining:

Croatia, Democratic Republic of the Congo, Ethiopia, Georgia, Germany, Hungary, Japan, Kenya, Mexico, Panama, Republic of Korea, Rwanda, Slovakia, Spain, Ukraine]

H.R.C. Res. 37/36, Israeli Settlements in the Occupied Palestinian Territory, including East Jerusalem, and in the Occupied Syrian Golan, A/HRC/RES/37/36 (Mar. 23, 2018)

United Nations
General Assembly
A/HRC/RES/37/36
Distr.: General
13 April 2018
Original: English
Human Rights Council
Thirty-seventh session
26 February–23 March 2018
Agenda item 7

Resolution adopted by the Human Rights Council on 23 March 2018

37/36. Israeli settlements in the Occupied Palestinian Territory, including East Jerusalem, and in the occupied Syrian Golan

The Human Rights Council,

Guided by the principles of the Charter of the United Nations, and affirming the inadmissibility of the acquisition of territory by force,

Reaffirming that all States have an obligation to promote and protect human rights and fundamental freedoms, as stated in the Charter and elaborated in the Universal Declaration of Human Rights, the International Covenants on Human Rights and other applicable instruments,

Recalling relevant resolutions of the Commission on Human Rights, the Human Rights Council, the Security Council and the General Assembly reaffirming, inter alia, the illegality of the Israeli settlements in the occupied territories, including in East Jerusalem,

Recalling also Human Rights Council resolution 19/17 of 22 March 2012, in which the Council decided to establish an independent international fact-finding mission to investigate the implications of the Israeli settlements on the human rights of the Palestinian people throughout the Occupied Palestinian Territory, including East Jerusalem,

Noting the accession by the State of Palestine to several human rights treaties and the core humanitarian law conventions, and its accession on 2 January 2015 to the Rome Statute of the International Criminal Court,

Reaffirming the applicability of the Geneva Convention relative to the Protection of Civilian Persons in Time of War, of 12 August 1949, to the Occupied Palestinian Territory, including East Jerusalem, and to the occupied Syrian Golan,

Recalling the declarations adopted at the Conferences of High Contracting Parties to the Fourth Geneva Convention, held in Geneva on 5 December 2001 and 17 December 2014, and reaffirming that States should not recognize an unlawful situation arising from breaches of peremptory norms of international law,

Affirming that the transfer by the occupying Power of parts of its own civilian population to the territory it occupies constitutes a breach of the Fourth Geneva Convention and relevant provisions of customary law, including those codified in Additional Protocol I to the four Geneva Conventions, [p. 2]

Recalling the advisory opinion rendered on 9 July 2004 by the International Court of Justice on the legal consequences of the construction of a wall in the Occupied Palestinian Territory, and recalling also General Assembly resolutions ES-10/15 of 20 July 2004 and ES-10/17 of 15 December 2006,

Noting that the International Court of Justice concluded, inter alia, that the Israeli settlements in the Occupied Palestinian Territory, including East Jerusalem, had been established in breach of international law,

Taking note of the recent relevant reports of the Secretary-General, the Office of the United Nations High Commissioner for Human Rights, the Special Committee to Investigate Israeli Practices Affecting the Human Rights of the Palestinian People and Other Arabs of the Occupied Territories and the treaty bodies monitoring compliance with the human rights treaties to which Israel is a party, and the recent reports of the Special Rapporteur on the situation of human rights in the Palestinian territories occupied since 1967,

Recalling the report of the independent international fact-finding mission to investigate the implications of the Israeli settlements on the civil, political, economic, social and cultural rights of the Palestinian people throughout the Occupied Palestinian Territory, including East Jerusalem,[1]

---

1 A/HRC/22/63.

Expressing its grave concern at any action taken by any body, governmental or non-governmental, in violation of the Security Council and General Assembly resolutions relevant to Jerusalem,

Noting that Israel has been planning, implementing, supporting and encouraging the establishment and expansion of settlements in the Occupied Palestinian Territory, including East Jerusalem, since 1967, through, inter alia, the granting of benefits and incentives to settlements and settlers,

Recalling the Quartet road map to a permanent two-State solution to the Israeli-Palestinian conflict, and emphasizing specifically its call for a freeze on all settlement activity, including so-called natural growth, and the dismantlement of all settlement outposts erected since March 2001, and the need for Israel to uphold its obligations and commitments in this regard,

Taking note of General Assembly resolution 67/19 of 29 November 2012, by which, inter alia, Palestine was accorded the status of non-member observer State in the United Nations, and also of the follow-up report thereon of the Secretary-General,[2]

Aware that Israeli settlement activities involve, inter alia, the transfer of nationals of the occupying Power into the occupied territories, the confiscation of land, the destruction of property, including homes and projects funded by the international community, the forcible displacement of Palestinian civilians, including Bedouin families, the exploitation of natural resources, the conduct of economic activity for the benefit of the occupying Power, disruption to the livelihood of protected persons, the de facto annexation of land and other actions against the Palestinian civilian population and the civilian population in the occupied Syrian Golan that are contrary to international law,

Affirming that the Israeli settlement policies and practices in the Occupied Palestinian Territory, including East Jerusalem, seriously endanger the viability of the two-State solution, undermining the physical possibility of its realization and entrenching a one-State reality of unequal rights, [p. 3]

Noting in this regard that the Israeli settlements fragment the West Bank, including East Jerusalem, into isolated geographical units, severely limiting the possibility of a contiguous territory and the ability to dispose freely of natural resources, both of which are required for the meaningful exercise of Palestinian self-determination,

Noting that the settlement enterprise and the impunity associated with its persistence, expansion and related violence continue to be a root cause of many violations of the Palestinians' human rights, and constitute the main

---

2 A/67/738.

factors perpetuating Israel's belligerent occupation of the Palestinian Territory, including East Jerusalem, since 1967,

Deploring in particular the construction and expansion of settlements by Israel in and around occupied East Jerusalem, including its so-called E-1 plan, which aims to connect its illegal settlements around and further isolate occupied East Jerusalem, the continuing demolition of Palestinian homes and eviction of Palestinian families from the city, the revocation of Palestinian residency rights in the city, and ongoing settlement activities in the Jordan Valley, all of which further fragment and undermine the contiguity of the Occupied Palestinian Territory,

Expressing grave concern at the continuing construction by Israel of the wall inside the Occupied Palestinian Territory, including in and around East Jerusalem, in violation of international law, and expressing its concern in particular at the route of the wall in departure from the Armistice Line of 1949, which is causing humanitarian hardship and a serious decline in socioeconomic conditions for the Palestinian people, fragmenting the territorial contiguity of the Territory and undermining its viability, creating a fait accompli on the ground that could be tantamount to de facto annexation in departure from the Armistice Line of 1949, and making the two-State solution physically impossible to implement,

Deeply concerned that the wall's route has been traced in such a way to include the great majority of the Israeli settlements in the Occupied Palestinian Territory, including East Jerusalem,

Gravely concerned at all acts of violence, destruction, harassment, provocation and incitement by extremist Israeli settlers and groups of armed settlers in the Occupied Palestinian Territory, including East Jerusalem, against Palestinian civilians, including children, and their properties, including homes, agricultural lands and historic and religious sites, and the acts of terror carried out by several extremist Israeli settlers, which are a long-standing phenomenon aimed at, inter alia, displacing the occupied population and facilitating the expansion of settlements,

Expressing concern at ongoing impunity for acts of settler violence against Palestinian civilians and their properties, and stressing the need for Israel to investigate and to ensure accountability for all of these acts,

Aware of the detrimental impact of the Israeli settlements on Palestinian and other Arab natural resources, especially as a result of the confiscation of land and the forced diversion of water resources, including the destruction of orchards and crops and the seizure of water wells by Israeli settlers, and of the dire socioeconomic consequences in this regard, which precludes the

Palestinian people from being able to exercise permanent sovereignty over their natural resources,

Noting that the agricultural sector, considered the cornerstone of Palestinian economic development, has not been able to play its strategic role because of the dispossession of land and the denial of access for farmers to agricultural areas, water resources and domestic and external markets owing to the construction, consolidation and expansion of Israeli settlements,

Aware that numerous Israeli policies and practices related to settlement activity in the Occupied Palestinian Territory, including East Jerusalem, amount to blatant discrimination, including through the creation of a system privileging Israeli settlements and settlers, against the Palestinian people and in violation of their human rights, [p. 4]

Recalling Human Rights Council resolution 22/29 of 22 March 2013, in follow-up to the report of the independent international fact-finding mission to investigate the implications of Israeli settlements on the civil, political, economic, social and cultural rights of the Palestinian people throughout the Occupied Palestinian Territory, including East Jerusalem,

Recalling also the Guiding Principles on Business and Human Rights, which place responsibilities on all business enterprises to respect human rights by, inter alia, refraining from contributing to human rights abuses arising from conflict, and call upon States to provide adequate assistance to business enterprises to assess and address the heightened risks of abuses in conflict-affected areas, including by ensuring that their current policies, legislation, regulations and enforcement measures are effective in addressing the risk of business involvement in gross human rights abuses,

Noting that, in situations of armed conflict, business enterprises should respect the standards of international humanitarian law, and concerned that some business enterprises have, directly and indirectly, enabled, facilitated and profited from the construction and growth of the Israeli settlements in the Occupied Palestinian Territory,

Emphasizing the importance for States to act in accordance with their own national legislation on promoting compliance with international humanitarian law with regard to business activities that result in human rights abuses,

Concerned that economic activities facilitate the expansion and entrenchment of settlements, aware that the conditions of harvesting and production of products made in settlements involve, inter alia, the exploitation of the natural resources of the Occupied Palestinian Territory, including East Jerusalem, and calling upon all States to respect their legal obligations in this regard,

Aware that products wholly or partially produced in settlements have been labelled as originating from Israel, and concerned about the significant role that the production and trade of such products plays in helping to support and maintain the settlements,

Aware also of the role of private individuals, associations and charities in third States that are involved in providing funding to Israeli settlements and settlement-based entities, contributing to the maintenance and expansion of settlements,

Noting that a number of business enterprises have decided to disengage from relationships or activities associated with the Israeli settlements owing to the risks involved,

Expressing its concern at the failure of Israel, the occupying Power, to cooperate fully with the relevant United Nations mechanisms, in particular the Special Rapporteur on the situation of human rights in the Palestinian territories occupied since 1967,

1. *Reaffirms* that the Israeli settlements established since 1967 in the Occupied Palestinian Territory, including East Jerusalem, and in the occupied Syrian Golan are illegal under international law, and constitute a major obstacle to the achievement of the two-State solution and a just, lasting and comprehensive peace, and to economic and social development;

2. *Calls upon* Israel to accept the de jure applicability of the Geneva Convention relative to the Protection of Civilian Persons in Time of War, of 12 August 1949, to the Occupied Palestinian Territory, including East Jerusalem, and to the occupied Syrian Golan, to abide scrupulously by the provisions of the Convention, in particular article 49 thereof, and to comply with all its obligations under international law and cease immediately all actions causing the alteration of the character, status and demographic composition of the Occupied Palestinian Territory, including East Jerusalem, and the occupied Syrian Golan;

3. *Demands* that Israel, the occupying Power, immediately cease all settlement activities in all the Occupied Palestinian Territory, including East Jerusalem, and in the occupied Syrian Golan, and calls in this regard for the full implementation of all relevant resolutions of the Security Council, including, inter alia, resolutions 446 (1979) of 22 March 1979, 452 (1979) of 20 July 1979, 465 (1980) of 1 March 1980, 476 (1980) of 30 June 1980, 497 (1981) of 17 December 1981, 1515 (2003) of 19 November 2003 and 2334 (2016) of 23 December 2016; [p. 5]

4. *Also demands* that Israel, the occupying Power, comply fully with its legal obligations, as mentioned in the advisory opinion rendered on 9 July 2004 by the International Court of Justice, including to cease forthwith the works of construction of the wall being built in the Occupied Palestinian Territory, including in and around East Jerusalem, to dismantle forthwith the structure therein situated, to repeal or render ineffective forthwith all legislative and

regulatory acts relating thereto, and to make reparation for the damage caused to all natural or legal persons affected by the construction of the wall;

5. *Condemns* the continuing settlement and related activities by Israel, including the construction and expansion of settlements, the expropriation of land, the demolition of houses, the confiscation and destruction of property, the forcible transfer of Palestinians, including entire communities, and the construction of bypass roads, which change the physical character and demographic composition of the occupied territories, including East Jerusalem and the Syrian Golan, constitute a violation of international humanitarian law, in particular article 49 of the Fourth Geneva Convention, and of international human rights law, and undermine the viability of the two-State solution;

6. *Expresses its grave concern* at declarations by Israeli officials calling for the annexation of Palestinian land, and reaffirms the prohibition of acquisition of territory resulting from the use of force;

7. *Also expresses its grave concern* at and calls for the cessation of:

(a) The operation by Israel of a tramway linking the settlements with West Jerusalem, which is in clear violation of international law and relevant United Nations resolutions;

(b) The expropriation of Palestinian land, the demolition of Palestinian homes, demolition orders, forced evictions and "relocation" plans, the obstruction and destruction of humanitarian assistance and the creation of a coercive environment and unbearable living conditions by Israel in areas identified for the expansion and construction of settlements, and other practices aimed at the forcible transfer of the Palestinian civilian population, including Bedouin communities and herders, and further settlement activities, including the denial of access to water and other basic services by Israel to Palestinians in the Occupied Palestinian Territory, including East Jerusalem, particularly in areas slated for settlement expansion, and including the appropriation of Palestinian property through, inter alia, the declaration of "State lands", closed "military zones", "national parks" and "archaeological" sites to facilitate and advance the expansion or construction of settlements and related infrastructure, in violation of Israel's obligations under international humanitarian law and international human rights law;

(c) Israeli measures in the form of policies, laws and practices that have the effect of preventing the full participation of Palestinians in the political, social, economic and cultural life of the Occupied Palestinian Territory, including East Jerusalem, and prevent their full development in both the West Bank and the Gaza Strip;

8. *Calls upon* Israel, the occupying Power:
(a) To end without delay its occupation of the territories occupied since 1967, to reverse the settlement policy in the occupied territories, including East Jerusalem and the Syrian Golan, and, as a first step towards the dismantlement of the settlement enterprise, to stop immediately the expansion of existing settlements, including so-called natural growth and related activities, to prevent any new installation of settlers in the occupied territories, including in East Jerusalem, and to discard its so-called E-1 plan;
(b) To put an end to all of the human rights violations linked to the presence of settlements, especially of the right to self-determination, and to fulfil its international obligations to provide effective remedy for victims;
(c) To take immediate measures to prohibit and eradicate all policies and practices that discriminate against and disproportionately affect the Palestinian population in the Occupied Palestinian Territory, including East Jerusalem, by, inter alia, putting an end to the system of separate roads for the exclusive use of Israeli settlers, who reside illegally in the said territory, the complex combination of movement restrictions consisting of the wall, roadblocks and a permit regime that only affects the Palestinian population, the [p. 6] application of a two-tier legal system that has facilitated the establishment and consolidation of the settlements, and other violations and forms of institutionalized discrimination;
(d) To cease the requisition and all other forms of unlawful appropriation of Palestinian land, including so-called State land, and its allocation for the establishment and expansion of settlements, and to halt the granting of benefits and incentives to settlements and settlers;
(e) To put an end to all practices and policies resulting in the territorial fragmentation of the Occupied Palestinian Territory, including East Jerusalem, and which are isolating Palestinian communities into separate enclaves and deliberately changing the demographic composition of the Occupied Palestinian Territory;
(f) To take and implement serious measures, including the confiscation of arms and enforcement of criminal sanctions, with the aim of ensuring full accountability for and preventing all acts of violence by Israeli settlers, and to take other measures to guarantee the safety and protection of Palestinian civilians and Palestinian properties in the Occupied Palestinian Territory, including East Jerusalem;
(g) To bring to a halt all actions, including those perpetrated by Israeli settlers, harming the environment, including the dumping of all kinds of waste materials in the Occupied Palestinian Territory, including East

Jerusalem, and in the occupied Syrian Golan, which gravely threaten their natural resources, namely water and land resources, and which pose an environmental, sanitation and health threat to the civilian population;

(h) To cease the exploitation, damage, cause of loss or depletion and endangerment of the natural resources of the Occupied Palestinian Territory, including East Jerusalem, and of the occupied Syrian Golan;

9. *Welcomes* the adoption of the European Union Guidelines on the eligibility of Israeli entities and their activities in the territories occupied by Israel since June 1967 for grants, prizes and financial instruments funded by the European Union since 2014;

10. *Urges* all States and international organizations to ensure that they are not taking actions that either recognize, aid or assist the expansion of settlements or the construction of the wall in the Occupied Palestinian Territory, including East Jerusalem, and to continue to actively pursue policies that ensure respect for their obligations under international law with regard to these and all other illegal Israeli practices and measures in the Occupied Palestinian Territory, including East Jerusalem;

11. *Reminds* all States of their legal obligations as mentioned in the advisory opinion of the International Court of Justice of 9 July 2004 on the legal consequences of the construction of a wall in the Occupied Palestinian Territory, including not to recognize the illegal situation resulting from the construction of the wall, not to render aid or assistance in maintaining the situation created by such construction, and to ensure compliance by Israel with international humanitarian law as embodied in the Fourth Geneva Convention;

12. *Calls upon* all States:

(a) To distinguish, in their relevant dealings, between the territory of the State of Israel and the territories occupied since 1967, including not to provide Israel with any assistance to be used specifically in connection with settlements in these territories with regard to, inter alia, the issue of trade with settlements, consistent with their obligations under international law;

(b) To implement the Guiding Principles on Business and Human Rights in relation to the Occupied Palestinian Territory, including East Jerusalem, and to take appropriate measures to help to ensure that businesses domiciled in their territory and/or under their jurisdiction, including those owned or controlled by them, refrain from committing, contributing to, enabling or benefiting from the human rights abuses of Palestinians, in accordance with the expected standard of conduct in the Guiding Principles and relevant international laws and standards, by taking appropriate steps in view of the immitigable nature of the adverse impact of their activities on human rights;

(c) To provide guidance to individuals and businesses on the financial, reputational and legal risks, including the possibility of liability for corporate involvement [p. 7] in gross human rights abuses and the abuses of the rights of individuals, of becoming involved in settlement-related activities, including through financial transactions, investments, purchases, procurements, loans, the provision of services, and other economic and financial activities in or benefiting Israeli settlements, to inform businesses of these risks in the formulation of their national action plans for the implementation of the Guiding Principles on Business and Human Rights, and to ensure that their policies, legislation, regulations and enforcement measures effectively address the heightened risks of operating a business in the Occupied Palestinian Territory, including East Jerusalem;

(d) To increase monitoring of settler violence with a view to promoting accountability;

13. *Calls upon* business enterprises to take all measures necessary to comply with their responsibilities under the Guiding Principles on Business and Human Rights and other relevant international laws and standards with respect to their activities in or in relation to the Israeli settlements and the wall in the Occupied Palestinian Territory, including East Jerusalem, to avoid the adverse impact of such activities on human rights, and to avoid contributing to the establishment, maintenance, development or consolidation of Israeli settlements or the exploitation of the natural resources of the Occupied Palestinian Territory;

14. *Requests* that all parties concerned, including United Nations bodies, implement and ensure the implementation of the recommendations contained in the report of the independent international fact-finding mission to investigate the implications of Israeli settlements on the civil, political, economic, social and cultural rights of the Palestinian people throughout the Occupied Palestinian Territory, including East Jerusalem, and endorsed by the Human Rights Council through its resolution 22/29, in accordance with their respective mandates;

15. *Calls upon* the relevant United Nations bodies to take all necessary measures and actions within their mandates to ensure full respect for and compliance with Human Rights Council resolution 17/4 of 16 June 2011, on the Guiding Principles on Business and Human Rights and other relevant international laws and standards, and to ensure the implementation of the United Nations "Protect, Respect and Remedy" Framework, which provides a global standard for upholding human rights in relation to business activities that are connected with Israeli settlements in the Occupied Palestinian Territory, including East Jerusalem;

16. *Requests* the United Nations High Commissioner for Human Rights to report to the Human Rights Council on the implementation of the provisions of the present resolution at its fortieth session;

17. *Decides* to remain seized of the matter.

56th meeting
23 March 2018

[Adopted by a recorded vote of 34 to 4, with 8 abstentions. The voting was as follows:

In favour:

Afghanistan, Angola, Belgium, Brazil, Burundi, Chile, China, Côte d'Ivoire, Cuba, Ecuador, Egypt, Ethiopia, Germany, Iraq, Japan, Kenya, Kyrgyzstan, Mexico, Nepal, Nigeria, Pakistan, Peru, Philippines, Qatar, Republic of Korea, Saudi Arabia, Senegal, Slovenia, South Africa, Spain, Switzerland, Tunisia, United Arab Emirates, Venezuela (Bolivarian Republic of)

Against:

Australia, Hungary, Togo, United States of America

Abstaining:

Croatia, Democratic Republic of the Congo, Georgia, Panama, Rwanda, Slovakia, Ukraine, United Kingdom of Great Britain and Northern Ireland]

H.R.C. Res. 37/35, Human Rights Situation in the Occupied Palestinian Territory, including East Jerusalem (Mar. 23, 2018)

United Nations
General Assembly
A/HRC/RES/37/35
Distr.: General
13 April 2018
Original: English
Human Rights Council
Thirty-seventh session
26 February–23 March 2018
Agenda item 7

Resolution adopted by the Human Rights Council on 23 March 2018

37/35. Human rights situation in the Occupied Palestinian Territory, including East Jerusalem

The Human Rights Council,

Recalling the Universal Declaration of Human Rights, the International Covenant on Civil and Political Rights, the International Covenant on Economic, Social and Cultural Rights, the Convention on the Rights of the Child and the Optional Protocol thereto on the involvement of children in armed conflict, the Convention on the Elimination of All Forms of Discrimination against Women, the Convention against Torture and Other Cruel, Inhuman or Degrading Treatment or Punishment and the International Convention on the Elimination of All Forms of Racial Discrimination, and affirming that these human rights instruments, among others, are applicable to and must be respected in the Occupied Palestinian Territory, including East Jerusalem,

Recalling also relevant resolutions of the Human Rights Council,

Taking note of the recent reports of the Special Rapporteur on the situation of human rights in the Palestinian territories occupied since 1967,[1] and other relevant recent reports of the Human Rights Council,

Stressing the urgent need for efforts to reverse the negative trends on the ground and to restore a political horizon for advancing and accelerating meaningful negotiations aimed at the achievement of a peace agreement that will bring a complete end to the Israeli occupation that began in 1967 and the resolution of all core final status issues, without exception, leading to a peaceful, just, lasting and comprehensive solution of the question of Palestine,

Noting the accession by the State of Palestine to several human rights treaties and the core humanitarian law conventions, and its accession on 2 January 2015 to the Rome Statute of the International Criminal Court,

Recalling the advisory opinion rendered on 9 July 2004 by the International Court of Justice, and recalling also General Assembly resolutions ES-10/15 of 20 July 2004 and ES-10/17 of 15 December 2006, [p. 2]

Noting in particular the Court's reply, including that the construction of the wall being built by Israel, the occupying Power, in the Occupied Palestinian Territory, including in and around East Jerusalem, and its associated regime are contrary to international law,

Reaffirming the principle of the inadmissibility of the acquisition of territory by force, and deeply concerned at the fragmentation of the Occupied Palestinian Territory, including East Jerusalem, through the construction of settlements, settler roads, the wall and other measures that are tantamount to de facto annexation of Palestinian land,

Emphasizing the applicability of the Geneva Convention relative to the Protection of Civilian Persons in Time of War, of 12 August 1949, to the Occupied Palestinian Territory, including East Jerusalem, and reaffirming the obligation of the States parties to the Fourth Geneva Convention under articles 146, 147 and 148 with regard to penal sanctions, grave breaches and responsibilities of the High Contracting Parties and to ensure respect for international humanitarian law,

Stressing the importance of accountability in preventing future conflicts and ensuring that there is no impunity for violations and abuses, thereby contributing to peace efforts and avoiding the recurrence of violations of international law, including international humanitarian law and international human rights law,

Expressing grave concern at the continuing violation of international humanitarian law and the systematic violation of the human rights of the

---

1 A/72/556 and A/HRC/37/75.

Palestinian people by Israel, the occupying Power, including that arising from the excessive use of force and military operations causing death and injury to Palestinian civilians, including children and women, and to non-violent, peaceful demonstrators and to journalists, including through the use of live ammunition; the arbitrary detention of Palestinians, some of whom have been detained for decades; the use of collective punishment; the closure of areas; the confiscation of land; the establishment and expansion of settlements; the construction of a wall in the Occupied Palestinian Territory in departure from the Armistice Line of 1949; the forcible displacement of civilians, including of Bedouin communities; the policies and practices that discriminate against and disproportionately affect the Palestinian population in the Occupied Palestinian Territory, including East Jerusalem; the discriminatory allocation of water resources between Israeli settlers, who reside illegally in the Occupied Palestinian Territory, and the Palestinian population of the said Territory; the violation of the basic right to adequate housing, which is a component of the right to an adequate standard of living; the revocation of residency permits from Palestinians of East Jerusalem and their eviction from their city; the destruction of property and infrastructure, inter alia, homes of Palestinians; the hampering of humanitarian assistance and the destruction of, inter alia, structures provided as humanitarian aid, contributing to a coercive environment that leads to the forcible transfer of Palestinian civilians in the Occupied Palestinian Territory, including when carried out as an act of collective punishment in violation of international humanitarian law; incidents of harassment of and attacks on school children and attacks on educational facilities by Israeli settlers and as a result of Israeli military action; and all other actions designed to change the legal status, geographical nature and demographic composition of the Occupied Palestinian Territory, including East Jerusalem,

Deploring all conflicts in and around the Gaza Strip and the civilian casualties caused, including the killing and injury of thousands of Palestinian civilians, including children, women and elderly persons, the widespread destruction of thousands of homes and of civilian infrastructure, including schools, hospitals, water sanitation and electricity networks, economic, industrial and agricultural properties, public institutions, religious sites and United Nations schools and facilities, the internal displacement of hundreds of thousands of civilians, and all violations of international law, including humanitarian and human rights law, in this regard,

Gravely concerned in particular about the disastrous humanitarian situation and the critical socioeconomic and security situations in the Gaza Strip, including that resulting from the prolonged continuous closures and severe economic and movement restrictions that in effect amount to a blockade, and from the continuing and vastly negative repercussions of previous Israeli military operations, and about the firing of rockets into Israel, [p. 3]

Expressing deep concern at the detrimental impact of continued impediments to the reconstruction process on the human rights situation and on the socioeconomic and humanitarian conditions of the Palestinian civilian population, and calling upon the international community to step up its efforts to provide the Gaza Strip with the assistance that it requires,

Stressing the need for all parties, in conformity with the relevant provisions of international humanitarian law, to cooperate fully with the United Nations and other humanitarian agencies and organizations and to ensure the safe and unhindered access of humanitarian personnel, and the delivery of supplies and equipment, in order to allow such personnel to perform efficiently their task of assisting affected civilian populations, including refugees and internally displaced persons,

Stressing the need also to end immediately the closure of the Gaza Strip and for the full implementation of the Agreement on Movement and Access and the Agreed Principles for the Rafah Crossing, both of 15 November 2005, to allow for the freedom of movement of the Palestinian civilian population within and into and out of the Gaza Strip, while taking into account Israeli concerns,

Expressing deep concern at the Israeli policy of closures and the imposition of severe restrictions and checkpoints, several of which have been transformed into structures akin to permanent border crossings, other physical obstacles and a permit regime, which are applied in a discriminatory manner affecting the Palestinian population only and all of which obstruct the freedom of movement of persons and goods, including medical and humanitarian goods, throughout the Occupied Palestinian Territory, including East Jerusalem, and impair the Territory's contiguity, violating the human rights of the Palestinian people,

Convinced that the Israeli occupation has gravely impeded the efforts made to achieve sustainable development and a sound economic environment in the Occupied Palestinian Territory, including East Jerusalem, and expressing grave concern at the consequent deterioration of economic and living conditions,

Deploring all policies and practices whereby Israeli settlers, who reside illegally in the Occupied Palestinian Territory, including East Jerusalem, are accorded preferential treatment over the Palestinian population in terms of access to roads, infrastructure, land, property, housing, natural resources and judicial mechanisms, resulting in widespread human rights violations of Palestinians,

Expressing deep concern that thousands of Palestinians, including many children and women and elected members of the Palestinian Legislative Council, continue to be detained and held in Israeli prisons or detention centres under harsh conditions, including unhygienic conditions, solitary confinement, lack of proper medical care, denial of family visits and denial of due process, that impair their well-being, and expressing deep concern also at the ill-treatment and harassment of Palestinian prisoners and all reports of torture,

Recalling the United Nations Standard Minimum Rules for the Treatment of Prisoners (the Nelson Mandela Rules) and the United Nations Rules for the Treatment of Women Prisoners and Non-custodial Measures for Women Offenders (the Bangkok Rules), and calling for respect for those rules,

Recalling also the prohibition under international humanitarian law of the deportation of civilians from occupied territories,

Deploring the practice of withholding the bodies of those killed, and calling for the release of the bodies that have not yet been returned to their relatives, in accordance with international humanitarian law and human rights law,

Stressing the need for the protection of human rights defenders engaged in the promotion of human rights issues in the Occupied Palestinian Territory, including East Jerusalem, to allow them to carry out their work freely and without fear of attack, harassment, arbitrary detention or criminal prosecution,

Convinced of the need for an international presence to monitor the situation, to contribute to ending the violence and protecting the Palestinian civilian population and to [p. 4] help the parties to implement the agreements reached, and in this regard recalling the positive contribution of the Temporary International Presence in Hebron,

Emphasizing the right of all people in the region to the enjoyment of human rights as enshrined in the international human rights covenants,

1. *Stresses* the need for Israel, the occupying Power, to withdraw from the Palestinian territory occupied since 1967, including East Jerusalem, so as to enable the Palestinian people to exercise its universally recognized right to self-determination;

2. *Reiterates* that all measures and actions taken by Israel, the occupying Power, in the Occupied Palestinian Territory, including East Jerusalem, in violation of the relevant provisions of the Geneva Convention relative to the Protection of Civilian Persons in Time of War, of 12 August 1949, and contrary to the relevant resolutions of the Security Council are illegal and have no validity;

3. *Demands* that Israel, the occupying Power, comply fully with the provisions of the Fourth Geneva Convention of 1949 and cease immediately all measures and actions taken in violation and in breach of the Convention;

4. *Also demands* that Israel, the occupying Power, cease all practices and actions that violate the human rights of the Palestinian people, and that it fully respect human rights law and comply with its legal obligations in this regard, including in accordance with relevant United Nations resolutions;

5. *Calls for* urgent measures to ensure the safety and protection of the Palestinian civilian population in the Occupied Palestinian Territory, including East Jerusalem, in accordance with the relevant provisions of international humanitarian law and as called for by the Security Council in its resolution 904 (1994) of 18 March 1994;

6. *Deplores* the persistent non-cooperation of Israel with special procedure mandate holders and other United Nations mechanisms, and calls for full cooperation by Israel with the Human Rights Council and all its special procedures, relevant mechanisms and inquiries, and with the Office of the United Nations High Commissioner for Human Rights;

7. *Demands* that Israel, the occupying Power, cease all of its settlement activities, the construction of the wall and any other measures aimed at altering the character, status and demographic composition of the Occupied Palestinian Territory, including in and around East Jerusalem, all of which have, inter alia, a grave and detrimental impact on the human rights of the Palestinian people and the prospects for a peaceful settlement;

8. *Also demands* that Israel, the occupying Power, comply with its legal obligations under international law, as mentioned in the advisory opinion rendered on 9 July 2004 by the International Court of Justice and as demanded by the General Assembly in its resolutions ES-10/15 of 20 July 2004 and ES-10/13 of 21 October 2003, and that it immediately cease the construction of the wall in the Occupied Palestinian Territory, including in and around East Jerusalem, dismantle forthwith the structure situated therein, repeal or render ineffective all legislative and regulatory acts relating thereto, and make reparation for all damage caused by the construction of the wall, which has had a grave impact on the human rights and the socioeconomic living conditions of the Palestinian people;

9. *Calls upon* Israel to immediately cease any demolitions or plans for demolitions that would result in the forcible transfer or forced eviction of Palestinians, particularly in the vulnerable areas of the Jordan Valley, the periphery of Jerusalem and the South Hebron Hills, to facilitate the return of those Palestinian communities already subjected to forcible transfer or eviction to their original dwellings and to ensure adequate housing and legal security of tenure;

10. *Deplores* the illegal Israeli actions in occupied East Jerusalem, including the construction of settlements in various areas; the demolition of residential structures, the forced eviction of Palestinian inhabitants and the application of the policy of punitive home demolitions, in violation of their basic right to adequate housing and in violation of [p. 5] international humanitarian law; the ongoing policy of revoking the residency permits of Palestinians living in East Jerusalem through various discriminatory laws; excavations in and around religious and historic sites; and all other unilateral measures aimed at altering the character, status and demographic composition of the city and of the territory as a whole, including those stemming from attempts aimed at illegally changing the status quo of holy sites;

11. *Expresses grave concern* at the restrictions imposed by Israel that impede the access of Christian and Muslim worshippers to holy sites in the Occupied Palestinian Territory, including East Jerusalem, and calls upon Israel to include guarantees for non-discrimination on grounds of religion or belief as well as for the preservation and peaceful access to all religious sites;

12. *Urges* Israel to ensure that water resource allocation in the Occupied Palestinian Territory is not discriminatory and does not result in water shortages disproportionately affecting the Palestinian population of the West Bank, and to take urgent steps to facilitate the restoration of the water infrastructure of the West Bank, including in the Jordan Valley, affected by the destruction of the wells of local civilians, roof water tanks and other water and irrigation facilities under military and settler operation since 1967;

13. *Expresses concern* at the Citizenship and Entry into Israel Law adopted by the Knesset, which suspends the possibility, with certain rare exceptions, of family reunification between Israeli citizens and persons residing in the Occupied Palestinian Territory, including East Jerusalem, thus adversely affecting the lives of many families;

14. *Reiterates* the need for respect for the territorial unity, contiguity and integrity of all of the Occupied Palestinian Territory and for guarantees of the freedom of movement of persons and goods within the Palestinian territory, including movement into and from East Jerusalem, into and from the Gaza Strip, between the West Bank and the Gaza Strip, and to and from the outside world;

15. *Demands* that Israel, the occupying Power, cease immediately its imposition of prolonged closures and economic and movement restrictions, including those amounting to a blockade on the Gaza Strip, which severely restricts the freedom of movement of Palestinians within, into and out of Gaza and

their access to basic utilities, housing, education, work, health and an adequate standard of living via various measures, including import and export restrictions, that have a direct impact on livelihoods, economic sustainability and development throughout Gaza, aggravating the state of de-development in Gaza, and in this regard calls upon Israel to implement fully the Agreement on Movement and Access and the Agreed Principles for the Rafah Crossing in order to allow for the sustained and regular movement of persons and goods and for the acceleration of long overdue reconstruction in the Gaza Strip;

16. *Condemns* all acts of violence, including all acts of terror, provocation, incitement and destruction, especially the excessive use of force by the Israeli occupying forces against Palestinian civilians, particularly in the Gaza Strip, where the bombardment of populated areas has caused extensive loss of life and a vast number of injuries, including among thousands of children and women, massive damage and destruction to homes, economic, industrial and agricultural properties, vital infrastructure, including water, sanitation and electricity networks, religious sites and public institutions, including hospitals and schools, United Nations facilities, and agricultural lands, the large-scale internal displacement of civilians, and the excessive use of force by the Israeli occupying forces against Palestinian civilians in the context of peaceful protests in the West Bank;

17. *Also condemns* the firing of rockets against Israeli civilian areas resulting in loss of life and injury;

18. *Reiterates* the responsibility of Israel, the occupying Power, to respect the right to health of all persons within the Occupied Palestinian Territory and to facilitate the immediate, sustained and unfettered passage of humanitarian relief, including the access of medical personnel, their equipment, transport and supplies to all areas under occupation, including the Gaza Strip, and the granting of exit permits for patients in need of medical [p. 6] treatment outside the Gaza Strip, and stresses the need for the unhindered passage of ambulances at checkpoints, especially in times of conflict;

19. *Urges* Member States to continue to provide emergency assistance to the Palestinian people to alleviate the financial crisis and the dire socioeconomic and humanitarian situation, particularly in the Gaza Strip;

20. *Calls upon* Israel to end all harassment, threats, intimidation and reprisals against human rights defenders and civil society actors who peacefully advocate for the rights of Palestinians in the Occupied Palestinian Territory, including by cooperating with United Nations human rights bodies, and underscores the need to investigate all such acts, ensure accountability and effective remedies, and to take steps to prevent any further such threats, attacks, reprisals or acts of intimidation;

21. *Expresses deep concern* at the conditions of the Palestinian prisoners and detainees, including minors, in Israeli jails and detention centres, calls upon Israel to explicitly prohibit torture, including psychological torture and other cruel, inhuman or degrading treatment or punishment, demands that Israel, the occupying Power, fully respect and abide by its international law obligations towards all Palestinian prisoners and detainees in its custody, expresses its concern at the continued extensive use of administrative detention, calls for the full implementation of the agreement reached in May 2012 for a prompt and independent investigation into all cases of death in custody, and calls upon Israel to immediately release all Palestinian prisoners, including Palestinian legislators, detained in violation of international law;

22. *Calls for* urgent attention to be paid to the plight and the rights, in accordance with international law, of Palestinian prisoners and detainees in Israeli jails, and also calls for respect for the United Nations Standard Minimum Rules for the Treatment of Prisoners (the Nelson Mandela Rules) and the United Nations Rules for the Treatment of Women Prisoners and Non-custodial Measures for Women Offenders (the Bangkok Rules);

23. *Demands* that Israel cease its policy of transferring prisoners from the Occupied Palestinian Territory into the territory of Israel, and respect fully its obligations under article 76 of the Fourth Geneva Convention;

24. *Urges* Israel to ensure that any arrest, detention and/or trial of Palestinian children is in line with the Convention on the Rights of the Child, including by refraining from holding criminal proceedings against them in military courts that, by definition, fall short of providing the necessary guarantees to ensure respect for their rights and that infringe upon their right to non-discrimination;

25. *Emphasizes* the need to preserve and develop Palestinian institutions and infrastructure for the provision of vital public services to the Palestinian civilian population and the promotion of human rights, including civil, political, economic, social and cultural rights;

26. *Urges* all States and the specialized agencies and organizations of the United Nations system to continue to support and assist the Palestinian people in the early realization of their inalienable human rights, including their right to self-determination, as a matter of urgency, in the light of the onset of the fiftieth year of the Israeli occupation and the continued denial and violation of the human rights of the Palestinian people;

27. *Decides* to remain seized of the matter.

56th meeting
23 March 2018

[Adopted by a recorded vote of 41 to 3, with 2 abstentions. The voting was as follows:

In favour:

Afghanistan, Angola, Belgium, Brazil, Burundi, Chile, China, Côte d'Ivoire, Croatia, Cuba, Ecuador, Egypt, Ethiopia, Georgia, Germany, Hungary, Iraq, Japan, Kenya, Kyrgyzstan, Mexico, Nepal, Nigeria, Pakistan, Panama, Peru, Philippines, Qatar, Republic of Korea, Saudi Arabia, Senegal, Slovakia, Slovenia, South Africa, Spain, Switzerland, Tunisia, Ukraine, United Arab [p. 7] Emirates, United Kingdom of Great Britain and Northern Ireland, Venezuela (Bolivarian Republic of)

Against:

Australia, Togo, United States of America

Abstaining:

Democratic Republic of the Congo, Rwanda]

H.R.C. Res. 37/34, Right of the Palestinian People to Self-Determination (Mar. 23, 2018)

United Nations
General Assembly
A/HRC/RES/37/34
Distr.: General
13 April 2018
Original: English
Human Rights Council
Thirty-seventh session
26 February–23 March 2018
Agenda item 7

Resolution adopted by the Human Rights Council on 23 March 2018

37/34. Right of the Palestinian people to self-determination

The Human Rights Council,

Guided by the purposes and principles of the Charter of the United Nations, in particular the provisions of Articles 1 and 55 thereof, which affirm the right of peoples to self-determination, reaffirming the need for the scrupulous respect of the principle of refraining in international relations from the threat or use of force, as specified in the Declaration on Principles of International Law concerning Friendly Relations and Cooperation among States in accordance with the Charter of the United Nations, adopted by the General Assembly in its resolution 2625 (XXV) of 24 October 1970, and affirming the inadmissibility of acquisition of territory resulting from the threat or use of force,

Guided also by the provisions of article 1 of the International Covenant on Economic, Social and Cultural Rights and article 1 of the International Covenant on Civil and Political Rights, which affirm that all peoples have the right to self-determination,

Guided further by the International Covenants on Human Rights, the Universal Declaration of Human Rights and the Declaration on the Granting of Independence to Colonial Countries and Peoples, in particular article 1 thereof, and by the provisions of the Vienna Declaration and Programme of Action, adopted on 25 June 1993 by the World Conference on Human Rights, and in particular Part I, paragraphs 2 and 3, relating to the right of self-determination of all peoples and especially those subject to foreign occupation,

Recalling General Assembly resolutions 181 A and B (II) of 29 November 1947 and 194 (III) of 11 December 1948, and all other relevant United Nations resolutions, including those adopted by the Assembly, the Commission on Human Rights and the Human Rights Council, that confirm and define the inalienable rights of the Palestinian people, particularly their right to self-determination,

Recalling also Security Council resolutions 242 (1967) of 22 November 1967, 338 (1973) of 22 October 1973, 1397 (2002) of 12 March 2002 and 1402 (2002) of 30 March 2002,

Recalling further General Assembly resolution 67/19 of 29 November 2012,

Reaffirming the right of the Palestinian people to self-determination in accordance with the provisions of the Charter, relevant United Nations resolutions and declarations, [p. 2] and the provisions of international covenants and instruments relating to the right to self-determination as an international principle and as a right of all peoples in the world, and emphasizing that this *jus cogens* norm of international law is a basic prerequisite for achieving a just, lasting and comprehensive peace in the Middle East,

Deploring the plight of millions of Palestine refugees and displaced persons who have been uprooted from their homes, and expressing deep regret about the fact that more than half of the Palestinian people continue to live in exile in refugee camps throughout the region and in the diaspora,

Affirming the applicability of the principle of permanent sovereignty over natural resources to the Palestinian situation as an integral component of the right to self-determination,

Recalling the conclusion of the International Court of Justice, in its advisory opinion of 9 July 2004, that the right to self-determination of the Palestinian people, which is a right *erga omnes*, is severely impeded by Israel, the occupying Power, through the construction of the wall in the Occupied Palestinian Territory, including East Jerusalem, which, together with the Israeli settlement enterprise and measures previously taken, results in serious violations of international humanitarian and human rights law, including the forcible transfer of Palestinians and Israeli acquisition of Palestinian land,

Considering that the right to self-determination of the Palestinian people is being violated further by Israel through the existence and ongoing expansion of settlements in the Occupied Palestinian Territory, including East Jerusalem,

Noting that the failure to bring the occupation to an end after 50 years heightens the international responsibility to uphold the human rights of the Palestinian people, and expressing its deep regret that the question of Palestine remains unresolved 70 years since the resolution on partition,

Reaffirming that the United Nations will continue to be engaged on the question of Palestine until the question is resolved in all its aspects in accordance with international law,

1. *Reaffirms* the inalienable, permanent and unqualified right of the Palestinian people to self-determination, including their right to live in freedom, justice and dignity and the right to their independent State of Palestine;

2. *Calls upon* Israel, the occupying Power, to immediately end its occupation of the Occupied Palestinian Territory, including East Jerusalem, and further reaffirms its support for the solution of two States, Palestine and Israel, living side by side in peace and security;

3. *Expresses grave concern* at any action taken by any body, governmental or non-governmental, in violation of the General Assembly and Security Council resolutions relevant to Jerusalem;

4. *Expresses grave concern* at the fragmentation and the changes in the demographic composition of the Occupied Palestinian Territory, including East Jerusalem, which are resulting from Israel's continuing construction and expansion of settlements, forcible transfer of Palestinians and construction of the wall, stresses that this fragmentation, which undermines the possibility of the Palestinian people realizing their right to self-determination, is incompatible with the purposes and principles of the Charter of the United Nations, and emphasizes in this regard the need for respect for and preservation of the territorial unity, contiguity and integrity of all of the Occupied Palestinian Territory, including East Jerusalem;

5. *Confirms* that the right of the Palestinian people to permanent sovereignty over their natural wealth and resources must be used in the interest of their national development, the well-being of the Palestinian people and as part of the realization of their right to self-determination;

6. *Calls upon* all States to ensure their obligations of non-recognition, non-aid or assistance with regard to the serious breaches of peremptory norms of international law [p. 3] by Israel, in particular of the prohibition of the acquisition of territory by force, in order to ensure the exercise of the right to self-determination, and also calls upon them to cooperate further to bring, through lawful means, an end to these serious breaches and a reversal of Israel's illegal policies and practices;

7. *Urges* all States to adopt measures as required to promote the realization of the right to self-determination of the Palestinian people, and to render assistance to the United Nations in carrying out the responsibilities entrusted to it by the Charter regarding the implementation of this right;

8. *Decides* to remain seized of the matter.

56th meeting
23 March 2018

[Adopted by a recorded vote of 43 to 2, with 1 abstention. The voting was as follows:

In favour:

Afghanistan, Angola, Belgium, Brazil, Burundi, Chile, China, Côte d'Ivoire, Croatia, Cuba, Ecuador, Egypt, Ethiopia, Georgia, Germany, Hungary, Iraq, Japan, Kenya, Kyrgyzstan, Mexico, Nepal, Nigeria, Pakistan, Panama, Peru, Philippines, Qatar, Republic of Korea, Rwanda, Saudi Arabia, Senegal, Slovakia, Slovenia, South Africa, Spain, Switzerland, Togo, Tunisia, Ukraine, United Arab Emirates, United Kingdom of Great Britain and Northern Ireland, Venezuela (Bolivarian Republic of)

Against:

Australia, United States of America

Abstaining:

Democratic Republic of the Congo]

SECTION B

United Nations Reports

Right of Peoples to Self-Determination, Report of the Secretary-General, U.N. Doc. A/73/329 (2018)

United Nations
General Assembly
A/73/329
Distr.: General
20 August 2018
Original: English
Seventy-third session
Item 73 of the provisional agenda
Right of peoples to self-determination

Right of peoples to self-determination

* A/73/100

Report of the Secretary-General

Summary

In its resolution 72/159, the General Assembly requested the Secretary-General to submit a report to the Assembly at its seventy-third session on the universal realization of the right of peoples to self-determination. The present report is submitted in accordance with that request.

The report provides a summary of the main developments relating to the realization of the right to self-determination within the framework of the activities of the main organs of the United Nations since the submission of the previous report on the question (A/72/317).

[p. 2] I   Introduction

1. The General Assembly, in paragraph 1 of its resolution 72/159, reaffirmed that the universal realization of the right of all peoples to self-determination was a fundamental condition for the effective guarantee and observance of human rights and for the preservation and promotion of such rights.

2. The present report is submitted in accordance with paragraph six of resolution 72/159, in which the General Assembly requested the Secretary-General to report on the question at its seventy-third session.

3. The report provides a summary of the main developments relating to the realization of the right of all peoples to self-determination within the framework of the activities of the main organs of the United Nations since the submission of the previous report (A/72/317).

4. The report also includes reference to the consideration of the issue within the framework of the Human Rights Council, both in its resolutions and in the reports submitted to the Council by special procedures mandate holders and the Expert Mechanism on the Rights of Indigenous Peoples.

5. In addition, it includes reference to concluding observations issued by the Human Rights Committee and the Committee on Economic, Social and Cultural Rights, which are based on their consideration of periodic reports submitted by the States parties to the International Covenant on Civil and Political Rights and the International Covenant on Economic, Social and Cultural Rights in respect of the implementation of the right of all peoples to self-determination guaranteed in common article 1 of the two Covenants.

II   Security Council

6. During the reporting period, in accordance with Security Council resolution 2351 (2017), the Secretary-General submitted to the Council a report on the situation concerning Western Sahara (S/2018/277). The report covered developments since the previous report (S/2017/307) and provided a description of the situation on the ground, the status and progress of the political negotiations on Western Sahara, the implementation of Council resolution 2351 (2017) and the challenges to the operations of the United Nations Mission for the Referendum in Western Sahara and steps taken to address them. In his current report, the Secretary-General noted that, in his report of 2017, he had proposed that negotiating efforts be relaunched with a new dynamic and a new spirit, reflecting the Council's guidance, with the aim of reaching a "just, durable and mutually

acceptable solution to the conflict in Western Sahara that will provide for the self-determination of the people of Western Sahara" (see S/2018/277, para. 77).

7. Having considered the report of the Secretary-General, the Security Council adopted resolution 2414 (2018). In paragraph 3 of the resolution, the Council called upon the parties to resume negotiations under the auspices of the Secretary-General without preconditions and in good faith, taking into account the efforts made since 2006 and subsequent developments, with a view to achieving a just, lasting and mutually acceptable political solution, which would provide for the self-determination of the people of Western Sahara in the context of arrangements consistent with the principles and purposes of the Charter of the United Nations, and noted the role and responsibilities of the parties in that respect. [p. 3]

III General Assembly

8. During the reporting period, in addition to its resolution on the universal realization of the right of peoples to self-determination (resolution 72/159), the General Assembly adopted a number of resolutions in which it addressed the issue of self-determination. The resolutions concerned Non-Self-Governing Territories, the use of mercenaries as a means of violating human rights and impeding the exercise of the right of peoples to self-determination, and the right of the Palestinian people to self-determination. In addition, in paragraph 7 (a) of its resolution 72/172, the Assembly affirmed that a democratic and equitable international order required, inter alia, the realization of the right of all peoples to self-determination, by virtue of which they could freely determine their political status and freely pursue their economic, social and cultural development.

A *Non-Self-Governing Territories*

9. In its resolution 72/92, the General Assembly reaffirmed the right of the peoples of Non-Self-Governing Territories to self-determination and their right to the enjoyment of their natural resources and to dispose of those resources in their best interest. It affirmed the value of foreign economic investment undertaken in collaboration with the peoples of the Non-Self-Governing Territories and in accordance with their wishes in order to make a valid contribution to the socioeconomic development of the Territories, especially during times of economic and financial crisis. It reaffirmed the responsibility of the administering Powers under the Charter to promote the political,

economic, social and educational advancement of the Non-Self-Governing Territories and reaffirmed the legitimate rights of their peoples over their natural resources. The Assembly reaffirmed its concern about any activities aimed at the exploitation of the natural resources that were the heritage of the peoples of the Non-Self-Governing Territories, including the indigenous populations, in the Caribbean, the Pacific and other regions, and of their human resources, to the detriment of their interests, and in such a way as to deprive them of their right to dispose of those resources. It reaffirmed the need to avoid any economic and other activities that adversely affected the interests of the peoples of the Non-Self-Governing Territories, and reminded the administering Powers of their responsibility and accountability vis-à-vis any detriment to the interests of the peoples of those Territories. The Assembly invited all Governments and organizations of the United Nations system to take all possible measures to ensure that the permanent sovereignty of the peoples of the Non-Self-Governing Territories over their natural resources was fully respected and safeguarded. It urged the administering Powers concerned to take effective measures to safeguard and guarantee the inalienable right of the peoples of the Non-Self-Governing Territories to their natural resources and to establish and maintain control over the future development of those resources, and requested the administering Powers to take all steps necessary to protect the property rights of the peoples of those Territories.

10. In its resolution 72/111, the General Assembly called upon the administering Powers, in accordance with resolutions on decolonization, to take all steps necessary to enable the peoples of the Non-Self-Governing Territories to exercise fully, as soon as possible, their right to self-determination, including independence, on a case-by-case basis. In its resolution 72/94, the Assembly invited all States to make, or continue to make, offers of study and training facilities to the inhabitants of those Territories that had not yet attained self-government or independence and, wherever possible, to provide travel funds to prospective students. [p. 4]

11. In its resolution 72/95 on the question of Western Sahara, the General Assembly expressed support for the process of negotiations initiated by the Security Council to achieve a just, lasting and mutually acceptable political solution, which would provide for the self-determination of the people of Western Sahara, and commended the efforts undertaken by the Secretary-General and his Personal Envoy for Western Sahara in that respect. It welcomed the commitment of the parties to continue to show political will and work in an atmosphere propitious for dialogue in order to enter into a more intensive phase of negotiations, in good faith and without preconditions.

12. In its resolution 72/96 on the question of American Samoa, the General Assembly reaffirmed the inalienable right of the people of American Samoa to self-determination, and also reaffirmed that it was ultimately for the people of American Samoa to determine freely their future political status. In that connection, the Assembly called upon the administering Power, in cooperation with the territorial Government and appropriate bodies of the United Nations system, to develop political education programmes for the Territory in order to foster an awareness among the people of their right to self-determination. It took note of the work of the territorial Government with respect to moving forward on political status, local autonomy and self-governance issues with a view to making political and economic progress.

13. In its resolution 72/97 on the question of Anguilla, the General Assembly reaffirmed the inalienable right of the people of Anguilla to self-determination, and also reaffirmed that it was ultimately for the people of Anguilla to determine freely their future political status. In that connection, the Assembly called upon the administering Power, in cooperation with the territorial Government and appropriate bodies of the United Nations system, to develop political education programmes for the Territory in order to foster an awareness among the people of their right to self-determination.

14. In its resolution 72/98 on the question of Bermuda, the General Assembly reaffirmed the inalienable right of the people of Bermuda to self-determination, and also reaffirmed that it was ultimately for the people of Bermuda to determine freely their future political status. In that connection, the Assembly called upon the administering Power, in cooperation with the territorial Government and appropriate bodies of the United Nations system, to develop political education programmes for the Territory in order to foster an awareness among the people of their right to self-determination.

15. In its resolution 72/99 on the question of the British Virgin Islands, the General Assembly reaffirmed the inalienable right of the people of the British Virgin Islands to self-determination, and also reaffirmed that it was ultimately for the people of the British Virgin Islands to determine freely their future political status. In that connection, the Assembly called upon the administering Power, in cooperation with the territorial Government and appropriate bodies of the United Nations system, to develop political education programmes for the Territory in order to foster an awareness among the people of their right to self-determination.

16. In its resolution 72/100 on the question of the Cayman Islands, the General Assembly reaffirmed the inalienable right of the people of the Cayman Islands to self-determination, and also reaffirmed that it was ultimately for the people

of the Cayman Islands to determine freely their future political status. In that connection, the Assembly called upon the administering Power, in cooperation with the territorial Government and appropriate bodies of the United Nations system, to develop political education programmes for the Territory in order to foster an awareness among the people of their right to self-determination.

17. In its resolution 72/101 on the question of French Polynesia, the General Assembly reaffirmed the inalienable right of the people of French Polynesia to self-[p. 5]determination, and also reaffirmed that it was ultimately for the people of French Polynesia to determine freely their future political status. In that connection, the Assembly called upon the administering Power, in cooperation with the territorial Government and appropriate bodies of the United Nations system, to develop political education programmes for the Territory in order to foster an awareness among the people of French Polynesia of their right to self-determination in conformity with the legitimate political status options and to intensify its dialogue with French Polynesia in order to facilitate rapid progress towards a fair and effective self-determination process, under which the terms and timelines for an act of self-determination would be agreed.

18. In its resolution 72/102 on the question of Guam, the General Assembly reaffirmed the inalienable right of the people of Guam to self-determination, and also reaffirmed that it was ultimately for the people of Guam to determine freely their future political status. In that connection, the Assembly called upon the administering Power, in cooperation with the territorial Government and appropriate bodies of the United Nations system, to develop political education programmes for the Territory in order to foster an awareness among the people of their right to self-determination. It called once again on the administering Power to take into consideration the expressed will of the Chamorro people as supported by Guam voters in the referendum of 1987 and as subsequently provided for in Guam law regarding Chamorro self-determination efforts, encouraged the administering Power and the territorial Government to enter into negotiations on the matter and stressed the need for continued close monitoring of the overall situation in the Territory.

19. In its resolution 72/103 on the question of Montserrat, the General Assembly reaffirmed the inalienable right of the people of Montserrat to self-determination, and also reaffirmed that it was ultimately for the people of Montserrat to determine freely their future political status. In that connection, the Assembly called upon the administering Power, in cooperation with the territorial Government and appropriate bodies of the United Nations system, to develop political education programmes for the Territory in order to foster an awareness among the people of their right to self-determination.

20. In its resolution 72/104 on the question of New Caledonia, the General Assembly reaffirmed that it was ultimately for the people of New Caledonia

to determine freely and fairly their future political status, and in that connection called upon the administering Power, in cooperation with the territorial Government and appropriate bodies of the United Nations system, to develop political education programmes for the Territory in order to foster an awareness among the people of their right to self-determination in conformity with the legitimate political status options. The Assembly expressed the view that adequate measures for conducting the upcoming consultations on access to full sovereignty, including a just, fair, credible and transparent electoral roll, as provided for in the Nouméa Accord, were essential for the conduct of a free, fair and genuine act of self-determination consistent with the Charter and United Nations principles and practices. In that respect, it welcomed the continuous dialogue undertaken by the parties within the framework of the Committee of Signatories to the Nouméa Accord to establish the parameters for the conduct of a conclusive act of self-determination, including the setting of an electoral roll, as provided for in the Accord. It called upon the administering Power to consider developing an education programme to inform the people of New Caledonia about the nature of self-determination so that they might be better prepared to face a future decision on the matter. The Assembly urged all the parties involved, in the interest of the people of New Caledonia and within the framework of the Nouméa Accord, to maintain their dialogue in a spirit of harmony and mutual respect in order to continue to promote a framework for the peaceful progress of the Territory towards an act of [p. 6] self-determination in which all options were open and the rights of all sectors of the population would be safeguarded, based on the principle that it was for the people of New Caledonia to choose how to determine their destiny.

21. In its resolution 72/105 on the question of Pitcairn, the General Assembly reaffirmed the inalienable right of the people of Pitcairn to self-determination, and also reaffirmed that it was ultimately for the people of Pitcairn to determine freely their future political status. In that connection, the Assembly called upon the administering Power, in cooperation with the territorial Government and appropriate bodies of the United Nations system, to develop political education programmes for the Territory in order to foster an awareness among the people of their right to self-determination. It welcomed all efforts by the administering Power and the territorial Government to further devolve operational responsibilities to the Territory, with a view to gradually expanding self-government, including through the training of local personnel.

22. In its resolution 72/106 on the question of Saint Helena, the General Assembly reaffirmed the inalienable right of the people of Saint Helena to self-determination, and also reaffirmed that it was ultimately for the people of Saint Helena to determine freely their future political status. In that connection, the Assembly called upon the administering Power, in cooperation

with the territorial Government and appropriate bodies of the United Nations system, to develop political education programmes for the Territory in order to foster an awareness among the people of their right to self-determination.

23. In its resolution 72/107 on the question of Tokelau, the General Assembly acknowledged the decision of the General Fono in 2008 that consideration of any future act of self-determination by Tokelau would be deferred. It welcomed the cooperative attitude of the other States and territories in the region towards Tokelau and their support for its economic and political aspirations and its increasing participation in regional and international affairs.

24. In its resolution 72/108 on the question of the Turks and Caicos Islands, the General Assembly reaffirmed the inalienable right of the people of the Turks and Caicos Islands to self-determination, and also reaffirmed that it was ultimately for the people of the Turks and Caicos Islands to determine freely their future political status. In that connection, the Assembly called upon the administering Power, in cooperation with the territorial Government and appropriate bodies of the United Nations system, to develop political education programmes for the Territory in order to foster an awareness among the people of their right to self-determination.

25. In its resolution 72/109 on the question of the United States Virgin Islands, the General Assembly reaffirmed the inalienable right of the people of the United States Virgin Islands to self-determination, and also reaffirmed that it was ultimately for the people of the United States Virgin Islands to determine freely their future political status. In that connection, the Assembly called upon the administering Power, in cooperation with the territorial Government and appropriate bodies of the United Nations system, to develop political education programmes for the Territory in order to foster an awareness among the people of their right to self-determination.

B   *Use of Mercenaries as a Means of Violating Human Rights and Impeding the Exercise of the Right of Peoples to Self-Determination*

26. In its resolution 72/158, the General Assembly urged all States to take the steps necessary and to exercise the utmost vigilance against the menace posed by the activities of mercenaries, and to take legislative measures to ensure that their [p. 7] territories and other territories under their control were not used for, and that their nationals did not take part in, the recruitment, assembly, financing, training, protection or transit of mercenaries for the planning of activities designed to impede the right of peoples to self-determination, to destabilize or overthrow the Government of any State or to dismember or impair,

totally or in part, the territorial integrity or political unity of sovereign and independent States conducting themselves in accordance with the right of peoples to self-determination. It requested the Working Group of the Human Rights Council on the use of mercenaries as a means of violating human rights and impeding the exercise of the right of peoples to self-determination to continue to study and identify sources and causes, emerging issues, manifestations and trends regarding mercenaries or mercenary-related activities and private military and security companies and their impact on human rights, particularly on the right of peoples to self-determination. It also requested the Office of the United Nations High Commissioner for Human Rights to publicize the adverse effects of the activities of mercenaries on the right of peoples to self-determination and to render advisory services to States that were affected by those activities.

C *Right of the Palestinian People to Self-Determination*

27. The right of the Palestinian people to self-determination, including the right to their independent State of Palestine, was reaffirmed by the General Assembly in its resolution 72/160. In the resolution, the Assembly also urged States and the specialized agencies and organizations of the United Nations system to continue to support and assist the Palestinian people in the early realization of their right to self-determination. The Assembly also called for the realization of the Palestinian people's human rights, including the right to self-determination, in its resolutions 72/14, 72/84 and 72/87.

28. In its resolution 72/13, the General Assembly, having considered the report of the Committee on the Exercise of the Inalienable Rights of the Palestinian People (A/72/35), requested the Committee, inter alia, to continue to exert all efforts to promote the realization of the inalienable rights of the Palestinian people, including their right to self-determination. The Assembly invited all Governments and organizations to extend their cooperation and support to the Committee in the performance of its tasks, recalling its repeated call for all States and the specialized agencies and organizations of the United Nations system to continue to support and assist the Palestinian people in the early realization of their right to self-determination, including the right to their independent State of Palestine.

29. The economic aspect of the right to self-determination, namely, the right of peoples to sovereignty over their natural resources, was reaffirmed by the General Assembly with regard to the Palestinian people in its resolution 72/240.

IV   Economic and Social Council

30. In its resolution 2017/31, the Economic and Social Council either recommended or requested a number of measures that specialized agencies and other organizations of the United Nations system should adopt in support of Non-Self-Governing Territories. The Council reaffirmed that the recognition by the General Assembly, the Security Council and other United Nations organs of the legitimacy of the aspirations of the peoples of the Non-Self-Governing Territories to exercise their right to self-determination entailed, as a corollary, the extension of all appropriate assistance to those peoples, on a case-by-case basis. [p. 8]

V   Human Rights Council

A   *Resolutions*

31. At its thirty-fifth session, held from 6 to 23 June 2017, the Human Rights Council adopted resolution 35/20 on human rights and climate change. In the resolution, the Council emphasized that the adverse effects of climate change had a range of implications, both direct and indirect, for the effective enjoyment of human rights, including for the right to self-determination.

32. At its thirty-sixth session, held from 11 to 29 September 2017, the Human Rights Council adopted resolution 36/3 on the use of mercenaries as a means of violating human rights and impeding the exercise of the right of peoples to self-determination. In the resolution, the Council condemned mercenary activities in developing countries in various parts of the world, in particular in areas of conflict, and the threat those activities posed to the integrity of and respect for the constitutional order of countries and the exercise of the right to self-determination. It urged all States to take the necessary steps and to exercise the utmost vigilance against the threat posed by the activities of mercenaries, and to take legislative measures to ensure that their territories and other territories under their control, as well as their nationals, were not used for the recruitment, assembly, financing, training, protection and transit of mercenaries for the planning of activities designed to impede the right to self-determination, to overthrow the Government of any State or to dismember or impair, totally or in part, the territorial integrity or political unity of sovereign and independent States conducting themselves in compliance with the right of peoples to self-determination.

33. At its thirty-seventh session, held from 26 February to 23 March 2018, the Human Rights Council addressed the question of the realization of the right of

the Palestinian people to self-determination in its resolutions 37/34, 37/35 and 37/36. In its resolution 37/34, the Council reaffirmed the inalienable, permanent and unqualified right of the Palestinian people to self-determination, including their right to live in freedom, justice and dignity and the right to their independent State of Palestine. It confirmed that the right of the Palestinian people to permanent sovereignty over their natural wealth and resources must be used in the interest of their national development, the well-being of the Palestinian people and as part of the realization of their right to self-determination, and urged all States to adopt measures, as required, to promote the realization of the right to self-determination of the Palestinian people and to render assistance to the United Nations in carrying out the responsibilities entrusted to it by the Charter regarding the implementation of that right. In its resolution 37/35, the Council stressed the need for the occupying Power to withdraw from the Palestinian territory occupied since 1967, including East Jerusalem, so as to enable the Palestinian people to exercise their universally recognized right to self-determination. In its resolution 37/36, the Council called upon the occupying Power to put an end to all of the human rights violations linked to the presence of settlements, especially of the right to self-determination, and to fulfil its international obligations to provide effective remedy for victims.

B   *Special Procedures and the Expert Mechanism on the Rights of Indigenous Peoples*

34. In her report to the General Assembly at its seventy-second session (A/72/186), the Special Rapporteur of the Human Rights Council on the rights of indigenous peoples provided an assessment on the status of implementation of the United Nations Declaration on the Rights of Indigenous Peoples. The Special Rapporteur concluded [p. 9] that there had been limited progress in the actual implementation of the rights of indigenous peoples. That was observed in particular with regard to the core rights of indigenous peoples to self-determination and their rights to their lands, territories and resources (ibid., para. 86). In her report to the Council at its thirty-sixth session (A/HRC/36/46), the Special Rapporteur provided an analysis of the impacts of climate change and climate finance on indigenous peoples' rights. She noted that the denial of indigenous peoples' right to self-determination and to their economic, social and cultural rights was strongly linked to indigenous peoples' historical experiences of marginalization, dispossession, the environmental destruction of their ancestral lands and their lack of autonomy, and warned that unless climate finance recognized that inequality, it could contribute to

the causes of poverty and further denial of the right to self-determination among indigenous communities (ibid., para. 41).

35. In his report to the Human Rights Council at its thirty-seventh session, the Independent Expert on the promotion of a democratic and equitable international order noted that a democratic and equitable international order was one in which peoples and nations enjoyed equitable representation, not only in the General Assembly, but also in regional and international financial institutions, in which, inter alia, they exercised their right to self-determination (see A/HRC/37/63, para. 12). He recalled that the right of peoples to self-determination was a fundamental principle of the international order affirmed in the Charter and in the International Covenant on Civil and Political Rights and the International Covenant on Economic, Social and Cultural Rights and that timely dialogue for the realization of self-determination was an effective conflict-prevention measure (ibid., para. 14 (d)). He noted that the implementation of the right to self-determination was not exclusively within the domestic jurisdiction of the State concerned but was a legitimate concern of the international community (ibid., para. 33) and that any process aimed at self-determination should be accompanied by the participation and consent of the peoples concerned (ibid., para. 35).

36. In its report to the General Assembly at its seventy-second session, the Working Group on the use of mercenaries as a means of violating human rights and impeding the exercise of the right of peoples to self-determination noted that in certain crises around the world, such as in occupied territories, the use of private security contractors to limit and prohibit people's right to liberty and free movement through deprivation of liberty was a means of deliberately undermining a people's right to self-determination (see A/72/286, para. 36). In its report to the Human Rights Council at its thirty-sixth session (A/HRC/36/47), the Working Group provided an overview of the findings of a global study conducted from 2013 to 2016 on the national legislation on private military and security companies in 60 States from all the regions of the world. The report concluded that it was necessary to fill existing gaps and promote international, regional and subregional agreements for the regulation of private military and security companies to effectively protect the rule of law, human rights and, especially in conjunction with the use of private military and security companies in extractive industries, the exercise of the right of peoples to self-determination (ibid., para. 64).

37. In his report to the seventy-second session of the General Assembly, the Special Rapporteur on the situation of human rights in the Palestinian territories occupied since 1967 stated that international human rights law, including the overarching right to self-determination, was integral to the application of

the laws of occupation (see A/72/556, para. 23) and that the right of peoples to self-determination, recognized as a right *erga omnes* in international law, applied to all peoples under occupation and other forms of alien rule (ibid., para. 24). He added that the entrenched and unaccountable occupation – through its denial of territorial integrity, genuine self-governance, a sustainable economy and a viable path to independence – [p. 10] substantively violated, and undermined, the right of the Palestinians to self-determination, the platform right that enabled the realization of many other rights (ibid., para. 62).

38. In his report to the Human Rights Council at its thirty-sixth session, the Special Rapporteur on the right to development recalled that Articles 1, 55 and 56 of the Charter established the foundations of the right to development by stating that the creation of conditions of stability and well-being were necessary for peaceful and friendly relations among nations based on respect for the principle of equal rights and self-determination of peoples (see A/HRC/36/49, para. 8). He also recalled that the Declaration on the Right to Development stated that the human right to development implied the full realization of the right of peoples to self-determination, which includes, subject to the relevant provisions of the International Covenant on Civil and Political Rights and the International Covenant on Economic, Social and Cultural Rights, the exercise of their inalienable right to full sovereignty over all their natural wealth and resources (ibid., para. 9).

39. The Expert Mechanism on the Rights of Indigenous Peoples presented to the Human Rights Council at its thirty-sixth session a report (A/HRC/36/56) intended to highlight the main legal and policy trends in the past 10 years in the application of the United Nations Declaration on the Rights of Indigenous Peoples across the United Nations and regional and national human rights systems, and to contribute to its further implementation. The report noted that, despite many good practices, indigenous peoples in some regions, including in a number of States in Asia and Africa, still struggled for legal recognition and respect for self-determination, and recommended that States refrain from hindering or limiting self-determination initiatives and recognize and learn from indigenous peoples' own initiatives to advance the implementation of the Declaration at the national level (ibid., para. 74).

VI Human Rights Treaty Bodies

40. The right of all peoples to self-determination is affirmed in article 1, paragraph 1, of both the International Covenant on Civil and Political Rights and the International Covenant on Economic, Social and Cultural Rights. It is in

that context that the right to self-determination has been addressed by the Committee on Economic, Social and Cultural Rights and the Human Rights Committee[1] in their consideration of the periodic reports of States parties. The relevant concluding observations adopted during the reporting period are highlighted below.

A *Concluding Observations by the Committee on Economic, Social and Cultural Rights*

41. In its concluding observations on the fifth periodic report of Australia (E/C.12/AUS/CO/5), adopted at its sixty-first session, held from 29 May to 23 June 2017, the Committee on Economic, Social and Cultural Rights expressed concern about insufficient compliance with the principle of free, prior and informed consent of indigenous peoples, including in the context of developing the white paper on the development of northern Australia and of the approval of extractive projects on lands owned or traditionally used by indigenous peoples (ibid., para. 15 (d)). The Committee recommended that Australia ensure that the principle of free, prior and informed consent was incorporated into the Native Title Act 1993 and into other legislation as appropriate and was fully implemented in practice (ibid., para. 16 (e)). [p. 11]

42. In its concluding observations on the sixth periodic report of Colombia (E/C.12/COL/CO/6), adopted at its sixty-second session, held from 18 September to 6 October 2017, the Committee noted the efforts made to ensure the enjoyment of economic, social and cultural rights by indigenous peoples and Afro-Colombians, but expressed remaining concern regarding reports of inadequate implementation of the process of prior consultation with a view to obtaining free, prior and informed consent, particularly in relation to natural resource development and exploitation projects likely to affect their territories (ibid., para. 17). The Committee recommended that Colombia carry out a broad process of consultation and participation in the drafting and adoption of the draft statutory act on prior consultation; ensure that the legislation complied with international standards, including the Indigenous and Tribal Peoples Convention, 1989 (No. 169) of the International Labour Organization and the United Nations Declaration on the Rights of Indigenous Peoples; and ensure that consultations held with a view to obtaining indigenous and Afro-Colombian peoples' free, prior and informed consent to decisions that might affect the exercise of their economic, social and cultural rights were conducted as an unavoidable and timely step, taking into account the cultural

---

1 See also Human Rights Committee, general comment No. 12 (see HRI/GEN/1/Rev.9 (Vol. I)).

differences of each people and carrying out studies of the impact that such measures might have on the exercise of their rights (ibid., para. 18 (a)–(b)).

43. In its concluding observations on the combined fifth and sixth periodic reports of Mexico (E/C.12/MEX/CO/5-6), adopted at its sixty-second session, the Committee expressed concern at the fact that protocols on prior consultation were not followed systematically, partly because they were non-binding, and that therefore the right of indigenous peoples to prior consultation with a view to obtaining their free, prior and informed consent was not fully respected, particularly when it came to the execution of economic projects and the development of natural resources. In addition, the Committee was concerned by the negative impact of such projects on the effective enjoyment of economic, social and cultural rights by the indigenous peoples concerned (ibid., para. 12). The Committee recommended that Mexico ensure that indigenous peoples were consulted in advance in a systematic and transparent manner with a view to obtaining their free, prior and informed consent with respect to decisions likely to affect them, especially before it granted permits for economic activities in territories that they had traditionally owned, occupied or used. In that regard, the Committee encouraged Mexico to establish, in consultation with indigenous peoples, effective, appropriate and legally binding protocols that fully guaranteed respect for that right or, where appropriate, to apply existing protocols, taking into account the cultural characteristics and customs and practices of each indigenous community and in accordance with applicable international standards (ibid., para. 13 (a)).

44. In its concluding observations on the sixth periodic report of the Russian Federation (E/C.12/RUS/CO/6), adopted at its sixty-second session, the Committee expressed concern at the limited prior consultation with indigenous peoples, especially in the context of extractive activities carried out on lands owned or traditionally used by them. The Committee was concerned that the requirement of free, prior and informed consent of indigenous peoples was rarely complied with in practice (ibid., para. 14). It recommended that the Russian Federation, inter alia, take effective measures to ensure compliance with the requirement of free, prior and informed consent of indigenous peoples, notably in the context of extractive activities, improve the legislative and institutional provisions relating to projects for the exploitation of natural resources, in consultation with indigenous peoples, and strengthen its capacity to oversee extractive industries to ensure that they did not have a negative impact on the rights of indigenous peoples and their territories and natural resources (ibid., para. 15 (b)–(c)). [p. 12]

45. In its concluding observations on the initial report of Bangladesh (E/C.12/BGD/CO/1), adopted at its sixty-third session, held from 12 to 29 March 2018,

the Committee expressed concern about the absence of explicit constitutional and legislative recognition of the rights of those who self-identified as indigenous peoples in the State, at repeated reports of expropriation of ancestral land of indigenous peoples where the requirements of free, prior and informed consent were not met and at the lack of appropriate mechanisms to enable affected indigenous persons and communities to take part in decision-making processes (ibid., para. 15). It recommended that Bangladesh, inter alia, ensure that the requirements of free, prior and informed consent were met in all cases of expropriation of land of indigenous peoples and provide effective mechanisms through which indigenous peoples could seek remedies for the deprivation of ancestral lands (ibid., para. 16 (c)–(d)).

46. In its concluding observations on the fourth periodic report of New Zealand (E/C.12/NZL/CO/4), adopted at its sixty-third session, the Committee expressed concern at the limited efforts that had been made to ensure the meaningful participation of the Maori people in decision-making concerning laws that affected their rights, including land and water rights. It was also concerned that the principle of free, prior and informed consent was not systematically implemented, in particular in the context of development and extractive activities carried out on territories owned or traditionally used by the Maori population (ibid., para. 8). The Committee recommended that New Zealand, inter alia, take effective measures to ensure compliance with the requirement of obtaining the free, prior and informed consent of indigenous peoples, notably in the context of extractive and development activities, and conduct social, environmental and human rights impact assessments prior to granting licences for extractive and development activities and during operations (ibid., para. 9 (e)).

B   *Concluding Observations by the Human Rights Committee*

47. At its 122nd session, held from 12 March to 6 April 2018, the Human Rights Committee adopted concluding observations on the seventh periodic report of Norway (CCPR/C/NOR/CO/7). The Committee expressed concern that, inter alia, the right to effective participation through consultations to obtain free, prior and informed consent was not yet granted in law or ensured in practice; a strong legislative framework ensuring land and resource rights to the Sami peoples, including fishing and reindeer husbandry, was lacking; and the Government had not yet followed up on the proposals of the Sami Rights Committee from 2007 on land and resource rights outside of Finnmark (ibid., para. 36). The Committee recommended that Norway, inter alia, ensure meaningful consultation with the Sami peoples in practice and adopt a law for consultations with a view to obtaining their free, prior and informed consent,

in consultation with them; enhance the legal framework on Sami land, fishing and reindeer rights, ensuring in particular that fishing rights were recognized by law; and ensure effective and speedy follow-up to the proposals of the Sami Rights Committee of 2007 regarding land and resource rights in Sami areas outside of Finnmark (ibid., para. 37 (b) and (d)–(e)).

VII   Conclusions

48. It is among the purposes of the United Nations, elaborated in Article 1 of the Charter, "to develop friendly relations among nations based on respect for the principle of equal rights and self-determination of peoples, and to take other appropriate measures to strengthen universal peace". The right of peoples to self-determination is also enshrined in article 1 of both the International [p. 13] Covenant on Civil and Political Rights and the International Covenant on Economic, Social and Cultural Rights, which states that all peoples have the right to self-determination and that by virtue of that right they freely determine their political status and freely pursue their economic, social and cultural development.

49. During the reporting period, the main organs of the United Nations, including the Security Council, the General Assembly and the Economic and Social Council, continued to discuss and adopt resolutions that referred to the right to self-determination, including resolutions concerning Non-Self-Governing Territories, the use of mercenaries and the right of the Palestinian people to self-determination. The Human Rights Council, a subsidiary organ of the Assembly, also continued to discuss and adopt resolutions that referred to that right.

50. The special procedures of the Human Rights Council and the Expert Mechanism on the Rights of Indigenous Peoples also discussed the implementation of the right of peoples to self-determination, including in relation to the human rights challenges faced by indigenous peoples, and its importance as a fundamental principle of international order.

51. The human rights treaty bodies addressed the right of peoples to self-determination through concluding observations on the periodic reports submitted by States parties to relevant treaties.

52. All States have an obligation to promote the realization of the right to self-determination and to respect that right, in conformity with the provisions of the Charter of the United Nations. In addition, as noted by the Human Rights Committee in relation to the International Covenant on Civil and Political Rights, the current 171 States parties to the Covenant should take positive

action to facilitate the realization of and respect for the right of peoples to self-determination.[2] Such positive action must be consistent with the obligations of States under the Charter and international law. In particular, States must refrain from interfering in the internal affairs of other States and thereby adversely affecting the exercise of the right to self-determination. The effective implementation of the right of peoples to self-determination will contribute to greater enjoyment of human rights, peace and stability, and thereby prevent conflict.

---

[2] See Human Rights Committee, general comment No. 12, para. 6 (see HRI/GEN/1/Rev.9 (Vol. I)); see also Committee on the Elimination of Racial Discrimination, general recommendation XXI, para. 3 (see HRI/GEN/1/Rev.9 (Vol. II)).

Report of the Special Rapporteur on the Situation of Human Rights in the Palestinian Territories Occupied since 1967, U.N. Doc. A/HRC/37/75 (June 14, 2018)

United Nations
General Assembly
A/HRC/37/75
Distr.: General
14 June 2018
Human Rights Council
Thirty-seventh session
26 February–23 March 2018
Agenda item 7
Human rights situation in Palestine and other occupied Arab territories

Report of the Special Rapporteur on the situation of human rights in the Palestinian territories occupied since 1967[*]

Note by the Secretariat

The Secretariat has the honour to transmit to the Human Rights Council the report of the Special Rapporteur on the situation of human rights in the Palestinian territories occupied since 1967, submitted pursuant to Commission on Human Rights resolution 1993/2 A and Human Rights Council resolution 5/1. In it, the Special Rapporteur examines the current human rights situation in the Occupied Palestinian Territory, with a particular emphasis on the right to health. [p. 2]

---

[*] The present report was submitted after the deadline in order to reflect the most recent developments.

Report of the Special Rapporteur on the situation of human rights in the Palestinian territories occupied since 1967

I   Introduction

1. The present report is submitted by the current Special Rapporteur to the Human Rights Council pursuant to Commission on Human Rights resolution 1993/2 A and Human Rights Council resolution 5/1.

2. The Special Rapporteur would like to draw attention once again to the fact that he has not been granted access to the Occupied Palestinian Territory, nor have his requests to meet with the Permanent Representative of Israel to the United Nations been accepted. The Special Rapporteur re-emphasizes that an open dialogue with all parties is an essential element of his work in support of the protection and promotion of human rights. He further notes that access to the Occupied Palestinian Territory is a key element in the development of a comprehensive understanding of the human rights situation on the ground. While he does wish to recognize the exemplary work of experienced and competent civil society organizations, which provide an excellent basis for his work, he laments the lack of opportunity to meet with many of those groups due both to his exclusion from the Territory and to the barriers many individuals face should they seek exit permits from the Israeli authorities, particularly from Gaza.

3. The present report is based primarily on written submissions and consultations with civil society representatives, victims, witnesses and United Nations representatives. The Special Rapporteur undertook his second annual mission to the region, to Amman, from 15 to 19 May 2017. In addition, throughout January 2018 he held several consultations with civil society by videoconference and received a number of written submissions, in particular related to the right to health.

4. In the present report, the Special Rapporteur focuses on the human rights and humanitarian law violations committed by Israel, in accordance with his mandate.[1] As the occupying Power, Israel has the legal obligation to ensure respect for and protection of the rights of Palestinians within its control.[2] The mandate of the Special Rapporteur therefore focuses on the responsibilities of the occupying Power, although he notes that human rights violations by any

---

1   As specified in the mandate of the Special Rapporteur set out in resolution 1993/2.
2   See Geneva Convention relative to the Protection of Civilian Persons in Time of War (Fourth Geneva Convention), art. 47.

State party or non-State actor are deplorable and only hinder the prospects for peace.

5. The Special Rapporteur wishes to express his appreciation for the full cooperation with his mandate extended by the Government of the State of Palestine. The Special Rapporteur also wishes to extend his thanks once again to all those who travelled to Amman in May 2017 to meet with him and to those who were unable to travel but made written or oral submissions. The Special Rapporteur acknowledges the essential work being done and the efforts undertaken by civil society organizations and human rights defenders to create an environment in which human rights are respected and violations of human rights and international humanitarian law are not committed with impunity and without witnesses. The Special Rapporteur will continue to support that work as much as possible.

6. The present report is set out in two parts. First, it provides an overview of the current human rights situation in the Occupied Palestinian Territory. This discussion, while not exhaustive, aims to highlight those human rights concerns the Special Rapporteur has identified as particularly pressing, with a focus on the human rights situation of children in the West Bank and in Gaza. In the second part of the report, the Special Rapporteur examines the right to health, with a particular focus on the increasingly dire humanitarian crisis in Gaza. It must be emphasized that the conditions in Gaza have been described as [p. 3] unliveable for many years now, and the people of Gaza have no choice but to persevere. The impact of the blockade on their right to health is explored in detail in the present report.

II   Current Human Rights Situation

7. Since the Special Rapporteur's previous report to the Human Rights Council, the human rights situation in the Occupied Palestinian Territory has continued to deteriorate. Palestinians in Gaza and the West Bank, including East Jerusalem, have faced demolitions of homes and schools, arrest and arbitrary detention and restrictions on freedom of movement. As the Rapporteur has noted in previous reports, the occupation by Israel affects all aspects of life for Palestinians, from access to medical care to building a home to seeking to travel abroad.

8. On 6 December 2017, the President of the United States of America, Donald Trump, announced that the United States recognized Jerusalem as the capital of Israel. The announcement specified that the United States was not taking any position on final status issues, including the specific boundaries of

Israeli sovereignty in Jerusalem or the resolution of contested borders. The announcement resulted in significant political backlash from the international community and the Palestinian authorities, and widespread protests broke out across the West Bank and Gaza. The feeling of hopelessness among Palestinians resulting from the announcement cannot be overstated, and it is against the background of 50 years of occupation that the announcement by the United States, and current concerns with respect to human rights, must be viewed.

A   *The West Bank, including East Jerusalem*

9. Over the course of 2017, the settlement enterprise steadily advanced after the start of the year saw a sharp rise in the number of new settlement units announced by the Government of Israel.[3] In June, the Prime Minister of Israel, Benjamin Netanyahu, announced that ground had been broken in the first new settlement established in 25 years, Amihai. The settlement was established for the families who were evacuated from the Amona outpost after the Israeli High Court of Justice declared the outpost to be illegal. The settlement is expected to include 102 housing units, although only 41 families were evicted from the Amona outpost (see A/72/564, para. 6). According to a report published by the European External Action Service of the European Union at the end of 2017, the first half of the year saw the development of settlement plans that would potentially enable more than 30,000 new settlers to move to the West Bank, including East Jerusalem.[4]

10. Settlements have been found to be at the centre of many recurrent human rights violations in the West Bank. Palestinians living in close proximity to settlements must regularly pass through checkpoints on their way to school or work, towns or villages are subject to closure by the Israeli military and night raids and arrests are frequent. According to data collected by Palestinian civil society organizations, night raids of Palestinian homes by the Israeli military predominately occur within 2 kilometres of settlements.[5] Night raids often result in the arrest and detention of Palestinians, including, in

---

3   See A/72/556, paras. 11–13, and A/72/564.

4   European External Action Service, "Six-month report on Israeli settlements in the occupied West Bank, including East Jerusalem (January–June 2017)", 15 December 2016. Available at https://eeas.europa.eu/delegations/palestine-occupied-palestinian-territory-west-bank-and-gaza-strip/37466/six-month-report-israeli-settlements-occupied-west-bank-including-east-jerusalem-january-june_en.

5   Women's Centre for Legal Aid and Counselling, "Israel military night-raids on Palestinian residences in the West Bank and East Jerusalem", June 2016. Available at: www.wclac.org/english/userfiles/NIGHT%20RAIDS.pdf.

many cases, Palestinian [p. 4] children. Data collected indicate that 98 per cent of Palestinian children arrested live within 1.02 kilometres of a settlement.[6]

Children

11. At the end of November 2017, figures released by the Israel Prison Service indicated that 313 Palestinian minors were being held in Israeli prisons, 2 of whom were being held on administrative detention orders, and 181 of whom were being held for ongoing legal proceedings.[7] It should also be noted that many Palestinian children are arrested and released during the course of a year. In 2017, the United Nations Children's Fund (UNICEF) reported that 729 children had been detained or arrested in East Jerusalem alone.[8] According to the Convention on the Rights of the Child, the deprivation of the liberty of a child should be used only as a last resort and for the shortest appropriate period of time.[9]

12. A 2013 UNICEF report noted that ill-treatment of Palestinian children in the Israeli military detention system appeared to be widespread, systematic and institutionalized, based on the volume of data the agency had collected in the 10 years preceding the publication of its report.[10] Concerns highlighted in that report, and which continue to be raised today by civil society based on numerous allegations, include reports of physical and verbal abuse, the regular use of hand ties and painful restraints, coerced confessions, a lack of access to lawyers and family members and the consistent use of night arrests.[11] The practices described by organizations working to protect and assist children in

---

6   Military Court Watch, "Briefing note: February 2018". Available at www.militarycourtwatch.org/files/server/BRIEFING%20PAPER%20-%20FEB%202018.pdf.

7   B'Tselem, Statistics on Palestinian minors in the custody of the Israeli security forces. Available at www.btselem.org/statistics/minors_in_custody.

8   United Nations Children's Fund (UNICEF), "State of Palestine: humanitarian situation report", January–December 2017. Available at: www.unicef.org/appeals/files/UNICEF_State_of_Palestine_Humanitarian_Situation_Report_Year_End_2017.pdf.

9   See Committee on the Rights of the Child, general comment No. 10 (2007) on children's rights in juvenile justice, para. 79.

10 See A/71/554, paras. 25–32; UNICEF, "Children in Israeli military detention: observations and recommendations", February 2013, p. 13, available at www.unicef.org/oPt/UNICEF_oPt_Children_in_Israeli_Military_Detention_Observations_and_Recommendations_-_6_March_2013.pdf.

11 Military Court Watch, "Briefing note: February 2018"; UNICEF, "Children in Israeli military detention", p. 14; Human Rights Watch, *World Report 2018: Events of 2017* (New York, 2017), available at www.hrw.org/world-report/2018/country-chapters/israel/palestine; Defense for Children International-Palestine, "Year-in-review: worst abuses against Palestinian children in 2017", 18 January 2018, available at: www.dci-palestine.org/year_in_review_worst_abuses_against_palestinian_children_in_2017.

detention not only fail to take into account the particularly vulnerable position of children, but also deny children their fundamental rights. The negative impact of those practices on the next generation of Palestinians is one of the greatest tragedies of the ongoing occupation.

13. This issue was brought to light once again at the start of 2018 by the arrest and detention of 17-year-old Ahed Tamimi. She was arrested after video footage showing her physically confronting two Israeli soldiers near her family's home in the West Bank was circulated in the media. The Office of the United Nations High Commissioner for Human Rights in the Occupied Palestinian Territory has called for Ms. Tamimi's best interests to be the primary consideration in her ongoing detention and trial. The Special Rapporteur, together with the Working Group on Arbitrary Detention, have raised concerns about her pre-trial detention and detention on remand.[12] Ms. Tamimi's case is emblematic of the issues arising from the practice of arrest and detention of children in the Occupied Palestinian Territory, and more broadly of the fact that children are bearing the brunt of the impact of [p. 5] the occupation and associated human rights violations. The importance of ensuring that the rights of children are respected and protected cannot be overstated.

14. Daily life in the West Bank is continually affected by the often heavy presence of Israeli security forces, for example at checkpoints and in relation to closures of roads and neighbourhoods – measures which in many cases may amount to collective punishment. Children continue to be affected by the restrictions on movement in the West Bank, which is particularly concerning when they are seeking to access hospitals and schools in East Jerusalem. To address the issue, UNICEF supports the provision of a protective presence to teachers and students going to and from school in the West Bank. In 2017, such support was provided to 8,123 children and 414 teachers.[13]

15. In addition to the difficulty children experience in accessing schools, the demolition of schools is also a concern, particularly in communities at risk of forcible transfer in the Jerusalem periphery. In 2017, the United Nations Relief and Works Agency for Palestinian Refugees in the Near East (UNRWA) reported on the situation of Khan al-Ahmar, a Bedouin community at risk of forcible transfer in the West Bank. The Israeli Civil Administration issued demolition orders for 44 structures, including the school, in Khan al-Ahmar in early 2017.

---

12 Office of the United Nations High Commissioner for Human Rights (OHCHR), "United Nations rights experts alarmed by detention of Palestinian girl for slapping Israeli soldier", 13 February 2018. Available at www.ohchr.org/EN/NewsEvents/Pages/DisplayNews.aspx?NewsID=22654&LangID=E.

13 UNICEF, "State of Palestine: humanitarian situation report".

The community received a temporary injunction in March 2017, but representatives of the nearby settlement of Kefar Adummim submitted a petition seeking to compel the Israeli Civil Administration to demolish the school, as it was built without required permits, which are nearly impossible for Palestinians to obtain (see A/71/554, para. 35). According to information submitted by UNRWA, the State response to the petition confirms that the community is expected to relocate to a site identified by the Government of Israel and that the State intends to demolish the school and structures in early 2018, proposing to build an alternative school at the relocation site. As of the start of 2018, the High Court of Justice had upheld those orders, although the demolitions had not yet been carried out.

16. In the West Bank, UNRWA has raised concerns regarding Israeli forces' repeated use of large amounts of tear gas, particularly in crowded areas and confined spaces, including refugee camps and homes within camps. The practice has a particularly detrimental effect on vulnerable populations such as children and the elderly, as the tear gas does not dissipate in densely populated or confined areas. UNRWA reported at least 48 incidents in 2016 in which tear-gas canisters, stun grenades, plastic-coated metal bullets or live ammunition used by Israeli forces landed in UNRWA compounds or damaged UNRWA installations. Those incidents resulted in one injury as well as lost school and work days for students and staff suffering from tear-gas inhalation. It should be noted that tear gas may only be used where strictly necessary in a law enforcement context, must be carefully controlled to minimize the risk to children and uninvolved persons[14] and must be used in proportion to the seriousness of the offence and the legitimate objective to be achieved.[15]

Legal Developments

17. The continued advancement of the settlement enterprise described above has been accompanied by a worrying number of legislative and legal policy developments, which, if continued, would have the effect of making the expropriation of private Palestinian land merely an administrative matter, occurring, in a sense, out of the public eye.

18. Legislative measures aimed at extending Israeli jurisdiction to the West Bank have proliferated recently, with a notable example being the recent passage of a bill which gives authority over institutions of higher education in the West Bank to an Israeli governmental body. The Knesset member who initiated

---

14   Basic Principles on the Use of Force and Firearms by Law Enforcement Officials, gen. provs. 3, 5 (c) and 14.
15   Ibid., gen. prov. 5 (a).

the legislation reportedly said when discussing the new legislation: "Alongside the academic importance of the law, there is a clear element [p. 6] here of applying sovereignty and I'm proud of both of these things."[16] The legislation comes after the passage last year of the Law for the Regularization of Settlement in Judea and Samaria, 5777-2017, referred to as the "regularization" law, which allowed for the retroactive legalization, under domestic law, of outposts built illegally on private Palestinian land. It should be noted that settlements of all kinds are considered illegal under international law (see A/72/564, para. 14). In addition to allowing for the confiscation of private Palestinian land, the passage of the law was the first time Israel extended its jurisdiction to matters involving private Palestinian land in the Occupied Palestinian Territory.

19. In addition to legislative moves seeking to extend Israeli control over the occupied West Bank, there are further policy shifts that have been described as attempts to "normalize" Israeli settlements in the West Bank. For example, in December 2017 the Attorney General of Israel issued a directive mandating that all Government-sponsored bills include a clause specifying whether or not the bill would also apply to the Occupied Palestinian Territory.[17]

20. The new laws and policy shifts, accompanied by the continued proposal of various legislative measures seeking to annex specific settlements and municipalities in the West Bank, represent what has been called a paradigm shift in the way the Israeli Government conducts the occupation. The legal framework of occupation, and the protections it provides, are being steadily eroded by the legislation, which seeks to regulate the West Bank as if it is a part of Israel.

B   Gaza

21. Despite widespread recognition that the situation in Gaza is unsustainable, unliveable and in many ways horrific, little progress has been made in improving the humanitarian situation of the people there. Many in Israel recognize the building crisis, and the Palestinian Authority is also well aware of the deteriorating conditions in which the residents of Gaza live. After 10 years of blockade, the population of Gaza is in a particularly vulnerable position, with

---

16 Yarden Zur, "Israel's creeping annexation: Knesset votes to extend Israeli law to academic institutions in the West Bank", *Haaretz*, 12 February 2018. Available at www.haaretz.com/israel-news/israel-votes-to-expand-israeli-law-to-academic-institutions-in-w-bank-1.5810994.

17 Revital Hovel, "New laws should also consider settlers in West Bank, says Israeli Attorney General", *Haaretz*, 31 December 2017. Available at www.haaretz.com/israel-news/.premium-new-draft-laws-must-also-consider-settlers-in-west-bank-says-israeli-ag-1.5630121.

as much as 70 per cent of the population dependent upon some form of humanitarian assistance. The electricity crisis, which intensified significantly in May 2017, although it has improved slightly in recent months, continues to have a negative impact on the situation of the residents of Gaza as of January 2018. The reconciliation process initiated in November 2017 between the authorities in Gaza and Fatah in the West Bank seems to have all but stopped, and punitive measures imposed on the authorities in Gaza by the Palestinian Authority continue to negatively impact the human rights and humanitarian situations of Gaza's residents. That, combined with 10 years of the Israeli blockade and continued restrictions on the movement of people and goods, have contributed to growing feelings of hopelessness and desperation for the people of Gaza.

Children

22. It must be noted that the impact of the occupation on children is not limited to the situation in the West Bank. In Gaza, restrictions on freedom of movement and the difficulty of importing goods critical for service delivery undermine economic prospects and the availability of essential services. The restrictions imposed by Israel continue to impede the realization of a broad range of human rights, including economic, social and cultural rights such as the rights to health and education and ultimately to an adequate standard of living. Children growing up in this environment face innumerable challenges. [p. 7]

23. Excessive use of force against Palestinians by Israeli forces is a concern in the area along the border fence, and often has an impact on children. In mid-February 2018, two Palestinian teenagers aged 14 and 16 were killed and two others were injured by Israeli forces, who fired what were reportedly artillery shells and live fire towards the boys as they approached the fence, although they were reportedly between 30 to 50 metres away when shot.[18] The incident raises concerns about the decision to use lethal force against young, unarmed boys as, according to the Basic Principles on the Use of Force and Firearms by Law Enforcement Officials, lethal force should be used only if other means are ineffective, and should be used with restraint and in proportion to the seriousness of the offence and the legitimate objective to be achieved. Not only in Gaza, but also in the West Bank, the use of force by Israeli forces has consistently been flagged as an issue of concern by the Special Rapporteur, the High

---

18 Defense for Children International – Palestine, "Israeli forces kill two teenagers on Gaza Strip border", 23 February 2018. Available at www.dci-palestine.org/israeli_forces_kill_two_teenagers_on_gaza_strip_border.

Commissioner for Human Rights and the Secretary-General. That concern is necessarily heightened when children are the victims.

24. In addition to actions that negatively affect the rights to life and to security of person, the conditions in Gaza have an untold effect on economic, social and cultural rights (for a detailed discussion of the right to development in Gaza, see A/71/554, paras. 45–48). Growing up in Gaza means growing up with limited access to health care. Schools and education suffer due to a lack of resources, travel restrictions, electricity cuts and crumbling infrastructure. UNICEF, Save the Children International and the Deputy Special Coordinator for the Middle East Peace Process and United Nations Coordinator for Humanitarian and Development Activities in the Occupied Palestinian Territory issued a joint statement in September 2017 highlighting the fact that Palestinian children continue to struggle to realize their right to education. In Gaza in particular, schools are overcrowded after the significant damage to infrastructure owing to escalations of hostilities, and reconstruction remains difficult given Israel's tight restrictions on the import of materials, in addition to the failing economy of Gaza and budget shortages. Two thirds of the schools in Gaza operate in double shifts, welcoming different groups of students in the morning and in the afternoon, and students who study at night often do so by candlelight as a result of the ongoing electricity crisis.[19] Education in Gaza is heavily dependent upon UNRWA, which operates more than 250 schools in the area. Due to travel restrictions and the near impossibility of obtaining a permit to exit Gaza, teachers, professors and students are unable to travel for needed training, and cannot access educational opportunities abroad.

25. The right to education is enshrined in article 13 of the International Covenant on Economic, Social and Cultural Rights, to which Israel is a party. Despite its position to the contrary, according to the Human Rights Committee and other United Nations treaty bodies, as well as the Advisory Opinion of the International Court of Justice in 2004,[20] Israel's human rights obligations extend to the Occupied Palestinian Territory and apply concurrently to its obligations under international humanitarian law (see A/HRC/34/38, paras. 6–9).

26. The Committee on Economic, Social and Cultural Rights, in its general comment No. 13, noted that education was both a human right in itself and an indispensable means of realizing other rights. The Committee also noted that,

---

[19] Office for the Coordination of Humanitarian Affairs, Occupied Palestinian Territory, "Right of education for 1 million Palestinian children at risk", 11 September 2017. Available at: www.ochaopt.org/content/right-education-1-million-palestinian-children-risk.

[20] *Legal Consequences of the Construction of a Wall in the Occupied Palestinian Territory, Advisory Opinion, I.C.J. Reports 2004*, p. 136.

with education, marginalized children and adults could gain the tools needed to lift themselves out of poverty and participate fully in their communities. Efforts to stymie that right are in turn efforts to ensure that a population remains trapped in a situation of poverty and desperation. For children growing up under the blockade and closure of Gaza, the importance of access to education is clear. A path by which to learn and grow and seek constructive ways to change their situation is an essential with which they must be provided. [p. 8]

III Right to Health

27. A 4-year-old girl in Gaza suffering from heart failure dies after Israeli authorities deny her permission to return to East Jerusalem for pediatric cardiology treatment that is unavailable in Gaza.[21] Access to safe and sufficient drinking water in the Occupied Palestinian Territory is severely compromised by the discriminatory access to sources of water in the West Bank, and by the depleted and contaminated water aquifers in Gaza.[22] The principal Palestinian hospital in East Jerusalem is raided repeatedly by heavily armed Israeli soldiers and police who fire stun and sponge grenades, resulting in mayhem and fear among patients and staff.[23] Significant stocks of essential drugs are exhausted in Gaza hospitals and are unable to be replaced, even as emergency services in local hospitals are reduced because of political decisions to cut electricity supplies to the territory.[24] Health workers in the West Bank are frequently impeded in their ability to reach patients and hospitals because of interference by Israeli security forces, including delays at checkpoints and the requirement to transfer patients from Palestinian ambulances to Israeli-registered ambulances before entering East Jerusalem.[25]

28. Those recent examples, among many others, raise serious concerns about the fulfilment of the right to health in the Occupied Palestinian Territory. In

---

21 Amira Hass, "For some Gazans in need of medical treatment, the wait for an exit permit ends in death", *Haaretz*, 4 December 2017. Available at: www.haaretz.com/middle-east-news/palestinians/.premium-for-some-sick-gazans-the-wait-for-an-exit-permit-ends-in-death-1.5627529.

22 Amnesty International, "The occupation of water", 30 November 2017. Available at www.amnesty.ca/blog/occupation-water.

23 B'Tselem, "Israeli security forces endangered patients' lives at al-Makassed hospital, East Jerusalem", 10 August 2017.

24 World Health Organization (WHO), "WHO special situation report: Occupied Palestinian Territory, Gaza – December 2017 to January 2018", 31 December 2017.

25 Medical Aid for Palestinians, "Health under occupation", September 2017. Available at www.map.org.uk/downloads/health-under-occupation---map-report-2017.pdf.

recent years, civil society organizations and international agencies have extensively documented the significant and chronic challenges to health care and well-being related to the occupation of the Palestinian territory. Relying upon the World Health Organization's (WHO) definition of health as "a state of complete physical, mental and social well-being and not merely the absence of disease or infirmity"[26] and understanding health within the context of human security and the enlargement of dignity and human choices,[27] this portion of the Special Rapporteur's report examines the impediments to the realization of the right to health in the Occupied Palestinian Territory.

A   *Right to Health under International Law*

29. The right to health is one of the most fundamental and widely recognized human rights. The right touches on everything that we do as humans, and its robust promotion is one of the most effective tools available to reduce the scourges of social and economic inequalities, gender disparities, discrimination and poverty. Reflecting the indivisibility and interdependence of all human rights, the right to health is inextricably linked to the realization of other recognized rights, including the rights to water, housing, food, work, education, life and human dignity. As WHO has stated: "Without health, other rights have little meaning."[28] [p. 9]

30. The right to health is well anchored within international law.[29] Article 25 of the Universal Declaration of Human Rights states that: "Everyone has the right to a standard of living adequate for the health and well-being of himself and his family." Article 12 (1) of the International Covenant on Economic, Social and Cultural Rights establishes the broad nature of States' obligations to ensure the availability of, access to, and acceptability and quality of health services in its proclamation of "the right of everyone to the enjoyment of the highest attainable standard of physical and mental health". In its general comment No. 14, the Committee on Economic, Social and Cultural Rights linked the right to health not only to the availability of quality health-care services but to a wide range of socioeconomic determinants that together promote the conditions by which people can lead a healthy life. The right to health is also

---

26   Constitution of the World Health Organization. Available at: www.who.int/governance/eb/who_constitution_en.pdf.
27   Rajaie Batniji and others, "Health as human security in the Occupied Palestinian Territory", *The Lancet*, vol. 373, No. 9669 (March 2009).
28   See Steven D. Jamar, "The international human right to health", *Southern University Law Review*, vol. 22, No. 1 (August 1994).
29   John Tobin, *The Right to Health in International Law* (Oxford, Oxford University Press, 2012).

expressly found in core international human rights instruments, including the Convention on the Rights of the Child, the Convention on the Elimination of All Forms of Discrimination against Women, the International Convention on the Elimination of All Forms of Racial Discrimination and the Convention on the Rights of Persons with Disabilities, as well as in important regional human rights instruments in Europe, the Americas and Africa.

31. The right to health creates a range of specific obligations upon States,[30] including:

(a) The progressive realization of the principle of enjoying the highest attainable standard of physical and mental health;

(b) Ensuring equality of access to health care and health services for all, without discrimination;

(c) The obligations to respect (to refrain from interfering with a right), protect (to prevent third parties from interfering with a right) and fulfill (to take steps to ensure the fullest possible realization of a right) the right to health;

(d) The protection of vulnerable and marginalized groups, including women, children, older persons, persons with disabilities, minorities and indigenous peoples;

(e) The provision and enhancement of the underlying social determinants of health, including food, housing, sanitation, safe water and physical security.

32. For protected peoples living under occupation, their right to health is also guaranteed by international humanitarian law and the laws of occupation. In particular, the Geneva Convention relative to the Protection of Civilian Persons in Time of War of 12 August 1949 (the Fourth Geneva Convention), together with the Additional Protocols and customary international law, places the overall responsibility for civilian access to health care in an occupied territory upon the occupying Power.[31] Among the extensive responsibilities assumed by the occupying Power for the civilian population are: the protection and respect for the wounded, sick and infirm;[32] the protection of civilian hospitals and their personnel;[33] the assurance that the medical supplies for the population

---

[30] Committee on Economic, Social and Cultural Rights, general comment No. 14 (2000) on the right to the highest attainable standard of health.

[31] See generally, Andrew Clapham, Paola Gaeta and Marco Sassòli, eds., *The 1949 Geneva Conventions: A Commentary* (Oxford, Oxford University Press, 2015), especially chaps. 37, 39 and 40.

[32] Fourth Geneva Convention, arts. 15 and 16.

[33] Ibid., arts. 18 and 20.

are adequate;[34] the maintenance of the medical and hospital establishment and services, public health and hygiene of the territory;[35] and the facilitation of medical personnel of all categories to fulfil their duties.[36] In addition, the Security Council has stated that all parties to a conflict must ensure that medical and humanitarian staff and health facilities are not attacked.[37] [p. 10]

33. Israel, as the occupying Power, has specific and significant obligations under international law to ensure the health and welfare of the Palestinian population under its control. As a State party to the International Covenant on Economic, Social and Cultural Rights and as an occupying Power, Israel is required to observe international human rights law throughout the Occupied Palestinian Territory.[38] And as a State party to the Geneva Conventions of 1949 and as the occupying Power, Israel is bound under international treaty and customary law to scrupulously apply the Fourth Geneva Convention and the other obligations of international humanitarian law.[39]

B *Situation of Health in the Occupied Palestinian Territory*

34. The unprecedented length and character of Israel's 50-year acquisitive occupation, driven by the logic of demographic engineering and territorial annexation, both de jure and de facto, has badly fragmented the Palestinian territory.[40] The consequence has been the political separation and geographic isolation of the West Bank, East Jerusalem and Gaza from one another, significantly impinging upon the Palestinians' internal freedom of movement. That fragmentation likewise splinters the delivery of Palestinian health services and deforms the social determinants of health throughout the Occupied Palestinian Territory.[41] Because the Occupied Palestinian Territory lacks any

---

34 Ibid., art. 55.
35 Ibid., art. 56.
36 Ibid., arts. 23 and 56.
37 Security Council resolution 2286 (2016).
38 International human rights law applies to a territory under occupation: see *Legal Consequences of the Construction of a Wall, Advisory Opinion*, paras. 111–113. See also CCPR/C/ISR/CO/4, para. 5.
39 Security Council resolution 2334 (2016). See also Aeyal Gross, "Litigating the right to strike under occupation: between bureaucracy and humanitarianism", *Minnesota Journal of International Law*, vol. 27 (forthcoming).
40 The report of the Special Rapporteur of October 2017 (A/72/556) submitted that Israel, as the occupying Power, had reached the status of an illegal occupier because of its violation of the fundamental principles of international law governing a belligerent occupation, including the principles of non-annexation, temporariness, good faith and compliance with international law and the directions of the international community.
41 Physicians for Human Rights – Israel, "Divide and conquer: inequality in health", January 2015.

reliable frontier with a neighbouring country, Israel completely controls the Palestinians' external freedom of movement as well.[42]

35. In the West Bank, health care is primarily delivered by the Palestinian Authority and UNRWA, while in Gaza, the governing authority and UNRWA are the principal providers of health services. Palestinian private health providers and Palestinian and international non-governmental organizations also play an important role in health delivery. Nonetheless, the extensive control exercised by the Israeli occupation over the daily lives and movements of the Palestinian population decisively and adversely affects the health services and health outcomes in those areas. In East Jerusalem, where the Israeli healthcare system is available to the resident Palestinians, their standard of living and their access to health services is considerably inferior to that enjoyed by Jewish Israeli residents.[43]

1   Gaza

36. As noted above, the health and humanitarian crisis in Gaza has become acute, bordering on a human calamity. Gaza has suffered grievously through three destructive wars in 2008–2009, 2012 and 2014. Israel has imposed a comprehensive blockade on Gaza's land, sea and air frontiers since 2007, which amounts to a form of collective punishment prohibited by international law.[44] The blockade comprehensively controls and restricts [p. 11] the movement of people and goods in and out of Gaza, resulting in economic suffocation, faltering reconstruction efforts, social and familial isolation from the outside world and a dire impact upon the territory's already anaemic living and health standards. The 12-year-old political schism between the Palestinian Authority and the authority governing Gaza has further compounded this misery. Given the critical state of health care in Gaza, the Special Rapporteur is devoting an outsized portion of the present report to the topic.

---

42   The only direct frontier between the Occupied Palestinian Territory and a State other than Israel is the Rafah crossing between Gaza and Egypt. The exit crossing is only open intermittently: in 2015, it was open for 24 days; in 2016, for 38 days; and in 2017, for only 21 days, see WHO, "Health access for referral patients from the Gaza Strip", monthly report, December 2017.

43   United Nations Conference on Trade and Development, "The Palestinian economy in East Jerusalem: enduring annexation, isolation and disintegration", document UNCTAD/GDS/APP/2012/1.

44   See A/HRC/34/36, para. 36, with references. Collective punishment is expressly prohibited by article 33 of the Fourth Geneva Convention as well as by customary international law. See Shane Darcy, "The prohibition of collective punishment", in Clapham, Gaeta and Sassòli, eds., *The 1949 Geneva Conventions*.

37. The 2 million people living in Gaza rely upon a health-care system that United Nations health officials have said is on the edge of collapse.[45] According to WHO, an estimated 206 (40 per cent) of the 516 listed essential medicines in its basic health basket were completely out of stock by the end of January 2018, and another 43 per cent of essential drugs had less than a month's supply remaining.[46] That included drugs required for treating cancer and autoimmune diseases and for performing dialysis and conducting cardiac angiographies.[47] The Office for the Coordination of Humanitarian Affairs of the Secretariat has noted that the funding, purchase and delivery of medicines is the responsibility of the Palestinian Authority and has observed a decline in the supply of essential drugs associated with internal Palestinian divisions, though it did note a slight improvement by the start of 2018.[48] Nonetheless, shortages of vital laboratory supplies has meant that hematology, culture and blood chemistry services can no longer be conducted at out-patient clinics, but only for patients who are hospitalized.[49] In addition, serious shortages of essential medical disposables such as syringes, line tubes, filters for dialysis and dressing materials have also been reported.[50]

38. The crippling electricity shortages in Gaza have forced many hospitals to shut down areas such as operating theatres, emergency departments and general medical wards, and ration essential services such as diagnostic services, instrument sterilization and the treatment of chronic illnesses.[51] At the beginning of 2018, 3 hospitals and 13 primary health-care clinics were temporarily closed, affecting health-care delivery to more than 300,000 people.[52] Neonatal intensive care units have become overcrowded in the face of maternal malnutrition and rising rates of premature and low-weight babies.[53] For

---

45 Amira Hass, "Gaza health system collapsing: 40 per cent of medicine runs out", *Haaretz*, 8 February 2018.
46 WHO, "WHO special situation report".
47 Physicians for Human Rights – Israel, "Overview of the Gaza health system: despite the reconciliation the situation keeps deteriorating", January 2018.
48 Office for the Coordination of Humanitarian Affairs, "Only marginal improvement in humanitarian situation in the Gaza Strip in wake of the intra-Palestinian reconciliation agreement", "Humanitarian bulletin: Occupied Palestinian Territory", January 2018. Available at www.ochaopt.org/content/only-marginal-improvement-humanitarian-situation-gaza-strip-wake-intra-palestinian.
49 Physicians for Human Rights – Israel, "Overview of the Gaza health system".
50 Ibid.
51 WHO, "WHO special situation report".
52 Ibid.
53 Ratcliffe, "Gaza's health system close to collapse as electricity crisis threatens total blackout".

the hospitals that remain open, bed occupancy rates are reported to be above 90 per cent. By December 2017, the waiting time for elective surgery stood at 52 weeks, well beyond the operative threshold of 24 weeks.[54] Compounding the problem of treatment services has been the inability of Gaza hospitals to obtain permission from Israel to import replacement parts for vital diagnostic imaging equipment, putting the equipment out of service for months and even years.[55] Serious funding shortages have affected the ability of hospitals to purchase fuel to power, maintain and repair their electrical generators during the endemic electricity cuts.

39. The dilapidated and failing Gaza health-care sector is overwhelmingly a human-made crisis. Notwithstanding the best efforts of the medical and health staff working in the [p. 12] territory, they have been unable to service Gaza's residents at anywhere near the health system's potential. One consequence of the acute crisis has been the compelling need to refer larger numbers of patients with serious or chronic health conditions to medical facilities outside Gaza for treatment that they should be able to, but cannot, receive in the territory. At that stage, another significant impediment to the fulfilment of the right to health in Gaza is encountered.

40. Israel administers a byzantine and opaque exit permit system imposed upon those patients who require specialized treatment in East Jerusalem (the location of the most advanced medical facilities within the Occupied Palestinian Territory), the rest of the West Bank or abroad.[56] Patients with complex disorders who are unable to be adequately treated in Gaza include: cancer patients requiring surgery, chemotherapy and/or radiotherapy; pediatric patients with metabolic disorders or congenital defects; heart patients requiring open-heart surgery or with post-operative complications; eye patients in need of specialized surgery or cornea transplants; bone-disease patients requiring hip or knee surgery; neurosurgical patients; patients requiring MRI scans; and patients with blood diseases.[57] For virtually all of those patients, time is of the essence, either because of the deteriorating nature of their serious or life-threatening disorders, or because life is at an absolute standstill as long as their chronic and debilitating health conditions remain unresolved.

41. Beyond the question of urgency, the non-governmental organization Physicians for Human Rights – Israel has criticized the Israeli authority's

---

54   WHO, "WHO special situation report".
55   Physicians for Human Rights – Israel, "Overview of the Gaza health system".
56   Anita Vitullo and others, "Barriers to the access to health services in the Occupied Palestinian Territory: a cohort study", *The Lancet*, vol. 380, Nos. S18–S19 (October 2012).
57   Al Mezan Center for Human Rights, "Medical care under siege: Israel's systematic violation of Gaza's patient rights", February 2018.

criteria for exit permit applications, which distinguishes between applications on the basis of whether the applicants require life-saving or disability-preventing medical treatments or whether their medical needs are less urgent, stating that this distinction is "at odds with the rules of medical ethics, according to which every patient must be allowed access to the best possible treatment available to him/her, regardless of its urgency or the severity of his/her medical condition".[58]

42. A patient with a complex disorder is first assessed by medical professionals in Gaza as to whether her or his condition can be adequately treated by the resources available within the local health system.[59] If the assessment determines that care must be sought outside of Gaza, the Palestinian Ministry of Health has the responsibility to approve the referral request. The patient's application is then forwarded to the Israeli authorities for permission for the patient and his or her travelling companion to exit the territory through the Erez crossing and travel to a hospital outside Gaza.

43. An application comes with no guarantee of success, and approval rates for travel outside Gaza have been steadily declining. Since WHO began collecting statistics for medical permit approvals in 2008, 2017 has marked the lowest annual approval rate. In 2012, the approval rate was 92 per cent; it declined to 82 per cent in 2014; and declined further to 62 per cent in 2016. According to WHO, the approval rate by Israeli authorities for the 25,812 health travel permit applications filed in Gaza in 2017 had tumbled to 52.4 per cent. While only 2.6 per cent of the applications were formally rejected by Israeli authorities (invariably with no clear reasons provided) in 2017, a large number – 45 per cent – were delayed, and no response was provided.[60] An estimated 11,000 medical [p. 13] appointments were missed in 2017 by patients from Gaza whose travel permit applications were either denied or delayed.[61]

44. WHO has documented that 54 patients who had applied for a medical travel permit and who had either been denied permission or who had not

---

58   Physicians for Human Rights – Israel, "Denied 2: harassment of Palestinian patients applying for exit permits", August 2016.

59   Al Mezan Center for Human Rights, "Medical care under siege"; WHO, "Timeline for Gaza patient referrals", available at https://unispal.un.org/DPA/DPR/unispal.nsf/0/ 604F89F84BAAA88085258169004FA797.

60   WHO, "WHO special situation report"; Al Mezan Center for Human Rights, "Medical care under siege".

61   Human Rights Watch, "Israel: record-low in Gaza medical permits", 13 February 2018.

received an answer to their application died in Gaza in 2017.[62] Three of those deaths are illustrative of that broader tragedy.[63]

45. Abeer Abu-Jayyad, 46, suffered from breast cancer, and required a treatment course of Herceptin. The drug was unavailable in Gaza, and she had applied for a health travel permit for treatment at Augusta Victoria Hospital in East Jerusalem. Her travel applications were denied on security grounds by the Israeli authorities, and she missed her scheduled appointments. Abeer died in Gaza on 8 June 2017 after the cancer metastasized. Abeer's case exemplifies a distressing trend: 46 of the 54 deaths in 2017 were cancer patients who were unable to receive adequate health treatment in Gaza. Ahmed Hasan Shbeir, 17, was born with a congenital heart defect. Because of the limited capacity to treat his condition in Gaza, Ahmed travelled regularly to hospitals in East Jerusalem and Israel for specialized treatment. However, beginning in September 2016, applications for a health travel permit filed by Ahmed's family were first not answered, and then formally refused, by Israeli authorities. His condition deteriorated, and he subsequently died in Gaza on 14 January 2017. Aya Khalil Abu Mutlaq, 5, was born with cerebral palsy and was initially treated in Gaza. In early February 2017, after obtaining a medical referral from the Palestinian Ministry of Health, Aya's family sought a medical travel permit from the Israeli authorities so that she could receive treatment at Al Makassed Hospital in East Jerusalem. She secured, but missed, three appointments at Al Makassed after her family received no responses to their repeated applications. While waiting for an answer to the third permit request, Aya died on 17 April 2017. It is not known whether any of the 54 patients would have either recovered or stabilized had permission to travel been granted, but the chances of their health improving were negligible without the opportunity to obtain the care they required outside Gaza.

46. The difficulties faced by cancer patients in Gaza in the face of the blockade has been recently reviewed by Physicians for Human Rights – Israel and by the Al Mezan Center for Human Rights.[64] In Gaza, only some chemotherapy treatments and auxiliary drugs are available. Operations to remove tumours are difficult in the face of electricity and fuel shortages. Radiation therapy and medical diagnostics requiring radioisotopes are non-existent because of the lack or non-functioning of necessary instruments such as linear accelerators

---

62 WHO, "WHO special situation report".
63 These profiles were collected by Al Mezan Center for Human Rights, see "Medical care under siege".
64 Physicians for Human Rights – Israel, "Overview of the Gaza health system"; Al Mezan Center for Human Rights, "Medical care under siege".

or PET-CT scanners, and the prohibition on the import of medical radioisotopes into Gaza. Cancer diagnosis in Gaza is frequently made at the end stage of the disease, and cancer patients report a low quality of life, reflecting the lack of adequate resources for detection and treatment.[65] Cancer patients are regularly referred for treatment outside Gaza, but a growing number are denied exit permits or face delays in receiving their exit permits from the Israeli authorities.

47. Physicians for Human Rights – Israel has observed that the Israeli authority which grants travel permission, the Coordinator of Government Activities in the Territories, has increasingly exceeded its own time limits for providing responses to health travel applications, sometimes by months. Referring specifically to the plight of female cancer patients from Gaza, the organization has stated that the decision-making delays by the Coordinator amount to "a policy of disparaging the suffering of those patients and shirking Israel's responsibility for the consequences of the restrictions it deliberately imposes".[66] [p. 14] Physicians for Human Rights – Israel has reported that a large number of exiting patients, many of whom are cancer patients, have been closely interrogated for intelligence information, which the organization deems to be unethical and immoral.[67]

48. Medical professionals and health delivery staff in Gaza, already underpaid, have been receiving only half to a quarter of their salaries, and in some cases no salary at all, in recent months.[68] Staff strikes protesting the salary suspensions have further impaired the delivery of health care.[69] The severe restrictions in movement imposed by the Israeli blockade have meant that doctors and nurses in Gaza face significant hurdles in receiving permission from the Coordinator to leave the territory to receive specialized professional training elsewhere in the Occupied Palestinian Territory or abroad: only 40 per cent of exit applications by health professionals were approved in 2017.[70] During the 2014 war, 23 health professionals in Gaza were killed and another

---

65 Ahmed Nimer Shamallakh and Asma M. Imam, "Quality of life in patients with cancer in the Gaza Strip: a cross-sectional study", *The Lancet*, vol. 390, No. S21 (August 2017).
66 Physicians for Human Rights – Israel, "Rapid response to applications by women cancer patients from Gaza" (November 2017). Available at www.phr.org.il/wp-content/uploads/2017/11/cogat-letter.pdf.
67 Physicians for Human Rights – Israel, "Denied 2"; Women's Centre for Legal Aid and Counselling, Communication with Special Rapporteur (February 2018).
68 Office for the Coordination of Humanitarian Affairs, "Only marginal improvement in humanitarian situation in the Gaza Strip in wake of the intra-Palestinian reconciliation agreement".
69 Physicians for Human Rights – Israel, "Denied 2".
70 WHO, "WHO special situation report".

78 were injured. An estimated 45 ambulances were damaged or destroyed and 73 hospitals and clinics were struck.[71]

49. Geographically, Gaza and Israel are cheek by jowl with each other. Gaza City is only 75 kilometres from Tel Aviv. However, there is an extraordinary gap in health outcomes between Gaza and Israel, according to some common international measuring sticks. The following statistics are provided by WHO:
– Life expectancy: 73.1 (Gaza) versus 82.1 (Israel)
– Infant mortality rate: 20 per 1,000 live births (Gaza) versus 3 (Israel)
– Maternal mortality rate: 31 per 100,000 births (Gaza) versus 2 (Israel)
– Breast cancer 5-year survival: 65 per cent (Gaza) versus 86 per cent (Israel)

50. The right to health is thus severely restricted for the residents of Gaza. Despite the fact that this is occurring in full view of the international community, the Palestinian authorities, and the Government of Israel, little has been done to alleviate the suffering of Gaza's people. The reconciliation agreement between Hamas in Gaza and Fatah in the West Bank signed in 2017 has all but ground to a halt.[72] Israel's obligations, as occupying Power, to the residents of Gaza remain far from fulfilled, and the international community takes note of the dire situation of Gaza's residents, yet fails to act.

2 Mental Health

51. Recent health studies in the Occupied Palestinian Territory have found that the cumulative threats to human security for its residents have had a significant and adverse impact upon psychological well-being among the population.[73] The cumulative threats include traumatic and anxiety-inducing experiences of warfare, home demolitions, imprisonment and beatings, land confiscation and violence arising from demonstrations and settler attacks, as well as the diminished character of life caused by the lack of freedom of movement, food insecurity, the lack of control over water resources, discrimination and [p. 15] statelessness, precarious work and the tottering economy and the mounting poverty rates, all of which serve to erode the social fabric of society

---

71 Medical Aid for Palestinians, "Health under occupation".
72 Nickolay Mladenov, Special Coordinator for the Middle East Peace Process, "Briefing to the Security Council on the situation in the Middle East", 25 January 2018. Available at https://reliefweb.int/report/occupied-palestinian-territory/nickolay-mladenov-special-coordinator-middle-east-peace-6.
73 WHO, "Health conditions in the Occupied Palestinian Territory, including East Jerusalem and in the occupied Syrian Golan", document A69/44, para. 15: "An increase in the burden of mental and psychosocial disorders can be expected in a population experiencing prolonged occupation, lack of personal security, severe restrictions on movement and violations of human rights, including displacement in a post-conflict situation". Available at http://apps.who.int/gb/ebwha/pdf_files/WHA69/A69_44-en.pdf.

in the Occupied Palestinian Territory.[74] Above all, Palestinians lack any collective control over the occupying authority that not only makes virtually all of the decisive political, economic and social decisions which govern their lives, but makes them in a fashion that thwarts their interests and disregards their well-being.

52. According to a 2013 regional study on mental health, the Occupied Palestinian Territory bore the largest burden of mental disorders among the examined countries in the Eastern Mediterranean region.[75] Mental health professionals in the Occupied Palestinian Territory have encountered a steady increase in visits to mental health clinics over the past several years, a rise in personality disorders and an increase in impulsive behaviours among the population.[76] A third of patients attending primary health clinics in the West Bank and Gaza were reported to be suffering from mental health issues, a rate that is higher than more politically stable countries.[77]

53. A recent WHO report has stated that mental health workers in the Occupied Palestinian Territory have found that the most common mental health issues are affective disorders, anxiety, depression, epilepsy, aggression, insomnia, neurosis, schizophrenia, total exhaustion, drug-induced conditions and post-traumatic stress disorder (PTSD).[78] Another health study estimated that the expected population prevalence of post-conflict PTSD and major depression would be close to 30 per cent among Palestinians in the West Bank and Gaza.[79] A noteworthy recent study found that residents of two Palestinian

---

74 Clea McNeely and others, "Human insecurity, chronic economic constraints and health in the Occupied Palestinian Territory", *Global Public Health*, vol. 9, No. 5 (2014); Stevan E. Hobfoll and others, "The limits of resilience: distress following chronic violence among Palestinians", *Social Science and Medicine*, vol. 72, No. 8 (April 2011); Batniji and others, "Health as human security in the Occupied Palestinian Territory".

75 Raghid Charara and others, "The burden of mental disorders in the Eastern Mediterranean region, 1990–2013", *PLoS One*, vol. 12, No. 1 (January 2017). The authors expressed caution about the full reliability of measurements on mental health in the Occupied Palestinian Territory, given the difficulties in data collection.

76 WHO, "Health conditions in the Occupied Palestinian Territory, including East Jerusalem and in the occupied Syrian Golan", document A70/39. Available at http://apps.who.int/gb/ebwha/pdf_files/WHA70/A70_39-en.pdf.

77 Ambrogio Manenti and others, "Report of a field assessment of health conditions in the Occupied Palestinian Territory", February 2016. Available at http://apps.who.int/gb/Statements/Report_Palestinian_territory/Report_Palestinian_territory-en.pdf.

78 Ibid.

79 Daphna Canetti and others, "Improving mental health is key to reduce violence in Israeli and Gaza", *The Lancet*, vol. 384, No. 9942 (August 2014). This study also noted that the promotion of the mental health of both Palestinians and Israelis is essential to laying the groundwork for peace.

refugee camps in the West Bank reported very high levels of profound psychological distress linked to regular raids by Israeli security forces and their frequent use of tear gas in close quarters against the residents.[80]

54. One significant feature is the relative lack of psychiatric, psychological and counselling services available. The West Bank, with 2.6 million Palestinians, has only one mental hospital, in Bethlehem, with 180 beds. Gaza, with 2 million people, has only a 40-bed hospital. There is only one psychiatric training programme in the Occupied Palestinian Territory and, as of May 2016, there was only 1 psychiatrist, along with approximately 30 psychologists.[81] A national mental health strategy has been developed by the Palestinian Ministry of Health, and among its goals are the enhancement of resources for the treatment of mental health, improvements in the measurement of mental illness and an increased [p. 16] focus on public education to challenge the social stigmatization related to mental health issues.[82]

3 Children

55. The health and social well-being of children are an apt barometer of the larger well-being of a society. Recent studies have reported that food insecurity in the Occupied Palestinian Territory has resulted in worrisome levels of child malnutrition. A 2013 study found disturbing levels of anaemia (26.5 per cent across the Occupied Palestinian Territory, and 30.8 per cent in Gaza), vitamin A deficiency (73 per cent across the Occupied Palestinian Territory) and vitamin D deficiency (60.1 per cent across the Occupied Palestinian Territory, and 64.4 per cent in Gaza) among children aged 6 months to 5 years. Those micronutrient deficiencies are strongly linked to poverty and poor nutrition. The study also found troubling levels of childhood stunting in the same age cohort: 10.3 per cent across the Occupied Palestinian Territory, and 11 per cent in Gaza. Stunting among young children is a consequence of chronic malnutrition, is irreversible and has adverse lifelong effects.[83]

---

80   Rohini Haar and Jess Ghannam, "No safe space: health consequences of tear gas exposure among Palestinian refugees, January 2018", Human Rights Center, University of California Berkeley School of Law. Available at www.law.berkeley.edu/wp-content/uploads/2017/12/NoSafeSpace_full_report22Dec2017.pdf.

81   WHO, "Health conditions in the Occupied Palestinian Territory, including East Jerusalem and in the occupied Syrian Golan", document A69/INF.6. Available at http://apps.who.int/gb/ebwha/pdf_files/WHA69/A69_INF6-en.pdf.

82   State of Palestine, Ministry of Health, "National mental health strategy: Palestine, 2015–2019", June 2015. Available at www.mindbank.info/item/6103.

83   State of Palestine, Ministry of Health, UNICEF and University of Vienna, "Palestine Micronutrient Survey", 2013.

56. A more recent study, conducted in 2014 and 2015, focused on levels of malnutrition among children and their mothers in the Jordan Valley. The study found that 16 per cent of children under 5 years of age surveyed were stunted. Half of all children surveyed (49.3 per cent) were anaemic. The study also observed that 87 per cent of the land in the Jordan Valley is under full Israeli military or settler jurisdiction, and Palestinian use of those lands is prohibited; it noted that the structural barriers associated with the occupation significantly affect the overall health status of the surveyed population.[84] While those levels of childhood stunting are highly concerning and are far too prevalent, other studies have indicated that there has been a general decline in the rates of wasting, stunting and underweight.[85] A recent study on water supplies and childhood development has drawn robust links between inadequate access to quality water, poverty and physical underdevelopment among Palestinian children living in 52 communities in the Occupied Palestinian Territory.[86]

57. Recent medical literature has focused on the mental well-being of children in the Occupied Palestinian Territory. A 2007 study that examined 3,415 adolescents living in the Ramallah District of the West Bank found a strong correlation between the humiliation induced by conflict conditions and a high number of subjective health complaints.[87] Chronic exposure to humiliation (defined as the subjective experiences felt by an individual who has been unjustly treated and debased) among Palestinians in the West Bank has been linked to higher levels of insecurity and depression, feelings of diminished personal freedom, poor health, higher levels of stress and feelings of being broken or destroyed.[88] The aftermath of intense warfare fought among dense civilian neighbourhoods has resulted [p. 17] in a high rate of PTSD among children in Gaza,[89] with one study estimating that the prevalence of PTSD among

---

[84] Palestinian National Institute of Public Health, "Prevalence and detriments of malnutrition and intestinal infections among children and their mothers in the Jordan Valley", 2016. Available at http://pniph.org/site/article/16.

[85] Manenti and others, "Report of a field assessment of health conditions in the Occupied Palestinian Territory".

[86] Ghassan N. Shakhshir, "Association between water supply and early childhood development in Palestine: a descriptive analysis of demographic and health survey data", *The Lancet*, vol. 390, No. S25 (August 2017).

[87] Rita Giacaman and others, "Humiliation: the invisible trauma of war for Palestinian youth", *Public Health*, vol. 121, No. 8 (August 2007).

[88] Brian K. Barber and others, "Effect of chronic exposure to humiliation on well-being in the Occupied Palestinian Territory: an event-history analysis", *The Lancet*, vol. 382, No. S7 (December 2017).

[89] A. Thabet, Omar El-Buhaisi and Panos Vostanis, "Trauma, PTSD, anxiety and coping strategies among Palestinian adolescents exposed to war on Gaza", *The Arab Journal of Psychiatry*, vol. 25, No. 1 (2014).

children in Gaza even before the destructive wars of the past decade ranged from 23 to 70 per cent.[90] After the 2012 war in Gaza, a study found exceptionally high numbers of children (aged 11 to 17) had experienced personal trauma (88 per cent), and had witnessed trauma experienced by others (84 per cent), all of which raised the potential for depression and PTSD.[91] In a related study, Palestinian mothers in the West Bank have reported that they feel a sense of helplessness, grief and strain on their mental well-being in the face of the anxiety and stress experienced by their children in an atmosphere of political violence, economic insecurity and frequent threats to their personal safety.[92]

4   Persons with Disabilities

58. Persons with disabilities in the Occupied Palestinian Territory include those who acquired their disability at birth or in childhood, through life activities or during war and conflict. A 2011 survey estimated that approximately 7 per cent of the population in the Occupied Palestinian Territory has a disability, as measured by the international definition of impairment and disability.[93]

59. One particular feature of the challenges of living with a disability in Palestine is the plight of those amputees in Gaza who lost a limb during the 2014 war. The war resulted in approximately 100 new amputees, adding to the 300 amputees in Gaza already wounded by conflict between 2009 and June 2014, according to one study.[94] The same study observed the diminished ability of the Gaza health-care system to provide quality care for the new amputees, including: (a) the lack of surgeons to adequately conduct proper limb amputations; (b) the lack of resources to provide quality prostheses for the amputees; (c) the destruction of the Al-Wafa rehabilitation hospital by Israeli munitions during the war and the subsequent diminishment of rehabilitation services; (d) the serious shortfall in rehabilitation beds; (e) the inadequate and insecure funding for rehabilitation services; and (f) the challenges in obtaining a health exit permit from the Israeli authorities to seek rehabilitation services outside Gaza.

---

90   A. Thabet and others, "Exposure to war trauma and PTSD among parents and children in the Gaza strip", *European Child and Adolescent Psychiatry*, vol. 17, No. 4 (2008).

91   Basel El-Khodary and Muthanna Samara, "The effect of exposure to war-traumatic events, stressful life events, and other variables on mental health of Palestinian children and adolescents in the 2012 Gaza war", *The Lancet*, vol. 391, No. S6 (February 2018).

92   Cindy Sousa and Mona El-Zuhairi, "Mothering within the context of political violence: an exploratory qualitative study of mental health risks and resilience", *The Lancet*, vol. 390, No. S36 (August 2017).

93   Palestinian Central Bureau of Statistics, "Press conference report: disability survey, 2011", June 2011.

94   Physicians for Human Rights – Israel, "Amputees: the challenges faced by Gaza-strip amputees in seeking medical treatment", May 2016.

60. In addition, amputees and others who rely upon wheelchairs or crutches for mobility face the challenges of navigating the ruined and crumbling infrastructure of Gaza. Those issues are further compounded by the recent worsening of the electricity crisis. As much of Gaza is densely populated, and has buildings with multiple floors, people with disabilities often rely on the use of elevators. Since electricity operates only a few hours a day in some cases, simply leaving one's home can be nearly impossible. Electricity is similarly essential for those who depend on motorized wheelchairs. The ability to participate in public life is seriously affected for those individuals. [p. 18]

5   Palestinian Prisoners in Israeli Detention

61. As of November 2017, nearly 6,000 Palestinians were being held in Israeli prisons for security-related offences, including 425 prisoners held under administrative detention.[95] The Special Rapporteur has previously expressed concern about Israel's use of administrative detention in contravention of international legal obligations, as well as the arrest and detention of children (see A/71/554, paras. 18–24).

62. Credible reports of ill-treatment and torture of Palestinian detainees have been made in recent years, including incidents in which detainees have been subjected to sleep deprivation, stress positions and physical beatings (see A/HRC/34/38, para. 49). A 2012 health study of a small cohort of prisoners released after long-term incarceration found that all of them had developed significant physical and psychological issues arising from their imprisonment. The former prisoners described overcrowding, poor nutrition, humidity, pest infestation, the denial of family visits and a general lack of hygiene at the prisons.[96] A 2016 study, which interviewed a large cohort of released prisoners, reported that they suffered long-term effects to their mental health, with depression, anxiety and psychological distress as the most commonly reported disorders.[97]

---

95   B'Tselem, Statistics on Palestinians in the custody of the Israeli security forces. Available at www.btselem.org/statistics/detainees_and_prisoners.

96   Randa May Wahbe, "Physical and mental health of long-term Palestinian political prisoners: a qualitative study", *The Lancet*, vol. 380, No. S23 (October 2012).

97   Manenti and others, "Report of a field assessment of health conditions in the Occupied Palestinian Territory".

IV   Conclusions

63. An occupying Power has the duty, under international law, to ensure that the right to health – the enjoyment by the protected population of the highest attainable standard of physical and mental health – is fulfilled during the temporary period of occupation, consistent with its reasonable security needs. While fully respecting its legal obligation not to act covetously towards the territory and resources of the occupied territory, it would actively work to restore and enhance the health-care system for the people under its effective control. It would not obstruct access by patients and medical staff to hospitals and health clinics, either physically or bureaucratically. It would strive to create conditions of stability and security, so that the social determinants of health can advance, rather than retard, the flourishing of physical and mental wellbeing. It would promote equality of access to health care for all, with particular attention paid to the vulnerable and marginalized. The occupying Power would actively work with the health institutions of the protected population to chart a progressive health-care strategy for the future that also respected the coming restoration of full sovereignty. It would not discriminate. It would not torture or mistreat prisoners and detainees. It would not impose collective punishments of any sort. As a priority, it would provide all the necessary health services and supplies that the medical institutions of the protected population were unable to deliver themselves. Ultimately, the occupying Power would understand that leaving behind a thriving health-care system, aligned with robust social determinants, at the end of the occupation provides the best opportunity for peace and prosperity to endure.

64. Measured against those obligations, Israel has been in profound breach of the right to health with respect to the Occupied Palestinian Territory. Its avaricious occupation – measured by the expanding settlement enterprise, the annexation of territory, the confiscation of private and public lands, the pillaging of resources, the publicly stated ambitions for permanent control over all or part of the Territory and the fragmentation of the lands left for the Palestinians – has had a highly disruptive impact upon health care and the broader social determinants for health for the Palestinians. While the Palestinian Authority (which governs in parts of the West Bank) and the authority in Gaza have some agency over the state of health care in the Occupied Palestinian Territory, Israel's conduct of the occupation bears the ultimate responsibility. At the heart of this chasm between the [p. 19] right to health and the harrowing conditions on the ground is what Dr. Paul Farmer has called the "pathologies of power": the enormous gap in situations of structured inequality between those who control the power to decide and those without power

who must bear the consequences of these rapacious decisions, until some combination of a vision for justice, an organized opposition and the display of an international conscience can bring these disparate relationships to an end.[98] Palestinian, Israeli and international human rights organizations have persuasively demonstrated both the inequities in the health and social conditions in the Occupied Palestinian Territory and their substantive relationship to Israel's occupation. That leaves to the rest of us the obligation to act decisively and effectively.

V   Recommendations

65. The Special Rapporteur recommends that the Government of Israel comply with international law and bring a complete end to its 50 years of occupation of the Palestinian territories occupied since 1967. The Special Rapporteur further recommends that the Government of Israel take the following immediate measures:
(a) Comply fully with Security Council resolution 2334 (2016) concerning the settlements;
(b) Ensure that Palestinian children are treated in accordance with the standards set forth in the Convention on the Rights of the Child, in particular with respect to arrest and detention;
(c) End the blockade of Gaza, lift all restrictions on imports and exports and facilitate the rebuilding of its housing and infrastructure, with due consideration given to justifiable security considerations.
66. With respect to the right to health, the Special Rapporteur recommends that the Government of Israel immediately take the following measures:
(a) Ensure regular and reliable access, at all times, for all Palestinian patients who require specialized health care outside of their jurisdictions, consistent with genuine Israeli security concerns;
(b) End the conditions which obstruct the free passage of Palestinian ambulances to access and transport patients to health-care facilities in an expeditious fashion;
(c) Ensure the respect and protection of medical personnel and medical facilities as required by international humanitarian law;

---

98   Paul Farmer, *Pathologies of Power: Health, Human Rights, and the New War on the Poor* (University of California Press, 2004).

(d) Substantially improve prison conditions and the provision of adequate health care for Palestinian prisoners and detainees;
(e) Remove the unnecessary barriers that prevent Palestinian health-care staff from acquiring professional training and specialization elsewhere in the Occupied Palestinian Territory and abroad, and allow them to receive training at their home institutions from international health professionals;
(f) Ensure that no one is subjected to torture or degrading treatment;
(g) Take meaningful steps to improve the many social determinants that influence health outcomes in the Occupied Palestinian Territory;
(h) Comply fully with its obligations under international human rights and humanitarian law with respect to fulfilling the health needs of the protected population.

Database of All Business Enterprises Involved in the Activities Detailed in Paragraph 96 of the Report of the Independent International Fact-Finding Mission to Investigate the Implications of the Israeli Settlements on the Civil, Political, Economic, Social and Cultural Rights of the Palestinian People throughout the Occupied Palestinian Territory, including East Jerusalem, U.N. Doc. A/HRC/37/39 (Feb. 1, 2018)

United Nations
General Assembly
A/HRC/37/39
Distr.: General
1 February 2018
Original: English
Human Rights Council
Thirty-seventh session
26 February–23 March 2018
Agenda items 2 and 7
Annual report of the United Nations High Commissioner for Human Rights and reports of the Office of the High Commissioner and the Secretary-General

Human rights situation in Palestine and other occupied Arab territories

Database of all business enterprises involved in the activities detailed in paragraph 96 of the report of the independent international fact-finding mission to investigate the implications of the Israeli settlements on the civil, political, economic, social and cultural rights of the Palestinian people throughout the Occupied Palestinian Territory, including East Jerusalem

Report of the United Nations High Commissioner for Human Rights

Summary

The Office of the United Nations High Commissioner for Human Rights (OHCHR) has prepared the present report, pursuant to Human Rights Council resolution 31/36 on Israeli settlements in the Occupied Palestinian Territory, including East Jerusalem, and in the occupied Syrian Golan, on producing a database of all business enterprises involved in the activities detailed in paragraph 96 of the report of the independent international fact-finding mission to investigate the implications of the Israeli settlements on the civil, political, economic, social and cultural rights of the Palestinian people throughout the Occupied Palestinian Territory, including East Jerusalem (A/HRC/22/63) ("listed activities"). It describes the state of progress made towards the consolidation of the database, including the methodology adopted by OHCHR, recalls the normative framework used, and makes a preliminary analysis of the most common explanations given by companies for their involvement in the listed activities, and makes recommendations.

[p. 2]   I   Introduction

A   *Background*

1. The present report of the United Nations High Commissioner for Human Rights is submitted to the Human Rights Council pursuant to resolution 31/36, on Israeli settlements in the Occupied Palestinian Territory, including East Jerusalem, and in the occupied Syrian Golan, adopted by the Council on 24 March 2016. In paragraph 17 of resolution 31/36, the Council requested the United Nations High Commissioner for Human Rights to produce a database of all business enterprises engaged in certain specified activities related to the Israeli settlements in the Occupied Palestinian Territory, in consultation with the Working Group on the issue of human rights and transnational corporations and other business enterprises, and to transmit the data therein in the form of a report to the Council at its thirty-fourth session. The Council also requested that the database be updated annually.

2. On 13 February 2017, the Human Rights Council, pursuant to the recommendation of the High Commissioner, decided to defer consideration of the

report to allow for additional time to consider the inputs received in the context of an open call for submissions, and to ensure a fair process for concerned stakeholders (see A/HRC/34/77).

B *Mandate*

3. Human Rights Council resolution 31/36 establishing the database follows up the report of the independent international fact-finding mission to investigate the implications of the Israeli settlements on the civil, political, economic, social and cultural rights of the Palestinian people throughout the Occupied Palestinian Territory, including East Jerusalem (A/HRC/22/63). In its report, the fact-finding mission found that business enterprises had directly and indirectly enabled, facilitated and profited from the construction and growth of the settlements; in paragraph 96 of the report, it provided a list of activities that raised particular human rights violations concerns ("listed activities"). In resolution 31/36, the Council defined the parameters of activities to be reflected in the database by reference to the list compiled by the mission in its report, which comprised:

(a) The supply of equipment and materials facilitating the construction and the expansion of settlements and the wall, and associated infrastructures;

(b) The supply of surveillance and identification equipment for settlements, the wall and checkpoints directly linked with settlements;

(c) The supply of equipment for the demolition of housing and property, the destruction of agricultural farms, greenhouses, olive groves and crops;

(d) The supply of security services, equipment and materials to enterprises operating in settlements;

(e) The provision of services and utilities supporting the maintenance and existence of settlements, including transport;

(f) Banking and financial operations helping to develop, expand or maintain settlements and their activities, including loans for housing and the development of businesses;

(g) The use of natural resources, in particular water and land, for business purposes;

(h) Pollution, and the dumping of waste in or its transfer to Palestinian villages;

(i) Use of benefits and reinvestments of enterprises owned totally or partially by settlers for developing, expanding and maintaining the settlements;

(j) Captivity of the Palestinian financial and economic markets, as well as practices that disadvantage Palestinian enterprises, including through restrictions on movement, administrative and legal constraints. [p. 3]

4. OHCHR notes that six of the 10 listed activities – (a), (b), (d), (e), (f) and (i) – refer to activities that are explicitly linked to the settlements, while the remaining four – (c), (g), (h) and (j) – refer to activities that may not be geographically connected to settlements, but form part of the processes that "enable and support the establishment, expansion and maintenance of Israeli residential communities beyond the Green Line".[1] For example, OHCHR notes that a company that is operating a quarry on Israeli-confiscated land in the West Bank will be considered to fall under category (g) regardless of whether it is located in or connected to a defined settlement community. Its presence in the Occupied Palestinian Territory and the use of its natural resources for business purposes is sufficient to fall within the scope of the database, as required by resolution 31/36.

5. The parameters of the database encompass local and international companies, whether domiciled in Israel, the Occupied Palestinian Territory or abroad, carrying out listed activities in relation to the Occupied Palestinian Territory. Companies engaged in activities related to the occupied Syrian Golan do not fall within the mandate.[2]

6. The mandate for producing the database established by resolution 31/36 is strictly confined to the 10 activities listed in paragraph 3 above. The database does not cover all corporate activity related to settlements, nor does it extend to all corporate activity in the Occupied Palestinian Territory that may raise human rights concerns.[3] In addition, while there may be other types of entities engaged in significant corporate activity related to the settlements, only those entities established as business enterprises are considered; non-governmental organizations, charities, sports associations or federations, and other entities are therefore excluded from consideration.

C   *Methods of Work*

7. As with all other mandates, in performing the present mandate assigned to it by the Human Rights Council in resolution 31/36, OHCHR was guided by

---

[1] The fact-finding mission defined Israeli settlements as encompassing "all physical and non-physical structures and processes that constitute, enable and support the establishment, expansion and maintenance of Israeli residential communities beyond the Green Line of 1949 in the Occupied Palestinian Territory" (see A/HRC/22/63, para. 4).

[2] While resolution 31/36 refers to the occupied Syrian Golan, paragraph 17 establishing the mandate to produce a database and the report of the fact-finding mission to which it refers pertain to the Occupied Palestinian Territory only.

[3] For instance, the mandate for the database does not extend to companies involved in supplying the Israel Defense Forces with weapons or other equipment used during military operations, nor does it encompass companies involved in controlling access to and from Gaza.

the principles of independence, impartiality, objectivity, credibility and professionalism. OHCHR formulated its methodology in accordance with these principles, based on best practices, the advice and guidance of the Working Group on the issue of human rights and transnational corporations and other business enterprises, and consultations with stakeholders (see paras. 23–25 below).

8. The work conducted by OHCHR in producing the database is in full compliance with resolution 31/36 and does not purport to constitute a judicial process of any kind. OHCHR is mandated to make factual determinations of whether businesses enterprises are engaged in the listed activities.

9. It is the view of OHCHR that the work performed in consolidating and also in communicating the information in the database to the Human Rights Council can assist both Member States and business enterprises in complying with their respective legal obligations and responsibilities under international law, including through constructive engagement and dialogue and by serving as a source of information to promote transparency. [p. 4]

1 Standard of Proof

10. OHCHR has determined that where there are reasonable grounds to believe based on the totality of the information reviewed by it that a business enterprise is engaged in one or more of the listed activities, such business enterprise will be included in the database. This standard is consistent with the practice of United Nations fact-finding bodies and is lower than a criminal standard. There are "reasonable grounds to believe" that a business enterprise is engaged in one or more of the listed activities where OHCHR has reviewed a reliable body of information, consistent with other material, based on which a reasonable and ordinarily prudent person would have reason to believe that the business enterprise is involved in such activities.

11. The same standard will be used to make determinations as to whether business enterprises are no longer engaged in one or more of the listed activities; thus, if subsequently, based on the totality of information reviewed by OHCHR, there are reasonable grounds to believe that a business enterprise is no longer engaged in the listed activities, the business enterprise will be removed from the database.

2 Information-Gathering Process

(a) *Initial Steps Taken to Collect Information*

12. OHCHR examined information relevant to the mandate that was available to it, initially gathered through the following methods:

- A desk review of publicly-available information, including reports by the United Nations, civil society organizations (Israeli, Palestinian and international), media reports, academic writings
- Information received in response to notes verbales sent on 11 October 2016 to all Member States inviting them to provide inputs relevant to the implementation of resolution 31/36
- Information received in response to an open invitation to all interested persons, entities and organizations to submit relevant information and documentation

(b)   *Screening Exercise*

13. OHCHR reviewed information pertaining to 307 companies that were named in the notes verbales or in the responses received through the open call for submissions. OHCHR excluded those that met the following criteria:

(a) Business enterprises that were not, on the face of the submissions, covered by the mandate; these included companies that were alleged to have engaged in human rights abuses or supported the occupation through their corporate activity, but were not alleged to have engaged in any of the listed activities;
(b) Business enterprises about which there were insufficient facts in the submissions or in the public domain to support allegations of involvement in the listed activities;
(c) Business enterprises that were no longer engaged in the alleged activities because of corporate restructuring (for example, if a part of the business had been sold), dissolution or other corporate action;
(d) Business enterprises with a minimal or remote connection to the listed activities.

14. Of the 307 companies reviewed, 115 companies were excluded on the basis of the criteria set out in paragraph 13 above. The 192 remaining companies formed the initial group of "screened" companies that were subject to further research and consideration. The majority of these 192 companies are domiciled in Israel or the settlements, followed by the United States of America, Germany, the Netherlands and France. [p. 5]

(c)   *Further Communications*

15. OHCHR sent notes verbales on 11 July 2017 to the 21 Member States in which the initial 192 screened companies were domiciled, identifying companies domiciled in that Member State. The purpose was to inform those Member States that information had been received alleging that business enterprises

domiciled in their territories and/or under their jurisdiction were engaged in one or more listed activities, and to invite any comments or observations concerning measures taken to ensure implementation of resolution 31/36. Fifteen of the 21 Member States responded by the deadline of 1 September 2017. Five of these Member States expressed a position in the notes verbales or in confidential meetings that supported OHCHR being in direct contact with companies. Six of the 15 Member States did not comment on this point, while four Member States expressed a position in the notes verbales or in confidential meetings that did not support direct contact between OHCHR and companies.[4]

16. In reviewing past practices, consulting with the Working Group on the issue of human rights and transnational corporations and other business enterprises, after having duly considered the responses and positions of Member States, considering the complexity of business relationships involved in each situation concerning listed activities, which often encompassed business enterprises domiciled in multiple States, and to offer a procedural safeguard designed to provide fairness, consistency, reasonableness and absence of arbitrariness of potential decisions that may affect the interests of business enterprises, OHCHR decided to communicate with the initial list of all 192 screened companies – not just those domiciled in the States that indicated they were in favour of such an approach – to provide them with an opportunity to respond to the information presented.

17. Of the 192 screened companies, OHCHR first contacted the companies concerning which the strongest allegations of a clear connection to listed activities had been received. To supplement information received in notes verbales from Member States and through the open call for submissions from interested stakeholders, OHCHR conducted further research into this subset of companies. This stage of the research included analysing public annual financial reports, official websites from companies in English and Hebrew, financial websites and media in English and Hebrew, the Israeli and other stock exchange markets, the websites of Israeli government offices[5] and websites of settlement industrial zones and settlement councils.

---

4   Notably, one Member State acknowledged awareness of the alleged activity of a company domiciled in its territory, and informed OHCHR that the Government had decided in August 2017 to conduct a baseline study to assess the degree of implementation of the Guiding Principles on Business and Human Rights in domestic legislation. OHCHR looks forward to the results of that study.

5   These included the Israeli Companies Registrar (http://havarot.justice.gov.il), the Bank of Israel (www.boi.org.il/heb/Pages/HomePage.aspx), the Knesset Research and Information Centre (www.knesset.gov.il/mmm/heb/index.asp), the Ministry of Environmental Protection

18. When contacting companies, OHCHR included in the communications, wherever possible, all relevant entities with respect to that particular situation of concern, including parent companies and their subsidiaries, franchisors and franchisees, local distributors of international companies, partners and other entities in relevant business relationships. In some of these cases, further research by OHCHR revealed relevant business entities, such as parent companies or subsidiaries, that were not initially named in the submissions received in notes verbales from Member States or through the open call for submissions from interested stakeholders. This necessitated adding 14 companies to the initial list of 192 screened companies, resulting in a total of 206 companies reviewed at the time of writing (see table below paragraph 22).

19. OHCHR was given limited resources to carry out the mandate within the anticipated time frame, which required it to calibrate its research and engagement with companies accordingly. Not all companies about which OHCHR had received information could be contacted by the time of submission of the present report. At the time of writing, OHCHR [p. 6] had contacted 64 of the 206 companies involved in 33 different situations concerning the listed activities.[6]

20. In the letters addressed to the companies concerned, OHCHR informed them of the listed activities that they appeared to be engaged in (based on the totality of information reviewed by OHCHR), and set out the basic facts of the companies' involvement in the listed activity or activities. Companies were requested to respond in writing within 60 days for an initial response, providing any clarification or update of the information. Companies were informed that they could request that the substance of their written responses be kept confidential; a number of companies made such a request.

21. OHCHR was also contacted by a number of companies that had not received letters from the Office, but had either seen news of the database in the media or had been informed by their governmental authorities of their inclusion in the notes verbales addressed to Member States on 11 July 2017.

22. Responses from companies included those that (a) objected to the mandate of OHCHR and declined to provide a substantive response to the information presented; (b) rejected the information presented and objected to being included in the database; (c) confirmed the information presented concerning

---

(www.sviva.gov.il) and the Ministry of National Infrastructures, Energy and Water Resources (http://energy.gov.il/).

6 Not all parent companies or other ownership structures were contacted. For instance, if a company was acquired by a hedge fund or private investment firm, these were not included for reasons of practicality, given the lack of publicly available information concerning their portfolios.

their involvement in one or more of the listed activities, and provided explanations; (d) provided updated information that indicated they were no longer engaged in one or more of the listed activities; and (e) provided additional information and clarifications that will require further discussion and analysis before a determination can be made. OHCHR is considering the responses received to date, and offers preliminary observations to the most common explanations put forth by companies for their involvement in the listed activities (see paras. 50–60 below). Where companies declined to provide a substantive response or failed to respond entirely, this will not prevent a determination as to their involvement in listed activities from being made. [p. 7]

Summary of screening exercise and communication with companies at the time of submission[a]

State concerned	*Screening exercise*				*Communication with companies*		
	Total number of companies reviewed	Number of companies screened from initial list	Number of companies excluded	Number of additional companies screened	Total number of screened companies[b]	Number of companies contacted to date	Number of companies not yet contacted
Israel or Israeli settlements	186	131	43	12	143	45	98
United States of America	54	20	32	2	22	7	15
Germany	21	7	14	–	7	1	6
Netherlands	7	5	2	–	5	3	2
France	8	4	4	–	4	2	2
Republic of Korea	3	3	0	–	3	1	2
Italy	3	3	0	–	3	0	3
United Kingdom of Great Britain and Northern Ireland	6	3	3	–	3	1	2
Canada	2	2	0	–	2	0	2
Japan	3	2	1	–	2	1	1
Switzerland	12	2	10	–	2	0	2
Ireland	2	1	1	–	1	0	1
Mexico	1	1	0	–	1	1	0
Denmark	1	1	0	–	1	0	1
Russian Federation	1	1	0	–	1	0	1
Singapore	1	1	0	–	1	0	1
Turkey	1	1	0	–	1	0	1

Summary of screening exercise and communication (*cont.*)

State concerned	Screening exercise					Communication with companies		
	Total number of companies reviewed	Number of companies screened from initial list	Number of companies excluded	Number of additional companies screened	Total number of screened companies[b]	Number of companies contacted to date	Number of companies not yet contacted
Sweden	2	1	1	–	1	1	0
Spain	2	1	1	–	1	0	1
Belgium	1	1	0	–	1	1	0
South Africa	1	1	0	–	1	0	1
Others	3	0	3	–	0	0	0
Total	321	192	115	14	206	64	142

a   Does not include companies that contacted OHCHR proactively (see para. 21 above).
b   Reflects the number of companies screened from the initial list plus the number of additional companies screened after further research (see para. 18 above).

(d)   *Consultations*

23. Throughout the process, as mandated by Human Rights Council resolution 31/36 and in preparation for the report, OHCHR carried out five in-person consultations with the Working Group on the issue of human rights and transnational corporations and other business enterprises and exchanged additional written correspondence. The feedback, guidance and advice from the Working Group were critical to the development of the methodology used to implement the mandate. [p. 8]

24. In addition, OHCHR held extensive discussions with Member States and was in regular contact with Israeli, Palestinian and international civil society, think tanks, academics, employer organizations, and other interested parties.

25. A number of Member States, civil society organizations and other entities have repeatedly voiced strong opposition, both publicly and privately, against Council resolution 31/36 mandating the High Commissioner to produce a database. Other Member States have expressed support, along with Israeli, Palestinian and international civil society, academics and think tanks. This includes a petition signed by over 400 members of Israeli civil society, including a former attorney general and former members of the Knesset, retired

diplomats, and other prominent individuals;[7] a joint statement by 56 non-governmental organizations;[8] and a letter signed by almost 60 Member States addressed to the High Commissioner.[9]

(e)   *Next Steps*

26. More resources are required for OHCHR to continue its dialogue with and issue communications to relevant business enterprises, adding information to the database and updating existing information in the database as required by resolution 31/36. Once OHCHR has been in contact with all 206 companies, and subject to determinations of their responses and non-responses, OHCHR expects to provide the names of the companies engaged in listed activities in a future update. Before the determinations on the companies are made public, OHCHR will notify the companies concerned.

II   Normative Framework

A   *The Obligations of Israel as the Occupying Power*

27. As stated above, the creation of the database is not a judicial process. In this respect, the work of OHCHR is guided by Council resolution 31/36, in which paragraph 17 sets out the tasks given to OHCHR. The preamble to resolution 31/36 reflects the normative framework with regard to Israel as the occupying Power.[10]

---

7   See "Hundreds of Israelis urge publication of UN settlement database", Middle East Monitor, 4 December 2017.

8   "Joint NGO Statement in Support of the UN Human Rights Database on Business Activities related to Settlements in the Occupied Palestinian Territory", Worldwide Movement for Human Rights, 30 November 2017.

9   On file with OHCHR.

10 In the preamble to resolution 31/36, the Human Rights Council recalls, inter alia, relevant reports of the Secretary-General, OHCHR and the fact-finding mission; relevant resolutions of the Commission on Human Rights, the General Assembly, the Human Rights Council and the Security Council reaffirming, inter alia, the illegality of the Israeli settlements in the occupied territories, including in East Jerusalem; the advisory opinion on the legal consequences of the construction of a wall in the Occupied Palestinian Territory rendered on 9 July 2004 by the International Court of Justice, which concluded that the Israeli settlements in the Occupied Palestinian Territory, including East Jerusalem, had been established in breach of international law; the treaty bodies monitoring compliance with the human rights treaties to which Israel is a party; relevant provisions of the Fourth Geneva Convention and customary law; and the Guiding Principles on Business and Human Rights.

28. Since the adoption by the Human Rights Council of resolution 31/36, the Security Council, on 23 December 2016, in its resolution 2334 (2016), reaffirmed its position that the establishment by Israel of settlements in the Occupied Palestinian Territory, including East Jerusalem, had no legal validity, and constituted a flagrant violation under international law. As recognized in numerous reports of the High Commissioner and the Secretary-General, continued expansion of settlements not only undermines the possibility of a two-State solution, but is also at the core of many human rights violations in the West Bank (see for example A/HRC/28/80, A/HRC/31/42, A/HRC/31/43 and A/HRC/34/39).

Human rights situation

29. The extensive human rights impact of settlements on the human rights of Palestinians has been well documented in successive reports of the High Commissioner, the [p. 9] Secretary-General and the fact-finding mission (see for example A/HRC/22/63, A/HRC/25/38, A/HRC/28/44, A/HRC/31/42 and A/HRC/34/39). The reports detailed how the settlements are extensively altering the demographic composition of the Occupied Palestinian Territory and fundamentally threatening the Palestinians' right to self-determination. The violations of human rights associated with the settlements are pervasive and devastating, reaching every facet of Palestinian life. Owing to settlement development and infrastructure, Palestinians suffer from restrictions on freedom of religion, movement and education; their rights to land and water; access to livelihoods and their right to an adequate standard of living; their rights to family life; and many other fundamental human rights.

B   *Obligations of States for Business and Human Rights in the Occupied Palestinian Territory*

30. The Guiding Principles on Business and Human Rights (A/HRC/17/31), which were unanimously endorsed by all States Members of the Human Rights Council in its resolution 17/4, set out the international human rights law obligations of States concerning business enterprises. They do not create new legal obligations, but rather clarify the implications of relevant existing international human rights standards, and provide practical guidance on how they can be operationalized.[11] These include the State duty to protect against human rights abuses by third parties, which includes business enterprises. States may be held responsible for abuse by business enterprises where the conduct can

---

11   See *Frequently Asked Questions about the Guiding Principles on Business and Human Rights* (OHCHR, New York and Geneva, 2014), p. 8.

be attributed to them (for example, in the case of a State-owned enterprise) or where States fail to take appropriate steps to prevent, investigate, punish and redress abuse.[12]

31. The Guiding Principles specifically address the issue of business operations in conflict-affected areas, which includes situations of occupation. In conflict-affected areas, the Guiding Principles recognize that the "host State"[13] may not be able to adequately protect human rights because of a lack of effective control or involvement in abuses itself.[14] In these situations, the Working Group on the issue of human rights and transnational corporations and other business enterprises acknowledges that "home States"[15] of transnational corporations have a crucial role to play. In the context of the Israeli settlements, Israel as the occupying Power is considered to have obligations equivalent to those of a "host State".[16] Given the direct involvement of Israel in establishing, maintaining and expanding the settlements, OHCHR considers that the role of homes States of transnational corporations is essential in assisting both corporations and Israel to ensure that businesses are not involved in human rights abuses.[17]

32. States' obligations specifically concerning business operations connected to Israeli settlements have been the subject of a number of United Nations reports and resolutions (for example, A/HRC/22/63, para. 117 and A/HRC/34/39, paras. 34–39, and Human Rights Council resolutions 28/26 and 34/31, para. 13 (*b*)). In its resolution 2334 (2016), the Security Council called upon all States to distinguish between the territory of Israel and the [p. 10] territories occupied since 1967. With regard to the role of home States, the fact-finding mission called upon all Member States to take appropriate measures to ensure that business enterprises domiciled in their territory and/or under their

---

12 Guiding Principle 1.
13 A "host State" is defined as the country in which a business operates. See *Frequently Asked Questions about the Guiding Principles* (see footnote 11), p. 23.
14 See Working Group on the issue of human rights and transnational corporations and other business enterprises, statement on the implications of the Guiding Principles on Business and Human Rights in the context of Israeli settlements in the Occupied Palestinian Territory, 6 June 2014, p. 3.
15 A "home State" is defined as a State where a company is incorporated or has its headquarters or primary seat. See *Frequently Asked Questions about the Guiding Principles* (see footnote 11), p. 23.
16 The Working Group recognized that the term "host State" is ambiguous in situations of occupation, and that it would be more accurate to refer to the State that exercises effective control over an occupied territory as having obligations equivalent to those of a "host State". See statement of the Working Group (see footnote 14), pp. 6–8.
17 In accordance with the statement of the Working Group, ibid., pp. 3–4 and 7.

jurisdiction, including those owned or controlled by them, that conduct activities in or related to the settlements respect human rights throughout their operations (A/HRC/22/63, para. 117).

33. Some States have taken steps towards fulfilling their obligations towards businesses operating in settlements. In November 2015, the European Union issued guidelines on the labelling of products made in Israeli settlements.[18] As at December 2017, 18 States members of the European Union had issued advisories warning businesses of the financial, legal and reputational risks incurred by becoming involved in settlement activities.[19]

34. Some States have argued that they do not have an obligation to regulate extraterritorial activities of businesses domiciled in their territory and/or jurisdiction. While States are not generally required under international human rights law to do so, according to the Guiding Principles on Business and Human Rights, there are "strong policy reasons" for homes States to clearly set out expectations that businesses respect human rights abroad. States also have additional obligations as economic actors in their own right when it comes to State-owned enterprises. In its report submitted to the Council at its thirty-second session, the Working Group on the issue of human rights and transnational corporations and other business enterprises stated that there were compelling reasons for "greater action on the part of States with regard to State-owned enterprises" so that they lead by example (A/HRC/32/45).

C   *Responsibilities of Businesses*

35. While States remain the primary duty bearers for the protection and promotion of human rights, international law has increasingly evolved to recognize that non-State actors – including business enterprises – also have responsibilities. The Guiding Principles on Business and Human Rights set out a "protect, respect and remedy" framework for business and human rights, which recognizes that while States have a duty to protect the rights of all against violations by third parties, there is an independent and complementary corporate responsibility to respect all internationally recognized human rights standards. In addition to human rights, humanitarian law standards also apply to business enterprises in situations of armed conflict.[20]

---

18   European Commission, Interpretative Notice on indication of origin of goods from the territories occupied by Israel since June 1967 (11 November 2015).

19   For excerpts of each State's advisory, see www.ecfr.eu/article/eu_member_state_business_advisories_on_israel_settlements.

20   International Committee of the Red Cross, *Business and International Humanitarian Law: an Introduction to the Rights and Obligations of Business Enterprises under International Humanitarian Law*, ICRC, Geneva, 2006).

36. Under the Guiding Principles, all companies, regardless of size, industry, location, ownership or legal structure, have a responsibility to conduct due diligence to identify, prevent, mitigate and account for how they address their adverse human rights impacts (principle 14). In its statement on the implications of the Guiding Principles in the context of Israeli settlements in the Occupied Palestinian Territory of 6 June 2014, the Working Group declared that businesses have a responsibility:

(a) To avoid causing or contributing to adverse human rights impacts through their own activities, and address such impacts when they occur;

(b) To seek to prevent or mitigate adverse human rights impacts that are directly linked to their operations, products or services by their business relationships, even if they have not contributed to those impacts.

37. The Guiding Principles recognize that businesses operating in conflict-affected areas – which include areas under occupation – face heightened risks of involvement in human rights abuses, including gross human rights abuses committed by other actors (Principle 7). [p. 11] In such situations, the Working Group clarified in the above-mentioned statement that where businesses have an increased risk, "enhanced" due diligence (namely, the "heightened care" with which due diligence processes should be executed) is required. The Working Group also highlighted a number of actions that enhanced due diligence may require, including formally integrating human rights principles into relevant contracts; exercising extreme caution in all business activities and relationships involving the acquisition of assets in conflict zones; and seeking advice from international organizations and mechanisms.

38. As part of the due diligence process, particularly in relation to a complex operating environment like the Occupied Palestinian Territory, businesses enterprises may need to consider whether it is possible to engage in such an environment in a manner that respects human rights. To do so, businesses would have to be able to show that they (in the words of the Working Group in its statement) do not "support the continuation of an international illegality nor are complicit in human rights abuses", and that they can effectively prevent or mitigate the risks to the human rights of Palestinians. This includes ensuring that businesses are not acquiring resources and property without the "freely given consent of the owner".[21]

39. In its report, the fact-finding mission emphasized that companies must assess the human rights impact of their activities and take all necessary steps – including by terminating their business interests in the settlements – to ensure that they do not have an adverse impact on the human rights of the Palestinian

---

21 Ibid., p. 22.

people, in conformity with international law and the Guiding Principles (A/HRC/22/63, para. 117).[22]

40. The scale, scope and immitigability of the human rights impacts caused by settlements must be taken into consideration as part of businesses' enhanced due diligence exercises.[23] The Guiding Principles do not explicitly require companies to terminate operations where they are involved in human rights abuses; they do stipulate, however, that such companies should be prepared to "accept any consequences – reputational, financial or legal – of the continuing connection."[24]

41. OHCHR notes that, considering the weight of the international legal consensus concerning the illegal nature of the settlements themselves, and the systemic and pervasive nature of the negative human rights impact caused by them, it is difficult to imagine a scenario in which a company could engage in listed activities in a way that is consistent with the Guiding Principles and international law. This view was reinforced in Human Rights Council resolution 34/31 on the Israeli settlements, in which the Council referred to the immitigable nature of the adverse impact of businesses' activities on human rights.

III   Involvement of Business in Settlements

A   *Overview*

42. Businesses play a central role in furthering the establishment, maintenance and expansion of Israeli settlements. They are involved in constructing and financing settlement homes and supporting infrastructure, providing services to the settlements, and operating out of them. In doing so, they are contributing to Israel's confiscation of land, facilitate the transfer of its population into the Occupied Palestinian Territory, and are involved in the exploitation of Palestine's natural resources (see A/HRC/34/39, para. 11). [p. 12]

B   *How Israeli Authorities Encourage Settlement Businesses*

43. The Government of Israel actively encourages economic development of and for the settlements through the Israeli and international private sector by creating an attractive financial business market, by providing key financial

---

22 See also the statement of the Working Group (see footnote 14) and Guiding Principles 17 to 19.
23 The commentary to Guiding Principle 14 provides that the severity of impact is judged by its scale, scope and irremediable character. See also Guiding Principle 17 on human rights due diligence.
24 Commentary to Guiding Principle 19.

incentives to companies to operate in the settlements. Ninety settlements have been designated as "national priority areas", which allows businesses operating within them to benefit from reductions in the price of land, grants for the development of infrastructure, and preferential tax treatment (A/HRC/34/39, para. 24). Businesses in settlements can also take advantage of functional immunity from labour law with respect to the treatment of Palestinian workers.[25] According to the fact-finding mission, business owners are able to cut their costs by paying lower rates to Palestinian workers than their Israeli counterparts, with substandard work conditions. This is largely due to a lack of supervision or regulation of employers in the settlements by Israeli officials (A/HRC/22/63, paras. 94–95).

44. Furthermore, Israeli authorities use their permit and licensing regime to encourage international and Israeli business engagement with the settlements. Permits and licenses are readily provided to businesses operating in or servicing settlements, but are rarely granted to companies engaged in providing similar services to Palestinians.[26] Israeli and international companies are regularly given quarrying licenses in Israeli-controlled territory in the West Bank, whereas, according to the Palestinian Union of Stone and Marble, no new permits have been issued to Palestinian businesses to open quarries in Area C[27] since 1994.[28]

45. Domestic laws and regulations in Israel also play a role in inducing businesses to serve individuals in the settlements. The Consumer Protection Law (1981) was amended in 2017 in response to alleged discrimination against consumers living in settlements. The revised law makes it mandatory for businesses to state clearly before any transaction is finalized whether they are not willing or able to provide services to settlements. The Prohibition of Discrimination in Products, Services and Entry into Places of Entertainment and Public Places Law (2000), was amended at the same time to include customers' "place of residence" to the list of prohibited grounds for discrimination. It applies to any business that provides public services, even if it is privately owned, such as

---

25 Human Rights Watch, "Occupation, Inc.: How Settlement Businesses Contribute to Israel's Violations of Palestinian Rights", 19 January 2016.
26 Ibid.
27 Under the Israeli-Palestinian Interim Agreement on the West Bank and the Gaza Strip (Oslo II) of 1995, the West Bank, excluding East Jerusalem, was divided into three temporary administrative zones, referred to as Areas A, B and C. Israel retains almost exclusive control over Area C, including control over law enforcement, building and planning (see www.ochaopt.org/location/area-c).
28 World Bank, "West Bank and Gaza: Area C and the Future of the Palestinian Economy", Washington, D.C., 2013, para. 30.

transportation services, communications services, entertainment, tourism or financial services intended for public use.[29] While these laws do not compel businesses to provide services to individuals in the settlements, they make it more difficult not to do so.

C   *How Businesses Contribute to and Benefit from the Establishment, Maintenance and Growth of Settlements*

46. OHCHR notes that businesses play a key role in facilitating the overall settlement enterprise, contributing to Israel's confiscation of land and the transfer of its population through commercial development. Some are directly involved in the confiscation of land by carrying out demolitions that make way for settlement residential communities or associated infrastructure, or by financing or executing settlement construction itself. Others provide services that ensure the sustainability of residential settlement communities, such [p. 13] as transport services that connect the settlements to Israel proper, tourism activities that contribute to the profitability of the settlements, and telecommunication services. Those that are located in the settlements help to perpetuate their existence through the payment of taxes to settlement regional councils and Israeli authorities and the provision of jobs to settlers, and by occupying confiscated land.

47. The involvement of businesses in the settlements extends across all main industries and sectors, including:
– The banking industry, which helps to finance construction and infrastructure projects in settlements, provide loans and financial services to settlement councils, and provide mortgage loans to home buyers[30]
– The tourism industry, including tour companies, online accommodation and travel booking sites, and rental car companies, all of which help to make the settlements profitable and sustainable[31]

---

29   According to articles 1 to 3 of the Prohibition of Discrimination in Products, Services and Entry into Places of Entertainment and Public Places Law (2000), "financial services" include banking services and the provision of credit and insurance.

30   See Who Profits, "Financing Land Grab: The Direct Involvement of Israeli Banks in the Israeli Settlement Enterprise", February 2017, and A/HRC/22/63, para. 97. Owing to the involvement of the banking industry in servicing and supporting the settlements, a number of pension funds in different countries have reportedly withdrawn their investments in Israeli banks; see for example PGGM, "Statement regarding exclusion of Israeli banks", 8 January 2014; Linda Bloom, "Israeli banks on ineligible list for pension agency", United Methodist Church, 13 January 2016; and Middle East Monitor, "Danish pension fund excludes four companies for role in Israeli occupation", 11 October 2017.

31   Who Profits, "Touring Israeli settlements: business and pleasure for the economy of occupation", flash report, September 2017.

- The private security industry, which includes companies involved in providing security for companies or residences in settlements, as well as those involved in the checkpoints throughout the West Bank, including East Jerusalem[32]
- The technology industry, which provides surveillance and identification equipment for use in the settlements, the wall and checkpoints
- The construction and demolition industries, including heavy machinery suppliers, which help to facilitate and entrench Israel's confiscation of Palestinian land for settlements and associated infrastructure[33]
- The real estate industry, including companies involved in marketing, renting and selling properties in settlements, which helps settlements to function as viable housing markets, enabling the transfer of Israel's population[34]
- The extractive industry, including mining and quarrying, which contribute financially to the sustainability of settlements through the payment of fees to settlement municipalities and the Israeli Civil Administration[35]
- The telecommunications industry, which includes mobile networks and Internet providers servicing settlements
- The agricultural industry, which includes companies involved in crop and livestock production, the wine industry and export companies
- The transportation industry
- The manufacturing industry, which includes companies that use raw materials from occupied territory
- Others [p. 14]

48. In addition to the financial benefits provided by the Israeli authorities for operating in the settlements, businesses engaged in certain sectors are able to take advantage of captive Palestinian markets for Israeli goods. According to the United Nations Conference on Trade and Development (UNCTAD), the Occupied Palestinian Territory operates as a captive market for Israeli exports due to the imbalanced customs arrangements enshrined in the Paris Protocol on Economic Relations and restrictions on movement and other obstacles to trade.[36] With regard to the economic consequences of situations of occupation, UNCTAD had noted that they always involved the exploitation, impoverishment, marginalization, displacement and appropriation of resources of

---

32   Who Profits, *Private Security Companies and the Israeli Occupation*, Tel Aviv, January 2016.
33   Who Profits, Facts on the Ground: Heavy Engineering Machinery and the Israeli Occupation, Tel Aviv, July 2014.
34   Human Rights Watch, "Occupation, Inc." (see footnote 27).
35   Ibid.
36   Report on UNCTAD assistance to the Palestinian people: Developments in the economy of the Occupied Palestinian Territory (UNCTAD/APP/2016/1), para. 20.

the occupied indigenous people. Such acts often deprived the people under colonial rule of the internationally recognized human right to development by confiscating their national resources, preventing them from accessing and utilizing those resources, depriving them of the ability to produce and thus forcing them to consume products produced by the occupier.[37]

49. An example of how Israeli companies are benefiting from a captive Palestinian market can be seen, for example, in the telecommunications industry. Palestinian mobile and landline companies are prevented from operating fully and effectively in the West Bank, including East Jerusalem, owing to restrictions on the import of necessary equipment, which is often identified by Israeli authorities as "dual use"; restrictions on the movement of goods and people; the inability to have independent access to international networks; restrictions on the building of the necessary infrastructure in Area C following the rejection of permit requests; and the provision of limited frequencies by the Israeli authorities.[38] Palestinian mobile providers are reportedly prohibited from operating inside Israel and annexed areas, including East Jerusalem, which forces users to rely on Israeli mobile providers.[39] Israeli telecommunications operators are authorized under the Oslo Agreement to provide services to settlements and settlement roads, but their infrastructure now covers large areas of the West Bank. According to World Bank estimates, between 10 and 20 per cent of the mobile market share in the West Bank has been captured by unauthorized Israeli operators, largely due to the fact that Palestinian companies do not have access to more than 60 per cent of Area C. In 2014, the Office of the Quartet Representative estimated that the quota captured by Israeli operators was even higher, between 20 and 40 per cent of total market share.[40]

IV Preliminary Observations of Responses of Business Enterprises

50. In communicating with companies and reviewing publicly available information, OHCHR encountered a number of companies that acknowledged

---

37 *Official Records of the General Assembly, Seventieth Session, Supplement No. 35* (A/70/35), annex, para. 6.

38 World Bank Group, *The Telecommunication Sector in the Palestinian Territories: A Missed Opportunity for Economic Development* (World Bank, Washington, D.C., 2016); see also World Bank, West Bank and Gaza: Area C and the Future of the Palestinian Economy, Washington, D.C., 2014, paras. 52–62.

39 "Israeli mobile companies banned from PA cities", Ma'an News Agency, 1 April 2010.

40 Office of the Quartet Representative, Initiative for the Palestinian Economy: Summary Overview, March 2014 (available at www.quartetrep.org/files/image/initiative.pdf).

some connection to the settlements and provided explanations of their involvement on a number of grounds. A summary of the most common explanations are set out below. OHCHR offers the following observations in response in the interest of continuing the dialogue with companies.

51. A major argument used by companies to explain their involvement in listed activities is that they provide jobs to Palestinian families and help to support the Palestinian economy.

52. OHCHR observes that this argument does not recognize that the presence of the settlements in the Occupied Palestinian Territory, which is unlawful, serves to depress the [p. 15] Palestinian economy and to reduce opportunities for Palestinian businesses to thrive. As pointed out by the fact-finding mission, the agricultural sector, which lies at the heart of the Palestinian economy, has been in a continuous decline since 1967 owing to the dispossession of land and the denial of access of Palestinian farmers to agricultural areas, water resources and trade markets (A/HRC/22/63, para. 89). According to the Office for the Coordination of Humanitarian Affairs, 70 per cent of Area C is "off limits for Palestinian use and development", as it falls within the boundaries of regional settlement councils. Palestinian construction is heavily restricted in 29 per cent of Area C, and only the remaining 1 per cent has been planned for Palestinian development.[41] The World Bank has acknowledged that the land allocated for settlement activity in Area C has "significantly reduced land available for use by the Palestinian private sector".[42] In East Jerusalem the situation is similar, as 35 per cent of land has been allocated to settlements and only 13 per cent is zoned for Palestinian construction.[43]

53. The depressed Palestinian economy has had a direct effect on the job market in the Occupied Palestinian Territory. According to UNCTAD, Israel's full control over Area C, which accounts for over 60 per cent of the area of the West Bank, has contributed to a "permanent unemployment crisis" in the Occupied Palestinian Territory that forces thousands of unemployed Palestinians to seek employment in Israel and in settlements in low-skill, low-wage manual activities (TD/B/63/3, para. 6). In 2017, the International Labour

---

41   Office for the Coordination of Humanitarian Affairs, Area C of the West Bank: Key Humanitarian Concerns, update August 2014.
42   World Bank Group, *Prospects for Growth and Jobs in the Palestinian Economy: A General Equilibrium Analysis*, November 2017.
43   Office for the Coordination of Humanitarian Affairs, East Jerusalem: Key Humanitarian Concerns, update August 2014.

Organization reported that the "stagnating labour market in the West Bank pushes Palestinians to take up work wherever it is to be found."[44]

54. OHCHR notes that the employment of Palestinians, even on favourable terms, does not exempt businesses of their responsibilities under the Guiding Principles concerning their overall engagement in or with the settlements. The Guiding Principles make clear that, while business enterprises may undertake certain commitments or activities to support and promote human rights, these "do not offset a failure to respect human rights throughout their operations."[45]

55. Another argument used by some business enterprises to explain their involvement in listed activities was that they did not take a political position in the conflict between Israel and the Occupied Palestinian Territory, nor did they actively support Israel's occupation of Palestine. OHCHR recalls, however, that the political position of business enterprises is not a relevant consideration in determining whether their actions are consistent with the Guiding Principles or whether their business activities fall within the ambit of Human Rights Council resolution 31/36.

56. Some companies that acknowledged operating in or with the settlements highlighted the fact that they were acting in compliance with Israeli national laws and in accordance with all required permits and authorizations.

57. According to the commentary to Guiding Principle 11, the corporate responsibility to respect human rights "exists over and above compliance with national laws and regulations protecting human rights".[46] Compliance with the national laws and regulations of a State does not necessarily equate to compliance with the Guiding Principles or international law. In the case of Israel, its national laws and regulations that allow for the establishment, maintenance and existence of the settlements are in direct conflict with [p. 16] international law, as settlements are widely recognized by the United Nations and the international community as being illegal.

58. Some companies indicated that they had no knowledge or control over the actions of other entities with which they had business relationships, such as distributors, partners or other entities in their value chains, and therefore they should not be held responsible for any harm caused by those entities.

59. According to the Guiding Principles, the responsibility of businesses to respect human rights extends to their business relationships. Guiding

---

44 International Labour Office, The situation of workers of the occupied Arab territories, report of the Director-General, International Labour Conference, 106th session, 2017, para. 21.

45 Commentary to Guiding Principle 11.

46 See also Working Group on the issue of human rights and transnational corporations and other business enterprises, statement (see footnote 14), pp. 11–12.

Principle 13 states that businesses are responsible for preventing or mitigating adverse human rights impacts directly linked to their operations, products or services through their business relationships, even if they have not contributed to them; this includes impacts caused by both actions and omissions.[47] The responsibility to conduct due diligence – and in the occupied territory this involves enhanced due diligence (see para. 37 above) – entails taking active steps to identify and assess any actual or potential adverse human rights impacts made as a result of business relationships.

60. Furthermore, in its report, the fact-finding mission stated that business enterprises conduct their activities in the settlements with "the full knowledge of the current situation and the related liability risks" and "contribute to their maintenance, development and consolidation" (A/HRC/22/63, para. 97).

V   Recommendations

61. The United Nations High Commissioner for Human Rights urges all businesses with which OHCHR has been or may be in contact in carrying out its mandate under Human Rights Council resolution 31/36 to cooperate with OHCHR with a view to engaging in constructive dialogue.

62. The High Commissioner acknowledges with appreciation the extension granted by the Human Rights Council for OHCHR to implement the mandate under resolution 31/36. Recognizing that this was the first time OHCHR has been tasked with such a mandate, the High Commissioner is satisfied that significant progress has been made. However, while the dialogue with concerned business enterprises is continuing, the work remains ongoing. For the High Commissioner to update the database as required by resolution 31/36, more resources are required.

---

47   Commentary to Guiding Principle 13.

SECTION C

International Criminal Court

Office of the Prosecutor, Report on Preliminary Examinations 2018 (Dec. 5, 2018) [Excerpts]

[p. 5]

III   Introduction

1. The Office of the Prosecutor ("Office" or "OTP") of the International Criminal Court ("Court" or "ICC") is responsible for determining whether a situation meets the legal criteria established by the Rome Statute ("Statute") to warrant investigation by the Office. For this purpose, the OTP conducts a preliminary examination of all communications and situations that come to its attention based on the statutory criteria and the information available.[1]

2. The preliminary examination of a situation by the Office may be initiated on the basis of: (i) information sent by individuals or groups, States, intergovernmental or non-governmental organisations; (ii) a referral from a State Party or the United Nations ("UN") Security Council; or (iii) a declaration lodged by a State accepting the exercise of jurisdiction by the Court pursuant to article 12(3) of the Statute.

3. Once a situation is thus identified, the factors set out in article 53(1)(a)–(c) of the Statute establish the legal framework for a preliminary examination.[2] This article provides that, in order to determine whether there is a reasonable basis to proceed with an investigation into the situation, the Prosecutor shall consider: jurisdiction (temporal, either territorial or personal, and material); admissibility (complementarity and gravity); and the interests of justice.

4. *Jurisdiction* relates to whether a crime within the jurisdiction of the Court has been or is being committed. It requires an assessment of (i) temporal jurisdiction (date of entry into force of the Statute, namely 1 July 2002 onwards, date of entry into force for an acceding State, date specified in a UN Security Council referral, or in a declaration lodged pursuant to

---

[1]   See ICC-OTP, Policy Paper on Preliminary Examinations, November 2013.
[2]   See also rule 48, ICC Rules of Procedure and Evidence.

article 12(3)); (ii) either territorial or personal jurisdiction, which entails that the crime has been or is being committed on the territory or by a national of a State Party or a State not Party that has lodged a declaration accepting the jurisdiction of the Court, or arises from a situation referred by the UN Security Council; and (iii) subject-matter jurisdiction as defined in article 5 of the Statute (genocide; crimes against humanity; war crimes, and aggression).

5. *Admissibility* comprises both complementarity and gravity.
6. *Complementarity* involves an examination of the existence of relevant national proceedings in relation to the potential cases being considered for investigation by the Office. This will be done bearing in mind the Office's prosecutorial strategy of investigating and prosecuting those most responsible for the most [p. 6] serious crimes.[3] Where relevant domestic investigations or prosecutions exist, the Office will assess their genuineness.
7. *Gravity* includes an assessment of the scale, nature, manner of commission of the crimes, and their impact, bearing in mind the potential cases that would likely arise from an investigation of the situation.
8. The *"interests of justice"* is a countervailing consideration. The Office must assess whether, taking into account the gravity of the crime and the interests of victims, there are nonetheless substantial reasons to believe that an investigation would not serve the interests of justice.
9. There are no other statutory criteria. Factors such as geographical or regional balance are not relevant criteria for a determination that a situation warrants investigation under the Statute. As long as universal ratification is not yet a reality, crimes in some situations may fall outside the territorial and personal jurisdiction of the ICC. This can be remedied only by the relevant State becoming a Party to the Statute or lodging a declaration accepting the exercise of jurisdiction by the Court or through a referral by the UN Security Council.
10. As required by the Statute, the Office's preliminary examination activities are conducted in the same manner irrespective of whether the Office receives a referral from a State Party or the UN Security Council, or acts on the basis of information on crimes obtained pursuant to article 15. In

---

3 See OTP Strategic Plan – 2016–2018, paras. 35–36. In appropriate cases the OTP will expand its general prosecutorial strategy to encompass mid- or high-level perpetrators, or even particularly notorious low- level perpetrators, with a view to building cases up to reach those most responsible for the most serious crimes. The Office may also consider prosecuting lower-level perpetrators where their conduct was particularly grave and has acquired extensive notoriety.

all circumstances, the Office analyses the seriousness of the information received and may seek additional information from States, organs of the UN, intergovernmental and non-governmental organisations and other reliable sources that are deemed appropriate. The Office may also receive oral testimony at the seat of the Court. All information gathered is subjected to a fully independent, impartial and thorough analysis.

11. It should be recalled that the Office does not possess investigative powers at the preliminary examination stage. Its findings are therefore preliminary in nature and may be reconsidered in the light of new facts or evidence. The preliminary examination process is conducted on the basis of the facts and information available. The goal of this process is to reach a fully informed determination of whether there is a reasonable basis to proceed with an investigation. The 'reasonable basis' standard has been interpreted by Pre-Trial Chamber ("PTC") II to require that "there exists a sensible or reasonable justification for a belief that a crime falling within the jurisdiction of the Court 'has been or is being [p. 7] committed'."[4] In this context, PTC II has indicated that all of the information need not necessarily "point towards only one conclusion."[5] This reflects the fact that the reasonable basis standard under article 53(1)(a) "has a different object, a more limited scope, and serves a different purpose" than other higher evidentiary standards provided for in the Statute.[6] In particular, at the preliminary examination stage, "the Prosecutor has limited powers which are not comparable to those provided for in article 54 of the Statute at the investigative stage" and the information available at such an early stage is "neither expected to be 'comprehensive' nor 'conclusive'."[7]

12. Before making a determination on whether to initiate an investigation, the Office also seeks to ensure that the States and other parties concerned

---

[4] Situation in the Republic of Kenya, "Decision Pursuant to Article 15 of the Rome Statute on the Authorization of an Investigation into the Situation in the Republic of Kenya", ICC-01/09-19-Corr, 31 March 2010, para. 35 ("Kenya Article 15 Decision").

[5] Kenya Article 15 Decision, para. 34. In this respect, it is further noted that even the higher "reasonable grounds" standard for arrest warrant applications under article 58 does not require that the conclusion reached on the facts be the only possible or reasonable one. Nor does it require that the Prosecutor disprove any other reasonable conclusions. Rather, it is sufficient to prove that there is a reasonable conclusion alongside others (not necessarily supporting the same finding), which can be supported on the basis of the evidence and information available. Situation in Darfur, Sudan, "Judgment on the appeal of the Prosecutor against the 'Decision on the Prosecution's Application for a Warrant of Arrest against Omar Hassan Ahmad Al Bashir", ICC-02/05-01/09-OA, 3 February 2010, para. 33.

[6] Kenya Article 15 Decision, para. 32.

[7] Kenya Article 15 Decision, para. 27.

have had the opportunity to provide the information they consider appropriate.

13. There are no timelines provided in the Statute for a decision on a preliminary examination. Depending on the facts and circumstances of each situation, the Office may decide either (i) to decline to initiate an investigation where the information manifestly fails to satisfy the factors set out in article 53(1) (a)–(c); (ii) to continue to collect information in order to establish a sufficient factual and legal basis to render a determination; or (iii) to initiate the investigation, subject to judicial review as appropriate.

14. In order to promote transparency of the preliminary examination process, the Office issues regular reports on its activities and provides reasons for its decisions either to proceed or not proceed with investigations.

15. In order to distinguish the situations that do warrant investigation from those that do not, and in order to manage the analysis of the factors set out in article 53(1), the Office has established a filtering process comprising four phases. While each phase focuses on a distinct statutory factor for analytical purposes, the Office applies a holistic approach throughout the preliminary examination process.

    – Phase 1 consists of an initial assessment of all information on alleged crimes received under article 15 ('communications'). The purpose is to analyse the [p. 8] seriousness of information received, filter out information on crimes that are outside the jurisdiction of the Court and identify those that appear to fall within the jurisdiction of the Court. In practice, the Office may occasionally encounter situations where alleged crimes are not manifestly outside the jurisdiction of the Court, but do not clearly fall within its subject-matter jurisdiction. In such situations, the Office will first consider whether the lack of clarity applies to most, or a limited set of allegations, and in the case of the latter, whether they are nevertheless of such gravity to justify further analysis. The Office will then consider whether the exercise of the Court's jurisdiction may be restricted due to factors such as a narrow geographic and/or personal scope of jurisdiction and/or the existence of national proceedings relating to the relevant conduct. In such limited situations, the Office will also take into account its prosecutorial strategy of focusing on those most responsible for the most serious crimes under the Court's jurisdiction, and as a general rule, will follow a conservative approach in terms of deciding whether to open a preliminary examination. It will, however, endeavour to give a more detailed response to the senders of such communications outlining the Office's reasoning for its decisions.

- Phase 2, represents the formal commencement of a preliminary examination, and focuses on whether the preconditions to the exercise of jurisdiction under article 12 are satisfied and whether there is a reasonable basis to believe that the alleged crimes fall within the subject-matter jurisdiction of the Court. Phase 2 analysis entails a thorough factual and legal assessment of the alleged crimes committed in the situation at hand, with a view to identifying potential cases falling within the jurisdiction of the Court. The Office may further gather information on relevant national proceedings if such information is available at this stage.
- Phase 3 focuses on the admissibility of potential cases in terms of complementarity and gravity. In this phase, the Office will also continue to collect information on subject-matter jurisdiction, in particular when new or ongoing crimes are alleged to have been committed within the situation.
- Phase 4 examines the interests of justice consideration in order to formulate the final recommendation to the Prosecutor on whether there is a reasonable basis to initiate an investigation.

16. In the course of its preliminary examination activities, the Office also seeks to contribute to two overarching goals of the Statute: the ending of impunity, by encouraging genuine national proceedings, and the prevention of crimes, thereby potentially obviating the need for the Court's intervention. Preliminary examination activities therefore constitute one of the most cost-effective ways for the Office to fulfil the Court's mission. [p. 9]

Summary of activities performed in 2018

17. This report summarises the preliminary examination activities conducted by the Office between 1 December 2017 and 30 November 2018.
18. Between 1 November 2017 and 31 October 2018, the Office received 673 communications pursuant to article 15 of the Statute. Of these, 443 were manifestly outside the Court's jurisdiction; 28 warranted further analysis; 158 were linked to a situation already under preliminary examination; and 44 were linked to an investigation or prosecution. The Office has received a total of 13,273 article 15 communications since July 2002.

***

20. During the reporting period, two situations were referred to the Office pursuant to article 14 of the Statute. On 22 May 2018, the Office received a

referral from the Government of the State of Palestine regarding the situation in Palestine since 13 June 2014 with no end date. On 27 September 2018, the Office received a referral from a group of States Parties, namely the Argentine Republic, Canada, the Republic of Colombia, the Republic of Chile, the Republic of Paraguay and the Republic of Peru, regarding the situation in Venezuela since 12 February 2014. At the time of receipt of these referrals, both situations were already subject to preliminary examination.

***

[p. 10]

23. The Office further continued its preliminary examinations of the situations in Colombia, Guinea, Iraq/United Kingdom ("UK"), Nigeria, Palestine, and Ukraine. During the reporting period, the Office sent preliminary examination missions to Abuja, Bogota, Conakry, and Kyiv and held numerous consultations at the seat of the Court with State authorities, representatives of international and non-government organisations, article 15 communication senders and other interested parties.

***

[p. 63]

III   Situations under Phase 3 (Subject-Matter Jurisdiction)

***

PALESTINE

Procedural History

251. The situation in Palestine has been under preliminary examination since 16 January 2015.[37] The Office has received a total of 125 communications pursuant to article 15 in relation to the situation in Palestine.

252. On 22 May 2018, the Office received a referral from the Government of the State of Palestine regarding the situation in Palestine since 13 June 2014 with no end date. In reference to articles 13(a) and 14 of the Statute, the State of Palestine requested the Prosecutor "to investigate, in accordance with the temporal jurisdiction of the Court, past, ongoing and future

---

37   The Prosecutor of the International Criminal Court, Fatou Bensouda, opens a preliminary examination of the situation in Palestine, 16 January 2015.

crimes within the court's jurisdiction, committed in all parts of the territory of the State of Palestine."[38]

253. On 24 May 2018, the Presidency of the Court assigned the Situation in Palestine to Pre-Trial Chamber I ("PTC I").[39]

254. On 13 July 2018, PTC I issued a decision concerning the establishment, by the Registry, of "a system of public information and outreach activities among the affected communities and particularly the victims of the situation in Palestine."[40]

Preliminary Jurisdictional Issues

255. On 1 January 2015, the Government of the State of Palestine lodged a declaration under article 12(3) of the Statute accepting the jurisdiction of the ICC over alleged crimes committed "in the occupied Palestinian territory, including East Jerusalem, since June 13, 2014." On 2 January 2015, the Government of the State of Palestine acceded to the Statute by depositing its instrument of accession with the UN Secretary-General. The Statute entered into force for the State of Palestine on 1 April 2015.

Contextual Background
West Bank and East Jerusalem

256. In June 1967, an international armed conflict (the Six-Day War) broke out between Israel and neighbouring states, as a result of which Israel acquired control over a number of territories including the West Bank and East Jerusalem. [p. 64] Immediately after the end of the Six-Day War, Israel established a military administration in the West Bank, and adopted laws and orders effectively extending Israeli law, jurisdiction and administration over East Jerusalem. In November 1981, a separate Civilian Administration was established to "run all regional civil matters" in the West Bank. On 30 July 1980, the Knesset passed a 'Basic Law' by which it established the city of Jerusalem "complete and united" as the capital of Israel.

257. Since 1967, the information available suggests that the Israeli civilian presence in the West Bank and East Jerusalem has reportedly grown to

---

38 Referral Pursuant to Article 13(a) and 14 of the Rome Statute, 15 May 2018, para. 9. See also Statement by ICC Prosecutor, Mrs Fatou Bensouda, on the referral submitted by Palestine, 22 May 2018.

39 Decision assigning the situation in the State of Palestine to Pre-Trial Chamber I, ICC-01/18-1, 24 May 2018.

40 Decision on Information and Outreach for the Victims of the Situation, ICC-01/18-2, 13 July 2018.

nearly 600,000 settlers, living in 137 settlements officially recognised by the Israeli authorities, including 12 large Israeli 'neighbourhoods' in the eastern part of Jerusalem, and some 100 unauthorised settlements or 'outposts'.

258. Pursuant to the Oslo Accords of 1993–1995, the Palestine Liberation Organization and the State of Israel formally recognised each other, and agreed on a progressive handover of certain Palestinian-populated areas in the West Bank to the Palestinian National Authority (or Palestinian Authority, "PA"). Under the 1995 Interim Agreement, the West Bank was divided into three administrative areas (Area A – full civil and security control by the PA; Area B – Palestinian civil control and joint Israeli-Palestinian security control; Area C – full civil and security control by Israel).

259. The peace talks between the parties ground to a halt in 1995 and were followed over the years by a number of rounds of negotiations including the Camp David Summit of 2000, the 2002/2003 Road Map for Peace, as well as intermittent peace talks and related initiatives since 2007. To date, no final peace agreement has been reached and a number of issues remain unresolved, including the determination of borders, security, water rights, control of the city of Jerusalem, Israeli settlements in the West Bank, refugees, and Palestinians' freedom of movement.

Gaza

260. On 7 July 2014, Israel launched 'Operation Protective Edge', which lasted 51 days. According to the Israeli authorities, the objective of the operation was to disable the military capabilities of Hamas and other groups operating in Gaza, neutralise their network of cross-border tunnels and halt their rocket and mortar attacks against Israel. The operation consisted of three phases: after an initial phase focussed on air strikes, Israel launched a ground operation on 17 July 2014; a third phase from 5 August onwards was characterised by alternating ceasefires and aerial strikes. Several Palestinian armed groups ("PAGs")_participated in the hostilities, most notably the respective armed wings of Hamas and the Palestinian Islamic Jihad as well as the al-Nasser Salah al-deen Brigades. The hostilities ended on 26 August 2014 when both sides agreed to an unconditional ceasefire. [p. 65]

261. Since the end of the 2014 hostilities, different national and international bodies have conducted inquiries and/or investigations into incidents that occurred during the 2014 Gaza conflict, such as, for example, the United Nations Independent Commission of Inquiry on the 2014 Gaza

Conflict, the UN Headquarters Board of Inquiry into certain incidents that occurred in the Gaza Strip between 8 July 2014 and 26 August 2014, the Israel Defense Forces ("IDF") Military Advocate General, and the Palestinian Independent National Committee.

262. On 30 March 2018, the 42nd anniversary of the Palestinian Land Day, tens of thousands of Palestinians participated in a protest, dubbed the "Great March of Return", near the border fence between the Gaza Strip and Israel. The demonstrations were reportedly organized to draw attention to the Palestinians' demands for an end of the Israeli occupation and its blockade on the Gaza Strip and the rights of refugees and their descendants to reclaim their ancestral lands in Israel. Although the protests were initially planned to last only six weeks, until 15 May ("Nakba Day"), they have ultimately continued to date.

263. In the context of these events, IDF soldiers have used non-lethal and lethal means against persons participating in the demonstrations, reportedly resulting in the killing of over 170 individuals, including over 30 children, and the wounding of more than 19,000 others. Reportedly, journalists and medical workers have been among those killed and injured.

264. While the majority of demonstrators reportedly engaged in non-violent protest and remained several hundred meters away from the border, some entered the immediate area of the border fence and engaged in violent acts, such as throwing rocks, Molotov cocktails and other explosive devices, deploying incendiary kites and balloons into Israel, and attempting to infiltrate into Israeli territory.

265. Israel has alleged that Hamas and other armed groups in Gaza have sought to instigate a violent confrontation and have exploited the protests as a cover for acts of terrorism against the State of Israel, using the presence of civilians to shield their military activities. However, the IDF's rules of engagement and the alleged use of excessive and deadly force by Israeli forces in the context of the demonstrations has been heavily criticized by, among others, UN officials and bodies and a number of international and regional NGOs.

266. On 18 May 2018, the UN Human Rights Council adopted Resolution S-28/1 establishing an independent international commission of inquiry to investigate alleged violations and abuses of international humanitarian law and international human rights law committed in the context of the demonstrations that began on 30 May 2018. The IDF has also announced that it is conducting its own examination and investigations of certain alleged incidents involving the shooting of demonstrators. [p. 66]

267. From 11 to 13 November 2018, there was also a marked increase in hostilities between Israel and Palestinian armed groups operating in Gaza. Reportedly, on 12–13 November, Palestinian armed groups fired over 400 rockets and mortar shells from Gaza towards Israel, killing at least one civilian and injuring dozens of others and causing damage to property. The IDF also launched strikes against over one hundred targets throughout Gaza – such attacks reportedly primarily targeted Palestinian armed group members and their infrastructure, though they also caused civilian casualties and damage in certain instances. On 13 November, a ceasefire was reached between the parties.

Subject-Matter Jurisdiction

268. The preliminary examination of the situation in Palestine has raised specific challenges relating to both factual and legal determinations. In the latter respect, the Office, in particular, has to consider the possible challenges to the Court's jurisdiction, and/or to the scope of any such jurisdiction. The following summary is without prejudice to any future determinations by the Office regarding the exercise of territorial or personal jurisdiction by the Court. It should not be taken as indicative of, or implying any particular legal qualifications or factual determinations regarding the alleged conduct. Additionally, the summary below is without prejudice to the identification of any further alleged crimes which may be made by the Office in the course of its continued analysis.

West Bank and East Jerusalem

269. The Office has focused its analysis on alleged war crimes committed in the West Bank, including East Jerusalem, since 13 June 2014. Namely, the Israeli authorities have allegedly been involved in the settlement of civilians onto the territory of the West Bank, including East Jerusalem, and the forced removal of Palestinians from their homes in the West Bank and East Jerusalem. Settlement-related activities have reportedly included the confiscation and appropriation of land; the planning and authorisation of settlement expansions; constructions of residential units and related infrastructures in the settlements; the regularisation of constructions built without the required authorisation from Israeli authorities (so-called outposts); and public subsidies, incentives and funding specifically allocated to settlers and settlements' local authorities to encourage migration to the settlements and boost their economic development.

270. Israeli authorities are also alleged to have been involved in the demolition of Palestinian property and eviction of Palestinian residents from

homes in the West Bank and East Jerusalem. Moreover, Israeli authorities have reportedly continued to advance plans to relocate Bedouin and other herder communities present in and around the so-called E1 area, including through the seizure and demolition of residential properties and related infrastructure.

271. The Office has also received information regarding other crimes allegedly committed by officials of the Israeli authorities in the West Bank, including East [p. 67] Jerusalem, which may fall under the purview of article 7 of the Statute on crimes against humanity. Specifically, these allegations relate to the crime of persecution, transfer and deportation of civilians, as well as the crime of apartheid.

272. In addition, the Office has also received allegations that Palestinian security and intelligence services in the West Bank have committed the crime against humanity of torture against civilians held in detention centres under their control. These and any other alleged crimes that may occur in the future, require further assessment.

Gaza 2014 Hostilities

273. Based on the information available, the hostilities that took place in Gaza between 7 July and 26 August 2014 may be classified as either an international or non-international armed conflict. Accordingly, the Office has taken into account the possible alternative available classifications of the 2014 armed conflict and the related possible alternative legal qualifications of the relevant alleged acts of the various perpetrators. Such an approach, however, has implications for any conclusions to be reached on the commission of particular alleged crimes of relevance, given that certain war crimes that are criminalised under the Statute provisions relevant to international armed conflicts, are by contrast not criminalised under the Statute in the case of a non-international armed conflict. Consequently, the Office's conclusions on the commission of alleged crimes in some instances depend on the qualification of the conflict as either international or non-international in character.

274. During the reporting period, the Office continued to analyse allegations of crimes committed by members of the IDF and members of PAGs, respectively, during the hostilities in Gaza in 2014. In conducting its analysis, the Office focused on a sample of illustrative incidents, out of the thousands previously documented by the Office and compiled in comprehensive databases. In this respect, the Office sought to: (i) select incidents which appear to be the most grave in terms of the alleged harm to civilians and damage to civilian objects and/or are representative of

the main types of alleged conduct, and (ii) prioritise incidents for which there is a range of sources and sufficient information available to enable an objective and thorough analysis.

Other Alleged Conduct since 30 March 2018

275. The Office has gathered information regarding other crimes allegedly committed by both sides in relation to the violence that has occurred in the context of the protests held along the Israel-Gaza border since 30 March 2018. These and any other alleged crimes that may occur require further assessment. [p. 68]

Admissibility Assessment

276. As set out in article 17(1), admissibility requires an assessment of complementarity and gravity.

West Bank and East Jerusalem

277. The information available does not seem to indicate the existence of any relevant national investigations or prosecutions being or having been conducted against the persons or groups of persons which are likely to be the focus of an investigation into the crimes allegedly committed in the West Bank, including East Jerusalem. This stems from the fact that on the one hand, the Palestinian authorities are unable to exercise jurisdiction over the alleged Israeli perpetrators, while, on the other hand, the Israeli government has consistently maintained that settlements-related activities are not unlawful and the High Court of Justice ("HCJ") has held that the issue of the Government's settlement policy was non-justiciable. The Office has nonetheless considered a number of decisions rendered by the HCJ pertaining to the legality of certain governmental actions connected to settlement activities.

278. In addition, the Office has considered whether, based on the information available, the crimes allegedly committed in the West Bank, including East Jerusalem, since 13 June 2014, are sufficiently grave within the meaning and requirements of the Statue to justify the opening of an investigation, in particular considering their scale, nature, manner of commission, and their impact on victims and affected communities.

Gaza 2014 Hostilities

279. With respect to the alleged crimes committed during the 2014 hostilities in Gaza, the Office has focussed on a sample of incidents that appear to be the gravest, most representative and best documented. With respect

to crimes allegedly committed by members of the IDF, the information available indicates that all of the relevant incidents are or have been the subject of some form of investigative activities at the national level within the IDF military justice system. With respect to crimes allegedly committed by Palestinian armed groups, the information available at this stage does not suggest any conflict of jurisdiction between the Court and any relevant States with jurisdiction

280. For the purpose of the gravity assessment, the Office has to consider whether the groups of persons that are likely to be the object of an investigation include those who appear to be most responsible for the most serious crimes, including persons with levels of responsibility in directing, ordering, facilitating or otherwise contributing to the commission of the alleged crimes.

281. Furthermore, taking into account both quantitative and qualitative factors, the crimes allegedly committed must be sufficiently grave considering their scale, [p. 69] nature, manner of commission, and their impact on victims and affected communities. Additionally, while the considerations outlined in article 8(1) are only meant to provide guidance that the Court should focus on cases meeting these requirements, the Office is also considering whether the alleged war crimes were committed on a large scale or as part of a plan or policy within the meaning of article 8(1) of the Statute.

OTP Activities

282. During the reporting period, the Office has reached an advanced stage of its assessment of statutory criteria for a determination whether there is a reasonable basis to proceed with an investigation into the situation in Palestine pursuant to article 53(1) of the Statute. In the course of this process, the Office engaged with a number of stakeholders – including officials of Palestine and Israel, intergovernmental and non-governmental organisations, and members of civil society – for the purpose of gathering additional information relevant to the Office's assessment.

283. On 8 April 2018, the Prosecutor issued a statement expressing grave concern at the violence and deteriorating situation in the Gaza Strip related to the events surrounding the Great March of Return demonstrations that began on 30 March 2018 and called for the violence to stop. In addition, on 17 October 2018, the Prosecutor issued a statement expressing concern in relation to the planned eviction of the Bedouin community of Khan al-Ahmar in the West Bank as well as the continued violence, perpetrated by actors on both sides, along the Gaza border with Israel.

Conclusion

284. During 2018, the Office has advanced and significantly progressed its analysis on all of the factors listed in article 53(1)(a)–(c), in line with its holistic approach. Given the detailed focus that the Office has given to this situation since 2015, the Prosecutor intends to complete the preliminary examination as early as possible.

Referral by the State of Palestine Pursuant to Articles 13(a) and 14 of the Rome Statute (May 15, 2018)

The State of Palestine

Referral by the State of Palestine Pursuant to Articles 13(a) and 14 of the Rome Statute.

15 May 2018

Ref: PAL-180515-Ref

[p. 2]

I General Considerations

1. On 16 January 2015, following the State of Palestine's article 12(3) declaration of 1 January 2015, the Prosecutor of the International Criminal Court announced the commencement of a preliminary examination of the Situation in Palestine to determine "whether there is a reasonable basis to proceed with an investigation".[1] This is the third preliminary examination that the Office of the Prosecutor ("OTP") has undertaken in relation to Palestine.[2] To date, none of these examinations has resulted in a decision to investigate.

---

1 Madam Fatou Bensouda, the Prosecutor of the International Criminal Court. Fatou Bensouda Opens a Preliminary Examination of the Situation in Palestine. ICC-OTP-20150116-PR1083, 16 January 2015.
2 Preliminary Examination I, opened 22 January 2009 following the 2009 article 12(3) Declaration, closed 3 April 2012; Preliminary Examination II relating to the Gaza Flotilla Situation, opened 14 May 2013 and the decision to not investigate was issued 6 November; Preliminary Examination III opened 16 January 2015 following the 2015 article 12 (3) declaration and currently in phase two of a four phase process.

2. Since the opening of the preliminary examination of the Situation in Palestine, Israel has continued unabated to commit crimes within the jurisdiction of the Court. It has done so brazenly in order to advance its settlement regime to an unprecedented level with the aim of pursuing its policy of displacement and replacement of the Palestinian people. This settlement policy has been carried out through the commission of multiple crimes within the Court's jurisdiction. It has been executed in the face of international condemnation of Israel's actions by the Secretary-General of the United Nations, the Security Council, and a wide range of other international fora.

3. The Israeli settlement regime represents much more than the physical structures that make up the actual housing units in a specific settlement. The physical structures are part of an entire settlement policy which is enacted, maintained, and expanded by top Israeli officials, governmental and military, and which encompasses a range of sub-policies and practices that allow for the [p. 3] planning, construction, expansion, maintenance, security and development of settlements. The unlawful occupation of the territory of the State of Palestine and the establishment and maintenance of settlements by Israel in Occupied Palestinian Territory ("OPT"), including East Jerusalem, has involved the enactment and maintenance of a multi-layered system of violence and intimidation against the Palestinian population, the destruction and unlawful appropriation of their properties, the severe violation of their fundamental rights on discriminatory grounds and the institutionalization of a separate structure of life and dual system of law and other measures deliberately intended to change the demographic composition of the OPT, including in particular in East Jerusalem. It has also involved the widespread and systematic attack on the Palestinian civilian population, through the commission of crimes, to create and perpetuate such a regime. These acts qualify under the Rome Statute as both war crimes and crimes against humanity.

4. As reflected in communications and twenty-five successive monthly reports submitted by the State of Palestine to the OTP,[3] war crimes and

---

[3] See, Submissions by the State of Palestine: Submission to the OTP Pursuant to Article 15(2) of the Statute (filed confidentially 25 June 2015); Communication to the ICC Prosecutor in follow-up to the Submission by the State of Palestine, with particular focus on Settler's Terrorist Attacks (filed confidentially 3 August 2015); Second Communication to the Office of the ICC Prosecutor by the State of Palestine in follow-up to the Submission of 24th of June 2015 (filed confidentially 30 October 2015); Answers to OTP Questions (filed confidentially 3 June 2016 and 2 September 2016); Communication on Present and Ongoing

crimes against humanity have continued to be committed on an aggravated basis throughout the period of the preliminary examination. The impunity of Israeli officials and [p. 4] Israeli nationals responsible for the commission of these crimes has contributed to the continuation, intensification and recurrence of these crimes.

5. The gravity and ongoing nature of this criminality, as well as the fact that State officials are involved in the commission of these crimes, calls for the Prosecution to conduct and finalise its investigation without delay, and with a view to bringing those responsible to justice.

6. It is thus necessary, on behalf of the citizens of the State of Palestine who have suffered for generations the consequences of crimes committed with impunity by Israeli officials and citizens, and who continue to suffer from ongoing, widespread and systematic crimes, for the State of Palestine to hereby exercise its right as a State Party to the Rome Statute to refer the Situation of Palestine for immediate investigation so that those most responsible for these crimes may be held accountable for their actions without further delay.

7. The State of Palestine stresses the importance of achieving justice for the victims of crimes, reaffirms its commitment to cooperate fully with the Court and maintains that ensuring justice and accountability is crucial to achieving peace, to deterring the commission of crimes, and to the integrity and credibility of the ICC itself. A failure to punish, let alone investigate, crimes associated with the unlawful occupation of Palestine has only emboldened perpetrators to carry on with their criminal deeds.

8. The present referral is without prejudice to the Prosecutor's ongoing duty and responsibility to continue and finalise her preliminary examination without delay in accordance with Article 53 of the Rome Statute regarding crimes currently the subject of her preliminary examination in the

---

Crimes Committed Against Palestinian Children (filed confidentially 16 November 2016); Observations by the State of Palestine on the Preliminary Examination after Two Years (filed confidentially 18 January 2017), Monthly reports (drawing on the findings of independent UN and other agencies) covering January, February and March 2016 (10 May 2016), April 2016 (10 May 2016), May 2016 (19 June 2016), June 2016 (21 July 2016, with corrigendum on 2 August 2016), July 2016 (27 August 2016), August 2016 (23 September 2016), September 2016 (24 October 2016), October 2016 (6 December 2016), November 2016 (28 December 2016), December 2016 (20 February 2017), January 2017 (170329-MR011), February 2017 (170409-MR012), March 2017 (170430-MR013), April 2017 (170528-MR014), May 2017 (170705-MR015), June 2017 (170905-MR016), July 2017 (171023-MR017), August 2017 (171109-MR018), September 2017 (180109-MR019), October 2017 (180111-MR020), November 2017 (180204-MR021), December 2017 (180211-MR022), January 2018 (180315-MR023), February (180402-MR024), and March (180503-MR025).

Situation of Palestine. However, given the acceleration of settlement-related crimes and their irreversible impact on the lives of Palestinians and on the prospects for a [p. 5] lasting peace, it is imperative that the OTP immediately commence an investigation into the crimes herein referred as its highest priority.

II   The Referral

9. The State of Palestine, pursuant to Articles 13(a) and 14 of the Rome Statute of the International Criminal Court, refers the Situation in Palestine for investigation by the Office of the Prosecutor and specifically requests the Prosecutor to investigate, in accordance with the temporal jurisdiction of the Court, past, ongoing and future crimes within the court's jurisdiction, committed in all parts of the territory of the State of Palestine.[4]
10. The State of Palestine respectfully requests, pursuant to Regulation 45 of the Regulations of the Court, that the Prosecutor immediately inform the Presidency of the ICC of this Referral so as to "facilitate the timely assignment of [the] situation to a Pre-Trial Chamber".[5]

Crimes within the Jurisdiction of the Court

11. Pursuant to Article 14(2) of the Rome Statute, the State of Palestine specifies that the circumstances relevant to the present referral include but are not limited to, all matters related to the Israeli settlement regime outlined in earlier communications, monthly reports and submissions by the Government of Palestine, confidentially filed with or conveyed to the Office of the Prosecutor.[6] In particular, the present referral incorporates as matters to be subject to [p. 6] investigation, any conduct, policies, laws, official decisions and practices that underlie, promote, encourage

---

[4] The State of Palestine comprises the Palestinian Territory occupied in 1967 by Israel, as defined by the 1949 Armistice Line, and includes the West Bank, including East Jerusalem, and the Gaza Strip.

[5] Regulation 45 of the Regulations of the Court provides:
The Prosecutor shall inform the Presidency in writing as soon as a situation has been referred to the Prosecutor by a State Party under article 14 or by the Security Council under article 13, sub-paragraph (b); and shall provide the Presidency with any other information that may facilitate the timely assignment of a situation to a Pre-Trial Chamber, including, in particular, the intention of the Prosecutor to submit a request under article 15, paragraph 3.

[6] The Government of Palestine hereby makes each and all of these (referenced previously above in footnote 3) a formal part of the present referral.

or otherwise make a contribution to the commission of these crimes in accordance with the terms of the Statute, including but not limited to those coming within the terms of the following Articles of the Statute: Articles 7(1)(a), (d), (e), (f), (h), (j) and (k), 8(2)(a)(i), (ii), (iii), (iv), (vi),' (vii), (b)(i), (ii), (iii), (iv), (viii), (ix), (xiii), (xvi) and (xxi) of the Rome Statute.

12. The Referral highlights certain categories of war crimes and crimes against humanity of particular seriousness and concern to the Palestinian people and the international community (as expressed in repeated Security Council Resolutions, including most recently Resolution 2334), to ensure that they form an integral part of the OTP's investigation. However, the crimes set forth below are not the only crimes committed within the jurisdiction of the ICC and are not intended to limit the scope of the OTP's investigation. For current purposes, and given the urgent need for an investigation to be opened without further delay, the State of Palestine hereby specifically identifies the following categories of crimes as being core to the *present* referral:

    i. Crimes involving the unlawful appropriation and destruction of private and public properties, including land, houses and buildings, as well as natural resources;

    ii. Crimes involving the forcible transfer of Palestinians, including by means of violence, compulsion, duress and the creation of inhumane living conditions;

    iii. Crimes involving the unlawful transfer of the Israeli Occupying Power's population into Occupied Palestinian Territory;

    iv. Crimes involving murders and unlawful attacks on civilians, including through excessive use of force and unlawful killings of Palestinians, including demonstrators exercising their right to protest;

    v. Crimes involving the torture, cruel and inhumane treatment of Palestinians;

    vi. Crimes involving persecution, including the grave, widespread and systematic denial or violation of basic human rights on discriminatory grounds against Palestinians, including those resulting in or intended to achieve the deportation or forcible transfer, directly or indirectly, of the Palestinian population, the re-populating of "cleansed" territories with Israeli settlers and the unlawful appropriation of Palestinian land and properties; and,

    vii. Crimes involving the establishment of a system of apartheid based in particular on the adoption of discriminatory laws, policies and practices as well as the commission of inhumane acts intended to establish an institutionalized regime of separation and advancement of Israeli settlements accompanied by the systematic oppression and domination by Israeli settlers over Palestinians.

13. The present referral pertains to all categories of criminal participation in the commission of the crimes described above, as provided for under the Statute of the Court, pursuant to Articles 25–28 of the Statute. This includes, but is not limited to, those who plan, prepare and implement policies linked to the settlements regime as well as those who enable it, whether through financial, military, or logistical support or otherwise aid and abet or encourage the commission of crimes connected to that regime. The referral includes, in particular, those civilian and military leaders who are in a position of command or authority towards those committing the underlying crimes and who, [p. 8] through their acts or omission, contribute to the commission of these crimes or fail to prevent, stop or punish them.

III The Rationale

14. This referral aims at securing justice for millions of Palestinian victims who look upon the ICC to provide justice and to help bring an end to, and prevent the recurrence of, such crimes against them. These crimes are among the most widely documented in contemporary history. In line with the *raison d'etre* of the ICC, they must be investigated and their perpetrators held to account without further delay.

15. The crimes committed by Israeli officials, including officials at the highest levels of the State, are entrenched as a matter of State policy, planned and perpetrated pervasively, systematically and on a widespread basis, attract no accountability, and have continued with impunity despite the OTP's preliminary examination. This state of affairs imposes unimaginable and long-lasting harm to victims and risks undermining the legitimacy of international law and international judicial institutions, including the ICC.

16. During the current preliminary examination, there has been an alarming intensification of Israeli crimes with an attendant and compounding impact on the Palestinian population and, in particular, on children. Such intensification is further evidenced, *inter alia,* by the following:

    a. There was a 70% surge in Israeli settlement construction starts on Occupied Palestinian Territory between April 2016 and March 2017, as compared to the same period in 2015–2016.[7] In 2017 alone, the Israeli [p. 9] government advanced plans for over 6,742 additional Israeli settler housing units.[8] "Israel's illegal settlement activities ... continued at a high rate, a consistent pattern" throughout the year.[9]

b. Israeli occupation forces and settlers killed or injured, with impunity, over 1,100 Palestinian children in 2017, worsening a child protection crisis in the territory of the Occupied Palestinian State. In total, members of Israeli forces murdered, unlawfully killed or injured over 7,300 Palestinian civilians throughout the course of the year.[10]

c. On 14 May 2018 alone, during peaceful demonstrations in the Gaza Strip, the Israeli Occupation Forces killed over 60 Palestinians, and injured thousands more, including with live ammunition and artillery fire.[11] The casualties included 6 children, a double amputee, and a paramedic. Hundreds were also injured, including 11 journalists. Since 30 March 2018, Israeli Occupation Forces killed over 110 peaceful demonstrators and other protected persons, including 2 journalists, 14 children, and 1 paramedic. During this period, the Israeli Occupation Forces repeatedly stated their knowledge of where every bullet fired on protestors landed,[12] while top Israeli officials congratulated the snipers on a job well done, including the

---

7   *Peace Now*, Central Bureau of Statistics: 70% Rise in Construction of Settlements during The Past Compared to Previous Year, 19 June 2017, available at: http://peacenow.org.il/en/central-bureau-statistics-70-rise-construction-settlements-past-year-compared-previous-year. Reported in State of Palestine Monthly Report for June (170905-MR016), para. 63.

8   *Peace Now*, Peace Now's Annual Settlement Construction Report for 2017, 28 March 2017.

9   Briefing to the Security Council on the Situation in the Middle East – Report on UNSCR 2334 (2016), 25 September 2017, available at: https://unsco.unmissions.org/security-council-briefing-25-september-2017-2334.

10 *OCHA*, Monthly Figures, available at: https://www.ochaopt.org/content/monthly-figures.

11 See, *Wafa*, Victim number 60 of Israeli massacre succumbs to wounds, 15 May 2018, available at: http://english.wafa.ps/page.aspx?id=DBMwz5a97707914733aDBMwz5.

12 See, *The Telegraph*, Israeli military defends tactics as video appears to show unarmed Gaza protestors shot by snipers, 31 March 2018, available at: https://www.telegraph.co.uk/news/2018/03/31/israeli-military-defends-tactics-video-appears-show-unarmed/.

Prime Minister[13] and Defense Minister, who declared that "there are no innocent people in the Gaza Strip".[14] [p. 10]

d. In 2017, Israeli occupation forces demolished or unlawfully appropriated 424 Palestinian homes and structures necessary to Palestinian livelihood.[15] In 2016, at least 1,054 Palestinian structures were demolished, marking the highest number of unlawful demolitions and appropriations of Palestinian homes and livelihood structures in the Occupied Palestinian Territory, including East Jerusalem, since 2009.[16]

e. Within the context of this deliberate pattern of destruction and appropriation of civilian property, Israeli occupation forces forcibly displaced 3,861 Palestinians, including 1,960 children, since 13 June 2014, the date from which the ICC's temporal jurisdiction over the matter began.[17] They also impacted the livelihood and access to services of a further 19,555 Palestinians.[18]

f. There was a record level of ratifications of "state land" declarations on Occupied Palestinian Territory by the Israeli government in 2016, which qualifies, *inter alia,* as pillage, unlawful appropriation of property and persecution;[19]

g. By the end of 2016, 7,000 Palestinians were being arbitrarily detained in Israeli jails, including 700 held under "administrative detention" (indefinitely renewable, without charge or trial or basic legal protections and on the basis of 'secret evidence' kept from

---

13 See, *Aljazeera*, 'Netanyahu praises Israeli army after killings of Palestinians', 31 March 2018, available at: https://www.aljazeera.com/news/2018/03/netanyahu-praises-israeli-army-killing-palestinians-180331183611045.html.

14 See, The Middle East Eye, 'No innocent people in Gaza' says Israeli defense minister, 8 April 2018, available at: http://www.middleeasteye.net/news/no-innocent-people-gaza-says-israeli-defence-minister-1155018849.

15 *OCHA*, West Bank – Online Demolitions Database, 1 January–31 December 2017, available at: http://data.ochaopt.org/dbs/demolition/demolition/index.aspx.

16 United Nations News Centre, UN study reveals record number of demolitions in occupied Palestinian territory in 2016. 29 December 2016.

17 *OCHA*, Demolition System, period of 13 June 2014 to 14 May 2018, accessed 14 May 2018, available at: http://data.ochaopt.Org/demolition-svs.aspx#close.

18 *OCHA*, Demolition System, period of 13 June 2014 to 14 May 2018, accessed 14 May 2018, available at: http://data.ochaopt.Org/demolition-svs.aspx#close.

19 According to the Colonization and Wall Resistance Commission, during 2016 the Israeli occupation authorities declared 3882 dunums as state land; Colonization and Wall Resistance Commission, 2016 Annual Report, 23 March 2017.

both detainee and [p. 11] attorney), the highest level since 2008.[20] With a bi-weekly average of 79 raids into the West Bank per week and 67 in total into the Gaza Strip in 2017,[21] the policy of mass arbitrary arrest and unlawful imprisonment by Israeli occupation forces continued.

17. In parallel, the Israeli government has guaranteed almost complete impunity to its leadership, occupying forces, settlers and other citizens responsible for crimes committed against the Palestinian population in the Occupied Palestinian Territory, demonstrating the discriminatory nature of the dual justice system applied there and the fact that it forms part of a State-sponsored policy of promoting, encouraging and authorizing the commission of such crimes.

18. Based on information already made available to the OTP, the State of Palestine submits that, in accordance with articles 14(1) and 53(1) of the Statute, there is clearly a "reasonable basis to proceed with an investigation" in relation to each and all of the above-mentioned crimes. The existence of a reasonable basis to conduct an investigation is also established by the following: [p. 12]

    a. Over the last 50 years, the United Nations Security Council,[22] the United Nations General Assembly[23] and the Human Rights

---

20 The United Nations Human Rights Council ("UNHRC"), Report of the Special Rapporteur on the situation of human rights in the Palestinian territories occupied since 1967, A/71/554. 19 October 2016, para. 18.

21 *OCHA*, Protection of Civilians – Reporting Period: 19 December 2017–1 January 2017, available at: https://www.ochaopt.org/content/protection-civilians-report-19-december-2017-1-ianuary-2018.

22 *See for example*, UN Security Council ("UNSC") Resolutions finding Israel in violation of international law: 242 (1967) ("Affirms that the fulfilment of [UN] Charter principles requires the establishment of a just and lasting peace in the Middle East which should include ... [withdrawal of Israel armed forces from territories occupied in the recent conflict...."); 446 (1979); 452(1979) ("[P]olicy of Israel in establishing settlements ... constitutes a violation of Geneva Convention"); 465 (1980) ("[M]easures taken by Israel to change the ... demographic composition ... of the Palestinian territories ... constitutes a flagrant violation of the Fourth Geneva Convention"); 476 (1980); 478 (1980) ("Affirms that the enactment of the 'basic law' [on Jerusalem] constitutes a violation of international law").

23 *See for example*, UN General Assembly ("UNGA") resolutions finding Israel in violation of international law: 1967: 2253; 1971: 2851; 1972: 3005 ("[T]he establishment of Israeli settlements in the occupied territories and the moving into the occupied territories of an alien population, contrary to the provisions of the Geneva Convention".); 1973: 3092; 1974: 3240 ("Expresses the gravest concern, at the continued and persistent disregard by Israel of the Geneva Convention ..."); 1975: 3525 ("Deplores the continued and persistent violation by Israel of the Geneva Conventions ..."); 1976: 31/106; 1977: 32/91; 1978: 33/113; 1979: 34/90 ("Deplores the continued and persistent violation by Israel of the Geneva Conventions

relative to the Protection of Civilian Persons in Time of War, of 12 August 1949, and other applicable international instruments, and condemns in particular those violations which that Convention designates as 'grave breaches'"); 1980: 35/122, 35/207 (1980) ("Deeply concerned that the Arab and Palestinian territories occupied since June 1967, including Jerusalem, still remain under illegal Israeli occupation"); 1981: 36/147; 1982: 37/88 ("Determines that all such measures and actions taken by Israel in the Palestinian ... including Jerusalem, are in violation of the relevant provisions of the Geneva Convention"); 37/222; 1983: 38/79; 38/166; 1984: 39/95; 1985: 40/201; 1986: 41/63; 1987: 42/160,42/190; 1988: 43/58; 1989: 44/48(Israel's actions constitute grave breaches of Geneva Convention). 1990: 45/74; 45/130; 1991: 46/47;46/82; 46/162; 46/199; 1992: 47/70; 1993: 48/41; 1994: 49/36; 1995: 50/29; 1996: 51/135; 51/132; 51/133; 1997: 51/223; 52/67; 52/65; 1998: ES-10/5 [Emergency Session]; 53/37 ("Determines that the decision of Israel to impose its laws, jurisdiction and administration on the Holy City of Jerusalem is illegal and therefore null and void and has no validity whatsoever"); 53/56; 53/57; 1999: ES-10/6 [Emergency Session]; 54/37; 54/76; 54/78; 54/79. 2000: ES-10/7; 55/130; 55/132; 55/134; 2001:55/61; 55/62; ES-10/9 [Emergency Session] ("Recalling relevant provisions of the Rome Statute of the International Criminal Court, Reaffirming the position of the international community on Israeli settlements in the Occupied Palestinian Territory, including East Jerusalem, as illegal and as an obstacle to peace, Expressing its concern at Israeli actions taken recently against the Orient House and other Palestinian institutions in Occupied East Jerusalem as well as other illegal Israeli actions aimed at altering the status of the city and its demographic composition"); 2002:ES-10/L.9/Rev.l ("Gravely concerned in particular at the reports of grave breaches of international humanitarian law committed in the Jenin refugee camp and other Palestinian cities by the Israeli occupying forces"); 57/127; 2003: 58/96; 2004: 59/123: 59/121; 2005: 60/108; 60/106; 2006: ES-10/16; 61/118; 2007: 62/84; 62/109; 2008: 63/98; 2009: 64/91; 64/94. 2010:65/17 ("Expressing its grave concern also, in particular, about the continuation by Israel, the occupying Power, of illegal settlement activities"); 65/102 ("Expresses grave concern about the critical situation in the Occupied Palestinian Territory, including East Jerusalem, particularly in the Gaza Strip, as a result of unlawful Israeli practices and measures...."); 65/103; 65/104 ("Affirming that the transfer by the occupying Power of parts of its own civilian population into the territory it occupies constitutes a breach of the Fourth Geneva Convention and relevant provisions of customary law, including those codified in Additional Protocol I to the four Geneva Conventions"); and 65/179. 2011: 66/18, 66/76 ("Convinced that occupation itself represents a gross and grave violation of human rights"); 66/225; 66/77; 66/78 ("Affirming transfer of Israeli citizens into occupied territory is a breach of the Fourth Geneva Convention and customary international law"); 66/79 ("Gravely concerned by reports regarding serious human rights violations and grave breaches of international humanitarian law committed during the military operations in the Gaza Strip between December 2008 and January 2009"). 2012: 67/24; 67/118 ("Convinced that occupation itself represents a gross and grave violation of human rights"); 67/119; 67/121 ("Expressing grave concern about the continuing systematic violation of the human rights of the Palestinian people by Israel"); 67/229 ("Expressing its grave concern about the extensive destruction by Israel, the occupying Power, of agricultural land and orchards in the Occupied Palestinian Territory, including the uprooting of a vast number of fruit-bearing trees and the destruction of farms and greenhouses, and the grave environmental and economic impact in this regard"). 2013:68/16; 68/80 ("Gravely concerned in particular by reports regarding serious human rights violations and grave breaches of international humanitarian law committed during the military operations

Council[24] have [p. 13] passed numerous resolutions recognizing that Israeli settlements in the Occupied Palestinian Territory are in violation of international law,[25] including the right of the Palestinian people to self-determination,[26] and calling on Israel, the occupying power, to abide by its obligations under international law;

b. On 8 December 2003, the General Assembly requested an advisory opinion from the International Court of Justice ("ICJ") on the legality of Israel's construction of a wall on and through the Occupied Palestinian Territory.[27] On 9 July 2004, after full deliberations, the ICJ ruled that Israel's building of a wall on occupied Palestinian

---

in the Gaza Strip between December 2008 and January 2009"); 68/81; 68/82 ("Affirming that the transfer by the occupying Power of parts of its own civilian population into the territory it occupies constitutes a breach of the Fourth Geneva Convention and relevant provisions of customary law, including those codified in Additional Protocol I to the four Geneva Conventions"); 68/83 ("Expressing grave concern about the continuing systematic violation of the human rights of the Palestinian people by Israel, the occupying Power"). 2014: 69/90; 69/91; 69/92 ("Aware that Israeli settlement activities involve, inter alia, the transfer of nationals of the occupying Power into the occupied territories, the confiscation of land, the forced transfer of Palestinian civilians ... that are contrary to international law"); 69/93. 2015: 70/87 ("Expressing grave concern about tensions, instability and violence in the Occupied Palestinian Territory, including East Jerusalem, due to the illegal policies and practices of Israel ..."); 70/88; 70/90. 2016:71/95; 71/96; 71/97; 71/98.

24 *See*, UNISPAL website for resolutions from the Human Rights Council (and Commission on Human Rights).

25 While the State of Palestine recognizes that the Prosecutor must make her own independent assessment of the facts and law, it also notes that never before has the ICC been seized of a situation that has been the subject of such intense scrutiny by the UN for such an extensive period. It is the firm belief of Palestine that such a corpus of material should facilitate the Prosecutor's work.

26 International Court of Justice ("ICJ"), Advisory Opinion, Legal Consequences of the Construction of a Wall in the Occupied Palestinian Territory ("Advisory Opinion on the Wall"), 9 July 2004, 2004 ICJ Reports, para. 122:

[...] In other terms, the route chosen for the wall gives expression *in loco* to the illegal measures taken by Israel with regard to Jerusalem and the settlements, as deplored by the Security Council (see paragraphs 75 and 120 above). There is also a risk of further alterations to the demographic composition of the Occupied Palestinian Territory resulting from the construction of the wall inasmuch as it is contributing, as will be further explained in paragraph 133 below, to the departure of Palestinian populations from certain areas. That construction, along with measures taken previously, thus severely impedes the exercise by the Palestinian people of its right to self-determination, and is therefore a breach of Israel's obligation to respect that right.

27 UNGA, ES-10/14, 8 December 2003.

territory is "contrary to international law".[28] In its Opinion the ICJ unanimously held that [p. 14] "Israeli settlements in the Occupied Palestinian Territory (including East Jerusalem) have been established in breach of international law".[29] In this opinion, the Court, after noting the illegality of settlements and fears that Israel may integrate these settlements and their means of access, stated "that the construction of the wall and its associated regime create *afait accompli* on the ground that could well become permanent, in which case, and notwithstanding the formal characterization of the wall by Israel, it would be tantamount to *de facto* annexation".[30] The Court also concluded that the establishment of Israeli settlements in the Occupied Palestinian Territory breached the prohibition under international law, whereby "the Occupying Power shall not deport or transfer parts of its own civilian population into the territory it occupies."[31]

c. On 23 December 2016, the United Nations Security Council adopted Resolution 2334 (2016) which, in line with the longstanding positions of [p. 15] the United Nations Security Council, condemned "all measures aimed at altering the demographic composition,

---

[28] Paragraph 163 of the Advisory Opinion on the Wall states in relevant part:
The construction of the wall being built by Israel, the occupying Power, in the Occupied Palestinian Territory, including in and around East Jerusalem, and its associated regime, are contrary to international law;

[29] ICJ, Advisory Opinion on the Wall, para 120 Judge Buergenthal (United States), who dissented on the finding of the illegality of the wall, agreed that settlements are unlawful: *See* Declaration by Judge Buergenthal on the Advisory opinion on the Wall, para. 9.

[30] ICJ, Advisory Opinion on the Wall, 9 July 2004, 2004 ICJ Reports, para. 121.

[31] ICJ, Advisory Opinion on the Wall, 9 July 2004, 2004 ICJ Reports, para. 120:
As regards these settlements, the Court notes that Article 49, paragraph 6, of the Fourth Geneva Convention provides: "The Occupying Power shall not deport or transfer parts of its own civilian population into the territory it occupies." That provision prohibits not only deportations or forced transfers of population such as those carried out during the Second World War, but also any measures taken by an occupying Power in order to organize or encourage transfers of parts of its own population into the occupied territory.

In this respect, the information provided to the Court shows that, since 1977, Israel has conducted a policy and developed practices involving the establishment of settlements in the Occupied Palestinian Territory, contrary to the terms of Article 49, paragraph 6, just cited. [...]

The Court concludes that the Israeli settlements in the Occupied Palestinian Territory (including East Jerusalem) have been established in breach of international law.

character and status of the Palestinian Territory occupied since 1967, including East Jerusalem, including *inter alia*, the construction and expansion of settlements, transfer of Israeli settlers, confiscation of land, demolition of homes and displacement of Palestinian civilians, in violation of international humanitarian law and relevant resolutions", and reaffirmed that the "establishment by Israel of settlements in the Palestinian territory occupied since 1967, including East Jerusalem, has no legal validity and constitutes a flagrant violation under international law and a major obstacle to the achievement of the two-State solution and a just, lasting and comprehensive peace". It also reiterated "its demand that Israel immediately and completely, cease all settlement activities in the occupied Palestinian territory, including East Jerusalem, and that it fully respect all of its legal obligations in this regard".[32] This and previous [p. 16] resolutions, by addressing Israel, acknowledge the Israeli State and officials' role in the planning, implementation, expansion and maintenance of the settlement regime and their responsibility in the ongoing criminality linked to this regime.[33]

---

32   UNSC, Resolution 2334 (2016). The resolution states in part:
Condemning all measures aimed at altering the demographic composition, character and status of the Palestinian Territory occupied since 1967, including East Jerusalem, including, inter alia, the construction and expansion of settlements, transfer of Israeli settlers, confiscation of land, demolition of homes and displacement of Palestinian civilians, in violation of international humanitarian law and relevant resolutions,
Reaffirms that the establishment by Israel of settlements in the Palestinian territory occupied since 1967, including East Jerusalem, has no legal validity and constitutes a flagrant violation under international law and a major obstacle to the achievement of the two-State solution and a just, lasting and comprehensive peace;
The United States abstained. On 28 December 2016, the US Secretary of State stated that: [T]he more outposts that are built, the more the settlements expand, the less possible it is to create a contiguous state. So in the end, a settlement is not just the land that it's on, it's also what the location does to the movement of people, what it does to the ability of a road to connect people, one community to another, what it does to the sense of statehood that is chipped away with each new construction. No one thinking seriously about peace can ignore the reality of what the settlements pose to that peace.
[T]here have been over 30,000 settlement units advanced through some stage of the planning process. That's right – over 30,000 settlement units advanced notwithstanding the positions of the United States and other countries. And if we had vetoed this resolution just the other day, the United States would have been giving license to further unfettered settlement construction that we fundamentally oppose.

33   *See for example*, UNGA Resolutions finding Israel in violation of international law: 1967: 2253; 1971:2851; 1972: 3005; 1973: 3092; 1974: 3240; 1975: 3525; 1976: 31/106; 1977: 32/91; 1978:

440   INTERNATIONAL CRIMINAL COURT

  d. Several United Nations fact-finding and inquiry commissions have found credible and reliable evidence establishing reasonable grounds to believe international crimes have been committed by Israeli forces and officials on the territory of the State of Palestine.[34]

  e. On 14 September 1967, shortly after the Six-Day War, Judge Theodor Meron,[35] then Legal Adviser of the Israel Ministry of Foreign Affairs,

---

33/113: 1979: 34/90: 1980: 35/122, 35/207 (1980); 1981: 36/147; 1982: 37/88; 37/222; 1983: 38/79; 38/166; 1984: 39/95; 1985: 40/201; 1986: 41/63; 1987: 42/160; 42/190; 1988: 43/58; 1989: 44/48; 1990: 45/74; 45/130; 1991: 46/47; 46/82; 46/162; 46/199; 1992: 47/70; 1993: 48/41; 1994: 49/36; 1995: 50/29; 1996: 51/135; 51/132; 51/133; 1997: 51/223; 52/67: 52/65; 1998: ES-10/5 [Emergency Session]; 53/37; 53/56; 53/57; 1999: ES-10/6 [Emergency Session]; 54/37; 54/76; 54/78; 54/79. 2000: ES-10/7: 55/130; 55/132; 55/134; 2001: 55/61; 55/62; ES-10/9 [Emergency Session]; 2002: ES-10/L.9/Rev.l; 57/127; 2003: 58/96; 2004: 59/123; 59/121; 2005: 60/108; 60/106; 2006: ES-10/16; 61/118; 2007: 62/84; 62/109; 2008: 63/98; 2009: 64/91; 64/94. 2010: 65/17; 65/102; 65/103; 65/104; and 65/179. 2011: 66/18; 66/76; 66/225; 66/77; 66/78; 66/79; 2012: 67/24; 67/118; 67/119; 67/121; 67/229; 2013: 68/16; 68/80; 68/81: 68/82; 68/83; 2014: 69/90; 69/91; 69/92; 69/93; 2015: 70/87; 70/88; 70/90. 2016:71/95; 71/96; 71/97; 71/98.

34 *See for example*, Human Rights In Palestine And Other Occupied Arab Territories: Report of the United Nations Fact-Finding Mission on the Gaza Conflict, A/HRC/12/48. 25 September 2009; Report of the Secretary-General on the Progress Made in the Implementation of the Recommendations of the Fact-Finding Mission on the Gaza Conflict, A/HRC/21/33. 21 September 2012; Report of the Secretary-General on the Human Rights Situation in the Occupied Palestinian Territory, including East Jerusalem, A/HRC/24/30, 22 August 2013; Implementation of the Recommendations Contained in the Report of the Independent Fact-finding Mission – Report of the United Nations High Commissioner for Human Rights, A/HRC/28/43, 12 January 2014; Israeli settlements in the Occupied Palestinian Territory, including East Jerusalem, and in the occupied Syrian Golan – Report of the Secretary-General, A/HRC/25/38, 12 February 2014; Report of the United Nations High Commissioner for Human Rights, Addendum on the Human Rights Situation in the Occupied Palestinian Territory between 12 June and 26 August 2014, including the Escalation in Hostilities Between the State of Israel and Palestinian Armed Groups in Gaza, A/HRC/28/80/Add. 1, 26 December 2014; Human Rights Situation in the Occupied Palestinian Territory, including East Jerusalem, A/HRC/28/45, 5 March 2015; Israeli Settlements in the Occupied Palestinian Territory – Report of the Secretary-General, A/HRC/28/44 9 March 2015); Report of the Independent Commission of Inquiry Established Pursuant to Human Rights Council Resolution S-21/1, A/HRC/29/52, 24 June 2015; Report of the detailed findings of the Commission of Inquiry on the 2014 Gaza Conflict, A/HRC/29/CRP.4, 24 June 2015; Annual report of the United Nations High Commissioner for Human Rights and reports of the Office of the High Commissioner and the Secretary-General. A/HRC/31/4420 January 2016; Israeli practices affecting the human rights of the Palestinian people in the Occupied Palestinian Territory, including East Jerusalem – Report of the Secretary-General, A/71/364, 30 August 2016.

35 Theodor Meron is a Judge in and President of the United Nations Mechanism for International Criminal Tribunals; Judge and Past President of the United Nations International Criminal Tribunal for the former Yugoslavia; former Judge of the United

[p. 17] issued a legal opinion "that the establishment of civilian settlements in the occupied West Bank and other conquered territories violates the Fourth Geneva Convention related to the protection of victims of war and, specifically, its prohibition on settlements (Article 49(6))".[36] Judge Meron reaffirmed this opinion on the fiftieth anniversary of the occupation:[37]

> But if the continuation of the settlement project on the West Bank has met with practically universal rejection by the international community, it is not just because of its illegality under the Fourth Geneva Convention or under international humanitarian law more generally. Nor is it only because, by preventing the establishment of a contiguous and viable Palestinian territory, the settlement project frustrates any prospect of serious negotiations aimed at a two state solution, and thus of reconciliation between the Israelis and the Palestinians. It is also because of the growing perception that individual Palestinians' human rights, as well as their rights under the Fourth Geneva Convention, are being violated and that the colonization of territories populated by other peoples can no longer be accepted in our time.

IV Cooperation

19. Throughout the period that the Prosecutor has been conducting her preliminary examination, the State of Palestine has fully cooperated with her Office.
20. Palestine pledges its continued support for, and cooperation with, the Prosecutor and the Court and maintains the hope that other States, including [p. 18] States Parties to the Rome Statute, will provide the

---

Nations International Criminal Tribunal for Rwanda; Charles L. Denison Professor Emeritus and Judicial Fellow, New York University School of Law; Visiting Professor, University of Oxford, since 2014; past Co-Editor-in-Chief of the American Journal of International Law; and the past Honorary President of the American Society of International Law.

36 Theodor Meron, The West Bank And International Humanitarian Law On The Eve Of The Fiftieth Anniversary Of The Six-Day War, AJIL (2017), p. 2.

37 Theodor Meron, The West Bank And International Humanitarian Law On The Eve Of The Fiftieth Anniversary Of The Six-Day War, AJIL (2017), p. 19.

cooperation and resources necessary for the Prosecutor to complete her investigation as expeditiously as possible, with a view to ensuring prompt accountability for the crimes committed in Palestine.

Respectfully Submitted,

SIGNED

Dr. Riad Malki
Minister of Foreign Affairs and Expatriates
The State of Palestine
Dated this 15 May 2018
At: Ramallah, Palestine

SECTION D

International Court of Justice

ICJ, Relocation of the United States Embassy to Jerusalem (Palestine v. United States of America), Application Instituting Proceedings, Sep. 28, 2018

APPLICATION INSTITUTING PROCEEDINGS IN THE INTERNATIONAL COURT OF JUSTICE

STATE OF PALESTINE V. UNITED STATES OF AMERICA

28 SEPTEMBER 2018 [p. 2]

To the Registrar of the International Court of Justice.

1. The undersigned, duly authorized by the Government of the State of Palestine, has the honour to submit to the International Court of Justice, in accordance with Security Council Resolution 9 (1946) and Article 35 (2) of the Statute of the Court, this Application instituting proceedings against the United States of America.

2. By the present Application, the State of Palestine requests the Court to settle the dispute it has with the United States of America over the relocation of the embassy of the United States of America in Israel to the Holy City of Jerusalem. In so doing, it places its faith in the Court to resolve the dispute in accordance with its Statute and jurisprudence, based on the Vienna Convention on Diplomatic Relations (VCDR) read in appropriate context.

I   Factual and Legal Background

3. The subject of the dispute being the relocation of the United States Embassy in Israel to the Holy City of Jerusalem, it is essential to explain the factual and legal context in which the decision to relocate the United States Embassy and its implementation took place.

4. The Holy City of Jerusalem is endowed with unique spiritual, religious and cultural dimensions. This special character of the city continues to prompt the United Nations to adopt numerous resolutions that aim to protect and preserve its unique and special status.

5. As early as 29 November 1947, the United Nations General Assembly adopted the Partition Plan in Resolution 181 (II), *Future Government of Palestine* providing for "Independent Arab and Jewish States and the Special International Regime for the City of Jerusalem" in Palestine. It further specified that:

> "The City of Jerusalem shall be established as a *corpus separatum* under a special international regime.
>
> [...]
>
> The City of Jerusalem shall include the present municipality of Jerusalem plus the surrounding villages and towns, the most eastern of which shall be Abu Dis; the most southern, Bethlehem; the most western, Ein Karim (including also the built-up area of Motsa); and the most northern Shu'fat." [p. 3]

6. The principles underlying this resolution, in particular, the need to protect the special character of the City and the recognition of a specific status within the set boundaries of the City, have continued to serve as a solid foundation for all subsequent resolutions relating to Jerusalem since then.

7. Despite the clear special protected status of the City of Jerusalem, Israel, the occupying power, adopted a set of illegal policies to gradually acquire control over the territory, including by the illegal use of force and by imposing illegal administrative and legislative measures, in an attempt to annex the city.

8. During the war that lasted between December 1947 and January 1949, Israeli Forces occupied West Jerusalem, in violation of Resolution 181. The Armistice agreement of 3 April 1949 lead to the *de facto* division of the city between East and West Jerusalem; meanwhile, the UN continued to advocate for the special status of the City.

9. On 9 December 1949, the General Assembly adopted Resolution 303 (IV), *Palestine: Question of an international regime for the Jerusalem area and the protection of the Holy Places*, in which it restated

> "its intention that Jerusalem should be placed under a permanent international regime, which should envisage appropriate guarantees for the protection of the Holy Place, both within and outside Jerusalem, and to confirm specifically the following provisions of General Assembly resolution 181 (II). (1) the City of Jerusalem shall be established as a *corpus separatum* under a special international regime and shall be administered by the United Nations".

10. In June 1967, Israel occupied the Gaza Strip and the West Bank, including East. Thereafter, Israel took a number of legislative and administrative measures in an attempt to extend its jurisdiction over the city of Jerusalem. It initially utilized local legislation to change the legal status of the entire area of Jerusalem.

11. In response, on 4 July 1967, the General Assembly held its fifth Emergency Special Session during which it adopted resolution 2253 (ES-V), *Measures taken by Israel to change the status of the City of Jerusalem*. In this resolution, the General Assembly, deeply concerned "at the situation prevailing in Jerusalem as a result of the measures taken by Israel to change the status of the City", considered that these measures were "invalid" and further [p. 4] called upon "Israel to rescind all measures already taken and to desist forthwith from taking any action which would alter the status of Jerusalem".

12. Subsequently, both the Security Council and General Assembly, while consistently reaffirming the inadmissibility of the acquisition of territory by use of force,[1] and the overriding necessity of the withdrawal of Israel's armed forces from occupied territories,[2] censured in the strongest terms all measures taken to change the status of the City of Jerusalem.

13. On 21 May 1968, the Security Council adopted Resolution 252 in which it *inter alia* stated that, "all legislative and administrative measures and actions taken by Israel, including expropriation of land and properties thereon which tend to change the legal status of Jerusalem are invalid and cannot change that status". The Security Council maintained its position and reaffirmed Resolution 252 in Resolutions 267 of 3 July 1969, 271 of 15 September 1969 and 298 of 25 September 1971.

14. In 1980, the Security Council, in the wake of and then by way of a response to Israel's adoption of the "Basic Law" that proclaims Jerusalem to be the "complete and united capital of Israel," adopted two very important resolutions concerning the status of the Holy City of Jerusalem. Resolution 476 (1980):

> "3. *Reconfirms* that all legislative and administrative measures and actions taken by Israel, the occupying Power, which purport to alter the character and status of the Holy City of Jerusalem have no legal validity and constitute a flagrant violation of the Geneva Convention relative to

---

[1] See, Security Council ('SC') Resolutions 242 (1967), 252 (1968), 267 (1969), 298 (1971), 476 (180), 478 (1980), and 2334 (2016); General Assembly ('GA') Resolutions 2628 (XXV), 2799 (XXVI), and 2949 (XXVII).

[2] See, SC Resolutions 242 (1967), 476 (180), GA Resolutions 2628 (XXV), 37/86 and 41/162.

the Protection of Civilian Persons in Time of War and also constitute a serious obstruction to achieving a comprehensive, just and lasting peace in the Middle East;

4. *Reiterates* that all such measures which have altered the geographic, demographic and historical character and status of the Holy City of Jerusalem are null and void and must be rescinded in compliance with the relevant resolutions of the Security Council;

5. *Urgently calls* on Israel, the occupying Power, to abide by the present and previous Security Council resolutions and to desist forthwith from persisting in the policy and measures affecting the character and status of the Holy City of Jerusalem." [p. 5]

15. Shortly later, the Security Council, in resolution 478, *noting* that Israel had not complied with resolution 476 (1980) *decided*

"(…) not to recognize the 'basic law' and such other actions by Israel that, as a result of this law, seek to alter the character and status of Jerusalem"

and, besides, called upon

"(a) All Member States to accept this decision;
(b) Those States that have established diplomatic missions at Jerusalem to withdraw such missions from the Holy City".

16. It is particularly worth noting that all those States that had in the meantime established their embassies in Jerusalem, decided to relocate them elsewhere, in compliance with that Security Council resolution.[3]

17. Chile, Ecuador and Venezuela had announced their decision to withdraw their diplomatic missions from Jerusalem, and at the time of the resolution's adoption, between 22 August and 9 September, Bolivia, Colombia, Costa Rica, the Dominican Republic, El Salvador, Guatemala, Haiti, the Netherlands, Panama, and Uruguay informed the Secretary General they had decided to also withdraw their respective embassies from Jerusalem.

---

3   *Yearbook of the United Nations*, 1980, Part 1, Section 1, Chapter 12: Questions relating to the Middle East, p. 405.

18. Most recently, the Republic of Paraguay, who had decided to move its embassy to Jerusalem at the same time the decision was taken by the United States, rescinded its decision and moved its embassy back to Tel Aviv on 5 September 2018. The Republic of Paraguay noted that it took this decision in line with its constitutional commitments to respect international law.[4]

19. In its more recent Resolution 2334 of 23 December 2016, the Security Council *inter alia* had reaffirmed its previous resolutions concerning Jerusalem, including resolution 478 (1980).

20. Both the General Assembly and the Security Council have consistently stated that actions or decisions purporting to alter the character, status or demographic composition [p. 6] of the Holy City of Jerusalem are deprived of legal effect and are null and void under international law.

II Statement of Facts

21. On 6 December 2017, the President of the United States of America unilaterally recognized the Holy City of Jerusalem as the capital of Israel and announced the relocation of the United States Embassy in Israel from Tel Aviv to the Holy City of Jerusalem.[5]

22. On 18 December 2017, due solely to the veto of the United States of America, the concerned party to the present dispute, the Security Council failed to adopt a resolution reiterating that

> "any decisions and actions which purport to have altered, the character, status or demographic composition of the Holy City of Jerusalem have no legal effect, are null and void and must be rescinded in compliance with relevant resolutions of the Security Council".[6]

---

4 Statement on the location of the Embassy of the Republic of Paraguay to the State of Israel, 5 September 2018, available at: http://www2.mre.gov.py/index.php/download_file/view/9576/3622.

5 Annex 5.

6 See, the meeting record of the Security Council meeting held on 18 December 2017, *The Situation in the Middle-East, including the Palestinian Question* (*S/PV.8139*) and the press release issued the same day (SC/13125). During this meeting, the Draft resolution S/2017/1060 was vetoed by the United States of America, there was no abstention during this vote and the 14 other States composing the Security Council voted in favour of the adoption.

23. The Security Council's failure to discharge its responsibilities on behalf of all the Member States to maintain international peace and security[7] led the General Assembly to hold an Emergency Special Session, in which it adopted Resolution ES-10/19 and affirmed

> "that any decisions and actions which purport to have altered the character, status or demographic composition of the Holy City of Jerusalem have no legal effect, are null and void and must be rescinded in compliance with relevant resolutions of the Security Council, and in this regard calls upon all States to refrain from the establishment of diplomatic missions in the Holy City of Jerusalem, pursuant to Council resolution 478 (1980)".

and further called upon

> "all States to refrain from the establishment of diplomatic missions in the Holy City of Jerusalem, pursuant to Council resolution 478 (1980)". [p. 7]

24. On 14 May 2018, the United States of America inaugurated its embassy in the Holy City of Jerusalem.[8]

III   Jurisdiction of the Court

25. The Court has jurisdiction over the issues addressed in this Application under Article 1 of the Optional Protocol to the Vienna Convention on Diplomatic Relations concerning the Compulsory Settlement of Disputes.[9]

26. The State of Palestine acceded to the Vienna Convention on Diplomatic Relations on 2 April 2014 and to the Optional Protocol on 22 March 2018 whereas the United States of America has been a party to both these instruments since 13 November 1972.

27. Article VII of the Optional Protocol provides that it

---

[7] Mechanisms established by the United Nations General Assembly in Resolution 377 (V), *Uniting for Peace*, adopted on 3 November 1950.

[8] See the Press Statement issued by the Secretary of State of the United States of America Mike Pompeo, issued on 14 May 2018, available at: https://www.state.gov/secretary/remarks/2018/05/282066.htm.

[9] Annex 2.

"(...) shall remain open for accession by all States which may become Parties to the Convention".

28. As for the Vienna Convention on Diplomatic Relations itself, its Article 48 provides that the Convention

"(...) shall be open for signature by all States Member of the United Nations or of any of the specialized agencies or Parties to the Statute of the International Court of Justice, and by any other State invited by the General Assembly of the United Nations to become a Party to the Convention".

29. Article 50 of the Vienna Convention on Diplomatic Relations in turn further provides that

"[t]he present Convention shall remain open for accession by any State belonging to any of the four categories mentioned in Article 48."[10] [p. 8]

30. The State of Palestine submitted on 4 July 2018, in accordance with Security Council Resolution 9 (1946) and Article 35 (2) of the Statute of the Court, a 'Declaration recognizing the Competence of the International Court of Justice' for the settlement of all disputes that may arise or that have already arisen covered by Articles I and II of the Optional Protocol.[11]

31. Article I of the Optional Protocol concerning the Compulsory Settlement of Disputes provides that:

"Disputes arising out of the interpretation or application of the Convention shall lie within the compulsory jurisdiction of the International Court of Justice and may accordingly be brought before the Court by an application made by any party to the dispute being a Party to the present Protocol."

32. This provision covers any dispute related to the interpretation or application of the Convention on Diplomatic Relations to which, as stated above, both the State of Palestine and the United States of America are contracting parties.

---

[10] It ought to be noted in that regard that the State of Palestine became a member of UNESCO effective 31 October 2011, UNESCO being such specialized agency within the meaning of Article 57 of the Charter of the United Nations.

[11] Annex 4.

33. Article II of the Optional Protocol concerning the Compulsory Settlement of Disputes provides that:

> "The parties may agree, within a period of two months after one party has notified its opinion to the other that a dispute exists, to resort not to the International Court of Justice but to an arbitral tribunal. After the expiry of the said period, either party may bring the dispute before the Court by an application."

34. Prior to the implementation of the decision to move the embassy, through a Note Verbale, dated 14 May 2018, the State of Palestine formally informed the State Department of the United States of America of its position that any steps taken to relocate the embassy constitute a violation of the VCDR, read in conjunction with the relevant UNSC resolutions and requested that the United States inform the State of Palestine of "any steps the United States is considering to ensure that its actions are in line with the Vienna Convention on Diplomatic Relations".[12] [p. 9]

35. Not having been informed of any steps taken as requested, the Ministry of Foreign Affairs and Expatriates of the State of Palestine[13] notified the State Department of the United States of America, through a Note Verbale dated 4 July 2018, of the existence of a dispute between the two Parties, pursuant to Articles I and II of the Optional Protocol concerning the Compulsory Settlement of Disputes, arising out of the interpretation or application of the Vienna Convention on Diplomatic Relations,[14] read in conjunction with relevant Security Council resolutions on the alteration of the status of the Holy City of Jerusalem, specifically resolution 478 (1980) adopted on 20 August 1980.

IV   Legal Grounds for the Claims

36. The relocation of the United States embassy in Israel to the Holy City of Jerusalem constitutes a breach of the Vienna Convention on Diplomatic Relations of 18 April 1961. It is undeniable that the Convention was conceived as a tool for the pacification of international relations. This is clear from the Preamble of the Convention in which the States Parties declare:

---

12   Annex 3.
13   Annex 3.
14   Annex 1.

> "*Having in mind* the purposes and principles of the Charter of the United Nations concerning the sovereign equality of States, the maintenance of international peace and security and the promotion of friendly relations among nations"

and

> "*Believing* that an international convention on diplomatic intercourse, privileges and immunities would contribute to the development of friendly relations among nations, irrespective of their differing constitutional and social systems"

37. Article 3, paragraph 1, of the Convention provides that:

> "1. The functions of a diplomatic mission consist, *inter alia*, in:
> (*a*) Representing the sending State in the receiving State;
> (*b*) Protecting in the receiving State the interests of the sending State and of its nationals, within the limits permitted by international law;
> (*c*) Negotiating with the Government of the receiving State;
> (*d*) Ascertaining by all lawful means conditions and developments in the receiving State, and reporting thereon to the Government of the sending State; [p. 10]
> (*e*) Promoting friendly relations between the sending State and the receiving State, and developing their economic, cultural and scientific relations".

38. It is clear from this article that one of the main functions of a diplomatic mission consists in "[r]epresenting the sending State *in the receiving State*".[15] The very wording of subparagraph (a) is self-explanatory and leaves no doubt on the fact that the representational function of any diplomatic mission should be performed on the territory of the receiving State.

39. In addition to that, out of the four other functions of diplomatic missions enumerated in Article 3 of the Vienna Convention on Diplomatic Relations, two functions are to be performed "in the receiving State".

40. This is true with regards to subparagraph (b), which deals with the function consisting in

---

15   Emphasis added.

> "[p]rotecting *in the receiving State* the interests of the sending State and of its nationals, within the limits permitted by international law",[16]

as well as with regards to subparagraph (d) which provides that one of the functions of a diplomatic mission consists in

> "[a]scertaining by all lawful means conditions and developments *in the receiving State*, and reporting thereon to the Government of the sending State".[17]

41. The only functions of a diplomatic mission that are not specifically required to be performed "in the receiving State" are the negotiation function of subparagraph (c) and the promotion of friendly relations with the receiving State mentioned in subparagraph (e).

42. The formula "in the receiving State" is not only used in Article 3 of the Vienna Convention on Diplomatic Relations. It is present in twelve other provisions of the Convention. This highlights the fact that the diplomatic mission of a sending State must be established on the territory of the receiving State.

[p. 11]

43. The fact that the sending State can only establish a diplomatic mission on the territory of the receiving State is confirmed by Article 21, paragraph 1, of the Convention which provides that

> "[t]he receiving State shall either facilitate the acquisition *on its territory*, in accordance with its laws, by the sending State of premises necessary for its mission or assist the latter in obtaining accommodation in some other way".[18]

44. A diplomatic mission may have to perform various functions on the territory of the receiving State, whether or not these functions are mentioned in the article. Nonetheless, there are clear limitations to the actions of such a mission, both under the Vienna Convention on Diplomatic Relations and general international law to which the Convention refers.

---

16   Emphasis added.
17   Emphasis added.
18   Emphasis added.

45. Subparagraphs (b) and (d) of Article 3, paragraph 1, of the Convention provide further limitations for the diplomatic mission of the sending State in performing specific functions that are expressly required to be performed "in the receiving State".

46. Thus, when a diplomatic mission protects the interests and the nationals of the sending State "in the receiving State", it may and must only do so "within the limits permitted by international law" as stated in subparagraph (b).

47. In a similar manner, when a diplomatic mission ascertains conditions and developments in the receiving State, it is bound to only use "all lawful means" as required by subparagraph (d).

48. Besides these specific limitations, Article 41, paragraph 3, of the Convention provides a general limitation and a framework for the action and purpose of a diplomatic mission. This article reads as follows:

> "The premises of the mission must not be used in any manner incompatible with the functions of the mission as laid down in the present Convention or by other rules of general international law or by any special agreement in force between the sending and the receiving State".
> [p. 12]

49. It is clear from the above provisions that the Convention on Diplomatic Relations requires the sending State to establish a diplomatic mission "in the receiving State" to perform its functions and demands that the diplomatic mission performs its functions while respecting the rule of law, especially international law.

50. The relocation of the US Embassy in Israel to the Holy City of Jerusalem is in breach of the provisions of the Convention on Diplomatic Relations mentioned above as well as, more generally, of its object and purpose and of "other rules of general international law" to which the Convention refers, including rights reiterated by the Court's Advisory Opinion of 4 July 2014.

V Decision Requested

51. By the present Application, the State of Palestine therefore requests the Court to declare that the relocation, to the Holy City of Jerusalem, of the United States embassy in Israel is in breach of the Vienna Convention on Diplomatic Relations.

52. The State of Palestine further requests the Court to order the United States of America to withdraw the diplomatic mission from the Holy City of Jerusalem and to conform to the international obligations flowing from the Vienna Convention on Diplomatic Relations.

53. In addition, the State of Palestine asks the Court to order the United States of America to take all necessary steps to comply with its obligations, to refrain from taking any future measures that would violate its obligations and to provide assurances and guarantees of non-repetition of its unlawful conduct.

VI   Reservation of Rights

54. The State of Palestine reserves its rights to supplement or amend the present Application. [p. 13]

VII   Appointment of Agent and Co-Agent

55. The State of Palestine hereby designates as its Agent Ambassador Ammar Hijazi, assistant Minister for Multilateral Affairs of the State of Palestine, and as its Co-Agent Ambassador Rawan Sulaiman, Head of the Palestinian Mission to the Kingdom of the Netherlands, Permanent Representative of the State of Palestine to the ICC, PCA and OPWC.

VIII   Ad Hoc Judge

56. In accordance with the provisions of Article 31(3) of the Statute of the Court, and Article 35(1) of the Rules of the Court, the State of Palestine declares its intention to exercise its right to choose a judge *ad hoc*.

Respectfully submitted,

Dr. Riad Malki
Minister of Foreign Affairs and Expatriates
State of Palestine [p. 14]

ANNEXES

Annex 1. Vienna Convention on Diplomatic Relations, 18 April 1961.

Annex 2. Optional Protocol to the Vienna Convention on Diplomatic Relations, concerning the Compulsory Settlement of Disputes, 18 April 1961.

Annex 3. Note Verbale of the Ministry of Foreign Affairs of the State of Palestine addressed to the Department of State of the United States of America, 14 May 2018.

Annex 4. Note Verbale of the Ministry of Foreign Affairs of the State of Palestine addressed to the Department of State of the United States of America, 4 July 2018.

Annex 5. Declaration recognizing the Competence of the International Court of Justice, 4 July 2018.

Annex 6. Presidential Proclamation Recognizing Jerusalem as the Capital of the State of Israel and Relocating the United States Embassy to Israel to Jerusalem, 6 December 2017.

ICJ, Relocation of the United States Embassy to Jerusalem (Palestine v. United States of America), Order, Sep. 28, 2018

INTERNATIONAL COURT OF JUSTICE

YEAR 2018

15 November 2018

RELOCATION OF THE UNITED STATES EMBASSY TO JERUSALEM (PALESTINE v. UNITED STATES OF AMERICA)

ORDER

2018
15 November
General List
No. 176

Present:

President YUSUF; *Vice-President* XUE; *Judges* TOMKA, ABRAHAM, BENNOUNA, CANÇADO TRINDADE, DONOGHUE, GAJA, SEBUTINDE, BHANDARI, ROBINSON, CRAWFORD, GEVORGIAN, SALAM, IWASAWA; *Registrar* COUVREUR.

The International Court of Justice,

Composed as above,

After deliberation,

Having regard to Article 48 of the Statute of the Court and to Articles 44, 48 and 79, paragraphs 2 and 3, of the Rules of Court,

Having regard to the "Declaration Recognizing the Competence of the International Court of Justice" deposited by the State of Palestine (hereinafter "Palestine") on 4 July 2018, whereby, pursuant to Security Council resolution 9 (1946) of 15 October 1946 adopted in virtue of the powers conferred upon the Council by Article 35, paragraph 2, of the Statute of the Court, Palestine "accept[ed] with immediate effect the competence of the International Court of Justice for the [p. 2] settlement of all disputes that may arise or that have already arisen covered by Article I of the Optional Protocol to the Vienna Convention on Diplomatic Relations Concerning the Compulsory Settlement of Disputes (1961), to which the State of Palestine acceded on 22 March 2018",

Having regard to the Application filed in the Registry of the Court on 28 September 2018, whereby Palestine instituted proceedings against the United States of America (hereinafter the "United States") concerning alleged violations of the Vienna Convention on Diplomatic Relations of 18 April 1961 (hereinafter the "Vienna Convention");

Whereas a certified copy of the Application was communicated to the United States on the day it was filed;

Whereas in its Application, Palestine seeks to found the jurisdiction of the Court on Article I of the Optional Protocol to the Vienna Convention on Diplomatic Relations concerning the Compulsory Settlement of Disputes (hereinafter the "Optional Protocol");

Whereas Palestine appointed H.E. Mr. Ammar Hijazi, as Agent, and H.E. Ms Rawan Sulaiman, as Co-Agent, for the purposes of the case; whereas the United States was invited to appoint an agent in the case, in accordance with Article 40, paragraph 2, of the Rules of Court; and whereas it has not appointed an agent to date;

Whereas, by a letter dated 11 October 2018, the Registrar invited the representatives of the Parties to a meeting with the President of the Court to be held on 5 November 2018, pursuant to Article 31 of the Rules of Court, in order for the President to ascertain the views of the Parties with regard to questions of procedure in the case;

Whereas, by a letter dated 2 November 2018, Ms Jennifer G. Newstead, Legal Adviser of the United States Department of State, informed the Court that, on 13 May 2014, following the Applicant's "purported accession" to the Vienna Convention, the United States had submitted a communication to the Secretary-General of the United Nations, declaring that the United States did not consider itself to be in a treaty relationship with the Applicant under the Vienna Convention; whereas she added that, on 1 May 2018, following the Applicant's "purported accession" to the Optional Protocol, the United States had submitted a similar communication to the Secretary-General of the United Nations, declaring that the United States did not consider itself to be in a treaty relationship with the Applicant under the Optional Protocol; whereas, in her letter, Ms Newstead observed that the Applicant had been aware of these communications by the United States before it submitted its Application to the Court; and whereas she concluded that, according to the United States, "it [was] manifest that the Court ha[d] no jurisdiction in respect of the Application" and that the case ought to be removed from the list;

Whereas, by a letter of the same date, Ms Newstead informed the Registrar that the United States would not participate in the proposed meeting to be held on 5 November 2018 by the President with the representatives of the Parties;

Whereas, on 5 November 2018, the President of the Court met with the representatives of Palestine; whereas, at that meeting, Palestine expressed the wish that the Court decide in favour of its claim and indicated a strong preference for the submission of a Memorial dealing both with jurisdiction and merits, on the grounds that these two aspects were, in its view, closely related, stating that Palestine would need six months for the preparation of the said pleading; whereas Palestine added that, if the Court were to order a first round of written pleadings dedicated solely to the question of its jurisdiction, a time-limit of six months would similarly be necessary for the preparation of a pleading on that question; [p. 3]

Whereas the Court considers, with reference to Article 79, paragraph 2, of its Rules, that, in the circumstances of the case, in particular in view of the fact that, according to the United States, the Court manifestly lacks jurisdiction to entertain Palestine's Application, it is necessary to resolve first of all the question of the Court's jurisdiction and that of the admissibility of the Application, and that these matters should accordingly be separately determined before any proceedings on the merits;

Whereas it is necessary for the Court to be informed of all the contentions and evidence on facts and law on which the Parties rely in relation to its jurisdiction and the admissibility of the Application,

Decides that the written pleadings shall first be addressed to the question of the jurisdiction of the Court and that of the admissibility of the Application;

Fixes the following time-limits for the filing of those pleadings:

15 May 2019 for the Memorial of the State of Palestine;

15 November 2019 for the Counter-Memorial of the United States of America; and

Reserves the subsequent procedure for further decision.

Done in French and in English, the French being authoritative, at the Peace Palace, The Hague, this fifteenth day of November, two thousand and eighteen, in three copies, one of which will be placed in the archives of the Court and the others transmitted to the Government of the State of Palestine and the Government of the United States of America, respectively.

(*Signed*) Abdulqawi Ahmed YUSUF, President.

(*Signed*) Philippe COUVREUR, Registrar.

SECTION E

Cases

United States, Koontz v. Watson, 283 F. Supp. 3d 1007 (D. Kan. 2018)

IN THE UNITED STATES DISTRICT COURT FOR THE DISTRICT OF KANSAS
ESTHER KOONTZ, Plaintiff,

v.

RANDALL D. WATSON, in his official capacity as Kansas Commission of Education, Defendant

Jan. 30, 2018

Case No. 17-4099-DDC-KGS

<u>MEMORANDUM AND ORDER</u>

In this lawsuit, plaintiff Esther Koontz seeks injunctive and declaratory relief under *42 U.S.C. § 1983*. She asks the court to enjoin enforcement of a Kansas law requiring all persons who enter into a contract with the State of Kansas to certify that they are not engaged in a boycott of Israel. Ms. Koontz claims that this law violates both the *First Amendment* and the *Fourteenth Amendment's Equal Protection Clause*. This matter comes before the court on Ms. Koontz's Motion for Preliminary Injunction (Doc. 3). The parties have briefed the issue fully and presented oral argument on it.

Judging the constitutionality of democratically enacted laws is among "the gravest and most delicate" enterprises a federal court ever undertakes. *Blodgett v. Holden*, 275 U.S. 142, 147–48 (1927) (Holmes, J., concurring). But just as surely, following precedent is a core component of the rule of law. When the Supreme Court or our Circuit has established a clear rule of law, our court must follow it. *Rodriguez de Quijas v. Shearson/Am. Express, Inc.*, 490 U.S. 477, 484 (1989). As this Order explains, the Supreme Court has held that the First Amendment protects the right to participate in a boycott like the one punished by the

Kansas law. The court thus grants plaintiff's motion and imposes the preliminary injunction specified at the end of this Order.

I   Facts

House Bill 2409

In June 2017, Kansas enacted House Bill 2409 ("the Kansas Law"). This law requires all state contractors to certify that they are not engaged in a boycott of Israel. Kan. Stat. Ann. § 75–3740f(a). The Kansas Law defines a "boycott" as:

> [E]ngaging in a refusal to deal, terminating business activities or performing other actions that are intended to limit commercial relations with persons or entities doing business in Israel or in territories controlled by Israel, if those actions are taken either: (1) In compliance with or adherence to calls for a boycott of Israel other than those boycotts to which 50 U.S.C. § 4607(c)[1] applies; or (2) in a manner that discriminates on the basis of nationality, national origin or religion, and that is not based on a valid business reason....

Id. § 75–3740e(a). The Kansas Law also allows the Secretary of Administration for the State of Kansas to waive this requirement "if the secretary determines that compliance is not practicable." *Id.* § 75–3740f(c). The Kansas Law took effect on July 1, 2017. 2017 Kan. Sess. Laws 1126.

Multiple legislators made statements during debate about the Kansas Law that its purpose was to stop people from antagonizing Israel. And multiple private individuals testified to the same effect. Several individuals emphasized the need to oppose "Boycott, Divestment, Sanctions" campaigns, which protest the Israeli government's treatment of Palestinians in the occupied Palestinian territories and Israel by applying economic pressure to Israel. During a committee hearing about the bill[2] that became the Kansas Law, the Director of Marketing and Research for the Kansas Department of Commerce testified that Israel and Kansas are substantial trading partners. The Department of Commerce calculated that in 2016, Kansas exported $56 million worth of commodities to Israel

---

1   This federal provision preempts state law from contradicting a federal statute prohibiting certain types of boycotts. *See* 50 U.S.C. § 4607(a)(1). Plaintiff does not assert that the Kansas Law conflicts with the federal provision.
2   House Bill 2409.

while importing $83 million from Israel. The Kansas Law's fiscal note asserted that the Kansas Law would not affect the Kansas state government fiscally.

Plaintiff's Boycott of Israel

In May 2017, plaintiff Esther Koontz began boycotting Israeli businesses. She first became motivated to boycott Israel in 2016 when she saw a presentation about conditions in Israel and Palestine. And on July 6, 2017, Mennonite Church USA passed a resolution calling on Mennonites to take steps to redress the injustice and violence that both Palestinians and Israelis have experienced. Ms. Koontz is a member of a Mennonite Church organization. Specifically, this organization's resolution called on Mennonites to boycott products associated with Israel's occupation of Palestine. As a consequence, plaintiff decided she would not buy any products or services from Israeli companies or from any company who operates in Israeli-occupied Palestine.

Plaintiff's Efforts to Contract with Kansas

Plaintiff is a curriculum coach at a public school in Wichita, Kansas. As part of her regular duties, she supports her school's curriculum and teaches teachers how to implement it. Before she began working in this position, plaintiff taught math in the Wichita public schools. During the 2016–17 academic year, the Kansas State Department of Education ("KSDE") selected plaintiff to participate as a teacher trainer in KSDE's Math and Science Partnership program. In this program, KSDE contracts with professional educators to provide coaching and training to public school math and science teachers throughout Kansas. Plaintiff wants to participate in the program, both to enhance her career and earn extra spending money. Plaintiff would have earned an extra $600 per day (plus travel expenses) for each training she gives.

On May 31, 2017, plaintiff successfully completed the requisite training to serve as trainer for the program. Shortly afterward, the program director for the Math and Science Partnership, Melissa Fast, began sending plaintiff travel requests asking her to lead training programs for other teachers. Plaintiff said she was willing to conduct three of the trainings that Ms. Fast initially offered her. In the future, plaintiff asserts, she would like to do as many training sessions as she can.

On July 10, 2017, the program director asked Ms. Koontz to sign a certification confirming that she was not participating in a boycott of Israel, as the Kansas Law requires. Initially, plaintiff did not respond because she wanted to consider her options. On August 9, 2017, plaintiff emailed the program director and told her that she had decided to refuse to sign the certification. The program director responded that Kansas could not pay plaintiff as a contractor unless she signed the certification.

Despite plaintiff's eligibility and interest in participating in the Math and Science Partnership program, the KSDE declined to contract with plaintiff because she would not sign the certification. But in this case, defendant Randall D. Watson[3] submitted an affidavit from the Secretary of Administration, Sarah Shipman. It asserts that Secretary Shipman would have waived the certification requirement if plaintiff had asked her to do so. It is undisputed that plaintiff did not apply for the waiver authorized by Kan. Stat. Ann. § 75–3740f(c).

II Ripeness

Before the court can reach the merits of plaintiff's motion, it must decide whether her claim is ripe for judicial review. *Kan. Judicial Review v. Stout*, 519 F.3d 1107, 1114 (10th Cir. 2008). This ripeness requirement is a component of justiciability. "In order for a claim to be justiciable under Article III [of the Constitution], it must present a live controversy, ripe for determination, advanced in a 'clean-cut and concrete form.'" *Id.* at 1116 (quoting *Renne v. Geary*, 501 U.S. 312, 322, 111 S. Ct. 2331, 115 L. Ed. 2d 288 (1991)).[4]

Typically, federal courts "apply a two-factor test to determine whether an issue is ripe." *Id.* These factors evaluate the fitness of "the issue for judicial resolution and the hardship to the parties of withholding judicial consideration." *Sierra Club v. Yeutter*, 911 F.2d 1405, 1415 (10th Cir. 1990). But when the claim presents a First Amendment facial challenge, the "ripeness analysis is 'relaxed

---

3 Randall Watson is the Kansas Commissioner of Education and the Chief Administrative Officer of the KSDE. He is charged with enforcing compliance with the Kansas Law for all KSDE independent contractors.

4 In a broader sense, the ripeness requirement implicates a federal court's subject matter jurisdiction under Article III's case and controversy clause. *Acorn v. City of Tulsa, Okla.*, 835 F.2d 735, 738 (10th Cir. 1987). When a defendant challenges a claim's ripeness, it is, in effect, a challenge to the court's subject matter jurisdiction. *New Mexicans for Bill Richardson v. Gonzales*, 64 F.3d 1495, 1498–99 (10th Cir. 1995). Typically, the federal courts view such a challenge as a motion under Fed. R. Civ. P. 12(b)(1). *Id.* at 1499. Here, defendant has not challenged the court's subject matter jurisdiction. Instead, he claims that plaintiff likely will not succeed on the merits because her claim is not ripe. Doc. 11 at 8. But because a claim's ripeness affects the court's subject matter jurisdiction, the court must consider it before deciding any substantive matter. *See Friends of Marolt Park v. U.S. Dep't of Transp.*, 382 F.3d 1088, 1093 (10th Cir. 2004) ("Before we reach the merits of appellant's claims, we must examine whether the issues raised in this case are ripe for review.").

somewhat'... because an unconstitutional law may chill free speech." *Stout*, 519 F.3d at 1116 (quoting *New Mexicans for Bill Richardson v. Gonzales*, 64 F.3d 1495, 1499 (10th Cir. 1995)).

The ripeness factors considered in a facial First Amendment challenge case are: "(1) hardship to the parties by withholding review; (2) the chilling effect the challenged law may have on First Amendment liberties; and (3) fitness of the controversy for judicial review." *Richardson*, 64 F.3d at 1500. Because these factors are not ones that apply themselves in a self-evident fashion, the next three subsections discuss them at some length.

A   *"Hardship to the Parties by Withholding Review"*

This first factor requires the court to "ask whether the [Kansas Law] create[s] a 'direct and immediate dilemma for the parties.'" *Stout*, 519 F.3d at 1117 (quoting *Richardson*, 64 F.3d at 1500). *Stout* illustrates how to apply this factor. There, two candidates for popularly elected judicial office challenged two provisions in the Kansas Code of Judicial Conduct. *Id.* at 1111. The provisions prohibited candidates for judicial office from making certain pledges and personally soliciting support for their campaigns. *Id.* Two candidates sued, presenting both a facial and as applied challenge asserting that these restrictions infringed their First Amendment rights of political expression. *Id.* Our court concluded that the claims were ripe and found that plaintiffs likely would succeed on the merits. *Id.* It thus entered a preliminary injunction forbidding enforcement of the provisions. *Id.*

On appeal, *Stout*'s defendants again challenged the ripeness of plaintiffs' claims. *Id.* at 1115–16. They argued that no one had initiated a disciplinary action against the judicial candidates for violating the restrictions and so, "plaintiffs' fears of prosecution are illusory." *Id.* at 1117. The Circuit rejected defendants' argument, reasoning: "So long as the [provisions] remain in effect in their current form, the state is free to initiate such action against candidates [for judicial office]." *Id.* at 1118 (citing *Grant v. Meyer*, 828 F.2d 1446, 1449 (10th Cir. 1987) (explaining that when fear of sanction "is not imaginary or wholly speculative, a plaintiff need not first expose himself to actual arrest or prosecution to be entitled to challenge [the] statute") (internal citation and quotation omitted)).

The Kansas Law challenged in the current case puts plaintiff in a different posture than the plaintiffs in *Richardson* and *Stout*. Ms. Koontz's boycott of Israel does not expose her to fear of prosecution (as in *Richardson*, 64 F.3d at 1501) or professional discipline (as in *Stout*, 519 F.3d at 1118). Instead, the Kansas Law simply disqualifies plaintiff from eligibility for reaping the benefits of a contract with the State of Kansas that she otherwise would have received, *i.e.*, a contract compensating plaintiff for serving as a trainer for the Math and

Science Partnership. But the court concludes that this difference is immaterial. The challenged Kansas Law still imposes a hardship on plaintiff and, potentially, others subject to its disqualifying provision. As long as the Kansas Law "remains in effect in [its] current form, the state is free" to use it to disqualify other contractual aspirants. *Stout*, 519 F.3d at 1118. As in *Stout*, this presents the requisite hardship for purposes of the ripeness analysis.

B   *Potential "Chilling Effect of the Challenged Law on First Amendment Liberties"*

The second factor of the relaxed ripeness test requires the court to assess "the chilling effect the challenged law may have on First Amendment liberties." *Id.* at 1116 (citing *Richardson*, 64 F.3d at 1499–1500). In its cases applying this factor, the Circuit has expressed an important corollary to it. When the challenged statute is unconstitutionally vague, that vagueness "greatly militates in favor of finding an otherwise premature controversy to be ripe." *Id.* at 1118 (citing *Richardson*, 64 F.3d at 1503). Indeed, the Circuit has observed that a plaintiff "should not have to risk prosecution, under a statute whose scope is unclear, before [her] challenge to the constitutionality of that statute is ripe." *Richardson*, 64 F.3d at 1503.

This corollary, then, frames the threshold question under this second factor: Is the Kansas Law challenged here vague? In one sense, it is not. It imposes a bright line rule. All prospective contractors must certify to Kansas that they are not boycotting Israel. *See* Kan. Stat. Ann § 75–3740f(a). If they don't so certify, they can't contract with the state. But a second aspect of the Kansas Law injects a significant degree of uncertainty. This provision authorizes the Kansas Secretary of Administration to waive the Kansas Law's certification requirement "if the secretary determines that compliance is not *practicable*." *Id.* § 75–3704f(c) (emphasis added).

When is compliance "not practicable?" The Kansas Law does not say. Indeed, it provides no guidance about the meaning intended for this important term. Defendant's Opposition to plaintiff's injunction motion (Doc. 11) is mum on the subject as well. It never mentions the issue at all. But at oral argument, defense counsel described the standard applied to date by Kansas's Secretary of Administration. The Secretary has received, defense counsel represented, a few requests to waive the certification requirement. Some requests were submitted by putative contractors who asserted that they just didn't "want to fill out another government form and deal with the state government to be a contractor." Counsel argued that the Secretary reasonably had determined it was "practicable" for these stubborn applicants to comply with the Kansas Law's certification requirement. Counsel contrasted this kind of contractor with Ms.

Koontz. He explained that the plaintiff is "a member of a church, a church [where] there's a religious belief that would oppose doing business with Israel." So, defense counsel asserted, the Secretary of Administration "would grant the waiver when presented with evidence; [but] not [grant a waiver to a contractor who] just [said,] 'I don't want to do it.'"

The court is not yet prepared to decide the constitutional sufficiency of such a malleable, uncertain definition for a term so central to the Kansas Law and to the ripeness analysis of plaintiff's claim. But the court has sufficient information to decide that "the arguable vagueness of [the Kansas Law] greatly militates in favor of a finding of ripeness." *Stout*, 519 F.3d at 1118. A potential contractor "should not have to risk [exclusion], under a statute whose scope is unclear, before [her] challenge to the constitutionality of that statute [becomes] ripe." *Richardson*, 64 F.3d at 1503. As in *Richardson* and *Stout*, this "potential vagueness" may increase the hardship to plaintiff and others, and the generalized chilling effect on speech. *Id.* The court thus concludes that this second factor also favors a finding that plaintiff's claim is ripe for adjudication.

C   *Fitness of the Controversy for Judicial Review*

The third and final factor of the relaxed ripeness test considers whether the controversy presented by plaintiff's claim is one fit for judicial review. *Stout*, 519 F.3d at 1116. Our Circuit explained that this factor focuses on "whether determination of the merits turns upon strictly legal issues or requires facts that may not yet be sufficiently developed." *Richardson*, 64 F.3d at 1499. Also, the Circuit has held, a "[F]irst [A]mendment challenge to the facial validity of a statute is a strictly legal question; it does not involve the application of the statute in a specific factual setting." *ACORN v. City of Tulsa, Okla.*, 835 F.2d 735, 740 (10th Cir. 1987); *accord Awad v. Ziriax*, 670 F.3d 1111, 1124–25 (10th Cir. 2012). And even when a case presents an as applied challenge, it is fit for judicial review if "the facts of the case are relatively uncontested." *Stout*, 519 F.3d at 1118.

Here, Ms. Koontz presents a facial challenge to the Kansas Law under the First Amendment. This brings it within the holding in *ACORN* and *Awad*. And even if one construed the case's claims as ones presenting only an as applied challenge – which the court does not – the facts controlling that analysis are not disputed materially.

D   *ACORN v. Tulsa*

While sections A, B, and C complete the analysis required by the three-part relaxed ripeness test, the court devotes a fourth section to the ripeness discussion in *ACORN v. Tulsa*. 835 F.2d 735. It does so because the Circuit's discussion there is particularly informative about the correct analysis here.

In *ACORN*, the plaintiffs brought a facial First Amendment challenge to an ordinance adopted by the City of Tulsa, Oklahoma. *Id.* at 738. The challenged ordinance prohibited public gatherings in public parks and also forbade posting signs in parks without approval by the Tulsa Park and Recreation Board. *Id.* at 736. Plaintiffs had made plans to protest in one of Tulsa's city parks but various city officials told them that only the Park and Recreation Board could approve their planned protest. *Id.* at 737–38. Plaintiffs never asked that board for permission to protest in the park and, instead, conducted their protest gathering on private property. *Id.* at 738. Afterward, plaintiffs sued the city, alleging that the ordinance violated the First Amendment on its face. *Id.* Their suit sought to recover damages for past harm and also asked to enjoin future enforcement of the ordinance. *Id.*

The district court held plaintiffs' challenge was not ripe for judicial review because the plaintiffs never had asked the Park and Recreation Board for permission to protest in the park. *Id.* The Tenth Circuit disagreed. It held that a request seeking the board's permission to protest in the park was not a prerequisite to filing suit. *Id.* at 739. It emphasized, "'applying for and being denied a license or an exemption is not a condition precedent to bringing a facial challenge to an unconstitutional law.'" *Id.* (quoting *ACORN v. Golden*, 744 F.2d 739, 744 (10th Cir. 1984)). *ACORN* also noted that Tulsa's ordinance was chilling plaintiffs' speech rights because the city could prosecute them for conduct that violated the ordinance. And the suit presented a clearly framed legal issue: whether the ordinance was unconstitutional, regardless of how Tulsa enforced it. *Id.* Reasoning that the case presented a strictly legal question and the ordinance could cause an irretrievable loss of speech rights, the Circuit held the case was ripe for review. *Id.* It thus reversed the district court's ripeness determination.

Defendant's ripeness argument here contradicts *ACORN*. He argues that plaintiff's challenge to the Kansas Law is not ripe because she never asked the Secretary of Administration to waive the certification requirement. He also supplies evidence – an affidavit from the Secretary of Administration – asserting that the Secretary would have granted the waiver if plaintiff only had asked. But *ACORN* squarely held that "applying for and being denied a license or exemption is not a condition precedent to bringing a facial challenge to an unconstitutional law." *Id.* Plaintiff's challenge presents a facial challenge to the Kansas Law and so, *ACORN*'s holding excuses plaintiff from applying for an exemption.[5]

---

5 Defendant primarily relies on *Levin v. South Carolina Department of Health & Human Services*, 12-CV-0007, 2015 U.S. Dist. LEXIS 31754, 2015 WL 1186370 (D.S.C. Mar. 16, 2015), for

E   Conclusion: Plaintiff's Claim is Ripe for Judicial Review

The court concludes that Ms. Koontz's First Amendment challenge to the Kansas Law is ripe for judicial review under the relaxed ripeness test applied to facial challenges under the First Amendment. It thus rejects defendant's arguments to the contrary.

III   Mootness

Defendant's memorandum opposing plaintiff's injunction motion also references mootness.[6] While it is not clear, it appears that he referenced mootness merely as an adjunct to his ripeness defense. *See* Doc. 11 at 10–11 (arguing that had plaintiff requested a waiver under the Kansas Law, the Secretary of Administration would have granted it and thus mooted the entire dispute).

The mootness doctrine is "grounded in the requirement that any case or dispute that is presented to a federal court be definite, concrete and amenable to specific relief." *Jordan v. Sosa*, 654 F.3d 1012, 1024 (10th Cir. 2011) (emphasis omitted). These requirements derive from Article III's case or controversy clause, which requires that "'an actual controversy must be extant at all stages of review, not merely at the time the complaint is filed.'" *Rio Grande Silvery Minnow v. Bureau of Reclamation*, 601 F.3d 1096, 1121 (10th Cir. 2010) (quoting *Arizonans for Official English v. Arizona*, 520 U.S. 43, 67, 117 S. Ct. 1055, 137 L. Ed. 2d 170 (1997)).

While it is not entirely clear, it seems that defendant may have intended to invoke the voluntary cessation doctrine. Under it, a defendant cannot moot a case by voluntary ceasing the allegedly wrongful conduct if the defendant could engage in the conduct again after a court would dismiss a case challenging it.

---

his ripeness argument. But it is of no consequence here. The plaintiff in *Levin* presented no First Amendment challenges – facial, as applied, or otherwise. So, as one would expect, *Levin* applied the two-part test generally applied to assess ripeness. *See id.* at *9 (considering "(1) fitness of the issues for judicial decision and (2) the hardship to the parties of withholding court consideration"); *see also Yeutter*, 911 F.2d at 1415 (summarizing the two-part ripeness test typically applied). *Levin* did not apply or even mention the relaxed ripeness test applied in First Amendment cases like this one.

6   Even if defendant does not present a mootness challenge, the court has a duty to assure itself that a case is not moot because, like ripeness, mootness is a jurisdictional prerequisite that the court must determine before proceeding. *Jordan v. Sosa*, 654 F.3d 1012, 1023 (10th Cir. 2011) ("The mootness doctrine provides that although there may be an actual and justiciable controversy at the time the litigation is commenced, once that controversy ceases to exist, the federal court must dismiss the action for want of jurisdiction." (internal quotation omitted)).

See Friends of the Earth, Inc. v. Laidlaw Envtl. Servs. (TOC), Inc., 528 U.S. 167, 189, 120 S. Ct. 693, 145 L. Ed. 2d 610 (2000).

Here, the affidavit from the Secretary of Administration asserts that she would have granted plaintiff a waiver of the certification requirement. But dismissing the case because defendant gave a waiver to plaintiff still would permit defendant to deny a waiver to others, or revoke a waiver given to plaintiff after the court dismisses her suit. These actions would prevent the court from reviewing the constitutionality of the Kansas Law, which is what the voluntary cessation doctrine aims to prevent. *See Already, LLC v. Nike, Inc.*, 568 U.S. 85, 91, 133 S. Ct. 721, 184 L. Ed. 2d 553 (2013) ("We have recognized, however, that a defendant cannot automatically moot a case simply by ending its unlawful conduct once sued. Otherwise, a defendant could engage in unlawful conduct, stop when sued to have the case declared moot, then pick up where he left off, repeating this cycle until he achieves all his unlawful ends." (internal citation omitted)).

Here, defendant never asserts that he permanently will abandon enforcement of the Kansas Law's certification requirement. Given this, the dispute presented by plaintiff's Complaint presents a "definite, concrete and amenable to specific relief" claim. *Jordan*, 654 F.3d at 1024. The claim is not moot.

IV   The Preliminary Injunction Analysis

Having concluded that Ms. Koontz's challenge to the Kansas Law presents a claim that is ripe but not moot, the court now turns to the merits of the pending motion. This motion seeks a preliminary injunction pending a final judgment in the case. Specifically, plaintiff asks for an order that temporarily enjoins defendant from enforcing the requirement established in Kan. Stat. Ann. § 75–3740f–or any other like Kansas law, policy, or practice – that state contractors must declare they are not boycotting Israel. The court begins its analysis of this request for relief with an overview of the requisite showing. It then applies that standard to the request made by plaintiff's motion.

A   *The Showing a Party Must Make to Deserve a Preliminary Injunction*

Federal Rule of Civil Procedure 65(a) authorizes district courts to issue preliminary injunctions. The relief afforded under this rule has a limited purpose – a preliminary injunction is "merely to preserve the relative positions of the parties until a trial on the merits can be held." *Univ. of Tex. v. Camenisch*, 451 U.S. 390, 395, 101 S. Ct. 1830, 68 L. Ed. 2d 175 (1981). The Tenth Circuit has specified the following standard for district courts to follow when deciding whether to issue a preliminary injunction:

> "To obtain a preliminary injunction the moving party must demonstrate: (1) a likelihood of success on the merits; (2) a likelihood that the moving party will suffer irreparable harm if the injunction is not granted; (3) the balance of equities is in the moving party's favor; and (4) the preliminary injunction is in the public interest."

Verlo v. Martinez, 820 F.3d 1113, 1126 (10th Cir. 2016) (quoting *Republican Party of N.M. v. King*, 741 F.3d 1089, 1092 (10th Cir. 2013)). The court has discretion to decide whether to grant a preliminary injunction. *Beltronics USA, Inc. v. Midwest Inventory Distrib., LLC*, 562 F.3d 1067, 1070 (10th Cir. 2009) (citations omitted). "[The Tenth Circuit] reviews a district court's grant of a preliminary injunction for abuse of discretion." *Verlo*, 820 F.3d at 1124 (internal quotation omitted). "A district court abuses its discretion when it commits an error of law or makes clearly erroneous factual findings.'" *Id.* (quoting *Moser*, 747 F.3d at 822).

A preliminary injunction is an extraordinary remedy. *Winter v. Nat. Res. Def. Council, Inc.*, 555 U.S. 7, 24, 129 S. Ct. 365, 172 L. Ed. 2d 249 (2008). So, the right to such relief must be "clear and unequivocal." *Petrella v. Brownback*, 787 F.3d 1242, 1256 (10th Cir. 2015) (quoting *Beltronics, USA, Inc.*, 562 F.3d at 1070). "In general, 'a preliminary injunction ... is the exception rather than the rule.'" *Gen. Motors Corp. v. Urban Gorilla, LLC*, 500 F.3d 1222, 1226 (10th Cir. 2007) (quoting *GTE Corp. v. Williams*, 731 F.2d 676, 678 (10th Cir. 1984)).

The parties here agree about some things. For example, they agree about the facts. They also agree that plaintiff must make the four showings required by *Verlo v. Martinez*, among other cases. But predictably, they disagree sharply about how the court should apply those four requirements.

For one, defendant argues that a preliminary injunction here would alter the status quo – not preserve it – thus increasing plaintiff's burden. Specifically, defendant contends, when a district court considers a preliminary injunction that would alter the status quo, the court must "closely scrutinize[] [the movant's request] to assure that the exigencies of the case support the granting of a remedy that is extraordinary even in the normal course." *O Centro Espirita Beneficente Uniao do Vegetal v. Ashcroft*, 389 F.3d 973, 975 (10th Cir. 2004) (en banc). While it is unclear whether the requested injunction would alter the status quo in the way the cases apply this term of art, the court need not resolve that question to decide the motion. As the following analysis explains, the court concludes that plaintiff meets even the heavier burden that defendant advocates. The court thus assumes, without deciding, that the requested preliminary injunction would alter the status quo. It thus "closely scrutinizes" Ms. Koontz's request for a preliminary injunction.

1. Is plaintiff likely to succeed on the merits of her claim?

Plaintiff asserts that by enforcing the Kansas Law, defendant is violating 42 U.S.C. § 1983. A defendant is liable under § 1983 if he deprives a person of a constitutional right under color of state law. 42 U.S.C. § 1983. Neither party contests that defendant is acting under color of state law. But the parties contest whether defendant has deprived plaintiff of a constitutional right.

Plaintiff asserts a variety of legal theories that show defendant is depriving plaintiff of a constitutional right. *See* Doc. 4 at 10–23. But the court concludes it must address just one of them to decide the current motion.

Under the First Amendment,[7] states cannot retaliate or impose conditions on an independent contractor "'on a basis that infringes his constitutionally protected freedom of speech.'" *Bd. of Cty. Comm'rs, Wabaunsee Cty., Kan. v. Umbehr*, 518 U.S. 668, 674, 116 S. Ct. 2342, 135 L. Ed. 2d 843 (1996) (quoting *Perry v. Sindermann*, 408 U.S. 593, 597, 92 S. Ct. 2694, 33 L. Ed. 2d 570 (1972)) (alteration omitted). To determine whether a state is infringing on an independent contractor's rights under the First Amendment, courts use the same guidelines developed in *Pickering v. Board of Education of Township High School District 205, Will County, Illinois*, 391 U.S. 563, 88 S. Ct. 1731, 20 L. Ed. 2d 811 (1968), and its progeny. *Umbehr*, 518 U.S. at 678.

The *Pickering* test requires plaintiff to show, first, that the First Amendment protects the conduct that she claims led to the state denying a benefit. *Id.* at 675. If the plaintiff succeeds on this showing, the government can justify its decision by showing that "legitimate countervailing government interests are sufficiently strong" to justify its encroachment. *Id.* Under the *Pickering* test, when a law has a widespread effect and the potential to chill speech before it happens, the government must show the speech's "'necessary impact on the actual operation'" of the government outweighs the interests of the speakers and their audiences. *United States v. Nat'l Treasury Emp. Union*, 513 U.S. 454, 468, 115 S. Ct. 1003, 130 L. Ed. 2d 964 (1995) (quoting *Pickering*, 391 U.S. at 571) (holding that a governmental ban on employees receiving academic honorary degrees was unconstitutional). To make this showing, the government must establish a real harm that the law will alleviate directly. *Id.* at 475.

---

7 The First Amendment applies to the states through the Fourteenth Amendment's Due Process Clause. *iMatter Utah v. Njord*, 774 F.3d 1258, 1263 (10th Cir. 2014) (citations omitted).

Plaintiff here has met her initial burden. The First Amendment protects the right to participate in a boycott as the Supreme Court held explicitly in *NAACP v. Claiborne Hardware Co.*, 458 U.S. 886, 907, 102 S. Ct. 3409, 73 L. Ed. 2d 1215 (1982).

In *Claiborne*, defendants – supporters of civil rights – organized a boycott of all white merchants after city and county officials had refused defendants' demands for racial equality. *Id.* at 899–900. Plaintiffs – a group of white merchants – sued in Mississippi state court seeking to recover damages they had lost because of the boycott. *Id.* at 889. After an eight-month trial, the judge imposed liability on the boycotters under three distinct conspiracy theories. *Id.* at 890–91. All three sounded in state law. *Id.* at 891. The state trial court also rejected the boycotters' argument that the First Amendment prohibited the court from imposing liability on them based on their boycott. *Id.* at 891–92. The Mississippi Supreme Court affirmed the trial court's imposition of liability and again rejected the defendants' argument that the First Amendment protected them from liability. *Id.* at 895.

The Supreme Court granted certiorari and reversed the Mississippi Supreme Court. *Id.* at 912. The Court emphasized, "[w]hile States have broad power to regulate economic activity, we do not find a comparable right to prohibit peaceful political activity such as that found in the boycott in this case." *Id.* at 913. While states broadly can regulate boycotts that aim to suppress competition or target companies involved with labor disputes, *id.* at 912, their regulatory power over boycotts is limited when the boycott's main purpose is to influence governmental action, *id.* at 914.

The Supreme Court explained that the boycott at issue in *Claiborne* included many elements. *Id.* at 907. Participants met with other likeminded individuals to organize and discuss the boycott. *Id.* They supported the boycott with speeches, nonviolent picketing, and encouragement to others to join their cause. *Id.* And all this was done to bring about change in society and government. *Id.* After reviewing the components of the *Claiborne* boycott, the Court noted:

> Each of these elements of the boycott is a form of speech or conduct that is ordinarily entitled to protection under the First and Fourteenth Amendments. The black citizens ... banded together and collectively expressed their dissatisfaction with a social structure that had denied them rights to equal treatment and respect.

Id. (footnote omitted). This, the Supreme Court held, is a key tenet of the First Amendment. *Id.* at 908.

The same analysis applies to the Kansas Law. The conduct prohibited by the Kansas Law is protected for the same reason as the boycotters' conduct in *Claiborne* was protected. Ms. Koontz, other members of the Mennonite Church, and others have "banded together" to express, collectively, their dissatisfaction with Israel and to influence governmental action. Namely, its organizers have banded together to express collectively their dissatisfaction with the injustice and violence they perceive, as experienced both by Palestinians and Israeli citizens. She and others participating in this boycott of Israel seek to amplify their voices to influence change, as did the boycotters in *Claiborne*. The court concludes that plaintiff has carried her burden on the current motion to establish that she and others are engaged in protected activity.[8]

Ms. Koontz's satisfaction of her initial burden shifts the burden to defendant. *Umbehr*, 518 U.S. at 675. He must show that Kansas has a strong, legitimate interest in enforcing the Kansas Law. *Id.* Defendant fails to meet his burden.

When evaluating whether a law serves a compelling governmental purpose, a court must inquire into the circumstances of the law's enactment. *Doe v. City of Albuquerque*, 667 F.3d 1111, 1132 (10th Cir. 2012). The Kansas Law's legislative history reveals that its goal is to undermine the message of those participating in a boycott of Israel. This is either viewpoint discrimination against the opinion that Israel mistreats Palestinians or subject matter discrimination on the topic of Israel. Both are impermissible goals under the First Amendment. *See Police Dep't of City of Chi. v. Mosley*, 408 U.S. 92, 95, 92 S. Ct. 2286, 33 L. Ed. 2d 212 (1972) ("[T]he First Amendment means that government has no power to restrict expression because of its message, its ideas, its subject matter, or its content.").

---

8   In some respects, the issue here is easier than the one in *Claiborne*. In that case, some of the boycotters had exerted discipline against persons who refused to join their boycott. *Id.* at 903–04. Some of this discipline directed illegal, violent conduct at persons who refused to join the boycott, *i.e.*, shots fired at a house, a brick thrown through a car's windshield, and some whiskey being stolen. *Id.* at 904–05. As the Court emphasized, "The First Amendment does not protect violence." *Id.* at 916 (citing *Samuels v. Mackell*, 401 U.S. 66, 75, 91 S. Ct. 764, 27 L. Ed. 2d 688 (1971) (Douglas, J., concurring) ("Certainly violence has no sanctuary in the First Amendment, and the use of weapons, gunpowder, and gasoline may not constitutionally masquerade under the guise of advocacy."). But violent, illegal, conduct by some boycotters did not strip other, legal conduct of its protected characteristic. *Id.* at 908 ("The right to associate does not lose all constitutional protection merely because some members of the group may have participated in conduct or advocated doctrine that itself is not protected."). Here, no one contends that Ms. Koontz or her fellow boycotters have done anything illegal or violent. To say it simply, the boycott here does not present any of the complicating facts present in *Claiborne*.

The Kansas Law also aims to minimize any discomfort that Israeli businesses may feel from the boycotts. This, too, is an impermissible goal. *See, e.g., Matal v. Tam*, 137 S. Ct. 1744, 1763, 198 L. Ed. 2d 366 (2017) ("We have said time and again that 'the public expression of ideas may not be prohibited merely because the ideas are themselves offensive to some of their hearers.'" (quoting *Street v. New York*, 394 U.S. 576, 592, 89 S. Ct. 1354, 22 L. Ed. 2d 572 (1969))).

But even if one assumed that Kansas had passed the law to achieve constitutionally permissible goals that would not change the outcome here. It is still unconstitutional because it is not narrowly tailored to achieve those permissive goals. If Kansas had passed its law to regulate boycotts intended to suppress economic competition coming from Israel – a goal that *Claiborne* permits[9] – the Kansas Law is overinclusive. It is overinclusive because it also bans political boycotts, which is impermissible. *See Garrison v. Louisiana*, 379 U.S. 64, 74–75, 85 S. Ct. 209, 13 L. Ed. 2d 125 (1964) ("[S]peech concerning public affairs is more than self-expression; it is the essence of self-government."). Likewise, if the Kansas Law's goal is to promote trade relations with Israel – also a permissible goal – the Kansas Law is underinclusive because it only regulates boycotts but does not regulate other conduct that affects trade.

The authority the Kansas Law grants the Secretary of Administration to waive the certification requirement also undermines any rationale offered by defendant. As the Supreme Court noted in *City of Ladue v. Gilleo*, 512 U.S. 43, 114 S. Ct. 2038, 129 L. Ed. 2d 36 (1994), "Exemptions from an otherwise legitimate regulation of a medium of speech … may diminish the credibility of the government's rationale for restricting speech in the first place." *Id.* at 52.

The defendant's written Opposition to plaintiff's injunction motion never argued the constitutionality of the Kansas Law. At the hearing on the motion, the court asked defense counsel to address this omission. He did. When asked whether there was an argument to be made that the Kansas Law is indeed constitutional, defense counsel said there was. He cited *Rumsfeld v. Forum for Academic & Institutional Rights, Inc.*, 547 U.S. 47, 126 S. Ct. 1297, 164 L. Ed. 2d 156 (2006).

In *Rumsfeld*, the Congress had enacted a law requiring a law school, to be eligible for federal funding, to "offer military recruiters the same access to its campus and students that it provides to the nonmilitary recruiter receiving the most favorable access." *Id.* at 55. Arguing that the law violated the First Amendment, a group of law schools sued. *Id.* at 51. They argued that the law made them choose between receiving federal funding and allowing the military

---

9 *See* 458 U.S. at 912 ("The right of business entities to 'associate' to suppress competition may be curtailed [by states].").

to recruit on campus. *Id.* at 53. According to the law schools, this amounted to the law compelling the schools to speak a certain message, in violation of the First Amendment. *Id.*

The Supreme Court disagreed. *Id.* at 60. The law schools argued that the law forced them to speak by "send[ing] e-mails or post[ing] notices on bulletin boards on an employer's behalf." *Id.* at 61. But the Supreme Court concluded that this speech was incidental to the law's regulation of conduct. *Id.* at 62. And the government can regulate conduct under the First Amendment so long as the conduct is not inherently expressive. *Id.* at 65–66. Conduct is inherently expressive when someone understands that the conduct is expressing an idea without any spoken or written explanation. *Id.* at 66 (citing *Texas v. Johnson*, 491 U.S. 397, 406, 109 S. Ct. 2533, 105 L. Ed. 2d 342 (1989) (holding that the First Amendment protects a person's right to burn the flag because a person understands this conduct expressed disdain of an idea)). The Court concluded that the law schools' refusal to allow military recruiters to recruit on campus was not expressive of an idea. *Id.* It reasoned that people could understand that the schools were expressing an idea only if the schools explicitly explained why the military recruiters were off-campus. *Id.* at 66.

The Supreme Court also concluded that the law did not force the law schools to host or accommodate the military's message. *Id.* at 64. The Court noted that in some circumstances, the Court had struck down laws that forced private parties to accommodate a message they opposed. *Id.* at 63. But the Supreme Court explained that in every one of those cases, the "speaker's own message was affected by the speech it was forced to accommodate." *Id.* For instance, a law requiring parade organizers to include a certain group altered the parade organizer's speech because "every participating [group] affects the message conveyed by the parade's private organizers...." *Id.* (internal bracket omitted) (quoting *Hurley v. Irish-American Gay, Lesbian and Bisexual Group of Bos.*, 515 U.S. 557, 572–73, 115 S. Ct. 2338, 132 L. Ed. 2d 487 (1995)). In contrast to parades, hosting employment interviews and holding recruiting receptions lacked an expressive quality. *Id.* at 64.

The Kansas Law here is different than the requirement at issue in *Rumsfeld*. The conduct the Kansas Law aims to regulate is inherently expressive. *See Claiborne*, 458 U.S. at 907–08. It is easy enough to associate plaintiff's conduct with the message that the boycotters believe Israel should improve its treatment of Palestinians. And boycotts – like parades – have an expressive quality. *Id.* Forcing plaintiff to disown her boycott is akin to forcing plaintiff to accommodate Kansas's message of support for Israel. Because the Kansas Law regulates inherently expressive conduct and forces plaintiff to accommodate

Kansas's message, it is unlike the law at issue in *Rumsfeld*. The court thus finds defendant's reliance on *Rumsfeld* misplaced.

In sum, the court holds that plaintiff is likely to succeed on the merits. This is so even if – as defendant contends – a preliminary injunction would alter the status quo. The court has "closely scrutinized [plaintiff's] request" and concludes "that the exigencies of the case support granting" this extraordinary remedy. *O Centro Espirita*, 389 F.3d at 975.

2. **Will plaintiff suffer irreparable harm if the court does not grant an injunction?**

Next, plaintiff must establish that she will sustain irreparable harm absent a preliminary injunction. *Verlo*, 820 F.3d at 1126. To show irreparable harm, plaintiff must show that her injury is certain, great, and not "merely serious or substantial." *Port City Props. v. Union Pac. R.R. Co.*, 518 F.3d 1186, 1190 (10th Cir. 2008). Economic loss "usually does not, in and of itself, constitute irreparable harm." *Id.* (internal quotation and citation omitted).

Ms. Koontz asserts that the analysis is simple. She is correct. The Supreme Court squarely has decided this point. "The loss of First Amendment freedoms, for even minimal periods of time, unquestionably constitutes irreparable injury." *Elrod v. Burns*, 427 U.S. 347, 373, 96 S. Ct. 2673, 49 L. Ed. 2d 547 (1976) (citing *N.Y. Times Co. v. United States*, 403 U.S. 713, 91 S. Ct. 2140, 29 L. Ed. 2d 822 (1971)). *Elrod* demonstrates this principle's vitality. In *Elrod*, the Republican Sheriff of Cook County, Illinois was replaced by a Democrat. *Id.* at 350. The new Sheriff discharged plaintiffs, all Republicans and non-civil service employees of the Sheriff's office and thus unprotected from arbitrary discharge. *Id.* at 351. This conformed to a long-standing practice where a newly installed Sheriff typically required such employees to join the new Sheriff's political party or face dismissal. *Id.* Plaintiffs challenged their dismissal – or, for one plaintiff, his looming dismissal – in federal court. They claimed that it encroached on freedoms protected by the First Amendment. *Id.* For relief, they sought a preliminary injunction. *Id.*

The district court declined to issue a preliminary injunction, reasoning that loss of employment did not constitute irreparable harm. *Id.* at 373. Such loss, if later proved to be unconstitutional, could be compensated with back pay, which would be an adequate remedy. *Id.* The Seventh Circuit disagreed, and directed the district court to issue the injunction. *Id.* The Supreme Court affirmed the Circuit's decision. *Id.* The Court explained, "[t]he loss of First Amendment freedoms, for even minimal periods of time, unquestionably constitutes irreparable injury." *Id.* The Court held that the plaintiffs lost those freedoms when the defendant fired them because of their political beliefs. *Id.* at 374.

Defendant here makes a similar argument to the one discredited in *Elrod.* He argues that Ms. Koontz will not sustain irreparable harm if the Kansas Law's certification requirement is left in place while the case is adjudicated on the merits. Defendant says that plaintiff can present evidence about the number of training sessions she would have conducted. And since each session fetches a payment of $600, simple math will permit a damage award to make her whole – assuming the court concludes that defendant has disenfranchised her constitutional rights.

While this argument has a pragmatic appeal, it is not one the First Amendment will abide. As referenced above, the Supreme Court already has decided the question. *See id.* at 373. This is so because "[t]he timeliness of political speech is particularly important …'[It] enable[s] every citizen at any time to bring the government and any person in authority to the bar of public opinion …" *Id.* at 373 n.29 (internal quotation and brackets omitted) (quoting *Wood v. Georgia*, 370 U.S. 375, 392, 82 S. Ct. 1364, 8 L. Ed. 2d 569 (1962) (further citation omitted)).

Nor will the pragmatic appeal of defendant's argument withstand closer scrutiny. Ms. Koontz has sued defendant in his official capacity. Doc. 1 ¶ 7. The Eleventh Amendment forbids recovery of damages in federal court suits against state officials sued in their official capacity. *See Chamber of Commerce of U.S. v. Edmondson*, 594 F.3d 742, 771 (10th Cir. 2010) (holding a movant for preliminary injunction would sustain irreparable harm because sovereign immunity would bar damage recovery). Our Circuit long has recognized that an award of money damages that the plaintiff cannot recover "for reasons such as sovereign immunity constitutes irreparable injury." *Crowe & Dunlevy, P.C. v. Stidham*, 640 F.3d 1140, 1157 (10th Cir. 2011) (collecting cases).

Defendant also argues that plaintiff's harm is not imminent because she already has refused to sign the certification. And, defendant argues, any future trainings plaintiff might give are speculative. To support his argument, defendant cites *Pinson v. Pacheco*, 397 F. App'x 488 (10th Cir. 2010), and *Schrier v. University of Colorado*, 427 F.3d 1253 (10th Cir. 2005). But his faith in those cases is misplaced. They are materially different.

In *Pinson*, the Tenth Circuit held that a movant for a preliminary injunction had failed to show irreparable harm. *Id.* at 492. The movant claimed that he would sustain irreparable harm because federal prison officials had refused to honor his request not to be housed in the same institution as prisoners "'who pose a known, specific risk of harm toward [p]laintiff.'" *Id.* (quoting the motion for preliminary injunction). Because plaintiff produced no specific evidence of any threats towards him in the institution where the officials placed him, *Pinson* held simply that the harm alleged by plaintiff was speculative. *Id.*

In *Schrier*, the district court denied plaintiff's preliminary injunction motion. 427 F.3d at 1267. The injunction he sought, if granted, would have required defendant to reinstate plaintiff in his former job after defendant had terminated plaintiff's employment, allegedly because of plaintiff's speech. *Id.* The Tenth Circuit affirmed the district court's decision not to grant the injunction, in part, because plaintiff had failed to show irreparable harm. *Id.* The Tenth Circuit concluded that the harms already had occurred and the injunction could not cure them. *Id.* And also, plaintiff failed to show that defendant's action violated his First Amendment rights. *Id.* at 1266. The harm thus was not imminent. *Id.* at 1267.

Here, defendant's argument focuses on the wrong harm. Plaintiff's harm stems not from her decision to refuse to sign the certification, but rather from the plainly unconstitutional choice the Kansas Law forces plaintiff to make: She either can contract with the state or she can support a boycott of Israel. Her harm is ongoing because the Kansas Law is currently chilling plaintiff's and other putative state contractors' speech rights.

In short, the court finds that Ms. Koontz has shown that she will sustain irreparable harm unless the court enjoins defendant from enforcing the Kansas Law's certification requirement. She thus has shouldered her burden on the second element of the injunction standard.

3. **Does plaintiff's irreparable harm outweigh any harm defendant will sustain if the court grants the preliminary injunction?**

Plaintiff next argues that her irreparable harm outweighs any harm defendant would bear if the court issued a preliminary injunction. Plaintiff asserts that defendant "does not have an interest in enforcing a law that is likely constitutionally infirm." *See Edmondson*, 594 F.3d at 771. Plaintiff also argues that a preliminary injunction against the Kansas Law would maintain the status quo because the Kansas Law is sufficiently new that any harm to the State of Kansas and defendant is minimal. On the other hand, plaintiff argues that she and other state contractors will suffer great harm because defendant is depriving them of a constitutional right.

Defendant argues that plaintiff has not shown any imminent or threatened injury and an injunction will harm Kansas and defendant greatly. Defendant notes that in 2016, Kansas exported more than $56 million worth of goods to Israel and imported more than $83 million worth of goods. Defendant fears that enjoining the Kansas Law will cause Israeli companies to refuse to do business in Kansas, or with Kansas companies, and thus harm the Kansas economy.

Defendant's argument is not persuasive. Defendant adduced no evidence that Israeli companies will refuse to do business in or with the State of Kansas unless its ban against Israeli boycotts is enforced. And defendant has not forwarded any evidence that Kansas commerce has increased because of, or in anticipation of, the boycott ban. If such evidence existed, one would expect the defense to have access to it and have presented it. It didn't.

After balancing the relative harms imposed by a preliminary injunction, the court finds that the continuing harm to plaintiff's First Amendment rights – and those of persons similarly situated – outweighs defendant's speculative suggestion that an injunction will harm him, the State of Kansas, or Kansas merchants. Ms. Koontz has carried her burden on this third part of the injunction test.

4. Is the requested injunction adverse to the public harm?

The fourth and final touchstone of the preliminary injunction standard requires the injunction's proponent to show that it will not be adverse to the public interest. Plaintiff argues that a preliminary injunction will serve the public interest because it will protect constitutional rights. *See Edmunson*, 594 F.3d at 771 ("'[T]he public interest will [certainly] be served by enjoining the enforcement of the invalid provisions of state law.'" (quoting *Bank One, Utah v. Guttau*, 190 F.3d 844, 848 (8th Cir. 1999))).

Defendant argues that an injunction will not serve the public interest because Israel is an important trade partner, as explained above. Defendant also argues that it is in the public interest to enforce a law that prevents Kansans from discriminating against foreign companies doing business in Kansas. Last, defendant argues that enforcing the Kansas Law is in the public interest because the Kansas Law passed the Kansas House 99 to 13 and the Kansas Senate 36 to 3.

Here, the court already has concluded that it is highly likely that the Kansas Law is invalid and thus enjoining it will protect a constitutional right. *See supra*, Part IV.A.1. Defendant has failed to produce evidence that an injunction will affect Kansas's relationship with Israeli companies. While the Kansas Law may have been passed by the legislature with flying colors, that showing merely would demonstrate that one state legislature had enacted a statute. Such a showing would not place the Kansas Law on the same level as an amendment to our Constitution – the very first amendment adopted by our founders and one ratified by three fourths of our states. *See* U.S. Const. art. V. A desire to prevent discrimination against Israeli businesses is an insufficient public interest to overcome the public's interest in protecting a constitutional right. The court finds that an injunction will serve the public interest.

IV   Conclusion

For reasons explained above, the court grants plaintiff's Motion for Preliminary Injunction (Doc. 3).

IT IS THEREFORE ORDERED THAT plaintiff's Motion for Preliminary Injunction (Doc. 3) is granted. Defendant is preliminarily enjoined from enforcing Kan. Stat. Ann. § 75-3740f and any other Kansas statute, law, policy, or practice that requires independent contractors to declare that they are not participating in a boycott of Israel. Pending further order from this court, the court enjoins defendant from requiring any independent contractor to sign a certification that they are not participating in a boycott of Israel as a condition of contracting with the State of Kansas.

IT IS FURTHER ORDERED THAT the parties must meet and confer to discuss a proposed schedule for the remainder of this case. Counsel for the parties are directed to contact the chambers of United States Magistrate Judge K. Gary Sebelius to request a Scheduling Conference to govern the remainder of the case. Counsel may either call his chambers at 785-338-5480 or email ksd_sebelius_chambers@ksd.uscourts.gov.

IT IS SO ORDERED.

Dated this 30th day of January, 2018, at Topeka, Kansas.

/s/ Daniel D. Crabtree
Daniel D. Crabtree
United States District Judge

United States, Jordahl v. Brnovich, 336 F Supp. 3d 1016 (D. Ariz. 2018)

UNITED STATES DISTRICT COURT FOR THE DISTRICT OF ARIZONA

MIKKEL JORDAHL, ET AL., Plaintiffs

v.

MARK BRNOVICH, ET AL., Plaintiffs

Sep. 27, 2018

Case No. CV-17-08263-PCT-DJH

ORDER

Introduction

In 2016, Arizona joined a growing number of states that enacted legislation "aimed at divesting state funding from companies that engage in a boycott of Israel." AZ S.F. Sheet, 2016 Reg. Sess. H.B. 2617. Arizona's House Bill 2617 was codified at Arizona Revised Statute § 35–393.01, and states in subsection (A) that:

> A public entity may not enter into a contract with a company to acquire or dispose of services, supplies, information technology or construction unless the contract includes a written certification that the company is not currently engaged in, and agrees for the duration of the contract to not engage in, a boycott of Israel.

A.R.S. § 35-393.01(A) (hereafter, "Certification Requirement" or "the Act").[1] The Act defines "boycott" as:

> ... engaging in a refusal to deal, terminating business activities or performing other actions that are intended to limit commercial relations with Israel or with persons or entitles doing business in Israel or in territories controlled by Israel, if those actions are taken either:
>
> (a) In compliance with or adherence to calls for a boycott of Israel other than those boycotts to which 50 United States Code § 4607(c) applies.[2]
>
> (b) In a matter that discriminates on the basis of nationality, national origin or religion and that is not based on a valid business reason.[3]

A.R.S. § 35-393(1).

Plaintiff Mikkel Jordahl ("Mr. Jordahl") is an attorney and sole owner of Plaintiff Mikkel (Mik) Jordahl, P.C. ("the Firm") (collectively, "Plaintiffs"). Mr. Jordahl personally participates in a boycott of consumer goods and services offered by businesses supporting Israel's occupation of the Palestinian territories. In doing so, Mr. Jordahl claims that he is moved by the Peace Not Walls campaign promoted by the Evangelical Lutheran Church in America ("ELCA"). The ELCA calls on "individuals to invest in Palestinian products to build their

---

[1] Subsection (B) separately prohibits public entities from "adopt[ing] a procurement, investment or other policy that has the effect of inducing or requiring a person or company to boycott Israel." A.R.S. § 35-393.01(B). Although Plaintiffs seek to enjoin A.R.S. § 35-393.01, the facts presented by Plaintiffs, as well as the arguments they have advanced, show that A.R.S. § 35-393.01(B) has no applicability here. (*See also* Doc. 20, First Amended Complaint ("FAC") (omitting any reference to A.R.S. § 35-393.01(B))). Accordingly, this Order will not address the constitutionality or enforceability of that subsection.

[2] 50 U.S.C. §4607(a)(1) is part of the Export Administration Act ("EAA"), which prohibits "any United States person, with respect to his activities in the interstate or foreign commerce of the United States, from taking or knowingly agreeing to take [certain enumerated actions] with intent to comply with, further, or support any boycott fostered or imposed by a foreign country against a country which is friendly to the United States and which is not itself the object of any form of boycott pursuant to United States law or regulation." Subsection 4607(c) states that this prohibition shall preempt any state law that "pertains to participation in, compliance with, implementation of, or the furnishing of information regarding restrictive trade practices or boycotts fostered or imposed by foreign countries against other countries." *Id.*

[3] The parties seem to agree that this subsection does not apply to Plaintiffs' desired boycotting activities. (*See* Doc. 28 at 13 and Doc. 39 at 22).

economy and to utilize selective purchasing to avoid buying products made in illegal Israeli settlements built on Palestinian land."[4] Mr. Jordahl is also a non-Jewish member of Jewish Voice for Peace ("JVP"), which "endorses the call from Palestinian civil society for Boycott, Divestment, and Sanctions campaigns to protest the Israeli government's occupation of Palestinian territories." (Doc. 6 at 4). Mr. Jordahl would like the Firm to participate in his boycott of "all businesses operating in Israeli settlements in the occupied Palestinian territories." (Doc. 57 at 6:6–7). He would also like his Firm "to be able to associate and provide financial resources and legal resources to Jewish Voice for Peace." (*Id.* at 6:8–10).

For the past twelve years, Mr. Jordahl's firm has contracted with the Coconino County Jail District ("the County") to provide legal advice to incarcerated individuals. In 2016, following the passage of A.R.S. § 35–393.01, the County asked Mr. Jordahl to execute a written certification, on the Firm's behalf, that the Firm "is not currently engaged in a boycott of Israel," that "no wholly owned subsidiaries, majority-owned subsidiaries, parent companies, or affiliates" of the Firm are "engaged in a boycott of Israel," and that neither the Firm nor any of the above-mentioned associated entities would "engage in a boycott of Israel" for the duration of the contract agreement. (Doc. 6–1, Ex. 1). The requested certification went on to state that "Any violation of this Certification by the Independent Contractor shall constitute an event of material breach of the Agreement." (*Id.*) Mr. Jordahl signed the 2016 certification under protest ("2016 Certification"), and sought confirmation with the County that the certification would not apply to his personal consumer decisions. (Doc. 6–1 at Exs. 1 & 2). The County did not respond to his inquiry but paid the Firm for its services during that year. During the contract year, Mr. Jordahl claims that he turned down opportunities for his Firm to provide administrative and pro bono services to organizations like JVP and he personally refrained from speaking out vocally about his personal boycott participation for fear that it might cast suspicion that his Firm was engaging in activity prohibited under the 2016 Certification. (Doc. 6–1 at 4–6).

The Firm's contract with the County came up for renewal in 2017, and the County again asked Mr. Jordahl to sign the required certification ("the 2017 Certification"), which by that time had been approved by the County's Jail Board of Directors. (Doc. 6 at 10; Doc. 6–1 at Ex. 5). The 2017 Certification was substantially unchanged from the 2016 Certification. This time, Mr. Jordahl refused to sign. (Doc. 6–1 at 5–6). Notwithstanding his refusal to sign, the Firm

---

4 Evangelical Lutheran Church in America, *Peace Not Walls*, https://www.elca.org/Our-Work/Publicly-Engaged-Church/Peace-Not-Walls (last visited Sept. 27, 2018).

has continued to provide representative services to the County under the contract; the County, however, has not paid the Firm for those services. Mr. Jordahl fears that he will lose approximately 10% of his total income if his Firm loses its contract with the County as a result of his refusal to sign the 2017 Certification.

In their Amended Complaint, Plaintiffs allege that section 35–393.01 violates the First and Fourteenth Amendments because it requires the Firm and other government contractors to disavow their participation in political boycotts or risk forfeiting the opportunity to work for the government. (Doc. 21 ¶ 1). Plaintiffs brought suit against the Arizona Attorney General ("the Attorney General"), the Coconino County Sheriff ("the Sheriff"), and various members of the Coconino County Jail District Board of Directors ("the Board") in their official capacities (collectively, "the Defendants"). (*Id.*) Thereafter, the parties consented to, and the Court granted, the State of Arizona's ("the State") request to intervene for the purpose of defending the facial constitutionality of the Act. (Docs. 24 & 48).

Plaintiffs have moved for a preliminary injunction in which they seek to have the Court enjoin Defendants from enforcing the Certification Requirement in A.R.S. § 35–393.01, or alternatively to enjoin Defendants from enforcing the Certification Requirement against them. (Doc. 6 at 1). Defendants oppose Plaintiffs' motion for injunctive relief and contend that Plaintiffs are unlikely to succeed on the merits and that their alleged injuries are insufficient to justify injunctive relief. (Doc. 28 at 37). The State, joined by the Attorney General ("Defendants" or "the State"), has also moved to dismiss Plaintiffs' complaint. (Doc. 28). In doing so, Defendants challenge Plaintiffs' standing and argue that to the extent the Act applies to Plaintiffs' conduct, the Court should abstain or certify the question of the scope of the Act to the Arizona Supreme Court. (*Id.*) Citing state sovereign immunity, standing, and ripeness issues, Defendants specifically seek to dismiss the Attorney General from the case. (*Id.* at 32–33).

The Court held oral argument on these issues on May 23, 2018. (Doc. 50). The parties continued to file documents with the Court after this hearing, including Plaintiffs' Notice that the State had misstated Arizona law during oral argument regarding the Attorney General's authority to offer opinions on the meaning of Arizona law (Doc. 58); Plaintiffs' Notice that Plaintiffs' counsel had misattributed a fact to the wrong authority during their oral argument (Doc. 59); and the State's Notice of Supplemental Authority regarding updates (1) to an Arizona Agency Handbook providing interpretative guidance on A.R.S. § 35–393 and (2) on *Koontz v. Watson*, 283 F. Supp. 3d 1007, 2018WL 617894 (D. Kan. 2018), a case relied upon by Plaintiffs, which since oral argument has been voluntary dismissed as a result of a settlement (Doc. 61). Defendants responded to Plaintiff's notice of misstatement (Doc. 60) and Plaintiffs have responded to the State's supplemental authority (Doc. 62). The Court has considered these filings in its decision, and where necessary, has addressed them below.

Discussion

The Court will first resolve the issues and concerns related to Plaintiffs' standing and the Court's retention of this case. The Court will then turn to the merits of Plaintiffs' Motion for Preliminary Injunction and ascertain whether Plaintiffs have met their burden of showing that the Certification Requirement runs afoul of First Amendment protections afforded to Arizona companies wishing to engage in "boycott[s] of Israel", as that term is defined in the Act.

I   *Standing*

In moving to dismiss the Plaintiffs' First Amended Complaint, the State argues that Plaintiffs do not have standing to challenge the constitutionality of the Act because their desired conduct is not covered by its terms. Defendants also contend that Plaintiffs do not have standing to sue the Attorney General because he has not enforced the Act, and does not have the authority to do so. Because a party that lacks standing divests the court of jurisdiction to hear the case, the Court will address the standing inquiries at the threshold. *See e.g., Fleck & Assocs., Inc. v. City of Phoenix*, 471 F.3d 1100, 1107 n. 4 (9th Cir. 2006) (noting that "no matter how important the issue, a court lacking jurisdiction is powerless to reach the merits under Article III of the Constitution"); *United States v. AVX Corp.*, 962 F.2d 108, 113 (1st Cir. 1992) ("If a party lacks standing to bring a matter before the court, the court lacks jurisdiction to decide the merits of the underlying case").

Federal Rule of Civil Procedure 12(b)(1) authorizes a court to dismiss claims over which it lacks subject-matter jurisdiction. A Rule 12(b)(1) challenge may be either facial or factual. *Safe Air for Everyone v. Meyer*, 373 F.3d 1035, 1039 (9th Cir. 2004). Article III of the Constitution limits federal court jurisdiction to "cases" and "controversies." *Lujan v. Defenders of Wildlife*, 504 U.S. 555, 559, 112 S. Ct. 2130, 119 L. Ed. 2d 351 (1992). To establish Article III standing, Plaintiffs must demonstrate that they "(1) suffered an injury in fact, (2) that is fairly traceable to the challenged conduct of the defendant, and (3) that is likely to be redressed by a favorable judicial decision." *Spokeo, Inc. v. Robins*, 136 S. Ct. 1540, 1547, 194 L. Ed. 2d 635 (2016). *Accord Lujan*, 504 U.S. at 560–61. Because the court's role is "neither to issue advisory opinions nor to declare rights in hypothetical cases," the case or controversy standard also requires that a claim be ripe for review. *Thomas v. Anchorage Equal Rights Comm'n*, 220 F.3d 1134,

1138 (9th Cir. 2000) (en banc) ("The constitutional component of the ripeness inquiry is often treated under the rubric of standing ...").

A plaintiff must prove standing "in the same way as any other matter on which the plaintiff bears the burden of proof, i.e., with the manner and degree of evidence required at the successive stages of the litigation." *Lujan*, 504 U.S. at 561. Ordinarily, "'[f]or purposes of ruling on a motion to dismiss for want of standing, both the trial and reviewing courts must accept as true all material allegations of the complaint and must construe the complaint in favor of the complaining party.'" *Maya v. Centex Corp.*, 658 F.3d 1060, 1068 (9th Cir. 2011) (quoting *Warth v. Seldin*, 422 U.S. 490, 501, 95 S. Ct. 2197, 45 L. Ed. 2d 343 (1975)). Here, however, Plaintiffs are also moving for a preliminary injunction, and as such, they must make "a clear showing of each element of standing." *Townley v. Miller*, 722 F.3d 1128, 1133 (9th Cir. 2013). *See also Lopez*, 630 F.3d at 785 ("[A]t the preliminary injunction stage, a plaintiff must make a 'clear showing' of his injury in fact") (internal citation omitted).

A   Plaintiffs Have Standing to Challenge the Constitutionality of the Act

The State first argues that Plaintiffs have no standing to challenge the constitutionality of the Certification Requirement because the conduct that Plaintiffs say they desire to engage in "does not fall within the narrow scope of the Act" and as a result, they "will suffer no irreparable injury absent an injunction." (Doc. 28 at 8). As far as the Court can tell, the State seems to think Plaintiffs are only harmed if they actually breach the contract by engaging in the prohibited activity. Thus, because Plaintiffs have not engaged in activity that falls within the statutory definition, Defendants say Plaintiffs cannot establish they have been injured by the Certification Requirement.

The Court first notes that "[s]tanding, or the lack of it, may be intertwined with whether the complaint states a claim upon which relief can be granted, but it is not the same thing. Standing is not about who wins the lawsuit; it is about who is allowed to have their case heard in court." *Catholic League for Religious and Civil Rights v. City and Cnty. of San. Fran.*, 624 F.3d 1043, 1048 (9th Cir. 2010). "'At bottom, the gist of the question of standing is whether petitioners have such a personal stake in the outcome of the controversy as to assure that concrete adverseness which sharpens the presentation of issues upon which the court so largely depends for illumination.'" *Id.* (quoting *Massachusetts v. E.P.A.*, 549 U.S. 497, 517, 127 S. Ct. 1438, 167 L. Ed. 2d 248 (2007)) (internal citation omitted).

Because sweeping restrictions on speech can have chilling effects on lawfully protected speech, "the Supreme Court has dispensed with rigid standing requirements" in First Amendment cases. *Cal. Pro – Life Council Inc. v. Getman*, 328 F.3d 1088, 1094 (9th Cir. 2003) ("*CPLC-I*"). *See also Ariz. Right to Life Pol. Action Comm. v. Bayless*, 320 F.3d 1002, 1006 (9th Cir. 2003) (First Amendment cases "present unique standing considerations"). For standing purposes, "[o]ne does not have to await the consummation of threatened injury to obtain preventative relief." *Bayless*, 320 F.3d at 1006. Plaintiffs alleging a violation of a First Amendment right must only show "a realistic danger of sustaining a direct injury as a result of the statute's operation or enforcement." *Id.* (internal quotation marks omitted) (noting that the "Supreme Court has endorsed what might be called a 'hold your tongue and challenge now' approach rather than requiring litigants to speak first and take their chances with the consequences") (citing *Dombrowski v. Pfister*, 380 U.S. 479, 486, 85 S. Ct. 1116, 14 L. Ed. 2d 22 (1965). *See also LSO, Ltd. v. Stroh*, 205 F.3d 1146, 1154–55 (9th Cir. 2000) ("[w]hen the threatened enforcement effort implicates First Amendment rights, the inquiry tilts dramatically toward a finding of standing").

The State's characterization of Plaintiffs' injury-in-fact presumes that Plaintiffs are only harmed if the Firm breaches its contract with the County by engaging in the conduct proscribed by the Act. The Court finds that the focus of the State's argument is misplaced, at least for purposes of standing. The Firm has been injured in at least two ways that suffice for standing to sue: one, when it was required to promise from refrain to engaging in arguably constitutionally protected activity; and two, when the County stopped paying it for services rendered.

First, the Firm was injured when it was asked to promise to refrain from engaging in a broad swath of boycotting activities, at least some of which is protected under the First Amendment, in exchange for receiving a government contract. The Supreme Court has made clear that corporations and other associations do not lose their First Amendment protections simply because they are not natural persons. *Citizens United v. FEC*, 558 U.S. 310, 342, 130 S. Ct. 876, 175 L. Ed. 2d 753 (2010). Defendants cannot dispute that as a "company" under A.R.S. § 35–393(2), the Certification Requirement applies to the Firm; after all, the County has twice asked Mr. Jordahl, on behalf of the Firm, to sign the Certification Requirement in order to receive the benefits of the County contracts. The substance of the Certifications required the Firm to promise to refrain from a "course of conduct arguably affected with a constitutional interest," or risk forfeiting a profitable government contract. *LSO, Ltd.*, 205 F.3d at 1154–55 (quoting *Babbitt v. United Farm Workers Nat'l Union*, 442 U.S. 289, 298, 99 S. Ct. 2301, 60 L. Ed. 2d 895 (1979)). *See also Alliance for Open Soc. Intern., Inc. v. U.S. Agency for Intern. Dev.*, 570 F. Supp. 2d 533 (S.D.N.Y. 2008) (finding the "fact that [] members are required to speak the Government's message in exchange for [the Government's] subsidy is a sufficient injury-in-fact for their compelled speech claim"). Mr. Jordahl has established that were it not for the Certification Requirement, he would extend his boycott participation to his Firm's consumer choices. (Doc. 6–1 ¶ 24). For example, he would "refuse to purchase Hewlett Packard equipment for [the Firm] because of Hewlett Packard's provision of information technology services used by Israeli checkpoints throughout the West Bank." (*Id.*) He would further like his Firm to provide administrative, financial, and pro bono legal services to organizations like JVP that "employ[] boycott, divestment, and sanctions tactics to put political pressure on Israel" but has not done so because he believes these actions will run afoul of the Certification. (*Id.* ¶ 25–6). The Firm thus sustained injuries-in-fact when the County conditioned the Firm's contracts on a promise to refrain from engaging in this protected course of conduct and the Firm refrained from engaging in such actions for fear of breaching the contract.

Moreover, when Mr. Jordahl refused to sign the 2017 Certification on behalf of the Firm, the County stopped paying the Firm for its services. In this regard, the Firm has not only experienced "a realistic danger of sustaining a direct injury as a result of the statute's operation or enforcement," it has actually sustained injury: it is not getting paid for services rendered due to its refusal to sign the certification. *Bayless*, 320 F.3d at 1006. The Firm has clearly shown it has standing to challenge the constitutionality of the Act.

Defendants also assert that Mr. Jordahl cannot establish injury for standing purposes because the Certification Requirement does not apply to Mr. Jordahl personally, and even if it did, the activities he wishes to engage in do not constitute a "boycott of Israel" as that term is defined in the Act. The Court finds, however, that Mr. Jordahl has sufficiently established his personal stake in the outcome of this controversy to challenge the constitutionality of the Certification Requirement. Although Mr. Jordahl is not a "company" under the Act, as the sole lawyer in a Firm that *is* required to sign the Certification to obtain the County contract, he has sufficiently established that his personal conduct, at least some of which would be prohibited by the Act, has been impermissibly chilled for fear that it may be confused with the Firm's conduct. For example, Mr. Jordahl has averred that in response to calls from JVP, the ELCA, and other "Boycott Divestment and Sanction" organizations, he has ceased purchasing products from Hewlett-Packard, Airbnb, and SodaStream, all which are companies that are "doing business ... in territories controlled by Israel." § 35–393.01(A). He says he has ceased some of these political activities for fear that they may be confused with those of his Firm's. Where a plaintiff has refrained from engaging in expressive activity for fear of prosecution under the challenged statute, such self-censorship is a "constitutionally sufficient injury" as long as it is based on "an actual and well-founded fear" that the challenged statute will be enforced. *Human Life of Wash., Inc. v. Brumsickle*, 624 F.3d 990, 1000 (9th Cir. 2010); *CPLC – I*, 328 F.3d at 1093, 1095. *See also Bayless*, 320 F.3d at 1006 (finding that an entity that was "forced to modify its speech and behavior to comply with the statute" had suffered injury even though it had "neither violated the statute nor been subject to penalties for doing so"). Relatedly, the fact that Mr. Jordahl has to affirmatively certify that his Firm is not participating in such activities is also sufficient injury for standing purposes. Requiring such an avowal undermines the expressive nature of collective political boycotts by chilling Plaintiffs' ability to join in larger calls for political change. The harm stemming from these chilling effects is sufficient injury for standing purposes.

Plaintiffs' injuries are plainly traceable to the Certification Requirement and would be alieved if the Act was found constitutionally unenforceable. *Spokeo*, 136 S. Ct. at 1547. Plaintiffs thus have standing to challenge the constitutionality of the Act.

B   Plaintiffs' Standing to Sue the Attorney General

The State and the Attorney General have also moved to dismiss Plaintiffs' claim against the Attorney General on the grounds that he has not acted to enforce the Act and thus that no alleged injury can be attributed to him. They contend that the lack of sufficient connection between Plaintiffs' injuries and the Attorney General's conduct render him an improper party under principles of standing and sovereign immunity.

The Ninth Circuit has noted how issues related to a plaintiff's standing overlap with issues related to a state official's immunity from suit. Whether a state official, acting in his official capacity, is a proper defendant to an action is

> really the common denominator of two separate inquiries: first, there is the requisite causal connection between their responsibilities and any injury that the plaintiffs *might* suffer, such that relief against the defendants would provide redress [i.e., Article III standing], and second, whether [ ] jurisdiction over the defendants is proper under the doctrine of *Ex parte Young*, 209 U.S. 123, 28 S. Ct. 441, 52 L. Ed. 714 [ ] (1908), which requires "some connection" between a named state officer and enforcement of a challenged state law.

Planned Parenthood of Idaho, Inc. v. Wasden, 376 F.3d 908, 919 (9th Cir. 2004) (citations omitted) (emphasis added). *See also Okpalobi v. Foster*, 190 F.3d 337, 347 (5th Cir. 1999) (observing that Article III standing and Eleventh Amendment immunity present "a closely related – indeed, overlapping – inquiry").

Causation for Article III standing requires that "the injury [] be fairly ... traceable to the challenged action of the defendant, and not ... the result of the independent action of some third party not before the court." *Lujan*, 504 U.S. at 560. The "line of causation" between a defendant's actions and a plaintiff's alleged harm must be more than "attenuated." *Allen v. Wright*, 468 U.S. 737, 757, 104 S. Ct. 3315, 82 L. Ed. 2d 556 (1984).

As stated in *Wasden*, courts determining whether an exception to the Eleventh Amendment applies in a given case assess causality - "the common denominator" - in a very similar manner. Typically, the Eleventh Amendment bars federal court lawsuits against a state "by Citizens of another State, or by Citizens or Subjects of any Foreign State," without the state's consent. U.S. Const. amend. XI. State agencies such as the Attorney General's Office fall within the protection of the Eleventh Amendment because a suit against that office is considered a suit against the State itself. *Will v. Michigan Dep't of State Police*, 491 U.S. 58, 71, 109 S. Ct. 2304, 105 L. Ed. 2d 45 (1989). There are, however, several exceptions to the protection of sovereign immunity. Sovereign immunity does not apply, for one, when lawsuits are brought against state officers in their official capacities for an injunction prohibiting future violations of federal law. *Ex parte Young*, 209 U.S. 123, 28 S. Ct. 441, 52 L. Ed. 714 (1908). "Official-capacity actions for prospective relief are not treated as actions against the State" for purposes of the Eleventh Amendment because state officers do not have the authority to violate the Constitution of the United States. *Will*, 491 U.S. at 71 n.10 (internal quotations omitted); Erwin Chemerinsky, *Federal Jurisdiction*, § 7.5 (6th ed. 2012).

But the *Ex parte Young* exception does not apply to all state officers. To enjoin the enforcement of an allegedly unconstitutional statute, the officer named in the suit "must have some connection with the enforcement of the act." 209 U.S. at 157. Moreover, the connection between the officer and the act "must be fairly direct; a generalized duty to enforce state law or general supervisory power over the persons responsible for enforcing the challenged provision will not subject an official to suit." *Coal. to Defend Affirmative Action v. Brown*, 674 F.3d 1128, 1134 (9th Cir. 2012) (quoting *L.A. Cty. Bar Ass'n v. Eu*, 979 F.2d 697, 704 (9th Cir. 1992)); *Sweat v. Hull*, 200 F. Supp. 2d 1162, 1167 (D. Ariz. 2001).

Plaintiffs have sued Mark Brnovich in his official capacity as the Arizona Attorney General. They allege that Mr. Brnovich is the chief law enforcement officer of Arizona under A.R.S. § 41–192(A). They further allege that under A.R.S. § 41–194.01, he has the authority to investigate, at the request of a state legislator, whether county actions violate state law; to initiate legal proceedings if he concludes that a county's actions do or may violate state law; and to notify the Arizona State Treasurer of his conclusions so that the Treasurer will withhold and redistribute state shared monies. They also allege that under A.R.S. § 41–193(A)(2), Mr. Brnovich has the authority to prosecute public officials and others for misappropriation of public monies.

The Arizona Attorney General is not directly responsible for enforcement of the Act, a fact that Plaintiffs acknowledge. But the lack of direct enforcement authority does not necessarily mean that the Attorney General's authority is unconnected to Plaintiffs' failure to be paid for their services, or the self-censorship Plaintiffs impose on their conduct. Courts have found a requisite connection for purposes of both standing and application of *Ex parte Young* not only where the law has specifically granted the defendant enforcement authority, *see, e.g., Ass'n des Eleveurs de Canards et d'Oies du Quebec v. Harris*, 729 F.3d 937, 943 (9th Cir. 2013), but also when there is a sufficient connection between the official's responsibilities and the injury that Plaintiffs might suffer, *see e.g., Wasden*, 376 F.3d at 919–20. Indeed, the Attorney General's conduct need not be the first or final step "in the chain of causation" in order to be fairly traceable to the enforcement of the Act from which Plaintiffs' injuries arise. *Bennett v. Spear*, 520 U.S. 154, 168–69, 117 S. Ct. 1154, 137 L. Ed. 2d 281 (1997). *See also Maya*, 658 F.3d at 1070 ("A causal chain does not fail simply because it has several 'links,' provided those links are 'not hypothetical or tenuous' and remain 'plausib[le].'") (*quoting Nat'l Audubon Soc'y*, 307 F.3d at 849). Notably, the Supreme Court has found sufficient connection where an "injury [is] produced by [the official's] determinative or coercive effect upon the action of someone else." *Bennett*, 520 U.S. at 169 (holding that although Fish and Wildlife Service's opinion statement to action agency was theoretically advisory, "in reality," it held "a powerful coercive effect" on agency's decision because disregarding it could expose the agency to civil and criminal penalties).

Sufficient causality exists here for both Article III standing purposes and *Ex Parte Young*. Specifically, a sufficient connection exists between the Attorney General's authority to prosecute persons illegally paying public contractors and Plaintiffs' injuries. *See* A.R.S. § 41–193(A)(2). Pursuant to A.R.S. § 35–301(1), the Attorney General is authorized to prosecute custodians of public funds who pay public funds to another person "[w]ithout authority of law." At the same time, the Act makes it unlawful for any public entity to enter into a contract for services unless the contracting company certifies that it is not and will not engage in a boycott of Israel. A.R.S. § 35–393.01. The County's decision to pay or not pay its government contractors is necessarily guided and determined in large part on whether that payment is authorized; if the payment is not authorized, but is nonetheless made, the Attorney General can prosecute the custodian of those funds. This authority to prosecute custodians of public funds for payment made in violation of the law imposes "a powerful coercive effect" on the County and entities charged with directly enforcing the Certification Requirement. *Bennett*, 520 U.S. at 169. Indeed, the County has ceased paying the Firm out of public funds presumably because to do so would expose it to prosecution under § 35–301(1).

The Attorney General's authority, together with the actions of the County, form a clear and plausible causal chain resulting in Plaintiffs' alleged constitutional injuries. The Attorney General is therefore a proper party to this suit and will not be dismissed for want of standing. Likewise, principles of sovereign immunity do not bar Plaintiffs' claim for injunctive relief against the Attorney General. The State's Motion to Dismiss the Attorney General from this action is therefore denied.

II   *Abstention and Certification*

Defendants next argue that given the lack of interpretative law on this recent state legislation, the Court should abstain from hearing this case or alternatively, "certify the legal question of the scope of the Act to the Arizona Supreme Court." (Doc. 28 at 14).

In order to avoid conflict with a state's legislature and the laws it enacts, federal cases raising constitutional issues sometimes warrant federal court abstention under the *Pullman* doctrine. *See R.R. Comm'n of Tex. v. Pullman Co.*, 312 U.S. 496, 498, 61 S. Ct. 643, 85 L. Ed. 971 (1941) ("*Pullman*"); *San Remo Hotel v. City & Cty. of San Francisco*, 145 F.3d 1095, 1105 (9th Cir. 1998). In order for a court to abstain from adjudicating a matter under *Pullman*, three requirements need to be met. Specifically, a court must find that:

(1)   the case touches on a sensitive area of social policy upon which the federal courts ought not enter unless no alternative to its adjudication is open, (2) constitutional adjudication plainly can be avoided if a definite ruling on the state issue would terminate the controversy, and (3) the proper resolution of the possible determinative issue of state law is uncertain.

Porter v. Jones, 319 F.3d 483, 492 (9th Cir. 2003) (internal alteration and quotation marks omitted) (referencing *Pullman*, 312 U.S at 498). A district court only has discretion to abstain under *Pullman* if all three of these requirements are met. Indeed, so as to "give due respect to a suitor's choice of a federal forum for the hearing and decision of his federal constitutional claims," courts have held that the doctrine should rarely apply. *Porter*, 319 F.3d at 492 (quoting *Zwickler v. Koota*, 389 U.S. 241, 248, 88 S. Ct. 391, 19 L. Ed. 2d 444 (1967)). Notably, the Ninth Circuit has stated that *Pullman* abstention is almost never appropriate in First Amendment cases "because the guarantee of free expression is always an area of particular federal concern." *Ripplinger v. Collins*, 868 F.2d 1043, 1048 (9th Cir. 1989).[5]

Unlike abstention, which entails a full round of litigation in the state court system before a plaintiff can resume proceedings in federal court, the certification process authorized by Arizona's statute enables a federal court to pose a question directly to the state's highest court. *Lehman Bros. v. Schein*, 416 U.S. 386, 391, 94 S. Ct. 1741, 40 L. Ed. 2d 215 (1973) (certification of novel or unsettled questions of state law may help save a federal court "time, energy, and resources and hel[p] build a cooperative judicial federalism"). To warrant certification, "[i]t is sufficient that the statute is susceptible of ... an interpretation [that] would avoid or substantially modify the federal constitutional challenge to the statute." *Bellotti v. Baird*, 428 U.S. 132, 148, 96 S. Ct. 2857, 49 L. Ed. 2d 844 (1976).

With regard to abstention, the Court finds that at least two of the requisite *Pullman* factors are not present, making abstention under that doctrine improper. This case squarely raises important questions surrounding First Amendment guarantees – "an area of particular federal concern" - that are not overridden by any sensitive area of social policy inappropriate for this Court. *Id.* The first requirement is therefore not met. The second requirement is also not met because Defendants have failed to show how a dispositive ruling on a "state issue" would avoid the need for constitutional adjudication. Defendants suggest that a state court ruling on the scope of what constitutes a "boycott of Israel" would resolve the need to reach the constitutional question. Defendants interpret "the Act's requirement not to engage in a 'boycott of Israel' to mean that the boycott is actually a general boycott of Israel – i.e., a broad or total boycott of Israel such as those called for by the Boycott, Divest and Sanctions ('BDS') movement, to which the Act is squarely addressed." (Doc. 28 at 7). They similarly contend that certification of this proposed scope of the phrase "boycott of Israel" to the Arizona Supreme Court would avoid or substantially modify the First Amendment concerns raised by Plaintiffs.

Defendants' proposed limiting construction of "boycott of Israel" does not, however, resolve the constitutionality of the Certification Requirement. As an initial matter, the proposed construction is contrary to the plain language of the Act. Courts should not apply limiting constructions when the proposed

---

5 The only First Amendment case in which the Ninth Circuit has ever held that a district court properly invoked *Pullman* abstention "was procedurally aberrational." *Courthouse News Serv. v. Planet*, 750 F.3d 776, 784 (9th Cir. 2014) (referencing *Almodovar v. Reiner*, 832 F.2d 1138 (9th Cir. 1987)).

construction is "contrary to the plain language of the statute." *Valle Del Sol v. Whiting*, 709 F.3d 808, n.3 (9th Cir. 2013) (citing *Bd. of Airport Comm'rs of L.A. v. Jews for Jesus, Inc.*, 482 U.S. 569, 575, 107 S. Ct. 2568, 96 L. Ed. 2d 500 (1987) (refusing to adopt a limiting construction because "the words of the resolution simply leave no room for a narrowing construction")). Under Defendants' interpretation, while adhering to a call to boycott Israel, a contracting company that refused to deal with another company that does business in Israel would *not* be in violation of 35–393.01 because such conduct would not be a "general boycott of Israel." This construction is belied by the plain language in § 35–393(1), which defines "boycott" to include actions against not only the country of Israel, but also of "persons or entities doing business in Israel or in territories controlled by Israel." A.R.S. § 35–393(1).[6]

Moreover, while interpretive guidance on the scope of "boycott of Israel" may help courts (and companies wishing to contract with a public entity in Arizona) determine whether certain activities constitute a breach of an avowal to refrain from the conduct prohibited by the Act, such an interpretation would not resolve the question of whether the Act's Certification Requirement unconstitutionally imposes a condition on receipt of a government contract. Indeed, this position presupposes that Arizona can constitutionally condition a company's right to engage in "a general boycott of Israel" that is taken in response to a larger call for such action on receipt of any public contract. But as the Court discusses *infra*, to justify such a broad restriction, regulation of activity that infringes on expressive boycotting activities must be "necessary" to the "actual operation of the government." *United States v. National Treasury Emples. Union*, 513 U.S. 454, 469 (1995), 115 S. Ct. 1003, 130 L. Ed. 2d 964 (hereafter,

---

6   Even under the Defendants' proposed meaning of "boycott of Israel", it remains unclear what a "broad or total boycott of Israel such as those called for the Boycott, Divest and Sanctions ("BDS") movement" constitutes. Although the Court does not find that the Act is unconstitutionally vague – the Act, after all, unambiguously defines "boycott" to include conduct other than just a "total boycott of Israel" - the Court notes that the vagueness inherent in the Defendants' proposed interpretation of "boycott of Israel" heightens, not lessens, the risk that protected conduct will be chilled, a factor that weighs against abstention. *See Grayned v. City of Rockford*, 408 U.S. 104, 109, 92 S. Ct. 2294, 33 L. Ed. 2d 222 (1972) ("Where a vague statute abuts upon sensitive areas of basic First Amendment freedoms, it operates to inhibit the exercise of those freedoms") (internal quotations and alterations omitted) (citations omitted)). Even assuming that the recently amended Arizona Agency Handbook ("Handbook") that was submitted with the State's Notice of Supplemental Authority (Doc. 61–1) has any binding or authoritative value, the same is true with regard to the purportedly clarifying interpretations of "boycott of Israel" therein. (*See* Doc. 61–1 at 5.4.18 (stating, in part, that "A boycott is not a "boycott of Israel" if it targets multiple countries and does not principally target Israel or those doing business with them [sic].")).

"Nat'l Treasury"). Defendants have failed to show that the government has such an interest here. Thus, the constitutional question would not be obviated even under Defendants' proposed interpretation of "boycott of Israel."

In sum, this case fails at least two of *Pullman's* requirements. This Court therefore lacks the discretion to abstain and the State's request for the same is denied. For similar reasons, Defendants' request to certify a question to the Arizona Supreme Court pursuant to A.R.S. § 12–8161 regarding the scope of "boycott of Israel" is also denied.

Having satisfied itself that this case is justiciable and abstention or certification to the Arizona Supreme Court would be improper, the Court will now turn to the merits of Plaintiffs' motion for injunctive relief.

III *Plaintiffs' Motion for Preliminary Injunction*

A preliminary injunction "is an extraordinary and drastic remedy, one that should not be granted unless the movant, by a clear showing, carries the burden of persuasion." *Mazurek v. Armstrong*, 520 U.S. 968, 972, 117 S. Ct. 1865, 138 L. Ed. 2d 162 (1997) (per curiam) (quoting 11A C. Wright, A. Miller, & M. Kane, Federal Practice and Procedure § 2948, 129–130 (2d ed. 1995)). An injunction may be granted when the movant shows that "'he is likely to succeed on the merits, that he is likely to suffer irreparable harm in the absence of preliminary relief, that the balance of equities tips in his favor, and that an injunction is in the public interest.'" *Am. Trucking Ass'ns, Inc. v. City of Los Angeles*, 559 F.3d 1046, 1052 (9th Cir. 2009) (quoting *Winter v. Natural Res. Def. Council, Inc.*, 555 U.S. 7, 20, 129 S. Ct. 365, 172 L. Ed. 2d 249 (2008)). In this circuit, a preliminary injunction may also be issued when a plaintiff shows that "'serious questions going to the merits were raised and the balance of hardships tips sharply in [plaintiff's] favor.'" *Alliance for the Wild Rockies v. Cottrell*, 632 F.3d 1127, 1134–35 (9th Cir. 2011) (quoting *Lands Council v. McNair*, 537 F.3d 981, 987 (9th Cir. 2008)). The movant has the burden of proof on each element of the test. *Envtl. Council of Sacramento v. Slater*, 184 F. Supp. 2d 1016, 1027 (E.D. Cal. 2000).

A Likelihood of Success on the Merits

Plaintiffs assert that they are likely to succeed in showing that the Certification Requirement unconstitutionally infringes on their First Amendment rights. In doing so, Plaintiffs contend that the Certification Requirement is an unconstitutional condition, is viewpoint and content discriminatory, and impermissibly compels protected speech. They further contend that the Certification Requirement is not justified by sufficiently legitimate government interests. Defendants argue that the activity that Plaintiffs wish to engage in is unexpressive commercial conduct that is not protected by the First Amendment, and that to the extent such conduct is protected, it is more than justified by the State's interest in regulating its "commercial activity to align commerce in the State with the State's policy objectives and values" as well as its interest in preventing discrimination on the basis of national origin. (Doc. 28 at 22–24). Accordingly, Defendants contend that "Plaintiffs are not likely to prevail on the merits and their Complaint should be dismissed." (Doc. 28 at 15).

The First Amendment, made applicable to the States by the Fourteenth Amendment, provides that "Congress shall make no law ... abridging the freedom of speech, or of the press; or the right of the people peaceably to assemble." U.S. Const. amend. I. "The First Amendment protects political association as well as political expression." *Buckley v. Valeo*, 424 U.S. 1, 15, 96 S. Ct. 612, 46 L. Ed. 2d 659 (1976); *Roberts v. U.S. Jaycees*, 468 U.S. 609, 622, 104 S. Ct. 3244, 82 L. Ed. 2d 462 (1984) ("An individual's freedom to speak, to worship, and to petition the government for the redress of grievances could not be vigorously protected from interference by the State unless a correlative freedom to engage in group effort toward those ends were not also guaranteed."). "The right to eschew association for expressive purposes is likewise protected." *Janus v. Am. Fed'n. of State, Cnty., and Mun. Emps., Council 31*, 138 S. Ct. 2448, 2463, 201 L. Ed. 2d 924 (2018) (citing *Roberts*, 468 U.S. at 623); *see also Pacific Gas & Elec. Co. v Public Utilities Com'n of California*, 475 U.S. 1, 12, 106 S. Ct. 903, 89 L. Ed. 2d 1 (1986) ("[F]orced associations that burden protected speech are impermissible"). Broad prohibitions of expressive activity on government employees that are not necessary to the operation of their service are also impermissible under the First Amendment. *Nat'l Treasury*, 513 U.S. at 469.

As the Supreme Court has observed, "[i]t is fundamental that the First Amendment was fashioned to assure an unfettered interchange of ideas for the bringing about of political and social changes desired by the people." *Legal Services Corp. v. Velazquez*, 531 U.S. 533, 548, 121 S. Ct. 1043, 149 L. Ed. 2d 63 (2001) (internal quotations omitted); *c.f. United States v. Associated Press*, 52 F. Supp. 362, 372 (S.D.N.Y. 1943) (noting that the interest protected by the First Amendment "presupposes that right conclusions are more likely to be gathered out of a multitude of tongues, than through any kind of authoritative selection"). "At the heart of the First Amendment lies the principle that each person should decide for himself or herself the ideas and beliefs deserving of expression, consideration, and adherence." *Turner Broadcasting System, Inc. v. FCC*, 512 U.S. 622, 641, 114 S. Ct. 2445, 129 L. Ed. 2d 497 (1994). *See also Knox v. SEIU, Local 1000*, 567 U.S. 298, 132 S. Ct. 2277, 2288, 183 L. Ed. 2d 281 (2012) ("The government may not ... compel the endorsement of ideas that it approves."). Indeed, "[i]f there is any fixed star in our constitutional constellation, it is that no official, high or petty, can prescribe what shall be orthodox in politics, nationalism, religion, or other matters of opinion or force citizens to confess by work or act their faith therein." *West Virginia Bd. of Ed. v. Barnette*, 319 U.S. 624, 642, 63 S. Ct. 1178, 87 L. Ed. 1628 (1943).

Plaintiffs advance various theories as to why the Certification Requirement is unconstitutional under the First Amendment.[7] The Court finds, however, that Plaintiffs would at least be able to meet their burden of showing that the Certification Requirement is an unconstitutional condition on government contractors. In reaching this conclusion, the Court will first discuss why the conduct implicated by the terms of the Act encompasses expressive activity that is protected under the First Amendment. The Court will then provide some background on the unconditional conditions doctrine in the context of government employment. Finally, the Court will explain why the State's proffered interests do not justify the infringement the Certification Requirement imposes on such expressive conduct.

1. The Act Burdens Expressive Conduct Protected by the First Amendment

Defendants argue that the Supreme Court's decision in *Int'l Longshoremen's Association, AFL-CIO v. Allied International, Inc.*, and the Seventh Circuit's decision in *Briggs & Stratton Corp. v. Baldrige* foreclose Plaintiffs' claims because they establish that economic boycotts are not protected under the First Amendment. 456 U.S. 212, 102 S. Ct. 1656, 72 L. Ed. 2d 21 (1982); 728 F.2d 915 (7th Cir. 1984). Alternatively, Defendants argue that a "boycott of Israel" should not be protected because banning such activity only prohibits non-expressive commercial conduct.

a. *Int'l Longshoremen's Association, AFL-CIO v. Allied International, Inc.*, 456 U.S. 212, 102 S. Ct. 1656, 72 L. Ed. 2d 21 (1982)

Defendants first contend that Plaintiffs cannot prevail on the merits of their claim because any alleged First Amendment right to engage in an economic boycott is foreclosed by the Supreme Court's decision in *Int'l Longshoremen*. In *Int'l Longshoremen*, the Supreme Court found that a labor organization's politically-motivated boycott of goods from the Soviet Union was an illegal

---

[7] "First Amendment doctrines are manifold, and their diverse facts and analyses may reveal but one consistent truth with respect to the amendment – each case is decided on its own merits." *Bishop v. Aronov*, 926 F.2d 1066, 1070 (11th Cir. 1991), cert. denied, 505 U.S. 1218, 112 S. Ct. 3026, 120 L. Ed. 2d 897 (1992).

secondary boycott under section 8(b)(4)(B) of the National Labor Relations Act ("NLRA"). *Id.* In so finding, the Court rejected the union's argument that section 8(b)(4)(B) unlawfully infringed on its First Amendment right to engage in a politically-motivated, secondary boycott of Russian goods. *Id.* at 226 (noting also that the Court has "consistently rejected the claim that secondary picketing by labor unions in violation of § 8(b)(4) is protected activity under the First Amendment"). Finding that "labor laws reflect a careful balancing of interests," the Court reasoned that the NLRA's prohibition against secondary boycotts was intended both to prevent imposing heavy financial burdens on neutral employers and the "widening of industrial strife." *Id.* at 223, 227.

Defendants overstate the meaning of *Int'l Longshoreman*, which was decided in the context of federal labor laws. *Int'l Longshoreman* does not purport to state that there is no constitutional right to engage in boycotting activities. It does, however, highlight the context in which this type of governmental infringement on the First Amendment rights of labor unions and their members is justified. *See NAACP v. Claiborne Hardware Co.*, 458 U.S. 886, 907, 102 S. Ct. 3409, 73 L. Ed. 2d 1215 (1982) ("Secondary boycotts and picketing by labor union may be prohibited, as part of Congress' striking of the delicate balance between union freedom of expression and the ability of neutral employers, employees, and consumers to remain free from coerced participation in industrial strife.") (internal quote omitted). Outside of the labor union context, however, the government has a much higher burden when it infringes on such activity. Indeed, only a few months after *Longshoreman* was decided, the Supreme Court in *Claiborne* expressly found that non-union boycotting activities aimed "to bring about political, social and economic change" were protected activities under the First Amendment. *Claiborne*, 458 U.S. at 907.

In *Claiborne*, civil rights activists called for a boycott of all white merchants in Claiborne County, Mississippi. *Id.* at 900. Several years later, those merchants filed suit in state court seeking to enjoin future boycott activities and to recover for the losses they had previously sustained. *Id.* at 889. In assessing whether the petitioners' boycotting activities were protected speech under the First Amendment, the Court looked at how and why the boycott originated, and the means by which it was supported. The Court noted that:

> The boycott was launched at a meeting of a local branch of the NAACP attended by several hundred persons. Its acknowledged purpose was to secure compliance by both civil and business leaders with a lengthy list of demands for equality and racial justice. The boycott was supported by speeches and nonviolent picketing. Participants repeatedly encouraged others to join its cause.

Id. at 906. The Court found that each "element[ ] of the boycott [was] a form of speech or conduct that is ordinarily entitled to protection under the First and Fourteenth Amendment." *Id.* In so finding, the Court reasoned that "'the practice of persons sharing common views banding together to achieve a common end is deeply embedded in the American political process.'" *Id.* at 907 (citing *Citizens Against Rent Control Coalition for Fair Housing v. Berkeley*, 454 U.S. 290, 294, 102 S. Ct. 434, 70 L. Ed. 2d 492 (1981) (recognizing that "by collective effort individuals can make their views known, when individually, their voices would be faint or lost")).

Claiborne stands for the proposition that collective boycotting activities undertaken to achieve social, political or economic ends is conduct that is protected by the First Amendment. *See also NAACP v. Alabama*, 357 U.S. 449, 78 S. Ct. 1163, 2 L. Ed. 2d 1488 (1959) (recognizing that the freedom of speech embraces the "freedom to engage in association for the advancement of beliefs and ideas"). Thus, the question for this Court is whether the Arizona legislature has infringed upon or restricted these types of boycotting activities.

The Arizona legislature has defined "boycott" to mean "engaging in a refusal to deal, terminating business activities or performing *other actions* that are intended to limited commercial relations with Israel or with persons or entities doing business in Israel or in territories controlled by Israel, *if those actions are taken ... in compliance with or adherence to calls for a boycott of Israel ...*" A.R.S. § 35–393(1)(a) (emphasis added). In accordance with *Claiborne*, these types of boycotting activities, which clearly include "the practice of persons sharing common views banding together to achieve a common end," are entitled constitutional protections. 458 U.S. at 907. The Act here specifically and generally enumerates certain activity companies cannot engage in if they wish to contract with a public entity. Specifically, the Act prohibits companies from "engaging in a refusal to deal," "terminating business activities" or "performing *other actions* that are intended to limit commercial relations." A.R.S. § 35–393(1) (emphasis added). These actions, however, are only prohibited when taken "in compliance with or adherence to calls for a boycott of Israel." *Id.* The language of the Act thus necessarily contemplates prohibiting collective conduct aimed "to achieve a common end"; here, a "boycott of Israel." 458 U.S. at 907–08.

Indeed, the collective element of the actions that are prohibited, together with the potential reach of what activities constitute "other actions," is what distinguishes this Act from those statutes that lawfully prohibit conduct that is not inherently expressive. *See e.g., Rumsfeld v. Forum for Academic & Institutional Rights, Inc.*, 547 U.S. 47, 126 S. Ct. 1297, 164 L. Ed. 2d 156 (2006)

("*FAIR*"). In *FAIR*, the Court rejected the argument that the law schools' decisions to exclude military recruiters from their campuses for purposes of expressing the schools' disagreement with the military's stance on homosexuals in the military was expressive conduct deserving protection under *United States v. O'Brien*, 391 U.S. 367, 88 S. Ct. 1673, 20 L. Ed. 2d 672 (1968). The Court held that the expressive component of the action was "not created by the conduct itself but by the speech that accompanie[d] it." *FAIR*, 547 U.S. at 66 ("The fact that such explanatory speech is necessary is strong evidence that the conduct at issue here is not so inherently expressive that it warrants protection under *O'Brien*"). Invoking this reasoning, Defendants argue that "[o]nly by talking about why Plaintiffs purchased an iPad or an HP printer would any observer discern any connection between that purchasing decision and Israeli government policies." (Doc. 28 at 21). The Court agrees that the commercial actions (or non-actions) of one person, e.g., the decision not to buy a particular brand of printer to show support for a political position, may not be deserving of First Amendment protections on the grounds that such action is typically only expressive when explanatory speech accompanies it. However, when a statute requires a company, in exchange for a government contract, to promise to refrain from engaging in certain actions that are taken in response to larger calls to action that the state opposes, the state is infringing on the very kind of expressive conduct at issue in *Claiborne*. Such a regulation squarely raises First Amendment concerns. Indeed, reasoning otherwise would completely undermine the First Amendment's long-held precedents protecting First Amendment rights to assemble so that citizens of this Country can collectively "secure compliance" with their political demands. *Claiborne*, 458 U.S. at 906.

"Effective advocacy of both public and private points of view, particularly controversial ones, is undeniably enhanced by group association, as this Court has more than once recognized by remarking upon the close nexus between the freedoms of speech and assembly." *NAACP*, 357 U.S. at 460. Mr. Jordahl was moved by calls by ELCA and JVP for individuals to collectively boycott products from companies doing business in Israeli-occupied settlements. Through this collective action, Mr. Jordahl and these organizations seek to promote the "equal human dignity and rights for all people in the Holy Land" and "an end to Israeli settlement building and the occupation of Palestinian land." (Doc. 6–1 at 3). A restriction of one's ability to participate in collective calls to oppose Israel unquestionably burdens the protected expression of companies wishing to engage in such a boycott. The type of collective action targeted by the Act specifically implicates the rights of assembly and association that Americans and Arizonans use "to bring about political, social, and economic change."

Claiborne, 458 U.S. at 911 (stating "[t]he established elements of speech, assembly, association, and petition, though not identical, are inseparable") (internal quotation omitted). *See also Lyng v. International Union, United Auto. Aerospace & Agricultural Implement Workers*, 485 U.S. 360, 367 n.5, 108 S. Ct. 1184, 99 L. Ed. 2d 380 (1988) ("[A]ssociational rights ... can be abridged even by government actions that do not directly restrict individuals' ability to associate freely"). Under *Claiborne*, this conduct is deserving of First Amendment protection. Plaintiffs claim is therefore not foreclosed by *Int'l Longshoremen*.

b. *Briggs & Stratton Corp. v. Baldrige*, 728 F.2d 915 (7th Cir. 1984)

Defendants also argue that Plaintiffs' First Amendment claim is precluded by the Seventh Circuit Court of Appeals' decision in *Briggs & Stratton Corp. v. Baldrige*. In *Briggs*, United States companies doing business with Arab League nations challenged the constitutionality of a section in the Federal Export Administration Act ("EAA") that prohibits United States companies from participating in a foreign government's request for a boycott against countries friendly to the United States. *See* 50 U.S.C. § 4607. The companies specifically argued that their inability to answer questionnaires propounded by the Arab countries for the purpose of ensuring compliance with those Arab countries' boycott of Israel unduly infringed on their First Amendment rights. *Briggs*, 728 F.2d at 917. The court rejected plaintiffs' claim, finding that their desired speech was commercial in nature and adequately justified by government interests in regulating international trade. *Id.* at 918. In characterizing the desired speech as commercial, and thus deserving of less protection under the First Amendment, the court noted that the companies' desire to answer the questionnaires was solely motivated by economics – not by their desire "to influence the Arabs' decision to conduct or enforce a trade boycott with Israel"; and the "proposed answers to boycott questionnaires would serve only to allow appellants to continue to maintain commercial dealings with the Arab world." *Id.*; *Briggs & Stratton Corp. v. Baldrige*, 539 F. Supp. 1307, 1319 (E. D. Wis. 1982) (finding that "[t]he state interest here is substantial, involving delicate foreign policy questions and the interest of the government in forestalling attempts by foreign governments to embroil American citizens in their battles against others by forcing them to participate in actions which are repugnant to American values and traditions"); *id.* at 1319 ("in passing this section of the EAA, "Congress concluded that supplying information to [foreign] boycott authorities has no legitimate business purpose and should be prohibited") (internal citations and quotations omitted)).

Briggs, as a result, is wholly distinguishable. First, unlike the activities Plaintiffs wish to engage in, and the politically-motivated actions that are contemplated by the plain language of the Act, the Court in *Briggs* found that the plaintiffs' desires to answer questions from their trade partners were not politically-motivated and thus not deserving of First Amendment protection. Second, the substantial state interests advanced by the government in *Briggs* – foreign policy and international trade relations – are simply not present here. Thus, even if *Briggs* were binding precedent on this Court, which it is not, the case does not stand for the proposition that the conduct prohibited under the Act falls outside the protections of the First Amendment.

c. Restriction of Purely Commercial Conduct

Finally, Defendants argue that the Certification Requirement does not implicate the First Amendment because it "only regulates commercial conduct." (Doc. 28 at 18). Defendants first maintain that "Plaintiffs may *say absolutely anything* they desire about Israel. Or they may maintain *complete and absolute silence* regarding their beliefs about the policies of Israel." (*Id.* (emphasis in original)). The Court again finds that Defendants interpret the protections of the First Amendment too narrowly. The fact that the Act does not expressly limit or restrain what Plaintiffs can *say* does not mean that protected conduct is not affected by its terms. The Supreme Court has held that even a facially speech-neutral statute or regulation may implicate expressive activity protected under the First Amendment. *See Nat'l Treasury*, 513 U.S. at 468–69 (noting that the honoraria ban in question, while "neither prohibit[ing] any speech nor discriminat[ing] among speakers based on the content or viewpoint of their message" nonetheless "unquestionably impose[d] a significant burden on expressive activity"). Even though the Act does not expressly limit speech, its terms limit collective engagement in types of political expression that the Supreme Court has found to fall within First Amendment protections. *See Claiborne*, 458 U.S. at 907.

The Act thus encompasses and contemplates elements of expressive political conduct protected under the Constitution. As such, the Court finds it highly likely that Plaintiffs will be able to establish that "boycott," as defined in the Arizona legislature, burdens expressive political activity protected under the First Amendment. The question then becomes whether the State has an adequate interest in restricting companies' rights to engage in boycotts of Israel by conditioning their government contracts on a promise to refrain from such activity.

2. Unconstitutional Conditions on Government Employment

"[C]itizens do not surrender their First Amendment rights by accepting public employment." *Lane v. Franks*, 573 U.S. 228, 134 S. Ct. 2369, 2374, 189 L. Ed. 2d 312 (2014). Thus, the premise that government employment contracts may be subjected to any condition "has been unequivocally rejected." *Pickering v. Bd of Edu. of Township High Sch. Dist. 205, Will Cty, Ill.*, 391 U.S. 563, 568, 88 S. Ct. 1731, 20 L. Ed. 2d 811 (1968). This premise has been extended to independent government contractors. *Bd. of Cnty. Comm'rs. Wabausee Cnty., Kan. v. Umbehr*, 518 U.S. 668, 674-5, 116 S. Ct. 2342, 135 L. Ed. 2d 843 (1996).

> Recognizing that "constitutional violations may arise from the deterrent, or 'chilling,' effect of governmental [efforts] that fall short of a direct prohibition against the exercise of First Amendment rights," [...] our modern "unconstitutional conditions" doctrine holds that the government "may not deny a benefit to a person on a basis that infringes his constitutionally protected ... freedom of speech" even if he has no entitlement to that benefit [...]

Umbehr, 518 U.S. at 674-5 (quoting *Laird v. Tatum*, 408 U.S. 1, 11, 92 S. Ct. 2318, 33 L. Ed. 2d 154 (1972) and *Perry v. Sindermann*, 408 U.S. 593, 597, 92 S. Ct. 2694, 33 L. Ed. 2d 570 (1972)). On the other hand, the rights guaranteed under the First Amendment, particularly in the context of government employment, are far from absolute. *Pickering*, 391 U.S. at 568. "The problem in any case is to arrive at a balance between the interests of the [government employee], as a citizen, in commenting upon matters of public concern and the interest of the State, as an employer, in promoting the efficiency of the public services it performs through its employees." *Id. Umbehr*, 518 U.S. at 677 (extending *Pickering*'s analytical framework to independent government contractors); *accord Alpha Energy Savers, Inc. Hansen*, 381 F.3d 917, 923 (9th Cir. 2004). In assessing the constitutionality of First Amendment restrictions imposed retroactively on individual government employees, courts engage in what has been referred to as the *Pickering* balancing test. In those scenarios, if the challenged restriction at issue reaches expression communicated in a government employee's capacity "as a citizen" and includes discussion of "matter[s] of public concern," "[t]he question becomes whether the relevant government entity had an adequate justification for treating the employee differently from any other member of the general public." *Garcetti v. Ceballos*, 547 U.S. 410, 418, 126 S. Ct. 1951, 164 L. Ed. 2d 689 (2006). *See e.g., Connick v. Myers*, 461 U.S. 138, 146, 103 S. Ct. 1684,

75 L. Ed. 2d 708 (1983) (dismissal of district attorney for circulating a questionnaire concerning internal office affairs did not violate her First Amendment rights because complaints about supervisors were matters of only private concern).

The State's burden in justifying a restriction of speech or expressive conduct is greater, however, when the restriction is not related to an isolated employee disciplinary action but instead has widespread prophylactic impact. *Moonin v. Tice*, 868 F.3d 853, 861 (9th Cir. 2017). *See Janus*, 138 S. Ct. at 2472 (noting that the adjustments made to the level of scrutiny in these contexts amounts to "a test that more closely resembles exacting scrutiny than the traditional *Pickering* analysis"); *Nat'l Treasury*, 513 U.S. at 467 n.11 (explaining that increased scrutiny is justified where the government's "ban deters an enormous quantity of speech before it is uttered, based only on speculation that the speech might threaten the Government's interests"). The burden is greater in this context because "'[u]nlike an adverse action taken in response to actual speech,'" which is the context in which the *Pickering* balancing framework developed, a prospective restriction or condition on government employment "'chills potential speech before it happens.'" *Moonin*, 868 F.3d at 861 (quoting *Nat'l Treasury*, 513 U.S. at 468). *See Nat'l Treasury*, 513 U.S. at 469 (finding provisions of the Ethics Reform Act that prohibited government employees from accepting honorarium for making speeches or writing articles unduly burdened public employee speech and the "public's right to read and hear what Government employees would otherwise have written and said" because it "induce[d] [employees] to curtail their expression if they wish to continue working for the Government").[8] Accordingly,

---

8 In this way, the prospective employment condition is akin to a prior restraint on speech. A prior restraint traditionally comes "bearing a heavy presumption against its constitutional validity." *Bantam Books, Inc. v. Sullivan*, 372 U.S. 58, 70, 83 S. Ct. 631, 9 L. Ed. 2d 584 (1963). Neither the Supreme Court nor the Ninth Circuit has analyzed an analogous government employment condition under the framework of a prior restraint, however. In *Moonin*, the Ninth Circuit distinguished an employer's policy that prospectively chilled employee speech from traditional prior restraints, noting, without expansion, that the former are "analytically distinct from claims involving archetypical prior restraints, like government licensing requirements affecting only citizen speech or judicial orders forbidding certain speech by private parties." *Moonin*, 868 F.3d at 858, n. 1 (citing *Alexander v. United States*, 509 U.S. 544, 550, 113 S. Ct. 2766, 125 L. Ed. 2d 441, (1993), *Forsyth Cty. v. Nationalist Movement*, 505 U.S. 123, 130, 112 S. Ct. 2395, 120 L. Ed. 2d 101 (1992), and *Near v. Minnesota*, 283 U.S. 697, 713, 51 S. Ct. 625, 75 L. Ed. 1357 (1931)). Here, the Certification Requirement is a condition imposed on all companies wishing to do business with a public entity in Arizona. A.R.S. § 35–393.01(A). As such, it is a restriction imposed only on independent government contractors, not the public

> Where a 'wholesale deterrent to a broad category of expression' rather than 'a post hoc analysis of one employee's speech and its impact on that employee's public responsibilities' is at issue ... the court weighs the impact of the ban as a whole – both on the employees whose speech may be curtailed and on the public interested in what they might say – against the restricted speech's 'necessary impact on the actual operation' of the Government.

Moonin, 868 F.3d at 861 (quoting *Nat'l Treasury*, 513 U.S. at 468) (quoting *Pickering*, 391 U.S. at 571, 88 S.Ct. 1731)).[9]

---

at large. The Court will accordingly follow the guidance of the *Moonin* court and analyze the constitutionality of the Certification Requirement under the employee speech framework in *Pickering* and *Nat'l Treasury*. *But see Janus*, 138 S. Ct. at 2473 (noting the "poor fit" of *Pickering* to the constitutionality of the labor union's agency-fee scheme in part because a hypothetical employee complaint regarding a raise would be a matter of "private concern" and unprotected under *Pickering*, whereas the same complaint raised by many employees speaking through their union would be of "public concern" and thus protected, despite the fact that the speech may have "a significant effect on the performance of government services").

9   The context of this case, which challenges the constitutionality of a condition imposed on companies wishing to contract with public entities in Arizona, falls somewhere between the unconstitutional condition employment cases and those cases that assess the constitutionality of conditions imposed on recipients of government funding. *See e.g., Agency for Intern. Dev. v. Alliance for Open Soc'y Int'l, Inc.*, 570 U.S. 205, 219, 133 S. Ct. 2321, 186 L. Ed. 2d 398 (2013) (finding government condition that international organization adopt its "view on an issue of public concern" in order to receive funding was an unconstitutional infringement on organization's First Amendment right because requirement went "beyond defining the limits of the federally funded program to defining the recipient"); *Rust v. Sullivan*, 500 U.S. 173, 197, 111 S. Ct. 1759, 114 L. Ed. 2d 233 (1991) (noting that cases in which a condition to federal funding has been found unconstitutional "involve situations in which the Government has placed a condition on the *recipient* of the subsidy rather than on a particular program or service, thus effectively prohibiting the recipient from engaging in the protected conduct outside the scope of the federally funded program") (emphasis in original); *FCC v. League of Women Voters of California*, 468 U.S. 364, 399–401, 104 S. Ct. 3106, 82 L. Ed. 2d 278 (1984) (prohibiting media stations from engaging in all editorializing, even with private funds, in order to receive federal assistance improperly leveraged federal funding to regulate the stations' speech outside the scope of the program); *Regan v. Taxation With Representation of Washington*, 461 U.S. 540, 546, 103 S. Ct. 1997, 76 L. Ed. 2d 129 (1983) (requirement that non-profit organizations seeking tax-exempt status not engage in substantial efforts to influence legislation was not "unduly burdensome" because condition did not prohibit organization from lobbying altogether). Although the Court analyzes the constitutionality of the Certification Requirement under *Nat'l Treasury* and other cases that condition government employment on broad speech bans, the Court also notes that in these government funding cases, the courts apply a similar level of scrutiny.

3. The Act Broadly Restricts Government Contractor's Expressive Conduct As Citizens Speaking on Matters of Public Concern

"The first prong of the employee speech analysis involves two inquiries: whether the restriction reaches only speech within the scope of a public employee's official duties, and whether it impacts speech on matters of public concern." *Pickering*, 391 U.S. at 571. In the context of a condition broadly banning certain expressive conduct, a court is to "focus on the text of the [statute] to determine the extent to which it implicates public employees' speech as citizens speaking on matters of public concern." *Id. See also Moonin*, 868 F.3d at 861.

The Court has little difficulty in finding that actions prohibited by the Act have no relation to Plaintiffs' official duties. The Ninth Circuit has found that communication "with individuals or entities outside of [an employee's] chain of command ...[is] unlikely" to be pursuant to the employee's official duties." *See Dahlia v. Rodriguez*, 735 F.3d 1060, 1074 (9th Cir. 2013) (en banc). For the past twelve years, Mr. Jordahl, through his Firm, has represented criminal defendants through a contract with the County. The State has not and cannot explain how preventing Plaintiffs' from engaging in a boycott of Israel as defined by the Act furthers or affects Plaintiffs' duty in representing his clients in relation to that contract. The Act requires contracting companies to promise to refrain from engaging in certain conduct if done at the behest of outside "calls" to boycott Israel. The Act thus clearly aims to suppress expressive conduct that may be "directed to community groups, to city and state legislators, to state and federal officials, and even to family members and friends," and is not limited – or even directed – to the Firm's legal representation of criminal defendants. *Moonin*, 868 F.3d at 863 (policy prohibiting "direct contact" between employee and "ANY nondepartmental and non-law enforcement entity or persons for the purpose of discussing [program]" covered speech outside the employees' official duties). There is no plausible relationship between the execution of the Firm's representation of their clients under the County contract and the Firm's avowal to refrain from engaging in a boycott of Israel.

The prohibited acts also have no relation to official contractors' duties in general. The Certification Requirement applies to any company that provides "services, supplies, information technology or construction" to a public entity in Arizona. A.R.S. § 35–393.01(A). The scope of "official duties" that are encompassed by the number and diversity of companies contracting with the State vary dramatically and the plain language of the Certification Requirement does not limit its scope to prohibit actions taken in furtherance of those duties. *See Moonin*, 868 F.3d at 861 n.5 (noting that the "focus in the prospective restraint context is on the chilling effect of the employer's policy on employee speech" which is "determined by the language of the policy – what an employee reading the policy would think the policy requires – not what [the employer] subjectively intended the [policy] to say"). The Court thus finds that the Act reaches beyond the scope of contractors' official duties.

The Act also unquestionably touches on matters of public concern. "Speech involves matters of public concern when it can be fairly considered as relating to any matter of political, social, or other concern to the community, or when it is a subject of legitimate news interest; that is, a subject of general interest and of value and concern to the public." *Lane*, 134 S.Ct. at 2380 (internal quotation marks and citation omitted). "This circuit and other courts have defined public concern speech broadly to include almost *any* matter other than speech that relates to internal power struggles within the workplace." *Tucker v. State of Cal. Dept. of Educ.*, 97 F.3d 1204, 1210 (9th Cir. 1996) (emphasis in original). *Gillette v. Delmore*, 886 F.2d 1194, 1197 (9th Cir. 1989) ("Speech that can fairly be considered as relating to any matter of political, social, or other concern to the community is constitutionally protected."); *see also McKinley v. City of Eloy*, 705 F.2d 1110, 1114 (9th Cir. 1983) ("Speech by public employees may be characterized as not of 'public concern' when it is clear that such speech deals with individual personnel disputes and grievances.") (citations omitted). "The Supreme Court has also made it clear that an employee need not address the public at large for his speech to be deemed to be on a matter of public concern." *Tucker*, 97 F.3d at 1210 (citing *Rankin v. McPherson*, 483 U.S. 378, 384–87, 107 S. Ct. 2891, 97 L. Ed. 2d 315 (1987) (finding that an employee's statement regarding President Reagan, although only made to co-worker, was on a matter of public concern).

As is evidenced by the parties' briefings, actions taken by Israel in relation to Palestine are matters of much political and public debate. Plaintiffs want to participate in collective economic boycotts of goods and products from companies doing business in Israeli-occupied settlements in order to show their political discontent with Israel's policies toward Palestine. Through their actions, Plaintiffs seek to promote "equal human dignity and rights for all people in the Holy Land" and "an end to Israeli settlement building and the occupation of Palestinian land." (Doc. 6–1 at 3). *See also Nat'l Treasury*, 513 U.S. at 461–62 (considering employees' past and intended speech in assessing the First Amendment consequences affecting employee speech). The State, however, finds such actions out of line with its values, stating that "the effect – and often goal – of BDS boycotts is to strengthen the hand of the Palestinian Authority ("PA") at the expense of Israel." (Doc. 28 at 23). Indeed, by prohibiting certain actions taken in compliance with larger calls for boycotts of Israel, the Arizona legislature's plain definition of "boycott" underscores the public nature of the conduct.

Plaintiffs have thus met their burden of showing not only that they and others are engaged in protected activities, but that the terms of the Act encompass such activities.

4. **The State Cannot Meet its Burden of Showing that the Certification Requirement Has a Necessary Impact on the Actual Operation of the State**

Of course, properly justified, the fact that the Act infringes on protected activity does not render the Act unconstitutional. Where a restriction prospectively limits government contractors' expressive conduct, the State can justify such interference by showing the restriction has a "necessary impact on the actual operation" of the State. *Nat'l Treasury*, 513 U.S. at 468. Here, the State has proffered two interests to justify the Certification Requirement: (1) an interest in regulating the State's "commercial activity to align commerce in the State with the State's policy objectives and values" and (2) an interest in preventing discrimination on the basis of national origin. (Doc. 28 at 22–24).

The legislative history of the Act calls these stated interests into doubt. The Act's history instead suggests that the goal of the Act is to penalize the efforts of those engaged in political boycotts of Israel and those doing business in Israeli-occupied territories because such boycotts are not aligned with the State's values. *See e.g.*, Ariz. House Republican Caucus News Release, Feb. 4, 2016 (representing that the purpose of the Act is to penalize "companies engaging in actions that are politically motivated and intended to penalize, inflict economic harm on, or otherwise limit commercial relations with Israel, its products, or partners"). If so, such an interest is constitutionally impermissible. *See Koontz v. Watson*, 283 F. Supp. 3d 1007, 1022 (D. Kan. 2018) (finding that goal behind Kansas law requiring that persons contracting with the state certify that they are not engaged in a boycott of Israel was "either viewpoint discrimination against the opinion that Israel mistreats Palestinians or subject matter discrimination on the topic of Israel" and that "[b]oth are impermissible goals under the First Amendment").

Assuming the legitimacy of the interests advanced by the State, the Court still finds that neither of the proffered interests justify the restriction because the Certification Requirement is not necessary to advance either of them. To meet its burden, the State "must demonstrate that the recited harms are real, not merely conjectural, and that the regulation will in fact alleviate these harms in a direct and material way." *Nat'l Treasury*, 513 U.S. at 475. The Arizona Fact Sheet to House Bill 2617 plainly states that "[t]here is no anticipated fiscal impact to the state General Fund associated with this legislation."

AZ S. F. Sheet, 2016 Reg. Sess. H.B. 2617. In line with that factual background, Defendants have failed to produce any evidence of Arizona's business dealings with Israel, Israeli entities, or entities that do business with Israel that would suggest the State was seeking to regulate boycotts of Israel that were intended to suppress economic competition. *See Claiborne*, 458 U.S. at 912 (noting that "[t]he right of business entities to 'associate' to suppress competition may be curtailed [by states]"). Instead, the State generally contends that "[a]bsent the Act's prohibitions, public monies will almost certainly be allocated to companies engaged in boycotts of Israel, thereby subsidizing those boycotts." (Doc. 28 at 25). But "'[f]ear of serious injury cannot alone justify suppression of free speech and assembly ... To justify suppression of free speech there must be reasonable ground to fear that serious evil will result if free speech is practiced.'" *Nat'l Treasury*, 513 U.S. at 471–72 (quoting *Whitney v. California*, 274 U.S. 357, 376, 47 S. Ct. 641, 71 L. Ed. 1095 (1927) (concurring opinion)). *Id.* at 471–72 (noting that though the government's interest in preventing misuse of power by accepting compensation was "undeniably powerful," the government failed to show the necessity of a total ban when it could not produce evidence of misconduct related to honoraria "in the vast rank and file of federal employees below grade GS-16"). The State's speculative fears of subsidizing boycotts of Israel, even assuming a legitimate one, does not justify the broad prospective restriction on boycotting activity that the Act prohibits. The State has similarly produced no evidence that Arizona businesses have or are engaged in discriminatory practices against Israel, Israeli entities, or entities that do business with Israel. And even if the State could make such a showing, by including politically-motivated boycotts of Israel within the activity that is prohibited, the Act is unconstitutionally over-inclusive. *Koontz*, 283 F. Supp. 3d at 1023 (finding certification requirement at issue was impermissibly over-inclusive because it banned political boycotts as well as acts arguably intended to suppress economic competition).

Beyond the conjecture noted above, the State has demonstrated no harms to Arizona, or its economic relationship with Israel, that would be alleviated by conditioning all public entity contracts on the contractors' promise to refrain from engaging in actions taken in response to larger calls to boycott of Israel. Defendants have failed to meet their burden of showing that restricting government contractors' right to boycott Israel is "necessary" to the State's operation.

B.   Likelihood of Irreparable Harm

Having established Plaintiffs' likelihood of success on the merits, the next issue is whether Plaintiffs are likely to suffer irreparable harm absent the protection of a preliminary injunction. Generally, courts of equity should not act when the moving party "will not suffer irreparable injury if denied equitable relief." *Younger v. Harris*, 401 U.S. 37, 43–44, 91 S. Ct. 746, 27 L. Ed. 2d 669 (1971). Plaintiffs have the burden of establishing that there is a likelihood, which is more than just a possibility, that they will suffer irreparable harm if a preliminary injunction is not entered. *See Winter*, 555 U.S. at 21–23.

The Court finds that Plaintiffs have met their burden here. Plaintiffs' objections to the Act implicate core protections of the First Amendment. "The loss of First Amendment freedoms, for even minimal periods of time, unquestionably constitutes irreparable injury." *Elrod v. Burns*, 427 U.S. 347, 373, 96 S. Ct. 2673, 49 L. Ed. 2d 547 (1976). Indeed, when the expressive conduct that is so burdened is political in nature, "[t]he harm is particularly irreparable." *Klein v. City of San Clemente*, 584 F.3d 1196, 1208 (9th Cir. 2009). As such, the harms that Plaintiffs and other companies wishing to contract with the state of Arizona are irreparable per se.

C.   Balance of the Equities and the Public Interest

The Court also finds that the balance of equities tips in favor of Plaintiffs. Defendants will experience little to no hardship by enjoining the enforcement of a law that does nothing to further any economic state interest and infringes on First Amendment protections. Although generally barring discrimination on the basis of national origin is a legitimate state interest, the State clearly has less intrusive and more viewpoint-neutral means to combat such discrimination. Plaintiffs, on the other hand, have shown a likelihood of irreparable harm if the Certification Requirement is not enjoined. Moreover, public interest favors an injunction as the public has little interest in enforcement of unconstitutional laws.

D.   Security

A court may issue a preliminary injunction "only if the movant gives security in an amount that the court considers proper to pay the costs and damages sustained by any party found to have been wrongfully enjoined or restrained." Fed. R. Civ. P. 65(c). Although the plain language of the rule suggests that a bond is mandatory, the Ninth Circuit has held that it "invests the district court with discretion as to the amount of security required, if any." *Johnson v. Couturier*, 572 F.3d 1067, 1086 (9th Cir. 2009). A district court need not require a bond "when it concludes there is no realistic likelihood of harm to the defendant from enjoining his or her conduct." *Jorgensen v. Cassiday*, 320 F.3d 906, 919 (9th Cir. 2003). There is no realistic likelihood that Defendants will be harmed by being enjoined from enforcing a law that violates the First Amendment on its face. No bond will be required.

Conclusion

Defendants' motion to dismiss Plaintiffs' Amended Complaint is denied, including their request to dismiss the Attorney General from this action. Moreover, Plaintiffs have shown that they are likely to succeed on the merits of their claim, that they are likely to suffer irreparable harm in the absence of a preliminary injunction, and that the balance of equities and public interest favor an injunction. The Court therefore will grant Plaintiffs' request for a preliminary injunction and enjoin Defendants from enforcing the Certification Requirement in A.R.S. § 35–393.01(A).

IT IS ORDERED that Plaintiffs' Motion for a Preliminary Injunction (Doc. 6) is **granted**. Until further order of the Court, Defendants are enjoined from enforcing A.R.S. § 35–393.01(A).

IT IS FURTHER ORDERED that Defendants' Motion to Dismiss Plaintiffs' Complaint (Doc. 28) is **denied**.

Dated this 27th day of September, 2018.
/s/ Diane J. Humetewa
Honorable Diane J. Humetewa
United States District Judge

SECTION F

Legislation

∴

Israel

Basic Law: Israel The Nation State of the Jewish People (July 25, 2018)

Translation provided by Adalah: The Legal Center for Arab Minority Rights in Israel (https://www.adalah.org/uploads/uploads/Basic_Law_Israel_as_the_Nation_State_of_the_Jewish_People_ENG_TRANSLATION_25072018.pdf)

Basic Law: Israel – The Nation State of the Jewish People

Unofficial translation – 25 July 2018

1 – Basic principles
A. The Land of Israel is the historic national home of the Jewish people, in which the State of Israel was established.
B. The State of Israel is the national state of the Jewish people, in which it exercises its natural, cultural, and historic right to self-determination.
C. Exercising the right to national self-determination in the State of Israel is unique to the Jewish people.

2 – The symbols of the state
A. The name of the state is "Israel."
B. The state flag is white with two blue stripes near the edges and a blue Star of David in the center.
C. The state emblem is a seven-branched menorah with olive leaves on both sides and the word "Israel" beneath it.
D. The state anthem is "Hatikva."
E. Details regarding state symbols shall be determined by law.

3 – The capital of the state
A greater, united Jerusalem is the capital of Israel.

4 – Language
A. The state's language is Hebrew.
B. The Arabic language has a special status; regulation of the use of the Arabic language in or with government institutions will be according to the law.

C. Nothing in this provision is intended to harm the practical status of the Arabic language prior to the enactment of this Basic Law.

5 – Ingathering of the exiles
The state will be open to Jewish immigration and the ingathering of the exiles.

6 – Connection with the Jewish people
A. The state shall foster the well-being of the Jewish people in trouble or in captivity due to the fact of their Jewishness or their citizenship.
B. The state shall act in the Diaspora to preserve the affinity between the state and the Jewish people.
C. The state shall act to preserve the cultural, historic, and religious heritage of the Jewish people in the Jewish Diaspora.

7 – Jewish settlement
The state views the development of Jewish settlement as a national value, and will act to encourage it and to promote and to consolidate its establishment.

8 – Official calendar
The Hebrew calendar is an official calendar of the state, and the foreign calendar shall be used concurrently as an official calendar; use of the Hebrew calendar and the foreign calendar shall be determined by law.

9 – Independence Day and memorial days
A. Independence Day is the national holiday of the state.
B. Memorial Day for the Fallen in Israel's Wars and Holocaust and Heroism Remembrance Day are official memorial days of the State.

10 – Days of rest and Sabbaths
The established days of rest in the state are the Sabbath and the festivals of Israel; non-Jews have the right to rest on their Sabbaths and their festivals; details of this issue shall be determined by law.

11 – Immutability
This Basic Law shall not be amended, unless by another Basic Law passed by a majority of Knesset members.

United States

S. 2946, Anti-Terrorism Clarification Act of 2018

[Congressional Bills 115th Congress]
[From the U.S. Government Publishing Office]
[S. 2946 Enrolled Bill (ENR)]

S.2946

One Hundred Fifteenth Congress of the United States of America

AT THE SECOND SESSION

Begun and held at the City of Washington on Wednesday, the third day of January, two thousand and eighteen

An Act

To amend title 18, United States Code, to clarify the meaning of the terms "act of war" and "blocked asset", and for other purposes.

Be it enacted by the Senate and House of Representatives of the United States of America in Congress assembled,

SECTION 1. SHORT TITLE.
    This Act may be cited as the "Anti-Terrorism Clarification Act of 2018".

SEC. 2. CLARIFICATION OF THE TERM "ACT OF WAR".
(a) IN GENERAL. – Section 2331 of title 18, United States Code, is amended –
    (1) in paragraph (4), by striking "and'" at the end;
    (2) in paragraph (5), by striking the period at the end and inserting "; and"; and
    (3) by adding at the end the following:
        "(6) the term 'military force' does not include any person that –
            "(A) has been designated as a –
                "(i) foreign terrorist organization by the Secretary of State under section 219 of the Immigration and Nationality Act (8 U.S.C. 1189); or

"(ii) specially designated global terrorist (as such term is defined in section 594.310 of title 31, Code of Federal Regulations) by the Secretary of State or the Secretary of the Treasury; or

"(B) has been determined by the court to not be a 'military force'.".

(b) APPLICABILITY. – The amendments made by this section shall apply to any civil action pending on or commenced after the date of the enactment of this Act.

SEC. 3. SATISFACTION OF JUDGMENTS AGAINST TERRORISTS.

(a) In General. – Section 2333 of title 18, United States Code, is amended by inserting at the end following:

"(e) Use of Blocked Assets to Satisfy Judgments of U.S. Nationals. – For purposes of section 201 of the Terrorism Risk Insurance Act of 2002 (28 U.S.C. 1610 note), in any action in which a national of the United States has obtained a judgment against a terrorist party pursuant to this section, the term 'blocked asset' shall include any asset of that terrorist party (including the blocked assets of any agency or instrumentality of that party) seized or frozen by the United States under section 805(b) of the Foreign Narcotics Kingpin Designation Act (21 U.S.C. 1904(b)).".

(b) Applicability. – The amendments made by this section shall apply to any judgment entered before, on, or after the date of enactment of this Act.

SEC. 4. CONSENT OF CERTAIN PARTIES TO PERSONAL JURISDICTION.

(a) IN GENERAL. – Section 2334 of title 18, United States Code, is amended by adding at the end the following:

"(e) Consent of Certain Parties to Personal Jurisdiction. –

"(1) IN GENERAL. – Except as provided in paragraph (2), for purposes of any civil action under section 2333 of this title, a defendant shall be deemed to have consented to personal jurisdiction in such civil action if, regardless of the date of the occurrence of the act of international terrorism upon which such civil action was filed, the defendant –

"(A) after the date that is 120 days after the date of enactment of this subsection, accepts –

"(i) any form of assistance, however provided, under chapter 4 of part II of the Foreign Assistance Act of 1961 (22 U.S.C. 2346 et seq.);

"(ii) any form of assistance, however provided, under section 481 of the Foreign Assistance Act of 1961 (22 U.S.C. 2291) for international narcotics control and law enforcement; or "(iii) any form of assistance, however provided, under chapter 9 of part II of the Foreign Assistance Act of 1961 (22 U.S.C. 2349bb et seq.); or

"(B) in the case of a defendant benefiting from a waiver or suspension of section 1003 of the Anti-Terrorism Act of 1987 (22 U.S.C. 5202) after the date that is 120 days after the date of enactment of this subsection –

"(i) continues to maintain any office, headquarters, premises, or other facilities or establishments within the jurisdiction of the United States; or

"(ii) establishes or procures any office, headquarters, premises, or other facilities or establishments within the jurisdiction of the United States.

"(2) APPLICABILITY. – Paragraph (1) shall not apply to any defendant who ceases to engage in the conduct described in paragraphs (1)(A) and (1)(B) for 5 consecutive calendar years.".

(b) APPLICABILITY. – The amendments made by this section shall take effect on the date of enactment of this Act.

Speaker of the House of Representatives.

Vice President of the United States and President of the Senate.

Index

Abandoned Areas Ordinance   91
Abandoned Property Ordinance   91
Abu Sitta, Salman   13
Abu-Jayyad, Abeer   377
accord Alpha Energy Savers, Inc. Hansen   508
accord Awad v. Ziriax   471
ACORN v. City of Tulsa, Okla.   471–472
Adl, Mostafa   131
admissibility assessment, of ICC   424–425
African Commission on Human and People's Rights   47
Afro-Asian States   36
Afro-Colombian peoples   354–355
Agency for Intern. Dev. v. Alliance for Open Soc'y Int'l, Inc.   492–493, 510n9
aggression   55
agriculture, in oPt   318, 408
   see also cultivation, of fallow land
Al Mezan Center for Human Rights   377
Aland Islands   35–36
Albania   165
Al-Khasawneh, Awn   68
All Palestine Government   123, 131–132, 134
Allen v. Wright   495
Alliance for Open Soc. Intern., Inc. v. U.S. Agency for Intern. Dev   492–493, 510n9
Alliance for the Wild Rockies v. Cottrell   500
Already, LLC v. Nike, Inc.   474
Am. Trucking Ass'ns, Inc. v. City of Los Angeles   500
American Samoa   345
American Society of International Law Proceedings (1971)   74
Amihai   362
Ammoun, Fouad   160
Amona outpost   362
amputees   383–384
Anglo-American cooperation
   in drafting Resolution 194
      in general   151–152, 175–177, 182–183
      disagreements in   127, 132, 138, 139, 174–175
Angola   62
Anguilla   345

Anti-Terrorism Clarification Act of 2018 (USA)   525–527
applicability, of Geneva Conventions   251–253
Arab countries
   constitutionalism in   201–202, 204–205, 211
   constitutions of   209
   revolutions of 2011 in   209
Arab Higher Committee   115
Arab League nations   506
Arab-Israeli conflict
   information on   286–288
   peaceful settlement of   289–300
   UN responsibilities in   111–112
   views on
      of Bernadotte   106, 110–111
      of UK   102–103, 104–105, 116, 132, 135–136, 145–147, 153–154
      of USA   117, 124–126, 127–129, 132–136, 137–139, 147, 150–152
Arab-Israeli War (1948)   6, 78–79
Arab-Israeli War (1967)   7, 79, 419
Arafat, Yasser   51, 52
Ariz. Right to Life Pol. Action Comm. v. Bayless   492, 493, 494
Arizonans for Official English v. Arizona   473
Arizona's House Bill 2617   486–516
   certfication requirements in   489, 491–494, 498–499, 500, 502, 507, 511, 513–514
   impermissible goals of   513–514
Armed Activities (Advisory Opinion ICJ)   55
Armistice Demarcation Line. *see* Green Line
Ass'n des Eleveurs de Canards et d'Oies du Quebec v. Harris   496
Association Agreement (EU-Israel AA)   4, 19, 20–21, 24
Association Agreement (EU-PA AA)   5, 19, 25
Attorney General, as party in lawsuit   494–497
Austin, Warren   121, 128–129
Australia
   on drafts of Resolution 194   143–144, 149, 154, 155n353, 156, 163, 194, 197

Australia (cont.)
   indigenous peoples in   354
autonomy   48, 75
Azkhoul, Karim   121, 133

Balfour Declaration   115n161
Bangladesh   355–356
Bantam Books, Inc. v. Sullivan   509n8
Barak, Aharon   207
al-Barazi, Muhsin   92
Basic Law (Israeli Constitution)
   in general   208, 419
   Israel Lands   8–9, 13–14
   Israel The Nation State of the Jewish People   521–522
   on Jerusalem   447
Bassiouni, Cherif   38
Bd. of Cnty. Comm'rs. Wabaunsee Cnty., Kan. v. Umbehr   476, 478, 508, 512
BDS movement   498, 499n6, 512
Bedouin communities   246–247, 364–365, 423, 425
Beeley, Harold   116, 117, 126, 128, 135, 150, 157, 161–162, 163, 174n436
Beersheba   106n117
Beith, John   135
Belgium   36
Bellotti v. Baird   498
Beltronics USA, Inc. v. Midwest Inventory Distrib.   475
Ben Gurion, David   6, 88, 119, 159n364, 186, 188
Bennett v. Spear   496, 497
Bermuda   345
Bernadotte, Folke
   death of   114
   and drafting of Resolution 194
      June suggestions   84, 85–95
      September Report   106–114
   negotiations of   85–86, 96
   views of
      on Arab-Israeli conflict   106, 110–111
      on Palestinian refugees   86–87, 89–91, 94–95, 107–110, 111–113, 173–174
Bevin, Ernest   105
Blodgett v. Holden   465
Boisson, Lawrence   23
Boling, Gail   177n450, 178–179n454, 179n456

Bourdieu, Pierre   206
Boycott, Divest and Sanctions (BDS) movement   498, 499n6, 512
boycotts
   in *Claiborne* case   477–478, 503–504
   economic   502–503
   of Israel
      in *Jordahl v. Bronvich* case   486–488, 493, 498–499, 504, 505, 512–514
      in *Koontz v. Watson* case   466–467, 469, 478–479, 480, 484, 485
   violence during   478n8
Briggs & Stratton Corp. v. Baldrige   502, 506–507
Brita v Hauptzollamt   25
British Middle East Office   98, 100, 106, 137
British Virgin Islands   345
Brnovich, Mark. see *Jordahl v. Bronvich*
Buckley v. Valeo   501
Bulgaria   165
Bunche, Ralph   85n26, 106, 120–126, 127–129, 157, 174, 191–192
Burkina Faso v. Mali   39
Burrows, Bernard   98–99
Bush administration   170–171n425
business
   involved in Israeli settlements. see under Israeli settlements

Cadogan, Alexander   97
Cal. Pro – Life Council Inc. v. Getman   492
cancer patients   377–378
captive markets   406–407
Cassese, Antonio   13, 15, 48, 71, 72
Catholic League for Religious and Civil Rights v. City and Cnty. of San. Fran   491
Cattan, Henry   146
Cayman Islands   345–346
CEIRPP (Committee on the Exercise of the Inalienable Rights of the Palestinian People)   286–288, 301–305, 349
Central Intelligence Agency (CIA)   104, 122
certification requirements
   in House Bill 2409   468, 470, 472, 474, 479, 482, 483
   in *Jordahl v. Bronvich* case   513–514
CESCR (Committee on Economic, Social and Cultural Rights)   354–356, 368–369, 370

INDEX 531

Chagos (Advisory Opinion ICJ)   33, 38, 47–48, 50, 60–61
Chagos Archipelago   33, 38, 47–48, 50
Chamber of Commerce of U.S. v. Edmondson   481–482, 483, 484
Charter of the Nuremberg Tribunal   165, 190
Chemerinsky, Erwin   495
children. *see* Palestinian children
China   95
CIA (Central Intelligence Agency)   104, 122
Cilento, Raphael   95, 131, 159n363
Citizens United v. FEC   492
City of Ladue v. Gilleo   479
civil war, in Israel   6
Clinton administration   170
Coal. to Defend Affirmative Action v. Brown   495
Colombia
  on drafts of Resolution 194   145, 163, 195
  indigenous peoples in   354–355
  on self-determination   36
  colonialism, and right to self-determination   37–39, 43, 45, 64, 67
Comay, Michael   141, 142
Committee on Economic, Social and Cultural Rights (CESCR)   354–356, 368–369, 370
Committee on the Exercise of the Inalienable Rights of the Palestinian People (CEIRPP)   286–288, 301–305, 349
Connick v. Myers   508–509
constitutionalism   201–202, 204–205, 211
constitutions
  in general   208–209
  in Arab countries   209
  of Israel. *see* Basic Law
  of USA. *see under* United States
Consumer Protection Law (1981)   404
Contini, Paolo   179
Convention on the Prevention and Punishment of the Crime of Genocide   131, 165
Coordinator of Government Activities in the Territories   378
Corfu Channel   56
Covenant of the League of Nations   35, 54
Crabtree, Daniel D.   465–485
Crawford, James   13, 14, 16, 17, 18, 21–22, 56, 65

Crimean Peninsula   52
Crimean people   52
crimes
  committing of
    by IDF
      in 2014   423–424, 425
      in 2018   421, 424, 433–434
      against children   367–368, 433
      in Palestinian Referral to ICC   430–432
      surge in   432–433
    by PAGs   423, 425
    by Palestinian security/intelligence services   423
    see also East Jerusalem; Gaza; West Bank
  gravity assessment by ICC of   414, 425
  referral by Palestine to ICC   427–442
Cristescu, Aureliu   67
critical legal theory   203–204
Cuba   130
cultivation, of fallow land   125
Cyprus   73, 92
Czechoslovakia   89, 100

DA (Development Authority)   8–9
Dabed, Emilio   201–212
Dahlia v. Rodriguez   511
database of all business enterprises involved in activities in Israeli settlements
  report UN Doc A/HRC/37/39 on. *see* report on database of all business enterprises involved in activities in Israeli settlements, UN Doc A/HRC/37/39
De Zayas, Alfred   179n454, 190n502
Declaration of Principles on Interim Self-Government Arrangements   170
Declaration on Principles of International Law Concerning Friendly Relations and Co-operation among States in Accordance with the Charter of the United Nations   40, 53, 56–57, 60, 64
decolonization
  in general   39, 43, 63
  and right to self-determination   49, 66
  unlawful process of   33, 47
Defense Emergency Regulations   125

Deir Yassin   102
Del Sarto, Raffaella   11, 25
demolition/destruction, of property
    364–365, 422–423, 434
demonstrations   421, 424, 433–434
destruction. *see* demolition/destruction
detention
    of men of military age   97
    of Palestinian children   363–364
    of Palestinians   239, 362–363, 384,
        434–435
Development Authority (DA)   8–9
Development Towns and Areas Law   10
Dewey, Thomas   132
diplomatic missions. *see* embassies
disabled persons   383–384
discrimination
    and Kansas Law   478, 484–485, 500–502,
        513, 514, 515
    of Palestinians   18, 159–160, 207–208,
        240, 321, 327, 331, 404
displacements
    after June 1967 hostilities   262–274
    direct/indirect   108–109
    forcible
        and genocide   131, 165
        of Palestinians   88, 95, 109, 120, 122,
            132, 134, 158n363
    Jewish   79n4
    see also exchanges/transfers
district courts, abstentions of   497–498
Doe v. City of Albuquerque   478
Douglas, Lewis   95, 102, 114, 127, 132, 138,
    141, 151
Dulles, John Foster   151, 164, 165–166, 167, 169
*The Dynamics of Exclusionary
    Constitutionalism: Israel as a Jewish and
    Democratic State* (Masri)   201–212

East Jerusalem
    agriculture in   408
    and applicability of Geneva
        Convention   251–253
    human rights situation in
        Special Rapporteur on   362–366
        UNHCR on   325–334
        violations of   234–243, 301–313
    Israeli civilian presence in   419–420
    Israeli settlements in
        UNGA on   244–250
        UNHCR on   314–324
    Palestinian refugees in, human rights
        violation of   301–313
    Palestinians in
        crimes committed against   422–423,
            424
        human rights violation of   234–243
        right to health in   369
        sovereignty of   226–231
    telecommunications industry in   407
    views on
        in report of ICC   419–420, 422–423,
            424
        of UNGA   281–283
    see also Jerusalem
Eban, Abba   141–142, 143, 148, 161, 163,
    184–189, 190
EC (European Commission)   20
ECJ (European Court of Justice). *see*
    European Court of Justice
Economic and Social Council
    (ECOSOC)   51, 350
Egypt
    and Israel, peace treaty with   7, 170
    judicial system in   209, 210
    on self-determination   40
Egypt-Israel Peace Treaty (1978)   7, 170
Elaraby, Nabil   62
electricity shortages   374–375
Eleventh Amendment (USA
    Constitution)   482, 495
Elrod v. Burns   481–482, 515
embassies
    functions of   453–454
    and 'in the receiving State'   453–455
    relocation of
        to Jerusalem   445–446, 449, 450,
            452–453
        from Jerusalem   448–449
Emergency Regulation 5727   9
Emergency Regulations Concerning
    Absentee Property   158–159
Emergency Regulations for the
    Cultivation of Fall Land
    125
enemy national concept   158

INDEX 533

Envtl. Council of Sacramento v. Slater   500
equal rights
   for Arabs and Jews   124, 126
   see also right to self-determination
ethnic Germans   89, 100, 131n233, 189
EU (European Union). *see* European Union
European Commission (EC)   20
European Council   21
European Court of Justice (ECJ)
   Brita v Hauptzollamt   19, 25
   Front Polisario v. Council of the European Union   65
   Rau v Smedt   20
European External Action Service (of EU)   362
European Jews   87–88
European Union (EU)
   European External Action Service of   362
   and trade with Israel
      and consistency in policies   21
      and differentiation polices   26–27, 28
      and EU-Israel AA   4, 19, 20–21, 24
      free-trade zone   4–5, 20
      options for sanctions on   4, 18, 21–22, 27, 28
      and Regulation 260/2009   21
      and territoriality   4, 19, 20–21, 24
      see also Israeli settlement goods
   and trade with oPt, and EU-PA AA   5, 19, 25
Evangelical Lutheran Church in America (ELCA)   487–488, 493, 505
Ex parte Young   495, 496
exchanges/transfers, of populations   88–89, 90, 93n54, 99–100, 131n233, 189, 190
Expert Mechanism on the Rights of Indigenous Peoples   353
Export Administration Act (EAA)   487n2, 506
exports   25–26
expressive conduct   480, 493–494, 501, 502, 504–505, 507, 509, 511, 513, 515
Eytan, Walter   89

faits accomplis   63, 89, 91, 111, 137, 186, 438
Fast, Melissa   467
Fawzi, Mahmoud   93, 119, 146, 160, 161, 163

FCC v. League of Women Voters of California   510n9
Federal Jurisdiction (Chemerinsky)   495
Federspiel, Per   185–187, 189
First Amendment (USA Constitution)   465, 468–473, 476–477, 478, 479–480, 481–483, 489, 492, 498, 501–504, 505, 506–509, 515
Fleck & Assocs., Inc. v. City of Phoenix   490
force, use of
   against civilians   421
   against Palestinian children   367–368, 433
   prohibitions on   54–63
   and right to self-determination. *see under* right to self-determination
Ford, Richard   23
Foucault, Michel   202
Fourteenth Amendment (USA Constitution)   465, 477, 489, 501, 504
Fourth Geneva Convention (GCIV)
   Article 49(6)   14, 17
   Article 53   14
   Article 147   13
   on deportation of civilians   190
Fourth Geneva Convention Relative to the Protection of Civilian Persons in Times of War (1949). *see* Fourth Geneva Convention (GCIV)
Framework for Peace in the Middle East (1978)   7, 170
Fraser, Peter   157n359, 169
freedom of movement   121, 125, 133, 178, 372–373
freedom of speech   476, 501, 504, 508, 509, 512, 514
freedoms, in First Amendment   470–471, 481–483, 515
free-trade zone   4–5, 20
French Polynesia   346
Frente Polisario   51
Friendly Relations Declaration   40, 53, 56–57, 60, 64
Friends of the Earth, Inc. v. Laidlaw Envtl. Servs.   474

Garcetti v. Ceballos   508
Garrison v. Louisiana   479

GATT (General Agreement on Tariffs and Trade)   21–22
Gaza
  blockade of   373
  cancer patients   377–378
  demonstrations in   421, 424, 433–434
  electricity shortages in   374–375
  health statistics for   379
  health-care system in   374, 375, 383
  hostilities in
    in 2014   423–425
    in 2018   421, 424, 433–434
    increase in   422
  human rights situation in
    in general   366–367
    of children   367–369
  medical exit permit system in   375–378
  medical professionals in   378
  Palestinians in
    crimes committed against   421, 422–423, 423–424, 425
    right to health of
      in general   369, 373–379
      of amputees   383–384
      of children   381–383
      mental health   380–381, 382–383
    views on, in report of ICC   420–422, 423–434
  water distribution in   369
  mention of   106n117
GCIV (Fourth Geneva Convention). *see* Fourth Geneva Convention
Gen. Motors Corp. v. Urban Gorilla, LLC   475
General Agreement on Tariffs and Trade (GATT)   21–22
Geneva Conventions (1949)
  applicability of   251–253
  Article 49(6) (GCIV)   440
  on prohibition of settlements   441
  on right of health   371
  travaux preparatoires   52
genocide, and forcible displacement   131, 165
Gillette v. Delmore   512
Gordon, Neve   24
government employment, unconstitutional conditions on   508–510
government funding, recipients of   510n9
Granados, Jorge García   144–145, 146, 147, 160, 161, 162

Grant v. Meyer   469
Grayned v. City of Rockford   499n6
Great Britain. *see* United Kingdom
"Great March of Return"   421, 424, 433–434
Greece   66–67, 89, 93n54, 165, 189
Green Line
  in general   5, 27–28
  and Israeli economy   24, 26–27
  legality of   4
  as legitimate international border   8, 28
  setting up of   6–7
  mention of   9, 11, 12, 18, 20
Griffiths, Anne M.O.   206
Guam   346
Guasti, Marco   3–28
Guatemala, on drafts of Resolution 194   144–145, 146, 147, 154, 156, 157, 160–162, 181, 195, 196, 197
Guinea-Bissau v. Senegal   39
Gurion, David Ben   102

Hague Regulations (1907)
  in general   178–179
  Article 23   121
  Article 25   121
  Article 43   17
  Article 49   14
  Article 53   14
  Article 55   13
  pillage in   12, 129
  violation by Israel of   12–13, 14, 17, 97, 178
Haifa   92n49
Hamas   420, 421
health
  definition of   370
  see also right to health
health-care system   374, 375
Hegel, Georg   22–23
Helsinki Conference   60
Henkin, Louis   64
Higgins, Rosalyn   38
High Court of Justice (HCJ)   424
Hood, John   166–168
House Bill 2409   465–516
  boycotts in. *see* boycotts
  certification requirements in   468, 470, 472, 474, 479, 482, 483
  constitutionality of   479

INDEX 535

and discrimination 478, 484–485, 500–502, 513, 514, 515
impermissible goals in 479
practicability of 466, 470
public interest of 484–485
see also Koontz v. Watson
Human Life of Wash., Inc. v. Brumsickle 494
Humetewa, Diane J. 516

ICC (International Criminal Court). see International Criminal Court
ICCPR (International Covenant on Civil and Political Rights). *see* International Covenant on Civil and Political Rights
ICESCR (International Covenant on Economic, Social and Cultural Rights). *see* International Covenant on Civil and Political Rights
ICJ (International Court of Justice). *see* International Court of Justice
IDF (Israel Defense Forces). *see* Israel Defense Forces
IHL (international humanitarian law) 22, 23, 27
IHRL (international human rights law) 22
illegality
of Israeli jurisdiction over oPt 12–15
and use of force in right to self-determination 71–75
see also under third-State obligations
impunity, of Israeli 435
inalienable rights
of Palestinian refugees 83, 90, 148, 186–187, 190, 286–288
see also Committee on the Exercise of the Inalienable Rights of the Palestinian People
India 95
Indigenous and Tribal Peoples Convention 354
indigenous peoples
rights of
in general 351–353
in Australia 354
in Bangladesh 355–356
in Colombia 354–355
in Mexico 355
in New Zealand 356
in Norway 356–357
in Russian Federation 355

individual rights. *see* inalienable rights
Indonesia 61
International Committee of the Red Cross 190
International Court of Justice (ICJ)
advisory opinions of
Armed Activities 55
Chagos 33, 38, 47–48, 50, 60–61
Kosovo 33, 46, 58, 59–60, 70, 73, 75
Namibia 16–17, 39, 46
Nicaragua 54
Reparation for Injuries Suffered in the Service of the United Nations 66
requests for 154, 163
Wall 14–16, 39, 56, 62, 68, 72, 437–438
Western Sahara 39
cases of
Burkina Faso v. Mali 39
Corfu Channel 56
Guinea-Bissau v. Senegal 39
Military and Paramilitary Activities in and against Nicaragua 56
North Sea Continental Shelf 67
Palestine v. United States of America. *see Palestine v. United States of America*
deliberations of, on *Palestine v. United States* 458–460
jurisdiction of 450–452, 460
views of
on human rights 13
on Israeli settlements 63
International Covenant on Civil and Political Rights (ICCPR)
Article 1.2 18
right to natural resources in 18
right to self-determination in 15, 40, 352, 353, 357
International Covenant on Economic, Social and Cultural Rights (ICESCR)
right of health in 370
right to eductation in 368
right to self-determination in 15, 40, 352, 353, 357
International Criminal Court (ICC)
admissibility assessment of 424–425
gravity assessment of crime by 414, 425

International Criminal Court (ICC) (cont.)
    jurisdiction of   419, 422–424
    preliminary examinations of
        on Palestine
            in general   427–428
            see also Report on Preliminary Examinations 2018
        Referral by Palestine to   427–442
            cooperation   441–442
            crimes in   430–432
            general considerations   427–430
            rationale of   432–441
International Declaration on Human Rights   90, 113, 121, 133
international human rights law (IHRL)   22
international humanitarian law (IHL)   22, 23, 27
International Labour Organization   354
international law
    Hegel on   22–23
    right to health in   370–372
    right to return in   178–179
    on use of force for self-determination   69
International Law Association   170–171n425
International Law Commission (ILC)
    Articles on State Responsibility   16, 17
    on right to self-determination   55
    Vienna Convention on the Law of Treaties   19, 83
international order   352
International Refugee Organization (IRO)   87, 123, 133–134n244, 143
Int'l Longshoremen's Association, AFL-CIO v. Allied International, Inc.   502–506
IRO (International Refugee Organization)   87, 123, 133–134n244, 143
irreparable harm
    in *Jordahl v. Bronvich* case   514–515
    in *Koontz v. Watson* case   481–485
Israel
    and Arab-Israeli War (1948)   6, 78–79
    and Arab-Israeli War (1967)   7, 79, 419
    boycotts of. *see under* boycotts
    breach of truce by   127–128
    citizenship of   188, 206–208
    civil war in   6
    as compact and homogenous state   98–99
    constitutional self-definition of   208
    constitutionalism in   201–202, 205
    economy of   24–25
    and Egypt   7, 170
    electoral system in   208
    establishment of state of   6, 78, 91, 111
    exports to EU of   25–26
    faits accomplis of   63, 89, 91, 111, 137, 186, 438
    free-trade zone with EU   4–5
    health statistics for   379
    human rights obligation of   368
    immigration to   207–208
    Jerusalem as capital of   361–362, 449
    and Jewish refugees, resettlement of   88, 92, 97–98, 113, 115, 133
    and Jordan   7
    jurisdiction over oPt. *see under* Occupied Palestinian Territories
    laws/regulations of
        constitution of. *see* Basic Law
        Consumer Protection Law   404
        Defense Emergency Regulations   125
        Emergency Regulations Concerning Absentee Property   158–159
        Emergency Regulations for the Cultivation of Fall Land   125
        Law for the Regularization of Settlement in Judea and Samaria   366
        Law of Return   9, 208
        Prohibition of Discrimination in Products, Services and Entry into Places of Entertainment and Public Places Law   404
    nationalism in   206–207
    and PA   8, 420
    and Palestinian refugees
        and compensation for property   91, 149, 158–159
        individual rights of   83, 90, 148, 186–187, 190
        opposition to return of   88–89, 98, 100, 102, 103–104, 119–120, 146, 149, 184–189
    and Palestinians, discriminatory treatment of   18, 159–160, 207–208, 240, 321, 327, 331, 404

INDEX 537

and PLO   170
settler-colonialism of   202, 205, 206–208
sovereignty of   99, 187, 190
territory of
   and Basic Law: Israel Lands   8–9
   borders and borderlands   5–12
   international borders of   5–8, 107, 138–139
   legal extent of   4
   and Palestinian land   5, 91
trade with EU
   and consistency in policies   21
   and differentiation polices   26–27, 28
   and EU-Israel AA   4, 19, 20–21, 24
   free-trade zone   4–5, 20
   and Regulation 260/2009   21
   and territoriality   4, 19, 20–21, 24
   see also Israeli settlement goods
and UN membership   148, 153, 166, 184
views of, on draft of Resolution 194   141–142, 148–149, 157
violations by
   of Hague Regulations   12–13, 14, 17, 97, 122, 178
   of international law, UNGA on   438–439
war crimes committed by   422–423
water distribution in   18
Israel Defense Forces (IDF)
   crimes committed by
     in 2014   423–424, 425
     in 2018   421, 424, 433–434
     against children   367–368, 433
     in Palestinian Referral to ICC   430–432
     surge in   432–433
Israel The Nation State of the Jewish People (Basic Law)   521–522
Israeli civilian courts, jurisdiction of   10
Israeli High Court of Justice   14
Israeli settlement goods (ISGs)
   certificates of origin   19–20
   and EU Law   19–23
   exports of   25–26
   import ban on   4, 18, 21–22
   labelling of   20
Israeli settlements
   business enterprises' involvement in
     contributions to and benefits for   405–407
     Israeli encouragement of   403–405
     responses to OHCHR of   407–410
   in East Jerusalem
     UNGA on   244–250
     UNHCR on   314–324
   illegality of   366
   Israeli policies on   428
   in oPt
     in general   8, 428
     and Article 49(6) (GCIV)   14, 17
     goods produced in. *see* Israeli settlement goods
     ICJ on   14–16, 63
     as National Priority Areas   10
     UNGA on   244–250
     UNHCR on   314–324
   report on database of all business enterprises involved in activities in. *see* report on database of all business enterprises involved in activities in Israeli settlements, UN Doc A/HRC/37/39
   in Syrian Golan
     UNGA on   244–250
     UNHCR on   314–324
   views on
     of ICJ   63, 438
     of UNSC   439
   in West Bank   362–363, 366
Israeli-Palestinian Interim Agreement on the West Bank and the Gaza Strip (Oslo Accord II)   8, 42, 68, 407
Israelis, definition of   9
Italian Court of Cassation   65

Jaffa   92n49, 106n117
Janus v. Am. Fed'n. of State, Cnty., and Mun. Emps., Council 31   501
Jennings, Robert   49n88
Jerusalem
   relocation of embassies
     of several countries from   448–449
     of USA to   445–446, 449, 450, 452–453
   status of
     in general   92n49, 446
     Israeli measures to change
       in general   446–447
       UNSC on   447–448
     recognition by USA as capital of Israel   361–362, 449

Jerusalem (cont.)
    UNGA on   446–447, 450
    see also East Jerusalem
Jessup, Philip   94, 96, 98, 100–101, 106,
    138–140, 147, 177–178
Jewish National Fund (JNF)   8–9
Jewish nationality   159
Jewish refugees, resettlement in Israel of
    88, 92, 97–98, 113, 115, 133
Jewish Voice for Peace (JVP)   487–488, 493,
    505
JNF (Jewish National Fund)   8–9
Johnson v. Couturier   515
Jordahl, Mikkel. *see Jordahl v. Bronvich*
Jordahl v. Bronvich   486–516
    abstention and certification   497–500
    boycotts in. *see under* boycotts
    introduction to   486–490
    motion for preliminary injunction in
        in general   500–502
        conclusion of   516
        and expressive conduct   502–507,
            511–512
        impact of certification
            requirements   513–514
        likelihood of harm in   513–514
        likelihood of success in   497–500
        public interest in   515
        restriction of commercial
            conduct   507
        security in   515
        unconstitutional condition on
            government employment   508
    plaintiff's standing in
        in general   490–491
        to challenge constitutionality of Act
            491–494
        to sue Attorney General   494–497
Jordan   7
Jordan v. Sosa   473, 474
Jorgensen v. Cassiday   515
judicial independence   210
judicial reform   209, 210
jurisdiction
    of ICC   419, 422–424
    of ICJ   450–452, 460
    of Israel over oPt. *see under* Occupied
        Palestinian Territories

jus ad bellum   54, 56, 69, 71, 74
jus cogens norm   15–16, 45–46
jus in bello   61, 66, 74

Kan. Judicial Review v. Stout   468–470, 471
Kansas Law. *see* House Bill 2409
Kansas State Department of Education
    (KSDE)   467–468
Kaplan, Eliezer   158, 159n364
Kashmir   49
Katangese Peoples' Congress v. Zaire   47
Keeley, James   115
Kefar Adummim   365
Kelly, Tobias   11, 23–24
Khan, Muhammad Zafrullah   112n143
Khan al-Ahmar   246–247, 364–365,
    425
el-Khouri, Faris   103, 127, 137, 148, 154, 160,
    161
Kimmerling, Baruch   11
Klein v. City of San Clemente   515
Knox v. SEIU, Local 1000   501
Koontz, Esther. *see Koontz v. Watson*
Koontz v. Watson   465–485
    in general   465–466
    boycotts in. *see* boycotts
    facts
        Kansas House Bill 2409   466–467
        plaintiff's boycott of Israel   467
        plaintiff's contract with Kansas
            467
    mootness in   473–474
    motion for preliminary injunction in
        in general   474
        conclusion of   484–485
        conditions to be met for
            in general   474–475
            harm to plaintiff   481–483
            harm to plaintiff vs. harm to
                defendant   483–484
            public harm in   484–485
            success of plaintiff   476–481
    quoting of   513, 514
    ripeness of motion in
        in general   468–469
        ACORN v. City of Tulsa, Okla.
            471–472
        conclusion of court on   473

INDEX

effect of challenged law on First
    Amendment liberties 470–471
effects on parties by withholding
    reviews 469–470
fitness for judicial review 471
Kosovo 42, 48, 49
Kosovo (Advisory Opinion ICJ) 33, 46, 58,
    59–60, 70, 73, 75
Kretzmer, David 13

Lachs, Manfred 47, 76
land, cultivation of fallow 125
Lane v. Franks 508, 512
Lauterpacht, Hersch 65, 71
law
    inconsistencies and indeterminacy in
        209–210
    role of 202–203, 206, 209–210
    as social and historical product 206
*Law and Revolution: Legitimacy and
    Constitutionalism after the Arab Spring*
    (Sultany) 201–212
Law for the Regularization of Settlement in
    Judea and Samaria 366
Law of Return 9, 208
legal capacity 65
Legal Services Corp. v. Velazquez 501
legalism 210
Lehman Bros. v. Schein 498
Lenin, Vladimir 34–35
*Levin v. South Carolina Department of Health
    & Human Services* 474–473n5
liberal Zionism 207
liberties. *see* freedoms
Libya 58
Lie, Trygve 97–98, 106, 114
Lien, Yehezkel 13
'live at peace,' in drafting of Resolution
    194 180
Lopez 491
Lotus judgement (PCIJ) 70
Lovett, Robert 124–125, 132, 142–143
LSO, Ltd. v. Stroh 492
Lujan v. Defenders of Wildlife 490, 495
Lydda 92n49, 122
*Lyng v. International Union, United Auto.
    Aerospace & Agricultural Implement
    Workers* 506

Malik, Charles 115
Malki, Riad 427–442, 445–457
Mallison, Sally V. 174n433, 183n465
Mallison, W. Thomas, Jr. 174n433, 183n465
malnutrition 381–382
Mandate Palestine 5–6
Marshall, George 95, 101, 103–104, 114, 121,
    132, 136, 140, 141, 165
Masri, Mazen 201–212
Matal v. Tam 479
Mauritius 48
Maya v. Centex Corp 491, 496
Mazurek v. Armstrong 500
McClintock, Robert 98, 104, 106, 138
McDonald, James 102, 128
McKinley v. City of Eloy 512
McNeil, Hector 78, 145, 150, 168–169
medical exit permit system 375–378
medical professionals 378
Mekorot 18
Mennonite Church 467, 478
mental health 379–381, 382
mercenaries 348–349, 352
Meron, Theodor 440–441
Mexico 355
Middle East
    peace in 280
    power in 202–203
    role of law in 202–203, 206, 209–210
*Military and Paramilitary Activities in and
    against Nicaragua* 56
minorities
    in general 161–162
    exchanges/transfers of 88–89, 93n54,
        131n233, 189
Moerenhout, Tom 15–16
Montserrat 346
Moonin v. Tice 509–510, 511
mootness doctrine 473
Muniz, Joao Carlos 167
Mutlaq, Aya Khalil Abu 377

NAACP v. Alabama 504
NAACP v. Claiborne Hardware Co. 477–478,
    503–504, 505, 506, 507, 513
Nagorno-Karabakh 73
Namibia (Advisory Opinion ICJ) 16–17,
    39, 46

Namibia (South West Africa)   16–17, 63
al-Nasser Salah al-Deen Brigades   420
national liberation movements   51
National Priority Areas   10
Native Title Act 1993 (Australia)   354
natural resources, right to   18
Nazareth   108n124
Negev   92, 110, 119–120, 127–128, 142
negotiations   67–68
Netanyahu, Benjamin   362
Netherlands   61
New Caledonia   346–347
New Mexicans for Bill Richardson v. Gonzales   469–471
New Zealand   156, 356
Nicaragua (Advisory Opinion ICJ)   54
Nisot, Joseph   187
non-assistance   17
non-recognition   16–17, 21
non-self-governing territories   49, 61, 74, 343–348
North Sea Continental Shelf   67
Norway   356–357
Nouméa Accord   347

O Centro Espirita Beneficente Uniao do Vegetal v. Ashcrof   475, 481
Occupied Palestinian Territories (oPt)
   in general   4, 5
   agriculture in   318, 408
   and applicability of Geneva Convention   251–253
   as captive market   406–407
   as closed military areas   9
   economy of   26, 408
   human rights situation in
      in general   352–353
      UNHCR on   325–334
      violations of
         in general   12–13
         accountability and justice for   301–313
         UNGA on   234–243
         UNHCR on   301–313
         and UNSCOP   254–259
   Israeli jurisdiction over
      in general   9–12, 23–26
      and HRs   12–13, 14, 17
      illegality of   12–15
      legislative measures to extend   365–366
      and non-assistance   17
      and non-recognition   16–17, 21
      and third-State responsiblities   16
   Israeli settlements in
      in general   8, 428
      and Article 49(6) (GCIV)   14, 17
      goods produced in. *see* Israeli settlement goods
      ICJ on   14–16, 63
      as National Priority Areas   10
      UNGA on   244–250
      UNHCR on   314–324
   Israeli settlers in   10–11
   Palestinians in. *see* Palestinians
   Segregation Wall in   14, 15
      see also Wall (Advisory Opinion ICJ)
   trade with EU
      in general   25–26
      and EU-PA AA   5, 19, 25
   UN fact finding missions to   440
   unemployment in   408–409
   water distribution in   18, 369
   see also East Jerusalem; Gaza; West Bank
Occupying Powers
   and claim of self-defense   61–62
   and human rights violations   12–13
   and right of health   371–372
   and transfer of own population   14
Office for the Coordination of Humanitarian Affairs (OCHA)   408
Office of the Prosecutor (OTP)
   report of. *see* Report on Preliminary Examinations 2018
Office of the United Nations High Commissioner for Human Rights (OHCHR)
      report on database of all business enterprises involved in activities in Israeli settlements. *see* report on database of all business enterprises involved in activities in Israeli settlements, UN Doc A/HRC/37/39
OHCHR (United Nations Human Rights Committee). *see* United Nations Human Rights Committee
Okpalobi v. Foster   494

INDEX 541

On Imperialism (Lenin) 34
Operation Protective Edge 420
Order Regarding Security 9
Oslo II Agreement (Israeli-Palestinian Interim Agreement) 8, 42, 407, 420

Pacific Gas & Elec. Co. v Public Utilities Com'n of California 501
Pakistan 95
Palestine
   and Convention on Diplomatic Relations 451
   ICC on
      report of OTP. *see* Report on Preliminary Examinations 2018
   partition plan for 6, 78
      see also Resolution 181
   refugee situation in 78–79, 94–95
   security and intelligence services of 423
   territorial integrity of 62–63
   and USA. *see Palestine v. United States of America*
Palestine Liberation Organization (PLO)
   and Israel 170
   on Palestinian refugees 170
   as representative of Palestinian people 51–52, 65
Palestine Mandate 78
Palestine Refugee Board 129
Palestine Refugee Compensation Committee 125, 129
Palestine v. United States of America (ICJ)
   Application of the State of Palestine 445–457
      annexes to 457
      background to 445–449
      decision requested 455–456
      ICJ's deliberations on 458–460
      jurisdiction of the court 450–452
      legal grounds for claims 452–455
      statement of facts 449–450
Palestinian armed groups (PAGs) 420, 423, 425
Palestinian children
   detention of 363–364
   human rights situation of
      in Gaza 367–369
      in West Bank 363–365

   right to education of 368
   right to health of
      in general 369, 381–383
      mental health 382–383
   and schooling, in West Bank 364–365
   UNICEF on 363–365
   use of force against 367–368, 433
   use of tear gas against 365
Palestinian Islamic Jihad 420
Palestinian Land Day 420–422
Palestinian National Authority (PA)
   and Israel 8, 420
   and trade with EU 5, 19, 25
Palestinian prisoners, right to health of 384
Palestinian refugees
   after Arab-Israeli wars 78–79
   assistance to, UNGA on 277–279
   and civilians/combatants distinction 108
   and direct/indirect displacement 108–109
   in East Jerusalem 301–313
   inalienable rights of 83, 90, 148, 186–187, 190, 286–288
   resettlement in Arab countries 98, 103n102
   right to compensation for property of. *see* right to compensation for property
   right to return of. *see* right to return
   right to self-determination of 150, 156, 352–353
   views on
      of Bernadotte 86–87, 89–91, 94–95, 107–110, 111–113, 173–174
      of PLO 170
      of UK 103, 115, 116–117, 118, 140–141, 145–146, 191, 193–194, 196–197
      of USA 100–102, 103–104, 114–115, 118, 124–125, 129–131, 139–140, 147, 150, 191, 194, 195, 196
   see also displacements; Palestinians; refugees
Palestinian security/intelligence services 423
Palestinians
   assistance to 219–225
   detention of 97, 239, 362–364, 384, 434–435

Palestinians (cont.)
  discriminatory treatment of   18, 159–160, 207–208, 240, 321, 327, 331, 404
  displacement of   88, 95, 109, 120, 122, 132, 134, 158n363
  in East Jerusalem. *see* East Jerusalem
  existence of   51
  in Gaza. *see* Gaza
  human rights of, violation by Israel of
    UNGA on   234–243
    and UNSCOP   254–259
  and Israeli economy   24–25
  and nationality   159, 207–208
  right to health of. *see* right to health
  right to independent state   349
  right to self-determination of   15, 25, 43–44, 79, 232–233, 335–338, 349
  sovereignty of   226–231
  in West Bank. *see* West Bank
  see also Palestinian children; Palestinian refugees
Pappé, Ilan   92n49, 108n127
Paraguay   449
Pardo, Sharon   24
partition plan. *see* Resolution 181 (UNGA)
Peace Not Walls campaign   487
Peace Treaty of Versailles   35
Pearson, Lester   148, 168, 169
peoples
  concept of   49–50
  representatives of   50–52
  as rightsholders in international law   65
  see also right to self-defense; right to self-determination
Permanent Court of International Justice (PCIJ)   70
Perry v. Sindermann   508
Petrella v. Brownback   475
Philosophy of Right (Hegel)   22–23
Physicians for Human Rights   375–376, 377, 378
Pickering v. Bd of Edu. of Township High Sch. Dist. 205, Will Cty, Ill.   508, 509
Pickering v. Board of Education of Township High School District 205, Will County, Illinois   476, 510n8, 511
pillage   12, 129, 149
Pinson v. Pacheco   482–483
Pitcairn Islands   347

Planned Parenthood of Idaho, Inc. v. Wasden   494, 495, 496
Poland   143, 154, 163, 195
Police Dep't of City of Chi. v. Mosley   478
political rights   107, 146, 148, 161
  see also inalienable rights
popular sovereignty   210–211
populations, exchanges/transfers of   88–89, 90, 93n54, 99–100, 131n233, 189, 190
Port City Props. v. Union Pac. R.R. Co   481
Porter v. Jones   497
Portugal   62
Prohibition of Discrimination in Products, Services and Entry into Places of Entertainment and Public Places Law (2000)   404
property
  demolition/destruction of   364–365, 422–423, 434
  right to compensation for. *see* right to compensation for property
puppet regimes   52–54

Quigley, John   182n465

Rabin, Yitzhak   52
Ramle   106n117, 110, 122
Rau v Smedt   20
reasonable grounds   392, 415, 417, 435, 440, 514
refugees
  after World War II   87–88
  definition of   157
  see also displacements; exchanges/transfers; Jewish refugees; Palestinian refugees
Regan v. Taxation With Representation of Washington   510n9
Regulation 260/2009 (EU)   21
Rempel, Terry   77–197
Renne v. Geary   468
Reparation for Injuries Suffered in the Service of the United Nations (Advisory Opinion ICJ)   66
repatriation. *see* right to return
Report of the Independent International Fact-Finding Mission to Investigate the Implications of the Israeli Settlements

INDEX

on the Civil, Political, Economic,
    Social and Cultural Rights of the
    Palestinian People throughout
    the Occupied Palestinian Territory,
    including East Jerusalem, UN Doc A/
    HRC/37/39
  on database of all business enterprises
    involved in activities in Israeli
    settlements. *see* report on database
    of all business enterprises involved in
    activities in Israeli settlements, UN
    Doc A/HRC/37/39
Report of the Secretary-General, UN Doc
    A/73/329   341–358
  Committee on Economic, Social and
    Cultural Rights in   354–356
  conclusion of   357–358
  Economic and Social Council in   350
  General Assembly in
    on mercenaries   348–349
    on non-self-governing
      territories   343–348
    on self-determination of Palestinian
      people   349
  Human Rights Committee in   356–357
  Human Rights Council in
    resolutions of   350–351
    rights of indigenous peoples
      in   351–353
  introduction in   342
  Security Council in, on Western
    Sahara   342–343
  summary of   341
report on database of all business
    enterprises involved in activities in Israeli
    settlements, UN Doc A/HRC/37/39
  activities listed   390–391
  background to   388–389
  and business enterprises in Israeli
    settlements
    contributions and benifits of   405–407
    Israeli encouragement of   403–405
    responses of   407–410
  mandate for   390–391
  methodology adopted for
    in general   391–392
    actvitities listed   390–391
    information gathering   392–398

consultations   397–398
    further communications   393–397
    next steps   398
    screening exercises   393, 396–397
  standards of proof   392
  normative framework for
    obligations of Israel   398–399
    obligations of other States   399–401
    responsibilities of businesses
      401–403
  recommendations in   410
  summary of   388
Report on Preliminary Examinations 2018
    (of OTP)
  introduction to   413–417
  on Palestine
    admissibility assessment
      East Jerusalem   424
      Gaza   424–425
      OTP activities   424–425
      West Bank   424
    conclusion of   426
    contextual background
      East Jerusalem   419–420
      Gaza   420–422
      West Bank   419–420
    preliminary jurisdictional issues   419
    procedural history   418–419
    subject-matter jurisdiction
      in general   422
      East Jerusalem   422–423
      Gaza   423–424
      West Bank   422–423
  summary of activities in   417–418
Report UN Doc A/HRC/37/75 of Special
    Rapporteur   359–387
  conclusion of   385–386
  on human rights situation
    in general   361–362
    of children   363–365, 367–369
    in East Jerusalem   362–366
    in Gaza   366–369
    legal developments in   365–366
    in West Bank   362–366
  introduction in   360–361
  recommendations in   386
  on right to health
    in general   369–370

Report UN Doc A/HRC/37/75 (cont.)
    of children   381–383
    under international law   370–372
    in oPt   372–384
    of Palestinian prisoners   384
    of persons with disabilities   383–384
Republika Srpska   73
Resolution 31/36 (UNHRC)   389–392, 397–399, 410
Resolution 32/14 (UNGA)   63
Resolution 33/15 (UNGA)   73
Resolution 34/30 (UNGA)   73
Resolution 34/92 (UNGA)   63
Resolution 35/20 (UNHCR)   350
Resolution 35/33 (UNGA)   63
Resolution 36/3 (UNHCR)   350
Resolution 37/34 (UNHCR)   335–338, 351
Resolution 37/35 (UNHCR)   325–334, 351
Resolution 37/36 (UNHCR)   314–324, 351
Resolution 37/37 (UNHCR)   301–313
Resolution 37/253 (UNGA)   73
Resolution 72/13 (UNGA)   349
Resolution 72/92 (UNGA)   343–344
Resolution 72/94 (UNGA)   344
Resolution 72/95 (UNGA)   344
Resolution 72/96 (UNGA)   345
Resolution 72/97 (UNGA)   345
Resolution 72/98 (UNGA)   345
Resolution 72/99 (UNGA)   345
Resolution 72/100 (UNGA)   345–346
Resolution 72/101 (UNGA)   346
Resolution 72/102 (UNGA)   346
Resolution 72/103 (UNGA)   346
Resolution 72/104 (UNGA)   346–347
Resolution 72/105 (UNGA)   347
Resolution 72/106 (UNGA)   347–348
Resolution 72/107 (UNGA)   348
Resolution 72/108 (UNGA)   348
Resolution 72/109 (UNGA)   348
Resolution 72/158 (UNGA)   348–349
Resolution 72/159 (UNGA)   341–342, 343
Resolution 72/160 (UNGA)   349
Resolution 72/172 (UNGA)   343
Resolution 73/18 (UNGA)   301–305
Resolution 73/19 (UNGA)   289–300
Resolution 73/20 (UNGA)   286–288
Resolution 73/21 (UNGA)   284–285
Resolution 73/22 (UNGA)   281–283
Resolution 73/89 (UNGA)   280
Resolution 73/92 (UNGA)   277–279
Resolution 73/93 (UNGA)   275–276
Resolution 73/94 (UNGA)   262–274
Resolution 73/95 (UNGA)   260–261
Resolution 73/96 (UNGA)   254–259
Resolution 73/97 (UNGA)   251–253
Resolution 73/98 (UNGA)   244–250
Resolution 73/158 (UNGA)   232–233
Resolution 73/255 (UNGA)   226–231
Resolution 73/256 (UNGA)   219–225
Resolution 79/99 (UNGA)   234–243
Resolution 180 (UNGA)   78
Resolution 181 (UNGA)
    in general   6, 78, 84, 446
    on Jerusalem   446
    on nationality/citizenship   89–90n42
    and Resolution 194   85, 132, 143–145, 147–148, 150, 152, 155–156, 164, 166–169, 174–177, 183
Resolution 194 (UNGA)
    in general   78–79
    drafting of
        in general   85
        Anglo-American-Acting Mediator Drafts   114–133
            in general   114–116
            American draft   117–118
            British draft   116–117
            Bunche draft   120–124, 191–192
            composite draft, first   118–120
            composite draft, second   124–127
            composite draft, third   127–133
        British provisional draft resolution   95–105
        First Committee Drafts
            in general   133–134
            American amendments   138–141
            American composite draft   149–151, 196
            American draft, first revised   134–136
            Australian amendments/resolutions   143–144, 149, 154, 155n353, 156, 163, 194, 197
            British draft resolution, first revised   145–148
            British draft resolution, second revised   151–155
            British draft resolution, second revised, discussions of   155–164

INDEX 545

British draft resolution, second
    revised, language of 196–197
British draft, revised 136–138
Colombian amendments/
    resolutions 145, 163, 195
Guatemalan amendments
    144–145, 146, 147, 154, 156, 157,
    160–162, 181, 195, 196, 197
Israeli observations on 148–149
Polish amendments/
    resolutions 143, 154, 163, 195
Syrian amendments/
    resolutions 154n349, 155n352,
    163
language on refugees in, overview
    191–197
and Mediator's June Suggestions
    in general 85–95
    language in 172, 173
and Mediator's September Report
    in general 106–114
    discussions of 115–127
    language in 172
and Resolution 181 85, 132, 143–145,
    147–148, 150, 152, 155–156, 164,
    166–169, 174–177, 183
Revisions in the General Assembly's
    Plenary Session, final amendments
    166–170
voting on 163–164, 165–166, 169–170
paragraph 11
    chapeau to 136, 156, 175, 176–177,
    183–184
    draft of
        approvement of 163
        changes to 162–163
        support for 156–162
    heightened interest in 170–171
    juridical effect of 171–173
    language of final version of 79,
    131n229, 168, 177, 179–180
    'live at peace' in 180
    refugee definition under 157
    removal of term 'right' from 82–83,
    177–182
political effects of 81–82
research on 83–84
significance for refugee situation
    80–82

Resolution 242 (UNSC) 7–8, 62, 79, 80, 171,
    182
Resolution 252 (UNSC) 447
Resolution 298 (UNSC) 62–63
Resolution 303(IV) (UNGA) 446
Resolution 476 (UNSC) 447–448
Resolution 478 (UNSC) 448
Resolution 1244 (UNSC) 42
Resolution 1514(XV) (UNGA) 37–38, 41
Resolution 1541(XV) (UNGA) 38, 39
Resolution 2253(ES-V) (UNSC) 446
Resolution 2334 (UNSC) 431, 438–439, 449
Resolution 2414 (UNSC) 343
Resolution 2625 (UNGA) 39–40
Resolution 3070(XXVIII) (UNGA) 64
Resolution 3210 (UNGA) 52
Resolution 3236 (UNGA) 52, 79–80
Resolution 3236(XXIX) (UNGA) 43
Resolution 3237 (UNGA) 52
Resolution 3246(XXIX) (UNGA) 64
Resolution ES-10/15 (UNGA) 15
Resolution ES-10/19 (UNGA) 450
Resolution S-28/1 (UNHRC) 421
Retroactive Transfer: A Scheme for the
    Solution of the Arab Question in the State
    of Israel 88–89
return. *see* right to return
right to compensation for property
    of Palestinian refugees
    in general 79, 109–110, 111–113, 123
    in Paragraph 11 168
    views on
        Anglo-American 152–153, 157–158
        Arabic 160
        of Bernadotte 90–91
        of Bunche 121–122
        of Israel 91, 149, 158–159
        of UK 136–137, 145–146
        of UNGA 260–261
        of USA 124–125, 129–130, 139, 140,
        147, 150
right to health
    in international law 370–372
    and obligations of States 371
    of Palestinians
        in general 369–370, 372–373
        of amputees 383–384
        of children 381–383
        of disabled persons 383–384

right to health (cont.)
    Gaza. *see* Gaza
    mental health   379–381, 382–383
    of prisoners in Israeli detention   384
    West Bank. *see* West Bank
right to return
    Constitution of IRO on   87
    in International Declaration on Human
        Rights   133
    in international law   178–179
    of Palestinian refugees
        in general   79–80, 81
        and civilians/combatants
            distinction   108, 158–159n363
        language about, in draft of Resolution
            194   191–197
        not exercising of   122
        and political rights   107, 146, 148, 161
        views on
            Anglo-American   152, 157, 175–177,
                182–183
            Arabic   161
            of Australia   197
            of Bernadotte   87, 89–90, 94–95,
                107–108, 111–113, 173–174
            of Bunche   120–121, 174, 191–192
            of Colombia   195
            of Conciliation Commission
                181–182
            of Guatemala   144–145, 160, 181,
                196, 197
            of Israel   88–89, 98, 100, 102,
                103–104, 119–120, 146, 149,
                184–189
            of PLO   170
            of UK   116–117, 118, 137, 140–141,
                146, 191, 193–194, 196–197
            of USA   118, 129, 139–140, 191, 194,
                195, 196
    in Universal Declaration of Human Rights
        83, 165, 171, 178
right to secession   46–47, 56, 72
right to self-defense   63–65, 70
right to self-determination
    in general   15, 33, 34
    in American Samoa   345
    in Anguilla   345
    CESCR on   354–356
    as collective right   51
    and colonialism   37–39, 43, 45, 64, 67
    contemporary relevance of   43–48, 75
    and decolonization   49, 66
    emergence of concept of   34–37
    as enforceable right   37–39
    general character of   44–46
    Human Rights Committee on   354–356
    of indigenous peoples. *see* indigenous
        peoples
    internal/external dimensions of   39–42,
        75
    mechanisms for implementation of
        65–66
    and mercenaries   348–349, 352
    of Palestinian people   15, 25, 43–44, 79,
        232–233, 335–338, 349
    of Palestinian refugees   150, 156, 352–353
    and right to secession   46–47
    in UN Charter   33, 36–37, 352
    U.N. Secretary-General's report on. *see*
        Report of the Secretary-General, UN
        Doc A/73/329
    UNGA resolutions on   345–347
    unlawful abolition of   48
    use of force for
        in general   33–34, 75–76
        and illegality   71–75
        as last resort   66–68
        by necessary implication   65–69
        neutrality of international law on
            69–71
        and people as beneficiaries   49–54
            in general   49–50
            and people's representatives
                50–52
            and puppet regimes   52–54
        reappraisal of   69–75
        and right to self-defense   63–65, 70
        and territory   54–63, 73–74
    in Western Sahara   342–343, 344
Rio Grande Silvery Minnow v. Bureau of
    Reclamation   473
ripeness requirements   468n4
Ripplinger v. Collins   498
Roberts v. U.S. Jaycees   501
Rodriguez de Quijas v. Shearson/Am. Express,
    Inc.   465
Rome Statute
    Article 7   423, 431

INDEX 547

Article 8   425, 431
Article 12   413, 414, 417, 419, 427
Article 14   416–417, 430, 435
Article 15   414–415, 416, 417, 418
Article 53   413, 415, 416, 435
Ronen, Yael   17
Roosevelt, Eleanor   133
Ross, John   106, 135
R.R. Comm'n of Tex. v. Pullman Co.   497–498, 500
Rules of Civil Procedure   10
Rumsfeld v. Forum for Academic & Institutional Rights, Inc.   479–481, 504–505
Rusk, Dean   104, 135, 149, 162
Russia   52, 59, 355
   see also Soviet Union

Safe Air for Everyone v. Meyer   490
Saint Helena   347–348
Sami peoples   356–357
San Francisco Conference (1945)   36
San Remo Hotel v. City & Cty. of San Francisco   497
Sassòli, Marco   16
Schechtman, Joseph B.   83n21
Schrier v. University of Colorado   483
Schuman, Robert   169
secession. *see* right to secession
security, in preliminary injunctions   515
Segregation Wall   14, 15
   see also Wall (Advisory Opinion ICJ)
self-defense. *see* right to self-determination
self-determination. *see* right to self-determination
Serbia   58
Settlement Councils   9
settler-colonialism   202, 205, 206–207
Sharett, Moshe   88–89, 97, 100, 119, 141, 142, 146, 149, 158, 184, 186, 189
Shaw, Malcolm   15
Shbeir, Ahmed Hasan   377
Shipman, Sarah   468, 470–471
Shuqayri, Ahmad   93
Sierra Club v. Yeutter   468
Simma, Bruno   70
Six Day War   7, 79, 419
Sloan, Blaine   78n3, 81n13, 83n22, 172n430, 177n450
soldiers of IDF. *see* Israel Defense Force

South Africa   16–17
sovereign immunity   495
sovereignty   58, 210–211, 226–231
Soviet Union   36, 40
   see also Russia
Special Rapporteur of the Human Rights Council   351, 353
Spokeo, Inc. v. Robins   490, 494
State of Kansas. *see* House Bill 2409; *Koontz v. Watson*
Sudeten Germans   89, 100, 131n233, 189
Sultany, Nimer   201–212
Supreme Court (US)
   on *Claiborne* boycott   477
   on loss of First Amendment freedoms   481–482
   Rumsfeld v. Forum for Academic & Institutional Rights, Inc.   480
Syrian Golan
   Israeli settlements in
      UNGA on   244–250
      UNHCR on   314–324
   Palestinian people in, sovereignty of   226–231

Tamimi, Ahed   364
Tawil-Souri, Helga   25
tear gas use   365
telecommunications industry   407
territorial integrity
   of Palestine   62–63
   and right to self-determination   56–62
territoriality
   clause in EU-Israel AA on   4, 19, 20–21, 24–25
   and concept of people   49–50
   of Israel   5–12
territory, forcible acquisition of   72, 103
TFEU (Treaty on the Functioning of the EU)   20–21
Theses on the Socialist Revolution and the Right of Nations to Self-Determination (Lenin)   34
third-State obligations
   and illegal situation in oPt
      in general   4, 16
      import ban on goods produced in
         in general   4, 18, 21–22
         lack of actions in   22

third-State obligations (cont.)
    lack of actions in   22
    and non-assistance   17
    and non-recognition   16–17
  and right to self-determination   52–54, 57
Thomas v. Anchorage Equal Rights Comm'n   490–491
Tiina Sanila-Aikio v. Finland case   51
Tokelau   348
torture   384, 423
Townley v. Miller   491
Trading with the Enemy Act   158n362
transfers, of populations. *see* exchanges/transfers
Transjordan   91–92, 103, 111, 138
travaux preparatoires
    of Article 2(4) of UN Charter   55
    of Friendly Relations Declaration   57, 64
    of Geneva Conventions   52
    and treaty rule   83n22
Treaty on the Functioning of the EU (TFEU)   20–21
Troutbeck, John   106
Truman, Harry   78, 101–102, 128, 130, 132–134, 140
Trump, Donald   342–343, 449
Tucker v. State of Cal. Dept. of Educ   512
Turkey   89, 93n54, 189
Turks and Caicos Islands   348
Turner Broadcasting System, Inc. v. FCC   501

UDHR (Universal Declaration of Human Rights). *see* Universal Declaration of Human Rights
Uganda   67
Ukraine   52
UNCTAD (United Nations Conference on Trade and Development)   406, 408
UNDPR (United Nations Division for Palestinian Rights)   284–285
UNDRIP (United Nations Declaration on the Rights of Indigenous Peoples)   351, 353, 354
unemployment   408–409
UNGA (United Nations General Assembly). *see* United Nations General Assembly
UNHCR (United Nations Human Rights Council). *see* United Nations Human Rights Council

United Kingdom (UK)
  and Chagos Archipelago   47–48
  and USA. *see* Anglo-American cooperation
  views of
    on Arab-Israeli conflict   102–103, 104–105, 116, 132, 135–136, 145–147, 153–154
    on Palestinian refugees   103, 115, 116–117, 118, 136–137, 140–141, 145–146, 191, 193–194, 196–197
    on territorial integrity   59
  see also British Middle East Office; British Virgin Islands
United Nations Charter
  Article 1   36–37, 38, 45, 69, 187
  Article 2(4)   54, 62, 64, 69
  Article 2(7)   75, 187, 189
  Article 33   67
  Article 51   62
  self-determination in   33, 36–37, 352
United Nations Children's Fund (UNICEF)   363–365
United Nations Conciliation Commission for Palestine (UNCCP)
  establishment of   112, 116, 194, 197
  powers of   135, 137, 147, 150
  relations with other UN agencies   163, 197
  on right to return   181–182
  subsidiary organs of   174n432
  tasks of   79, 116, 118, 120, 121, 122–123, 125, 128, 136, 143, 150, 156, 162, 176, 191–192, 194, 197
United Nations Conference on Trade and Development (UNCTAD)   406, 408
United Nations Declaration on the Rights of Indigenous Peoples (UNDRIP)   351, 353, 354
United Nations Division for Palestinian Rights (UNDPR)   284–285
United Nations Fiftieth Anniversary Declaration (1995)   65
United Nations General Assembly (UNGA)
  first peace plan of. *see* Resolution 181
  laws/regulations of
    Convention on the Prevention and Punishment of the Crime of Genocide   165
    Trading with the Enemy Act   158n362
  resolutions of

INDEX 549

Resolution 32/14   63
Resolution 33/15   73
Resolution 34/30   73
Resolution 34/92   63
Resolution 35/33   63
Resolution 37/253   73
Resolution 72/13   349
Resolution 72/92   343–344
Resolution 72/94   344
Resolution 72/95   344
Resolution 72/96   345
Resolution 72/97   345
Resolution 72/98   345
Resolution 72/99   345
Resolution 72/100   345–346
Resolution 72/101   346
Resolution 72/102   346
Resolution 72/103   346
Resolution 72/104   346–347
Resolution 72/105   347
Resolution 72/106   347–348
Resolution 72/107   348
Resolution 72/108   348
Resolution 72/109   348
Resolution 72/158   348–349
Resolution 72/159   341–342, 343
Resolution 72/160   349
Resolution 72/172   343
Resolution 73/18   301–305
Resolution 73/19   289–300
Resolution 73/20   286–288
Resolution 73/21   284–285
Resolution 73/22   281–283
Resolution 73/89   280
Resolution 73/92   277–279
Resolution 73/93   262–274
Resolution 73/94   262–274
Resolution 73/95   260–261
Resolution 73/96   254–259
Resolution 73/97   251–253
Resolution 73/98   244–250
Resolution 73/158   232–233
Resolution 73/255   226–231
Resolution 73/256   219–225
Resolution 79/99   234–243
Resolution 180   78
Resolution 181. *see* Resolution 181
Resolution 194. *see* Resolution 194
Resolution 303(IV)   446
Resolution 1514(XV)   37–38, 41
Resolution 1541(XV)   38, 39
Resolution 2625   39–40
Resolution 3070(XXVIII)   64
Resolution 3210   52
Resolution 3236   52, 79–80
Resolution 3236(XXIX)   43
Resolution 3237   52
Resolution 3246(XXIX)   64
Resolution ES-10/15   15
Resolution ES-10/19   450
second peace plan of. *see* Resolution 194
views of
    on applicability of Geneva
        Convention   251–253
    of displaced persons after June 1967
        hostilities   262–274
    on Israeli settlements in oPt   244–250
    on Jerusalem   281–283
    on national liberation movements   51
    on Palestinian people
        assistance to   219–225
        crimes commited against   435
        human rights violation in oPt
          of   234–243, 254–259
        right to self-determination   349
        right to self-determination of
          232–233
        sovereignty of   226–231
    on Palestinian refugees, assistence to
        277–279
    on peace in Middle East   280
    on right to self-determination   37–38,
        343–344
    on status of Jerusalem   446–447, 450
United Nations Guiding Principles on
    Business and Human Rights (UNGPs)
    409–410
United Nations High Commissioner for
    Human Rights   349
United Nations Human Rights Committee
    (OHCHR)
    on right to self-determination   15, 41, 51
    on rights of Sami peoples   356–357
United Nations Human Rights Council
    (UNHCR)
    resolutions of
        Resolution 31/36   389–392, 397–399,
          410

third-State obligations (cont.)
    Resolution 35/20   350
    Resolution 36/3   350
    Resolution 37/34   335–338, 351
    Resolution 37/35   325–334, 351
    Resolution 37/36   314–324, 351
    Resolution 37/37   301–313
    Resolution S-28/1   421
    views of
        on Israeli settlements in oPt   437
        on rights of indigenous peoples in
            351–353
    Working Group of   349, 352, 394
United Nations Interim Administration
    Mission in Kosovo (UNMIK)   42
United Nations Mediator on Palestine
    Progress Report (1948) of   82–83
    see also Bernadotte, Folke
United Nations Palestine Commission   85
United Nations Relief and Rehabilitation
    Administration (UNRRA)   87, 123
United Nations Relief and Works Agency
    for Palestine Refugees in the Near East
    (UNRWA)   174n432, 262–274,
    364–365
United Nations Relief for Palestine Refugees
    (UNRPR)   131, 142, 146, 150, 162,
    163, 197
United Nations Secretary-General
    report of, on right to self-determination.
        see Report of the Secretary-General,
        UN Doc A/73/329
United Nations Security Council (UNSC)
    resolutions of
        Resolution 242   7–8, 62, 79, 80, 171,
            182
        Resolution 252   447
        Resolution 298   62–63
        Resolution 476   447–448
        Resolution 478   448
        Resolution 1244   42
        Resolution 2253(ES-V)   447
        Resolution 2334   431, 438–439, 449
        Resolution 2414   343
    views of
        on crimes committed in oPt   435
        on military occupation of oPt   7–8
        on right of health   372
        on secessions   73
        on Western Sahara   342–343

United Nations Special Committee on
    Palestine (UNSCOP)   254–259
United Nations (UN)
    fact finding missions of   440
    membership of, Israel's request for   148,
        153, 166, 184
    responsibilities of, in Arab-Israeli
        conflict   111–112
    see also under specific organs of UN
United Nations Working Group on Arbitrary
    Detention   364
United States (USA)
    Anti-Terrorism Clarification Act of
        2018   525–527
    Bush administration of   170–171n425
    cases in
        Jordahl v. Bronvich. see Jordahl v.
            Bronvich
        Koontz v. Watson. see Koontz v. Watson
        see also under specific cases
    Clinton administration of   170
    Constitution of
        Eleventh Amendment to   482, 495
        First Amendment to   465, 468–473,
            476–477, 478, 479–480, 481–483,
            489, 492, 501–504, 505, 506–509,
            515
        Fourteenth Amendment to   465, 477,
            489, 501, 504
    and Convention on Diplomatic
        Relations   451
    Export Administration Act   487n2, 506
    and Palestine. see Palestine v. United States
        of America
    recognition of Jerusalem as capital of
        Israel   361–362
    relocation of embassy to
        Jerusalem   445–446, 449, 450,
        452–453
    and UK. see Anglo-American cooperation
    views of
        on Arab-Israeli conflict   117, 124–126,
            127–129, 132–136, 137–139, 147,
            150–152
        on Israel's sovereignty   99
        on Palestinian refugees   100–102,
            103–104, 114–115, 118, 124–125,
            129–131, 139–140, 147, 150, 191, 194,
            195, 196
        on territorial integrity   59

INDEX 551

United States v. AVX Corp.   490
United States v. National Treasury Emples. Union   476, 499–500, 501, 507, 509, 510n8, 510n9, 512, 513, 514
United States v. O'Brien   505
United States Virgin Islands   348
Univ. of Tex. v. Camenisch   474
Universal Declaration of Human Rights (UDHR)
   on right of health   370
   right to return in   83, 165, 171, 178
UNMIK (United Nations Interim Administration Mission in Kosovo)   42
UNRPR (United Nations Relief for Palestine Refugees)   131, 142, 146, 150, 162, 163, 197
UNRRA (United Nations Relief and Rehabilitation Administration)   87, 123
UNRWA (United Nations Relief and Works Agency for Palestine Refugees in the Near East)   174n432, 262–274, 364–365
UNSC (United Nations Security Council). *see* United Nations Security Council
UNSCOP (United Nations Special Committee on Palestine)   254–259
USA vs. Friedrich Flick   12–13
Use of Force and Firearms by Law Enforcement Officials   367
uti possidetis iure principle   73

Valle Del Sol v. Whiting   499
VCDR (Vienna Convention on Diplomatic Relations). *see* Vienna Convention on Diplomatic Relations
VCLT (Vienna Convention on the Law of Treaties)   19, 83
Verlo v. Martinez   475, 481
Versailles Peace Treaty   35
Vienna Convention on Diplomatic Relations (VCDR)
   Article 3   453–455
   Article 21   454
   Article 48   451
   Article 50   451
   breach of   452–455
   Optional Protocol of   450–452
   preamble of   452–453

Vienna Convention on the Law of Treaties (VCLT)   19, 83
Vienna Declaration (1993)   65
violence. *see* force, use of
Virgin Islands   345, 348
Voltolini, Benedetta   14, 20

Wall (Advisory Opinion ICJ)   14–16, 39, 56, 62, 68, 72, 437–438
war crimes. *see* crimes
Warren, George   134n244
water distribution   18, 369
Watson, Randall D. *see Koontz v. Watson*
Weizman, Chaim   97, 133
West Bank
   agriculture in   408
   human rights situation in
      in general   362–363
      of children   363–365
   Israeli civilian presence in   419–420
   Israeli settlements in
      in general   362–363
      normalization of   366
   legislative measures, to extend Israeli jurisdiction   365–366
   Palestinians in
      crimes committed against   422–423, 424
      right to health of
         in general   369
         of children   382–383
         mental health   380–381, 382–383
   telecommunications industry in   407
   two-tier system of laws in   11
   views on, in report of ICC   419–420, 422–423, 424
   water distribution in   369
West Bank barrier   14, 15
   see also Wall (Advisory Opinion ICJ)
West Virginia Bd. of Ed. v. Barnette   501.
Western Galilee   92, 99, 110, 128, 142
Western Sahara   51, 65, 342–343, 344
Western Sahara (Advisory Opinion ICJ)   39
WHO (World Health Organization). *see* World Health Organization
Will v. Michigan Dep't of State Police   495
Wilson, Woodrow   35

Winter v. Nat. Res. Def. Council, Inc. 475, 515
Working Group of the Human Rights
    Council 349, 352, 394
World Bank 407, 408
World Health Organization (WHO)
    on health-care system in Gaza 374
    on medical exit permit system in
        376–377
    on right of health 370
    on water distribution 18

World Trade Organization (WTO) 22
Wortley, B.A. 13–14

Yau, Sean Shun Ming 32–76
Younger v. Harris 515
Yugoslavia 64, 165
Yusuf, Abdulqawi Ahmed 458–460

Zionism 91, 207
Zorlu, Rifki 190